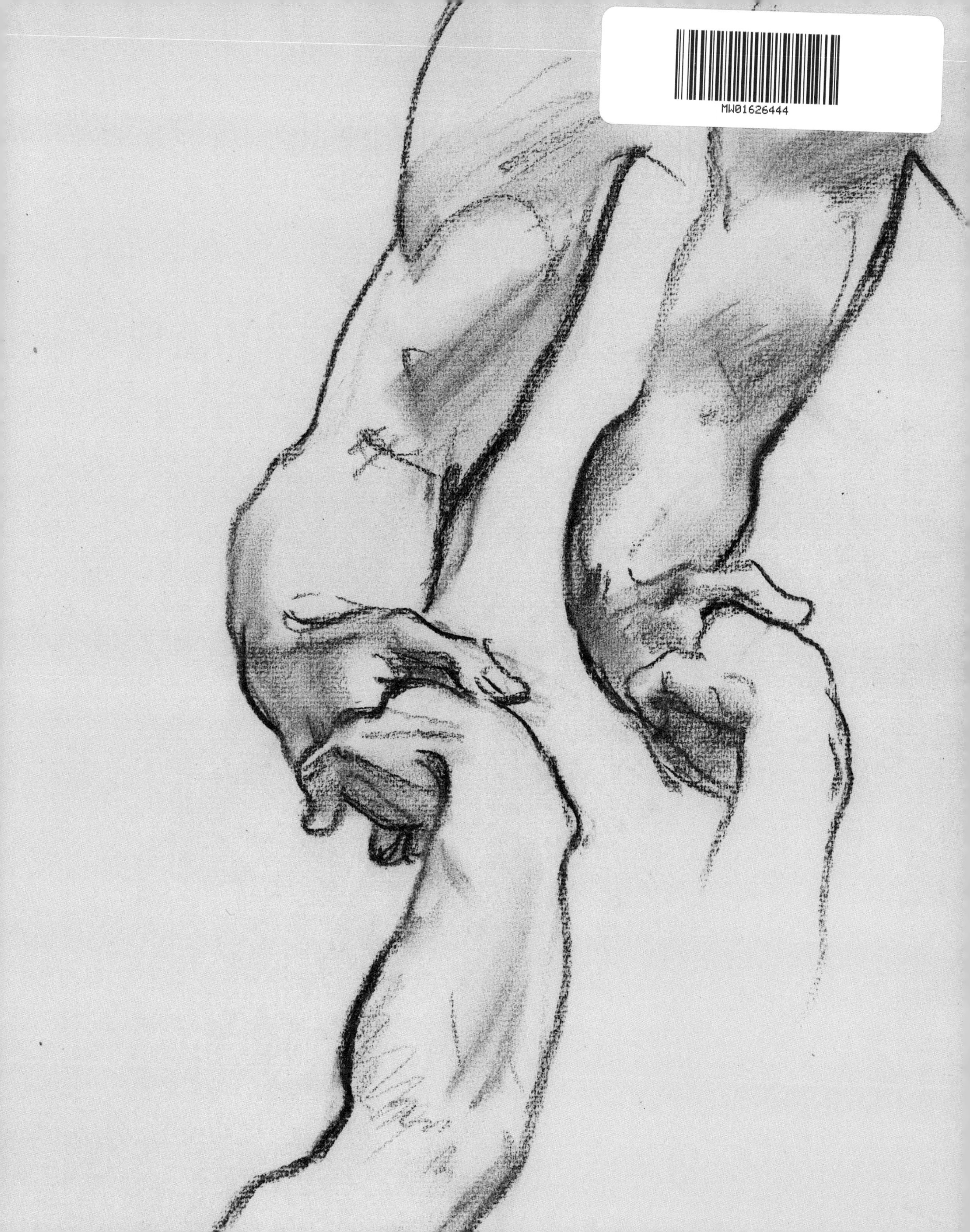

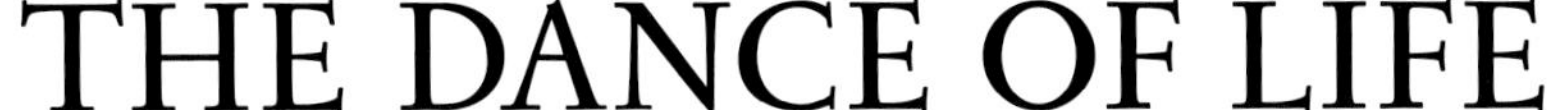

THE DANCE OF LIFE

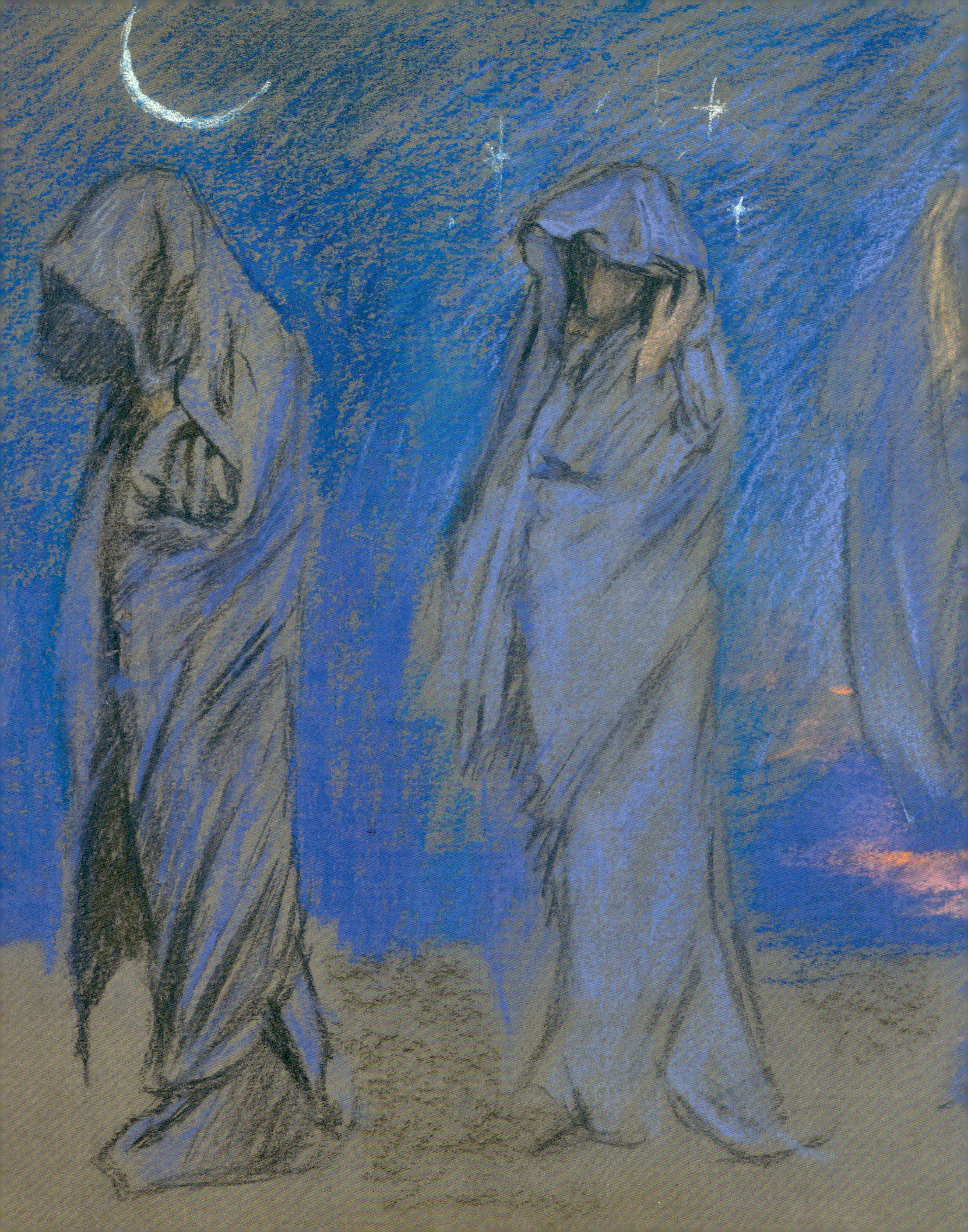

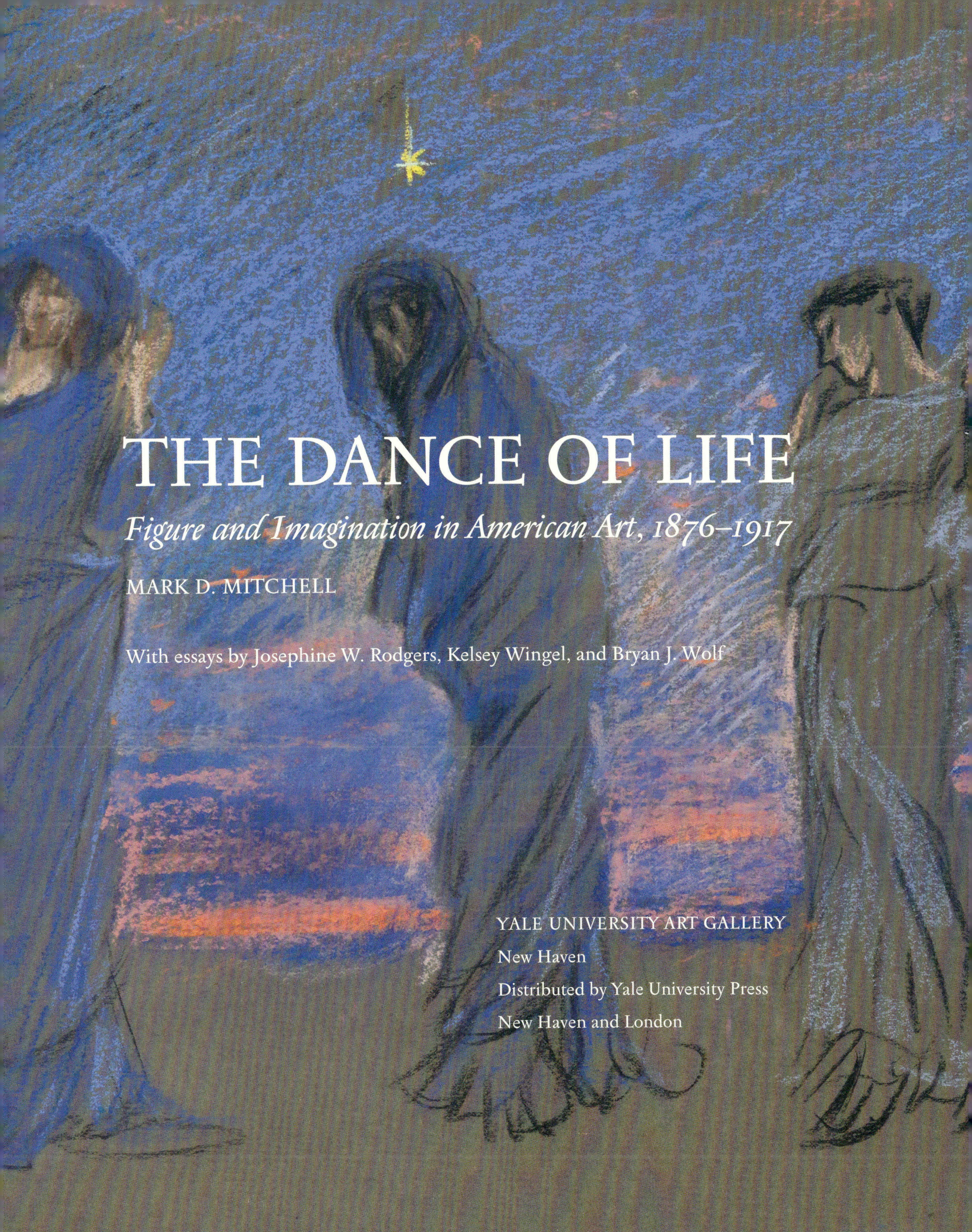

THE DANCE OF LIFE

Figure and Imagination in American Art, 1876–1917

MARK D. MITCHELL

With essays by Josephine W. Rodgers, Kelsey Wingel, and Bryan J. Wolf

YALE UNIVERSITY ART GALLERY
New Haven
Distributed by Yale University Press
New Haven and London

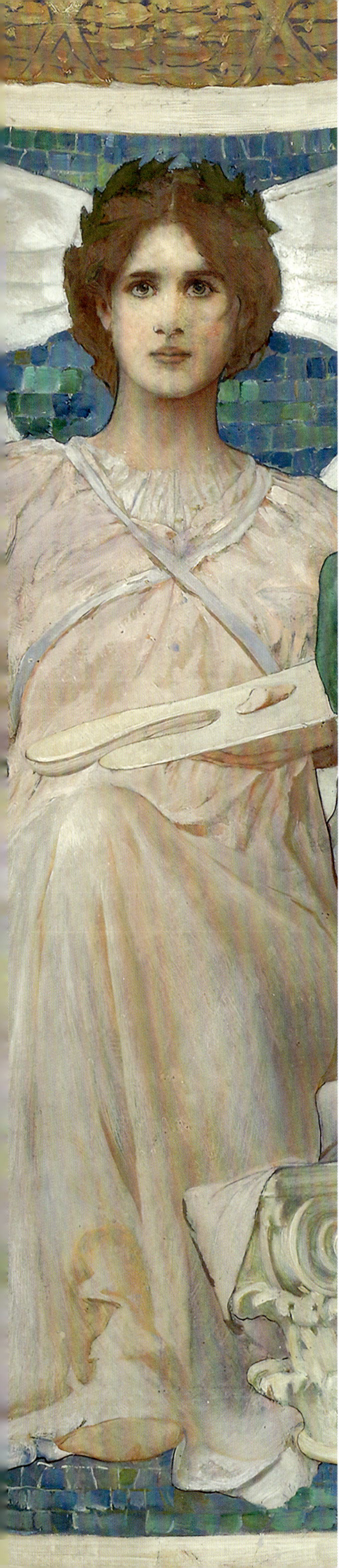

Contents

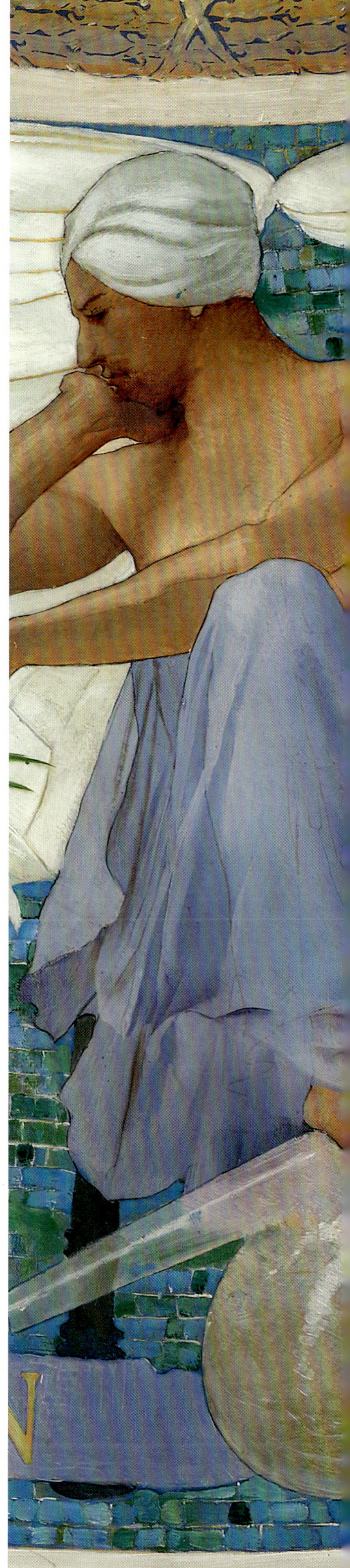

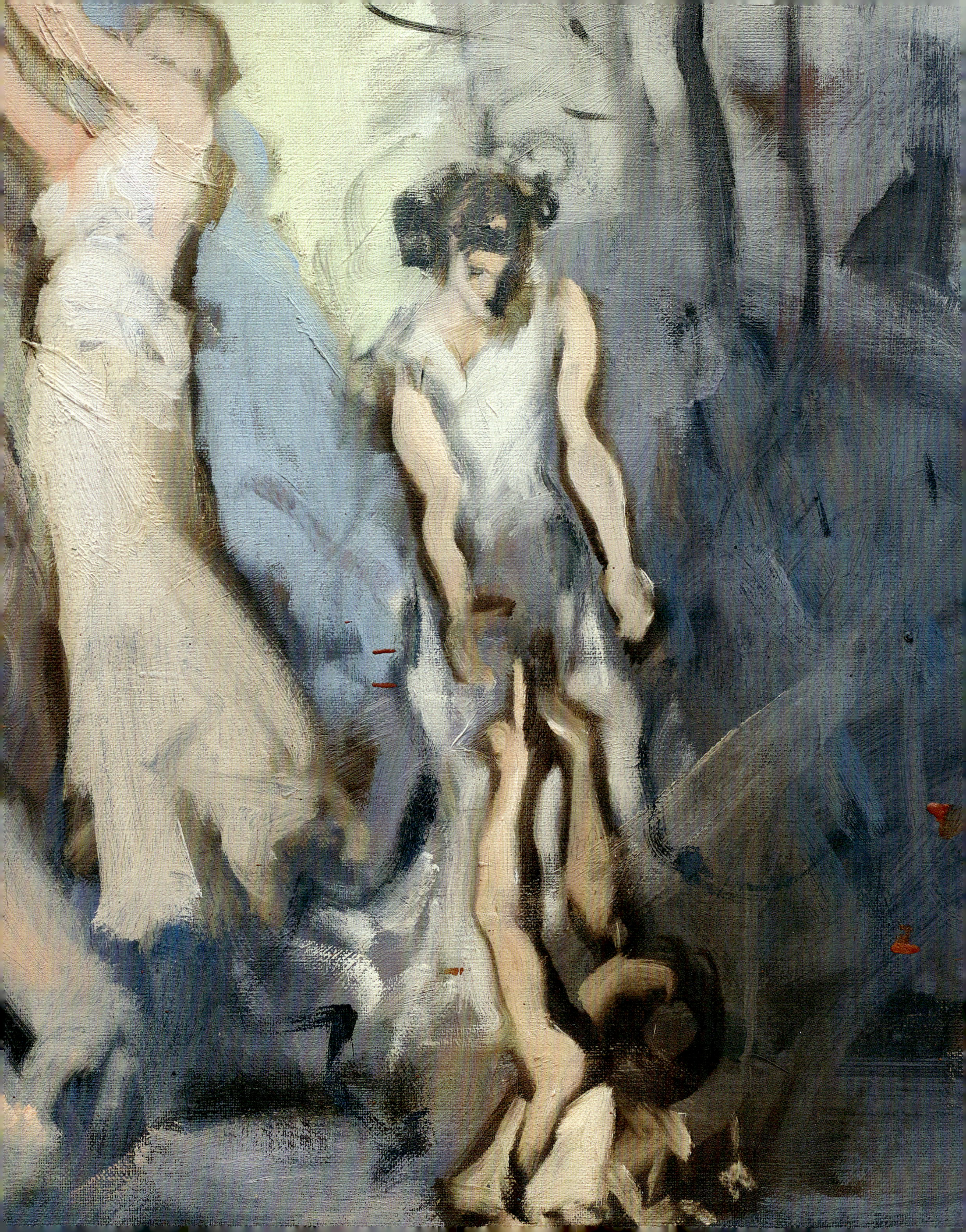

Director's Foreword

This book, and the exhibition that it accompanies, explores the creative process and artistic community active during a period in art and architecture known as the American Renaissance. Led by progressive ideals of democratic participation and opportunity made possible through education, these artists grappled with themes of shared humanity and collaboration to create works that would inspire and unite in an age of political division, class conflict, endemic racism, and technological transformation. The aesthetic they shaped in civic art in the post–Civil War nation remains ingrained in our collective visual imagination.

The evolution of these artists' personal yet highly public projects invites questions about how they developed their ideas. For some, the process was straightforward, consisting of a few preparatory studies in a single medium; for others, it involved ongoing experiments and revisions in a wide range of media, sometimes created over the course of several years. Studies and iterative variants were neither short-lived nor disposable; rather, they were part of an evolving practice of reflection and imaginative ferment. This exhibition seeks an understanding of the creative process and an appreciation for its meaning to the artists of this period.

The Dance of Life has its foundation in the 1937 bequest of Mary Gertrude Abbey, widow of the artist Edwin Austin Abbey, a leading mural painter of the American Renaissance. The estate included three thousand works created by Abbey as well as a few other artists. The resulting Edwin Austin Abbey Memorial Collection has been a central holding of the Yale University Art Gallery for nearly a century, though it has only occasionally been featured in exhibitions, the most recent in 1973 and 1994. In the present exhibition, Abbey's work is juxtaposed with that of his peers, including Edwin Howland Blashfield, John La Farge, Violet Oakley, and John Singer Sargent. These were among the most famous artists of their day, and the studies on the following pages are their statements of vision and ambition.

The Gallery's comprehensive collection presents an unparalleled opportunity to introduce Abbey's work—little known today—to the public in new and exciting ways. Mark D. Mitchell, the Holcombe T. Green Curator of American Paintings and Sculpture, has done so beautifully here, celebrating the sophistication of expression and sheer confidence of the artist's touch in quick sketches, exquisite pastels, and dramatic oils on canvas. With this monumental project that has its roots in collections stewardship and preservation, Mitchell and many colleagues at the Gallery, in particular our expert team of talented conservators, have brought the excitement and spirit of this period to life once again.

We are deeply grateful to the generous donors and foundations who have supported *The Dance of Life*. Jerald Dillon Fessenden, B.A. 1960, has been a steadfast friend of the project and ensured that our conservation team had the support needed to complete their work. An exceptional and timely gift from Clifford Ross, B.A. 1974, helped us reach our goal during the last stage of the exhibition's production. Major grants from the Henry Luce Foundation and the Mr. and Mrs. Raymond J. Horowitz Foundation for the Arts ensured that the exhibition would fulfill the richness of its vision. The Wyeth Foundation for American Art offered critical support for this catalogue. Through their extraordinary foresight, endowment donors, including Rosalee and David McCullough and Jan and Warren Adelson, have offered resources to make projects like this one possible. As with all of the Gallery's initiatives in American art, *The Dance of Life* also benefitted from the support of the devoted members of the Friends of American Arts at Yale through their Exhibition and Publication Endowment Funds.

Stephanie Wiles
The Henry J. Heinz II Director
Yale University Art Gallery

Acknowledgments

The Dance of Life began as a partnership with Elisabeth (Lisa) Hodermarsky, the Sutphin Family Curator of Prints and Drawings at the Yale University Art Gallery. Together, we surveyed the Edwin Austin Abbey Memorial Collection—three thousand works of art housed in the Gallery's collection—and thought about the contours of an exhibition. Lisa had been working on Abbey long before I arrived as curator in the Department of American Paintings and Sculpture in 2015, and she freely and generously shared the benefits of her research. Over the ensuing years, we shaped and refined the exhibition's themes and early checklist. Lisa coauthored the exhibition's first grant applications, helped persuade lenders, and traveled widely to see the major sites, collections, and archives. When the pandemic arrived, the Gallery had to adjust priorities and schedules, and Lisa reluctantly withdrew from the project to focus on other, more urgent projects, especially the landmark exhibition *On the Basis of Art: 150 Years of Women at Yale*, held in 2021. I remain deeply grateful for Lisa's defining contributions, which are embedded in this project, and her continued support.

The exhibition has also benefitted from the dedicated efforts of fellows and students at various stages of their academic journeys. During the project's early days, the brilliant organizational and research abilities of Molly K. Eckel, who worked with us for three years as the Marcia Brady Tucker Fellow in American Paintings and Sculpture, were invaluable. Molly maintained the exhibition's records, organized Abbey's studies, assembled research files on the show's primary artists and sites, and always took the long view, knowing that others would follow after her. Molly was succeeded in the role of Marcia Brady Tucker Fellow by Josephine (Jodi) Rodgers, who wholeheartedly embraced the project as her own and became an essential partner—and essayist—as the pandemic arrived and upended all our expectations. As Lisa stepped back, Jodi stepped forward and took on greater responsibility for the shape of the exhibition and its organization. Jodi's partnership through the ups and downs of the pandemic and final stages of exhibition development have been invaluable.

From the outset, this project would only ever be possible with extraordinary efforts from the Gallery's brilliant team of conservators. Even the survey of the Abbey estate—just to see everything—required the constant presence of our colleagues in the Conservation Department. Three conservators have made a special project of the exhibition, and Abbey in particular, over the years of its development: Kelsey Wingel and Cynthia (Cindy) Schwarz for the paintings and Theresa Fairbanks-Harris for the works on paper. They have invested years of effort to ensure that Abbey's art could be seen to best advantage. If we now all have the opportunity to see the art of this era in a new way, then it is because of their brilliant and diligent work. Kelsey's years of research on and care for Abbey's half-scale study for *The Hours* has resulted in not only its prominence as the project's culminating object but also her essay for this catalogue.

Many have joined Kelsey, Cindy, and Theresa in their work, overseen first by Ian McClure and more recently by Irma Passeri, the Gallery's Susan Morse Hilles Chief Conservator. Among their colleagues in Conservation, Olav Bjornerud, Kyler Brahmer, Łukasz Bratasz, Elizabeth Godcher, Tirza Harris, Amanda Kasman, Anna Krez, Julianna Ly, Sydney Nikolaus, Anne O'Connor, Katherine Peters, Sarah Schlick, Nikita Shah, and Anna Vesaluoma have made important contributions with collaboration from research scientists in Yale's Institute for the Preservation of Cultural Heritage, including Anikó Bezur, Richard Hark, Pablo Londero, Kate Schilling, and Marcie Wiggins. As the opening of the exhibition approached, Paul Panamarenko and Peter Cohen beautifully framed many of the conserved works to ensure that they are shown to best effect. The extensive framing needs of the exhibition presented a challenge that was greatly eased by the sage advice and hands-on participation offered by R. Wayne Reynolds and the assistance of Ryan Norman Cyr.

Advisers have helped steer the project from its inception. In the fall of 2016, students in the semester-long undergraduate seminar that I led, "Exhibiting America's Gilded Age," included Olivia Armandroff, Jessica Blau, Olivia Hamel, and Edward Maza. They vetted artists and themes for the exhibition, conducted research, examined artworks, and shared their ideas about what would make a compelling show. In January 2017 a group of graduate students, faculty, curators, and other scholars came together at Yale to look into the collection and share their perspectives; these included Tim Barringer, Rebecca (Ruthie) Dibble, Trevor Fairbrother, Lucy Oakley, Sally Promey, Rebecca Szantyr, Carol Troyen, Nicole Bass Williams, and Bryan Wolf. Several participants remained involved in different roles during the exhibition's development, but none more so than Bryan, who has been a cherished friend and fellow traveler for the length of the journey. His essay for this catalogue is just one of his many valued contributions. Along with Bryan, David Getsy, Jennifer Raab, Kirk Savage, and Marc Simpson contributed advice and perspective along the way.

The lenders to the exhibition are essential to its success, and we are deeply grateful to the private collectors and museum colleagues across the country who have volunteered their enthusiastic support. Special effort is gratefully acknowledged from Annelise Madsen and Sarah Kelly Oehler at the Art Institute of Chicago; Anne Collins Goodyear and Frank Goodyear at the Bowdoin College Museum of Art; Aleesa Pitchamarn Alexander and Kathryn Cua at the Cantor

Arts Center; Akemi May at the Carnegie Museum of Art; Caitlin Condell, Laura Fravel, and Caroline O'Connell at the Cooper Hewitt, Smithsonian Design Museum; Rachel Passannante and Jessica Roscio at the Danforth Art Museum; Joanna Catron at the Gari Melchers Home and Studio; Joachim Homann at the Harvard Art Museums; Katherine Blood and Sara Duke at the Library of Congress; Stephanie Herdrich, Thayer Tolles, and Sylvia Yount at the Metropolitan Museum of Art; Erica Hirshler, Ethan Lasser, Meghan Melvin, Patrick Murphy, and Katrina Newbury at the Museum of Fine Arts, Boston; Rena Hoisington and Shelley Langdale at the National Gallery of Art in Washington, D.C.; Danielle Carrabino at the Smith College Museum of Art; Randy Griffey, Eleanor Jones Harvey, and Karen Lemmey at the Smithsonian American Art Museum; Amy Hammond and Curt Miner at the State Museum of Pennsylvania; Erin Corrales-Diaz at the Toledo Museum of Art; Cynthia Staples at Trinity Church, Boston; Jeremiah McCarthy at the Westmoreland Museum of American Art; and Pamela Franks and Kevin Murphy at the Williams College Museum of Art.

Many individuals lent time and energy to the research behind the exhibition, for which we offer sincere thanks. Although there are far too many to name in full, some of those who have gone above and beyond to assist with our research both in the United States and in England include Vanessa Bell, Marisa Bourgoin, Janet Broske, Jay Clarke, David Peters Corbett, Abby Eron, Donna Hassler, Kate Howell, Marilyn Kushner, Alexandra Mazzitelli, Douglas Miller, Shirley Nicholson, Roberta J. M. Olson, Renee Pappous, Karen Parsons, Dana Pilson, Mark Pomeroy, Christopher Ridgway, Megan Schwenke, Jonathan R. Stayer, Julie Warchol, Sileas Wood, and Amanda Zehnder.

At the Yale University Art Gallery, nearly every member of the staff has contributed to the exhibition, and the organizers deeply appreciate their professionalism and expertise. I am indebted to the Gallery's former and current Henry J. Heinz II Directors, Jock Reynolds and Stephanie Wiles, as well as to our chief curator, Laurence Kanter, and former deputy directors Pam Franks and Heather Nolin, for their support and encouragement. I also owe special thanks to Michèle Wije, Curatorial Project Manager, for stewarding the project through its late stages of production. In the Department of American Paintings and Sculpture, Gabby Gervase and Janet Miller have brought critical organizational clarity to this complicated and ever-changing project, and our former Rose Herrick Jackson Fellows Gavriella Levy Haskell and Nicole Bass Williams provided essential research support. I am grateful to my colleagues Miranda Saylor and Royce Young Wolf, who have worked steadily to keep us moving forward while my attention has been focused on this project. Special efforts have been made by many others, including Emily Herberich, Brian McGovern, and Hilary Sierpinski in the Department of Advancement; Eric Litke in the

Department of American Decorative Arts; Jessica Labbé, Charlene Senical, and Catherine Sparer-Morales in the Business Office; Jason DeBlock, Anthony Florio, Mark Geist, David Norris, Vicki Onofrio, Tom Philips, and Anna Russell in the Department of Collections; Lisa Scilipote in the Office of the Director; Liz Harnett, Alice Matthews, Liliana Milkova, Jessica Sack, Sydney Simon, and Molleen Theodore in the Department of Education; Andrew Daubar, Grant Johnston, David Marshall, Christina Vergara, and Jeffrey Yoshimine in the Exhibitions Department; George Hagerty and Bradley Olson in the Facilities Department; Yer Vang-Cohen in the Information and Digital Services Department; Suzanne Boorsch, Diana Brownell, Evelyn Davis, Suzanne Greenawalt, Freyda Spira, and Alicia Van Campen in the Department of Prints and Drawings; Chris Chew, Tiffany Sprague, and Grace Zhou in the Department of Publications and Editorial Services; Lynne Addison, Amy Dowe, Ashley Kane, and Anne Moore in the Registrar's Office; Laurie Laliberte in Special Events; Leonor Barroso and Michael Moore in Visitor Services; and Al Harding, Rich House, Kathleen Mylen-Coulombe, Milan Russell, Jessie Smolinski, and David Whaples in the Department of Visual Resources. Among our many Gallery colleagues, Andrew Daubar and Amy Dowe have been coorganizers who made the exhibition both possible and special through their dedicated effort.

To our exhibition partners at the National Gallery in London, where a version of the exhibition will travel, we extend special thanks for their patience and dedication to finding the right configuration for their museum. Christopher Riopelle, the Neil Westreich Curator of Post-1800 Paintings, has been steadfast in his interest and engagement from the beginning. We are grateful for the support of director Gabriele Finaldi and assistance from colleagues Jane Knowles, Sunnifa Hope, and Katherine Miller. Our conversation might not have begun, however, if not for the generous collegiality of Katherine Bourguignon, Curator at the Terra Foundation for American Art, who first introduced us and shared our sense of the potential for a partnership.

Last, but certainly not least, a few colleagues and friends have been essential partners in the project. For them, a special word of thanks is in order. For Christine Boyle, who jumped in the car and cheerfully explored the English hinterlands together in search of Abbey's trail, I hope this is only the beginning of many future adventures. To Amy Meyers, who saw this as a transatlantic project from the start and made special introductions for Lisa and me to an array of trusted colleagues in England, there cannot be enough gratitude. To Keely Orgeman, who is a dear friend and admired colleague, personal thanks. For Jason Wilson, whose dedication and long service as historian to the state of Pennsylvania at its capitol is an inspiration, our deepest appreciation. We offer thanks to our gifted graphic designer Laura Lindgren, who set out to design a book and ended up creating the graphics for a whole exhibition, for so beautifully amplifying the artworks and helping us tell their stories visually. And to Mary Ellen Wilson, our beloved editor, who has worked steadily and painstakingly to keep us all on track with extraordinary positivity, please accept our heartfelt thanks and admiration.

Among the exhibition's generous donors, I would like to thank Jerald Fessenden for his enduring commitment to the project and to American art at Yale, as well as devoted friends of the Gallery Max Berry and Clifford Ross for their kindhearted and enthusiastic interest. I also gratefully acknowledge the Friends of American Art at Yale and their chair, Ulysses Dietz, for their dedicated support.

Finally, I would like to thank my family—my wife, Becca, and our daughters, Lucy and Emily—for their steadfast love and encouragement, which sustains me in all that I do.

Mark D. Mitchell
The Holcombe T. Green Curator of American Paintings and Sculpture
Yale University Art Gallery

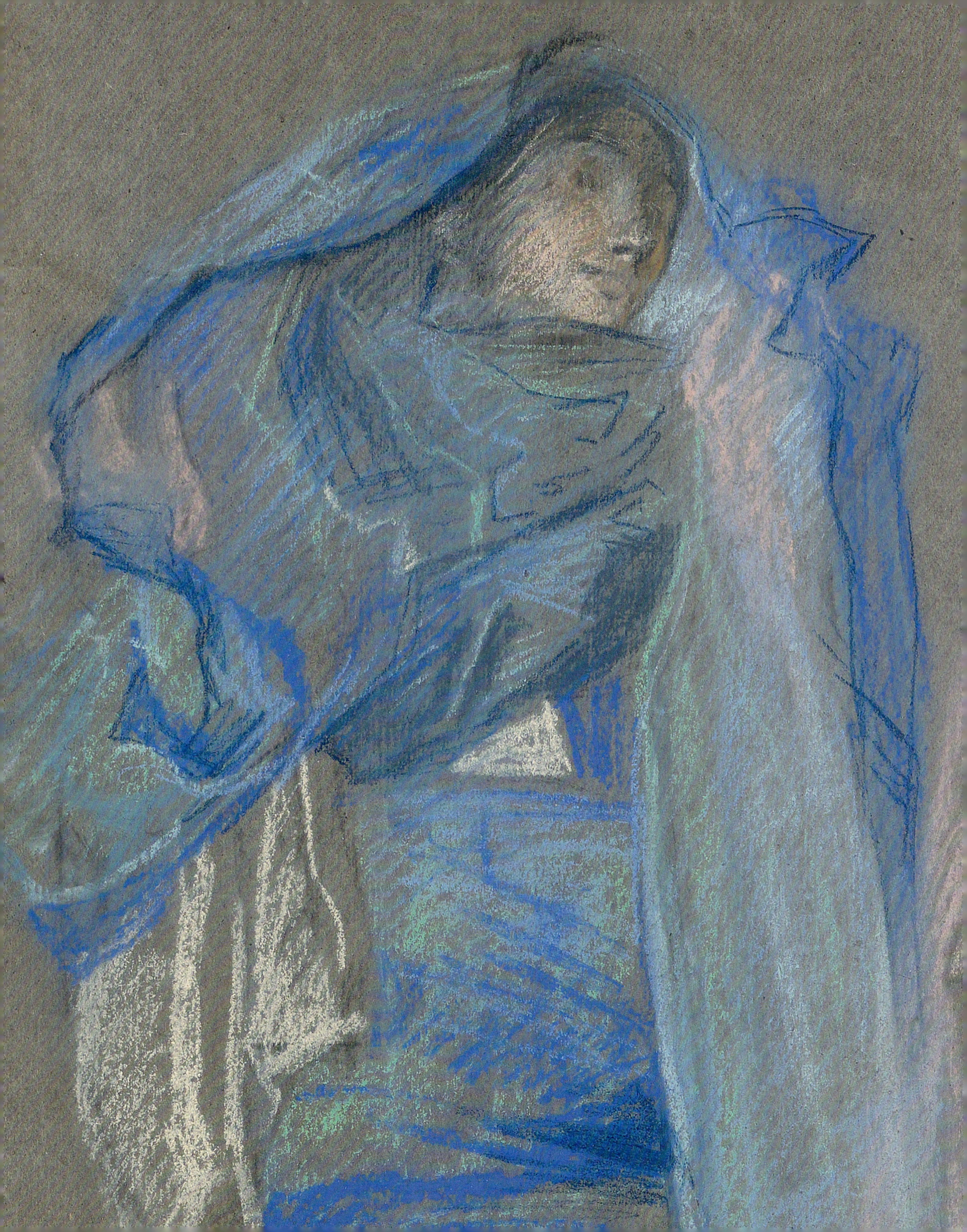

Lenders to the Exhibition

Anonymous
The Art Institute of Chicago
Bowdoin College Museum of Art, Brunswick, Maine
Cantor Arts Center at Stanford University, California
Carnegie Museum of Art, Pittsburgh
Cooper Hewitt, Smithsonian Design Museum, New York
Danforth Art Museum at Framingham State University, Massachusetts
Gari Melchers Home and Studio at the University of Mary Washington, Virginia
Harvard Art Museums, Cambridge, Massachusetts
Library of Congress, Washington, D.C.
The Metropolitan Museum of Art, New York
Museum of Fine Arts, Boston
National Gallery of Art, Washington, D.C.
Pennsylvania Capitol Preservation Committee, Harrisburg
Smith College Museum of Art, Northampton, Massachusetts
Smithsonian American Art Museum, Washington, D.C.
The State Museum of Pennsylvania, Harrisburg
Toledo Museum of Art, Ohio
Trinity Church, Boston
Westmoreland Museum of American Art, Greensburg, Pennsylvania
Williams College Museum of Art, Williamstown, Massachusetts

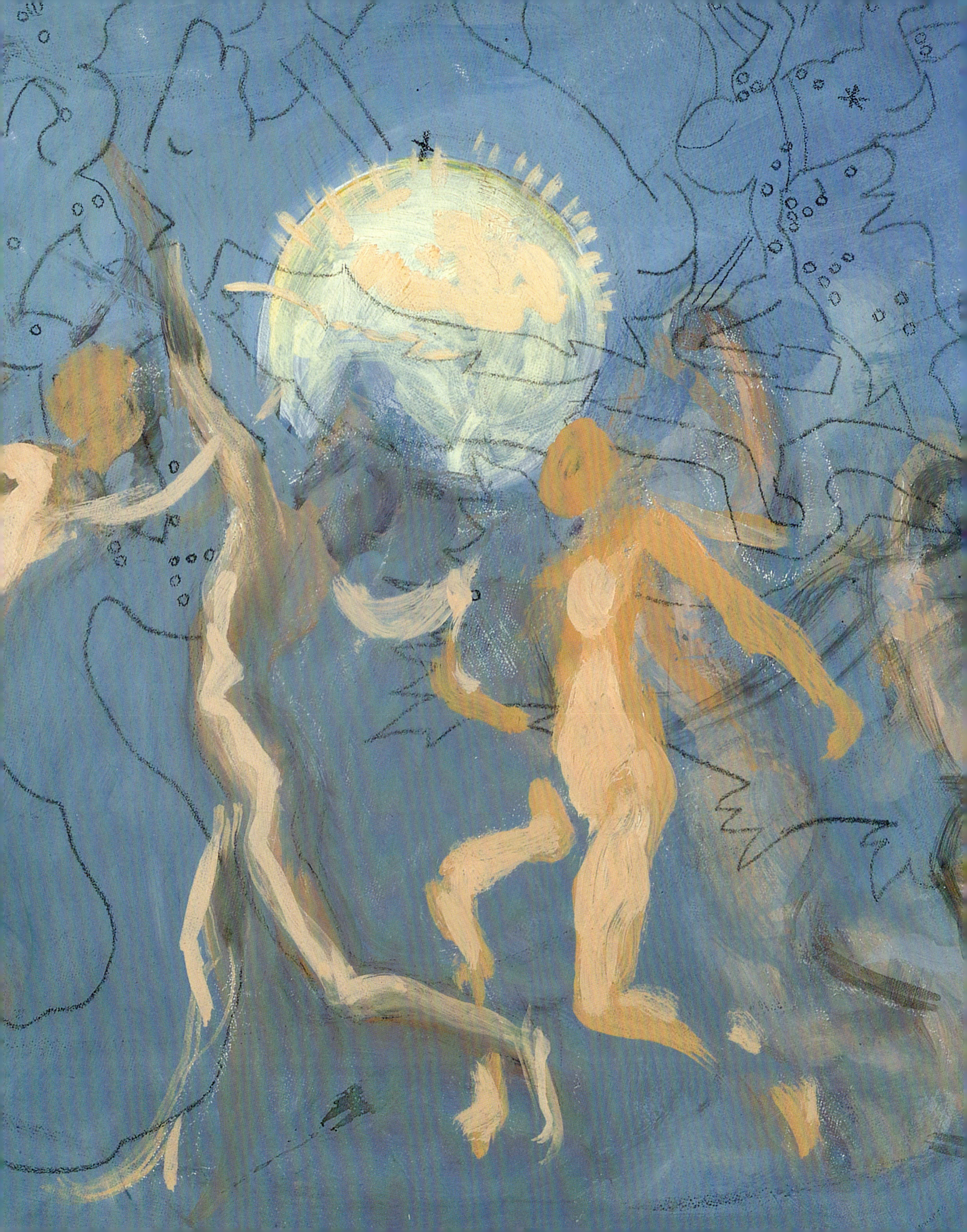

Introduction

MARK D. MITCHELL

Between the United States' Centennial in 1876 and its entry into World War I in 1917, American artists focused public attention on the human figure to an unparalleled extent. The period, known as the American Renaissance, was defined by progressivism and revitalization in the aftermath of the Civil War and Reconstruction. To decorate a wide variety of ambitious new civic structures—state capitols, libraries, churches, train stations, universities, museums, and courthouses, as well as more ephemeral projects like world's fairs and expositions—a new generation of American artists embraced the expressive human figure as a vehicle for collective imagination and social reform. For many, this was art's highest calling.

The American Renaissance gave form to some of the country's leading cultural institutions, many as we still know them today. A host of arts organizations were founded at the time, from ballets to museums, libraries to operas. These initiatives brought communities together, created opportunity and inspiration, and have, in several cases, grown into the firmament of American cultural life. In parallel, leading civic charities and advocacy groups—the United Way, the NAACP, the American Federation of Labor, and the predecessors of both the League of Women Voters and the ACLU—were founded to envision a more just and equitable future.

Yale also witnessed transformations during this period, including its transition from college to university in 1887. Among the first honorary degree recipients were the leading painters and sculptors of the American Renaissance, including Edwin Austin Abbey in 1897. For the arts at Yale, the period was bracketed on its early side by the creation of the Yale School of Art, the University's first coeducational program, and the Yale University Art Gallery's expansion into a second home, Street Hall, designed in the Gothic Revival style by Peter Bonnett Wight. At the center of the new School of Art's curriculum was, naturally, the human figure. At the far end of the period, in 1917, the University commissioned its Memorial Quadrangle and signature Harkness Tower, redefining the campus's architectural character. A decade later, the Gallery would begin construction on its third home, an ambitious Renaissance Revival building that reflected continued interest in Renaissance aesthetics. In the meantime, the University began a series of commissions for public spaces around its bicentennial celebration in 1901, which included public artworks, especially sculptures and stained glass, that remain campus landmarks. For the University as for the country, the American Renaissance era has had an enduring impact.

Beneath this era of progress and optimism, however, were realities of a culture undergoing transformation. Pseudoscientific thought rationalized racism and eugenics in evolutionary terms. Huge influxes of immigrants, rapid urbanization, revolutions in transportation, industrial monopolies, new technologies, and organized labor left no corner of society unchanged. Political corruption was rampant, and efforts to reconcile the North with the South led to the creation of troubling monuments to Confederate leaders that have been the subjects of protest in recent years. Yet despite its intractable challenges, the era's vertiginous growth and affluence emboldened grand, utopian visions of the nation's future that inspired reformers and attracted generations of hope-filled migrants from around the world.

Life would be the quintessential subject of American artists and the metric of critics for four decades. Despite Americans' long-held ambivalence about both art and the body, the human figure became ubiquitous in fine art as well as the nearly exclusive subject of a largely new form in America: public art. The body offered a universal medium of visual communication. In the minds of artists, their work aligned with the humanism of the Italian Renaissance of the fifteenth and sixteenth centuries, a period of unparalleled creative vibrance in Western culture. That comparison was made often during the period, beginning in 1880, and peaked at the World's Columbian Exposition in Chicago in 1893. The study and collecting of Italian Renaissance art also surged in America during this period, widening appreciation for the native artists' sources as part of what the cultural historian Oliver Larkin called "a Renaissance complex."[1]

Ironically, it was death that brought life into relief at the end of the nineteenth century. The Civil War lingered in the American imagination long after its end in 1865. Art seemed inadequate to the task of responding to the incalculable loss of life, likely greater than virtually every other military conflict in U.S. history combined.[2] At the Centennial Exposition in Philadelphia in 1876, a turning point in the history of American art and culture, depictions of the war were forbidden, for they served as "an unsuitable reminder, at this Centennial time, of discords that are past."[3] Despite the prohibition, Civil War subjects were included, as were landscapes, the genre that had dominated American artistic practice for a half century. Increasingly recognized as the product of antebellum culture, by 1877 such scenic works were on the decline as "the tide of artistic favor turned."[4]

For American audiences of the late nineteenth century, art remained a European idea. Among artists, the stigma of provincialism led to a divide between

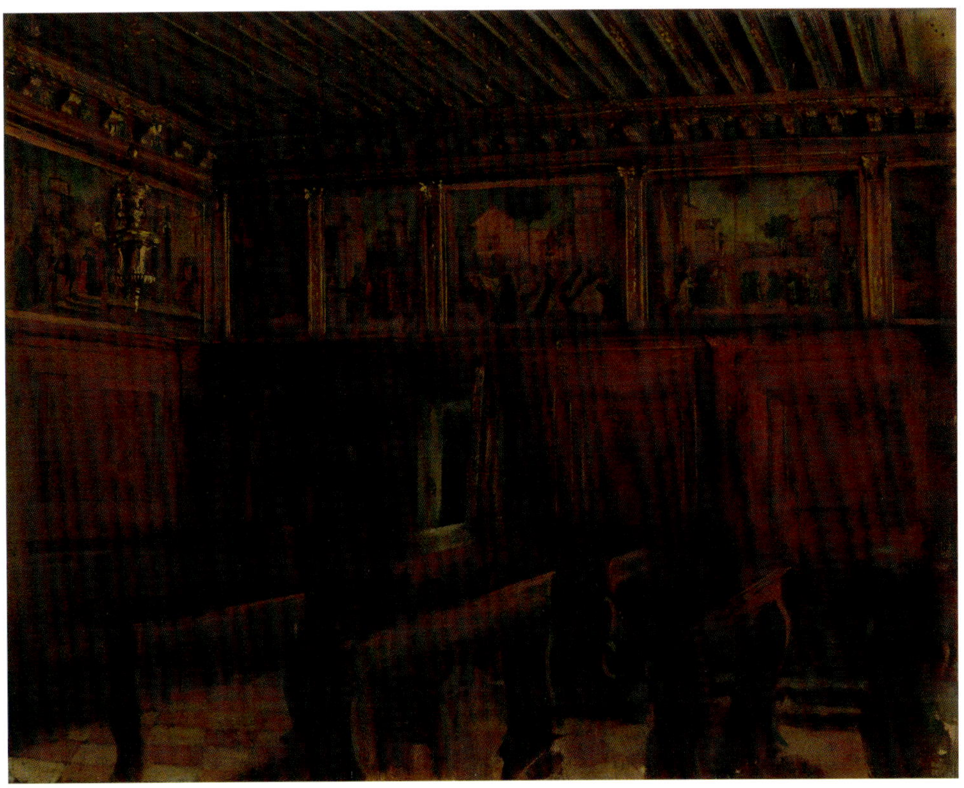

FIG. 1. Edwin Austin Abbey, *Interior Study of the Chapel of Scuola di San Giorgio degli Schiavoni, Venice, Italy*, ca. 1893. Oil on canvas, 15½ × 19½ in. (39.4 × 49.5 cm). Yale University Art Gallery, New Haven, Conn., Edwin Austin Abbey Memorial Collection, 1937.2657

those who proudly stayed in the United States and those who left in search of wider horizons. Even some of the largest murals and sculptures created during the American Renaissance were made by Americans working abroad. England, in particular, hosted many such artists, including Edwin Austin Abbey and John Singer Sargent, whose works and friendship are at the heart of this book and the exhibition. Both traveled widely from England, venturing across Europe and North Africa in search of regional inspiration and historical sources. In the Renaissance chapel of the Dalmatian School of Saint George of the Slavs in Venice, with its series of nine paintings by Vittore Carpaccio (fig. 1), Abbey found the model for his fifteen-part cycle *The Quest and Achievement of the Holy Grail* (1890–1902), created for the book delivery room of the Boston Public Library designed by Charles Follen McKim. With direct access to the sites and subjects of Western art's history and the finest works of its past and present, Europe offered American artists a font of inspiration.

For John La Farge, who helped initiate the American Renaissance at Trinity Church in Boston in 1876, the value in the Old Masters extended not just to their finished works but also to their studies. As he recalled, "If I copied the painting from which the drawing had been made I could only copy the surface, without knowing exactly how the master had made this result. But I knew that in the master's drawings and studies for a given work I met him intimately, saw into his mind, and learned his intentions and his character, and what was great and what was deficient."[5] Contemporary critics who admired studies by American Renaissance artists similarly did not associate them with the stylistic modernism of their time—such as Post-Impressionism or Fauvism—focusing instead on the animating ideas of their finished work in formation, "permanent records of their steps toward the goal," in the words of *Scribner's* magazine editor Russell Sturgis in 1907.[6]

This catalogue and the exhibition it accompanies highlight not only the artists' projects but also their dramatically different approaches to studies and creative processes. Two extant American Renaissance landmarks are touchstones of this project: the Boston Public Library and the Pennsylvania State Capitol in Harrisburg. Both are anchors of the career of Edwin Austin Abbey, whose artistic estate housed at the Gallery provides insight into his creative investment in studies as well as his developing practice. Each site also encompasses commissions by other painters and sculptors, reflecting their need to work around and in harmony with one another. These men and women worked in busy studios with models, apprentices, guests, and other artists coming and going. They lived in a sociable age, in which membership in organizations and clubs helped them gain commissions and provided venues to seek advice. The artists were in constant communication with one another, offering and receiving support for their work.

Although excluded from these social networks, a remarkable number of women contributed to the American Renaissance, especially Violet Oakley, whose murals are a centerpiece of the interior decoration at the Pennsylvania State Capitol. Artists of color, such as Meta Warrick Fuller and Henry Ossawa Tanner, rarely benefitted from civic commissions, despite public recognition for their art. Their work in adjacent forms is included here in order to invite comparative study of their contributions to art featuring the human figure. Models were more diverse than the artists, and several of their stories are included as well. An exhibition devoted to the Boston model Thomas McKeller (fig. 2), held at the Isabella Stewart Gardner Museum in 2020, has helped focus attention on his contributions. Impressed by the "deliberate completeness" of Sargent's drawings, the art historian Nikki A. Greene observed in the exhibition catalogue: "When I take in the beautiful set of drawings of Thomas E. McKeller by John Singer Sargent, I *see* Thomas E. McKeller . . . fully as a man and as a depiction of mythological figures."[7] The interactions between artist and model, and the importance of the latter in shaping the civic work of this period, are a key theme in this project as well.

Professional models were important inspiration, and their roles changed over time, reflecting a shifting visual paradigm in public art from narrative to symbolic and, for the model, from actor to dancer. The title *The Dance of Life* derives from a 1923 cultural study by the British social reformer Havelock Ellis, for whom dance provided a metaphor for human activity and creative experience.[8] The modern dance pioneer Ruth St. Denis enthusiastically reviewed Ellis's book, which she called the "Dancers' Bible" for "its power to feed and stimulate the mind of the dancer"; she hailed the author's understanding of the vibrant ties between dance and life.[9] In his book, Ellis pointed to St. Denis as well as to Isadora Duncan as contemporary exemplars of revivalism in modern American dance. Their sense of historical consciousness, reframed for the modern age, was as characteristic of the era's murals and sculpture as it was of dance.

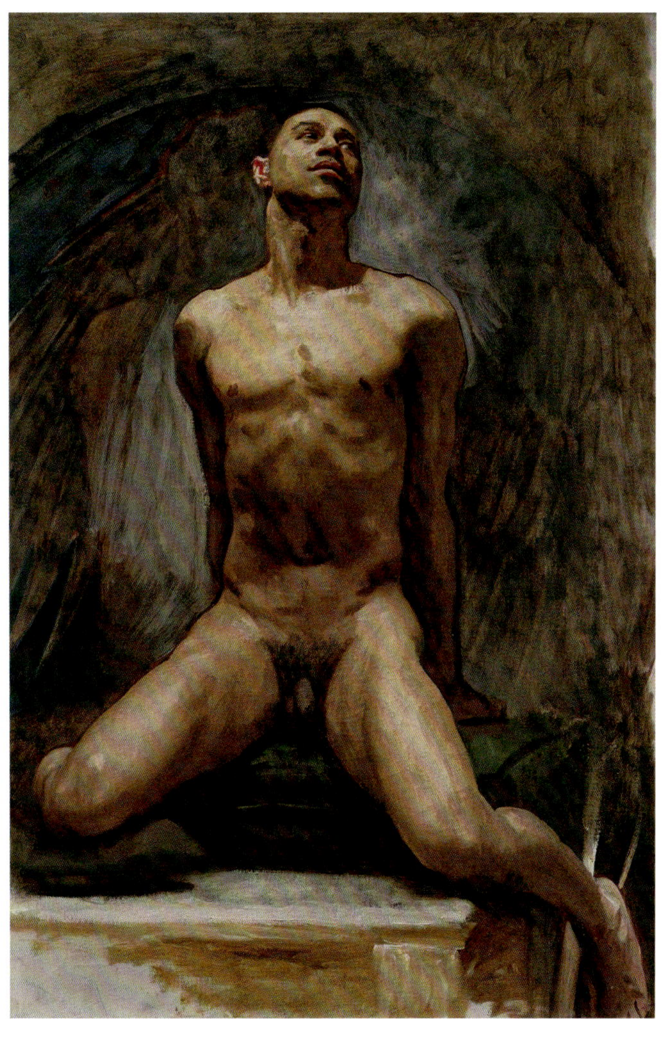

FIG. 2. John Singer Sargent, *Nude Study of Thomas E. McKeller,* ca. 1917–20. Oil on canvas, 49½ × 33¼ in. (125.73 × 84.45 cm). Museum of Fine Arts, Boston, Henry H. and Zoe Oliver Sherman Fund, 1986.60

The artists' awareness of contemporary artistic developments, coupled with their exclusive focus on modern bodies, is a reflection of their aspirations to address their own time. Although the humanism of the Italian Renaissance was a source of inspiration, its value lay in its relevance to their own era. As modern dance emerged simultaneously in the United States, it reflected a change in the performing arts that echoed the visual arts. Where theater of the late nineteenth century was characterized by lavishly produced spectacles of storytelling, the twentieth century brought natural, energetic movement to the American stage. St. Denis along with Duncan, Loïe Fuller, and Anna Pavlova introduced poetic forms of bodily expression, often hybrids of historic and popular dance that reached new audiences. Sharyn Udall has discussed how these dancers, especially Pavlova, were able to transform their appeal to artists into lasting fame as subjects of modern American art.[10] As the era progressed, the movements and meanings of the figures in civic murals (fig. 3) and sculptures reflected a change in prevailing idiom, from theater to dance, story to symbol.

Duncan, whose naturalism Ellis admired, conducted her own research in the British Museum's library at the same time that Abbey was there working on his studies for the Pennsylvania State Capitol. Abbey's figures in his final mural, *The Hours*—especially those of daylight—could be quotations from the work of Duncan's dance company, whose "living beauty" was a direct source for other murals at the time.[11] The parallels between the vital expressions of

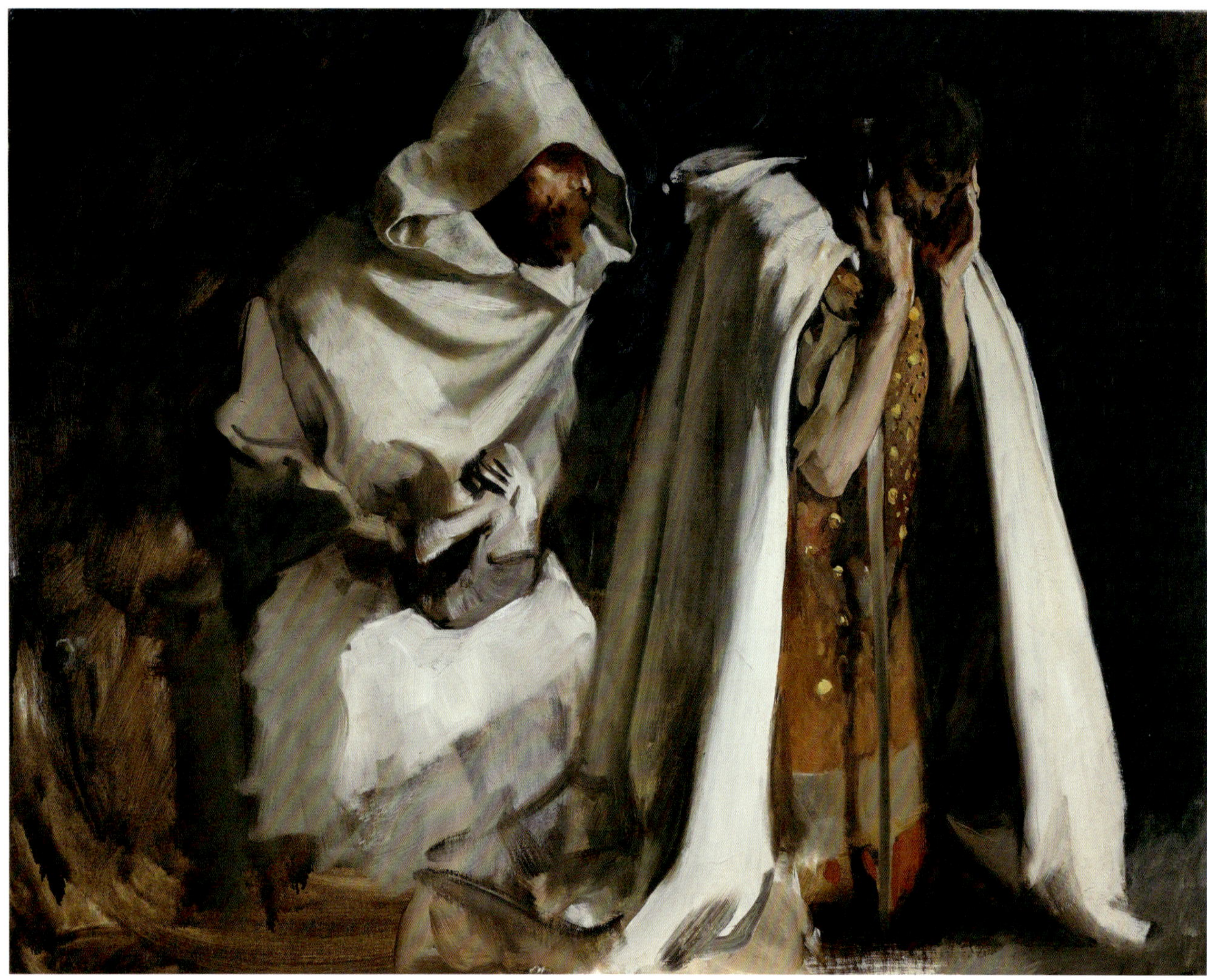

FIG. 3. Edwin Austin Abbey, Figure Study for *The Quest and Achievement of the Holy Grail* in the Boston Public Library, ca. 1890–1901. Oil on canvas, 28 × 35¾ in. (71.1 × 90.8 cm). Yale University Art Gallery, New Haven, Conn., Edwin Austin Abbey Memorial Collection, 1937.2092

American civic art at the turn of the twentieth century and the emerging vocabulary of modern dance are resonant, especially in the artists' working studies, in which the pose of a model and choreographed composition suggest performative acts of creative invention.

NOTES

1. Oliver W. Larkin, *Art and Life in America* (rev. ed.; New York: Holt, Rinehart and Winston, 1964), 295.
2. Drew Gilpin Faust, *This Republic of Suffering: Death and the American Civil War* (New York: Alfred A. Knopf, 2008), xi.
3. S.N.C. [Susan Nichols Carter], "Paintings at the Centennial Exhibition," *Art Journal* 2 (1876): 284.
4. Doreen Bolger Burke and Catherine Hoover Voorsanger, "The Hudson River School in Eclipse," in *American Paradise: The World of the Hudson River School*, ed. John K. Howat, exh. cat. (New York: The Metropolitan Museum of Art, 1987), 71, 89.

5. La Farge cited in Royal Cortissoz, *John La Farge: A Memoir and a Study* (Boston: Houghton Mifflin, 1911), 94.
6. Russell Sturgis, "The Field of Art—As to a Museum of Studies," *Scribner's* 42, no. 6 (December 1907): 765.
7. Nikki A. Greene, "Thomas McKeller *sous rature*: John Singer Sargent's Erasure of a ~~Black~~ Model," in *Boston's Apollo: Thomas McKeller and John Singer Sargent*, ed. Nathaniel Silver, exh. cat. (Boston: Isabella Stewart Gardner Museum, 2020).
8. Havelock Ellis, *The Dance of Life* (New York: Houghton Mifflin, 1923).
9. Ruth St. Denis, "The Dance of Life: An Appreciation of Havelock Ellis," *Birth Control Review* 8, no. 2 (February 1924): 53.
10. [Mary Fanton Roberts?], "Modern Dancing as an Inspiration for Mural Decoration," *Touchstone* 6, no. 3 (December 1919): 132.
11. Sharyn R. Udall, "Anna Pavlova in America: Performance, Popular Culture, and the Commodification of Desire," in *Dance: American Art, 1830–1960*, ed. Jane Dini, exh. cat. (Detroit: Detroit Institute of Arts, 2016), 149.

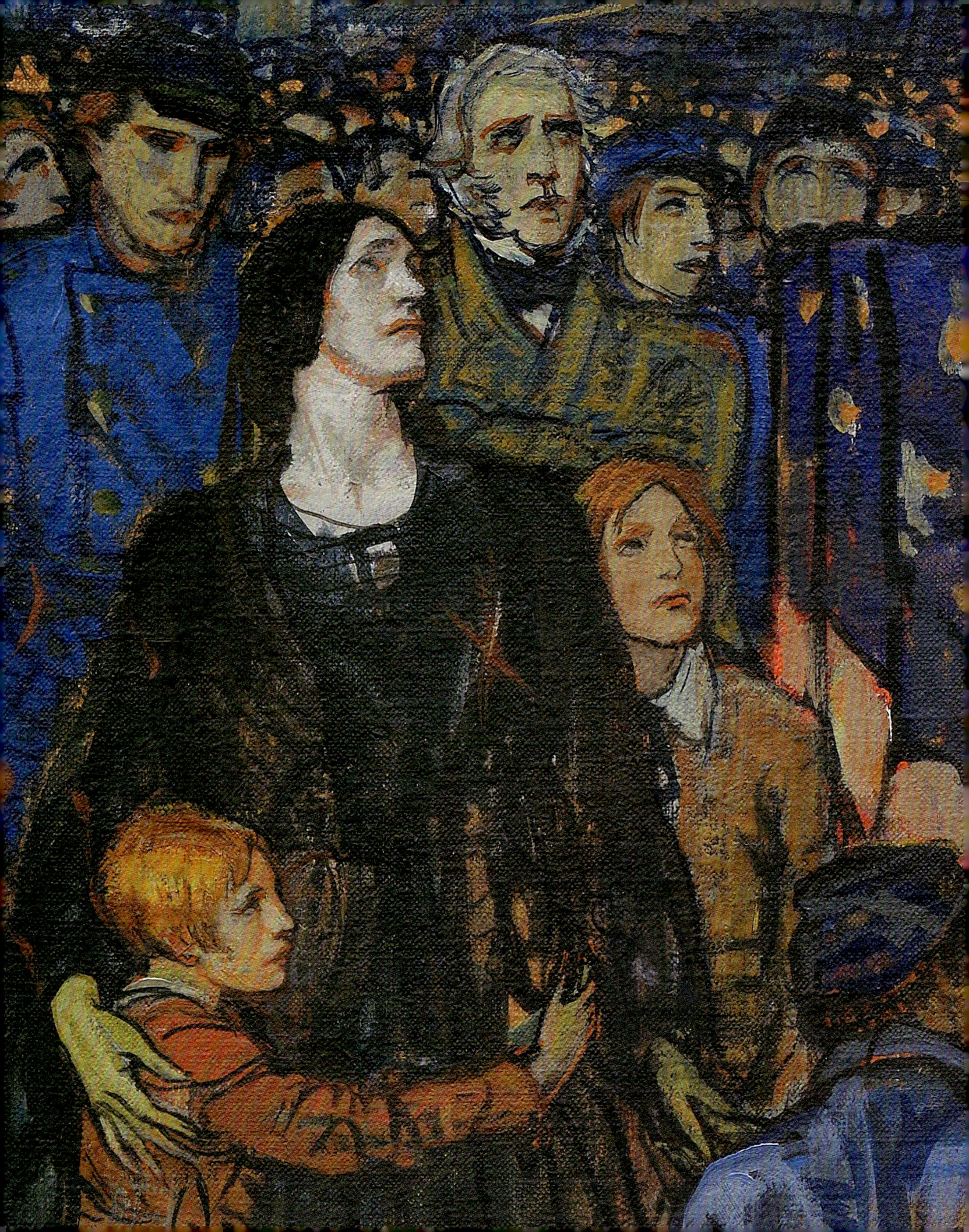

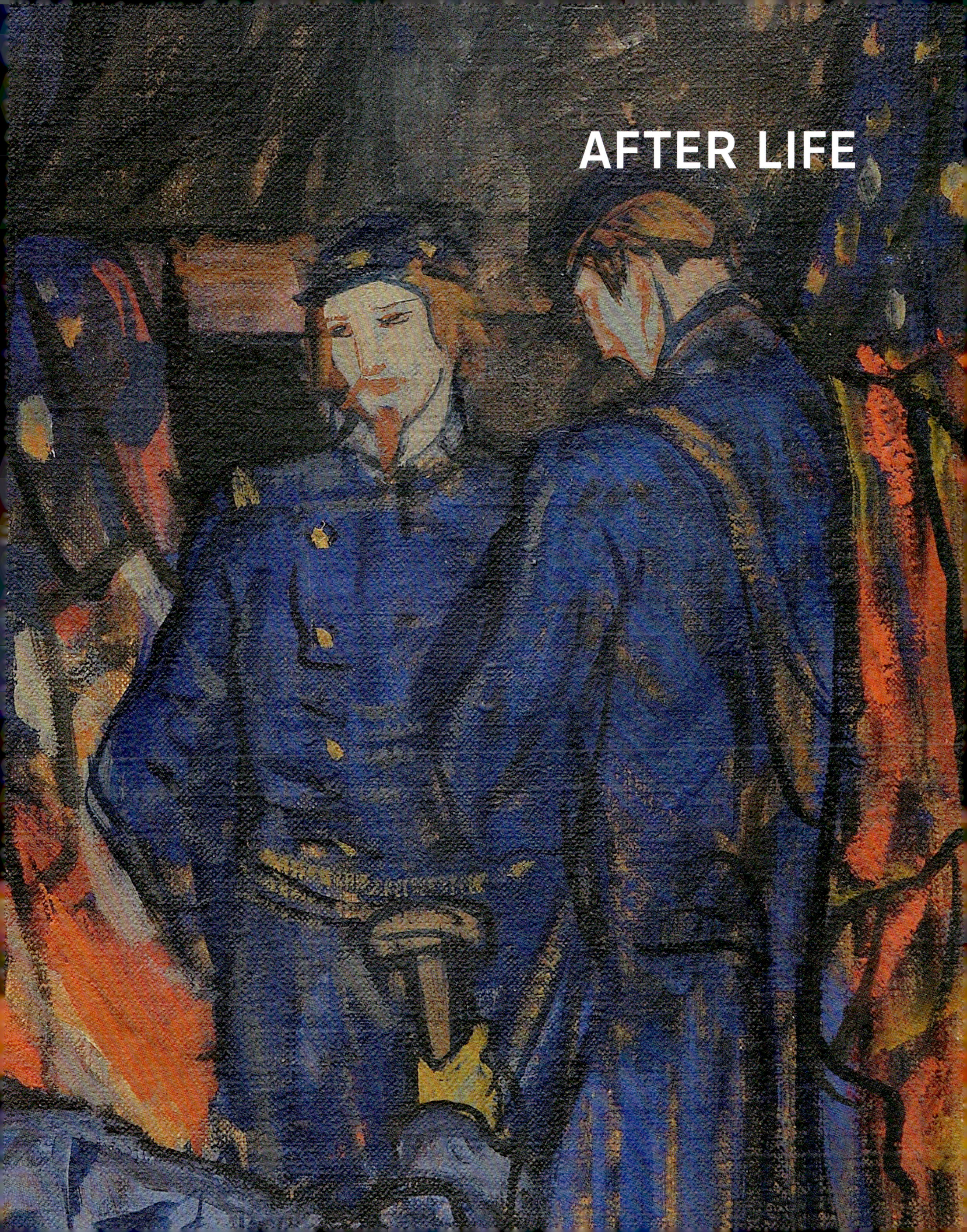

AFTER LIFE

Victory strides forward with right arm extended, reaching for something unseen but on which its eyes focus: "the seer of visions: peace is ahead and an end of war."[1] In the guise of an ancient Greek, the figure is dressed in a flowing chiton, with angel's wings, a laurel wreath atop the head, and a palm frond in the left hand (cat. 1). The laurel and palm represent victory, with the latter having the added symbolism of victory over death in the Christian tradition.[2] As a beginning to this volume and the exhibition it accompanies, such vital, determined movement into the future is emblematic of the hopes of this era as well as the ineffable presence of the recent past.

The sculpture was adapted from Augustus Saint-Gaudens's Sherman Monument in New York City, which features Victory leading the resolute Union general William Tecumseh Sherman, mounted on horseback, on the march through Georgia that destroyed the viability of the Confederacy in 1864. This would be Saint-Gaudens's most critically acclaimed work, gaining long-sought international recognition when versions were shown in Paris in 1899 and 1900. Scholars have identified the primary model for the figure of Victory as Hettie Anderson, a woman of mixed-race ancestry, and illuminated her story.[3] Choosing a woman of color to represent Victory in the war that ended slavery in America is significant for the artist who also created the Robert Gould Shaw and Massachusetts 54th Regiment Memorial (see cat. 16) in Boston, perhaps the best-known portrayal of African American soldiers in the country.

CAT. 1 Augustus Saint-Gaudens (American, born Ireland, 1848–1907, HON. 1905)
Victory, from the Sherman Monument, modeled ca. 1892–1903, cast by 1916
Gilded bronze, 42¾ × 24 × 33 in. (108.6 × 61 × 83.8 cm)
Toledo Museum of Art, Ohio, Purchased with funds from the Florence Scott Libbey Bequest in Memory of her Father, Maurice A. Scott, 1986.34

In *Victory*, the monumentality of the Sherman Monument is preserved not only in the refinement and detailed appearance of the figure but also in its remarkably animated and naturalistic movement through space: it feels finished and complete, not like a fragment. The sculpture is a full expression of an idea represented in the final monument, here extracted and inviting appreciation—a reflection of the artist's continued engagement with the subject after the unveiling of the Sherman Monument in 1903.[4]

Saint-Gaudens had trained in Paris, one of the first in a new, postwar generation of American artists to study abroad, and became America's most accomplished sculptor. Whereas earlier American artists and patrons had sought to present national identity in their work, those of the Centennial era looked outward, considering themselves part of a cosmopolitan world of art. Saint-Gaudens, in particular, would facilitate many of the early public commissions of his peers across the country. In an age of social connection, Saint-Gaudens was a well-known and well-liked tastemaker who embraced the opportunity to encourage other artists and expand the reach of art into American life.

Although widely interpreted as female and white, the gilded figure's presentation can be read as ambiguous—a recurring attribute of allegories during this period—because the artist masked the muscled torso and waist in clothing that historically had no primary gender association.[5] *Victory* invites consideration about the role of ambiguity in such works. Sculptors' conversion from white marble to dark bronze as their primary medium reflected the changing aesthetic emphasis from classicism to vitalism in rich tones of brown and gold. Admired and preserved in their own time,

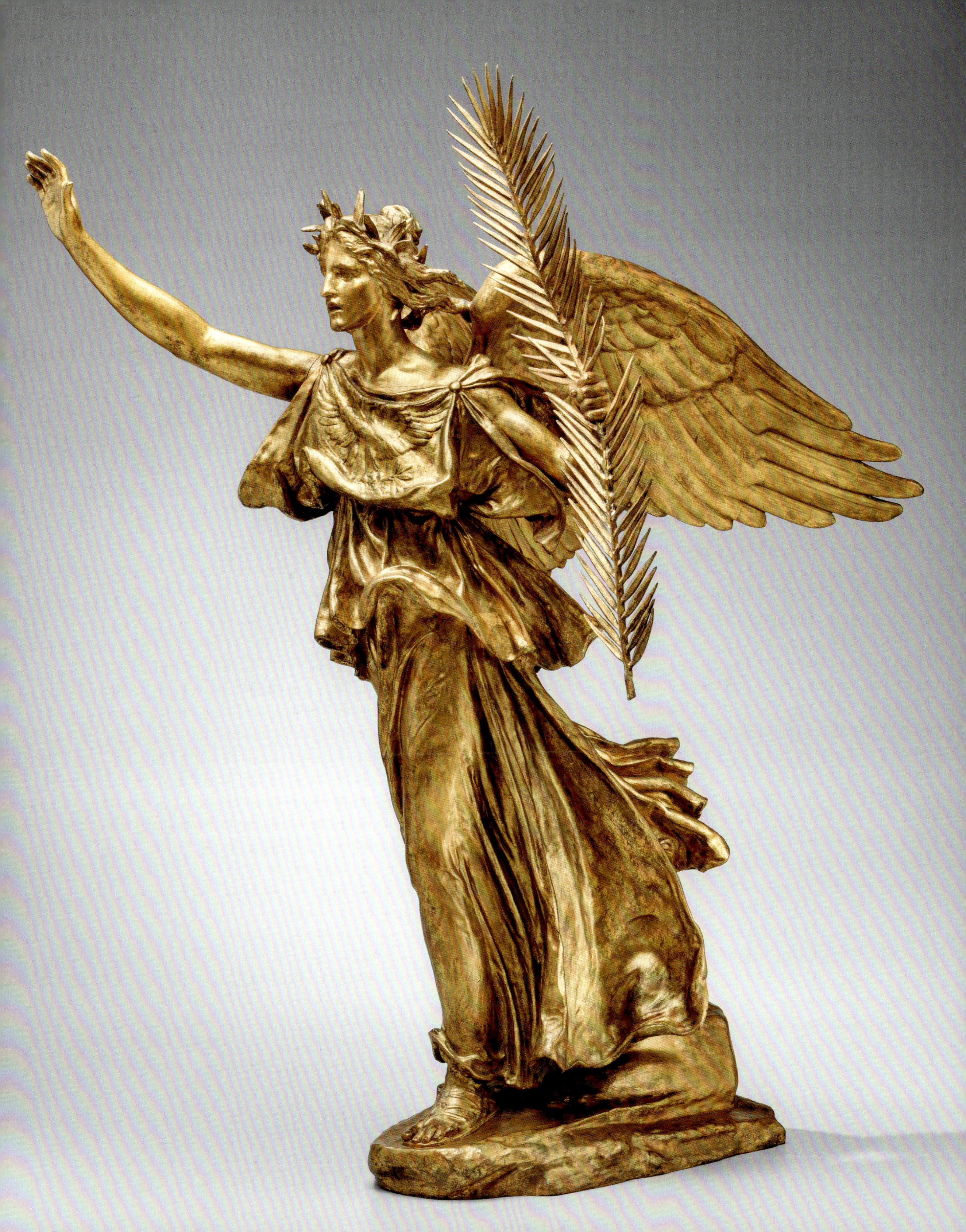

artworks such as *Victory* illuminate the concerns of a historic age that resound in the present.

Although the post-Reconstruction era was marked by widespread violence, oppression, retrenchment, and exploitation based on class, race, gender, and citizenship, it also experienced vertiginous economic development and social progressivism. In the northern states especially, artists like Saint-Gaudens used their work in dialogue with their time, not obedience to it. Their most compelling subjects struggle with the transformations and anxieties of the age, reckoning with the forces that threatened a society whose fragility was proven.

NOTES

1. Kenyon Cox, "The Sherman Statue," *Nation* 76 (June 18, 1903): 491; reprinted in Kenyon Cox, *Old Masters and New: Essays in Art Criticism* (New York: Duffield, 1908), 282.
2. James Hall, *Dictionary of Subjects and Symbols in Art*, rev. ed. (New York: Harper and Row, 1979), 231.
3. William E. Hagans, "Saint-Gaudens, Zorn, and the Goddesslike Miss Anderson," *American Art* 16, no. 2 (2002): 81; and Eve M. Kahn, "The Woman Who Was Victory . . . ," *Magazine Antiques* 188, no. 5 (September/October 2021): 68–75.
4. Based on a copyright mark found on the sculpture, the date of this Gorham cast has been revised to 1912 or after, as proposed by John H. Dryfhout in *The Work of Augustus Saint-Gaudens* (Hanover, N.H.: University Press of New England, 1982), 256, pl. 184. Also see the related object entry in Thayer Tolles, *Augustus Saint-Gaudens in the Metropolitan Museum of Art*, exh. cat. (New York: The Metropolitan Museum of Art, 2009), 74, pl. 44.
5. Scholar Renée Ater evocatively characterizes the identities of the "un-raced" figure and model as "subsumed under allegorical representation"; Ater, "Female Allegory, Race, and the Civil War Memorial," in *Monuments and Myths: The America of Sculptors Augustus Saint-Gaudens and Daniel Chester French*, ed. Andrew Eschelbacher, exh. cat. (New York: American Federation of Arts, 2023), 46.

Beginnings

The American Renaissance began at Boston's Trinity Church in the frigid winter of 1876–77, during a short—feverish—three-month mural campaign to decorate the new building. The work was led by the painter and designer John La Farge, who was supported by a team of promising assistants that included Augustus Saint-Gaudens. The ambitious designs and figurative subjects that resulted offered new inspiration animated by the "principle of life" sought by critics.[1] That a church in Boston could initiate a wider civic art movement, mostly in the northern states, reflected the community's self-image of moral authority and progressive leadership, espousing faith, public education, and civic investment. This vision extended to the blank slate of its newly filled Back Bay, where Trinity Church would later be joined by another American Renaissance landmark, the Boston Public Library, across Copley Square.

Overlooking the nave and transept from the base of the church's iconic central tower are monumental biblical figures, which occupy the broad arch spandrels of architect H. H. Richardson's Romanesque Revival structure. The Old Testament prophets Isaiah and Jeremiah share the south wall. Each is depicted swathed in luxuriant fabrics that incorporate areas of vivid color and broad form in a style inspired by the early Italian Renaissance. The weighty masses of the figures, with their full beards and large expressive hands, robustly fill the allotted space. Their size contrives with their sweeping forms to suggest volume, more sculptural than painterly, and complements the shape of the arch, though the studies "exceeded the finished work in grace and expression."[2] In the monochromatic drawing of Jeremiah (cat. 2), deep shadows and relief are evident. This sculptural quality contrasts with the more sensual aspect of the watercolor of Isaiah (cat. 3), which offers a dramatic play of light across the figure and the soft, worn textures of his robes.

At Trinity Church, La Farge struggled to address technical challenges that would influence future American mural practice. Seeking a durable and light-absorptive surface, he settled on wax-based encaustic to tone down the paintings and make them fit more easefully into the adjacent stone, wood, and plaster materials.[3] This was La Farge's first major commission, and his collaborators learned from their experiments together. Some would go on to distinguished careers in public art—most as muralists, including Will Hicok Low, George Willoughby Maynard, Francis Davis Millet, and Saint-Gaudens—and La Farge's vision provided a shared starting point.

The church and its charismatic rector, Phillips Brooks, would continue to engage La Farge for decades thereafter to add to its decorations, reflecting the artist's ongoing artistic development, including in stained glass. His *Christ in Majesty* window (1883) at the church's west end remains

CAT. 2 John La Farge (American, 1835–1910, HON. 1896)
Study for *Jeremiah* in Trinity Church, Boston, ca. 1876
Charcoal and graphite, 27 11/16 × 13 3/4 in. (70.3 × 35 cm) framed
Yale University Art Gallery, New Haven, Conn., The Gherardi Davis Fund, 1974.1

CAT. 3 John La Farge (American, 1835–1910, HON. 1896)
Study for *Isaiah* in Trinity Church, Boston, 1876
Watercolor on paper, 28 × 16 in. (71.1 × 40.6 cm)
Trinity Church, Boston

CAT. 4 John La Farge (American, 1835–1910, HON. 1896)
Visit of Nicodemus to Christ, 1880
Oil on canvas, 42 1/4 × 35 1/8 in. (107.3 × 89.2 cm)
Smithsonian American Art Museum, Washington, D.C., Gift of William T. Evans, 1909.7.37

one of the most admired stained-glass works in the country, offering Brooks a constant dialogue with and inspiration from the luminous, monumental figure of Christ as he looked out from the altar.[4] Of two later panels (1877–78) for the nave of Trinity, La Farge's *Visit of Nicodemus to Christ* drew praise for its sophistication while remaining true to the character of the earlier tower figures. The artist revisited the subject later, including in the version shown here (cat. 4), and exhibited a related tempera study, *Visit of Nicodemus to Our Lord: Study of Moonlight and Lamplight*.[5] The title captures the evocative combination of lighting—earthly and heavenly—that illuminates the figures and their respective natures, as well as the artist's participation in the contemporary Aesthetic movement.

NOTES

1. Henry Van Brunt, "The New Dispensation of Monumental Art," *Atlantic Monthly* 43, no. 259 (May 1879): 634.
2. H. Barbara Weinberg, *The Decorative Work of John La Farge* (New York: Garland, 1977), 112–13.
3. According to the architect, La Farge chose "an encaustic medium, consisting of wax, melted with turpentine, alcohol, and Venice turpentine, in certain proportions." Henry Hobson Richardson, "A Description of Trinity Church," in *Consecration Services of Trinity Church, Boston, February 9, 1877* (Boston: Vestry, Trinity Church, 1877), 10. See also H. Barbara Weinberg, "John La Farge: Pioneer of the American Mural Movement," in *John La Farge*, exh. cat. (New York: Abbeville, 1987), 165.
4. James L. Yarnall, *John La Farge, A Biographical and Critical Study* (Farnham, Surrey, Eng.: Ashgate, 2012), 116.
5. Weinberg, *Decorative Work*, 140.

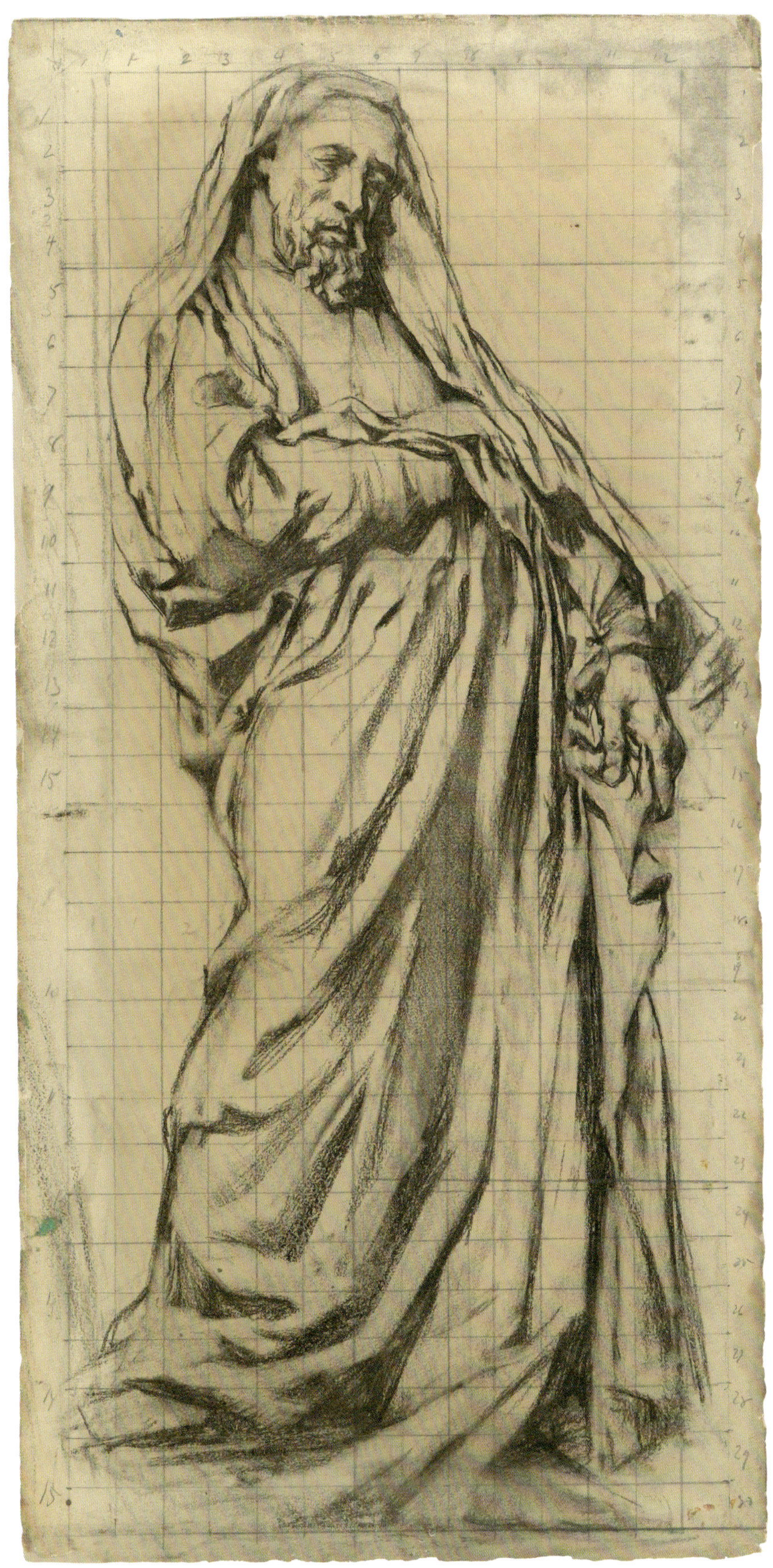

2

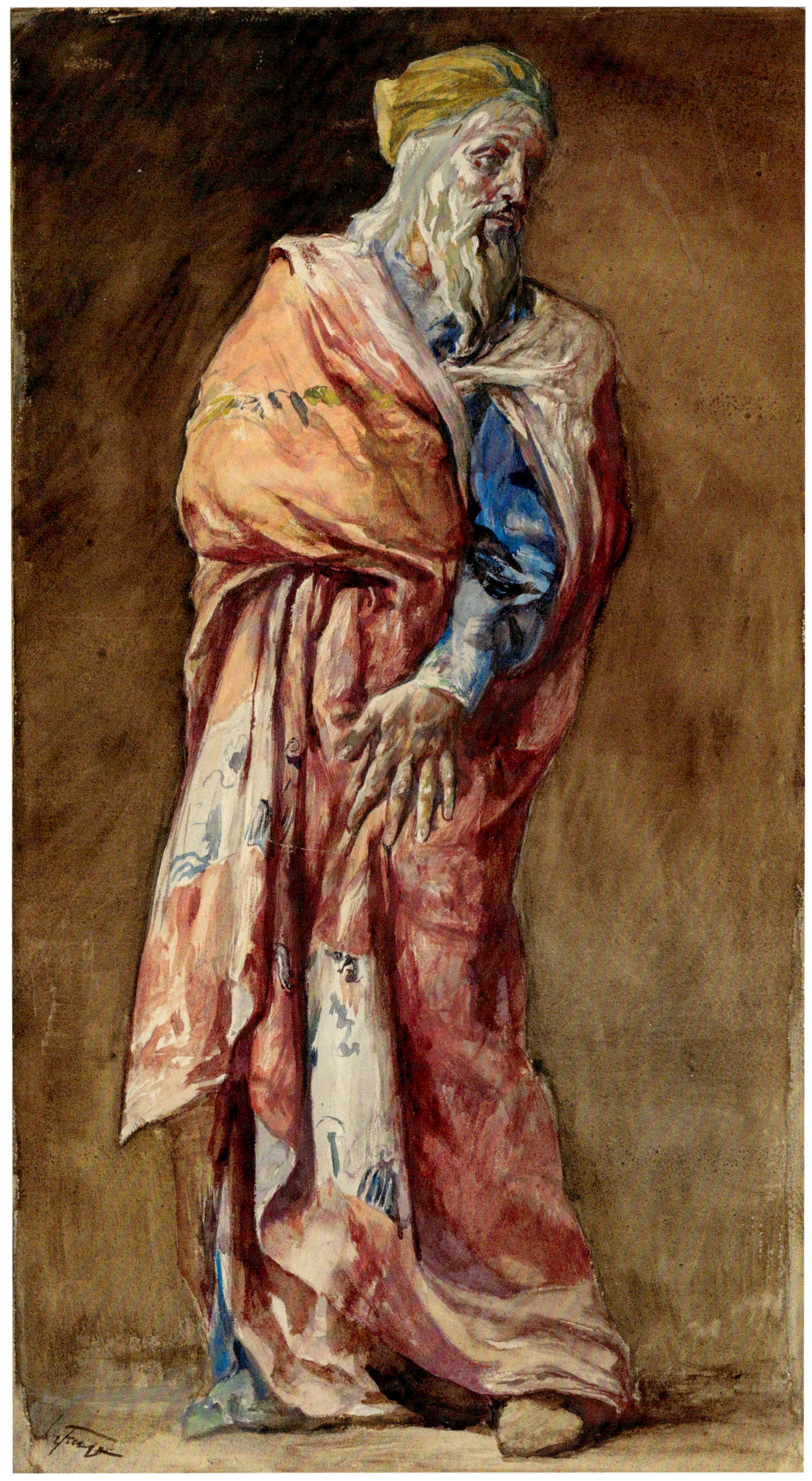

3

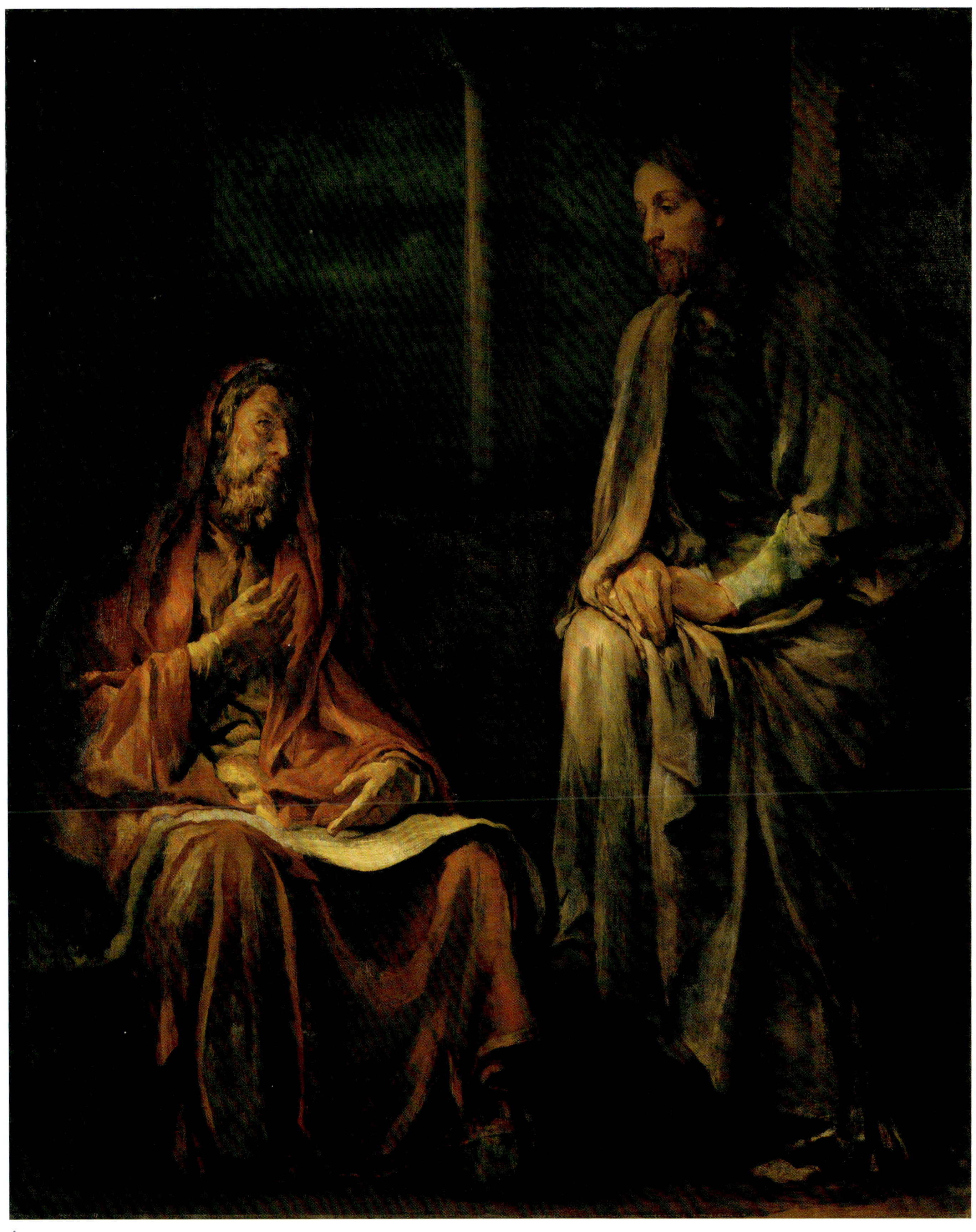

4

Inspiration

American artists' abiding fascination with the Italian Renaissance is encapsulated by the decorative program of the Walker Art Building at Bowdoin College in Brunswick, Maine. Commissioned as a permanent home for the college's museum, the building was designed by Charles Follen McKim, the New York architect responsible for many civic landmarks of the era who was equally inspired by Italian sources. The central rotunda features four large painted lunettes, each by a different artist and measuring twenty-four feet across, on the subjects of Venice, Florence, Rome, and Athens (the last painted by John La Farge, with Hettie Anderson as a model). For his depiction of Venice, Kenyon Cox celebrated the city's Renaissance masters—including Veronese, Titian, and Giorgione—in both style and subject, modeling his palette and figures on theirs.[1]

CAT. 5 Kenyon Cox (American, 1856–1919)
Study for *Venice* in the Walker Art Building, Bowdoin College, 1894
Oil and graphite on canvas, 29⅝ × 59⅝ in. (75.2 × 151.4 cm)
Bowdoin College Museum of Art, Brunswick, Maine, Gift of Colonel Leonard Cox, Mrs. Caroline Cox Lansing, and Mr. Allyn Cox

CAT. 6 Kenyon Cox (American, 1856–1919)
Study for *Venice* in the Walker Art Building, Bowdoin College, ca. 1893
Graphite on paper, 28 × 24 in. (61 × 45.7 cm)
Library of Congress, Washington, D.C.

CAT. 7 Kenyon Cox (American, 1856–1919)
Study after Michelangelo's *Night*, 1879
Charcoal and graphite on cream laid paper, 18 13/16 × 24⅝ in. (47.8 × 62.5 cm)
Cooper Hewitt, Smithsonian Design Museum, New York, Gift of Allyn Cox, 1960-83-349

Cox was one of several American artists to earn prominence in mural painting as a result of their work for the World's Columbian Exposition in Chicago in 1893, a showcase for the new generation of public artists. In Cox's case, it led directly to commissions for Bowdoin and the Library of Congress. Depicting Venice enthroned with allegories of commerce and art, alongside the landmarks and emblems of the city in the background, Cox's mural study (cat. 5) balances the strengths of his two primary types of preparatory work: pencil figure drawings and painted color studies. The meticulously—at times astonishingly—detailed pencil drawings of nudes and drapery that Cox created to refine his ideas are very close to his finished works. They describe his intended compositions and figures in an advanced stage of development, with little sense of improvisation but striking conviction and dedication to descriptive naturalism; they convey both understanding and authority.

The intense effort and pressure of application required by the drawings—they were hard work—is generally concealed in the finished murals by Cox's vivid color schemes and the sensuality when portraying a subject like Renaissance Venice (cat. 6), a place widely associated in art history with those traits. This study, however—his last before undertaking the final work—retains the crisp detail of the pencil drawings, as seen in the elaborate brocade patterns and lustrous silk drapery. Its diluted color only suggests the richness of the finished composition, invoking a tradition that Cox felt appealed to modern American tastes.[2] Cox's portrayal of Venice's reliance on the alliance of commerce and art was also significant to his and his peers' ambitions for civic art in the United States. The mural is prescriptive and didactic as well as historical. Only with the support of affluent patrons could American artists create works comparable in scale and significance to those of the Italian Renaissance.

Cox's approach reflected his education. Trained at the École des Beaux-Arts in Paris and a devoted student of art's history, he preserved for the rest of his life his own student drawing of Michelangelo's sculpture *Night* (cat. 7), created by the Italian master for the tomb of Giuliano de' Medici in Florence. The drawing earned Cox admission to the studio of Jean-Léon Gérôme at the École, where he would study for three years, and records an important, aspirational transition in his early career as he committed himself to a more disciplined approach to drawing.[3] Cox paired careful modeling of the sculpture's surface with vivid shadows to accentuate the volumetric presence of Michelangelo's reclining nude. The beauty in the figure is not conventional, but its energy and character were celebrated in Cox's time and remain among the most admired achievements of the Italian Renaissance. For Cox to take on such a challenging subject testifies to his seriousness and ambition. The study of the expressive body—which Michelangelo "pushed to its highest point," in Cox's words—would remain Cox's standard of excellence; as a muralist, it provided the grammar of his civic practice, as it would for many of his peers.[4]

NOTES

1. Richard V. West, "The Walker Art Building Murals," *Bowdoin College Museum of Art, Occasional Papers* 1 (1972): 7–13.
2. H. Wayne Morgan, *Kenyon Cox, 1856–1919: A Life in American Art* (Kent, Ohio: Kent State University Press, 1994), 141.
3. Ibid., 46; and Richard Murray, "Kenyon Cox and the Art of Drawing," *Drawing* 3, no. 1 (May–June 1981): 3.
4. Kenyon Cox, *Michelangelo* (New York: Mentor Association, 1914), 3.

"VENICE" DECORATION IN
BOWDOIN COLLEGE
SCALE-DRAWING -
KENYON COX

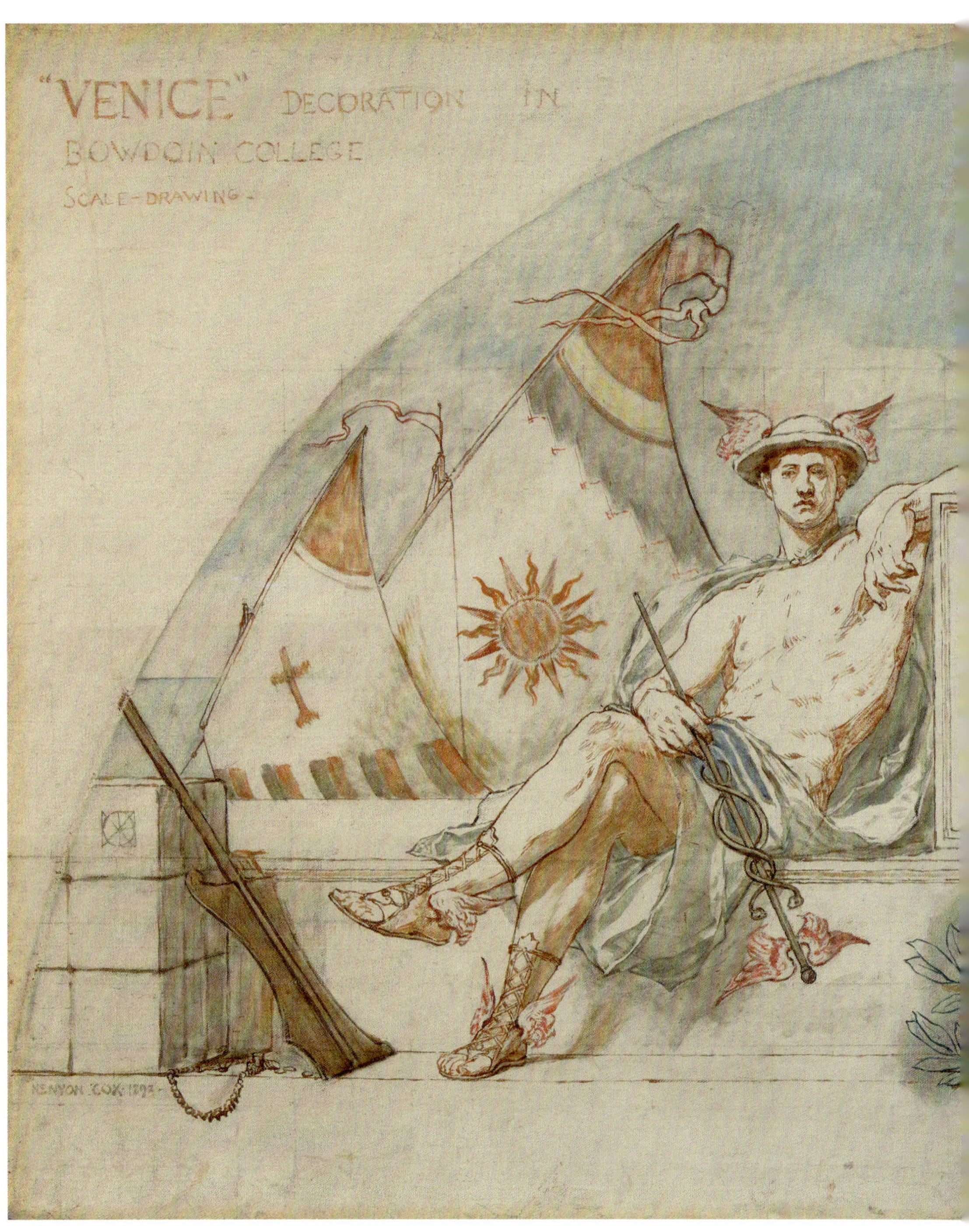

5

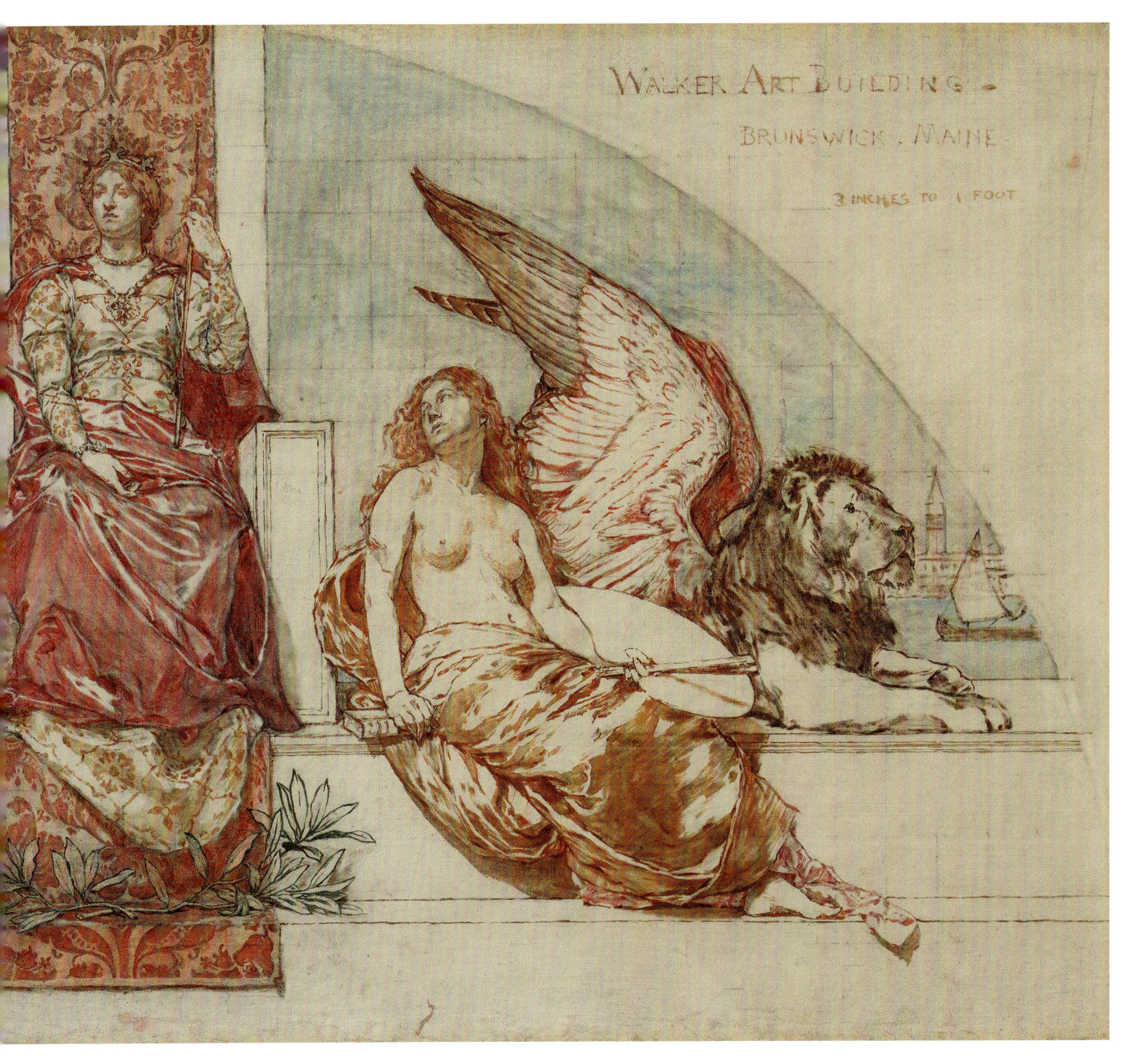
WALKER ART BUILDING
BRUNSWICK . MAINE
3 INCHES TO 1 FOOT

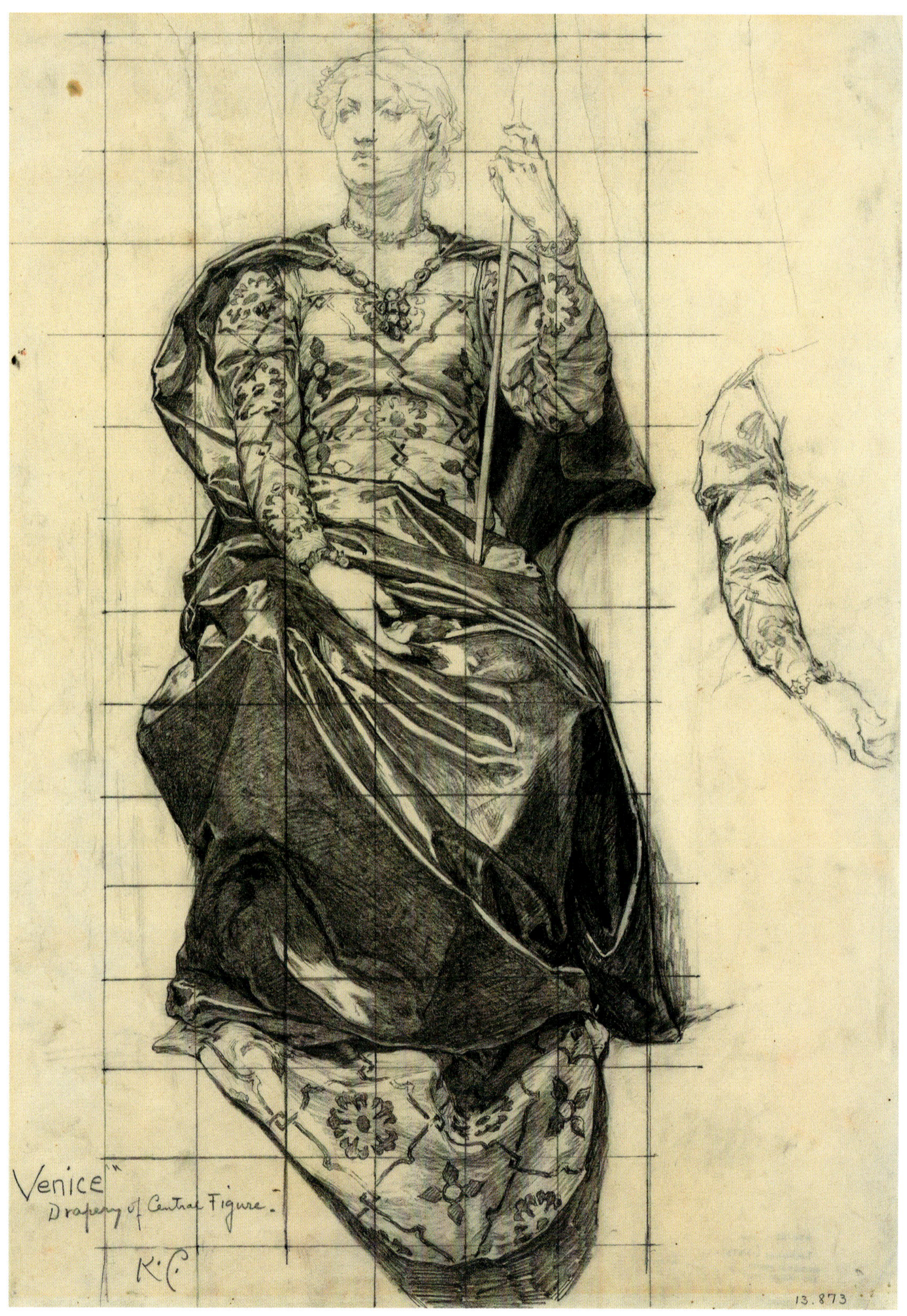

6

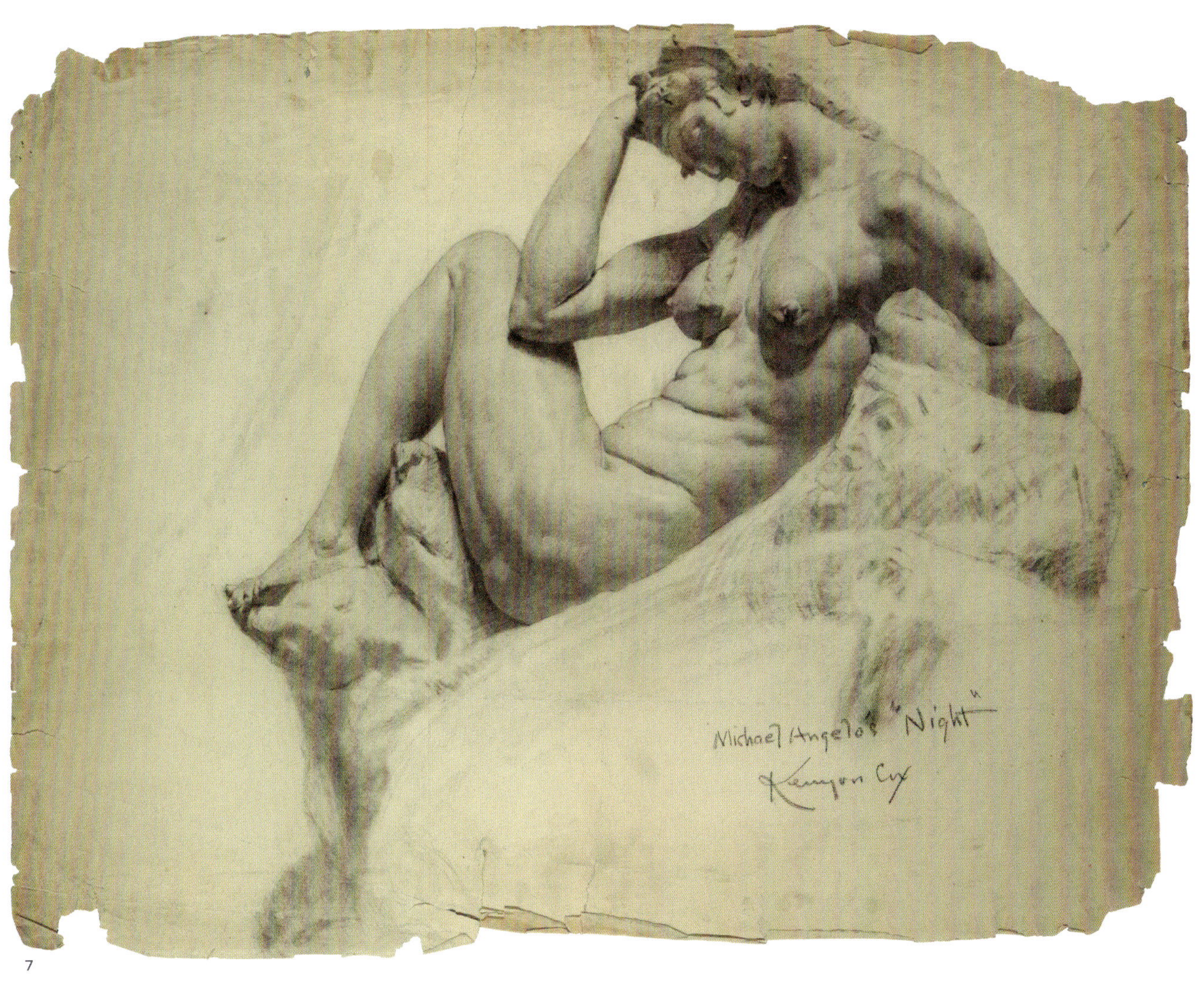

7

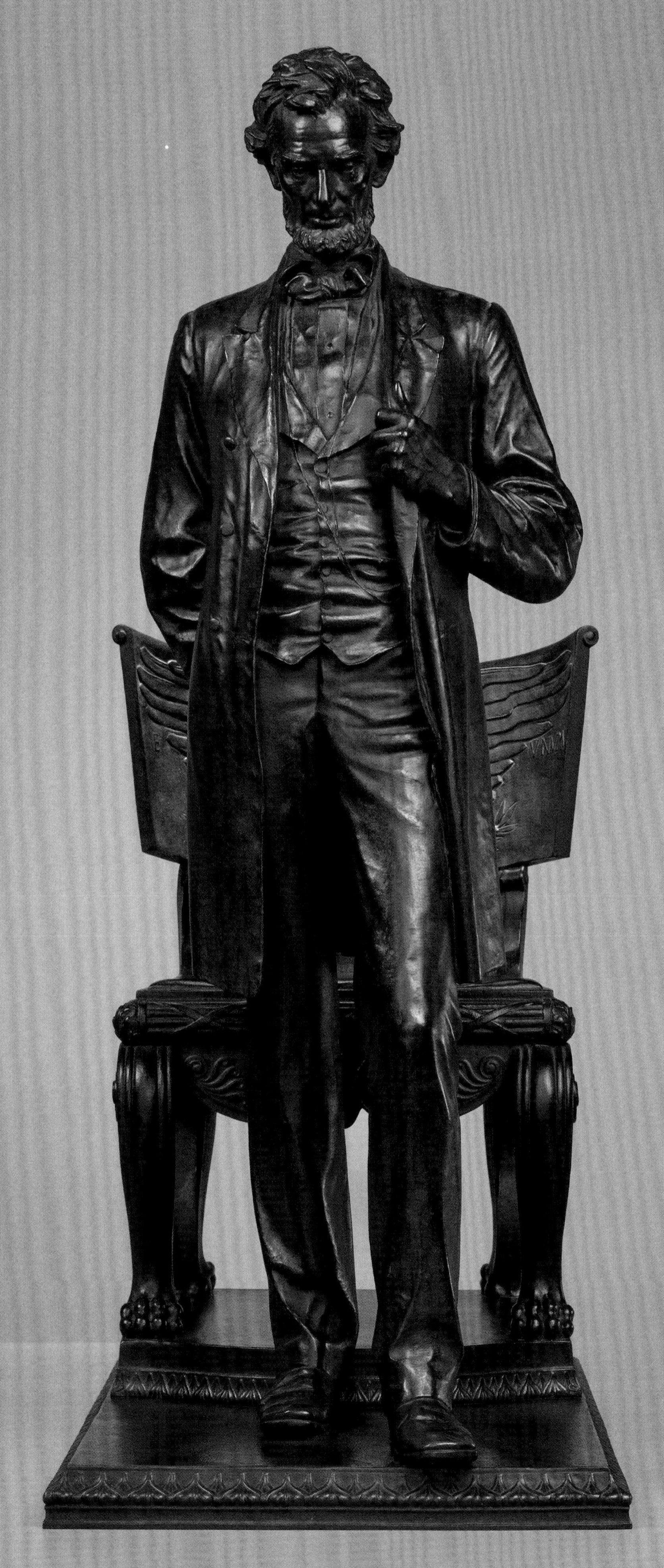

Lincoln's Body

The most famous and most recognized figure in American visual culture at the end of the nineteenth century was Abraham Lincoln. His assassination not only marked the end of the Civil War in 1865 but also fixed his image in the nation's imagination. Lincoln's ungainly features and expressive gravity had already reached the widest audience in American history during his first presidential campaign in 1860, thanks to the mass distribution of the iconic photograph by Mathew Brady on the day of his Cooper Institute speech.[1] After his death, Lincoln's likeness became nearly ubiquitous in the northern states. The prevalence of his image and its reach as a national icon established a different sort of figural ideal as Lincoln became synonymous with the Civil War and national unity. His lanky proportions made his body distinctive and easily recognized.

Unlike the active and expansive depictions of George Washington, whose image had largely dominated American visual culture until the Civil War, those of Lincoln tended to be introverted and contemplative. Augustus Saint-Gaudens's *Standing Lincoln* (cat. 8) presents the rumpled figure of the president standing apart from the oversized neoclassical chair of state. Developed from his own observation of Lincoln's standing posture in 1860 and plaster casts of Lincoln's face and hands taken by Leonard Volk that same year, Saint-Gaudens's portrait offers a sense of individual imperfection and direct observation, rather than idealization.[2] The distinctive upright pose reminds viewers of his stately presence. Lincoln, the sculpture insists, was singular, admired for the nobility of his spirit and mind, not his physical prowess.

Violet Oakley's depiction of Lincoln at Gettysburg (cat. 9; detail below), the town forty miles southwest of the Pennsylvania capitol in Harrisburg for which it was commissioned, shows the president in a posture strikingly similar to that in Saint-Gaudens's sculpture, elevated in a format recognized as a Christian apotheosis: a sainted figure raised to heaven. The Battle of Gettysburg

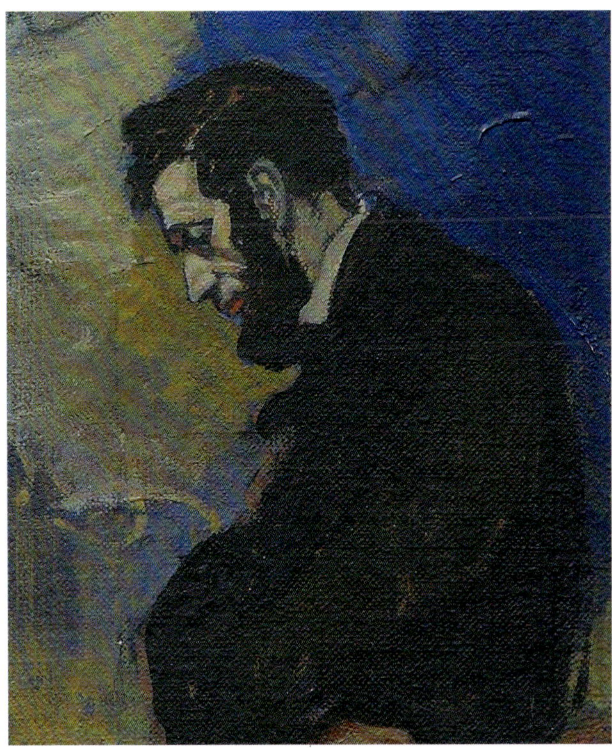

CAT. 8 Augustus Saint-Gaudens (American, born Ireland, 1848–1907, HON. 1905)
Abraham Lincoln: The Man (Standing Lincoln), modeled 1884–87, this cast ca. 1911–12
Bronze with dark reddish-brown patina, 40 × 30½ × 16¼ in. (101.6 × 77.5 × 41.3 cm)
Yale University Art Gallery, New Haven, Conn., Gift of Allison V. Armour, B.A. 1884, 1937.193

CAT. 9 Violet Oakley (American, 1874–1961)
Study for *Lincoln at Gettysburg—The Preservation of the Union* in the Pennsylvania State Capitol, ca. 1911
Oil on canvas, 40¼ × 26¼ in. (102.2 × 66.7 cm)
Pennsylvania Capitol Preservation Committee, Harrisburg

would prove to be the turning point of the war, and Lincoln's memorial address calling for the dedication of a national cemetery there remains a touchstone of American cultural memory. Oakley portrays Lincoln looking downward from a dais at a widow and her two sons, rather than addressing the assembled soldiers and citizens.[3] His profile, set against a dramatically illuminated sky, creates a symbolic register for the final mural painting, which is saturated in a rich blue, the color of the Union, rather than a more descriptive representation of the actual site.

NOTES

1. Harold Holzer, G. S. Boritt, and Mark E. Neely, *The Lincoln Image: Abraham Lincoln and the Popular Print* (New York: Scribner, 1984), 21.
2. Thayer Tolles, "'Refined Picturesqueness': Augustus Saint-Gaudens and the Concept of Finish," in Catherine Gaich and Anne Dopffer, *Augustus Saint-Gaudens, 1848–1907: A Master of American Sculpture*, exh. cat. (Paris: Éditions Somogy, 1999), 63–64, 126.
3. Unveiled on Lincoln's birthday in 1917, the painting is believed to adapt a scene from Elsie Singmaster's 1913 short-story collection, *Gettysburg: Stories of the Red Harvest and the Aftermath*, featuring its fictional widow Mary Bowman, for whom Lincoln's address is prophetic; Bailey Van Hook, *Violet Oakley: An Artist's Life* (Newark: University of Delaware Press, 2016), 219–21, 225. See also *A Sacred Challenge: Violet Oakley and the Pennsylvania Capitol Murals* (Harrisburg: Pennsylvania Capitol Preservation Committee, 2002), 72, 157n82.

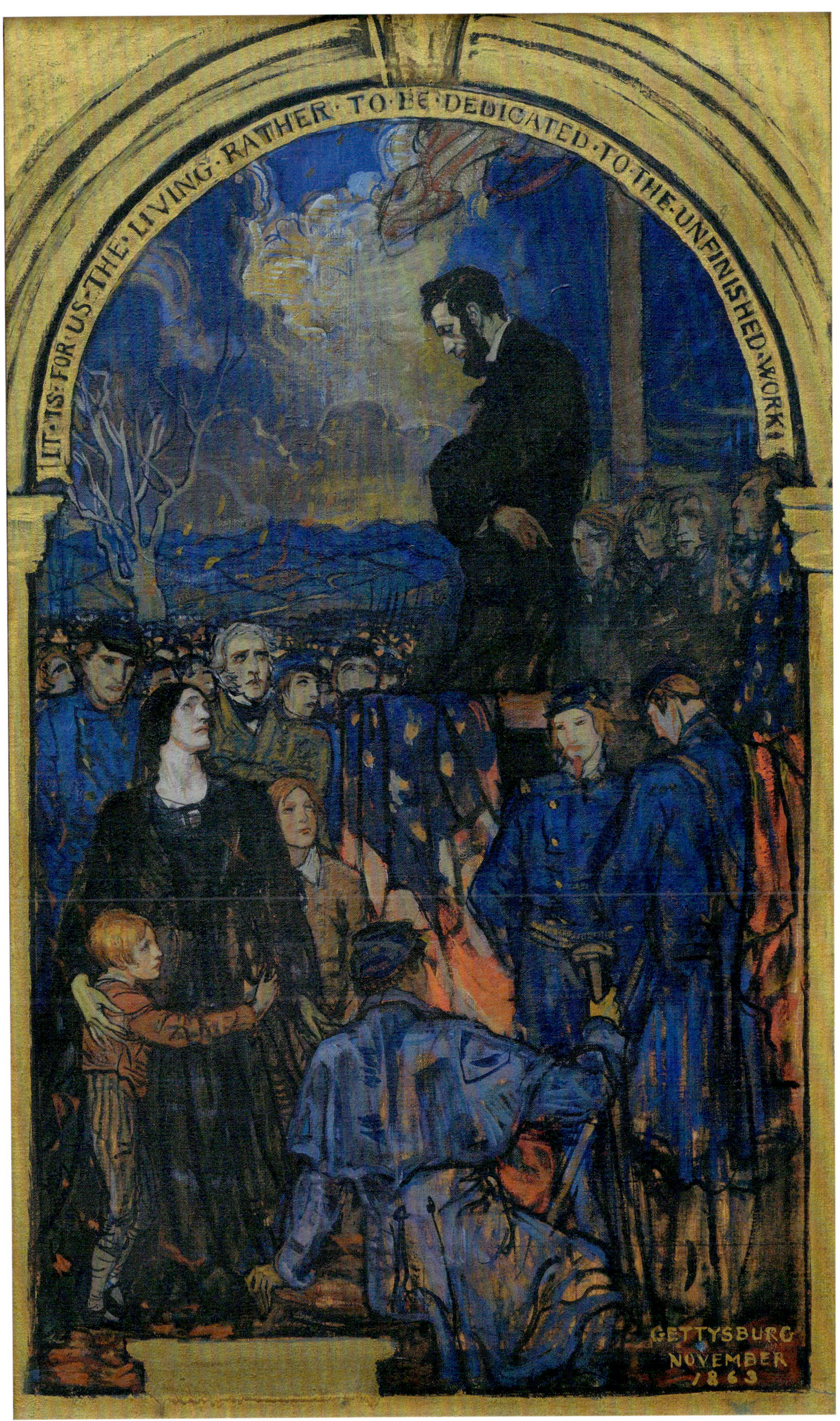
IT·IS·FOR·US·THE·LIVING·RATHER·TO·BE·DEDICATED·TO·THE·UNFINISHED·WORK·
GETTYSBURG
NOVEMBER
1863

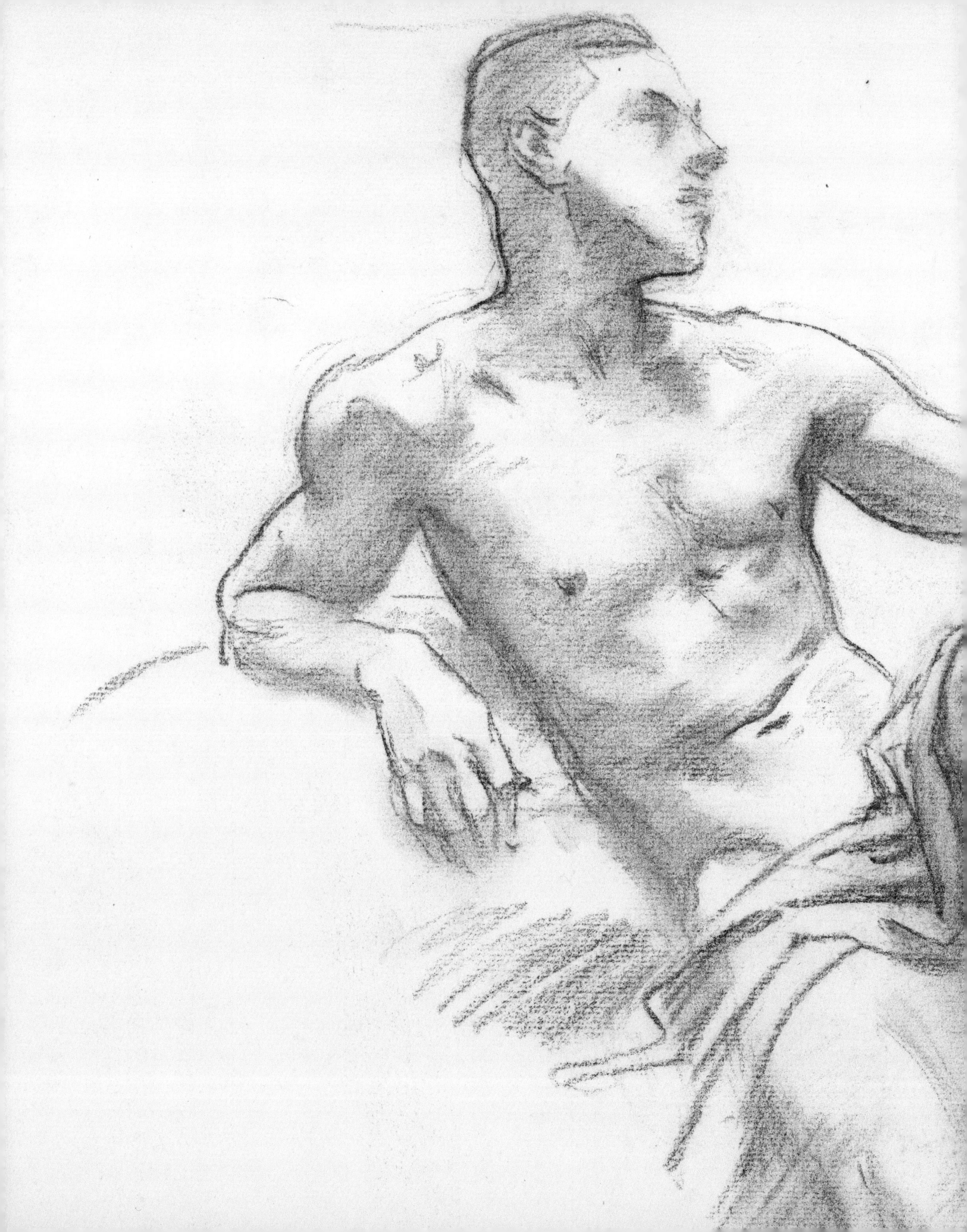

MODELS

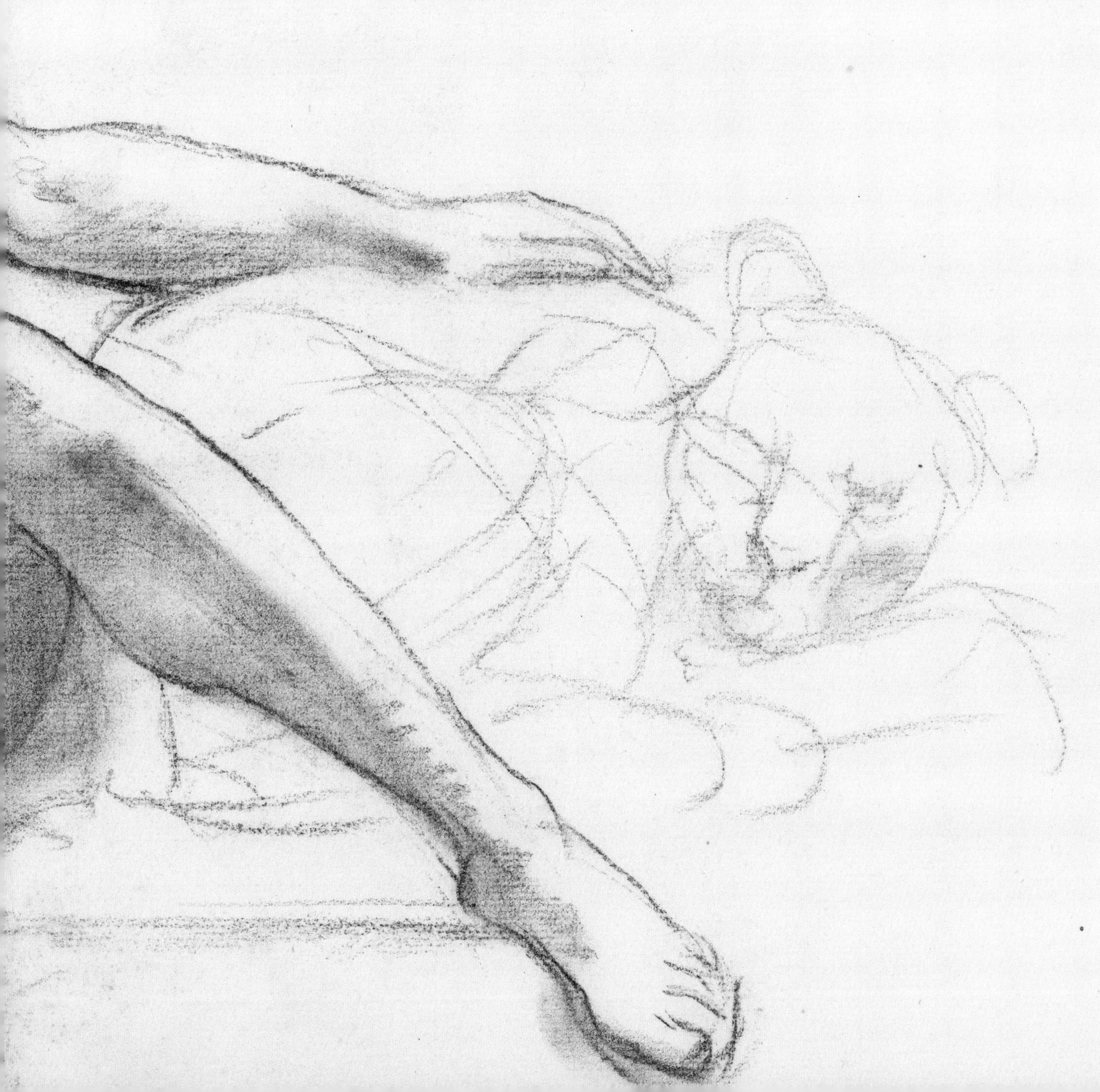

Henry James's short story "The Real Thing" (1892) describes the inability of amateur models to pose, even as themselves. In the story, a couple of poor aristocrats try to earn extra money as models only to discover that they have no inclination, even when cast as the very aristocrats they are. The artist's conundrum is resolved at last when he hires a professional model, Miss Churm, and discovers the fluidity of performance and character that he needs.[1]

An artist's model has to be many things, versatile especially. Models must occupy an almost unlimited repertoire of poses for long stretches of time, enduring discomfort, fatigue, and boredom. They must be able to assume virtually any role, great or small, divine or mortal, male or female, with the adaptability of an actor and the strength and flexibility of an athlete. At the turn of the twentieth century, talented models were difficult to find and retain, and they often worked for several artists and academies to sustain continuous employment.[2]

Despite the inscription on John Singer Sargent's oil study (cat. 10) identifying the sitter as Pietro Corsi, Antonio Corsi is believed to be the subject, his name perhaps misremembered in early acquaintance or hindsight. The latter enjoyed remarkable fame, which led him to a second career as an actor in silent films. He could well have been the inspiration for a poor Italian model, Oronte, described in James's story. The inscription may be in error, but no record of another model with the same last name is known. By his own account, he was the model for seventy different figures in Sargent's *Triumph of Religion* murals and sixty in Edwin Austin Abbey's *Holy Grail* cycle for the Boston Public Library.[3]

Corsi's value for artists was his ability to communicate ideas with his body. In many studies from this period, such as the drapery study by Sargent (cat. 11; detail below), the figure was developed separately from the face. In allegories, faces

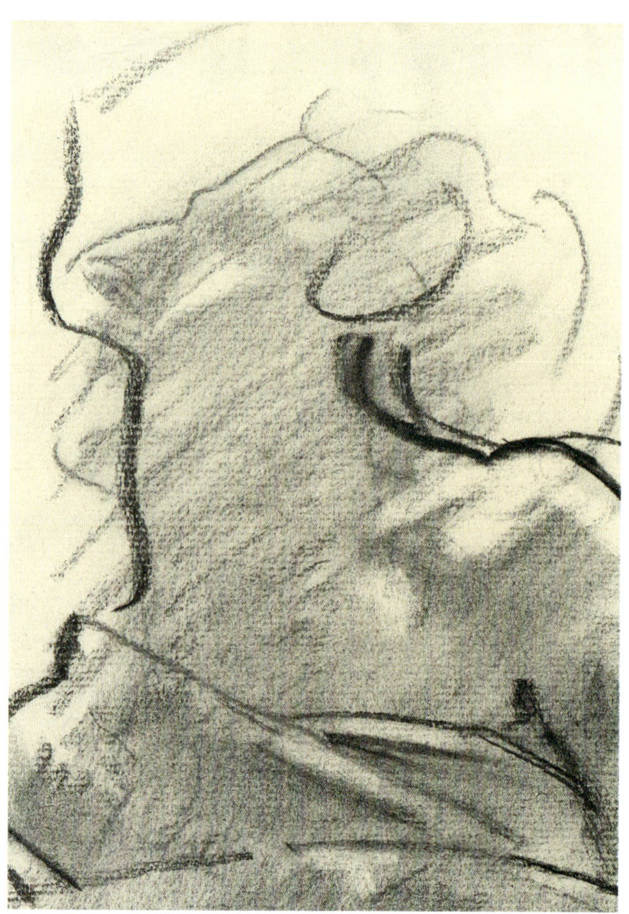

CAT. 10 John Singer Sargent (American, born Italy, 1856–1925, LL.D. 1916)

Pietro Corsi, ca. 1891–95

Oil on canvas, 35¾ × 25¾ in. (90.8 × 65.4 cm)
Yale University Art Gallery, New Haven, Conn., Edwin Austin Abbey Memorial Collection, 1937.2546

CAT. 11 John Singer Sargent (American, born Italy, 1856–1925, LL.D. 1916)

Drapery Study, n.d.

Crayon on paper, 18 11/16 × 24 9/16 in. (47.4 × 62.4 cm)
Yale University Art Gallery, New Haven, Conn., Gift of Miss Emily Sargent and Mrs. Francis Ormond (through Thomas A. Fox), 1932.29

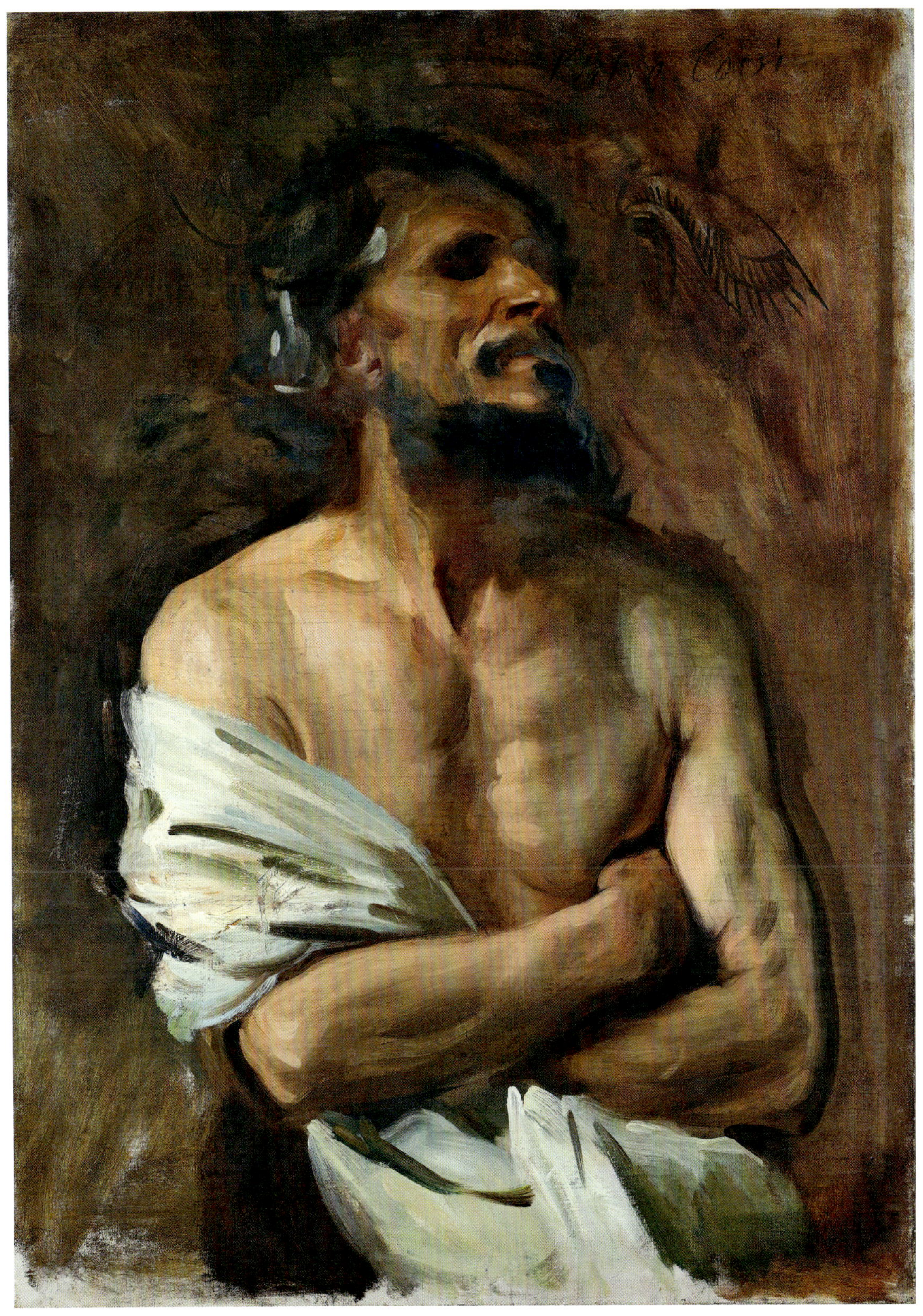

10

were often turned away to focus attention on poses and body movements. Age and gender, too, are often opaque and can change based on the value of the pose to particular roles—Corsi, for example, posed as both male and female characters of diverse ages. The flexibility of a pose, its ability to express different ideas in different contexts, speaks to its continuous refinement in series of studies, showing how artists sought to cast the body in one role and adapted a similar pose into others as well.

Sargent's oil study of Corsi is notable for its supple treatment of the body and rich tonal development.[4] The sitter's musculature and folded arms convey containment, reiterated by the white drape wrapped around his upper arm and held close. The right hand is tucked under the left bicep, pushing the arm muscle outward while pressing into the pectoral muscle. The richness and thickness of the white paint contrasts with the thinner application for the warm skin. Broad strokes describe the hollows of the neck and eye sockets as the raking light casts shadows that emphasize the undulations of Corsi's chest and face. The study's richly worked backdrop obscures an earlier design—perhaps the canvas had been reused—and creates a foil for the emergent figure. Despite the breadth of Sargent's treatment, the model remains close at hand. Character studies like this one were integral to compositional development, retaining a sense of the model's individuality that grounds the authority of the final works as true records of human experience.

NOTES

1. On the story's serial newspaper publication alongside articles related to the themes of the body and art that concern this exhibition, see Charles Johanningsmeier, "How Real American Readers Originally Experienced James's 'The Real Thing,'" *Henry James Review* 27, no. 1 (Winter 2006): 94–95.
2. A few, like Evelyn Nesbit and Audrey Munson, became well known or even notorious in the press.
3. Virginia Calhoun, "A Model for Many Famous Painters," *World's Work* 16 (1908): 10,342; according to Calhoun, Antonio Corsi did have brothers.
4. Formerly attributed to Abbey, this work has been reattributed in consultation with Sargent authorities Richard Ormond and Elaine Kilmurray.

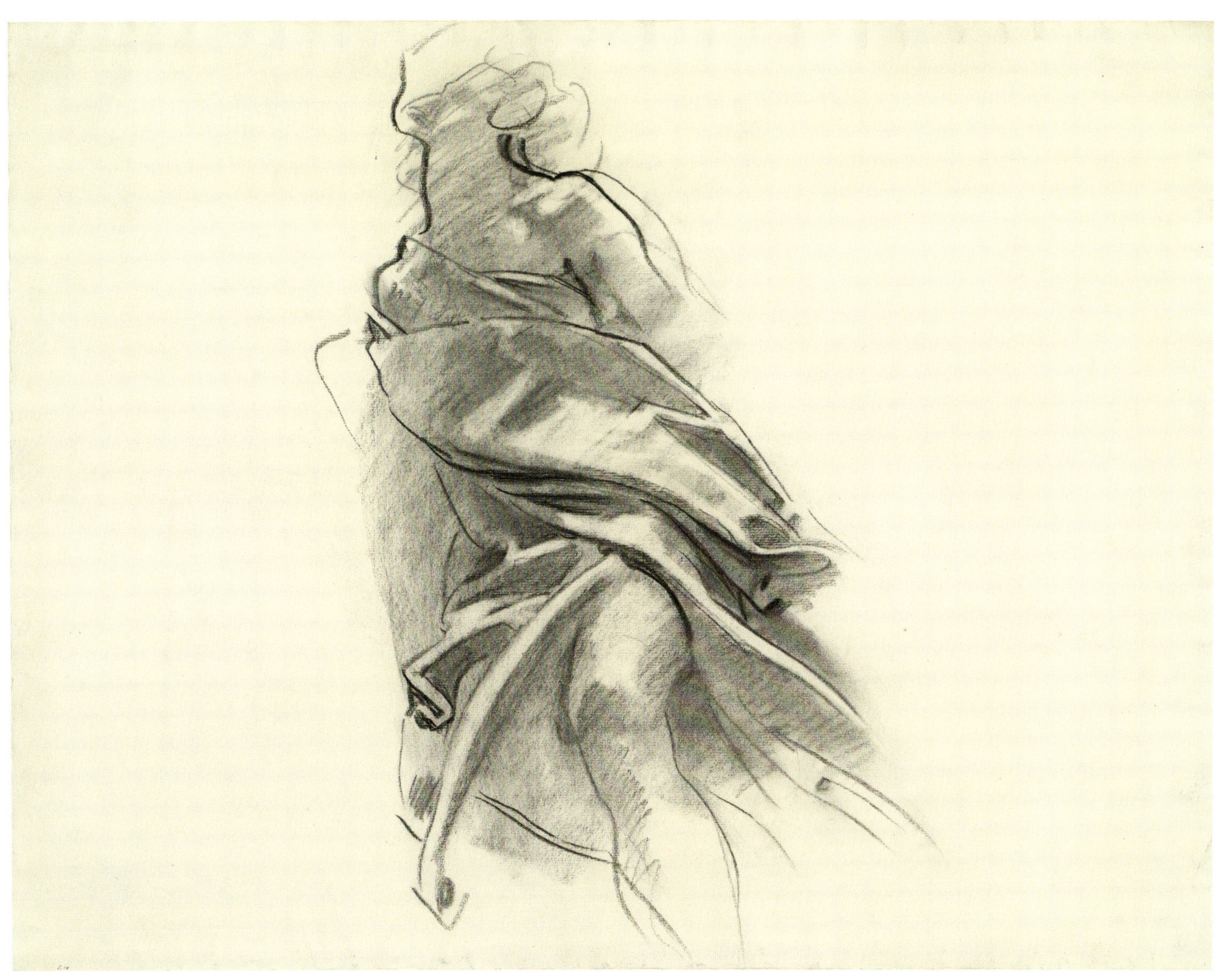

11

Life Class

Since the Renaissance, training to become a professional artist meant intensive study of the human figure in academies or private studios, including the Pennsylvania Academy of the Fine Arts in Philadelphia and National Academy of Design in New York. Full-sheet drawings of the body became known as "academies," such as Frederick MacMonnies's standing female nude (cat. 12), made by the future sculptor while he attended the École des Beaux-Arts in Paris. Despite receiving the same training as their European colleagues, American artists rarely applied such study beyond their student years because of American patrons' discomfort with the body as a subject.[1] That situation changed in the wake of the Civil War and the nation's Centennial, when American artists adopted the human figure, and audiences at last accepted its artistic potential.

Through their studies, aspiring artists learned about the body's mechanics as well as its integration as a whole. Class monitors, who were students themselves, would select the model's pose for the session, and then the students would draw or paint from their seats or easels. In often-packed rooms, the models were usually elevated so that everyone could see—training that proved to be excellent preparation for creating public murals and sculptures destined to be viewed from below.

Academy models were paid professionals. They used canes, wedges, straps, and other supports to help them hold poses. Most came from the working classes, and their bodies reflected their lived experience.[2] Rarely were they thin or heavyset, nor did they often represent classical ideals. In class, the students' aim was to depict what they saw, demonstrating their capacity for close observation rather than transformation. As a result, the drawings often show props or furniture as well as, occasionally, some of their peers—as seen in Julian Alden Weir's oil painting (cat. 13; detail below). This practice carried over into the artists' professional lives, with the individuality of models

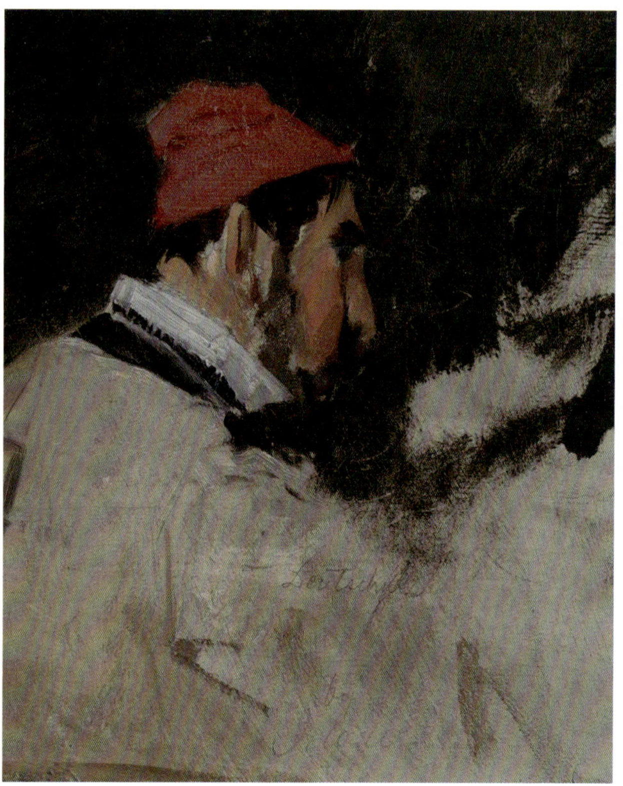

CAT. 12 Frederick William MacMonnies (American, 1863–1937)
Standing Female Nude, 1885
Charcoal on paper mounted on board, 21 11/16 × 12 in. (55.1 × 30.5 cm)
The Metropolitan Museum of Art, New York, Gift of Mrs. Gerret van S. Copeland, 1987.114.5

CAT. 13 Julian Alden Weir (American, 1852–1919)
Male Nude Leaning on a Staff, 1876
Oil on canvas, 31½ × 25½ in. (80 × 64.8 cm)
Yale University Art Gallery, New Haven, Conn., Gift of Julian Alden Weir, 1914.13

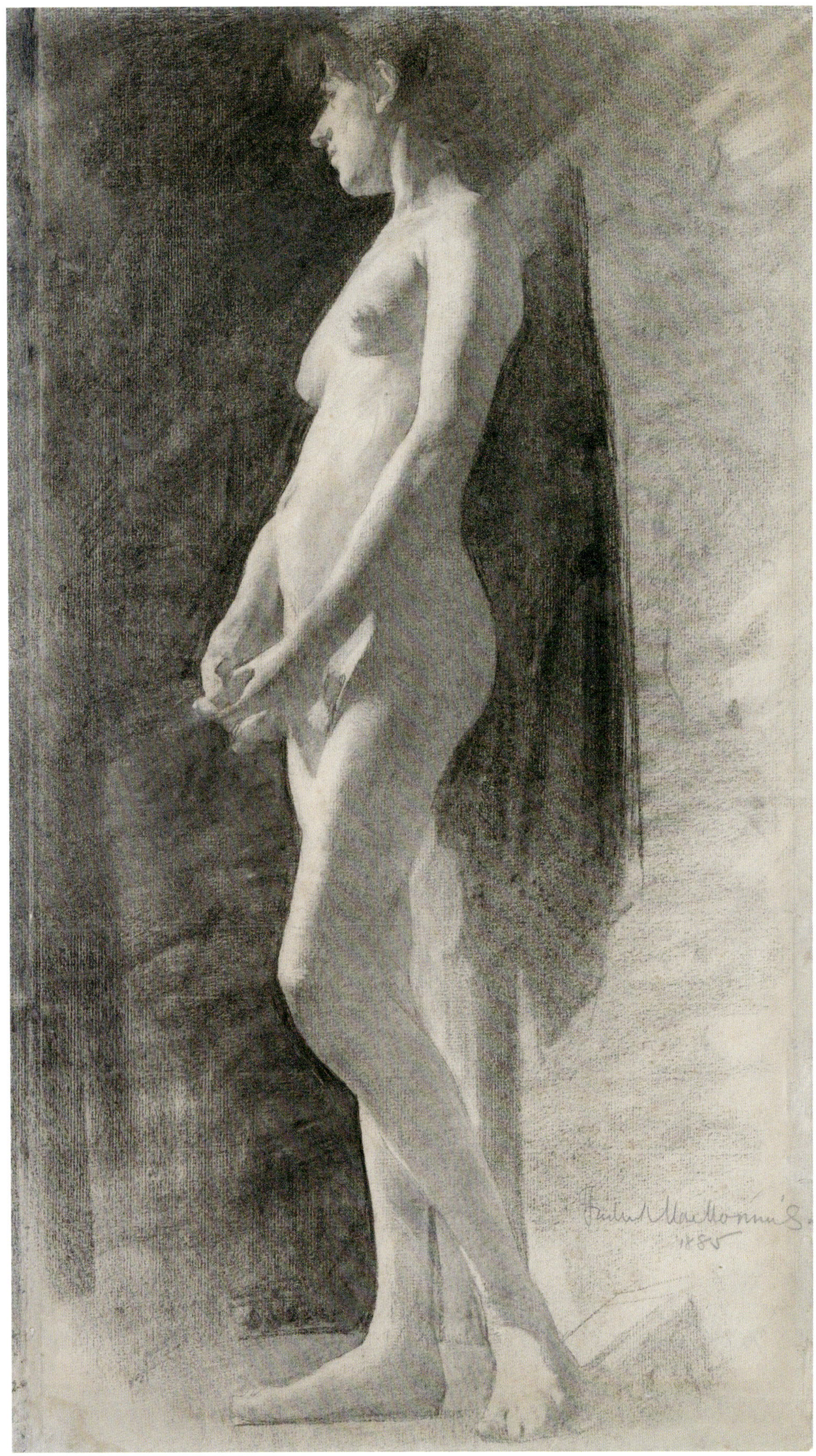

and their supports often included in figure studies made throughout their careers.

In its disciplined description and dramatic contrast, MacMonnies's charcoal drawing records his study in Munich and Paris, where he won awards for drawings like this one.[3] The cast shadows within and through the hands, as well as along the back and leg, are remarkable demonstrations of tonal control and detailed observation. Using the darkened background to accentuate the highlights increases the sense of the figure's dimensionality. The hair is up, focusing attention on the ear, neck, and shoulder. MacMonnies's vantage frames the body at a raking angle, making the integration of the hands and torso in space especially challenging.

Like MacMonnies, Weir studied in Paris. In his oil study, Weir, who came from a prominent family of artists, presents the body frontally but with similar care paid to volume and contrast. The artist gave this work to his brother, John Ferguson Weir, who directed the Yale School of Art, to use as a classroom demonstration piece.[4] The detailed study of models was considered the foundation of artistic practice, and its value to public art that centered the human figure was critical for American artists who wanted to participate in the new generation of commissions that emerged after the Centennial.

NOTES

1. Discomfort with the nude persisted well into the era of the American Renaissance, including at the Boston Public Library, which is a focus of the present exhibition. See Julia Rosenbaum, "Displaying Civic Culture: The Controversy over Frederick MacMonnies' 'Bacchante,'" *American Art* 14, no. 3 (2000): 41–57.
2. Later in life, Charlotte Eaton recalled her own experience as an artist's model, seeking to dispel misconceptions about the profession; Eaton, "Artists' Model on Her Occupation," *New York Herald* (1907), reprinted in *Artists and Models: An Exhibition of Photographs, Letters, and Other Documents from the Collections of the Archives of American Art, Smithsonian Institution*, exh. cat. (Washington, D.C.: Archives of American Art, Smithsonian Institution, 1975), n.p.
3. Working in Alexandre Falguière's studio in Paris in April 1887, at the end of his first year, MacMonnies surpassed more advanced students to receive first prize for a sculpted clay figure. He was rewarded with a display of his charcoal drawings around the studio, "such drawings as no other sculptor perhaps had ever shown in the Beaux Arts," recalled Lorado Taft in 1895. Cited in Mary Smart, *A Flight with Fame: The Life and Art of Frederick MacMonnies (1863–1937)* (Madison, Conn.: Sound View, 1996), 67.
4. Marian Wardle, ed., *The Weir Family, 1820–1920: Expanding the Traditions of American Art*, exh. cat. (Provo, Utah: Brigham Young University Museum of Art, 2011), 12–15, 62; Doreen Bolger Burke, *J. Alden Weir, An American Impressionist* (Newark: University of Delaware Press, 1983), 44–45; and Betsy Fahlman, *John Ferguson Weir, The Labor of Art* (Newark: University of Delaware Press, 1997), 135–36.

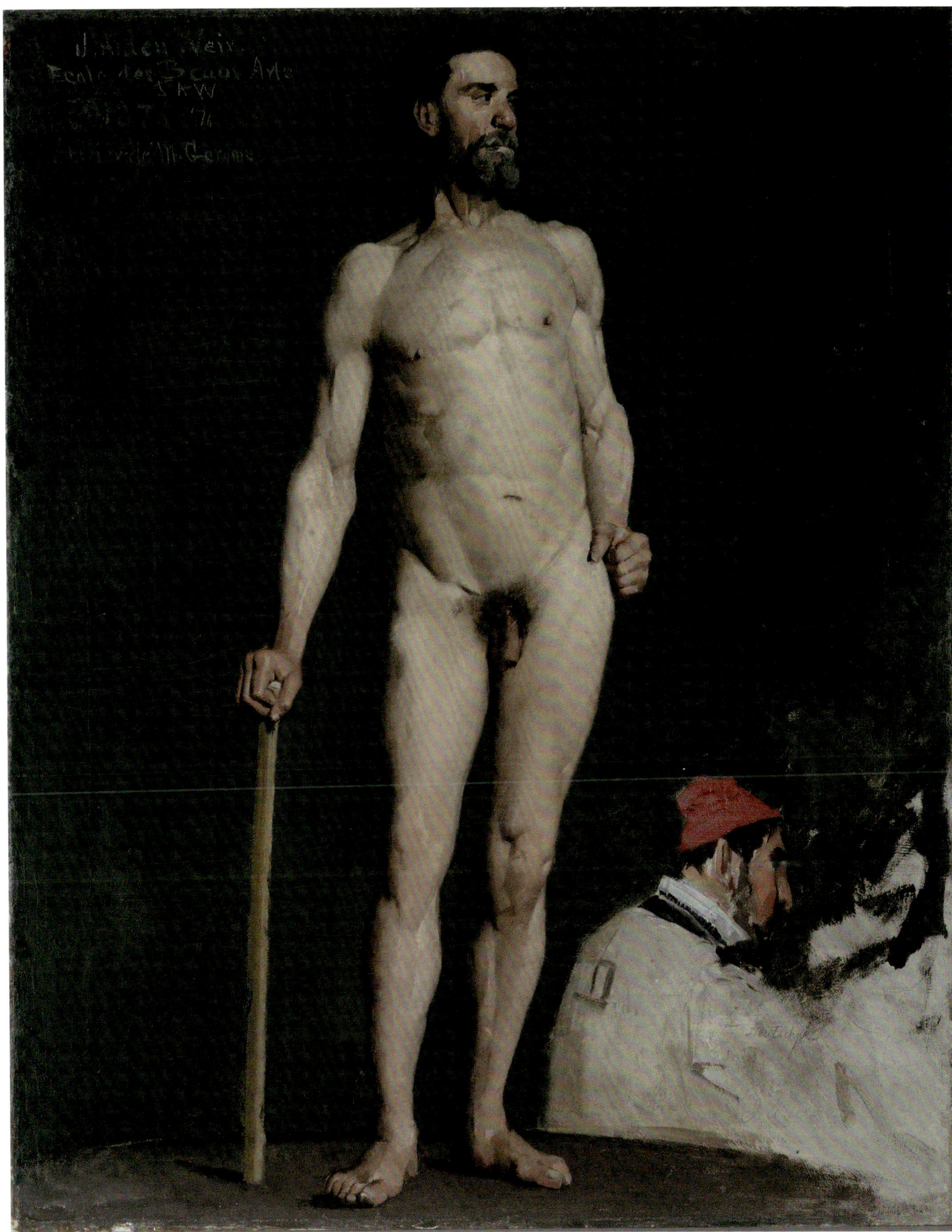

Real People

Expectations of realism prevailed for historical and allegorical subjects in public art during the American Renaissance. A significant dimension of the artists' success derived from their ability to establish authority through research. While developing murals for the Boston Public Library, both Edwin Austin Abbey and John Singer Sargent traveled extensively and researched their ideas. For *The Triumph of Religion*, Sargent traveled to the Middle East, as Henry Ossawa Tanner had before creating his oil painting *The Annunciation* of ca. 1898 (see cat. 34), seeking models and sites that would resemble those described in scripture.[1] In the two individualized oil studies shown here (cats. 14–15), Sargent focused on faces and clothing. He provides a sense of the color and texture of the fabrics and jewelry as well as the physical characteristics of residents of different ages, descendants of the historical cultures he hoped to portray. From such studies, Sargent could establish his documentary credentials.

For the Robert Gould Shaw Memorial commission in Boston, Augustus Saint-Gaudens sought to individualize images of African American soldiers in a Civil War regiment, developing study heads (cat. 16; detail below) based on the likenesses of several local men of military age—including John

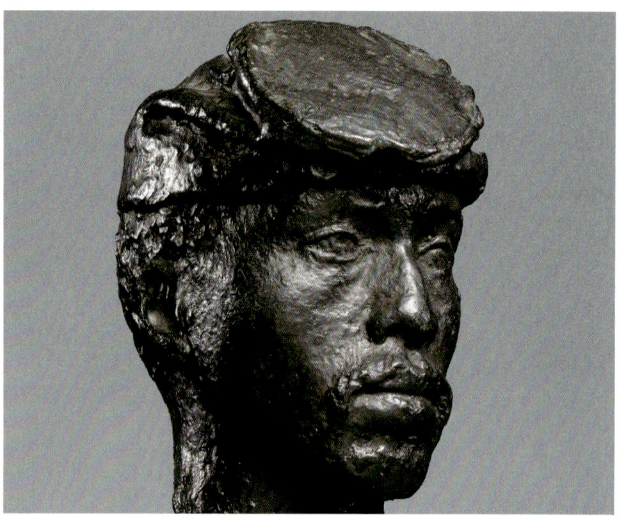

CAT. 14 John Singer Sargent (American, born Italy, 1856–1925, LL.D. 1916)

Egyptian Woman, Study for *The Triumph of Religion* in the Boston Public Library, 1890–91

Oil on canvas, 25½ × 21 in. (64.8 × 53.3 cm)
The Metropolitan Museum of Art, New York, Gift of Mrs. Francis Ormond, 1950, 50.130.21

CAT. 15 John Singer Sargent (American, born Italy, 1856–1925, LL.D. 1916)

Head of an Arab, Study for *The Triumph of Religion* in the Boston Public Library, 1891

Oil on canvas, 31½ × 23⅛ in. (80 × 58.7 cm)
Museum of Fine Arts, Boston, Gift of Mrs. Francis Ormond, 37.49

CAT. 16 Augustus Saint-Gaudens (American, born Ireland, 1848–1907, HON. 1905)

Studies of African American Soldiers' Heads for *Memorial to Robert Gould Shaw and the Massachusetts Fifty-Fourth Regiment*, modeled 1883–93, cast 1965

Bronze, MAX. 7 × 3½ × 4½ in. (17.8 × 8.9 × 11.4 cm)
Yale University Art Gallery, New Haven, Conn., Gift of the William Platt Family, 2015.4.1.1–.4

CAT. 17 John Singer Sargent (American, born Italy, 1856–1925, LL.D. 1916)

Figure Study, ca. 1916–21

Black chalk and charcoal on paper, 19$\frac{1}{16}$ × 24$\frac{15}{16}$ in. (48.4 × 63.4 cm)
Yale University Art Gallery, New Haven, Conn., Gift of Miss Emily Sargent and Mrs. Francis Ormond, through Thomas A. Fox, 1929.263

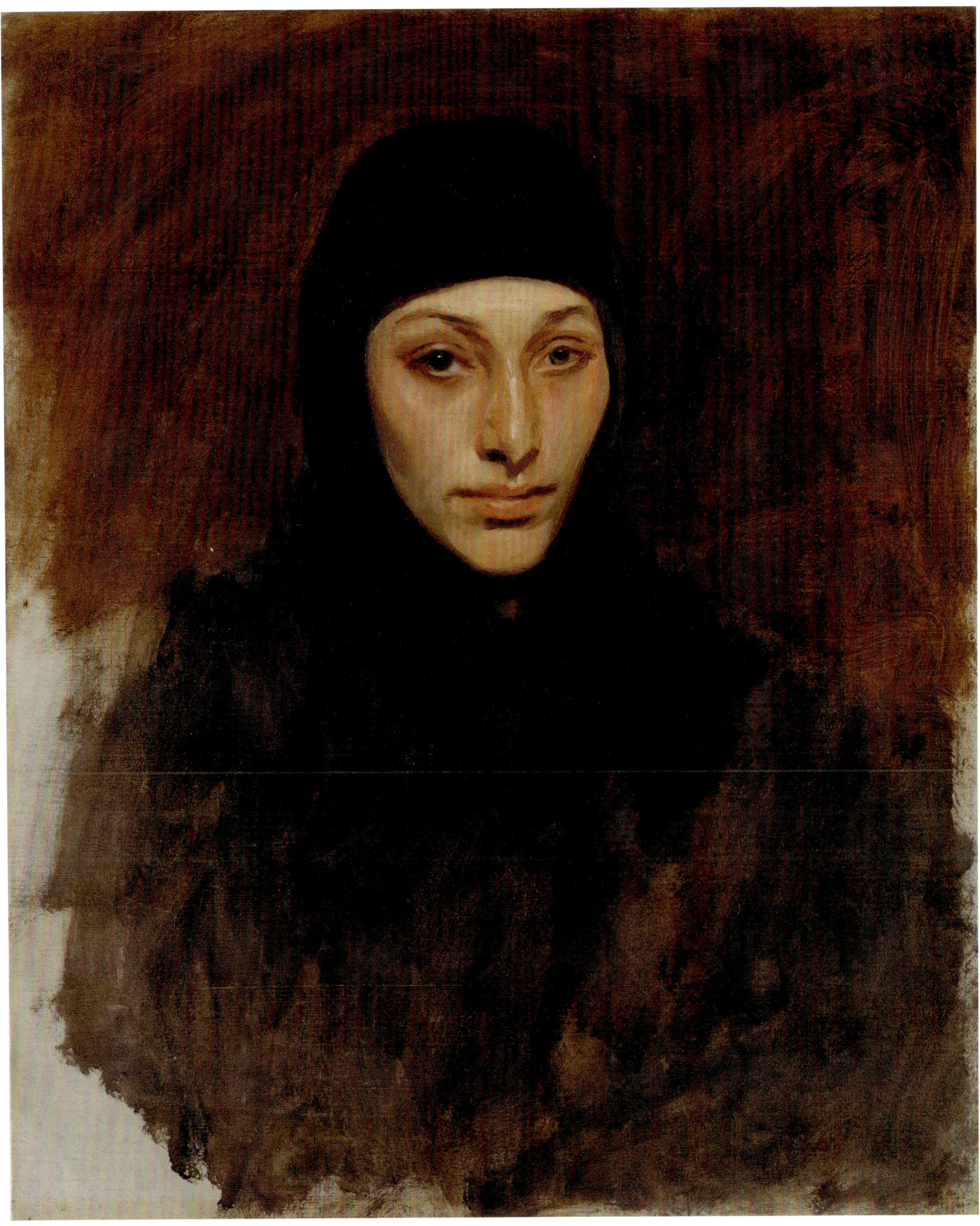

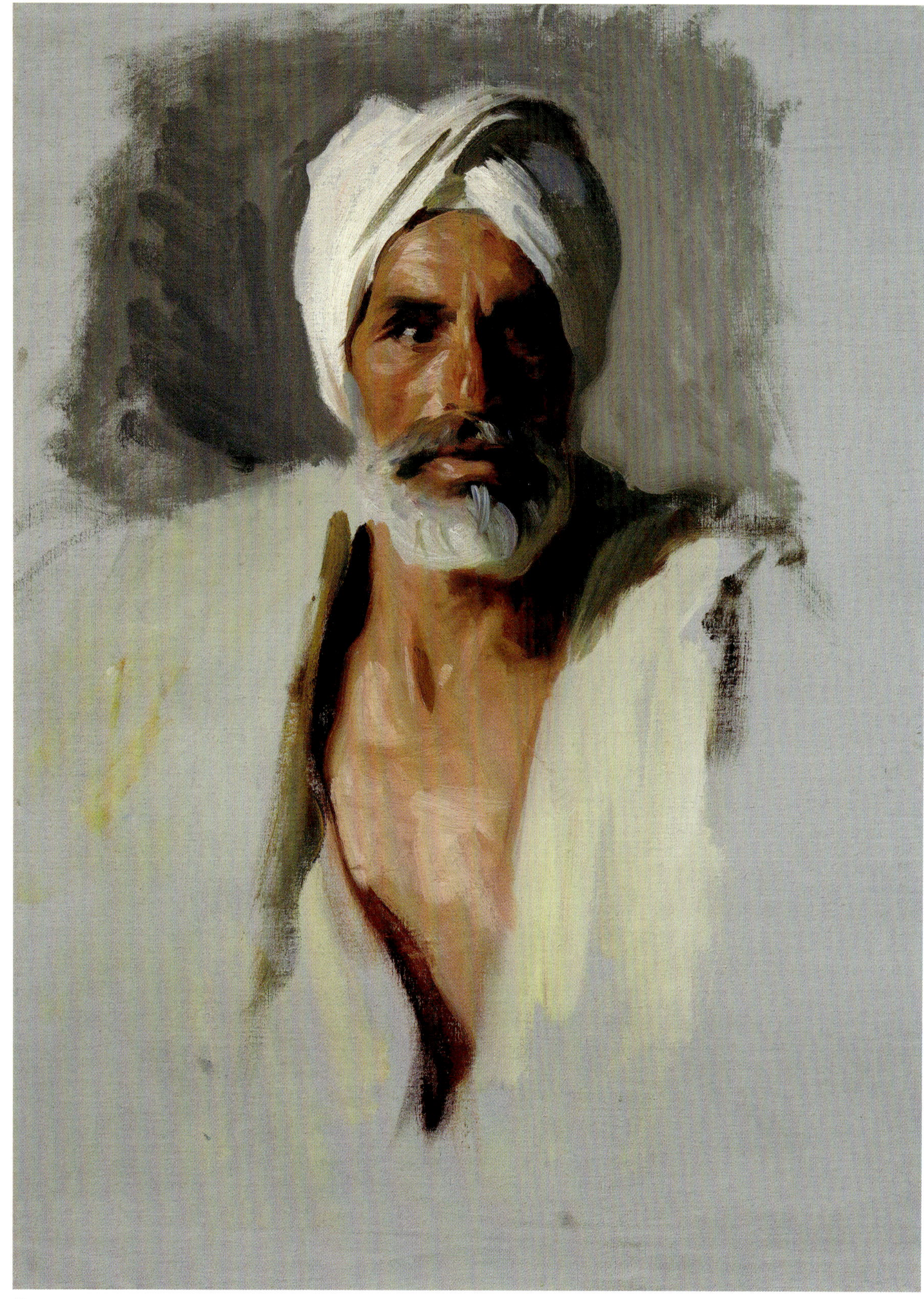

15

Lee and Riley Lee—whom he hired to pose twenty years after the events he portrayed.[2] These four casts from plaster studies preserve the remarkable individuality that Saint-Gaudens invested in the figures and later sustained in the commission. Although these likenesses have not been documented in the final monument, the artist's direct observation carried through and endowed the work with a sense of individuality among the marching troops.

Over time, more of the models from this period have been identified and their stories told, as is the case for Hettie Anderson (see cat. 1) and Thomas McKeller (cat. 17), who worked with Sargent. McKeller inspired figures in some of the most prominent commissions of the day and was himself the subject of a 2020 exhibition at the Isabella Stewart Gardner Museum in Boston.[3]

NOTES

1. Richard Ormond and Elaine Kilmurray, *John Singer Sargent: Complete Paintings* (New Haven, Conn.: Yale University Press for the Paul Mellon Centre for Studies in British Art, 2010), 5:214–19; Evan Charteris, *John Sargent* (New York: Charles Scribner's Sons, 1927), 114; and Darrel Sewell, "The Annunciation," in Dewey F. Mosby, *Henry Ossawa Tanner*, exh. cat. (Philadelphia: Philadelphia Museum of Art, 1991), 162.
2. Kirk Savage effectively describes the artist's ambivalence in working with African American models as well as the demands of artistic process that compelled attention to their individuality; Savage, *Standing Soldiers, Kneeling Slaves: Race, War, and Monument in Nineteenth-Century America* (Princeton, N.J.: Princeton University Press, 1997), 201–2. See also Molly K. Eckel, "Model Citizens: Four Studies for Augustus Saint-Gaudens's Robert Gould Shaw Memorial," *Yale University Art Gallery Bulletin* (2017): 49–55. For an opposing view, see Katie Mullis Kresser, "Power and Glory: Brahmin Identity and the Shaw Memorial," *American Art* 20, no. 3 (Fall 2006): 46–49.
3. In the exhibition's catalogue, Nikki A. Greene observed in her conclusion that the completeness of Sargent's study drawings of McKeller enabled her to see McKeller "fully as a man and as a depiction of mythological figures"; Greene, "Thomas McKeller *sous rature*: John Singer Sargent's Erasure of a ~~Black~~ Model," in *Boston's Apollo: Thomas McKeller and John Singer Sargent*, ed. Nathaniel Silver, exh. cat. (Boston: Isabella Stewart Gardner Museum, 2020), 78.

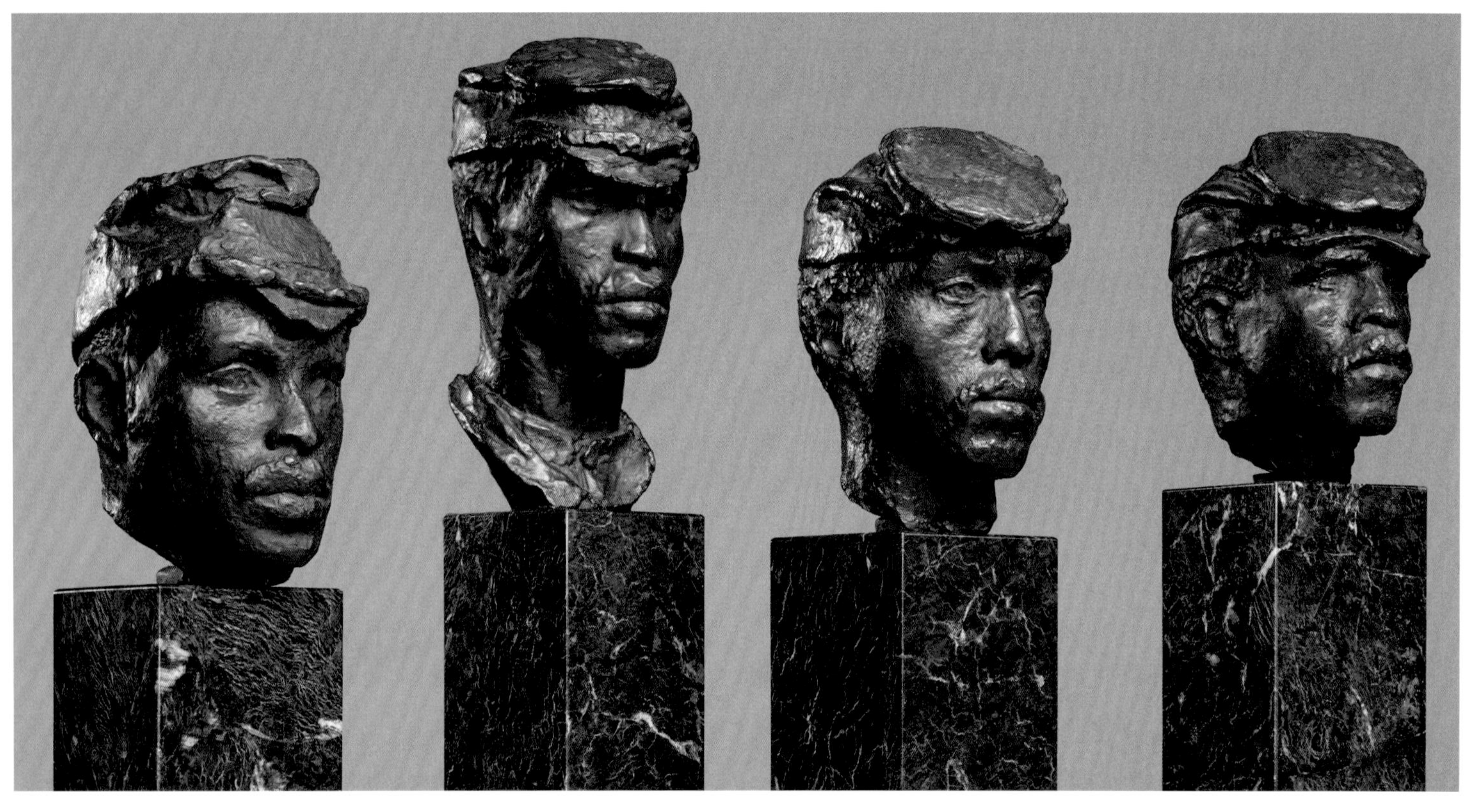
16

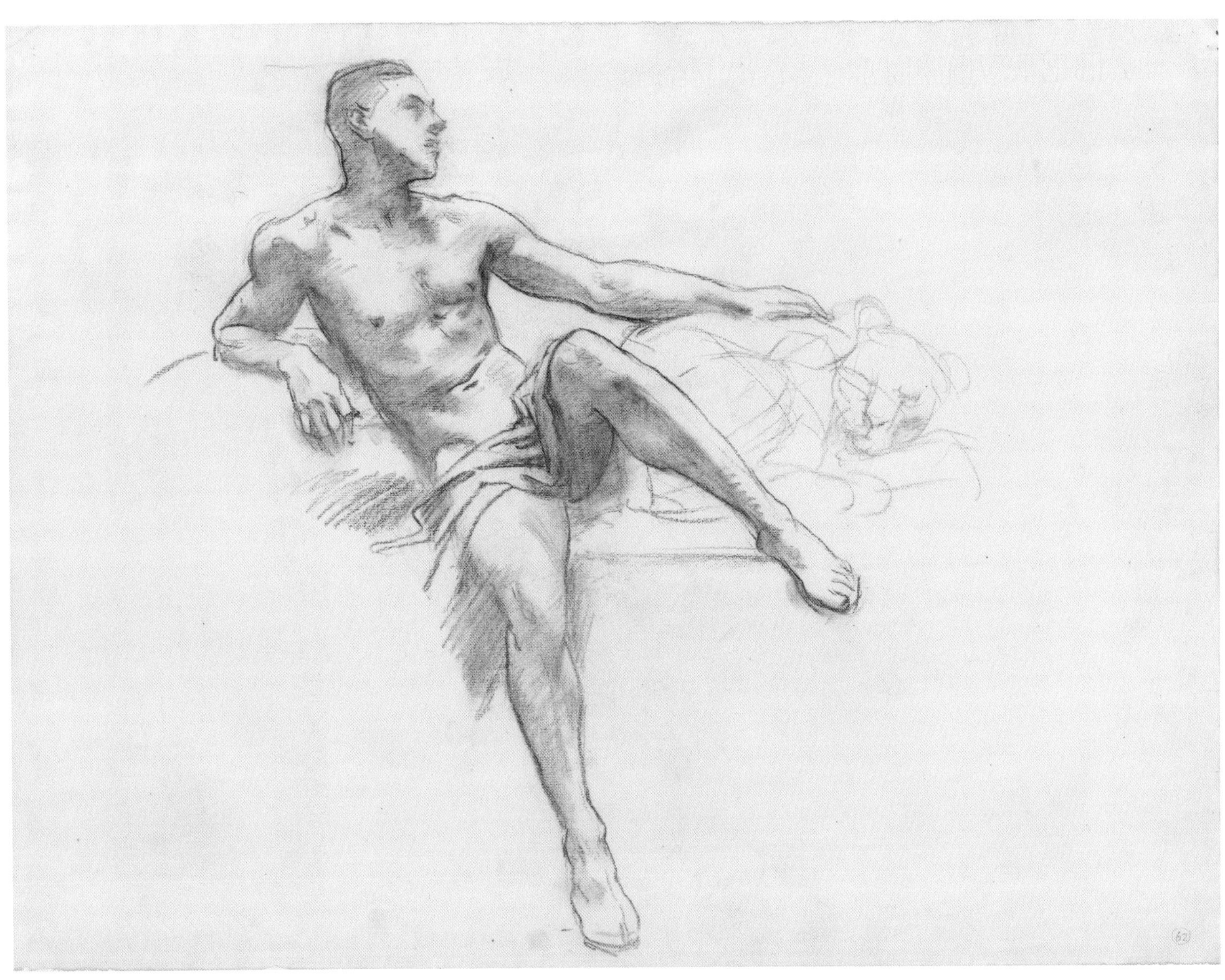

17

Literary Figures

Public libraries—thousands of which were established by the steel magnate Andrew Carnegie—provided environments for artists whose works would be seen, or perhaps read, by a secular, democratic audience.[1] After the World's Columbian Exposition in 1893, a subset of artists who were not otherwise committed to commissions—as were Edwin Austin Abbey and John Singer Sargent at the Boston Public Library—turned their attention to the ambitious project of a new home for the Library of Congress in Washington, D.C. Over one hundred murals by nineteen artists would be created to decorate the building.

Among them, Edwin Howland Blashfield was both a leader of the movement and one of its early historians. Soaring in the dome above the library's main reading room, Blashfield's collar of twelve iconic figures representing the contributions of historical cultures are the centerpiece of a vast program of public decorations that is a highwater mark of mural painting in America. Blashfield was one of the few who painted in true fresco or who had the technical ability to undertake such a challenging project. Among the six figures illustrated here (cats. 18–19), the most unexpected may be that of Islam, which was credited with the development of physics, "in its older and less restricted sense" as well as "mathematics and astronomy," according to the library's original handbook.[2]

NOTES

1. Wayne Craven, *Marble Halls: Beaux-Arts Classicism and Civic Architecture in the Gilded Age* (Newark: University of Delaware Press, 2017), 72–73. Derrick Cartwright proposed reading as a metaphor for the visual experience of library murals in this period; Cartwright, "Reading Rooms: Interpreting the American Public Library Mural, 1890–1930" (Ph.D. diss., University of Michigan, 1994), 12–13.
2. Herbert Small, *Handbook of the New Library of Congress in Washington* (1897), reprinted in John Y. Cole and Henry Hope Reed, eds., *The Library of Congress: The Art and Architecture of the Thomas Jefferson Building* (New York: W. W. Norton, 1997), 135–36. See also Annelise K. Madsen, "Mural Painting's New Education at the Library of Congress," *American Art* 26, no. 2 (Summer 2012): 74–80.

CAT. 18 Edwin Howland Blashfield (American, 1848–1936)

Study for *The Evolution of Civilization: Middle Ages, Italy, Germany* in the Library of Congress, 1895

Oil on canvas, 44⅝ × 93⅞ in. (113.4 × 238.4 cm)
Williams College Museum of Art, Williamstown, Mass., Gift of Grace Hall Blashfield, 37.1.1

CAT. 19 Edwin Howland Blashfield (American, 1848–1936)

Study for *The Evolution of Civilization: Greece, Rome, Islam* in the Library of Congress, 1895

Oil on canvas, 47⅜ × 95¼ in. (120.3 × 241.9 cm)
Williams College Museum of Art, Williamstown, Mass., Gift of Grace Hall Blashfield, 37.1.2

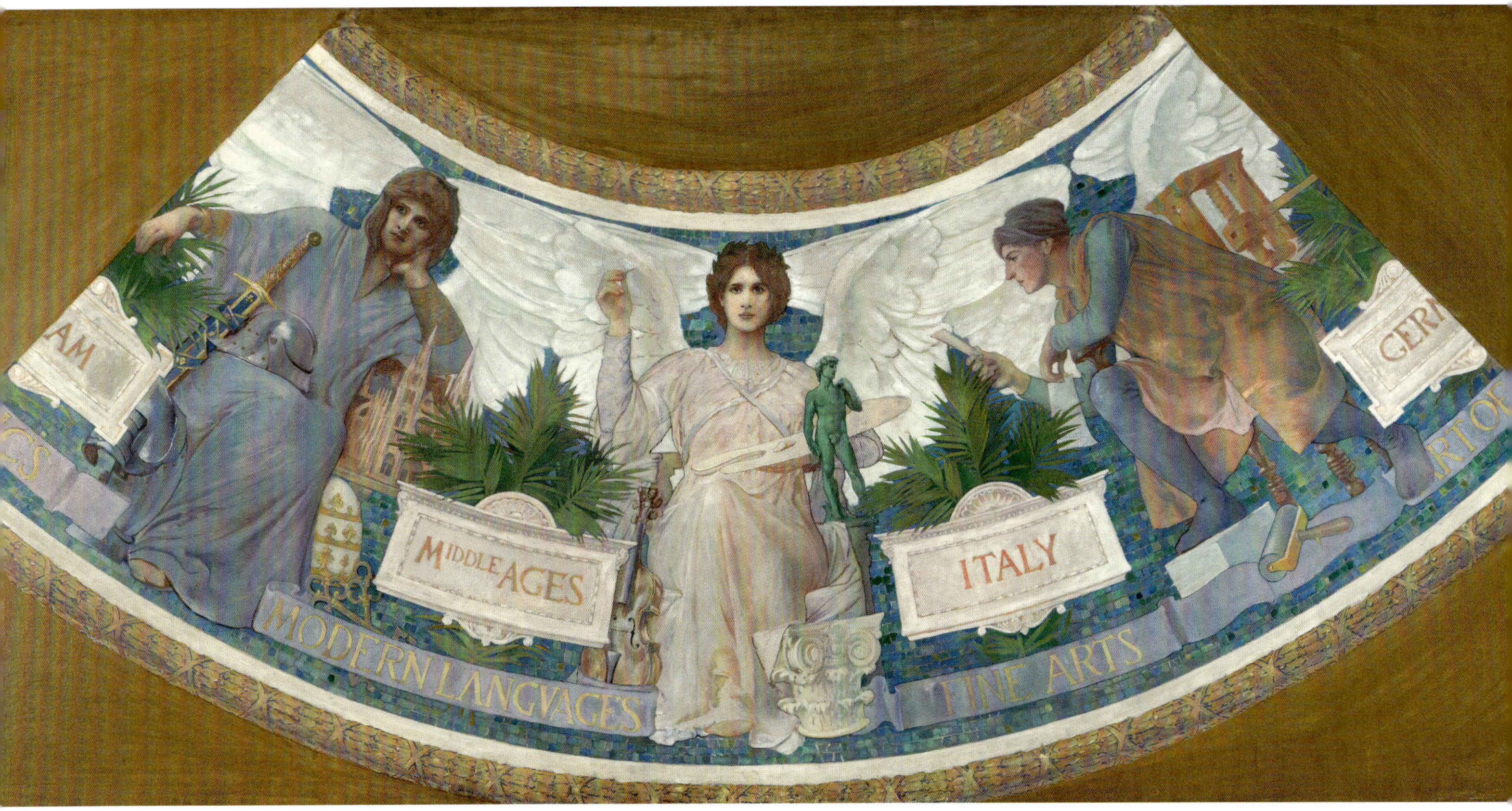

18

19

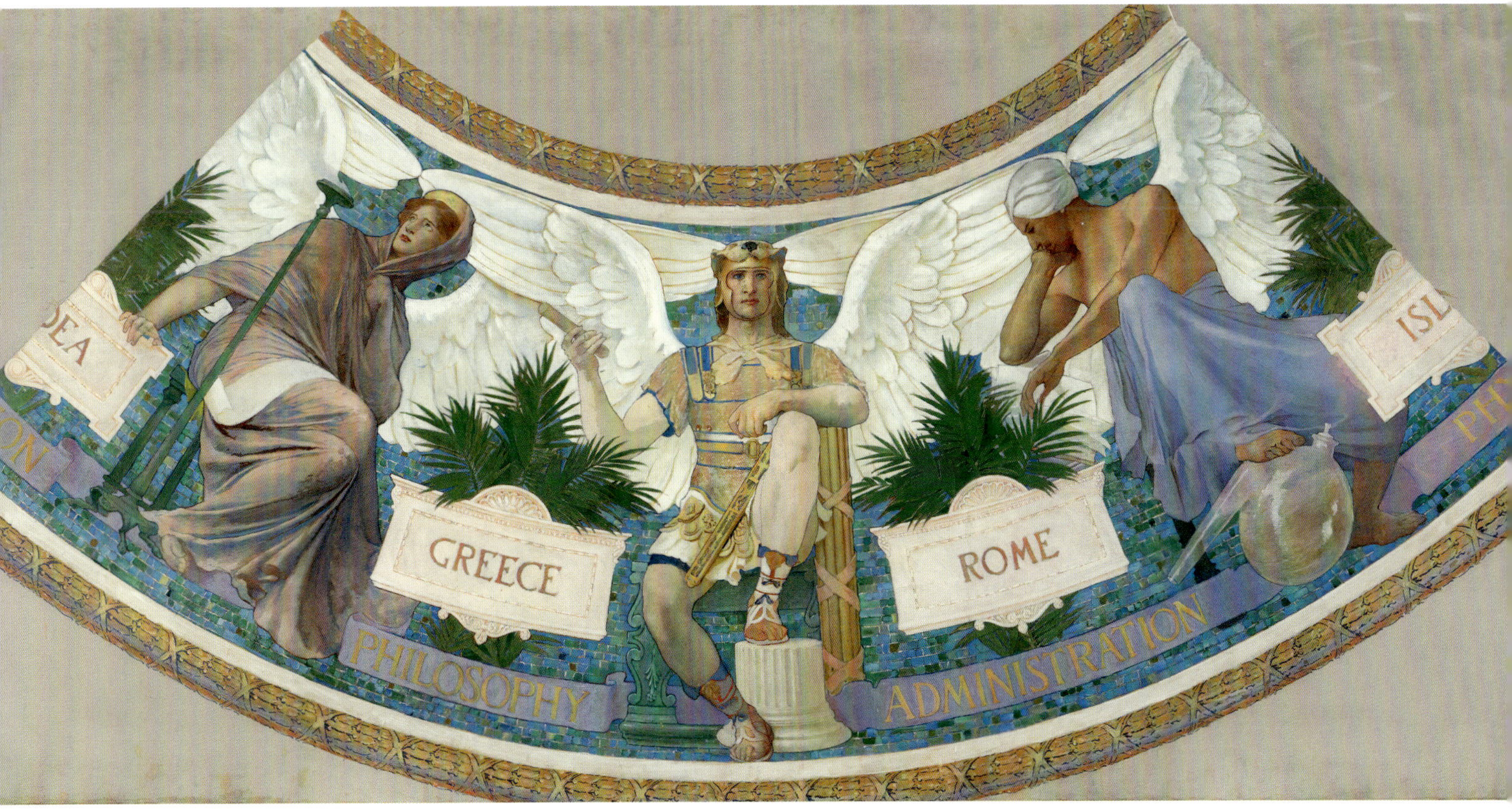

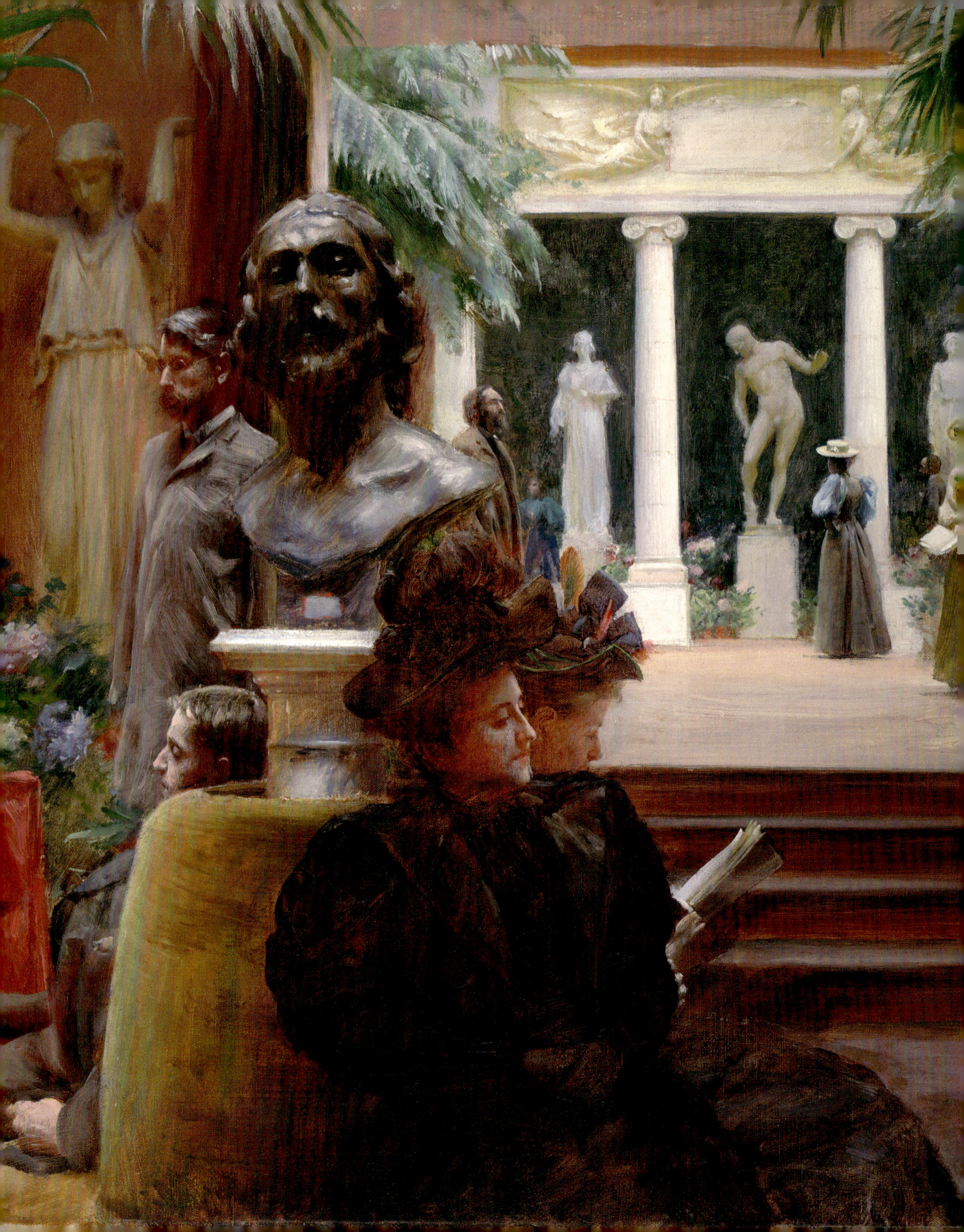

"Live One's Life as a Work of Art": A FABLE OF CLASS AND TASTE

BRYAN J. WOLF

Henry James was unhappy. He had just discovered that the Boston Public Library, newly opened in 1895, had placed the Main Reading Room next to the children's room. This was not to James's liking. Children, he felt, should be hustled off to a separate part of the building, where their shouts and cries could not be heard. For James, literate culture and barely literate children did not mix. High culture merited its own spaces, far from the hustle and bustle of street life and young urchins.

But the Boston Public Library had been designed, in part, to attract that bustle. Its ambitions were as much social as literary. The planners of the library hoped to provide immigrant and working-class visitors with a form of uplift. Patrons were greeted with an inscription on the main facade that heralded the dedication of this civic building to the "Advancement of Learning." And learning, in turn, was not a goal to be achieved for its own sake. The library offered more than a space to read. It functioned as a place where contact with the great works of Western culture would produce, it was hoped, an engaged and enlightened citizenry, a public mindful of the grand achievements of Western civilization. What it provided, therefore, was more than shelves overflowing with books. It offered a civic education. As one journalist of the period remarked, the "range and scope of the Boston Library go very much beyond the gratuitous circulation of literature. They aim at the general culture of the people, and the raising of the standard of artistic feeling of the entire town."[1]

Note the terms here: "culture" and "artistic feeling." The language of uplift has been hijacked from a social and economic context to an aesthetic one. What soothes the soul and, in effect, washes the great "unwashed" masses is art. Not adequate housing, nor sanitary living conditions, nor decent employment, but books as well as, implicitly, operas, symphonies, ballet, and theater.

Our journalist's choice of words is not innocent. He speaks a language that had been developing in America since the end of the Civil War: the discourse of

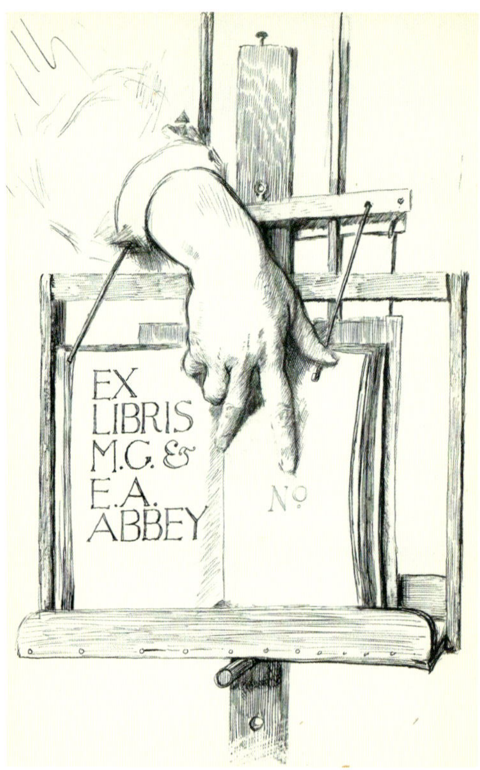

FIG. 1. Edwin Austin Abbey, Sketch for Ex Libris: M. G. & E. A. Abbey, n.d. Pen and ink on wove paper, 13⅛ × 8$\frac{9}{16}$ in. (33.4 × 21.7 cm). Yale University Art Gallery, New Haven, Conn., Edwin Austin Abbey Memorial Collection, 1937.2717

what we might term "high culture." To understand that language, we need to examine its inventors and purveyors: an emergent social elite in the late nineteenth century that defined itself less in terms of birth, inheritance, wealth, or property—though any of these might also be present—and more according to what the scholar Pierre Bourdieu called "cultural capital."[2] In New York, for example, the financial center of the nation, the upper classes were divided among several overlapping, and occasionally adversarial, groups: merchants, financiers, industrialists, brokers, bankers, real estate speculators, rentiers, and, at one remove, an educational elite that included professionals, experts, and intellectuals.[3] What united them all, despite their divergent interests and allegiances, was their relation to—and reaction against—"proletarianization," the growth of a permanent unskilled or semiskilled class of workers whose differences of religion, or race, or ethnicity, or education set them in long-term opposition to the "better classes." Seen from above, these "dangerous classes" formed the lower tier of a social hierarchy that ranked everyone having "artistic feeling" at the top and anyone else below.

What the elites needed was a powerful glue to bind them together, a common vision or a shared language beyond their own whiteness that not only distinguished the upper classes from those lacking proper taste but also furnished them with legitimating social value. They found that glue in *culture*, a concept that provided a vocabulary of taste and refinement transcending the "numerous economic fault lines that market competition generated."[4]

When, for instance, Edwin Austin Abbey sketched a bookplate for the volumes in his library, he drew a double easel that filled the rectangular frame (fig. 1). The trope of doubling is repeated several times in the image: in the two sides of the easel, in the extended fingers of the hand holding open the book, and, somewhat more abstractly, in the larger relation of reading to painting. What we see is a bookplate (the world of words), but what we get is a drawing (the world of images). Abbey is defining the visual arts as more than a parallel endeavor, a kindred spirit, to literary efforts. He is insisting that painting, at its best, represents a synthesis of the two, a mode of visual discourse that, like literature, tells stories, opens up new vistas, and in this way brings culture itself to life. The bookplate makes two claims. The first is that Abbey's art—his studies, drawings, canvases, and mural paintings—stands in the tradition of what the poet Matthew Arnold earlier described as the central mission of art: to represent the "best that has been thought and said."[5] And second, that this fusion of art and literature defines a culture of refinement that—like those rectangles within rectangles—frames not only Abbey's aesthetic world but his social world as well. This second claim is about *class* rather than art. Abbey's bookplate functions as a badge of elite privilege, a visual confirmation of his participation in the rituals of high culture.

It also proclaims, through its emphasis on hands and the handmade, its opposition to an emergent modernity and its effects on everyday life. As Sarah Burns notes, the contemporary world that defined Abbey's generation was characterized by "its sensationalism, its consumerism, its heterogeneity, its cult of the momentary."[6] Abbey's bookplate, by its very quiet and decorum—its rectilinear elegance—signals its opposition to the brave new world of fin-de-siècle America. It substitutes symmetry for the helter-skelter, stillness for motion, traditional modes of art for the new inventions of the age: electricity, cinema, the automobile. The writer Henry Adams would attend the World's Columbian Exposition in Chicago in 1893 and find himself marveling at the dynamo, a machine so central to modern life that it rivaled in influence the social and emotional power of the Virgin Mary in medieval times. Abbey, in an image as simple as a bookplate, affirms a parallel position: his allegiance to (or perhaps longing for) a world resistant to the abrasive incursions of modernity. In his hands, the quiet humanism of his image, with its symmetrical forms, determined gesture, and insistence that books be opened, becomes a mode of social critique. His art, like his library, represents a rebuff to the rising commercialism of his time.

Or again, in a different vein, Charles Courtney Curran's painting *At the Sculpture Exhibition* (1895) unites a jumble of well-dressed people, classical statuary, and potted plants (see page 62 and cat. 62). Though the gentleman leaning against the circular chair on the left appears to be sleeping—culture, after all, does not appeal to everyone—the painting as a whole defines the figures through their educated taste: they read guidebooks, dress fashionably, and surround themselves with classical works of art. Curran links refinement to a proper taste for the values and achievements of the past as embodied in the world of Greek nymphs and maidens as well as one male nude standing in contrapposto at the apex of the painting.[7] We should remember that this emulation of the past is precisely what the Boston Public Library (also dated 1895) hoped

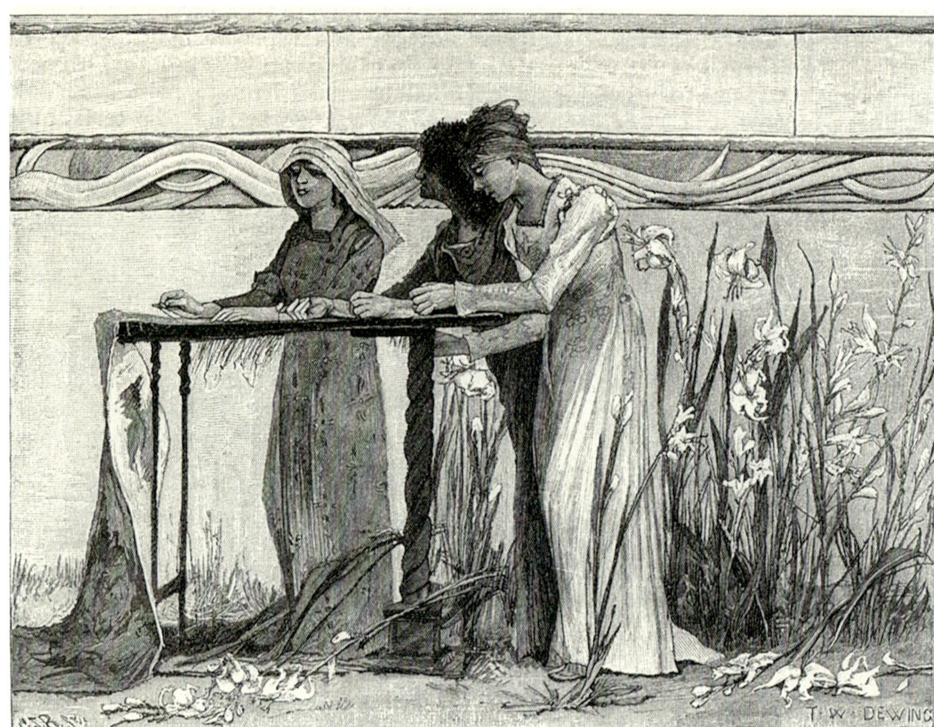

FIG. 2. "Decorative Panel, by Thomas Wilmer Dewing," *Harper's New Monthly Magazine*, vol. 64 (April 1882)

to achieve through its outreach to the general public: social uplift defined as cultural appetite. Except Curran's painting does not feature the general public. It is a portrait of an elite class defined by members' aesthetic sensitivity.

That central nude sculpture in the back gallery raises the issue of the heroic male body and its relation to the very different nineteenth-century world in which it is set. The question is: What is that heroic body reacting *against*? What lies on the other side of the appetite for an art of ideal forms during this era? Or to phrase the matter differently: In what ways might we treat the taste for things classical as a *symptom* rather than an achievement—a hint of untoward forces just below the surface of respectability?

The answer comes in the form of an illustration made in 1882 by Thomas Wilmer Dewing for *Harper's New Monthly Magazine* (fig. 2).[8] The image portrays a trio of women who might be mistaken for the Three Graces: female figures standing elegantly around an embroidery table as they decorate a cloth runner that the viewer cannot see. What we observe instead is a "Decorative Panel" (the work's title) running along the back wall—a hint, perhaps, at what their labors, when completed, might resemble. The figures, intent upon their work, embody virtues that late Victorian society expected of proper womanhood: a dutiful attention to domestic tasks, shared bonds of sympathy and cordiality, and an innocence as unassuming as their endeavors. They display, through their activities, a form of conspicuous leisure, a mode of upper-class behavior designed to highlight the noncommercial, nonutilitarian nature of their work.[9]

These graceful poses contrast dramatically with the lone figure who appears in Winslow Homer's wood engraving of a woman winding shuttle bobbins, published the previous decade (fig. 3).[10] She, too, is working with her hands, but her work is not her own. She performs a single, repetitive task over and over, focusing intently and, judging from her expression, unhappily on one small step in an industrialized form of labor that bears little resemblance to the artisanal work of Dewing's figures. Homer's woman functions as a cog in a machine; her labor has been de-skilled and depersonalized. She is an anonymous worker within New England's burgeoning textile industry.

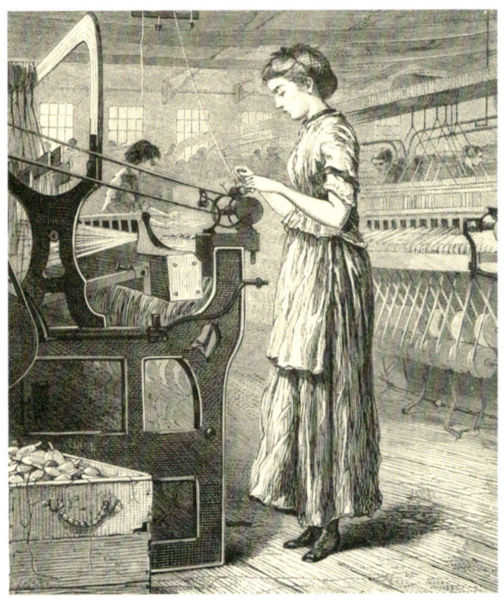

FIG. 3. Winslow Homer, "Industry. Women in Textile Mills: Woman Winding Shuttle Bobbins," in William Cullen Bryant, *The Song of the Sower* (New York: Appleton, 1871)

The problem is that she is present, like a ghost, in Dewing's illustration. The two images are related like night and day; they form the flip sides of a single coin. Note, for instance, the way the hands of Dewing's women align as they work. The viewer sees five hands (the sixth is below the embroidery table). Each is engaged in the same task, echoing and repeating the gestures of the others, and all forming a unidirectional workflow that reproduces, without intending to, the linear movement of the assembly line. Unlike traditional images of middle-class women of the era sewing or embroidering from the comfort of their home, Dewing's figures take part in a collective form of work that requires them to stand rather than sit. The woman behind the table on the left wears a headdress that is anything but fashionable. She resembles a laboring woman—a mill worker—whose dress is less gownlike than utilitarian. Even the lilies—traditional symbols of female virtue and beauty—lie fallen and disheveled on the floor.

The point is not that Dewing intended his figures to suggest, however remotely, factory workers. To the contrary, they appear to labor in ways that we might characterize as artisanal and domestic rather than impersonal and industrial. But even in its innocence, Dewing's image cannot escape the deeper and more pervasive logic that quietly invades it: the factory-like rhythm of shared tasks performed by a group of women working at repetitive labors. In this way, the illustration echoes a very different and monumental work, Abbey's study for *The Hours*, which—for all its attention to female grace and beauty—situates its figures within a world similarly defined by serialized forms, repetitive gestures, and standardized units of time (see cat. 104). Here, too, Abbey's industrialized workers have slipped, like Alice through the rabbit hole, into the fantasy of a preindustrial world.

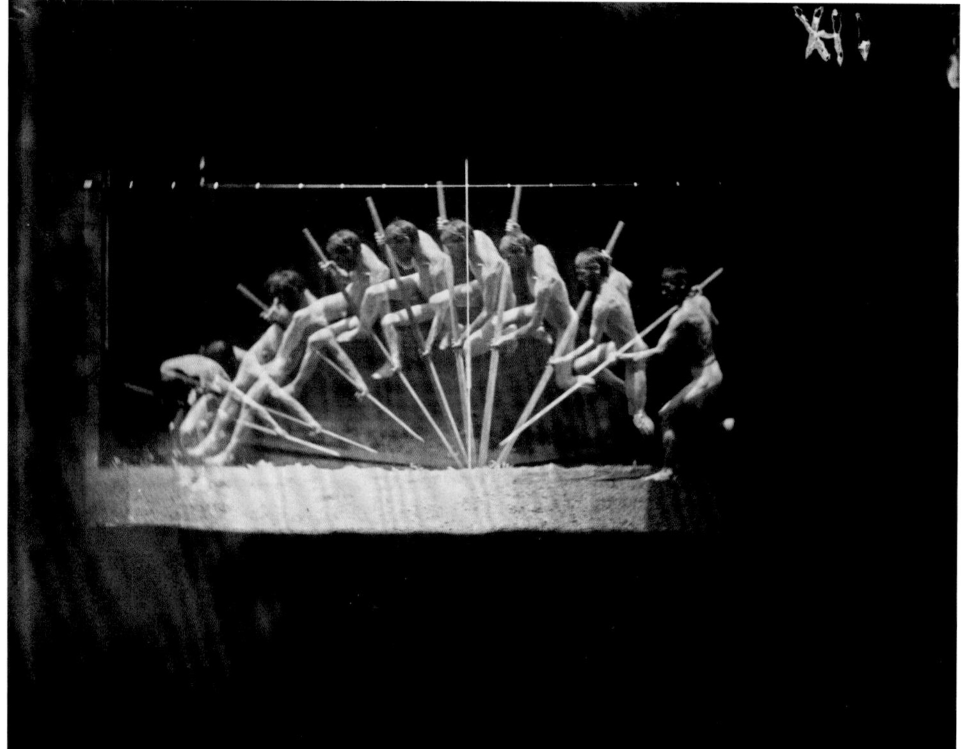

FIG. 4. Thomas Eakins and Eadweard Muybridge, *Motion Study: George Reynolds Nude, Pole-Vaulting to Left*, 1885. Dry-plate negative, 3⅞ × 4⅝ in. (9.8 × 11.7 cm). Charles Bregler's Thomas Eakins Collection, purchased with the partial support of the Pew Memorial Trust, Pennsylvania Academy of the Fine Arts, Philadelphia, 1985.68.2.996

And that returns us to the question of the body. Artists of this period, including Thomas Eakins and Eadweard Muybridge, were determined to understand the science of the body. They abandoned the Romantic notions of the human form as an organic whole and sought instead to analyze the physics behind what the scholar Mark Seltzer has termed the "body machine."[11] In a collaboration from 1884–85, Eakins and Muybridge combined sequential images taken by several cameras into an early version of stop-action photography (fig. 4). In what we might think of as an act of visual dissection, they sliced through time itself, creating a series of cross sections of a pole-vaulter leaping through space. The pole-vaulter could just as well have been an antelope. The artists were not concerned about the athlete's psychology or inner life. Instead, they wanted to understand how his body, as a physical instrument, responded to gravity. They termed their project "animal locomotion."

Several decades later, a mechanical engineer and industrial consultant named Frederick Winslow Taylor attempted to map the moment-by-moment movements of a group of ironworkers at the Bethlehem Steel Company. His goal was to enhance the laborers' productivity by a twofold process: optimizing their movements and simplifying their tasks. In 1911 he published the results of his studies in *The Principles of Scientific Management*, a treatise whose premise was the machinelike nature of the workers' bodies. Efficiency in one (the laboring body) produced measurable gains in the other (industrial output). When Taylor referred to a worker named Schmidt as resembling "the ox," he was attempting a compliment. Schmidt was valuable because his body, like that of a beast of burden or a machine, could be engineered toward ever-higher levels of productivity.

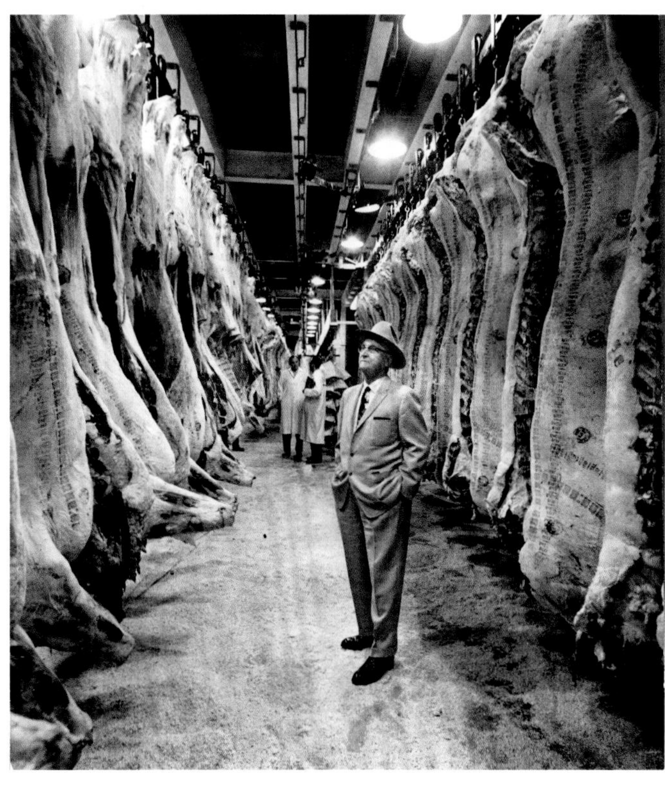

FIG. 5. Otto Hagel, Untitled, 1959. Gelatin silver print, 11¾ × 10½ in. (29.9 × 26.7 cm). Center for Creative Photography, University of Arizona, Hansel Mieth/Otto Hagel Archive, 98.120.115

It's not far, then, from Schmidt's oxlike body to Abbey's study of five male torsos for the dome of the Pennsylvania State Capitol in Harrisburg (see cat. 54). We might think of Abbey's figures—somewhat unkindly—as a portrait of "men as meat." Their taut and stretched chest muscles, their recessed abdomens, and their upstretched arms define them as miners toiling in the state's coal industry. They swing their upraised hammers at veins of the valuable rock, hinted at in the black recesses surrounding them. But those same postures echo something else, something a bit more untoward: hanging slabs of beef in a refrigerated meat container. An untitled photograph by Otto Hagel dated 1959 resonates uncomfortably with the figures and composition of Abbey's study (fig. 5). The comparison is not a gratuitous one: it follows directly from the logic that governs the photography of Eakins and Muybridge and the materialism of late Gilded Age society. Whether the body is presented as a machine or as a slab of meat, it performs as a physical object measured and judged by empirical criteria. The heroic male torso, the classicized body seen in Curran's painting and in so many of Abbey's studies, must be read not only as a confirmation of an elite class's cultural nostalgia for a preindustrial past but also as their response to—and refusal of—the proletarianization of the body in a rapidly industrializing era, a response both anguished and urgent.

For Abbey, the body as "meat" or as ideal form served as an object of nostalgia as well as an agent of resistance. In its elemental dimensions—as flesh, as sinews, as bare musculature—it provided an image of beauty and endurance that stood outside or beyond the degradations of the modern social world: a realm of class conflict, ethnic and racial division, and de-skilled labor. Abbey's bodies return us to an idealized era so distant from our own as to seem timeless—the world of the High Renaissance and, at one remove, Greek and Roman culture. Abbey immerses his viewers in the fantasy of heroic torsos as a way of enlisting

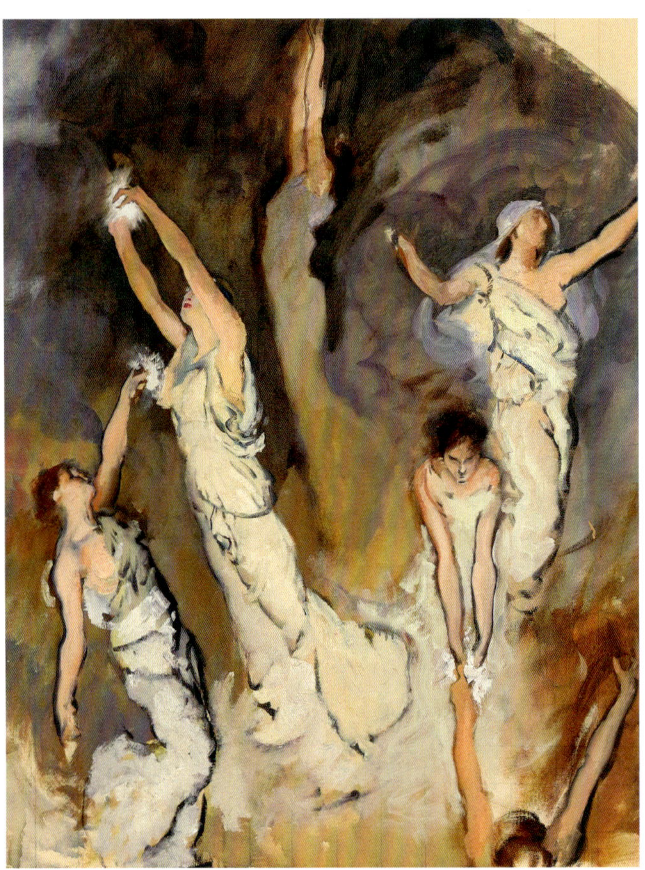

FIG. 6. Detail of cat. 35

his audience in a battle against the opposite: the deformation of the body into mere machine. The flip side of nostalgia, therefore, is not a withdrawal from the hard realities of daily life but an embrace of alternative realities: past worlds where the body once served as the measure of the beautiful, the ideal, and the harmonious. Abbey idealizes the body because he insists on its elemental ability to step outside the present and to imagine instead something more utopian: a world beyond the distortions of late nineteenth-century society.

The same artists who turned men into meat also converted women into angels. In a study for Abbey's *Spirit of Light* mural, destined for the rotunda of the Pennsylvania State Capitol, a group of white-gowned women flutter and ascend their way to heaven (fig. 6). They appear to be weightless, floating against the dark and foreboding forms of oil derricks in the background. The juxtaposition is jarring—spiritual, delicate, and torch-bearing creatures set against the heavy machinery of Pennsylvania oil fields (which, ironically, also point upward, more phallic than angelic). To understand the women's ascent, we need to compare them with two lunettes that John Singer Sargent painted for the Boston Public Library several years later. The first, *The Passing of Souls into Heaven*, brings together white-gowned women, discreetly nude men, and four harps as they all jointly ascend skyward (fig. 7).[12] Each figure looks longingly toward the heavens as if anticipating a long-awaited rapture.

Sargent's language of ascent and spiritualization reflects a larger transformation that occurred in Protestant culture toward the close of the nineteenth century. As Sally Promey notes, the religion of elite Boston was less a matter of dogma and institutions than a more generalized discourse—a set of spiritual values rather than beliefs—that privileged subjective experience over sectarian creed. The Church Triumphant was imagined as a nondenominational mode of liberal Protestant Christianity, where the interior life of the individual, "disconnected . . . from institutions and the dogma," stood as the measure of all true religion.[13] For those Boston elites, religion bled quietly into culture, and both were imagined as heightened—and enlightened—forms of human experience. In their upward flight, Abbey's figures embody the spiritualization of religious practice defining that culture. The women are nonsectarian avatars of a religion

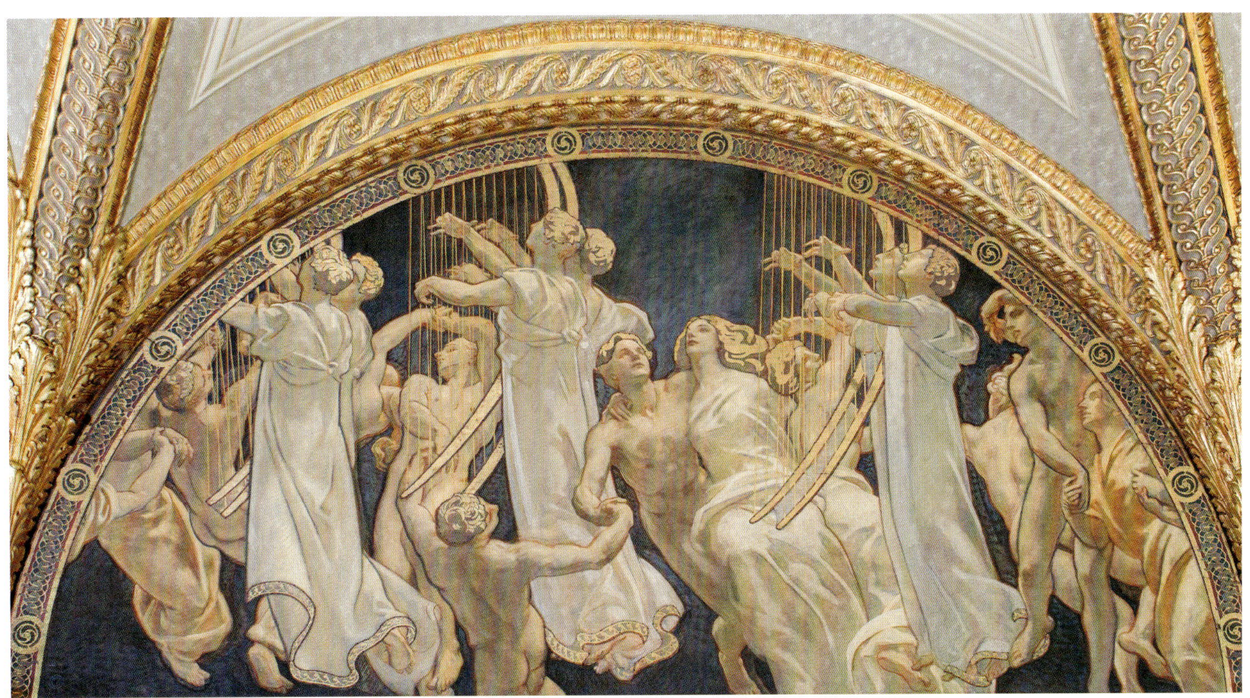

FIG. 7. John Singer Sargent, *The Passing of Souls into Heaven*, installed 1916. Oil and gilded or painted Lincrusta Walton on canvas, w. approx. 16 ft. 10 in. (513 cm). Trustees of the Boston Public Library

of feeling, a world wherein subjective life and personal emotion replace any and all creedal claims.

They exist in a world apart from that inhabited by the earthbound ballet dancer in a sketch by Edgar Degas (fig. 8). On the other side of the Atlantic in this same period, Degas was painting female figures defined not by their spiritual ambitions or balletic beauty but by their bodily struggles: that left leg in need of stretching, that torso bent forward, that downturned face. For Degas, ballet as a mode for artistic endeavor has less to do with form and spirit than with pain and discipline. In this way his dancers are no different from Muybridge's pole-vaulter: material bodies governed by the laws of physics as they move through space. They bear the weight of modernity in their bodies, and in their fraught physicality they bear little relation to Abbey's gravity-defying women.

At the south end of the library, on the east wall, Sargent painted his version of the endpoint of humankind's questlike adventure for salvation. In his mural titled *Messianic Era*, a young boy strides forward from the middle of

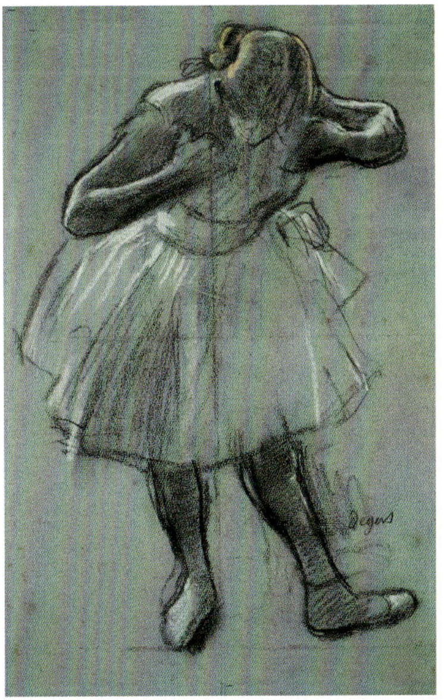

FIG. 8. Edgar Degas, *Dancer Bending Forward*, 1874/79. Charcoal with stumping and pastel on blue laid paper, 18¼ × 12 in. (46.2 × 30.4 cm). The Art Institute of Chicago, 1933.1230

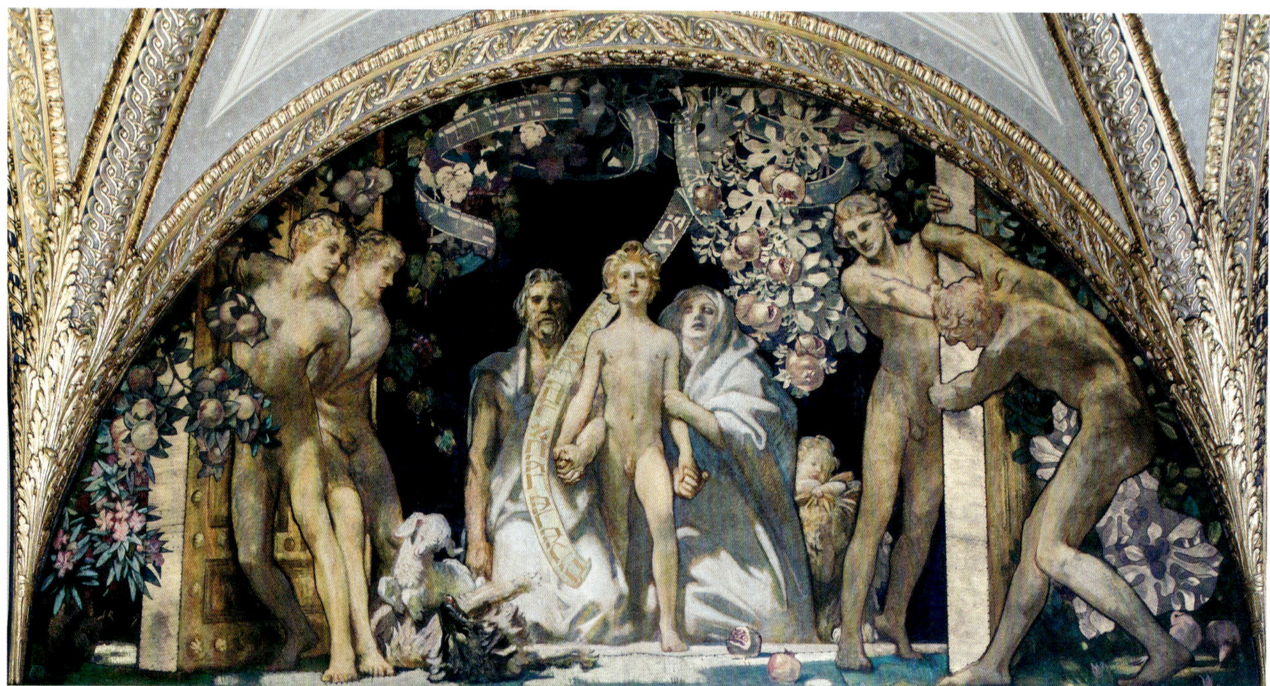

FIG. 9. John Singer Sargent, *The Messianic Era*, East Wall Lunette, South End, installed 1916. Oil and gilded or painted Lincrusta Walton on canvas, w. approx. 16 ft. 10 in. (513 cm). Trustees of the Boston Public Library

the scene (fig. 9). He gazes upward, as do the two adults behind him, each holding one of his hands while gently urging him onward. Four Michelangelo-like figures—a pair on each side—help usher the child into the future. They hold open doorlike frames flanking the central image. A small lamb romps on the ground in front of the boy, and a floral arrangement of leaves and fruits frames the upper crescent of the lunette. The boy commences his journey confident of his goal: a spiritual odyssey toward redemption not only for himself but for all humanity. What matters here is the venturing forth.

This language of questing, and with it an implicit faith in the heavenly reward to follow, reinforces the larger confidence of this era in its own religious advancement. The motif of questing operated at several levels: it suggested the individual's passage toward personal enlightenment; it presaged the efforts of an aspiring middle class toward its own cultural uplift; and it heralded the imagined progress of society in its march toward spiritual freedom and subjective fulfillment. On a more private level for Sargent, as a painter and muralist, the language of questing created an equation between the progress of civilization and his own aesthetic maturation. His murals proclaim, in effect, that the artist has arrived—he has achieved a new level of public prominence visible to all.[14] The metaphor of questing—a motif present everywhere in the state capitols and public works constructed during the American Renaissance—stitches together the social aspirations of cultural elites with an imagined (and often Arthurian) past of great and universal value.[15]

There is a paradox here, an irony worth attending to. At the same time that religion is being privatized and reconceived as a quest for heightened subjectivity, it is also being presented publicly through abstract and allegorical modes of visual address. The former removes it from the realm of public discourse, while the latter eschews the private and relies instead on conventionalized modes of instruction. How do we reconcile the two, and why the apparent contradiction?

The answer lies in an extraordinary set of stained-glass windows created by Louis Comfort Tiffany for Chittenden Hall, then the new library at Yale University (fig. 10). The windows were installed in 1889 as a memorial to the young Mary Lusk, who had died nineteen years earlier. Lusk was the wife of a Yale graduate and the mother of a future Yale professor who later married the daughter of Louis Tiffany. The window features allegorical figures of Art, Science, Religion, and Music, each personified as an angel. All four are accompanied by a retinue of retainers whose halos identify the ideal properties associated with their particular endeavor. Art, for example, is surrounded by personifications of Form, Color, and Imagination. She holds in her hand—as an example of her craft—a sample of stained glass looking very much like a Tiffany window (a humorously self-serving moment on Tiffany's part). At the other end of the window, Music sits surrounded by a chorus of Rhythm, Melody, Harmony, Verse, and Voice.

The power of the window—beyond its sensuality, color, opulence, and variety—lies in its location. Overlooking what was then the University library, high above the heads of the students, the window performed its visual magic like a preacher addressing an attentive congregation. It instructed spectators in the virtues that attend a university education, summarizing in a single, extended image—it is thirty feet wide—the necessary components of a morally lived and intellectually resplendent life. Each personification stands (or sits) as the embodiment of universal values. Each derives legitimacy from an implicitly divine sanction (all four personifications gaze heavenward). And each addresses its audience as if its value were self-evident.

Tiffany's windows, for all their visual majesty, might be understood as the soft side of power—not the threatening stick that Teddy Roosevelt would soon brandish as the ultimate enforcer of American authority but a more persuasive mode—kinder and gentler, attached to art, culture, and education. As Jonathan Freedman notes, "Instruction in the touchstones of Western civilization—classical music, literature, high art, with their ostensibly universal subjects and timeless significance—was seen by those in power as a means of keeping social order, and by those aspiring to power as a means of achieving middle class security."[16] Or to return once more to the Boston Public Library, the "Advancement of Learning" that the library offered, like the allegory of Tiffany's window, proffers both a promise of art and advancement as well as something more than that: an insistence that those wishing to enter its precincts must first drink the Kool-Aid of high culture.[17]

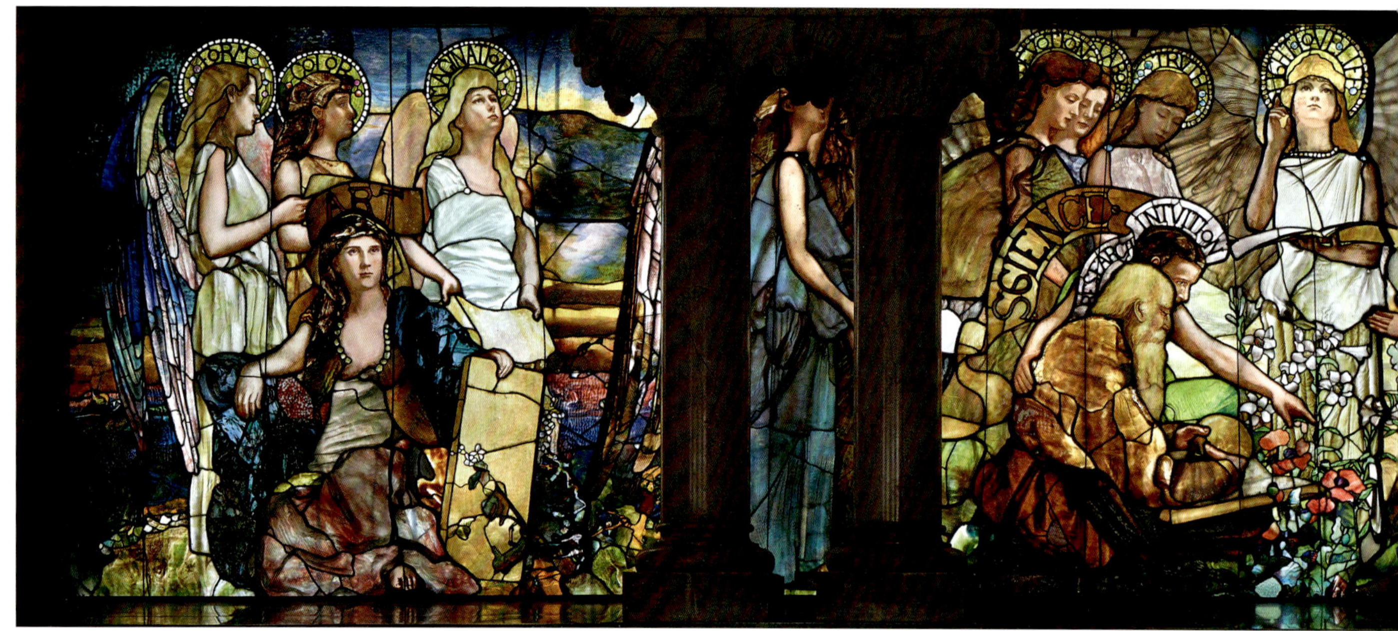

What endures today—more than a century later—from the art of the American Renaissance is not its allegorical language, nor its quiet battle with proletarianization, nor its heroic vision of the classical body (an option that Pablo Picasso would soon bring to a screeching halt with his fractured torsos and fragmented spaces). What survives is a modern mode of art that mixes beauty, power, class, and identity in equal portions. Ultimately, the last word belongs to Henry James. In *The Portrait of a Lady*, Gilbert Osmond admonishes Isabel Archer that one "must live one's life as a work of art."[18] That is the same lesson that Tiffany's windows, two decades later, will offer Yale students entering Chittenden Hall. Tiffany imagines education as a one-way passage into a sacred space, a realm of beauty, taste, and class. And as James might have whispered, keep the children in a separate room.

NOTES

1. Quoted in Sally M. Promey, *Painting Religion in Public: John Singer Sargent's "Triumph of Religion" at the Boston Public Library* (Princeton, N.J.: Princeton University Press, 1999), 159.
2. Pierre Bourdieu, "Cultural Reproduction and Social Reproduction," in *Knowledge, Education, and Cultural Change*, ed. Richard Brown (London: Tavistock, 1973), 71–112.
3. Sven Beckert, *The Monied Metropolis: New York City and the Consolidation of the American Bourgeoisie, 1850–1896* (New York: Cambridge University Press, 2001), 4–8. See also Margaret R. Laster and Chelsea Bruner, eds., *New York: Art and Cultural Capital of the Gilded Age* (New York: Routledge, 2019).
4. Beckert, *Monied Metropolis*, 257.
5. Matthew Arnold, *Culture and Anarchy: An Essay in Political and Social Criticism* (New York: Thomas Nelson and Sons, 1869), 11.

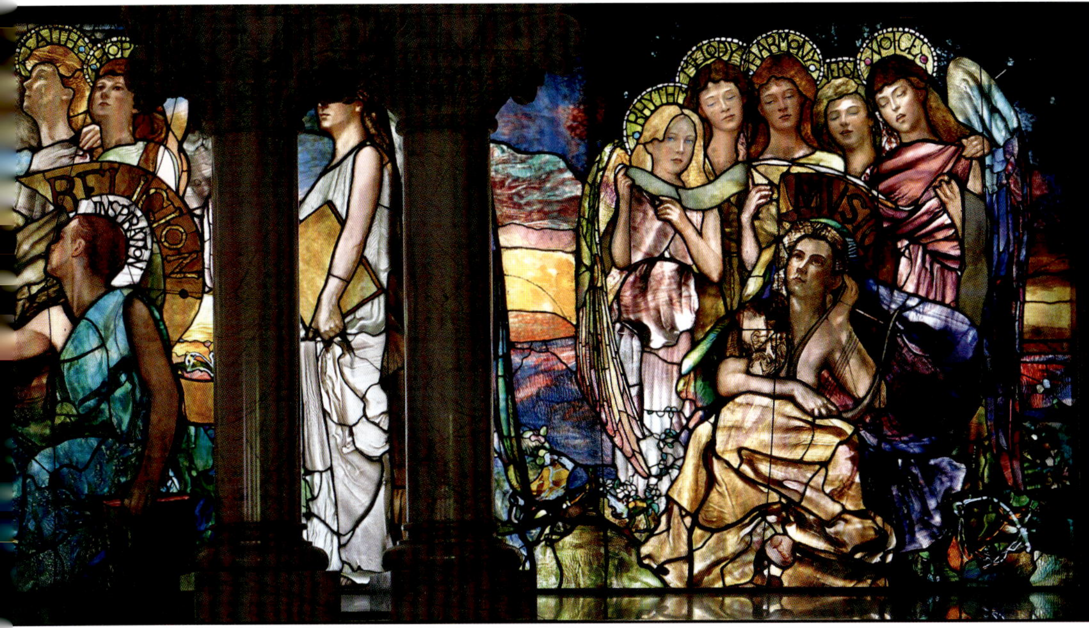

FIG. 10. Louis Comfort Tiffany, designer, and Tiffany Glass Company, manufacturer, *Education: Mary Hartwell Lusk Memorial Window*, designed 1888, dedicated 1889. Leaded opalescent, sheet, and crown glass, 5 ft. 1 in. × 30 ft. (156.2 × 916.9 cm). Linsly-Chittenden Hall, Yale University, New Haven, Conn.

6. Sarah Burns, *Inventing the Modern Artist: Art and Culture in Gilded Age America* (New Haven, Conn.: Yale University Press, 1996), 326. Burns references Bailey Van Hook, "Clear-Eyed Justice: Edward Simmons's Mural in the Criminal Courts Building, Manhattan," *New York History* 73 (October 1992): 457.
7. Kenneth Silver has identified the central male statue in Curran's painting as *The Scraper* by Charles Niehaus, a figure based on ancient Greek sculpture. The scene represents an almost "documentary account" of the National Sculpture Society's second annual exhibition of 1895 in New York. See "*At the Sculpture Exhibition* by Charles Curran," *Yale University Art Gallery Bulletin* 35, no. 1 (Summer 1974): 20–25.
8. *Harper's New Monthly Magazine* 64, no. 383 (April 1882): 740.
9. For a discussion of the high social status attached to embroidery in the late nineteenth century, see Ronald G. Pisano, *Idle Hours: Americans at Leisure, 1865–1914* (Boston: Little Brown, 1988), 43–44.
10. William Cullen Bryant, *The Song of the Sower* (New York: Appleton, 1871), 29.
11. Mark Seltzer, *Bodies and Machines* (New York: Routledge, 1992).
12. Promey, *Painting Religion*, 94. See also Kristin Schwain, *Signs of Grace: Religion and American Art in the Gilded Age* (Ithaca, N.Y.: Cornell University Press, 2008), 104–32.
13. Promey, *Painting Religion*, 7.
14. Ibid., 36.
15. Ibid., 154.
16. Jonathan Freedman, "Jews and the Making of Middlebrow American Culture," *Chronicle of Higher Education* 45 (September 18, 1988); quoted in Promey, *Painting Religion*, 154.
17. Lawrence Levine traces what he terms the "sacralization of culture" during the nineteenth century in his now-classic study *Highbrow/Lowbrow: The Emergence of Cultural Hierarchy in America* (Cambridge, Mass.: Harvard University Press, 1988), 81.
18. Henry James, *Novels and Tales*, vols. 3–4, *The Portrait of a Lady* (New York: Charles Scribner's Sons, 1908), 3:375.

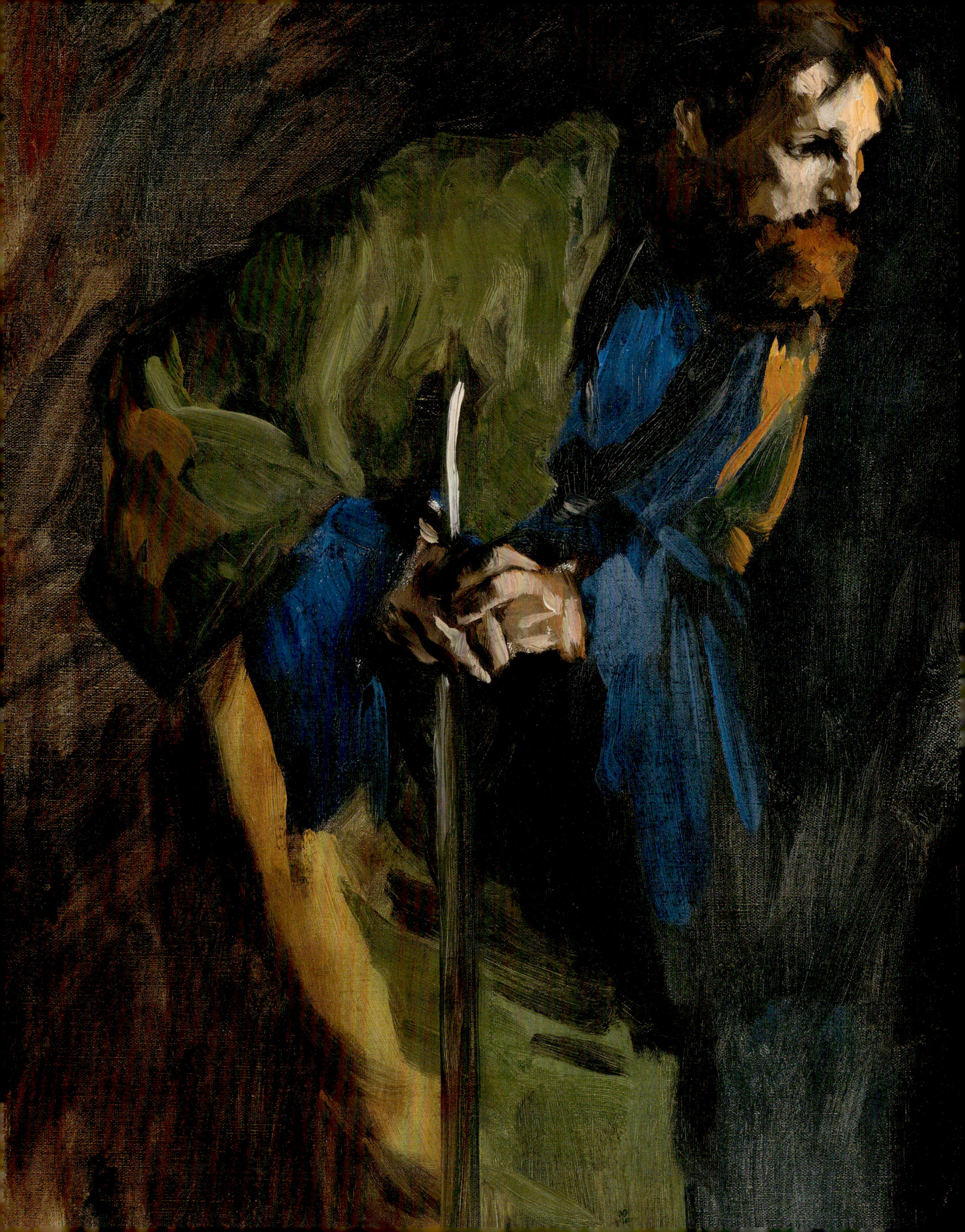

THE BOSTON PUBLIC LIBRARY

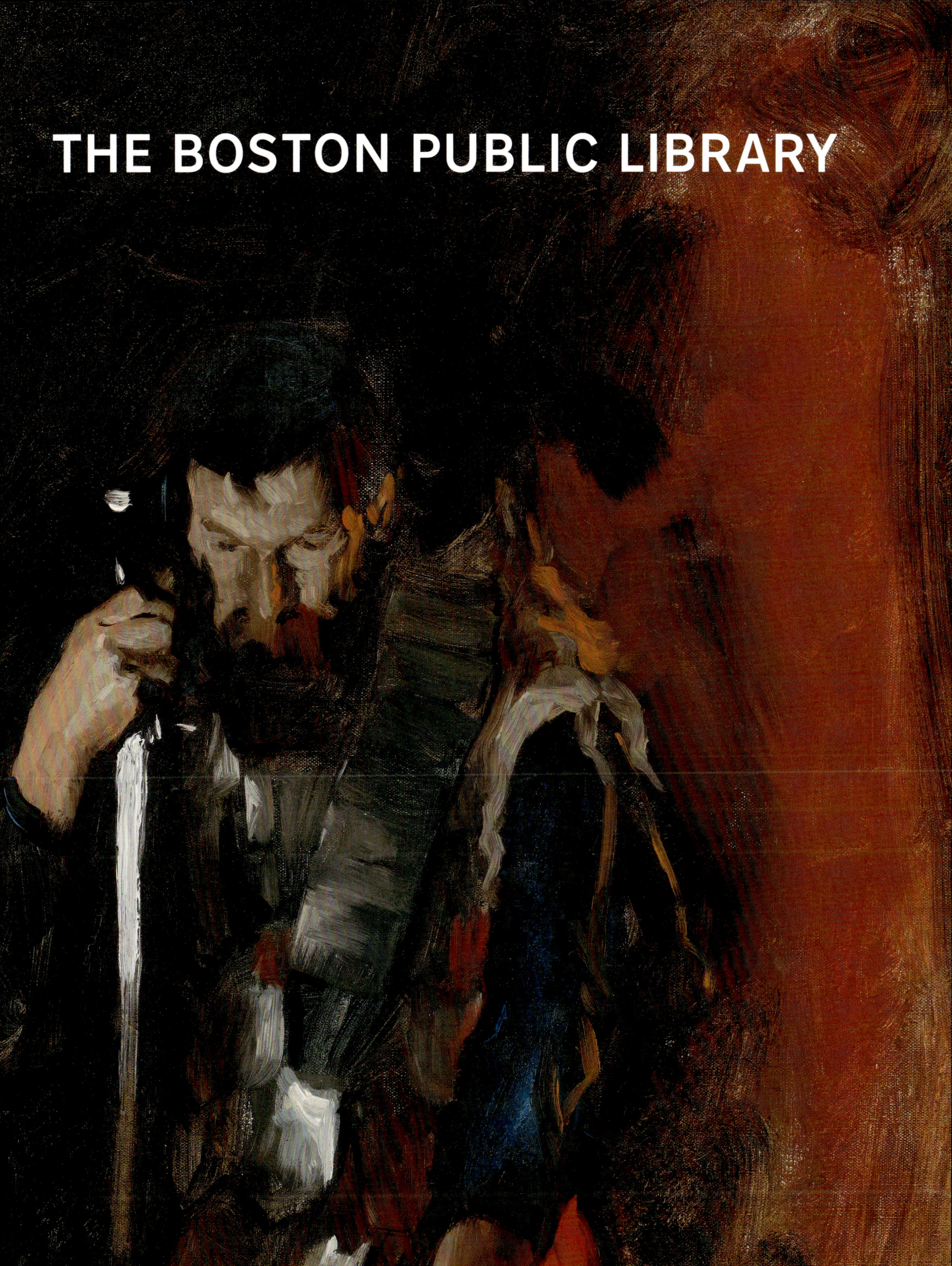

Like Trinity Church across Copley Square, the Boston Public Library (1888–95) was a widely admired centerpiece of the American Renaissance from the moment of its dedication, and it remains so today. Designed by Charles Follen McKim of the New York architectural firm McKim, Mead, and White in the style of an Italian Renaissance palazzo, the library was intended to integrate the arts into a unified aesthetic environment.[1] Ornate bronze doors and sculpture fill the building and are set amid richly colored Italian marble stonework. Among the murals decorating key interior spaces are *The Muses of Inspiration* by the French symbolist Pierre Puvis de Chavannes (see pages 82–83), which surrounds the great staircase, and a cycle on the history of religion by John Singer Sargent in the hall leading to special collections. The book delivery room features a cycle titled *The Quest and Achievement of the Holy Grail* by Edwin Austin Abbey (see pages 100–101).

Monographic scholarship has focused attention on Sargent and the public controversies surrounding his unfinished *Triumph of Religion*, but left unaddressed are the adjacent works by his friend Abbey and their more famous elder, Puvis, for whom this would be his only work in the United States.[2] Puvis had a well-established studio and experience with projects on the scale of the Boston Public Library, which made his commission move relatively quickly.

For Abbey and Sargent, however, their commissions were of a different order than had been their practice—mural painting was new to both artists—and challenged them in ambition and complexity for many years. Begun in 1890, Abbey's series was completed in 1902; Sargent's remained unfinished at his death in 1925. From November 1891 until 1895, the two Americans worked together on their respective commissions for the library at Abbey's rented home, Morgan Hall, in rural Fairford, England, where Abbey had a vast studio built for the purpose.[3]

Both men focused their work on the body. For Abbey, large-scale oil painting was a significant change from his early career as creator of Shakespearean illustrations in pen and ink. His remarkable aptitude for other media is apparent in his studies, for which he used a wide variety of materials and approaches. Here, a loose

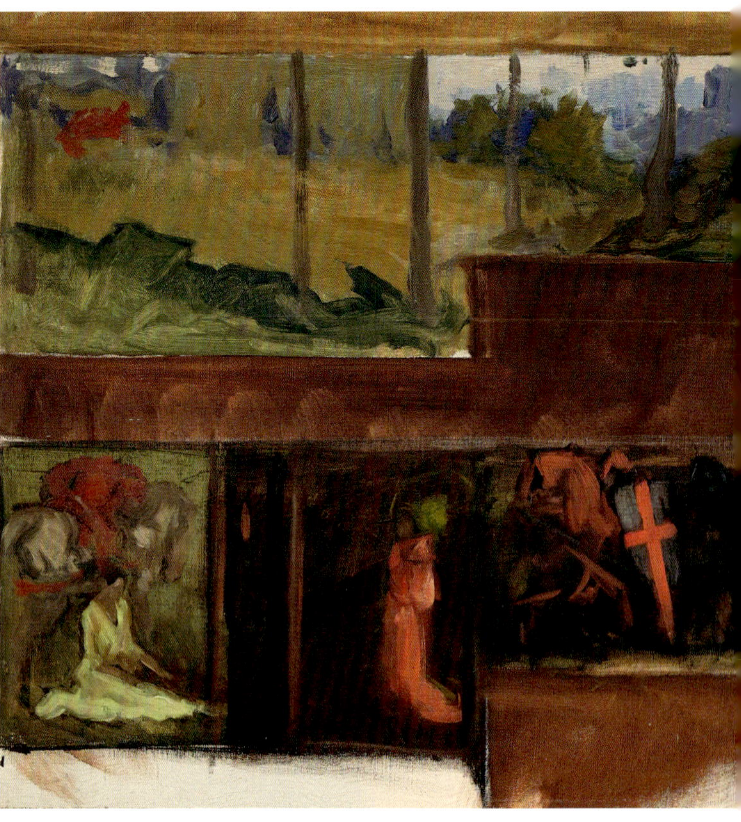

CAT. 20 Edwin Austin Abbey (American, 1852–1911, HON. 1897)

Study for *The Quest and Achievement of the Holy Grail* in the Boston Public Library, ca. 1890–93

Oil on canvas, 23¾ × 70½ in. (60.3 × 179.1 cm)
Yale University Art Gallery, New Haven, Conn., Edwin Austin Abbey Memorial Collection, 1937.2084

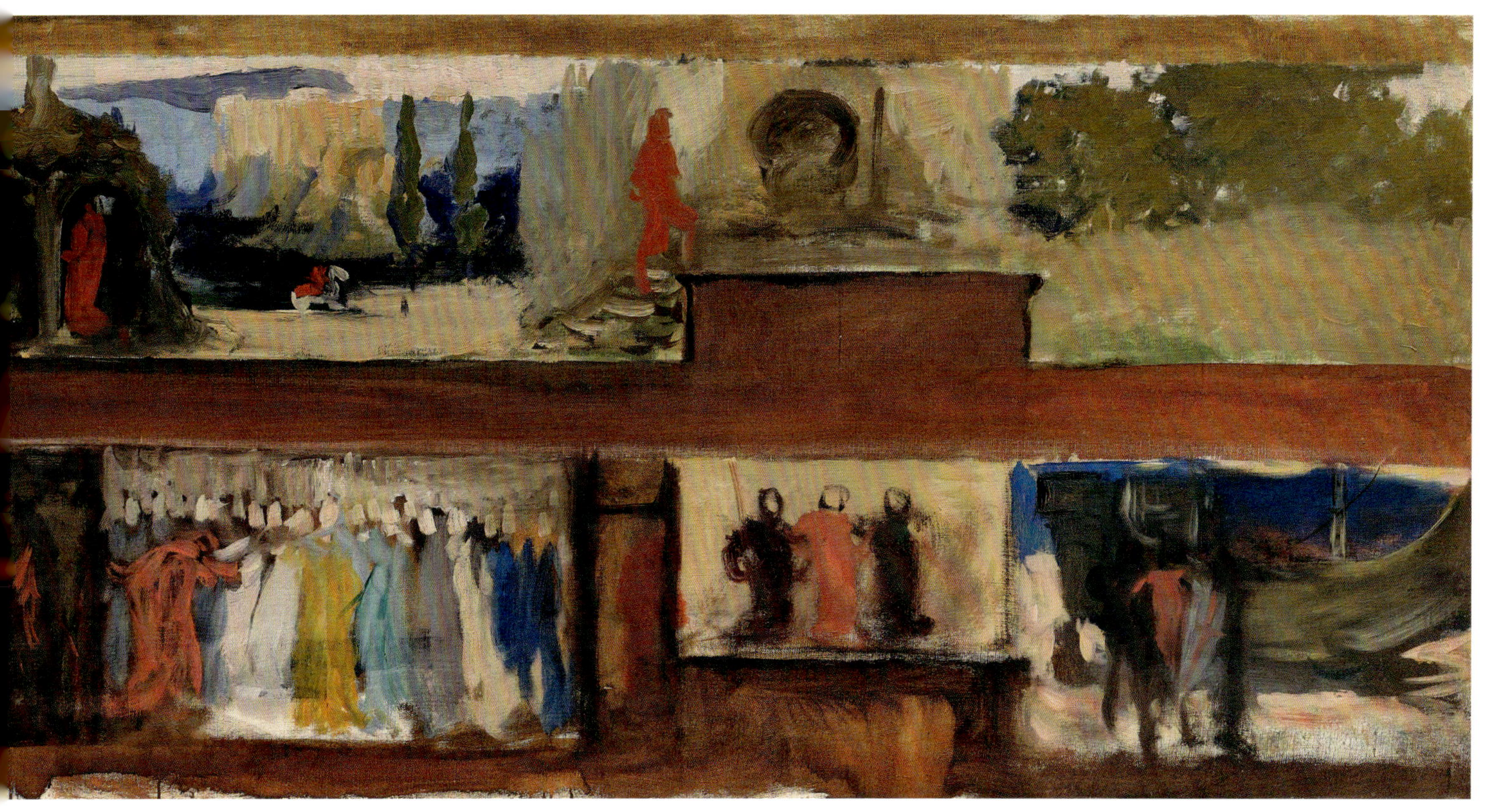

storyboard of the panels—or, perhaps, two alternate proposals—circles the book delivery room (cat. 20), developing a unified narrative and aesthetic effect for the ensemble as the tale navigates the doorways that break into its register.[4] Abbey had earned a reputation for careful research, an extension of the aesthetic practices and historical affinities of the British Pre-Raphaelites who inspired him. Sargent had come to London from Paris, where his sensual virtuosity in oil paint had gained fame that approached infamy.

Both Americans sought a new start in the Boston commissions. Each invested heavily in research to inform their subjects and methods. Sargent's cycle portrayed art history as much as religious history, adapting representations of gods and goddesses from other religions and visual traditions into a compendium of dynamic energy. Abbey was initially hired to portray scenes from Shakespeare's plays, building on his strength and familiarity with their subjects. Instead, he settled on the legend of the Holy Grail, which he embraced as a story with roots and variations in all Western traditions, such that it could be visually adapted for a modern audience.

Wending around the upper register of the elaborate Renaissance-inspired room of dark wood paneling, Abbey's final series distills the legend of Galahad's search for the Holy Grail into fifteen panels, recasting different versions of the narrative for scenes. When complete, a new, summary version of the story was written, possibly with support from his friend Henry James, to accompany the paintings as a key.[5] Reviews of Abbey's work,

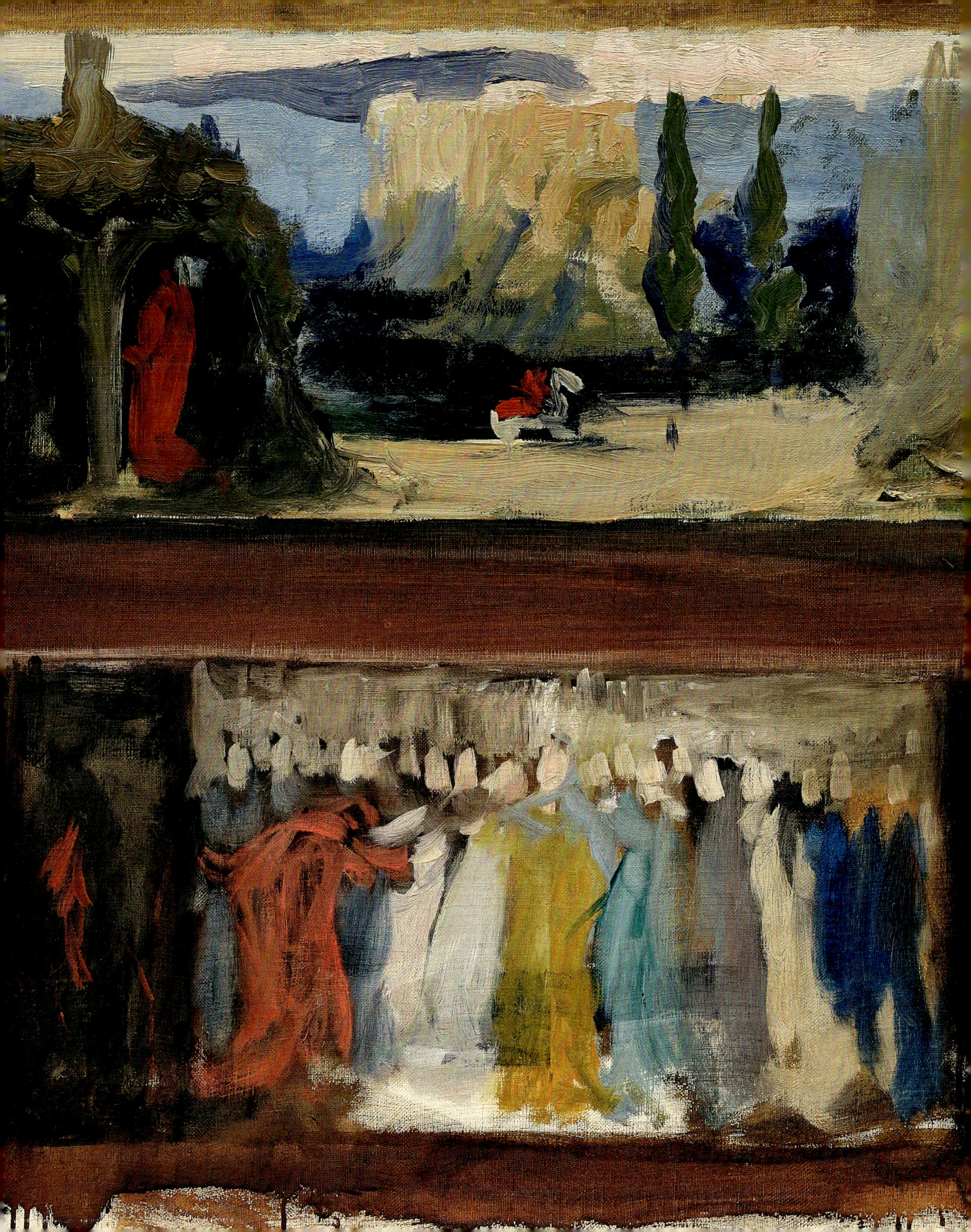

completed and installed in two parts, the first in 1895 and the second in 1902, were euphoric.

As in his illustrations, Abbey invested tremendous detail and narrative orchestration into the compositions. He employed theatrical gestures and lighting to transport viewers to a world of magic and mysticism. Accustomed to the popular theatrical adaptions of his day, in which texts, including Shakespeare, were amended, abbreviated, or omitted to amplify dramatic action and elaborate settings and costumes, Abbey was able to create a grail legend for his own time.[6] In this rendition, the virtuous knight would accept his fated role, resist temptation, battle evil, and sacrifice love, all in the name of his calling. In an age of unsurpassed greed and notorious corruption, Abbey's dramatic tale was widely embraced, reproduced, and emulated. His was not a history of histories, as was Sargent's, but the reinvention of a shared and popular storybook for a new age.

Abbey did not miss the opportunity to display his murals separately before they were installed in Boston, including diverting the scene of the *Castle of the Maidens* to the Paris Salon in 1901, and he exhibited both the finished paintings and related studies in exhibitions and publications. He, more than Sargent, created studies as independent works of art. After Abbey's early death in 1911, Sargent selected several of the studies as illustrations for the defining biography of his friend, which was written by Edward Verrall Lucas and published in 1921.

Detail of cat. 20

NOTES

1. Notably, McKim had also worked on the drawings for Trinity Church in 1870 while in the office of H. H. Richardson; Walter Muir Whitehill, "The Making of an Architectural Masterpiece: The Boston Public Library," *American Art Journal* 2, no. 2 (Autumn 1970): 15.
2. On Sargent, see esp. the scholarship of Sally M. Promey, which examines the drawings for Sargent's final panel of Christ's Sermon on the Mount as expressions of the culminating spiritual ideal of the uncompleted panel; Promey, "Sargent's Truncated Triumph: Art and Religion at the Boston Public Library, 1890–1925," *Art Bulletin* 79, no. 2 (June 1997): 224–32; and Promey, *Painting Religion in Public: John Singer Sargent's "Triumph of Religion" at the Boston Public Library* (Princeton: Princeton University Press, 1999), 42–51.
3. Abbey's studio, believed by his biographer to be the largest in England, was 64 × 40 × 25 ft.; Edward Verrall Lucas, *Edwin Austin Abbey, Royal Academician: The Record of His Life and Work* (London: Methuen, 1921), 1:241–49. See also Evan Charteris, *John Sargent* (New York: Charles Scribner's Sons, 1927), 116. An unlikely coincidence lies in the close resemblance between the dimensions of Abbey's studio and those of the Book Delivery Room at the Boston Public Library, which measures 64 × 33 ft.
4. Unity of effect in his decorative schemes would be a career-long priority for Abbey. His later experience in the uncoordinated decoration of London's Royal Exchange (completed 1904) led, in his view, to a "hideous result" and was a cautionary tale that he cited to others; Abbey to Lord Carlisle, MSS, July 17, 1908, series J33/84, Castle Howard Archive, York, England.
5. Leon Edel and Dan H. Laurence, *A Bibliography of Henry James*, 3rd ed. (Oxford: Clarendon, 1982), 218–22.
6. In the Grail legend, Abbey found a subject "treating generally of the sources of romances or the beginning of modern literature . . . offering great scope for the exercise of imagination"; Abbey, undated typescript, Trustees Records: Art and Architecture Records (MS Bos Li), box 1, folder 1A, Abbey Mural, Boston Public Library.

PAGES 82–83: The Puvis de Chavannes Gallery in the Boston Public Library

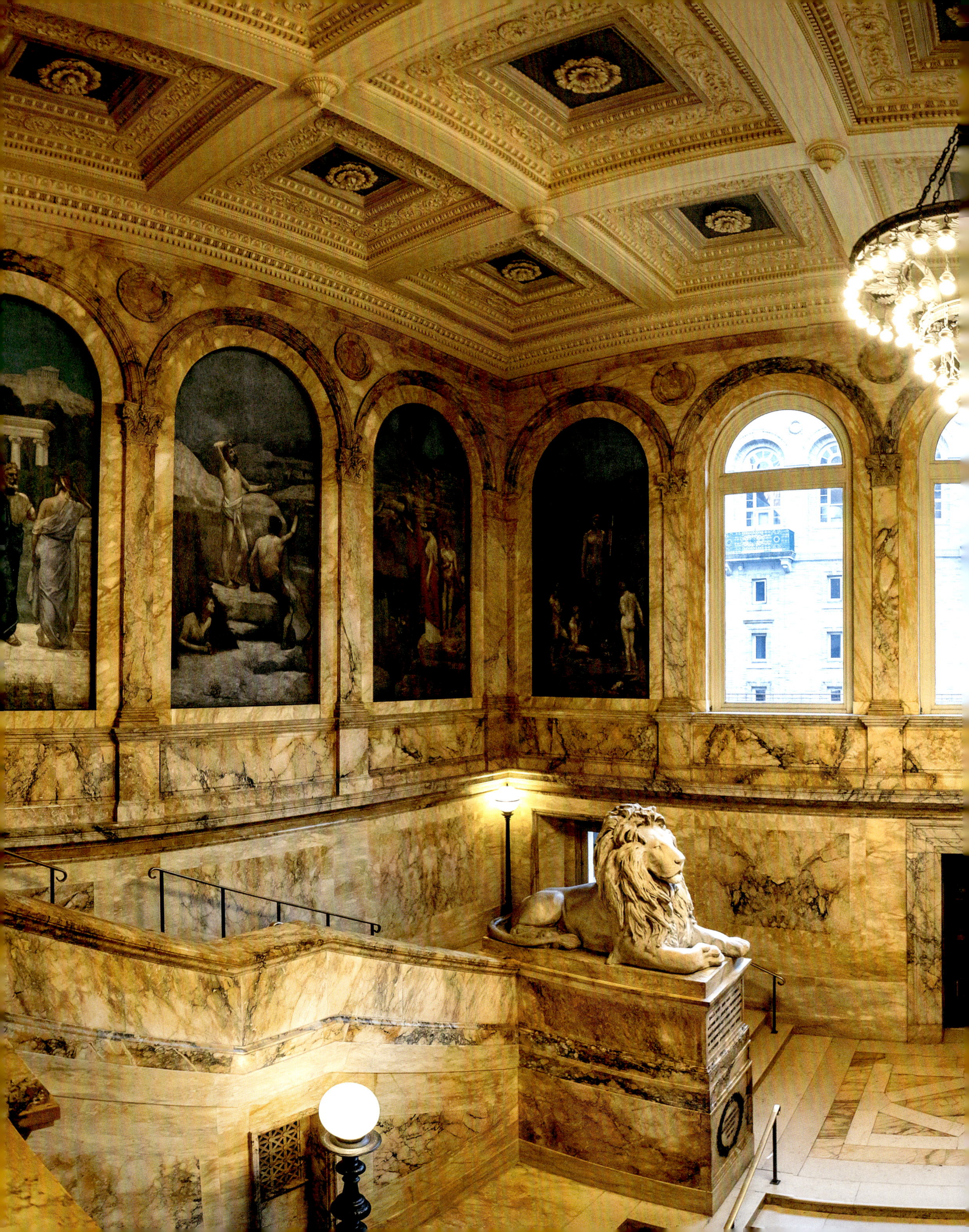

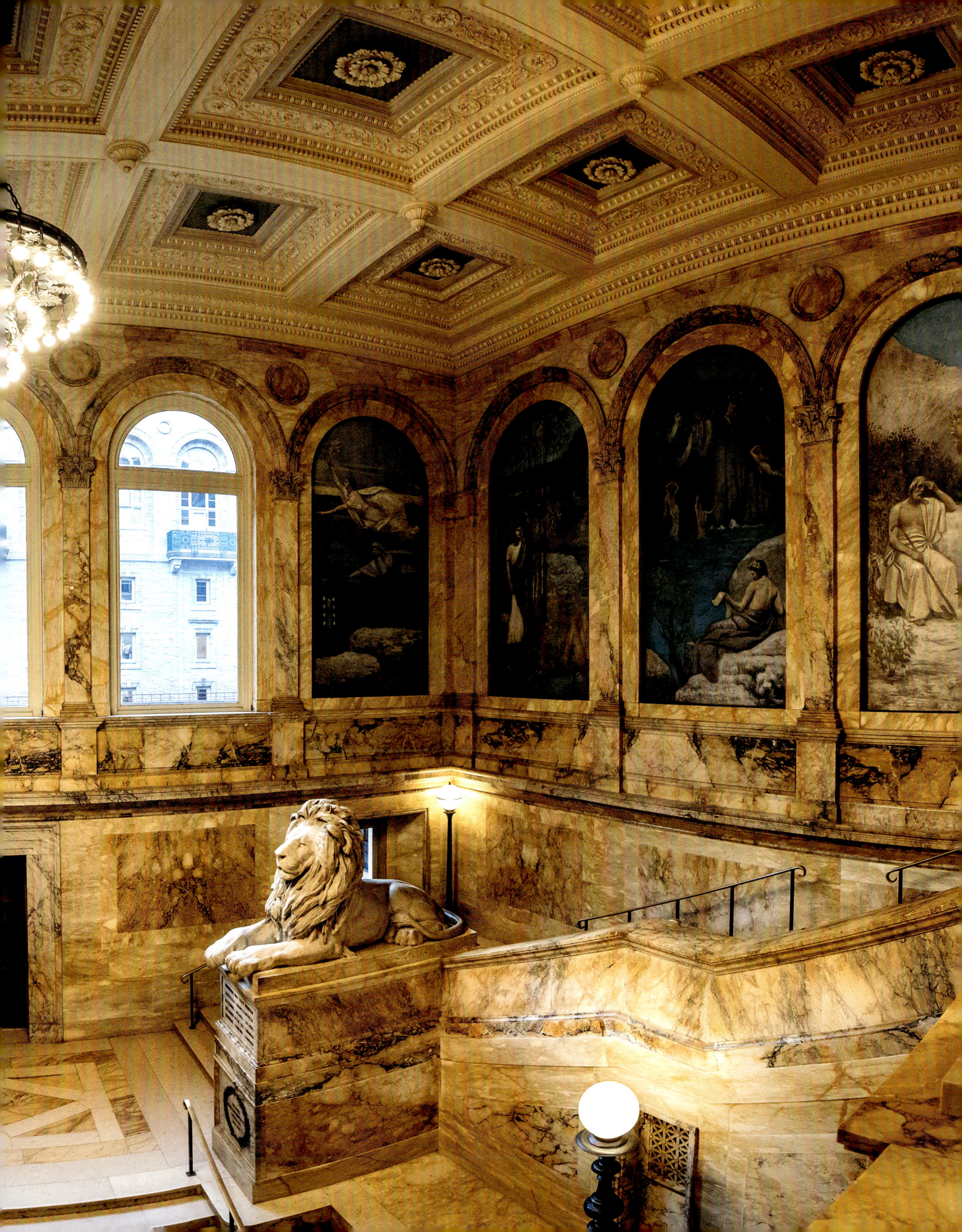

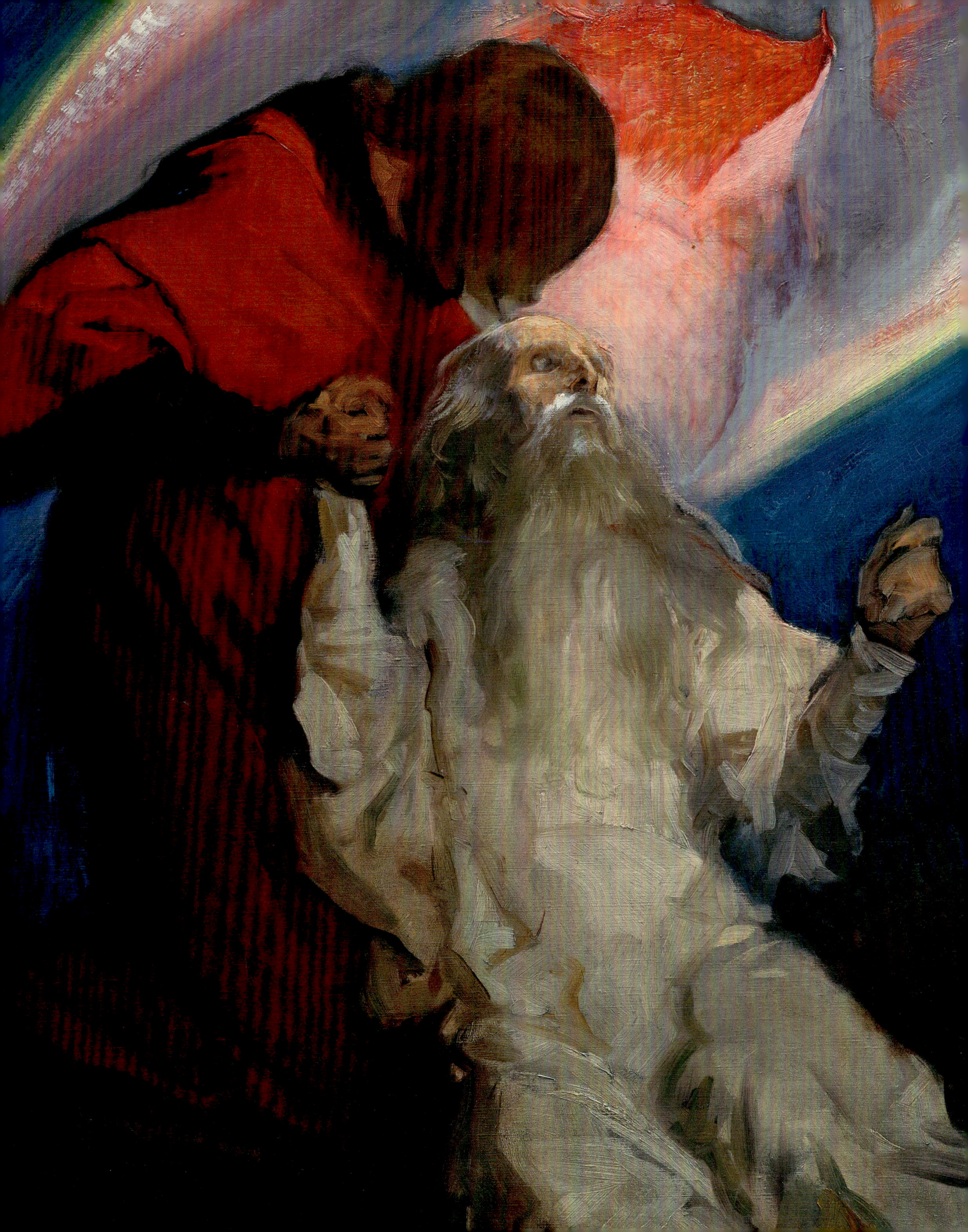

Passing Generations

These two studies of King Amfortas, created by Edwin Austin Abbey for his *Holy Grail* mural cycle at the Boston Public Library, center on the dying king's face at the moment of his release from the spell that has held him captive. Galahad cradles him gently and appears to support the falling figure. Abbey's studies embellish the psychological focus of the scene and balance between an emphasis on transcendence or fear. In the oil version (cat. 21), the shrouded Grail casts a stark, bright light that amplifies color to an otherworldly saturation, which Abbey would eventually tone down to align with the rest of the scenes. In a related way, the charcoal and chalk study (cat. 22) presents a wide-eyed and dazed king, well-suited to the emphatic lines and expressive contrasts of the drawing. In medium and style, each work accentuates different aspects of the composition and expands its expressive potential, presenting a possibility for the finished mural.

Abbey's scene of Amfortas's death highlights a generational transition similar to that of his own time as memory of the Civil War ebbed. After his trials and sacrifices, Galahad has at last broken the spell that bound the king in thrall, earning the Grail as well as his own throne. The old king, having lived in a distant age and asleep since then, offered an appropriate symbol of an earlier, defining time that seems to pass away. Abbey's experiments with Amfortas's feelings suggest ambivalence, however: a dark era has passed, but the future may not be better, and the Grail is not yet in hand.

CAT. 21 Edwin Austin Abbey (American, 1852–1911, HON. 1897)

Study for *The Passing of King Amfortas* in *The Quest and Achievement of the Holy Grail* in the Boston Public Library, ca. 1895–1900

Oil on canvas, 75 7/16 × 30 in. (191.6 × 76.2 cm)
Yale University Art Gallery, New Haven, Conn., Edwin Austin Abbey Memorial Collection, 1937.2050

CAT. 22 Edwin Austin Abbey (American, 1852–1911, HON. 1897)

Study for *The Passing of King Amfortas* in *The Quest and Achievement of the Holy Grail* in the Boston Public Library, ca. 1895–1900

Charcoal and chalk on paper, 30 7/8 × 22 1/8 in. (78.4 × 56.2 cm)
Yale University Art Gallery, New Haven, Conn., Edwin Austin Abbey Memorial Collection, 1937.2055

Detail of cat. 21

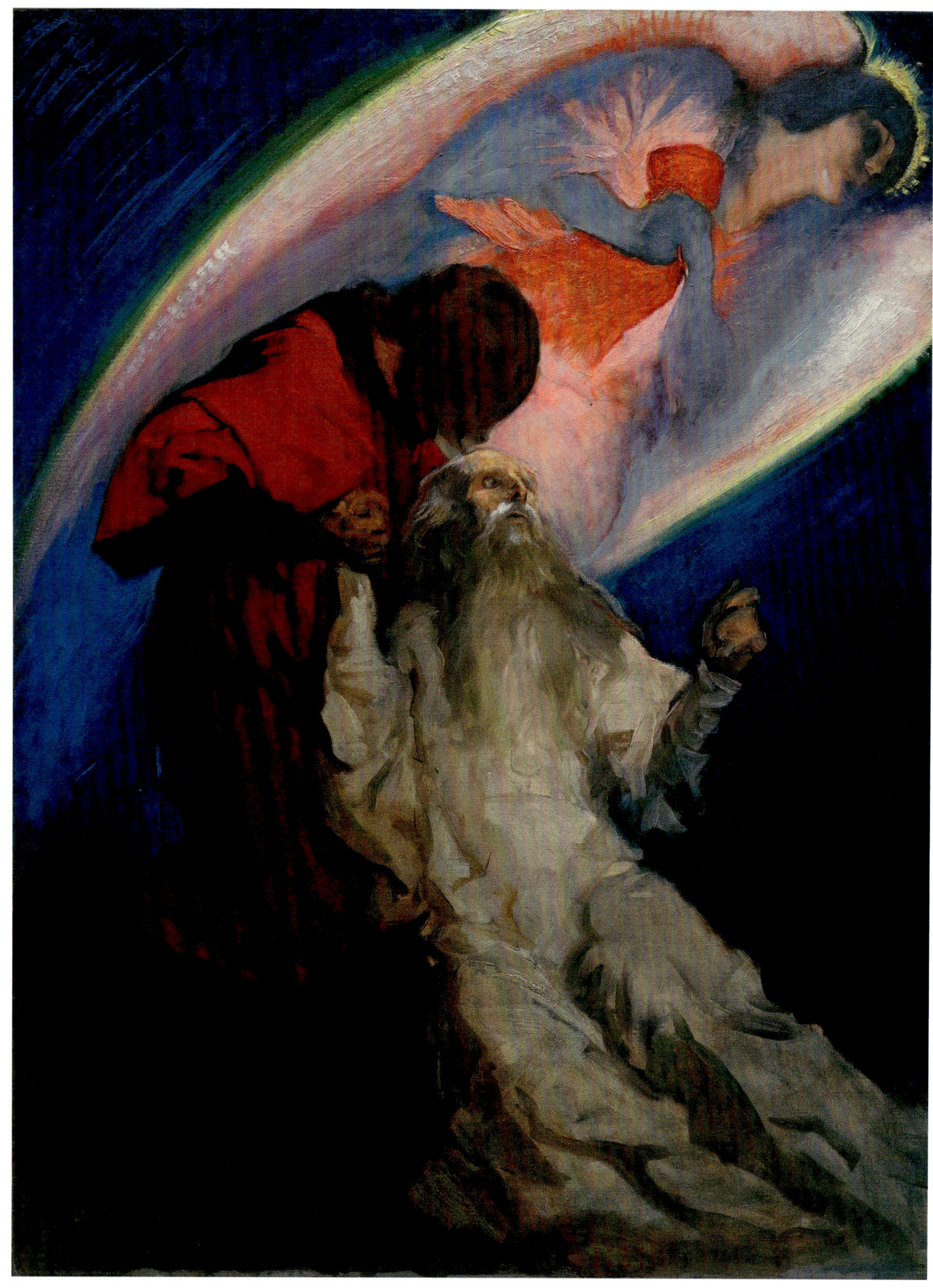

21

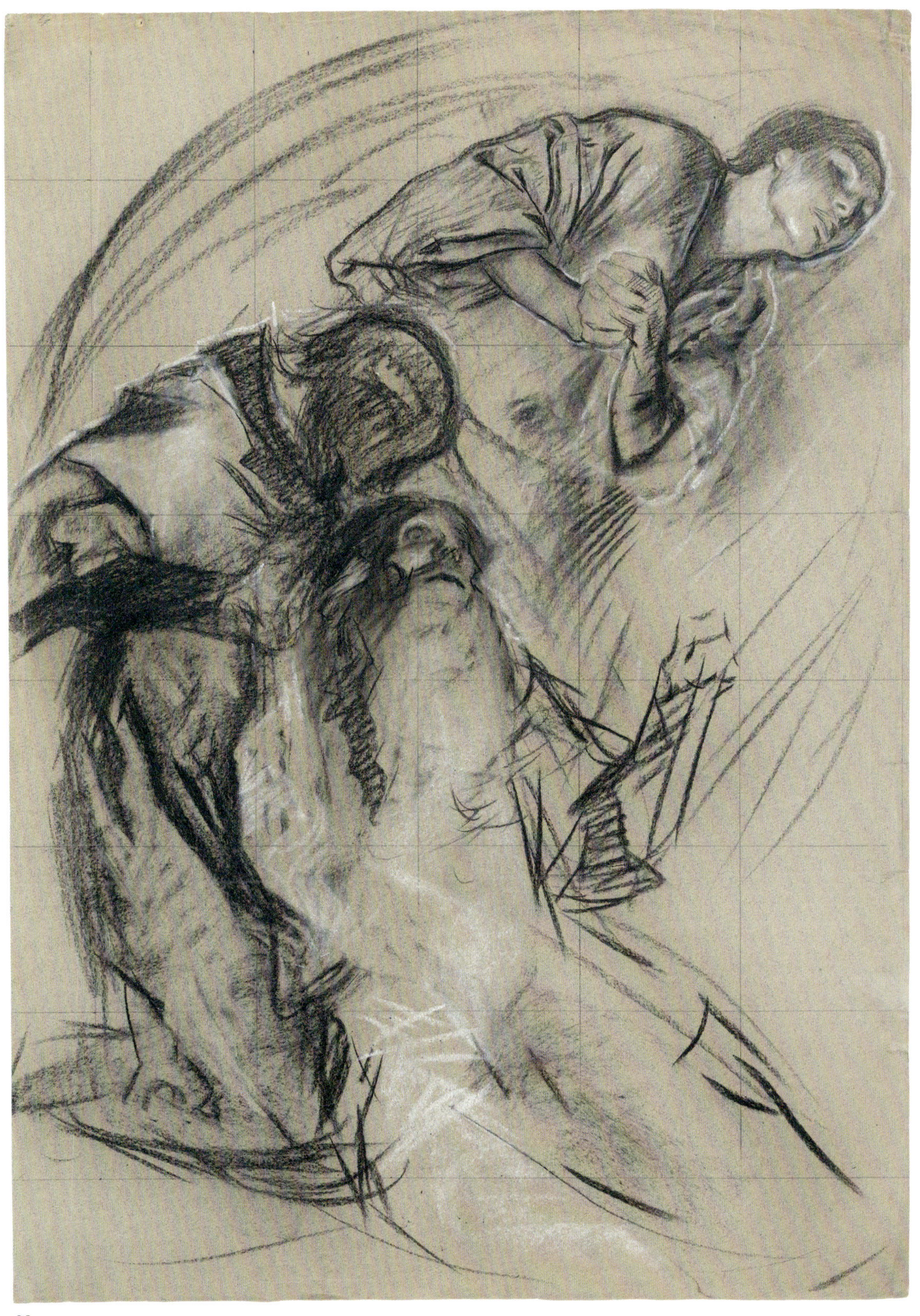

22

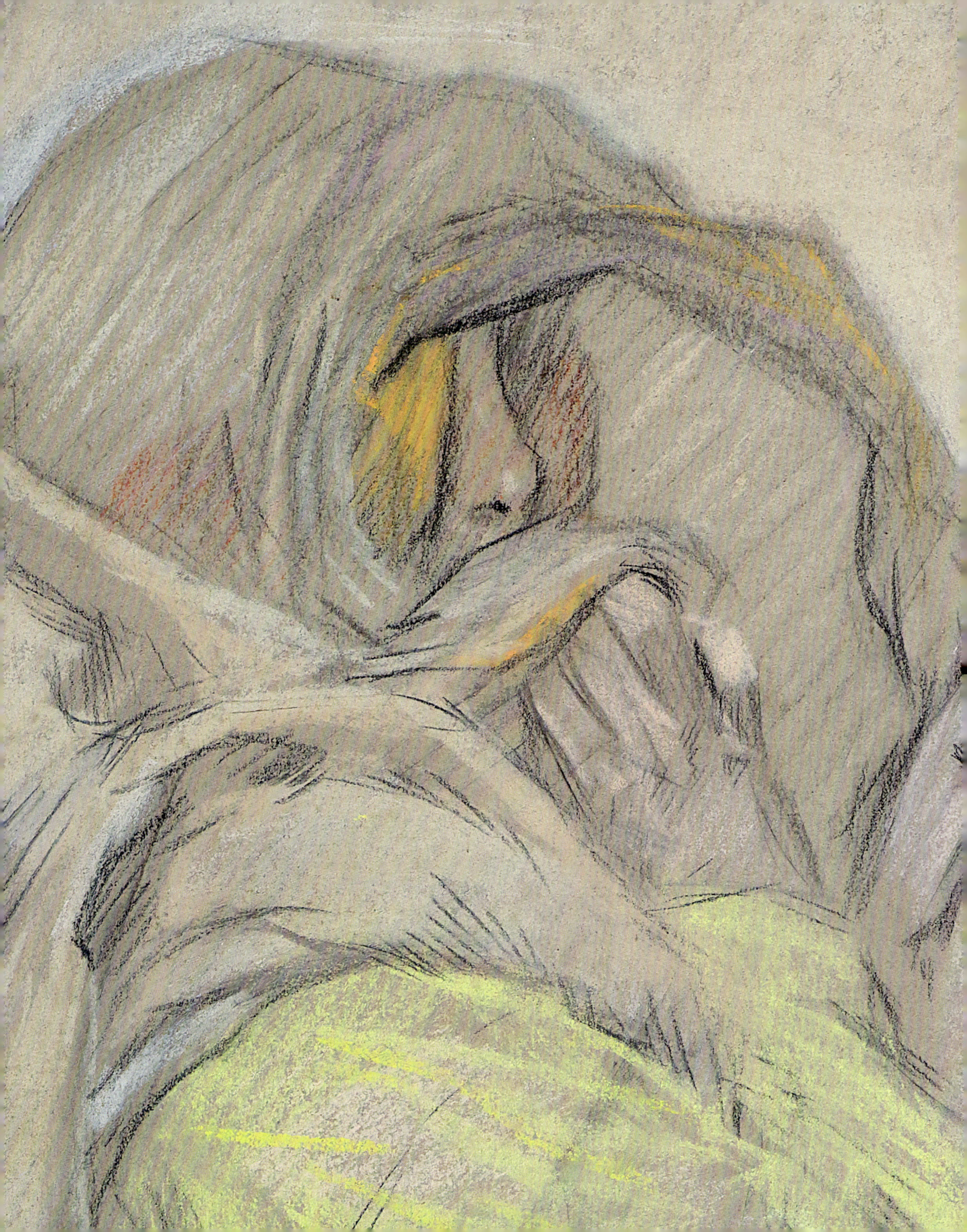

Ghosts

Cloaked and veiled figures were central to Edwin Austin Abbey's mural projects, as they were to many European and American Expressionist and Symbolist artists at the turn of the twentieth century. The figures' hidden features, like the ghost of King Hamlet, are both specters and chorus, representing the lingering past as well as the collective present. In these two studies, Abbey portrays them as heavily draped priests, monks, nuns, and angels (cats. 23–24). Like those religious roles, the figures suggest physical absence and spiritual presence.

In Abbey's early study for the *Arthurian Round Table* in the *Holy Grail* cycle, Joseph of Arimathea leads Galahad to his appointed seat, identifying him as the prophesied hero. Joseph is a caretaker of the Grail, the sacred cup from which Jesus drank at the Last Supper before his crucifixion. In Abbey's composition, even Joseph's identification is uncertain, for lack of information; his role is more as a facilitator than protector. He leads Galahad to his destiny.

Abbey's ghosts haunt his scenes and bridge disconnected narrative elements. They often stand in for multiple characters from the various historic renditions of the Grail legend that the artist elided for visual effect. By masking the body, Abbey is able to fold together multiple roles and identities and make the figure perform different functions. Without being told, the viewer has no means of identifying the figures specifically, though knowing any of the most popular versions of the story would enable them to identify a plausible candidate for the cloaked figure, thereby sustaining the integrity and consistency of their preferred narrative.

More broadly, the haunting of Abbey's characters suggests a subconscious, unspoken presence, a past that continues to act in the unfolding drama. At the end of the nineteenth century, the nation was haunted by many things, including retrenchment after the abolition of slavery, sectional conflict of the Civil War, continuing displacement of Native American communities, and increasingly oppressive treatment of industrial laborers. All of these echo in the hauntings of Abbey's work, hidden but present on the allegorical stage of history.

CAT. 23 Edwin Austin Abbey (American, 1852–1911, HON. 1897)

Study for Joseph of Arimathea for *The Arthurian Round Table and the Fable of the Seat Perilous* in *The Quest and Achievement of the Holy Grail* in the Boston Public Library, ca. 1890–94

Charcoal and white chalk on brown paper, 28¼ × 19⅜ in. (71.8 × 49.2 cm)
Yale University Art Gallery, New Haven, Conn., Edwin Austin Abbey Memorial Collection, 1937.4357

CAT. 24 Edwin Austin Abbey (American, 1852–1911, HON. 1897)

Study for *The Castle of the Maidens* in *The Quest and Achievement of the Holy Grail* in the Boston Public Library, ca. 1895–1900

Pastel on paper, 32¾ × 13 in. (83.2 × 33 cm)
Yale University Art Gallery, New Haven, Conn., Edwin Austin Abbey Memorial Collection, 1937.1346

Detail of cat. 24

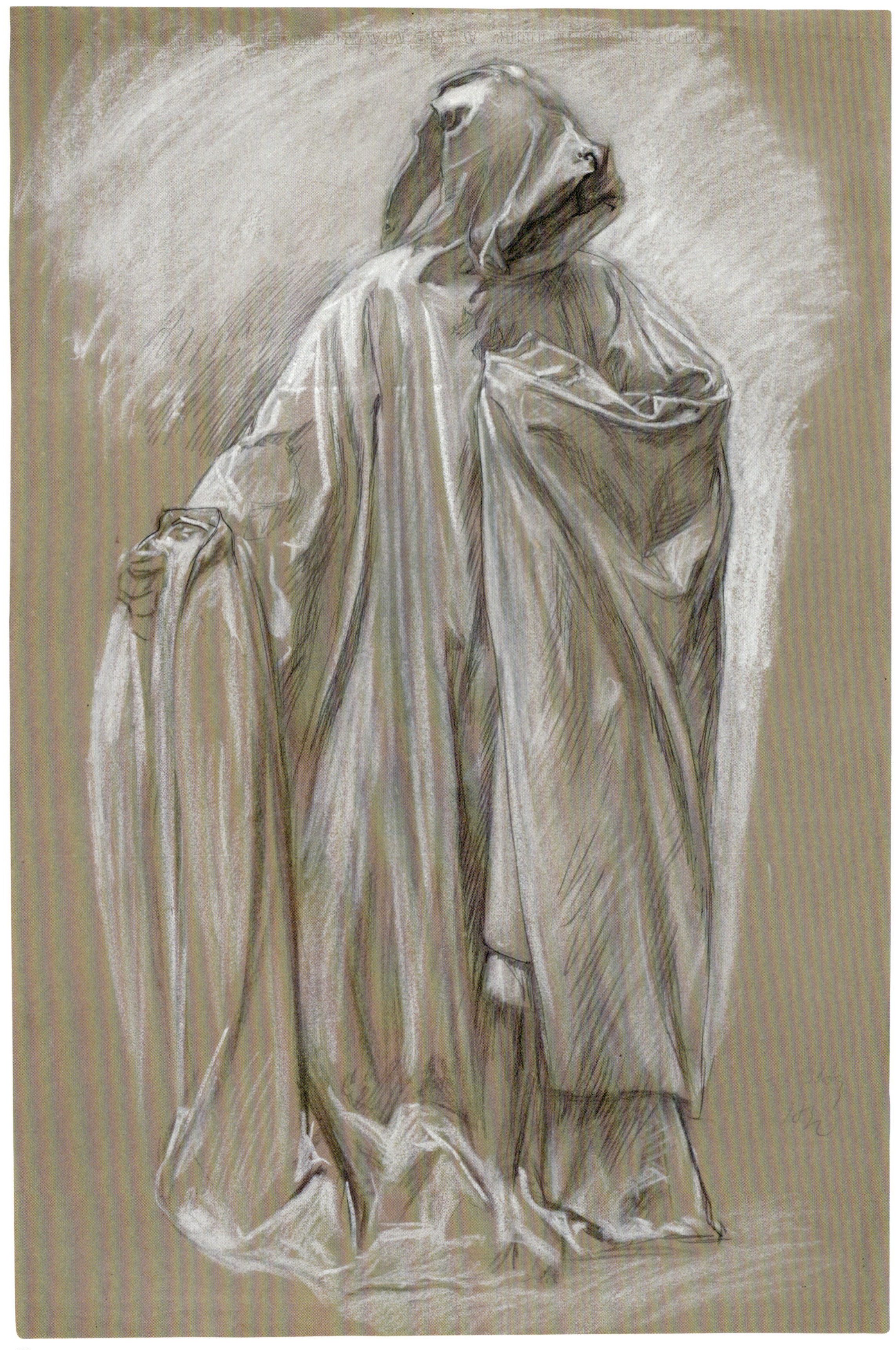

23

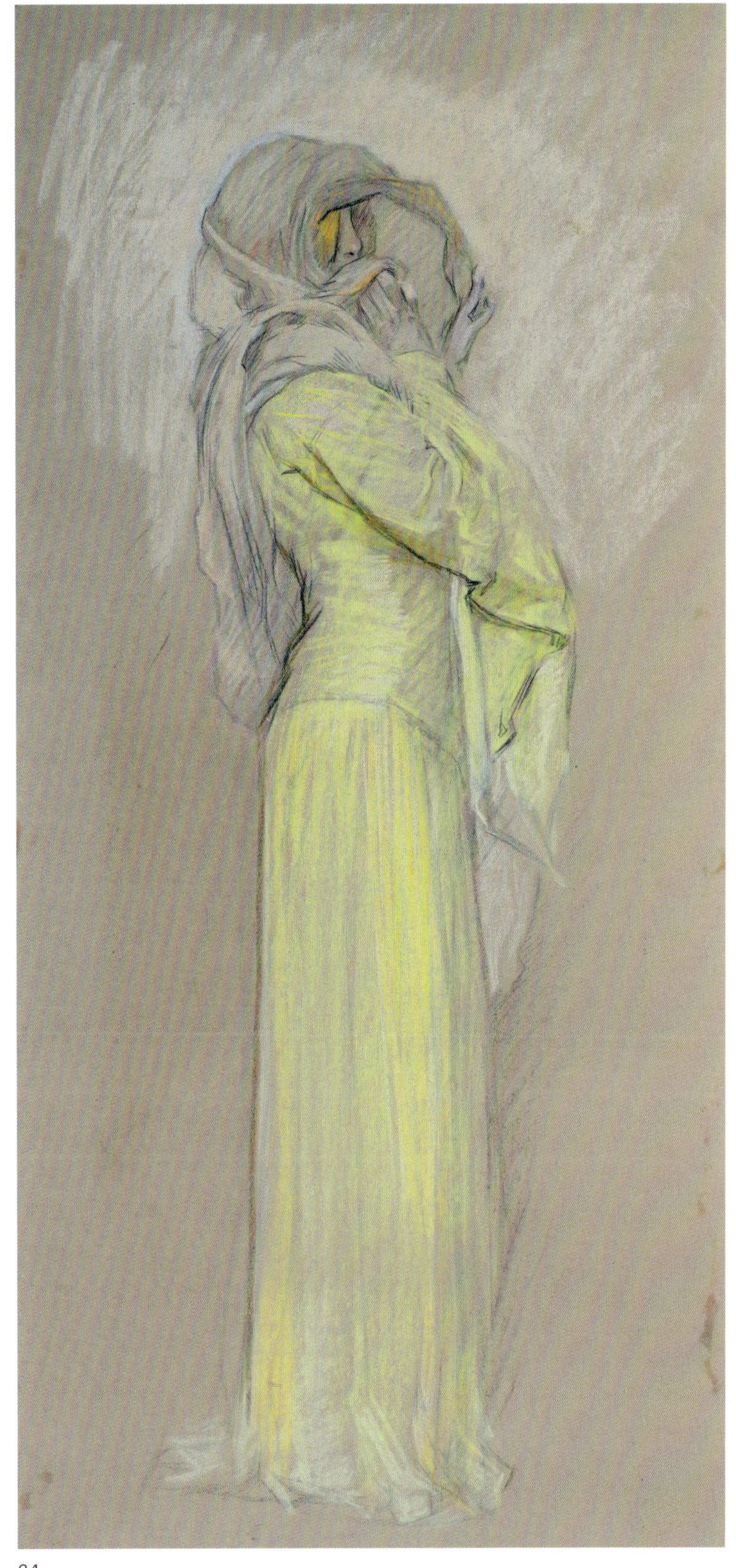

24

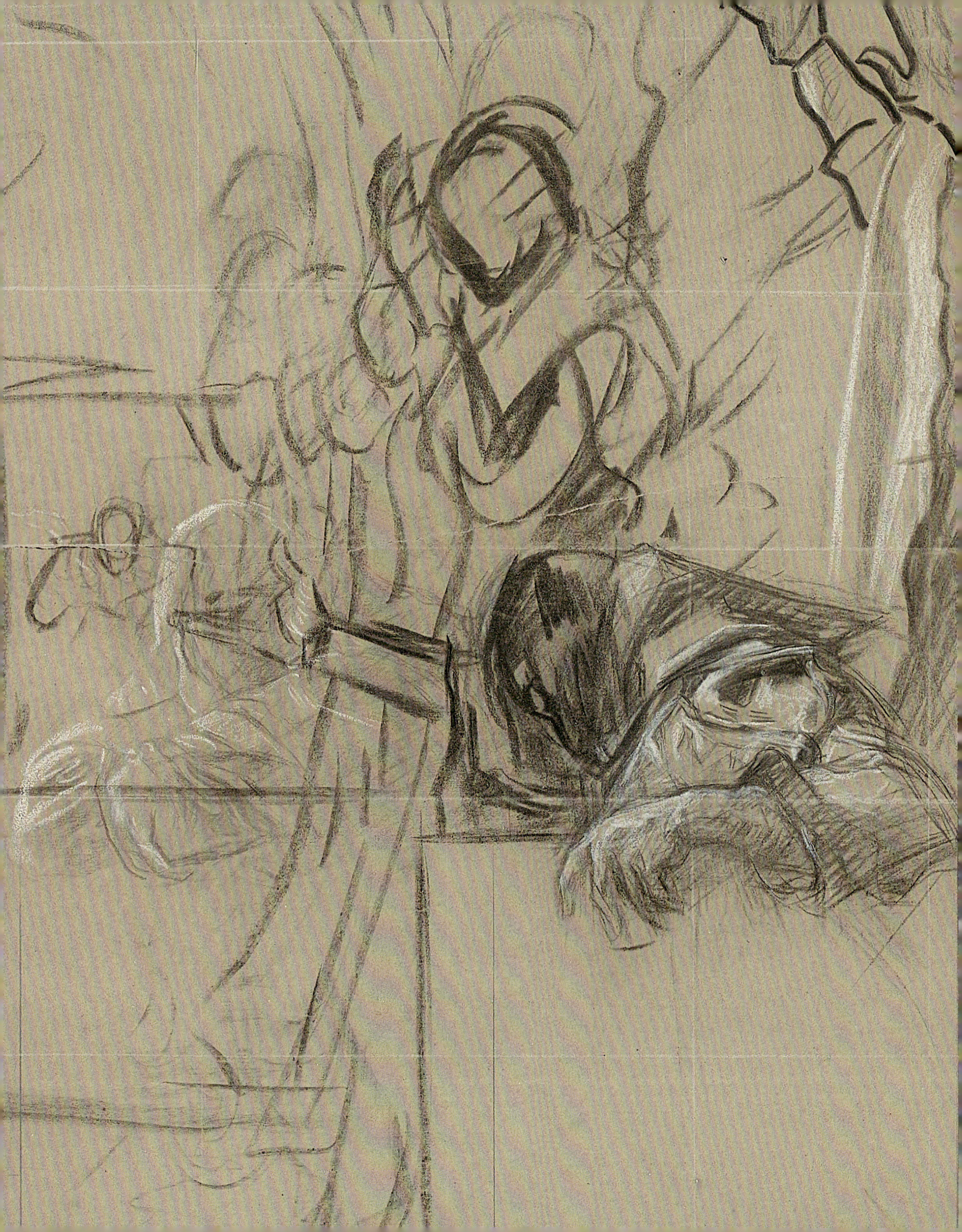

Knights

Edwin Austin Abbey's knights offer a range of expressions. Contemplating the fate of Galahad if he fails the test of the Siege Perilous—a seat that only the virtuous may occupy—the assembled group offers a mixture of dramatic responses, all disbelieving and fearful. Their lack of faith resounds in Christian tradition and leaves Galahad's fate to his own conviction. Rather than evoking certainty and devotion, Abbey's knights more often meditate on death, contemplate by firelight, or kneel in submission. Like many of William Shakespeare's characters, their exaggerated gestures and fatalism highlight the protagonist's determination by contrast.

In the aftermath of the Civil War, Abbey's knights and their search for salvation recast recent history and ongoing conflicts in moral terms. Abbey's interpretation of the Grail legend focuses on the single knight, Galahad, rather than his army. Clad in vivid red, Galahad stands apart from his peers; he moves away from their inadequacies and failings, which have left the world in moral suspension. The knights are depicted in darkness, contemplating their mortality, while Galahad alone moves forward, a beacon in an age of moral turpitude. He breaks with the knights' traditions and history, leading them to a new order illuminated by divine approbation and accompanied by a host of angels, his coming foretold.

CAT. 25 Edwin Austin Abbey (American, 1852–1911, HON. 1897)

Compositional Study for *The Arthurian Round Table and the Fable of the Seat Perilous* in *The Quest and Achievement of the Holy Grail* in the Boston Public Library, ca. 1890–95

Black and white chalk on gray wove paper, 52¾ × 86 in. (134 × 218.4 cm)
Yale University Art Gallery, New Haven, Conn., Edwin Austin Abbey Memorial Collection, 1937.1925

CAT. 26 Edwin Austin Abbey (American, 1852–1911, HON. 1897)

Figure Study, possibly for *The Quest and Achievement of the Holy Grail* in the Boston Public Library, ca. 1890–1902

Oil on canvas, 28 × 36 in. (71.1 × 91.4 cm)
Yale University Art Gallery, New Haven, Conn., Edwin Austin Abbey Memorial Collection, 1937.2094

Detail of cat. 25

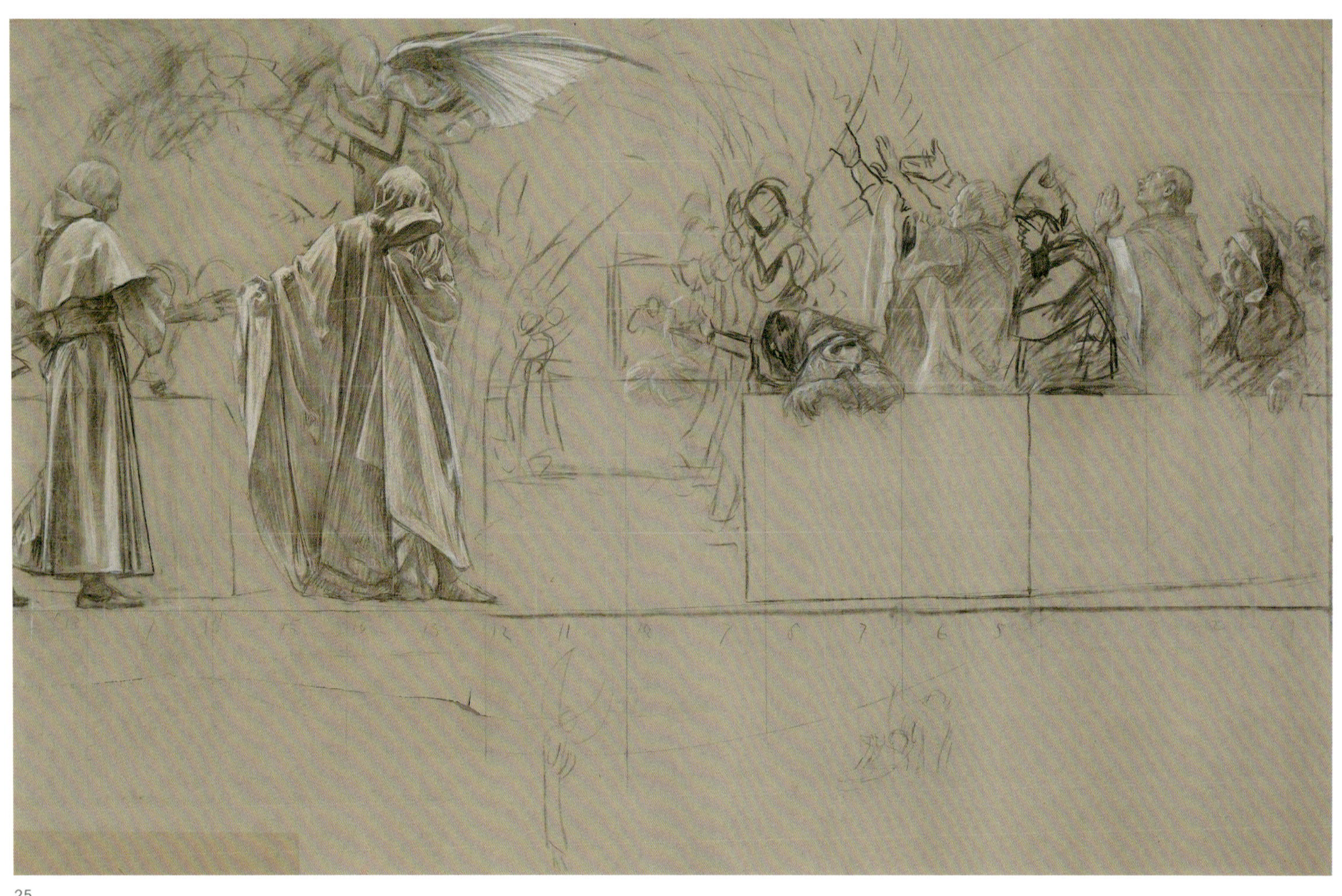

25

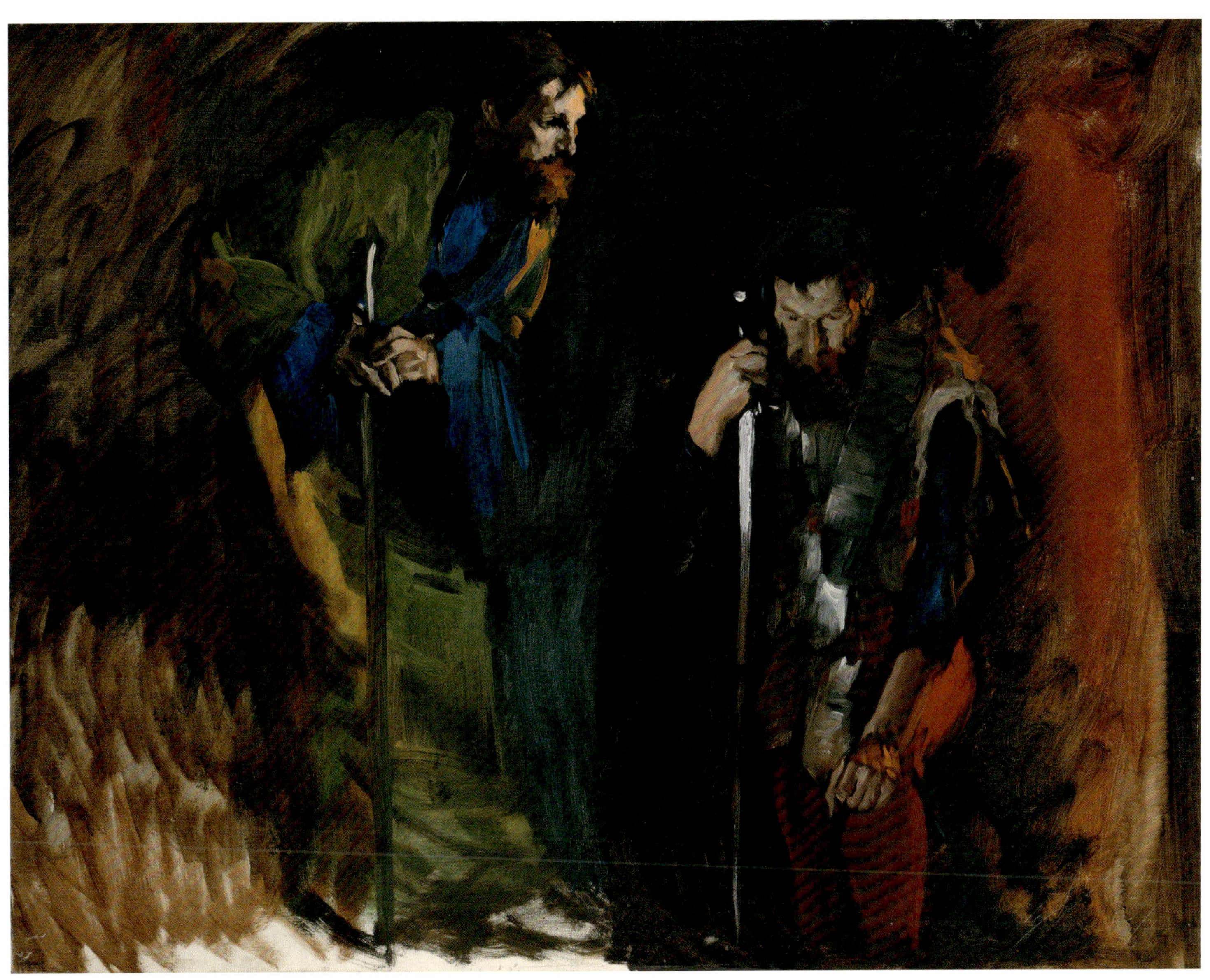

26

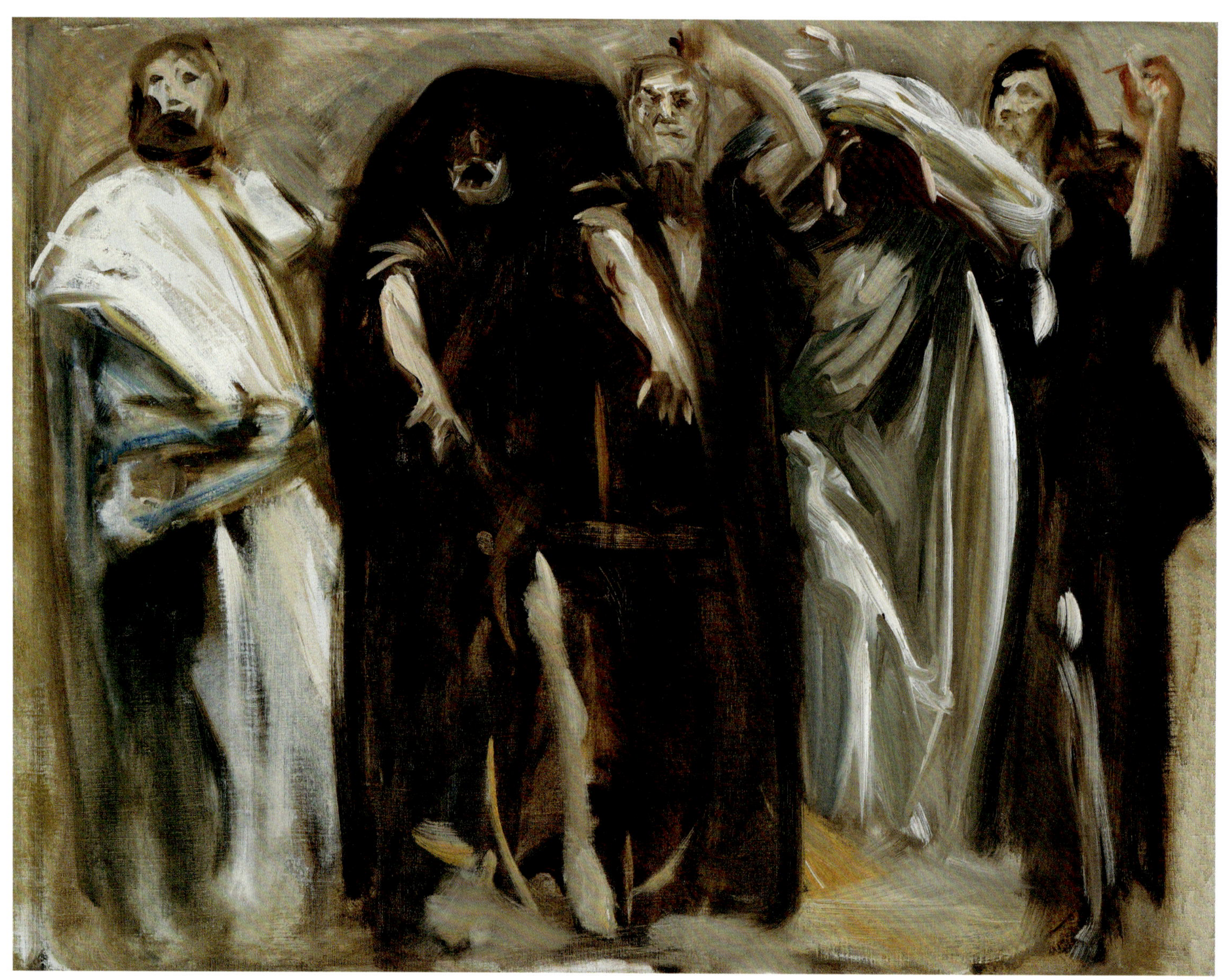

27

Group Dynamics

The coordinated action of groups of figures was a special focus of Edwin Austin Abbey and John Singer Sargent in their commissions for the Boston Public Library. With remarkable investment and effort, both artists articulated their ambitions in their studies of complex ensembles. In Sargent's study for *Frieze of the Prophets* (cat. 27), the choreography of gestures and confrontation of the Old Testament figures is as striking in its psychological energy as in its dramatic gestures. The figures fill the space and move forward with decisive thrust. Each has a vision of the future, though not the same one, and is gripped by divine spirit that manifests as possession.

Abbey, by contrast, arranges the coordinated extension of the figures in his *Castle of the Maidens* in a chromatic register that evokes musical lyricism (cat. 28). He and Sargent, along with most of their peers, admired the consuming passion of the Romantic composer Richard Wagner, and they employ groups of figures to suggest musical resonance and rhythm. Sargent's prophets are typically Wagnerian in their power and intensity, but Abbey's pastel is more nuanced and suggestive of the tonalities of other contemporary composers, such as Claude Debussy and Camille Saint-Saëns, aligning his work with the Aesthetic movement, which sought synesthetic associations across forms. The coordination of gesture and tone in these theatrical and narrative works set the foundation for a turn to more active, rhythmic movement and, ultimately, dance over the ensuing years.

CAT. 27 John Singer Sargent (American, born Italy, 1856–1925, LL.D. 1916)

Study for *Frieze of the Prophets* in *The Triumph of Religion* in the Boston Public Library, ca. 1892

Oil on canvas, 22⅛ × 28 in. (56.2 × 71.1 cm)
Museum of Fine Arts, Boston, Gift of Mrs. Francis Ormond, 37.45

CAT. 28 Edwin Austin Abbey (American, 1852–1911, HON. 1897)

Study for *The Castle of the Maidens* in *The Quest of the Holy Grail* in the Boston Public Library, ca. 1895–1900

Pastel on gray paper, 28 × 39¼ in. (71.1 × 99.7 cm)
Yale University Art Gallery, New Haven, Conn., Edwin Austin Abbey Memorial Collection, 1937.2035

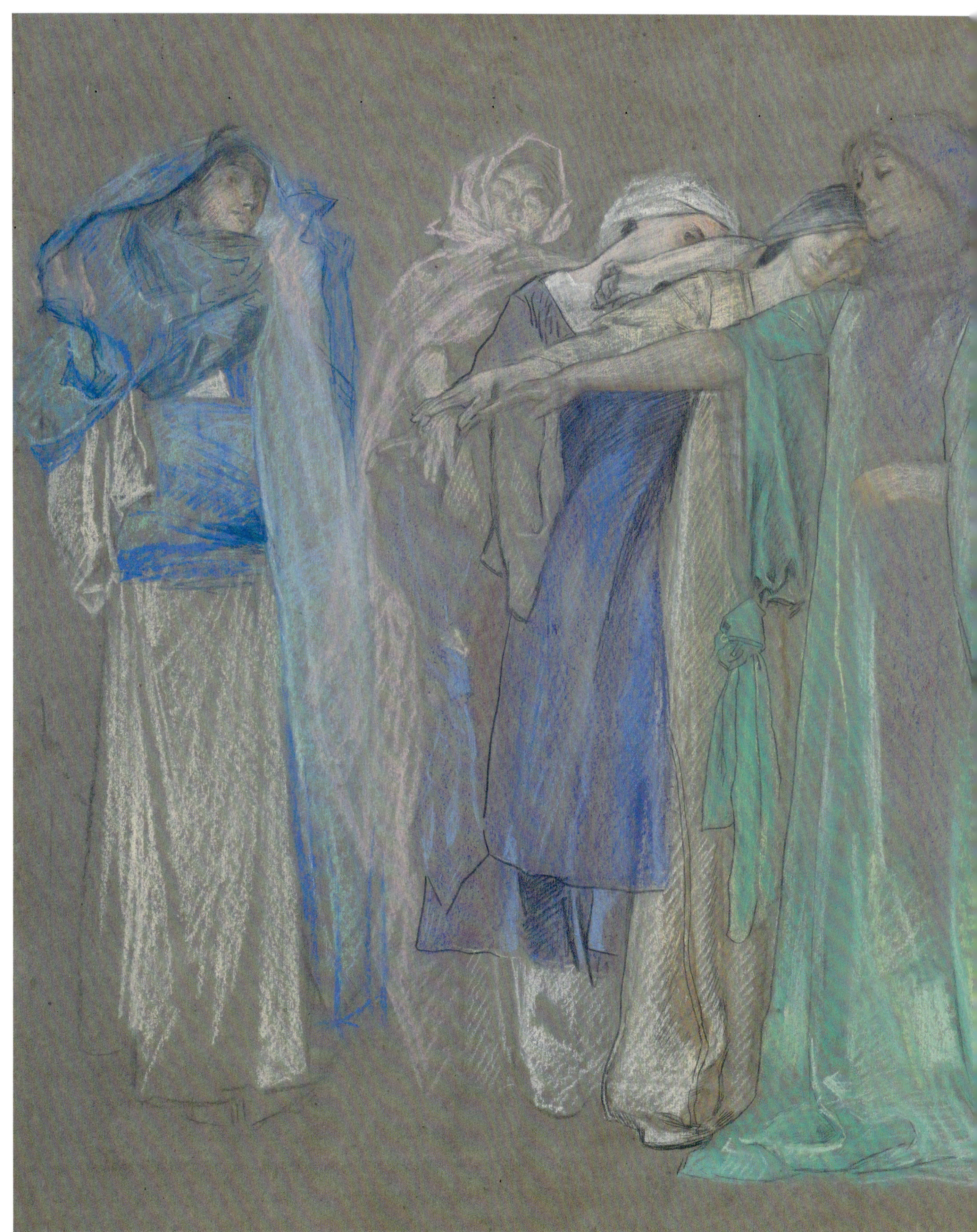

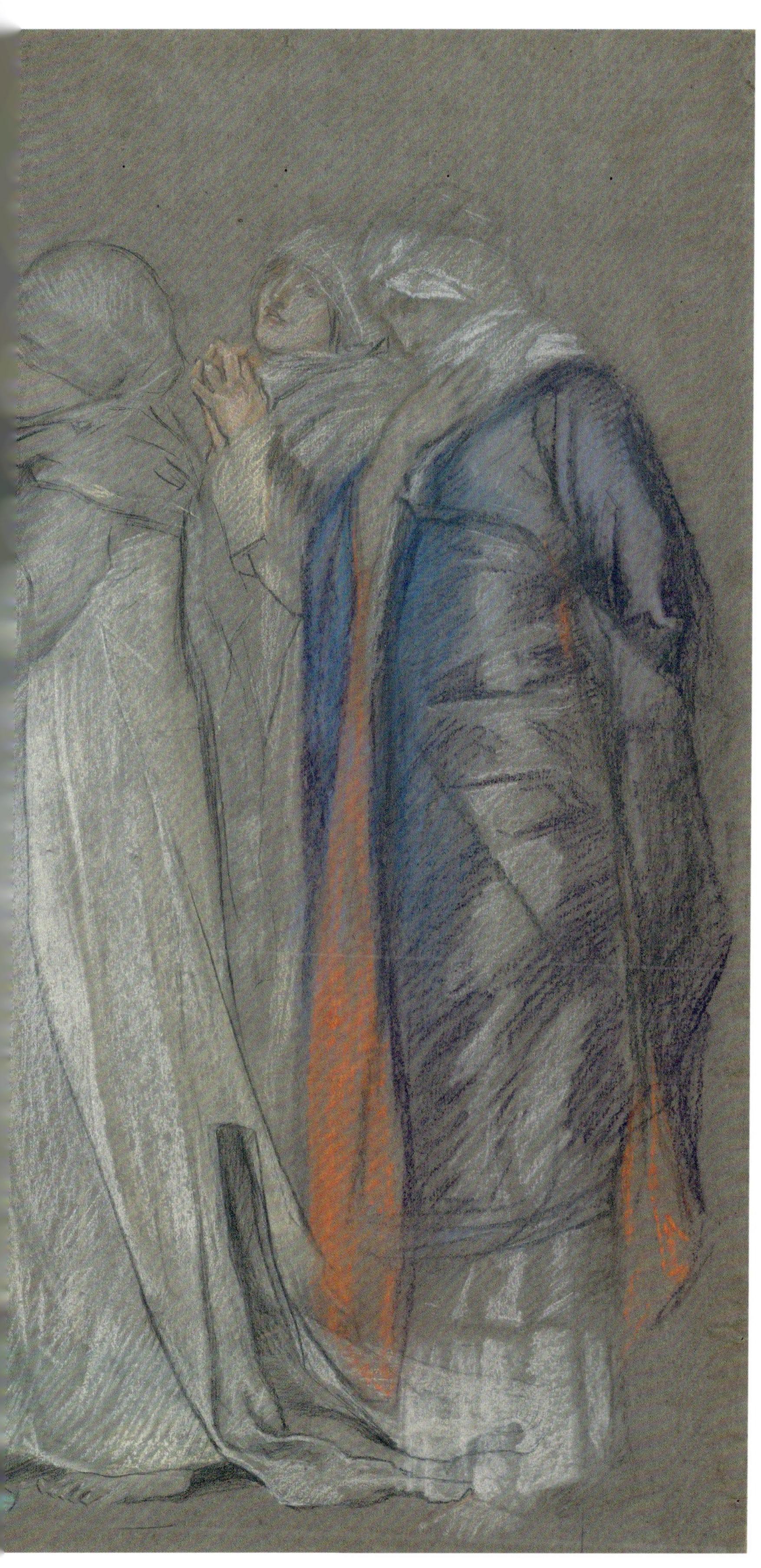

PAGES 100–101: The Abbey Room in the Boston Public Library, showing Edwin Austin Abbey's *Castle of the Maidens* from the *Quest and Achievement of the Holy Grail* cycle

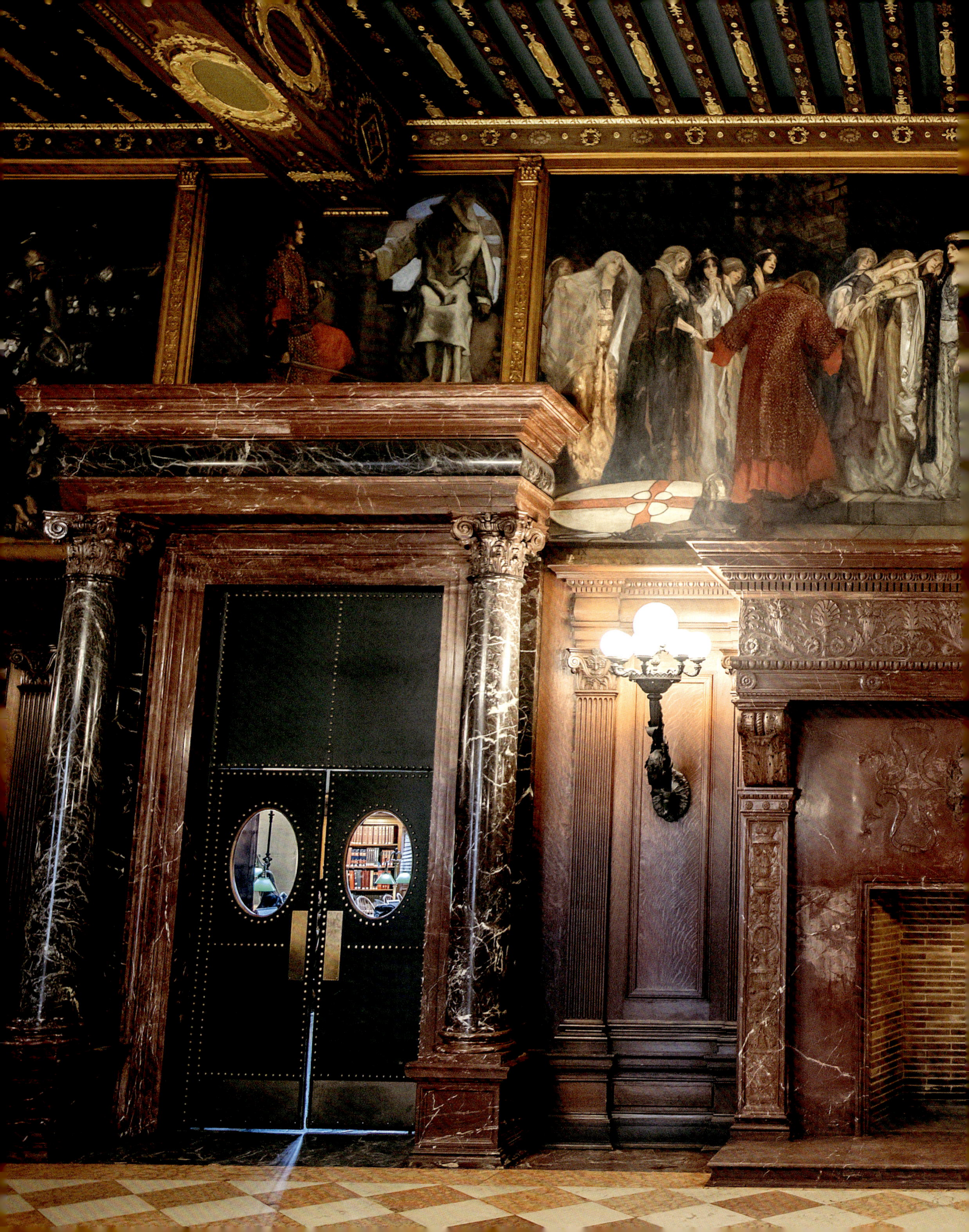

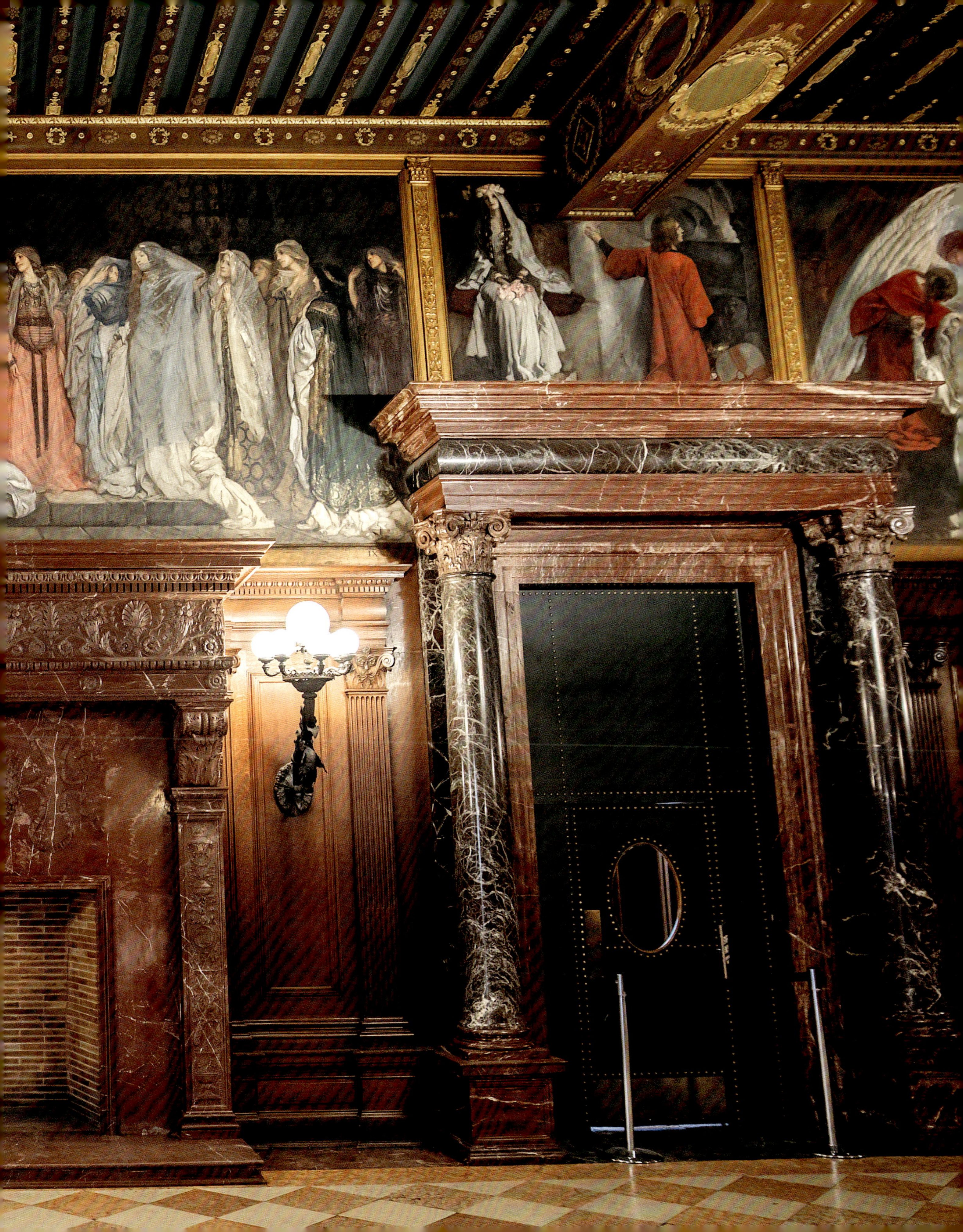

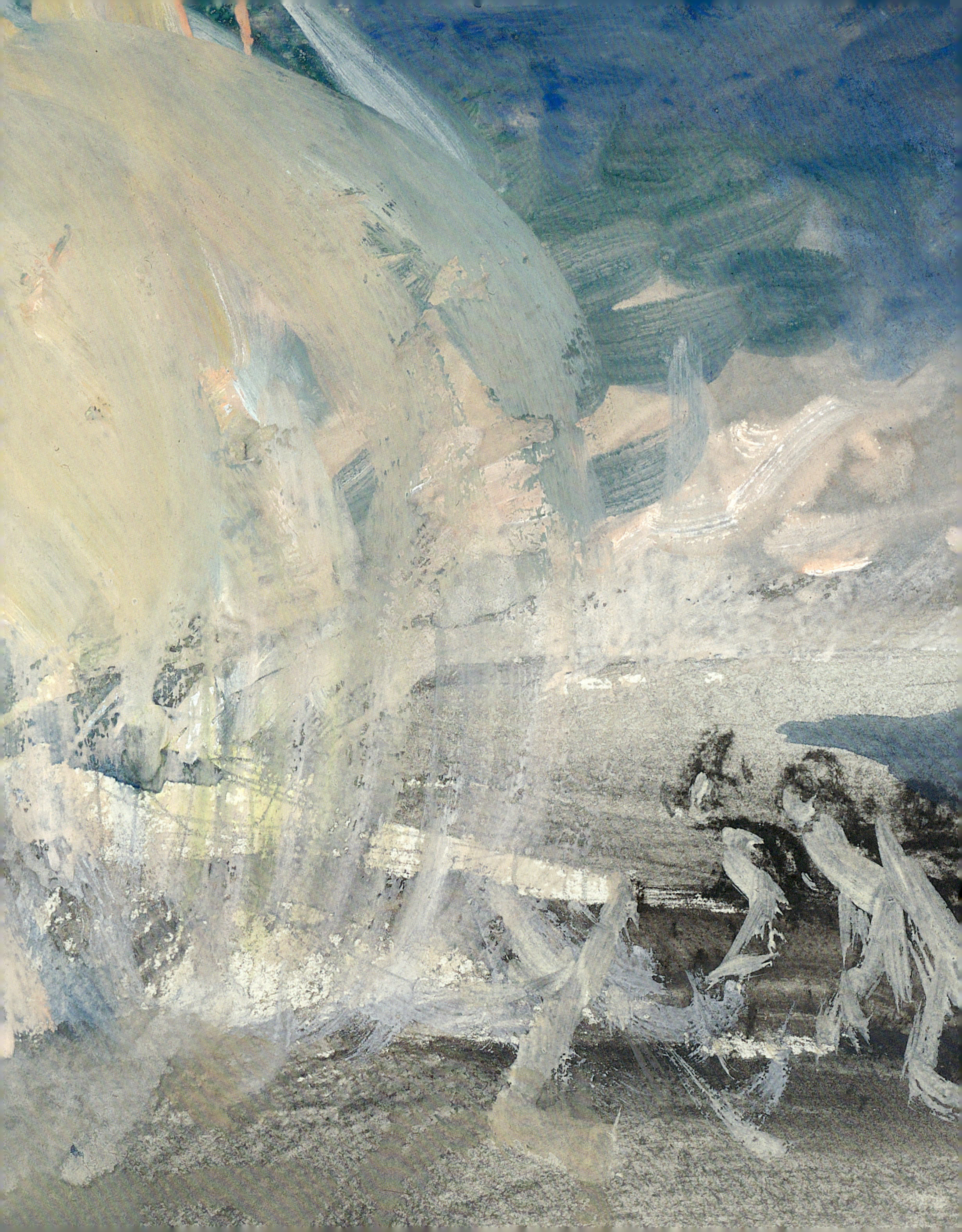

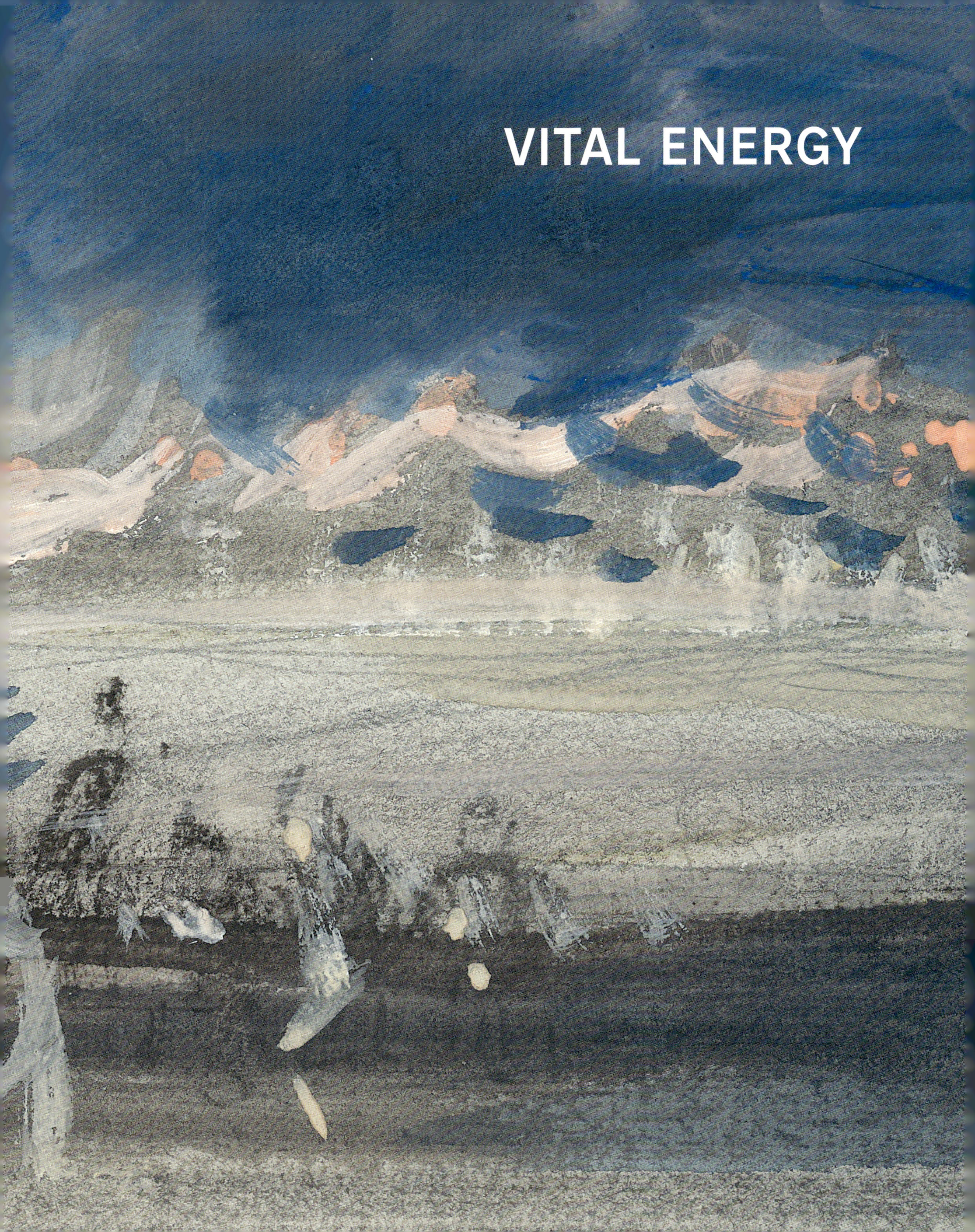

VITAL ENERGY

THE ESSENCE OF THE AMERICAN RENAISSANCE IS affirmation of life. The ecstatic energy of Edwin Austin Abbey's watercolor study for his scene of Arthur's round table for the Boston Public Library offers a remarkable expression of life force (cat. 29). The twin prismatic compositions burst beyond their edges, thwarting containment and conveying a special illusionism. Here, instead of describing a table or figures in a conventional sense, Abbey conveys forces at work in the room as vivid centrifugal energy. His prismatic brilliance provides the affective backdrop of his later composition but bears little resemblance to the final scene, much as his early studies underlie the night skyscape of *The Hours* (cat. 30), for the ceiling in the House of Representatives chamber of the Pennsylvania State Capitol in Harrisburg. Both portray the motivating force in the orientation and movement of energy that he hoped to translate. There is energy behind and among Abbey's figures and their actions, as well as inside them.

The energy highlighted in these studies is modern and responsive to its time. Daniel Chester French's *Spirit of Life* (cat. 31), which was cast from a reduced-scale study for the Spencer Trask Memorial in Saratoga Springs, New York, is remarkable for its exceptional naturalism and lyricism of movement in defiance of gravity. Yet the expectation for public art to have a finished, or refined, representational appearance remained, often depriving the completed commissions of the freedom visible in such studies. Public commissions required a degree of conventionality that bound the artists to more prosaic effect, and French specifically expressed his gratitude to the Trask monument's commissioner, George Foster Peabody, for the license to work freely and produce a satisfying result.[1] Often behind, within, and beneath the vast final murals and monumental sculptures of the American Renaissance rushes the animation of studies like these, which the artists kept, published, exhibited, and left behind.

CAT. 29 Edwin Austin Abbey (American, 1852–1911, HON. 1897)

Compositional Study for *The Arthurian Round Table* and *The Fable of the Seat Perilous* in *The Quest and Achievement of the Holy Grail* in the Boston Public Library, ca. 1890–94

Graphite, watercolor, and gouache on paper, 13⅞ × 19¹⁵⁄₁₆ in. (35.2 × 50.6 cm)
Yale University Art Gallery, New Haven, Conn., Edwin Austin Abbey Memorial Collection, 1937.1931

CAT. 30 Edwin Austin Abbey (American, 1852–1911, HON. 1897)

Study for *The Hours* in the Pennsylvania State Capitol, ca. 1904–11

Oil on composition board, 21³⁄₁₆ × 28⁹⁄₁₆ in. (53.8 × 72.5 cm)
Yale University Art Gallery, New Haven, Conn., Edwin Austin Abbey Memorial Collection, 1937.1718

CAT. 31 Daniel Chester French (American, 1850–1931)

Spirit of Life, 1914

Bronze, 30 × 34⅞ in. (76.2 × 88.6 cm)
Smithsonian American Art Museum, Washington, D.C., Museum purchase through the Luisita L. and Franz H. Denghausen Endowment, 2000.99

NOTE

1. Michael Tingley Richman, *Daniel Chester French, an American Sculptor*, exh. cat. (New York: The Metropolitan Museum of Art for the National Trust for Historic Preservation, 1976), 135.

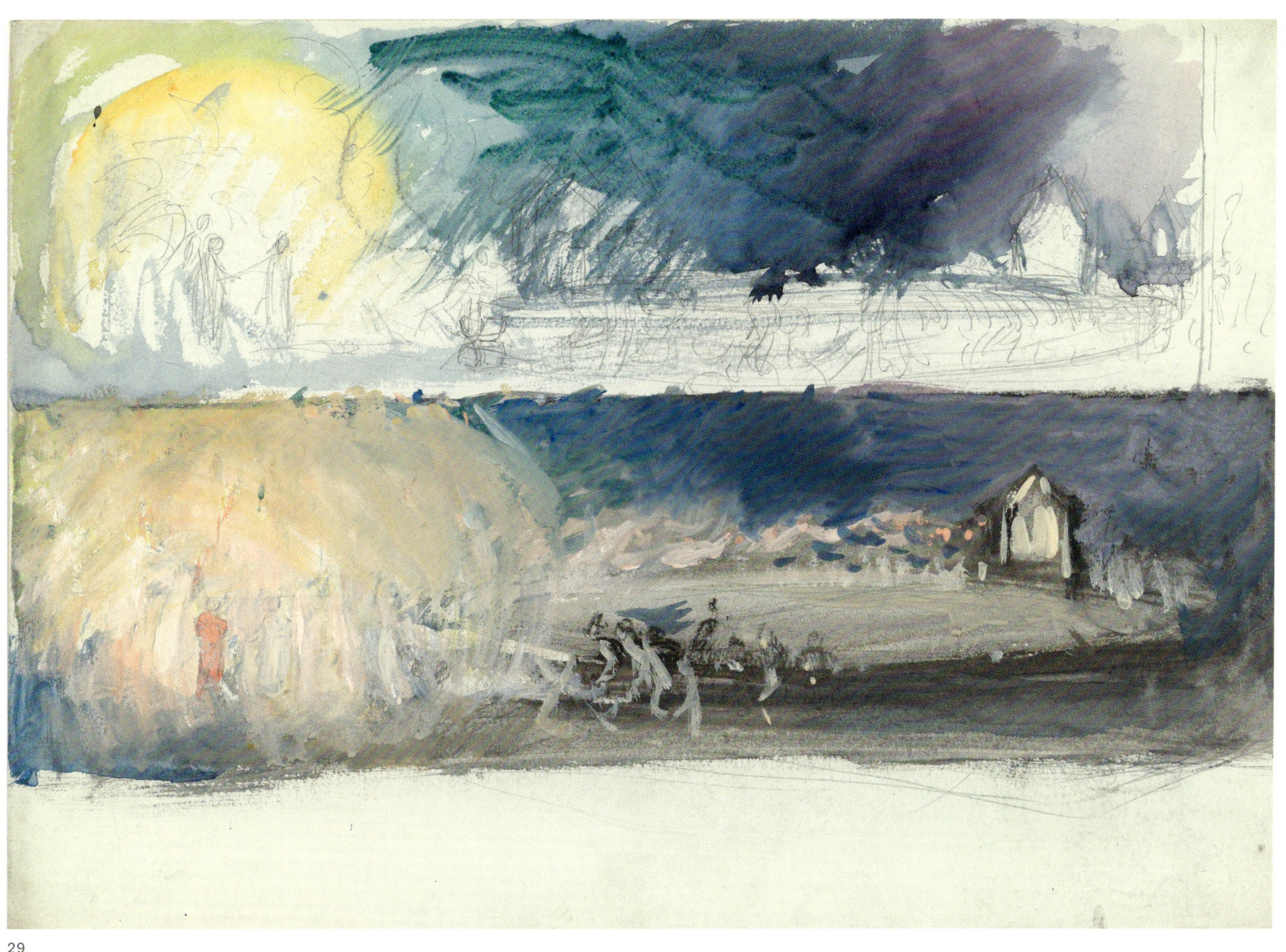

29

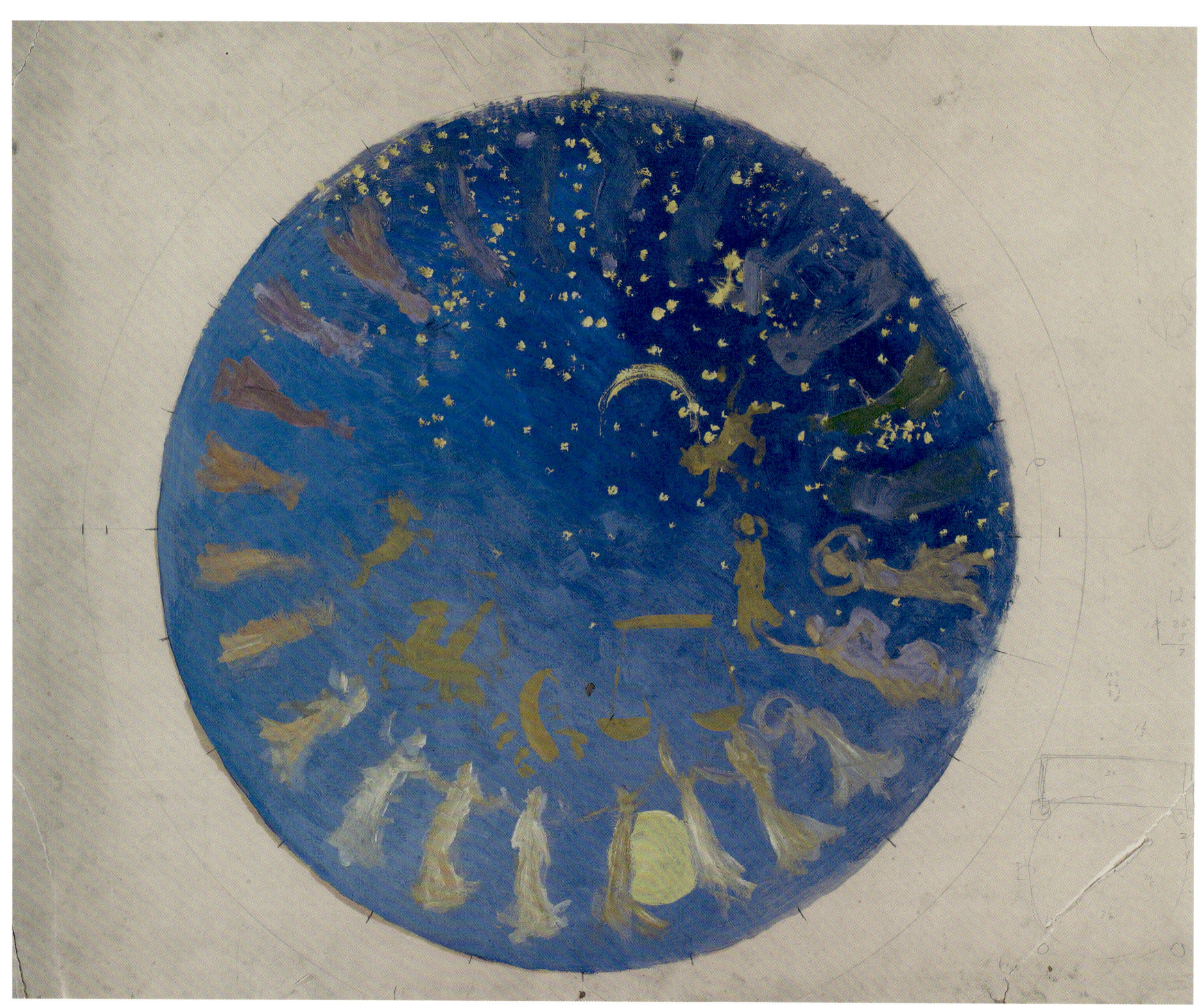

30

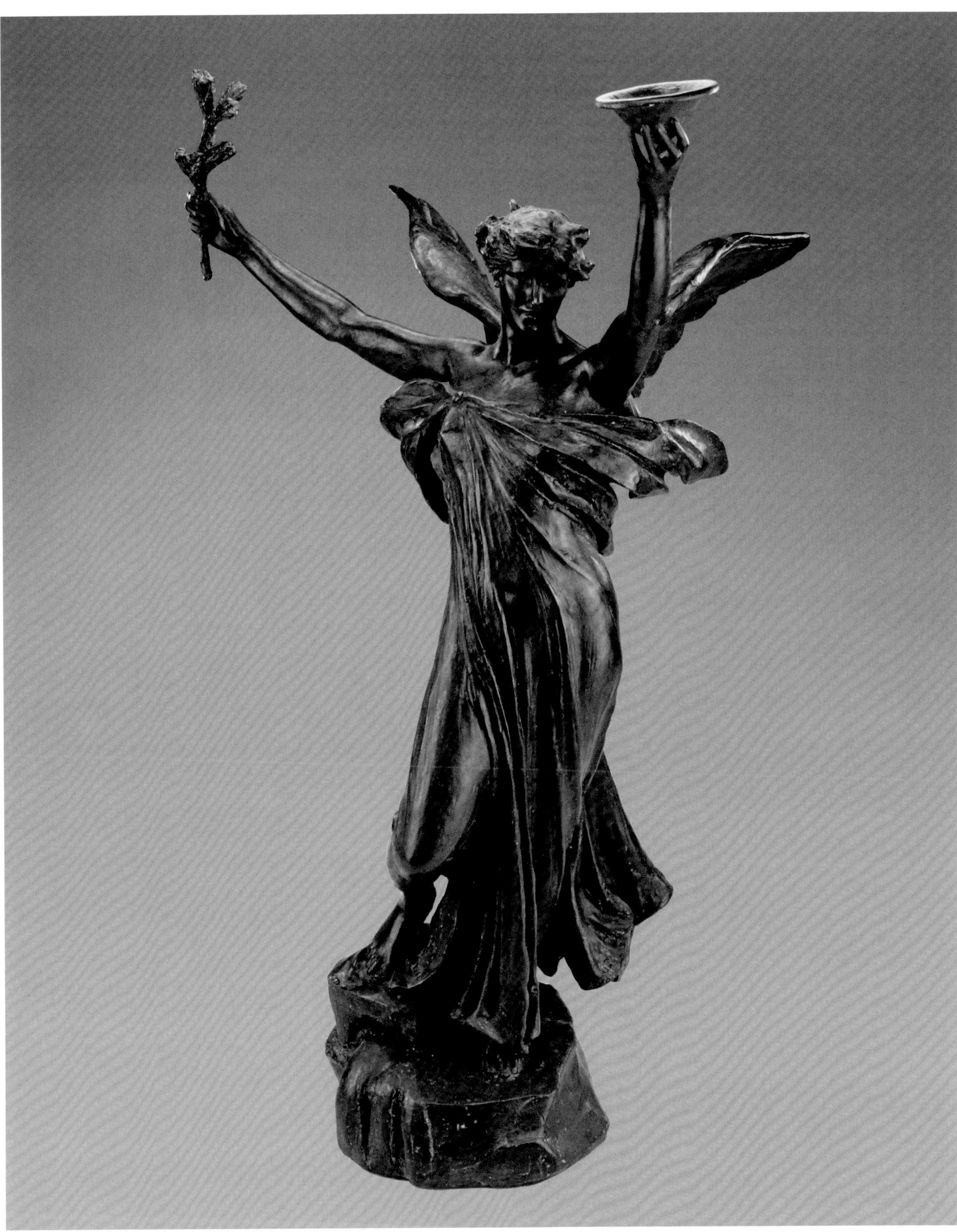

31

Light

Light defines form, and its absence creates void. Light is aligned with life and associated with it, in all its properties: a candle's delicate flame, the warmth of the sun, the powerful heat of the forge. In the late nineteenth century, with new technology transforming the night—especially in cities—light increasingly controlled darkness and chased away its threat.[1] The cycles of day and night were disrupted, and work continued around the clock, a device that increasingly regulated both time and life in place of the rising and setting sun. In art, light took on new meaning as well, becoming a symbolic motif.[2]

Abbey's studies for the nun who holds the infant Galahad in the first scene of his Holy Grail series for the Boston Public Library accentuate the potential of both light and shadow (cats. 32–33). The ability to construct form is evident in the brighter, more lushly painted study, like whipped cream on the canvas. In the darker study, the opposite is true: predominant shadows deepen the space and recede from the surface. Abbey's highlights rise up on the surface of the canvas; the shadows recede and become illusions of depth.

For Henry Ossawa Tanner, an artist of African descent from Pittsburgh and Philadelphia who worked abroad in Paris, opportunities for public commissions in America were unavailable. As a Pennsylvanian, like Abbey and Violet Oakley, Tanner should have been eligible for commissions in the new Pennsylvania State Capitol but was likely not considered because of racial prejudice, despite his international prominence. Instead, Tanner's public reputation was formed at the annual French Salon. There, in 1898, he exhibited his landmark painting *The Annunciation*, which was

CAT. 32 Edwin Austin Abbey (American, 1852–1911, HON. 1897)
Figure Study of a Nun for *The Infancy of Galahad* in *The Quest and Achievement of the Holy Grail* in the Boston Public Library, ca. 1890–95
Oil on canvas, 30 × 25 in. (76.2 × 63.5 cm)
Yale University Art Gallery, New Haven, Conn., Edwin Austin Abbey Memorial Collection, 1937.1896

CAT. 33 Edwin Austin Abbey (American, 1852–1911, HON. 1897)
Figure Study of a Nun for *The Infancy of Galahad* in *The Quest and Achievement of the Holy Grail* in the Boston Public Library, ca. 1890–95
Oil on canvas, 30 × 20 in. (76.2 × 50.8 cm)
Yale University Art Gallery, New Haven, Conn., Edwin Austin Abbey Memorial Collection, 1937.1897

CAT. 34 Henry Ossawa Tanner (American, 1859–1937)
Study for *The Annunciation*, ca. 1898
Oil on wood, 8½ × 10¾ in. (21.6 × 27.3 cm)
Smithsonian American Art Museum, Washington, D.C., Gift of Mr. and Mrs. Norman Robbins, 1983.95.187

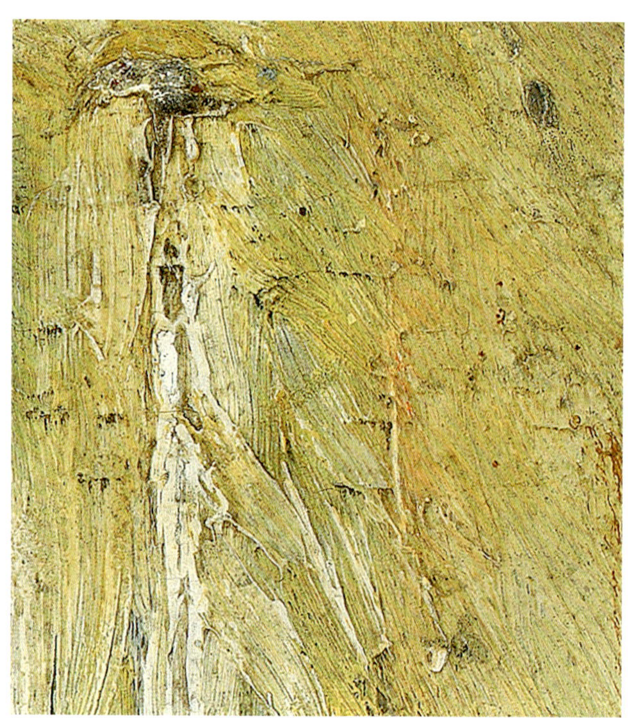

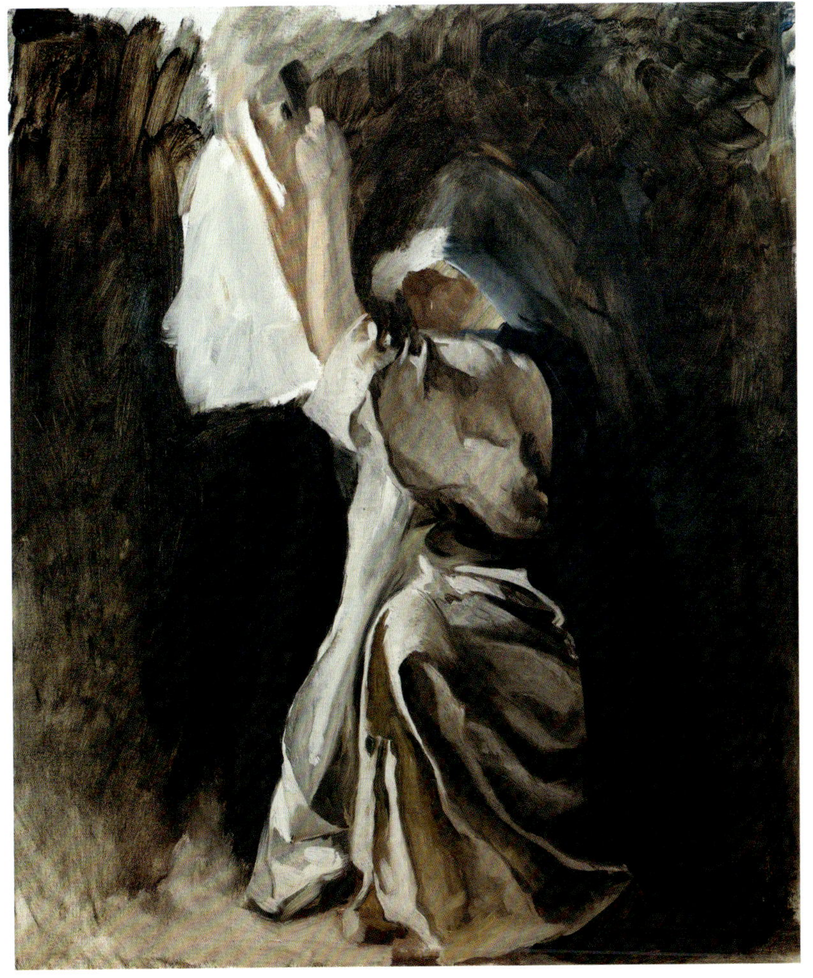

32

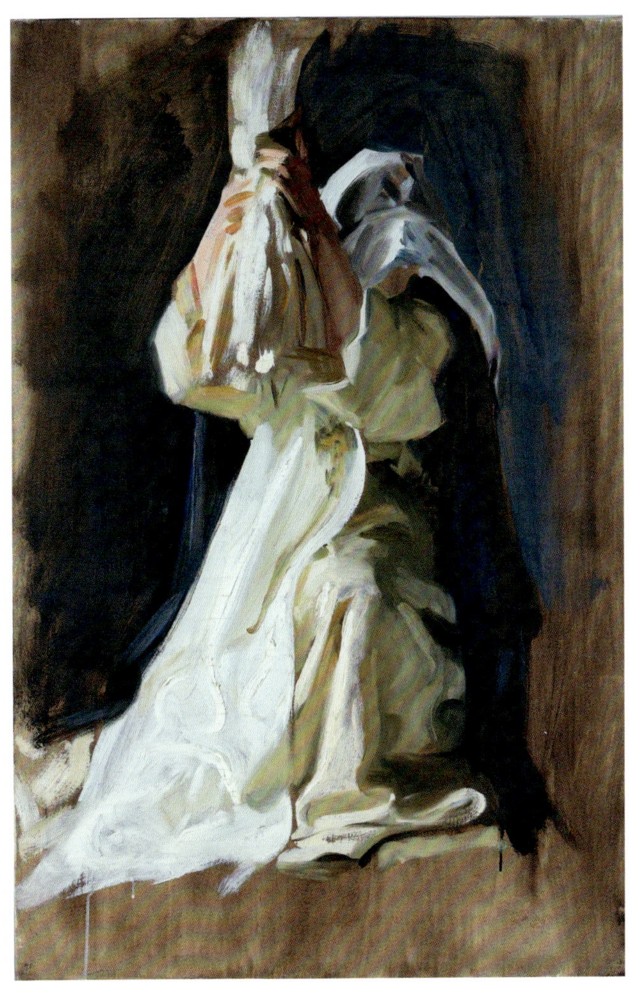

33

immediately purchased and donated to the Philadelphia Museum of Art.[3]

For this work, Tanner developed a new approach to portraying angels: representing Gabriel as a column of light in the room in which Mary rests, filling it with divine energy. In his preparatory oil study (cat. 34; detail on page 108), Tanner transmutes the angel's body into light, a remarkable abstraction that he would sustain in the final composition. Integrating research into the environment and the appearance of the region along with the figure of Mary, Tanner carried out the biblical historicism that was admired in this period. Light, however, was his tool of innovation, and he used it to convert a familiar story into something new and striking.[4]

NOTES

1. Hélène Valance, *Nocturne: Night in American Art, 1890–1917* (New Haven, Conn.: Yale University Press, 2018), 147–49.
2. For American artists influenced by European Symbolism, including Henry Ossawa Tanner and the sculptor George Grey Barnard, light offered a basis for philosophical reflection and creative practice; see Abby R. Eron, "The Symbolist Impulse in American Art across Media circa 1900" (Ph.D. diss., University of Maryland, 2020), 238.
3. Darrel Sewell, "The Annunciation," in Dewey F. Mosby, *Henry Ossawa Tanner*, exh. cat. (Philadelphia: Philadelphia Museum of Art, 1991), 162–65.
4. On Tanner's inspiration from and relationship with modern dance and lighting, see Hélène Valance, "'The Dynamo and the Virgin': Henry Ossawa Tanner's Religious Nocturnes," in Anna O. Marley, *Henry Ossawa Tanner: Modern Spirit*, exh. cat. (Philadelphia: Pennsylvania Academy of the Fine Arts; Berkeley: University of California Press, 2012), 129–31.

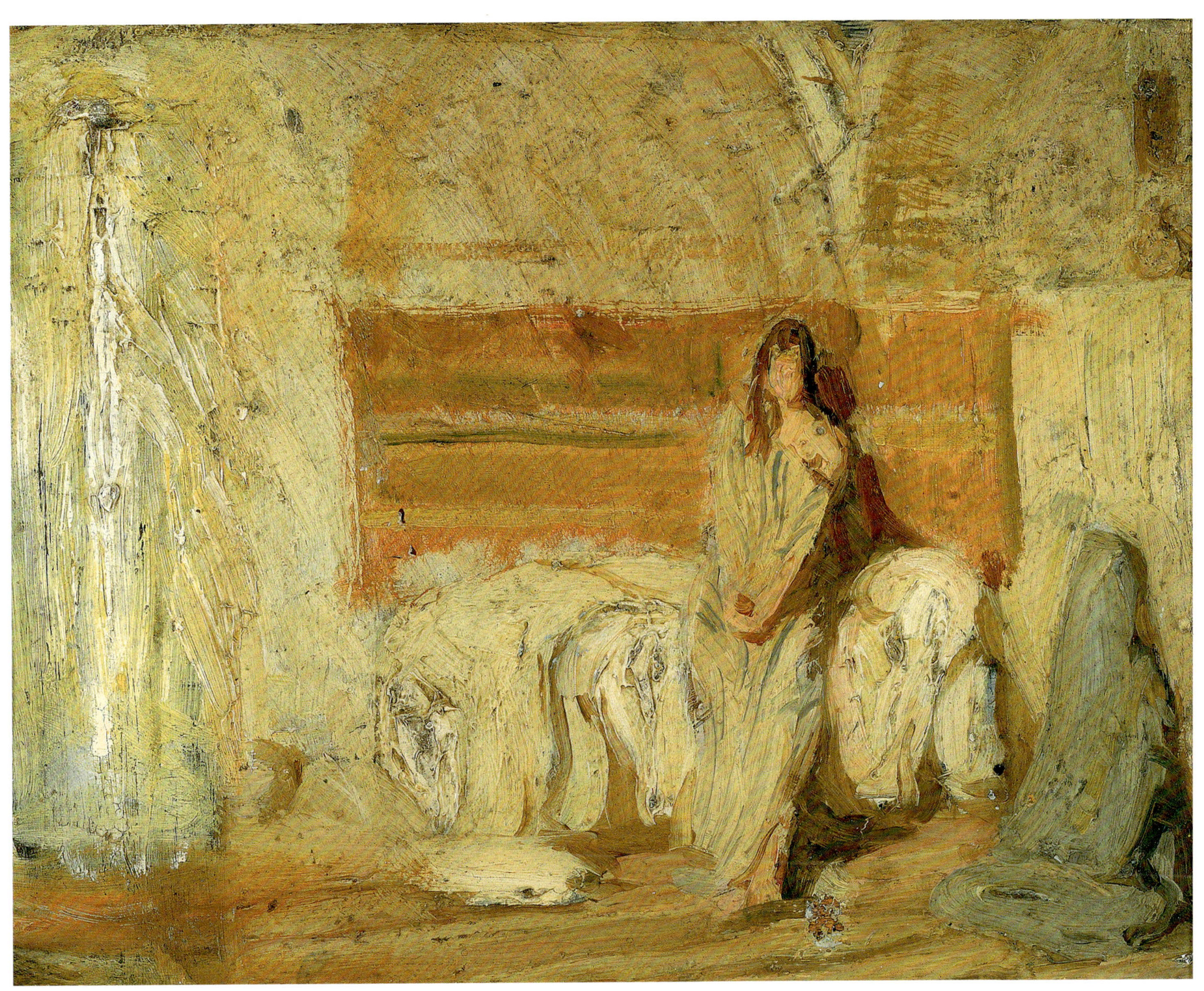

34

Clouds

During the industrial age, clouds took on new meaning as factory smoke soared skyward. Infused with chemical fumes, the surging banks of colored haze that feature in many murals from the turn of the twentieth century reflected not just the wonders of nature at sunset but also the work of humanity. Coal smoke had darkened urban skies and caked surfaces with fallen ash for most of the 1800s. By century's end, cleaner-burning oil derivatives promised brighter light and less pollution, although in cities with heavy industry, like Pittsburgh and Philadelphia, emissions from factory furnaces remained choking. Nevertheless, industry promised jobs and economic security to a new generation; in their eyes, dark plumes of soot transformed into light clouds of water vapor. Industrial smoke and steam were the backdrops for progress and hope—for life itself.

Edwin Austin Abbey's oil study for *The Spirit of Light* lunette in the rotunda of the Pennsylvania State Capitol is filled with colored clouds (cat. 35). Their vigor and energy seem to buffet the bodies floating in front of them. The forms and colors of the figures, allegories of light produced by oil flames, complement the skies. They seem to share the same softness and undulating movement, creating a resonance between subject and medium that extends to the runs of paint in the margin below

CAT. 35 Edwin Austin Abbey (American, 1852–1911, HON. 1897)

Compositional Study for *The Spirit of Light* in the Pennsylvania State Capitol, ca. 1902–8

Oil on canvas, 43½ × 74½ in. (110.5 × 189.2 cm)
Yale University Art Gallery, New Haven, Conn., Edwin Austin Abbey Memorial Collection, 1937.1509

CAT. 36 John La Farge (American, 1835–1910, HON. 1896)

Study for *Faith* and *Hope,* ca. 1890

Watercolor and gouache over graphite on illustration board, 9¹¹⁄₁₆ × 6⁷⁄₁₆ in. (24.6 × 16.4 cm)
National Gallery of Art, Washington, D.C., Corcoran Collection (Bequest of James Parmelee), 2015.19.506

CAT. 37 John La Farge (American, 1835–1910, HON. 1896)

Color Study for *The Moral and Divine Law: Moses Receives the Law on Mount Sinai* in the Minnesota State Capitol, 1903

Watercolor, gouache, and graphite on olive-green wove paper, 7⅜ × 10⅝ in. (18.7 × 27 cm)
The Metropolitan Museum of Art, New York, Bequest of Susan Dwight Bliss, 1966, 67.55.166

CAT. 38 William Morris Hunt (American, 1824–1879)

Study for *The Discoverer* in the New York State Capitol, 1878

Charcoal on cream laid paper, 11⁵⁄₁₆ × 17⅜ in. (28.7 × 44.1 cm)
Harvard Art Museums/Fogg Museum, Cambridge, Mass., Gifts for Special Uses Fund, through the generosity of Mrs. George R. Agassiz, Mrs. Raymond Emerson, Dr. Alexander Forbes, Mr. Edward W. Forbes, Mrs. Isabella Grandin, The Honorable and Mrs. John F. Perkins, and Mr. Quincy A. Shaw, 1956.240

CAT. 39 William Morris Hunt (American, 1824–1879)

Study for *The Discoverer* in the New York State Capitol, 1878

Pastel on brown wove paper, 12½ × 18⁵⁄₁₆ in. (31.8 × 46.5 cm)
Harvard Art Museums/Fogg Museum, Cambridge, Mass., Gifts for Special Uses Fund, through the generosity of Mrs. George R. Agassiz, Mrs. Raymond Emerson, Dr. Alexander Forbes, Mr. Edward W. Forbes, Mrs. Isabella Grandin, The Honorable and Mrs. John F. Perkins, and Mr. Quincy A. Shaw, 1956.237

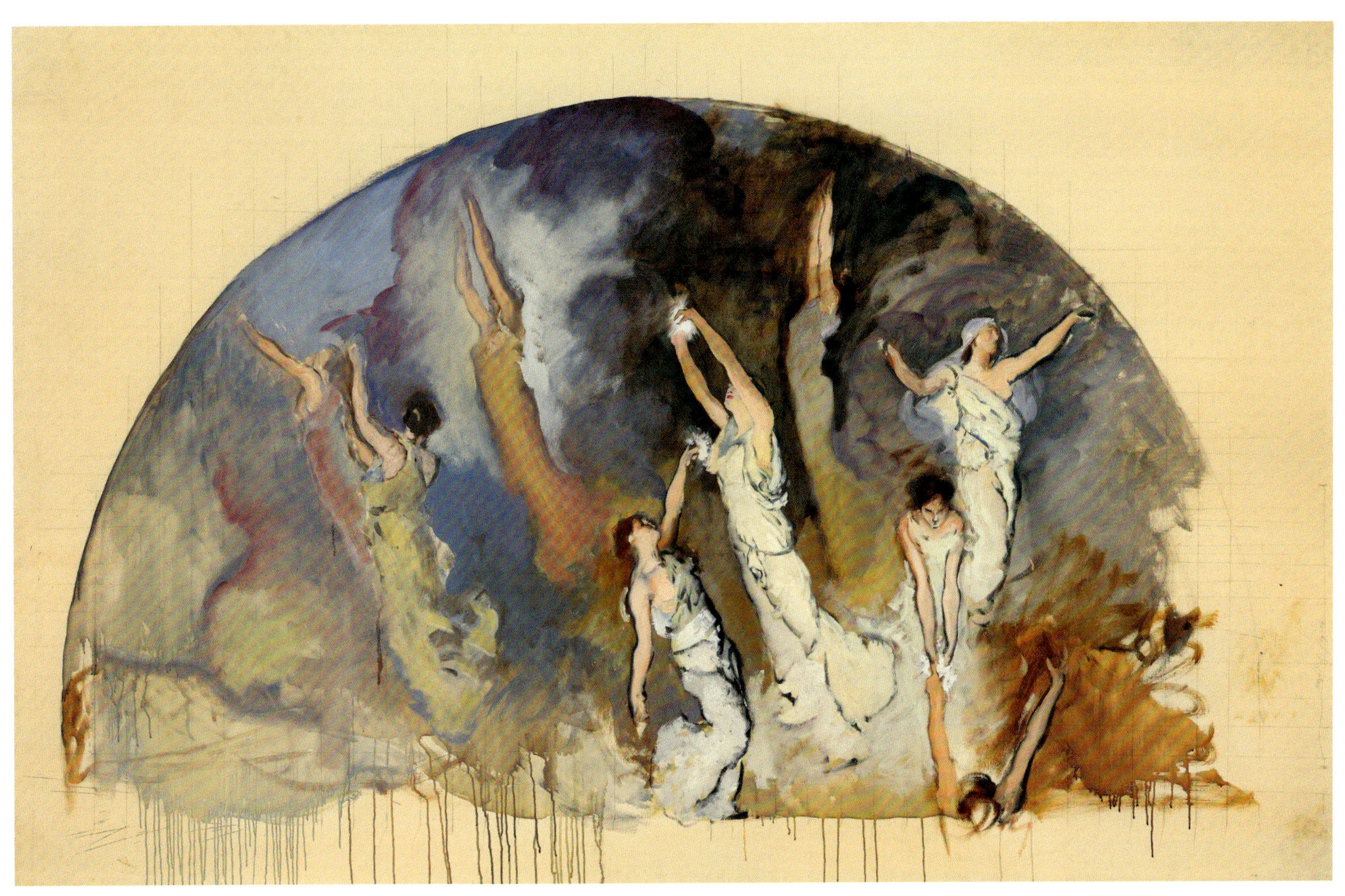

35

the image. The women appear to retrieve bright white clumps of light from beneath the composition at lower right and then launch upward toward the sky in the upper left. In later iterations, Abbey would move away from the progression of retrieving light from the earth, repurposing that anecdote in the neighboring lunette *Science Revealing the Treasures of the Earth*. The final version of *The Spirit of Light* favors a more unified action of the group moving as one, as if the figures are wisps of flame.

Although clouds resonated with contemporary themes of industry, science, and technology, their long history as symbols of the divine remained integral. The home of the gods and resting place of the virtuous is often among the clouds. In both John La Farge's watercolor study for the *Faith and Hope* stained-glass window (cat. 36) and a later watercolor study for *The Moral and Divine Law: Moses Receives the Law on Mount Sinai* (cat. 37), the artist tonally integrates the figures' robes with the sky as an allusion to the divine and harmony with the natural world. Each has a luxuriant colorism that reflects the artist's interest in the effects of his experiments with materials as well as his study of the history of Christian imagery. These were the associations to which artists' oily clouds of progress aspired; yet even at their most engaging, a sense of foreboding lurks, inescapable and urgent.

Natural backdrops such as these and their emotive effect appeared early in the American Renaissance, including in William Morris Hunt's influential murals for the New York capitol in Albany, often described by critics and historians of the time, alongside La Farge's work for Trinity Church, as the foundations of the new public art movement.[1] Including echoes of the meditative form of Abraham Lincoln as well as the emotive skies characteristic of the period, Hunt's charcoal and pastel studies for *The Discoverer* fresco of 1878 set the new course. The heaviness of the dark sky in the charcoal drawing (cat. 38) is especially resonant, appearing to weigh down the central figure, which stands implausibly above his small, vulnerable boat just as dawn breaks at the distant horizon, revealing land at last. The pastel study (cat. 39), like the finished mural, is more evocative, leavening the scene's mood with a lightening sky and greatly increasing the scale of the figures so that they dominate the composition. Hunt's change in focus from landscape to figure reflects the wider shift of artistic practice during the 1870s and helps accentuate the continued importance of natural settings to muralists.

NOTE

1. Pauline King, *American Mural Painting: A Study of the Important Decorations by Distinguished Artists in the United States* (Boston: Noyes, Platt, 1902), 41, 55.

Detail of cat. 39

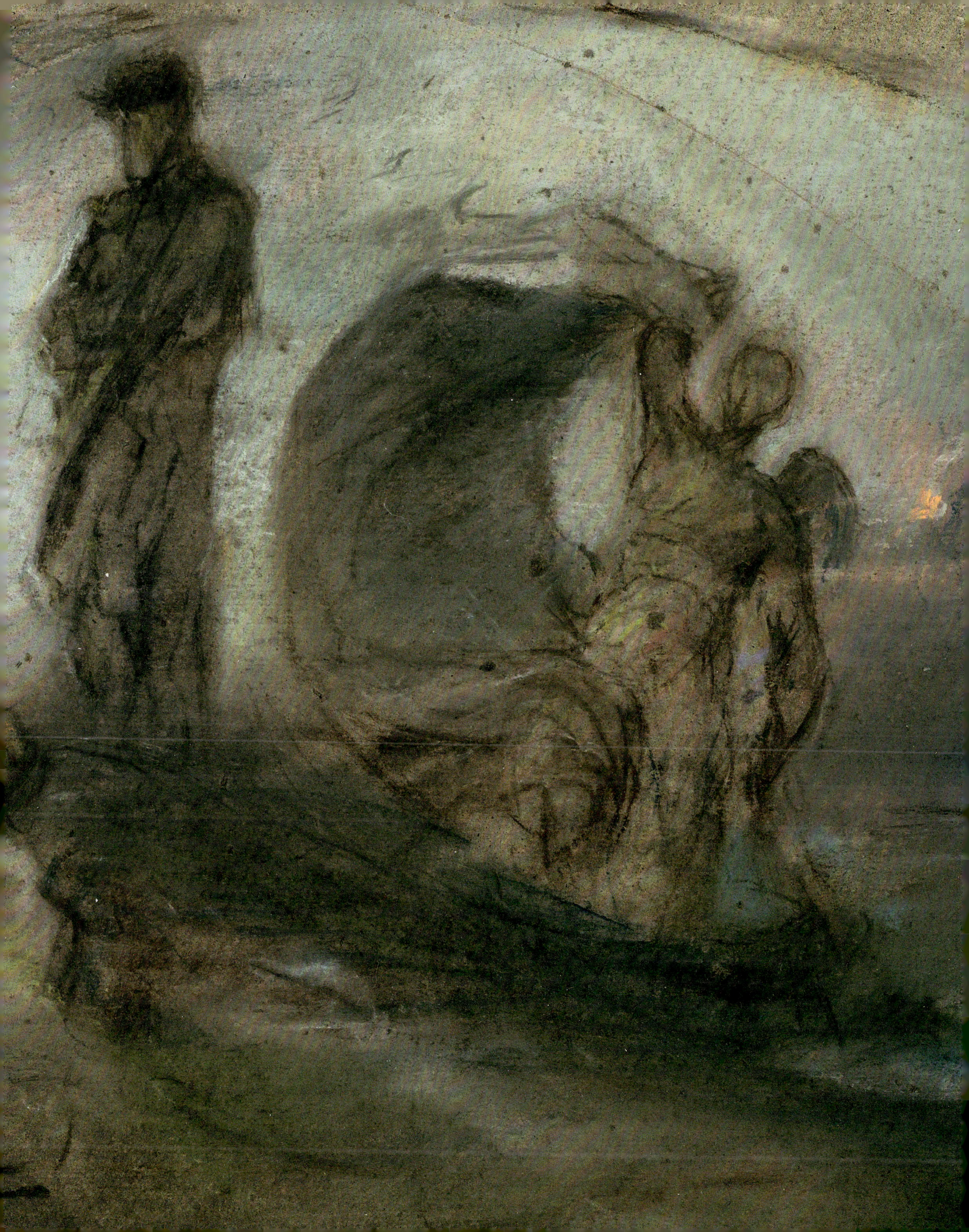

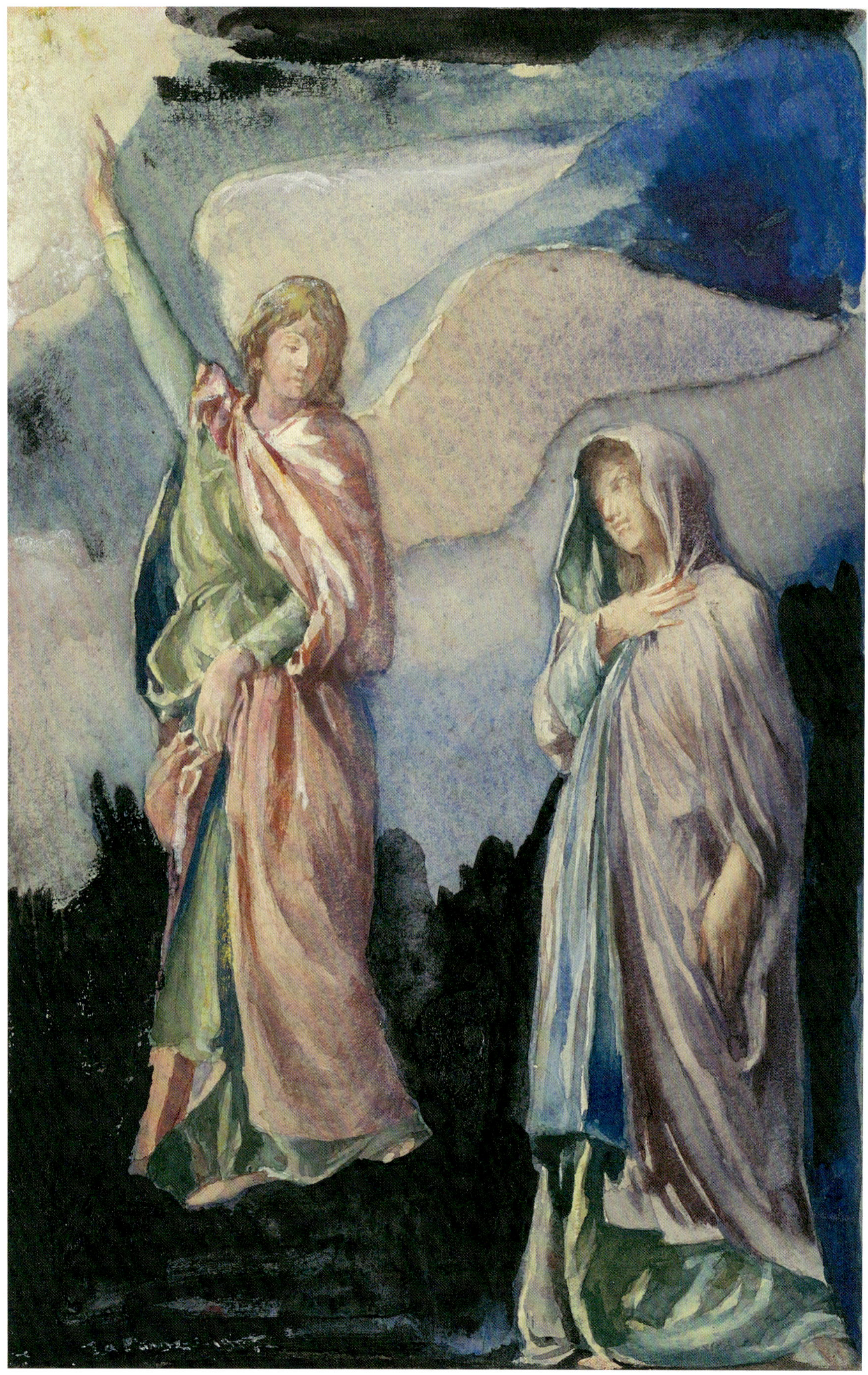

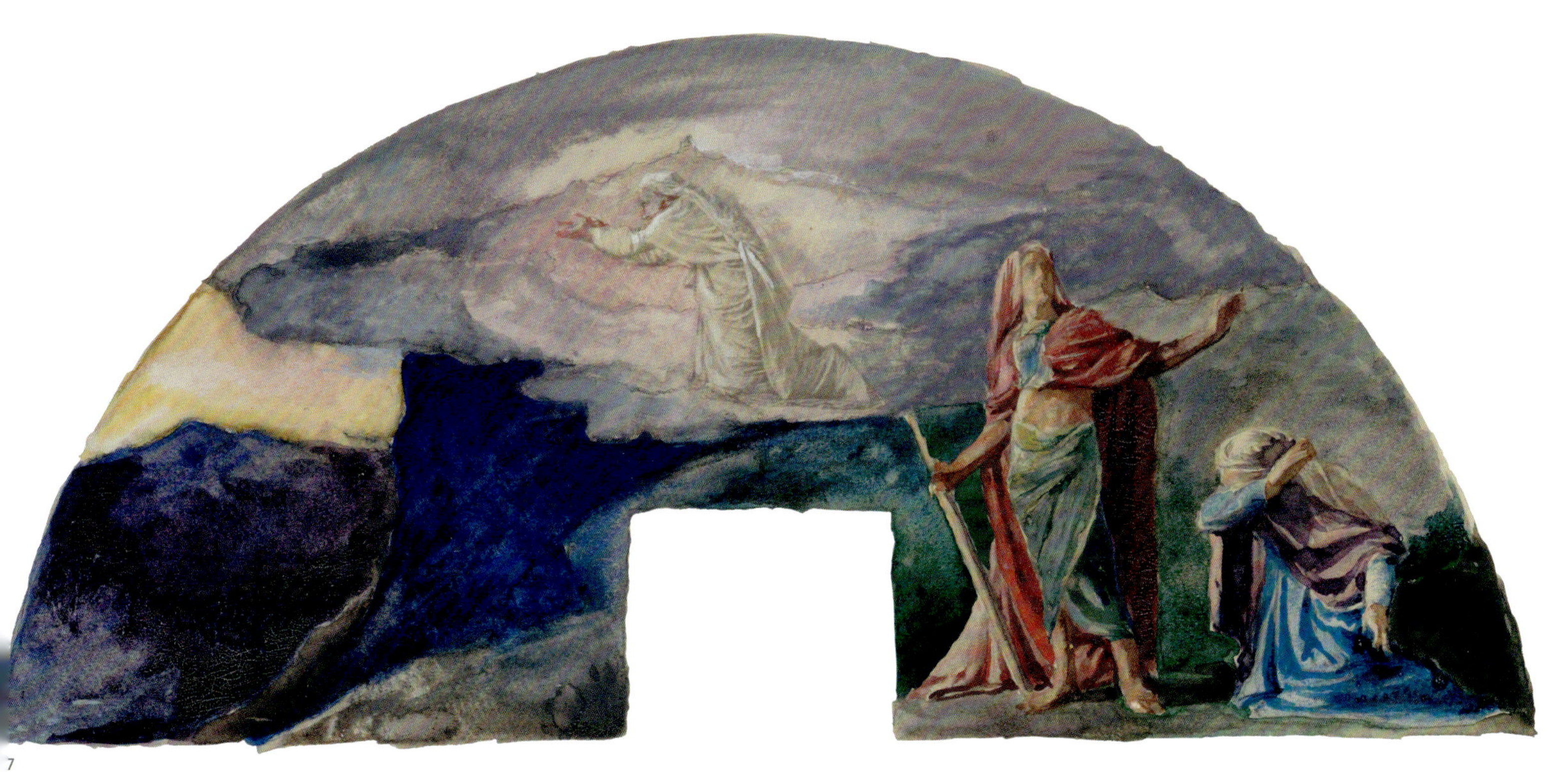

7

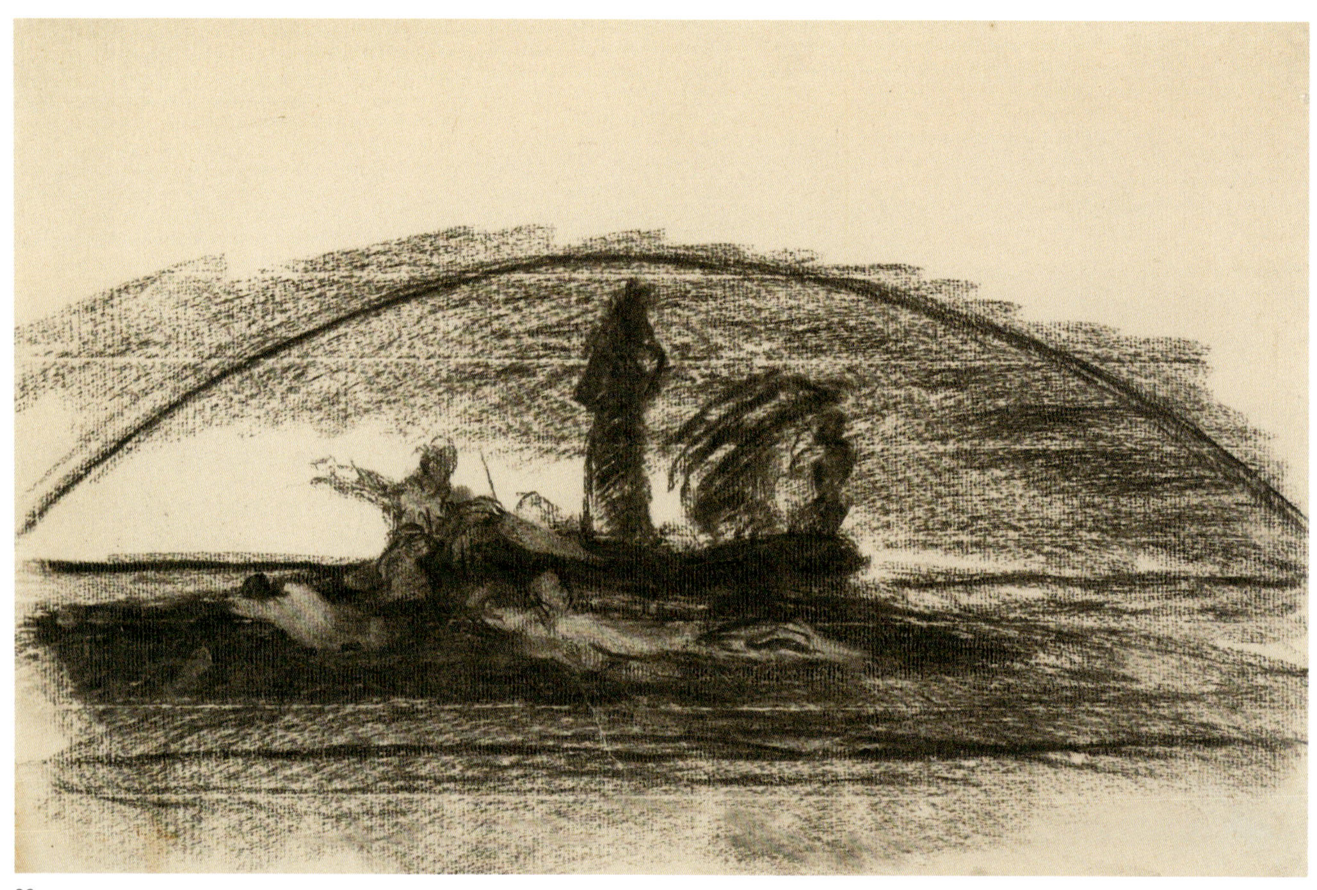

38

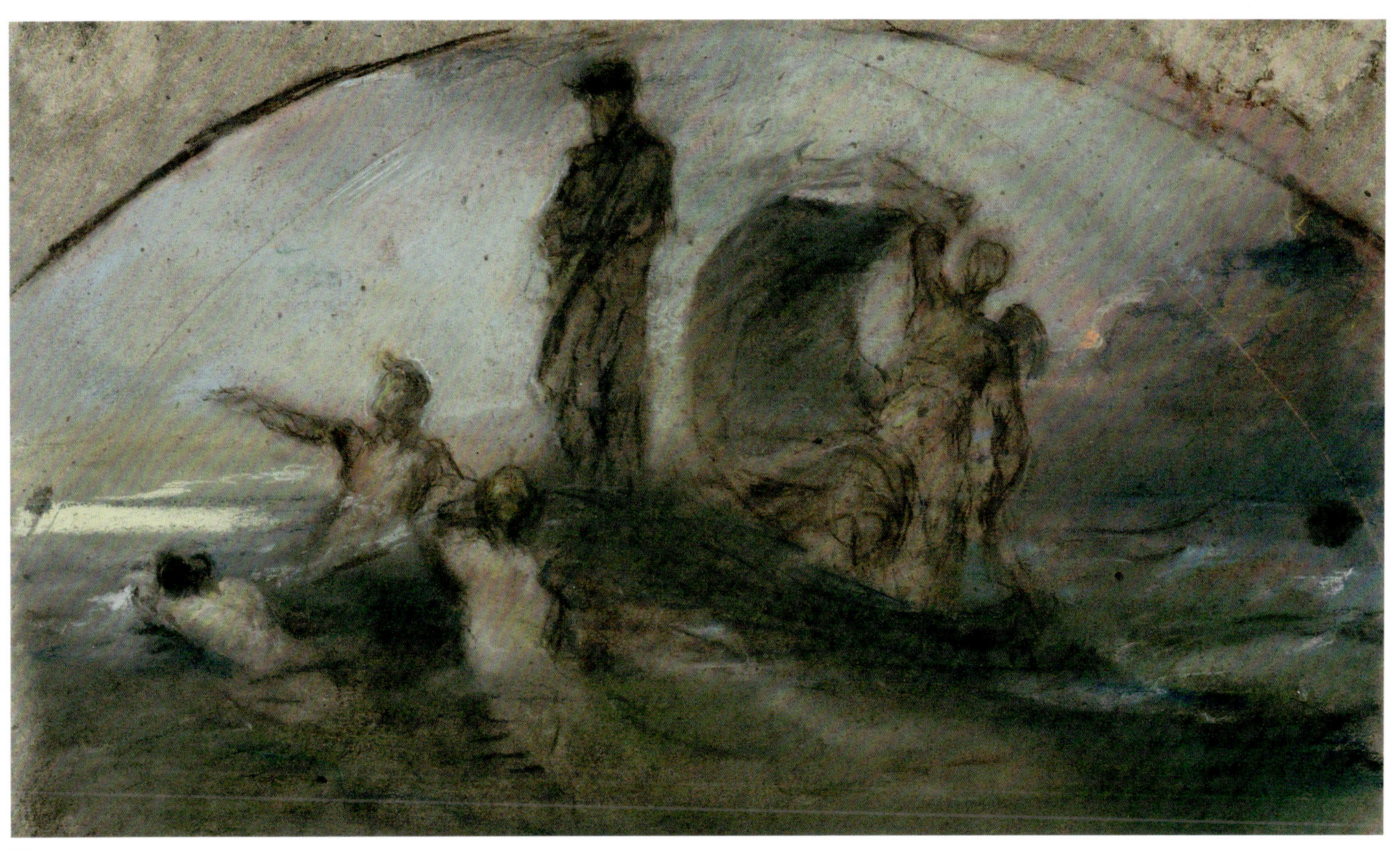

39

Figure and Ground

Looming figures dominate these three studies, each describing a dynamic relationship with its background. Here, the purpose of monumentality—filling the field of vision—is emergence. The figures overtake their own space and project into the viewer's, at times crowding the edge of the composition and engaging the audience in a different, more involved form of visual experience.

The figure of Fortune (cat. 40), William Morris Hunt's oil study for *The Discoverer* (1878), his mural commission for the New York State Capitol in Albany, is silhouetted by a brightening sky, reflecting Hunt's academic training in Paris with the figure painter Thomas Couture and, later, in rural Barbizon with the landscape and genre painter Jean-François Millet. The elongated body resembles the bowed form of the sail that Fortune holds to catch the wind and propel the raft forward.

CAT. 40 William Morris Hunt (American, 1824–1879)
Fortune, Study for *The Discoverer* in the New York State Capitol, 1878

Oil on paper, 37 × 25½ in. (94 × 64.8 cm)
The Metropolitan Museum of Art, New York, Rogers Fund, 11.34.1

CAT. 41 Edwin Austin Abbey (American, 1852–1911, HON. 1897)
Figure Study for *The Spirit of Light* in the Pennsylvania State Capitol, ca. 1900

Oil and gold leaf on canvas, 37 × 32 in. (94 × 81.3 cm)
Yale University Art Gallery, New Haven, Conn., Edwin Austin Abbey Memorial Collection, 1937.2459

CAT. 42 Edwin Austin Abbey (American, 1852–1911, HON. 1897)
Figure Study for *The Spirit of Light* in the Pennsylvania State Capitol, ca. 1902–8

Pastel on speckled wove paper, 52¾ × 31⅜ in. (134 × 79.7 cm)
Yale University Art Gallery, New Haven, Conn., Edwin Austin Abbey Memorial Collection, 1937.1514

Shrouded in shadow, she offers a rare reversal of the usual emphasis in mural painting during the American Renaissance. To cast lead figures in shadow is unexpected; typically, they would be bathed in bright light, the main actors on stage. Instead, Hunt focuses on the lifting of fear and uncertainty as dawn breaks. The composition was an early and widely admired template of success for later projects, and its break with convention was a strategy emulated by other artists, including Edwin Austin Abbey.[1]

Dramatic contrast is Hunt's vehicle for the advancement of the figure, to push it forward from its setting. Abbey's study of a draped figure against a gilded background adapts a more traditional method, drawing on the medieval and early Renaissance use of golden backdrops for biblical scenes (cat. 41). The gold denies space altogether, moving the subject forward from a shimmering wall. Despite the enveloping brown clothing, the figure emerges with remarkable grace and volume. The pose suggests the Virgin Mary holding the infant Jesus, but the study prioritizes the relationship between a demure woman and her reflective backdrop. The gold leaf does not extend beneath the figure, indicating that the setting was created after, as a necessary complement to the humble subject. Abbey would repeatedly use gold backdrops, sometimes painted, sometimes gilded, throughout his career, including in studies for the Pennsylvania State Capitol (see, for example, cat. 76), evidence of his continued exploration of figure–ground dynamics over time.

Abbey's studies for Harrisburg demonstrate special investment in the body as a vehicle for symbolic expression. Newly focused on the nude as the basis of his murals for the massive project, he began a dialogue with the priorities of Symbolism in the contemporary art of Germany and France.

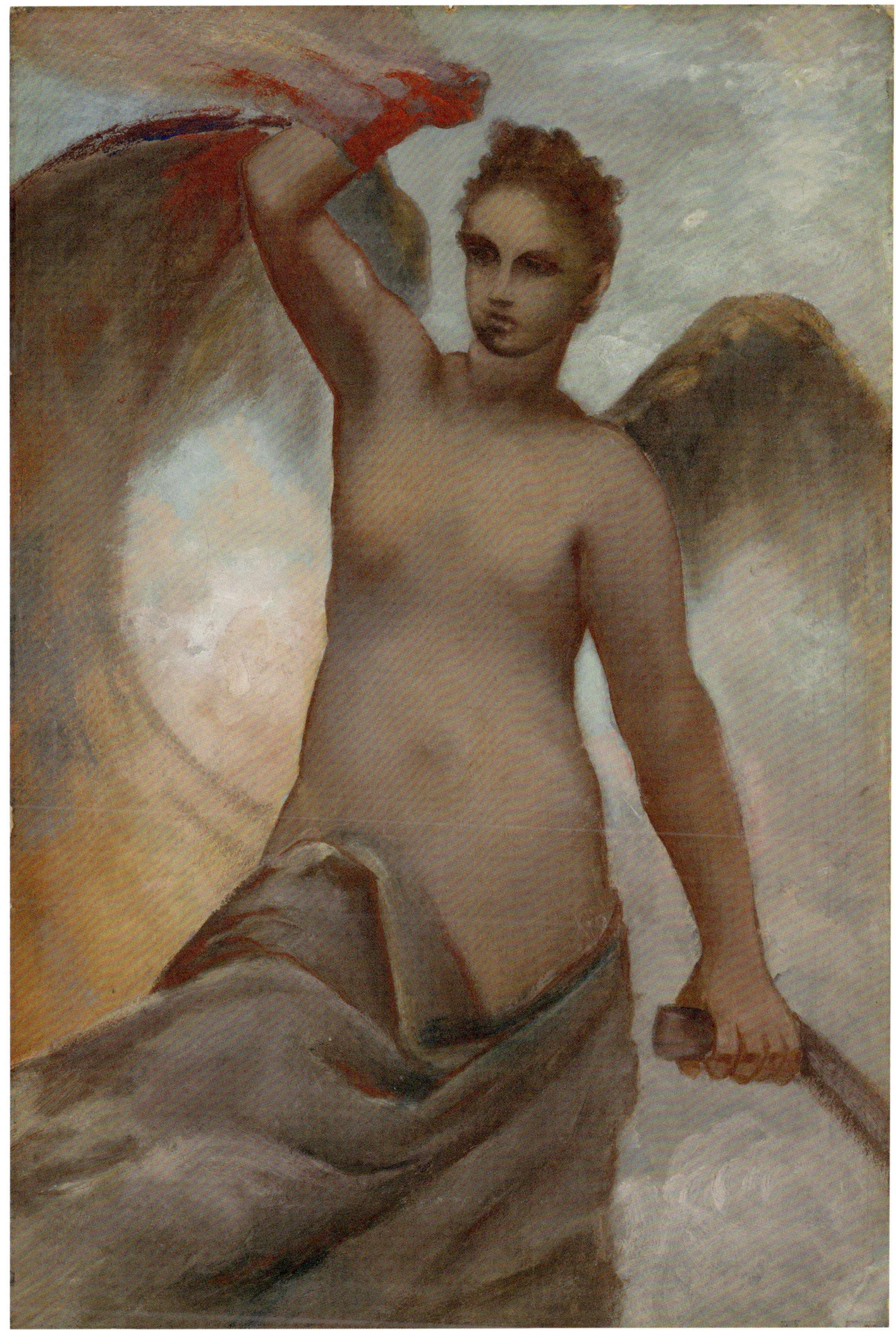

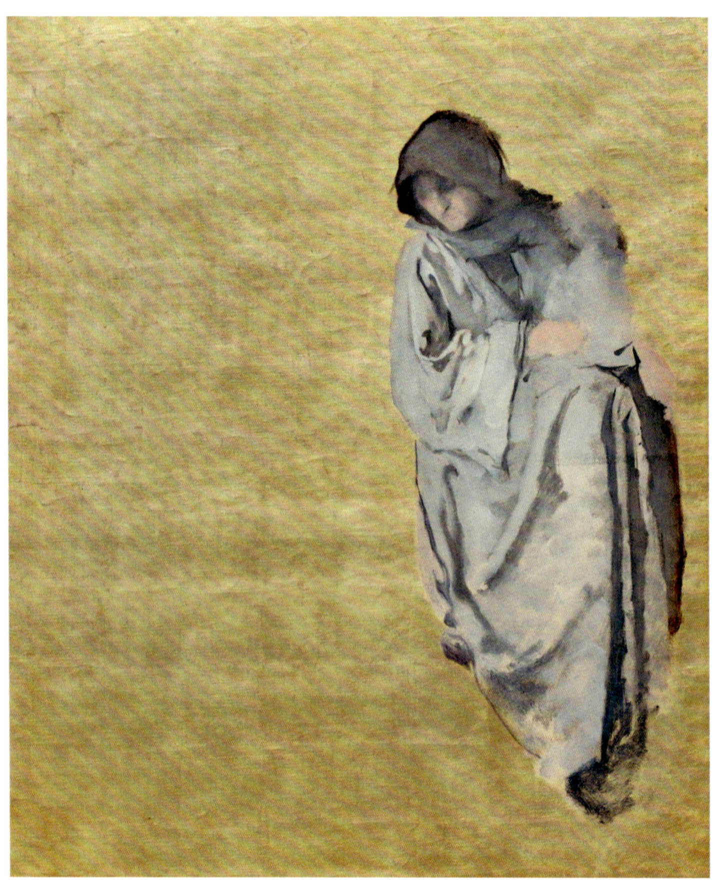

41

He used nude studies in different media—pencil, charcoal and chalk (black and white), colored pastel, translucent watercolor, and dense or thinned oil—to develop a vocabulary of movement and expression beneath the final, clothed figures. Rarely does the extent of his investment in the studies, including the extraordinary effort in this pastel for the *The Spirit of Light* (cat. 42), correlate directly to prominence in the final composition; instead, the studies suggest meditations on their respective roles and meanings in the murals. This pastel offers a lavish portrayal of the body against a vivid blue backdrop that exceeds basic description, amplifying the stark contrast between skin and sky. The difference of tone and texture between body and blue background describes a counterpoint present in the final composition, though Abbey eventually settled on a gold sunset.

NOTE

1. Abbey's allegories of religious freedom guiding settlers across the Atlantic Ocean for his lunette *The Spirit of Religious Freedom*, in the Pennsylvania State Capitol, owe much to Hunt's model.

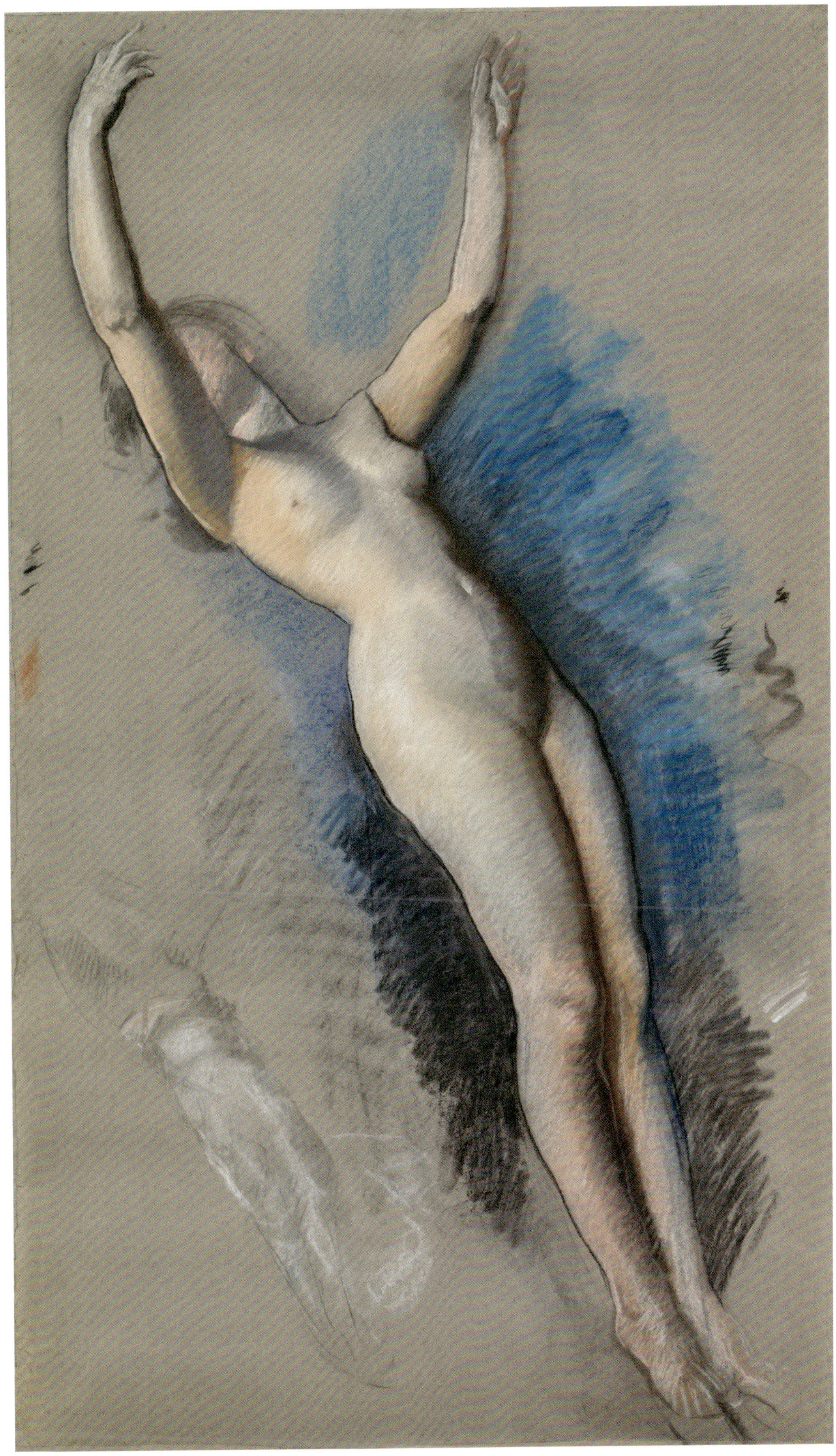

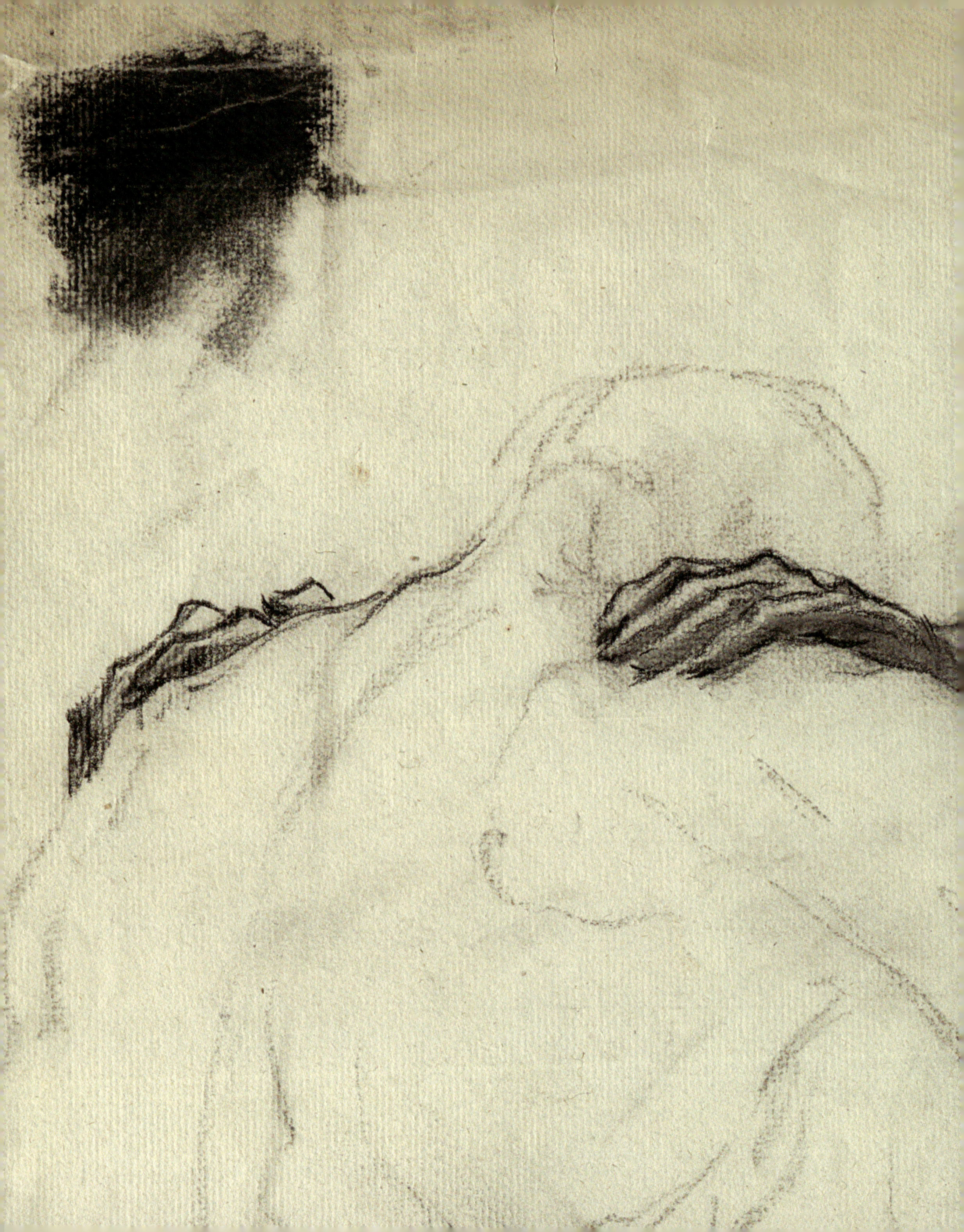

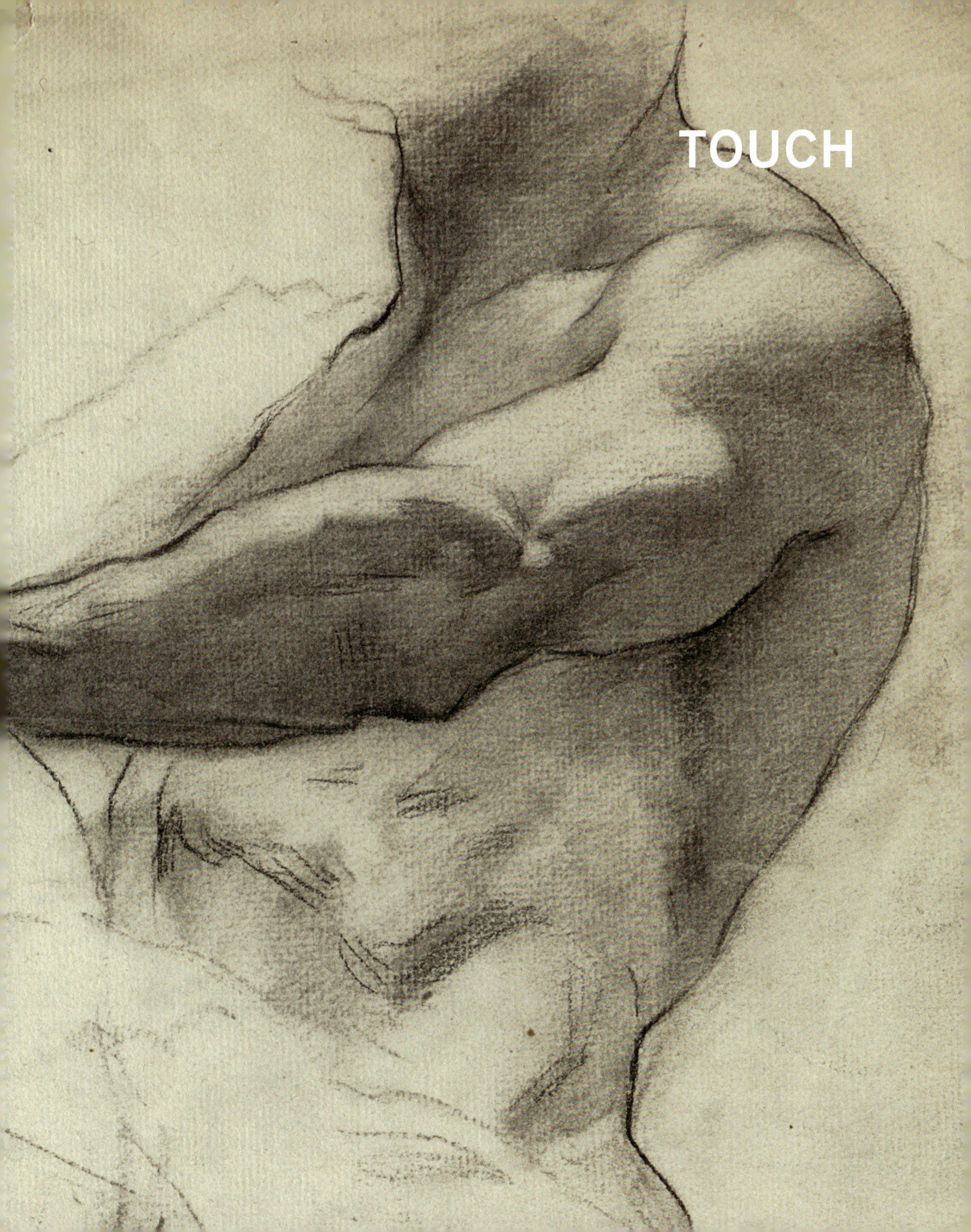

TOUCH

Touch was an especially frequent subject of the studies created for public commissions during the American Renaissance. Exemplified most sensually by the charcoal figure drawings of John Singer Sargent, the sense of tactile contact takes on both literal and figurative significance in these works.[1] Although sensualism—and its associations with desire and sexuality—is prominent in Sargent's practice, it assumes broader significance and range when compared with the work of other artists.

Why is touch important, and what work did it do? In this age of industry, labor became increasingly dehumanized and mechanical. Assembly lines transformed the worker into a cog in a machine, distant from the craftsmanship, quality, and pride often associated with preindustrial creation. Artists of the period also recognized the potential of their work to engage viewers physically, enlivening their sense of presence, contact, and connection and reminding them of their capacity for community.

Sargent's drawing of joined hands for his lunette *The Passing of Souls into Heaven* in the Boston Public Library is emblematic, even exemplary, of this dynamic (cat. 43). Initially, there is the connection of the hands, rendering aid and support to lift another person upward. The outreach is agreeable and mutual; both wrists arch and pull toward each other. The varying strength and slippage of their relationship is natural and harmonious. In the final composition (see page 71, fig. 7), the figures wrap around and between pairs of dressed harpists and accompany clothed individuals, presumably on their way to heaven. These interactions preoccupied the artist and highlight the theme of cooperation.

In his choice of medium and its application in drawings like this one, Sargent further deepened his exploration of touch. The varied contours and tones produce a richness that invites metaphor. Flowing outlines define the arms and sensuously draw the eye to trace the skin's surface. Similarly, rubbed areas show the movement of the artist's hand as he shaped the impression of musculature, likely using a combination of paper stumps, rags, erasers, and his fingers. To draw with charcoal is a combination of calligraphically describing contour and actively working the carbon material across the surface. The medium involves a tactile performance by the artist, especially one such as Sargent, that synesthetically invokes the sense of touch for viewers as well.

Such tactile studies are especially evocative. They brought artists closer to the experience of human connection and contact and accentuate their embrace of observation that is both immediate and intimate. Often lost in their final form on the walls of a library, church, or statehouse, the artists' original ideas can be difficult to perceive. And yet touch is prominent, even predominant, as in studies like this. It is here that the artists seek their own sense of connection, extending a hand to the viewer.

CAT. 43 John Singer Sargent (American, born Italy, 1856–1925, LL.D. 1916)

Study of Clasped Hands for *Heaven* in *The Triumph of Religion* in the Boston Public Library, ca. 1895–1916

Charcoal on off-white laid paper, 18¾ × 24½ in. (47.6 × 62.2 cm)
Harvard Art Museums/Fogg Museum, Cambridge, Mass., Gift of Miss Emily Sargent and Mrs. Francis Ormond in memory of their brother, John Singer Sargent, 1929.274

NOTE

1. This discussion is indebted to the work of Trevor Fairbrother, including his study *John Singer Sargent: The Sensualist*, exh. cat. (Seattle: Seattle Art Museum, 2000).

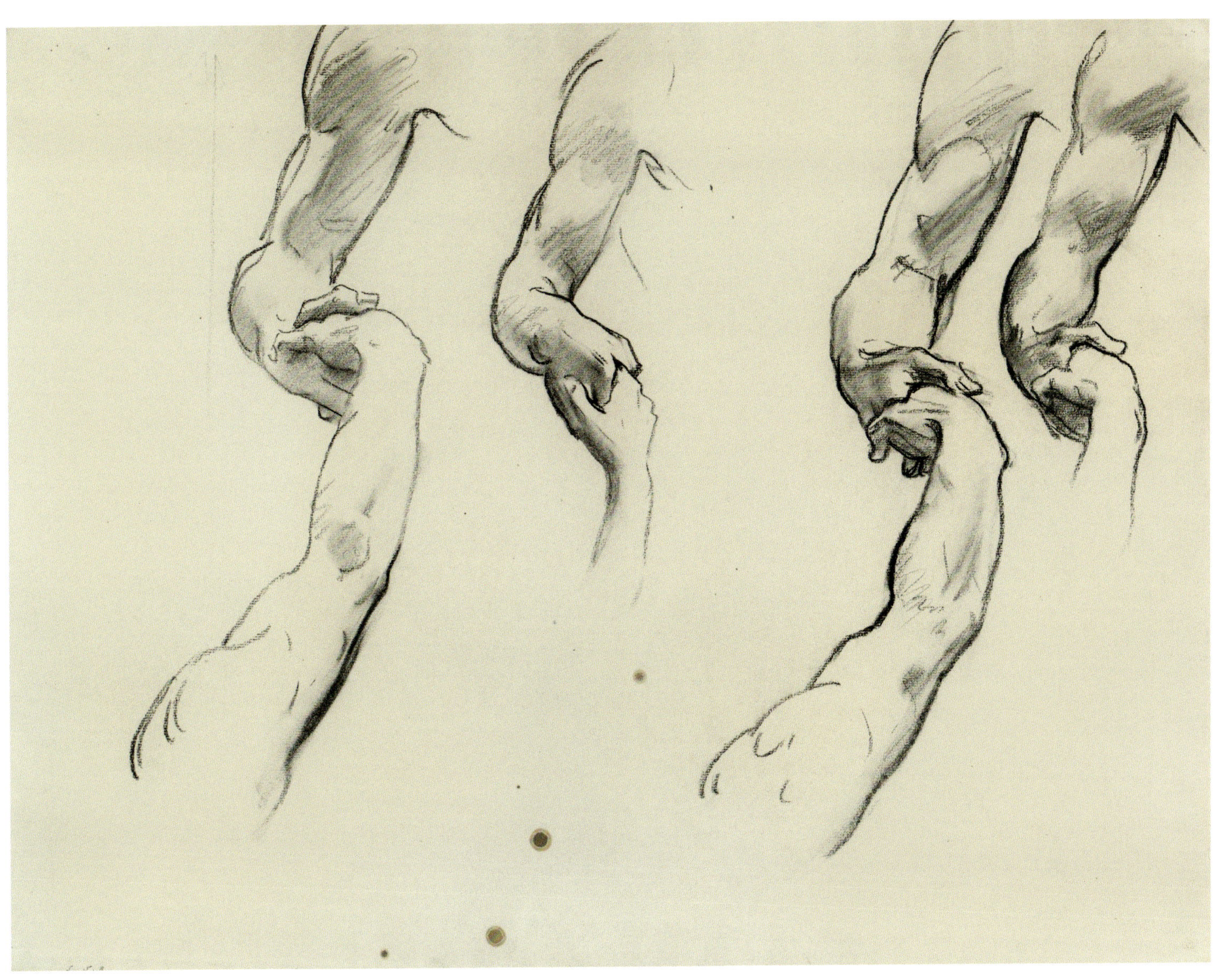

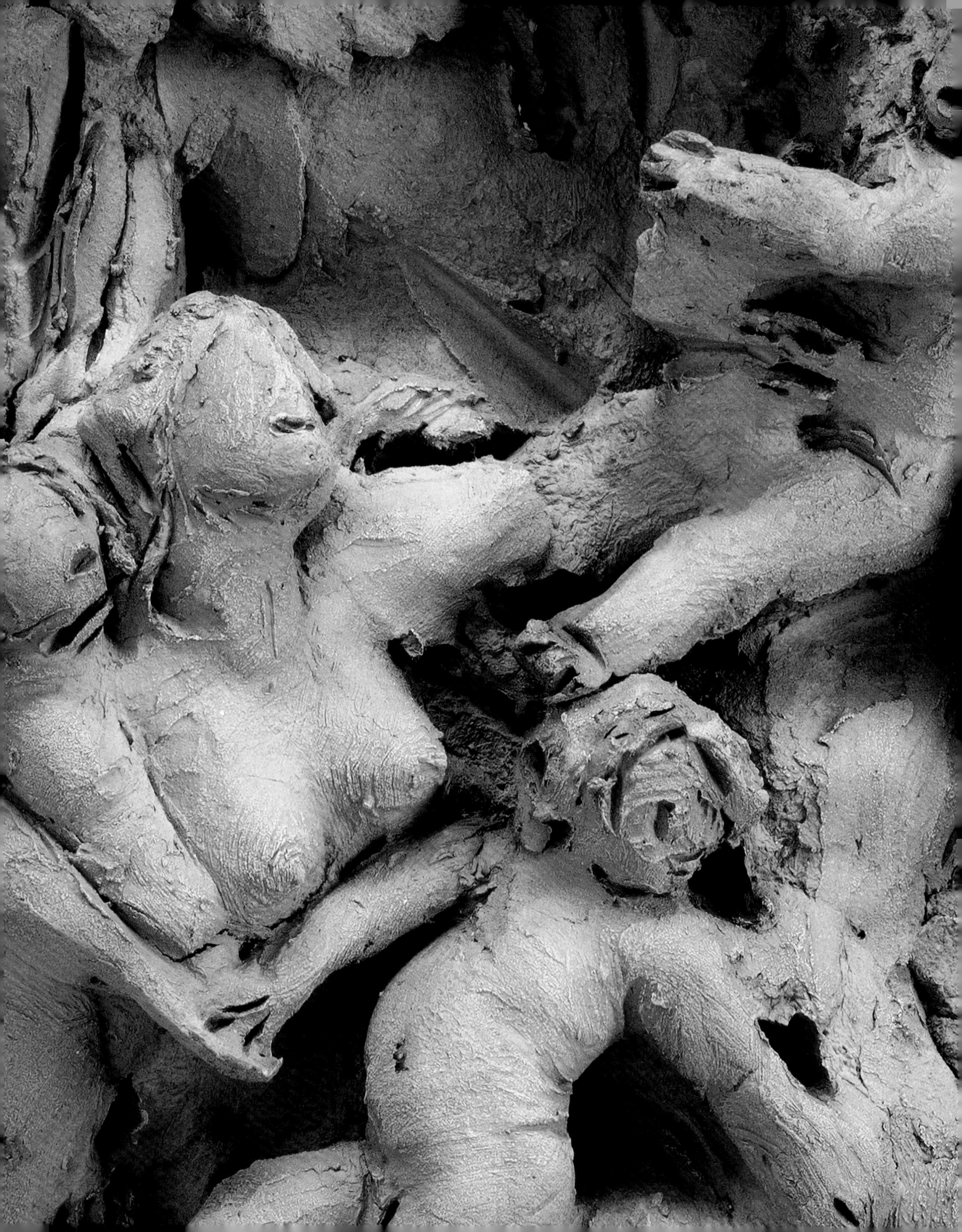

Holding Tight

A clinging grasp was a recurring motif for artists of the American Renaissance. Stolid, immovable forms (and figures) provide anchors for holding, suggesting a metaphor for wider social stability. A tight hold bonds individuals and illuminates the nature of their relationship, be it dependency or struggle. At times, embrace itself is a primary subject, especially in studies. Rather than light or artificially symbolic, the connection is usually firm and physical.

For the Symbolist sculptor George Grey Barnard—best remembered for his large-scale figural sculptures for the Pennsylvania State Capitol—this study for an unidentified group (cat. 44) portrays the defensive grasp of an adult woman in response to threat: she seizes two infants and reaches for a third being pulled away, even as her own body falls back. Her protective hold reflects fear of loss and projects intense emotion. Despite an unstable arrangement, the figures are densely interwoven in mutual protection. Such powerful, expressive scenes were typical of Barnard, who was a catalyst for Romantic sensualism in American sculpture at the end of the nineteenth century, inspired by the work of the French modernist Auguste Rodin.[1]

In contrast to Barnard's broad effects stands Kenyon Cox's study for *Jacob Wrestling with the Angel* (cat. 45), which portrays the massive, unyielding angel in great detail, as if he is made of stone. The struggling Jacob is shown only lightly, in motion, and ineffectual in his efforts to move the divine figure. In this study, Cox's two forms defy physical comparison, despite their similar proportions. Jacob's entire weight is apparently insufficient to move his opponent through their night-long struggle. The drawing manifests their difference of type—human and divine—as well as their intimate bond, suggesting the struggle of faith.[2]

NOTES

1. Wayne Craven, *Sculpture in America* (rev. ed.; Newark: University of Delaware Press, 1984), 442.
2. Cox's father, Jacob, was a brigadier general during the Civil War and served as governor of Ohio, among other offices, just after the war's end, so the young artist had a special view of the era's major conflicts. See H. Wayne Morgan, *Kenyon Cox, 1856–1919: A Life in American Art* (Kent, Ohio: Kent State University Press, 1994), 3–7.

CAT. 44 George Grey Barnard (American, 1863–1938)
Group, ca. 1903–11
Terracotta, 5 9/16 × 5 3/4 × 3 7/8 in. (14 × 14.5 × 9.8 cm)
The Art Institute of Chicago, Gift of Caroline D. Wade, 1938.252

CAT. 45 Kenyon Cox (American, 1856–1919)
Figure Study for *Jacob Wrestling with the Angel*, 1886
Charcoal on cream laid paper, 24 3/16 × 18 5/8 in. (61.4 × 47.3 cm)
Cooper Hewitt, Smithsonian Design Museum, New York, Gift of Allyn Cox, 1960-83-182

Detail of cat. 44

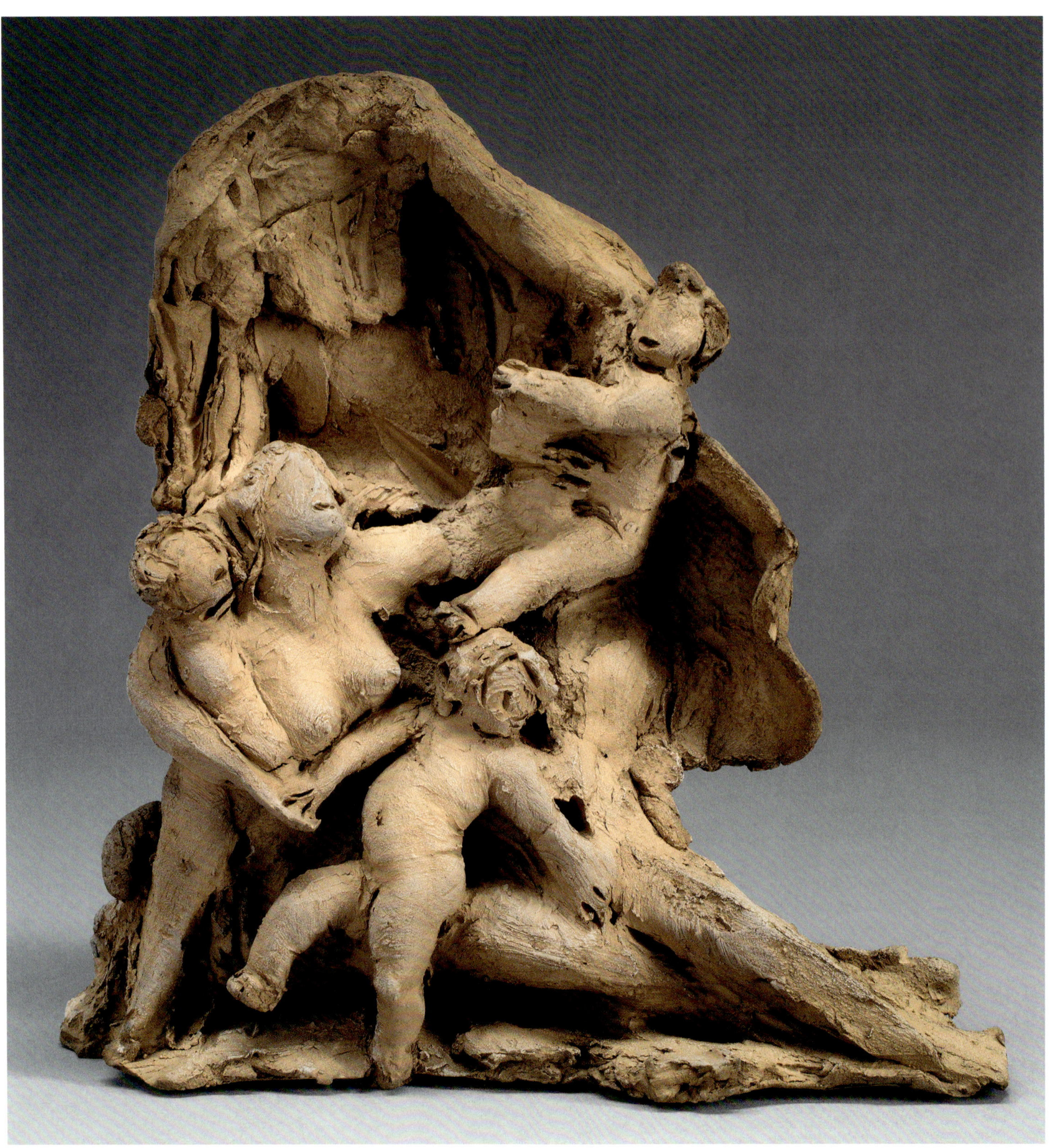

44

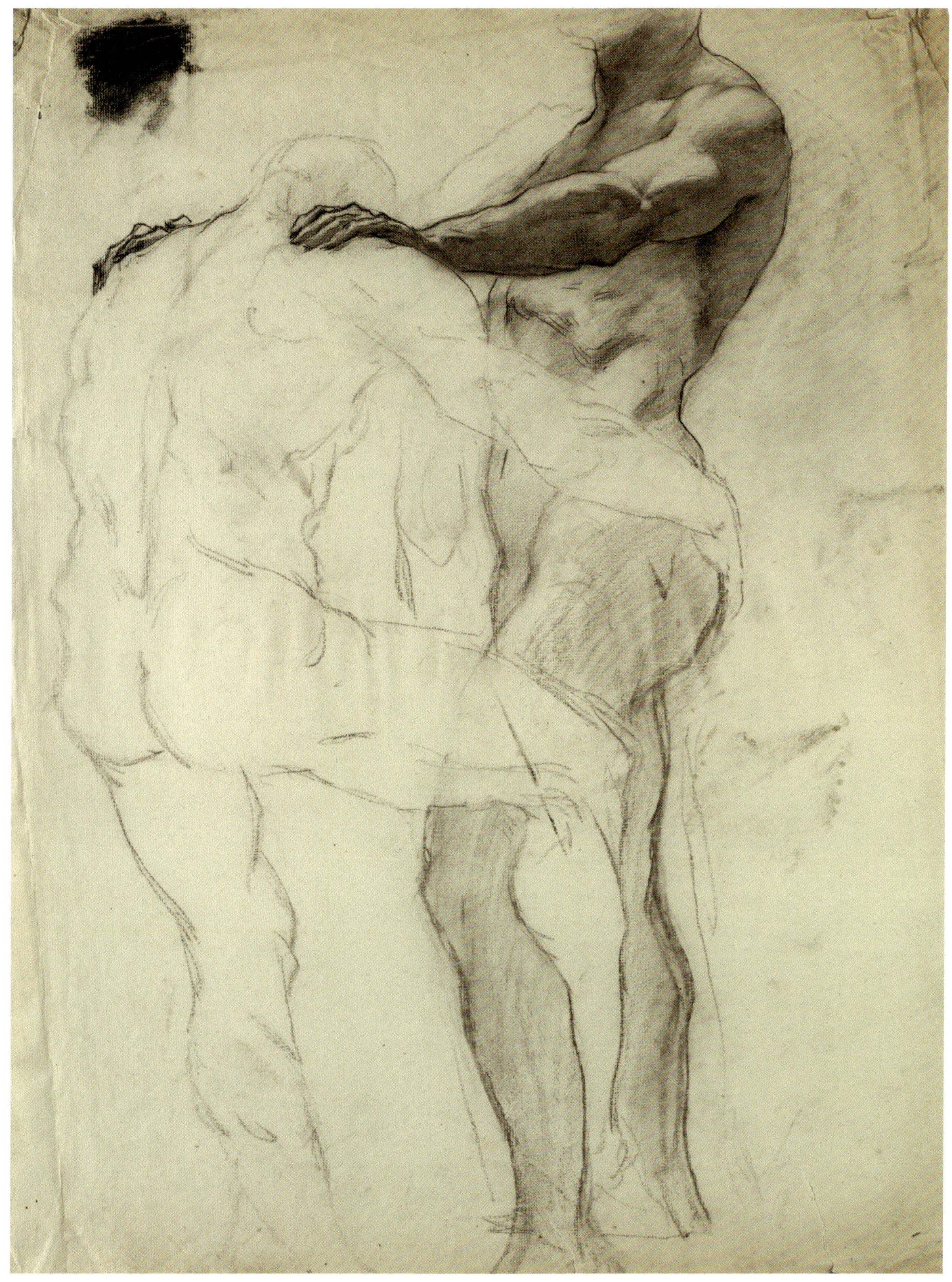

45

Reaching Out

As much as a tight grasp can seize attention, thwarted touch can provoke a comparable sense of vexation, which became a motif during the American Renaissance. Two figures, such as Jesus and Mary Magdalen in the Garden of Gethsemane in the drawing by John La Farge (cat. 46), can present anticipation as well as desire across space. Figures reaching toward one another to embrace, hold hands, or otherwise join together describe connection, which became a prominent expressive strategy during this period.

John Singer Sargent created frequent visual plays with and manipulations of touch in his works. In a study for the mural *The Crucifixion and Death of Our Lord* in the Boston Public Library, he presents the remarkable illusion of a figure stretching outward from the paper (cat. 47; detail right). With palms reversed, his oversized hands extend into the viewer's space and partially mask his face. The dramatic power of the gesture is greatly amplified in this concentrated image, accentuating the

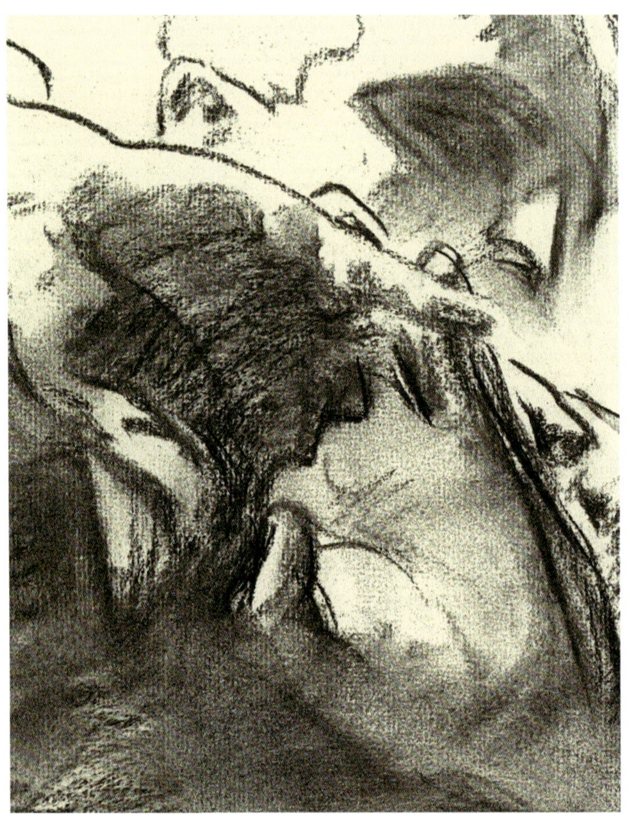

CAT. 46 John La Farge (American, 1835–1910, HON. 1896)
Study for *Christ Appearing to Mary*, 1877–78
Graphite on wove paper mounted to paperboard, 10⅛ × 11 13/16 in. (25.72 × 30 cm)
National Gallery of Art, Washington, D.C., Corcoran Collection (Museum Purchase, Membership Association Fund), 2015.19.742

CAT. 47 John Singer Sargent (American, born Italy, 1856–1925, LL.D. 1916)
Study for *The Crucifixion and Death of Our Lord* in *The Triumph of Religion* in the Boston Public Library, ca. 1909–16
Charcoal on laid paper, 24 9/16 × 18 15/16 in. (62.4 × 48.1 cm)
National Gallery of Art, Washington, D.C., Corcoran Collection (Gift of Miss Emily Sargent and Mrs. Francis Ormond, sisters of the artist), 2015.19.673

CAT. 48 Violet Oakley (American, 1874–1961)
Figure Study for *Revealed Law: The Beatitudes* in the Pennsylvania State Capitol, ca. 1922
Charcoal and chalk on paper, 18¾ × 12 in. (47.6 × 30.5 cm)
Pennsylvania Capitol Preservation Committee, Harrisburg, 82.78.274

CAT. 49 John La Farge (American, 1835–1910, HON. 1896)
Madonna, ca. 1886–87
Graphite on paper, 7⅜ × 3¾ in. (18.7 × 9.5 cm)
Carnegie Museum of Art, Pittsburgh, Purchase, 13.9.1

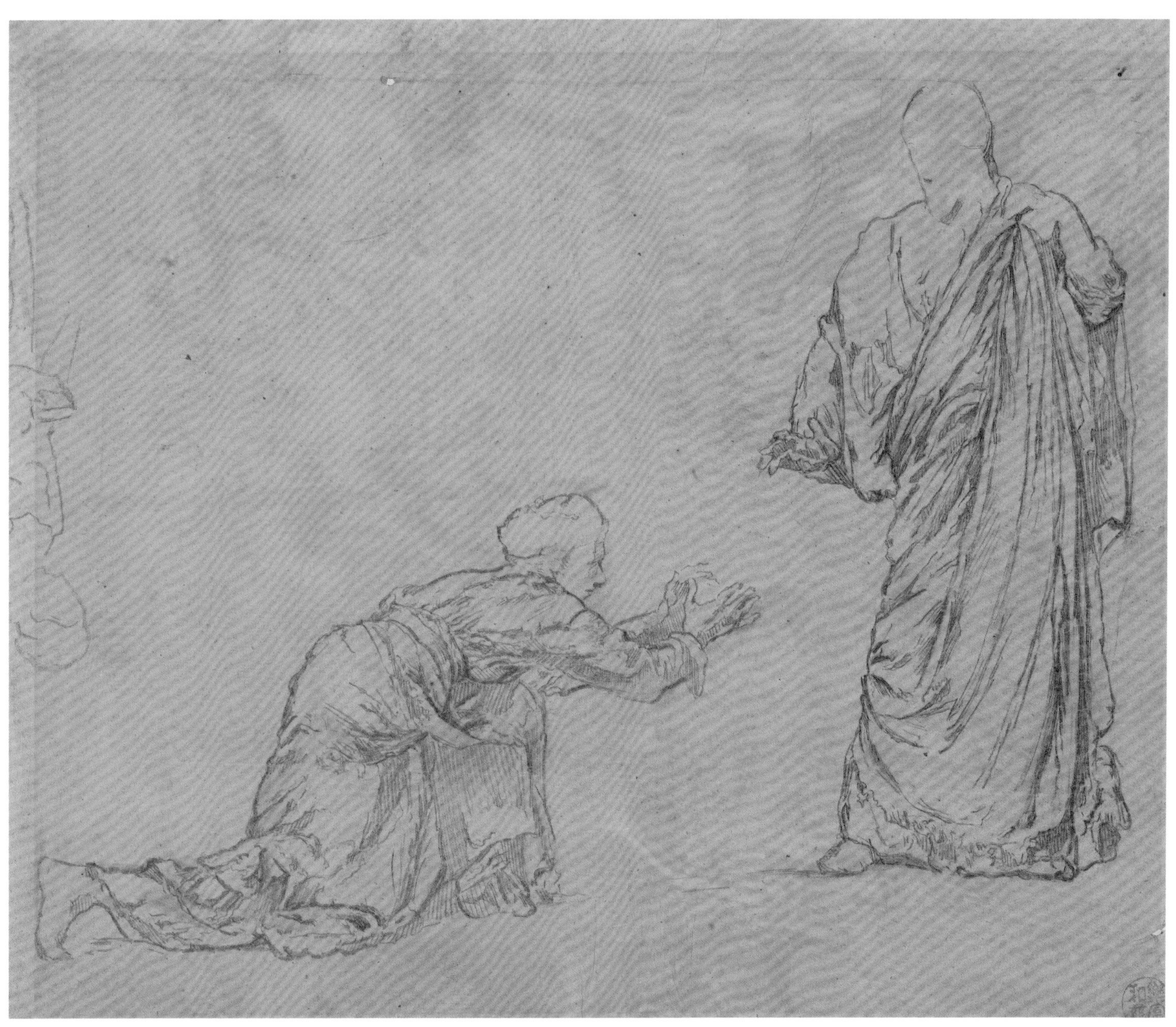

46

artist's delight in such visual anecdotes within the broader final composition. The power of the design derives from its illusionism, involving the viewer in a spatial relationship not just laterally across the scene but also outward into space. That the figure reaches forth so directly—not just toward us but toward the artist conceiving it—effectively repels our experience spatially, blocking sight of the figure even as it resists touch; the knitted fingers push us away. This formal confection is a virtuosic technical challenge, embraced by an artist eager to demonstrate mastery in draftsmanship and create a rewarding, dynamic composition that engages visual experience on several levels.

Violet Oakley's study for one of the figures in her murals for the Supreme Court chamber in the Pennsylvania State Capitol significantly decontextualizes the arms to create a communicative gesture of appeal (cat. 48). The figure points upward, akin to the gaze of John La Farge's *Madonna* (cat. 49), appealing to the untouchable heaven, outside the frame, outside of vision, and outside of touch. The sense of implied presence relates to external authority. Oakley's tandem gesture combines the experience of tactile grip with the figure's clothing alongside the decisive pointed finger, contrasting concrete touch with what lies beyond reach.

Vexed touch is a sign of dislocation. To clutch oneself is an external expression of inner feeling. Reaching out to heaven is an aspect of faith to that which is not present or possible but sought and hoped for. Outward reach in the art of the American Renaissance accentuates disconnection and the forces of disruption that threatened social order. Jesus resists Mary Magdalen's touch, pushing away as Sargent's figure does to the viewer, preventing the very thing that would confirm both sight and faith: touch.

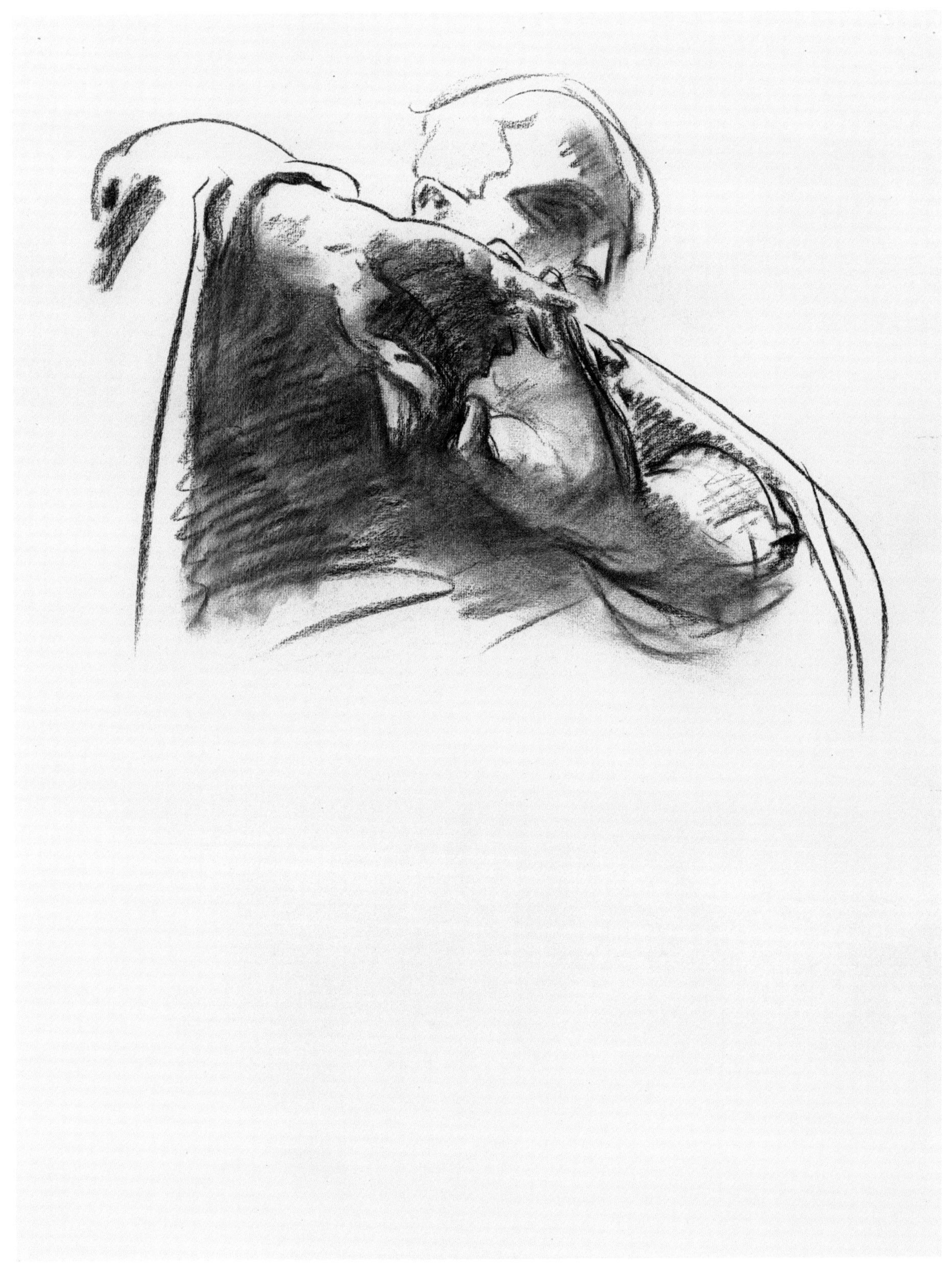

47

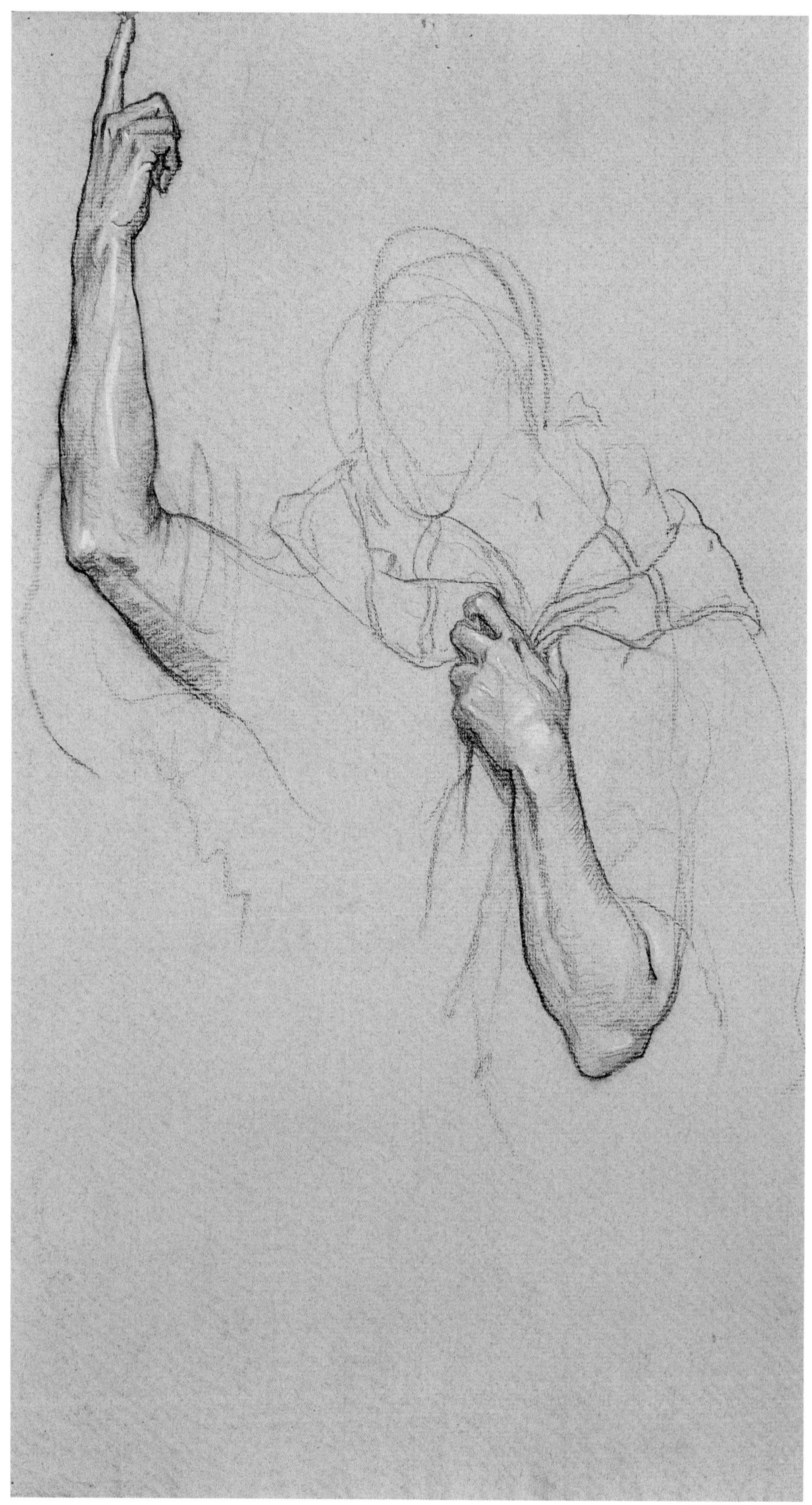

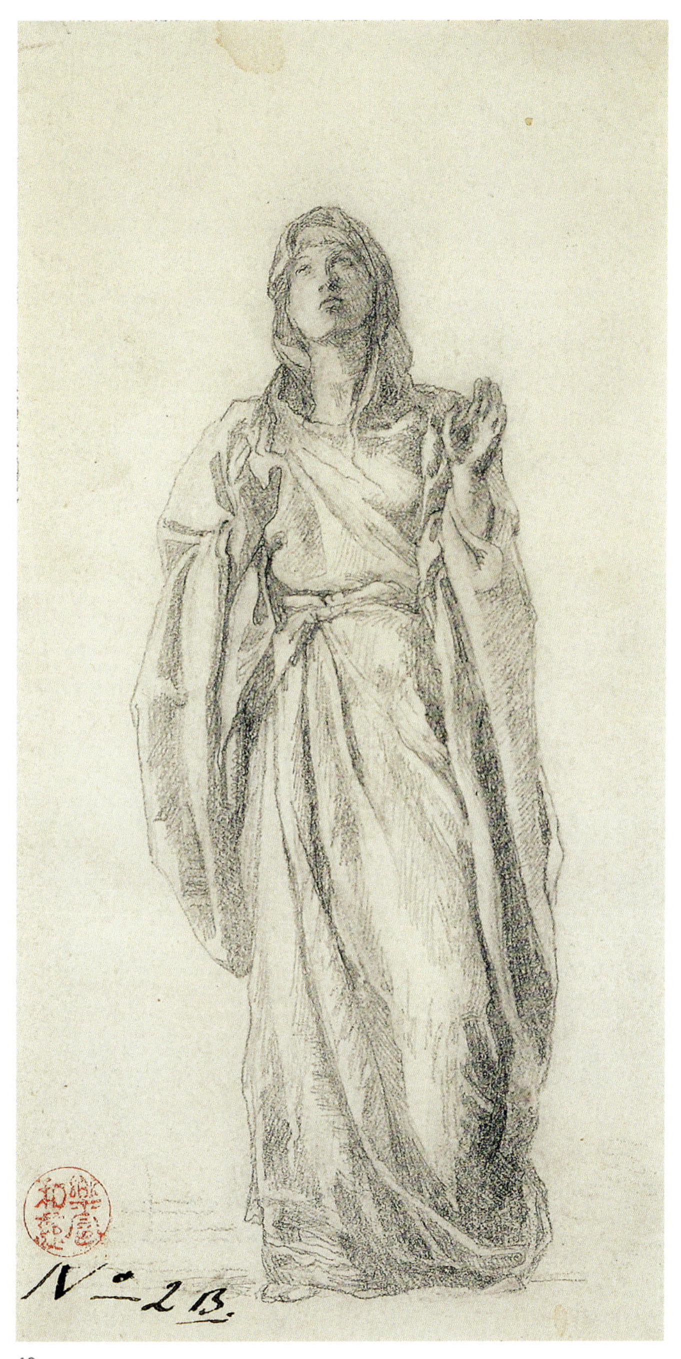

49

Tactile Materials

Artistic media can be visceral as well as vividly evocative of touch. This group of studies directs attention to a range of techniques by which artists of the American Renaissance involved the medium itself as a vehicle for discovery of and engagement with their own and the viewer's sense of touch. Of course for the artist, making art is a physical action in which touch and movement are primary, but inviting viewers to experience that sensation is unusual in the history of art. The immediacy of the studies mostly did not translate to the final large-scale works; but as a reflection of the artists' process and aspirations, the contribution of such works was integral and heuristic.

For the expatriate realist Gari Melchers, representing masculinity offered special interest, as seen in his public commissions for the World's Columbian Exposition and the Library of Congress. Within Melchers's documented work, men convey a distinct, gendered aesthetic. He depicted men more often than women and with a higher degree of effort, facility, and experimentation. He seems to have wanted to understand and investigate masculinity per se, a subject of wider public interest (and insecurity) during the period as well. In terms of media, densely applied oil paint such as in his study of a man's head (cat. 50) is typically associated with smoothness, languor, and lingering contact, but the figure exhibits none of those qualities. Instead, Melchers has roughly knifed on paint in a terse series of abbreviated strokes. No long or gentle contours or modeling appears. Rather, a faceted, sculptural aesthetic prevails, resembling a form built of masses and angles. Melchers set out to present the body differently—chiseled, not lissome.

Kenyon Cox's seated male nude (cat. 51), almost certainly a student work, offers a striking comparison to Melchers's painted bust. Densely described, this male body presents the infirmities and marks of toilsome life. Cox does not conceal them, instead emphasizing a dramatic interplay of shadows across the receding volume of the model's

CAT. 50 Gari Melchers (American, 1860–1932)
Study of a Man's Head, 1912

Oil on paper, 20 × 10 in. (50.8 × 25.4 cm)
Gari Melchers Home and Studio at the University of Mary Washington, Va., 1942.1.1595

CAT. 51 Kenyon Cox (American, 1856–1919)
Nude Study of a Seated Man, 1880–84

Charcoal and graphite on cream paper, 25 3/16 × 19 1/2 in. (64 × 49.5 cm)
Cooper Hewitt, Smithsonian Design Museum, New York, Gift of Allyn Cox, 1960-83-339

CAT. 52 Edwin Austin Abbey (American, 1852–1911, HON. 1897)
Study for *The Hours* in the Pennsylvania State Capitol, ca. 1903

Colored chalk on black wove paper, 28 7/16 × 22 7/16 in. (72.2 × 57 cm)
Yale University Art Gallery, New Haven, Conn., Edwin Austin Abbey Memorial Collection, 1937.1795

CAT. 53 Edwin Austin Abbey (American, 1852–1911, HON. 1897)
Study for Ophelia in *The Play Scene in Hamlet, Act III, Scene II*, ca. 1896–97

Pastel on paper, approx. 20 3/16 × 26 1/4 in. (51.3 × 66.7 cm)
Yale University Art Gallery, New Haven, Conn., Edwin Austin Abbey Memorial Collection, 1937.2178

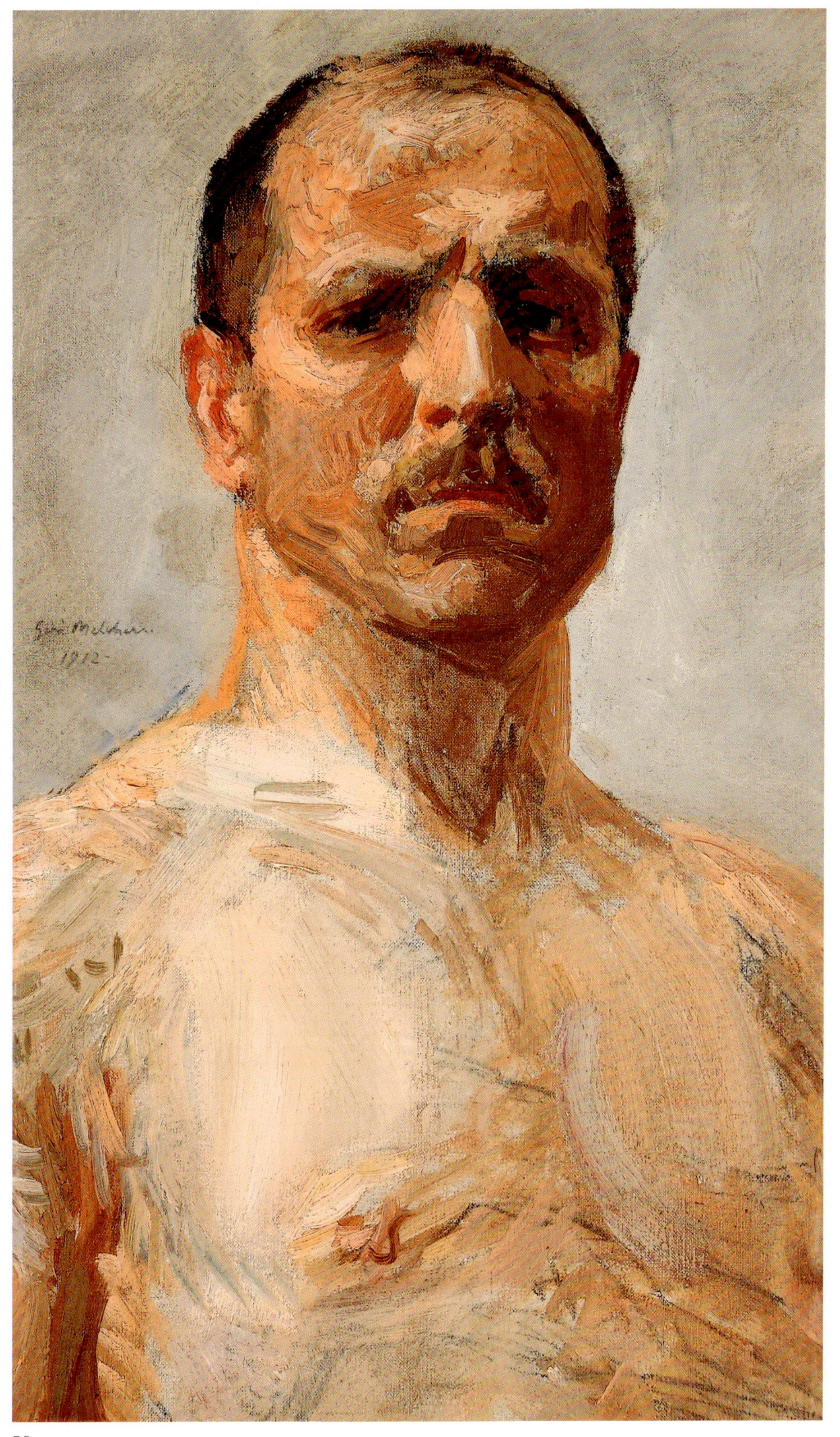

50

torso, left arm, and legs. The dark backdrop is painstakingly drawn, making the figure a bright, radiant highlight and adding to the sense of illusionistic volume—its brightness emerges from the dark. The body's folds and creases are no youthful idealizations, but rather emphasize the sagging flesh and wrinkled skin of an aging man. Like Melchers, Cox presents tactility and solid description. He focuses on a richly visceral sense of the lived experience of an individual.

Edwin Austin Abbey's more lyrical sense of touch in his charcoals, chalks, and pastels more closely approaches the sensuality of John Singer Sargent than that of Melchers or Cox. Abbey described his envy of Sargent's confident, effortless facility, finding his own art more workmanlike and strenuous.[1] His luminous figure study for *The Hours* (cat. 52) combines pastel and chalk to create a vaporous suggestion of fabric and skin set against a dark sheet of paper. The hues and material softness of the pastels replace description with luminosity and independent touches of pigment, emphasizing formal properties of representation and artistic technique. Abbey leads with the idea of an evanescent human experience in sensual tones and textures.

In his study for Ophelia (cat. 53), Abbey goes further, infusing cascading color and texture through the figure's vivid and layered red hair. Less a description of hair than a record of interwoven color and movement, the drawing is an expert demonstration of the medium's capacity. Abbey's method provokes the viewer's sense of touch, not with realistic description but with the poetic richness of the medium.

NOTE

1. Edward Verrall Lucas, *Edwin Austin Abbey, Royal Academician: The Record of His Life and Work* (London: Methuen, 1921), 1:199.

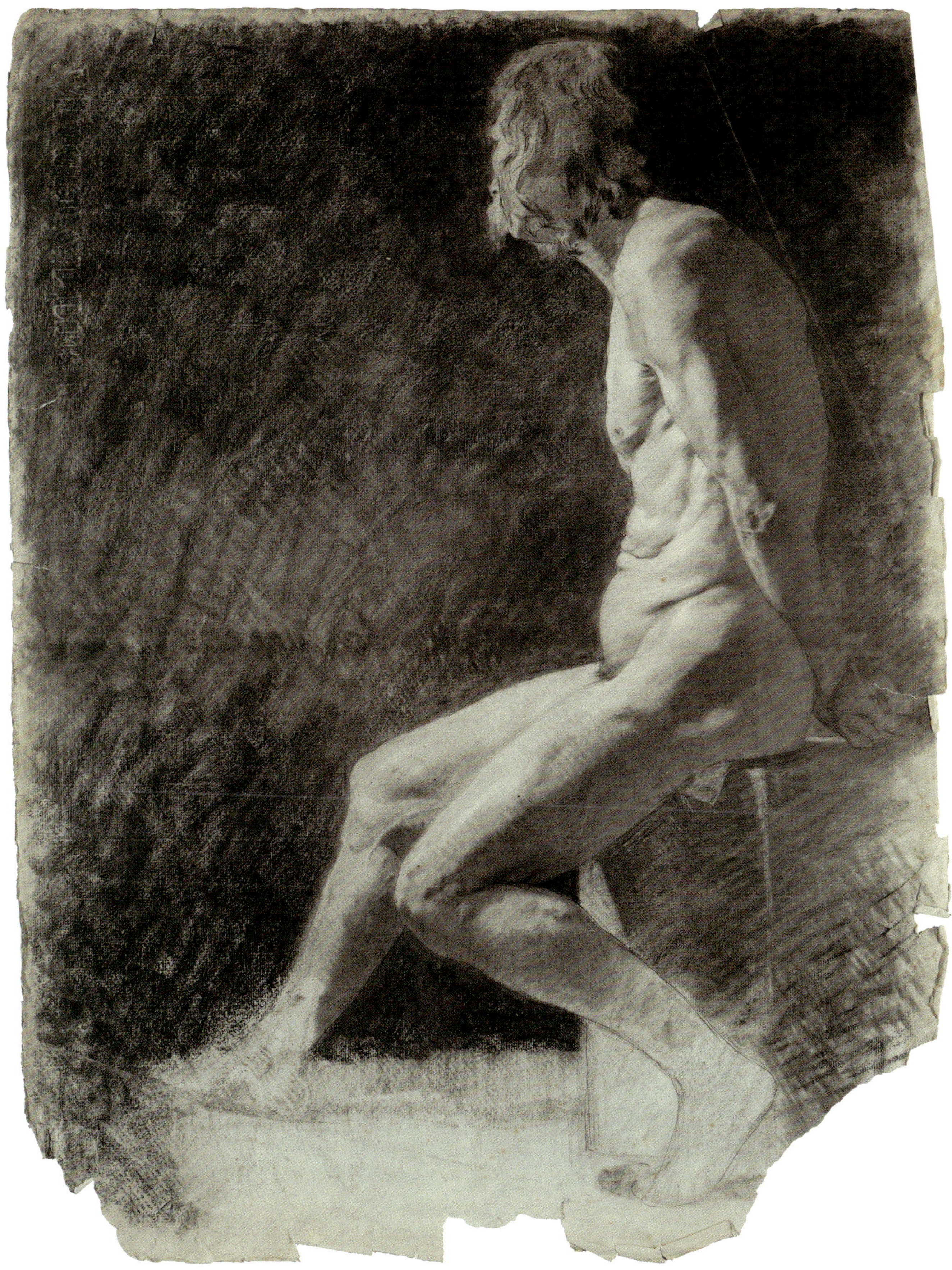

51

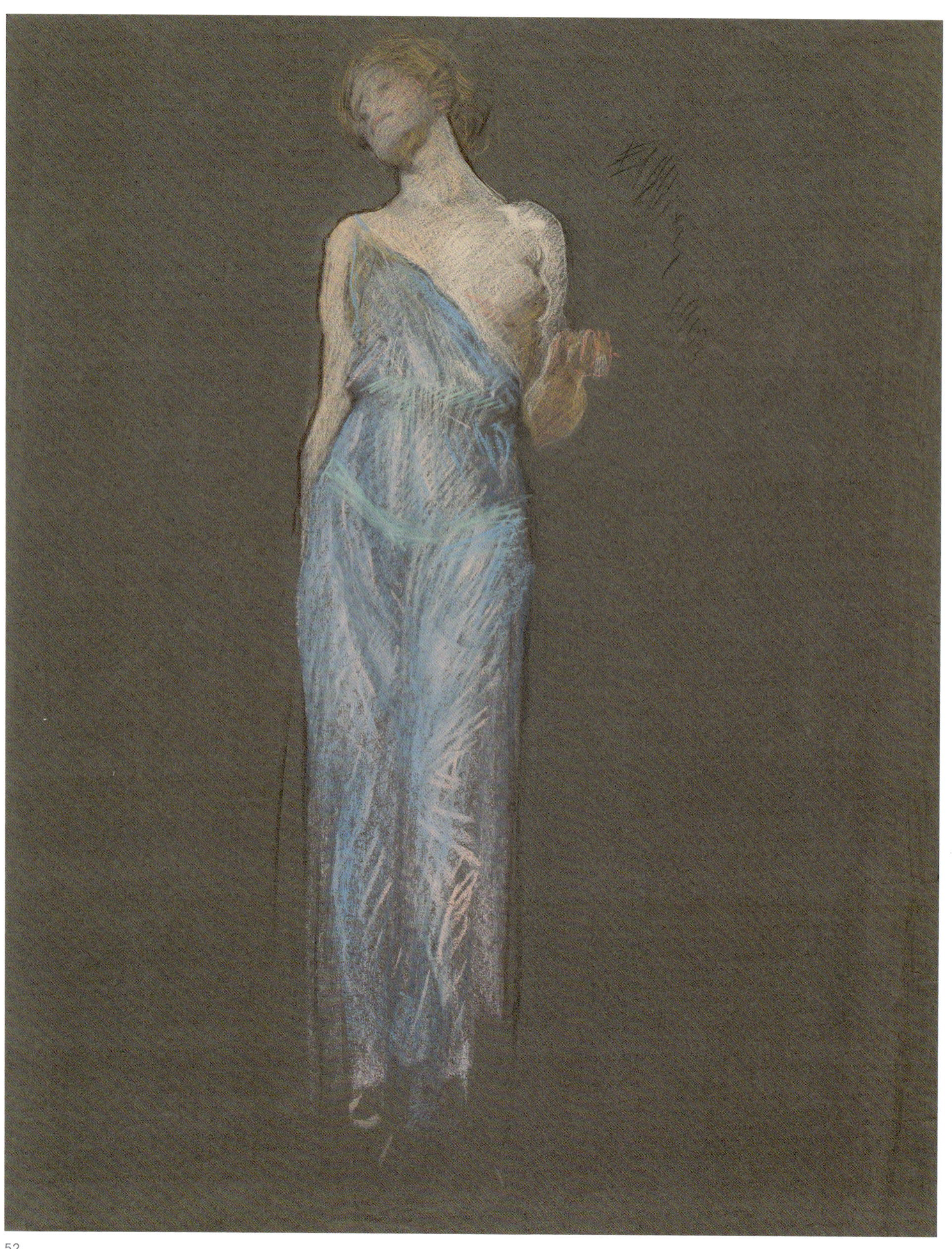

52

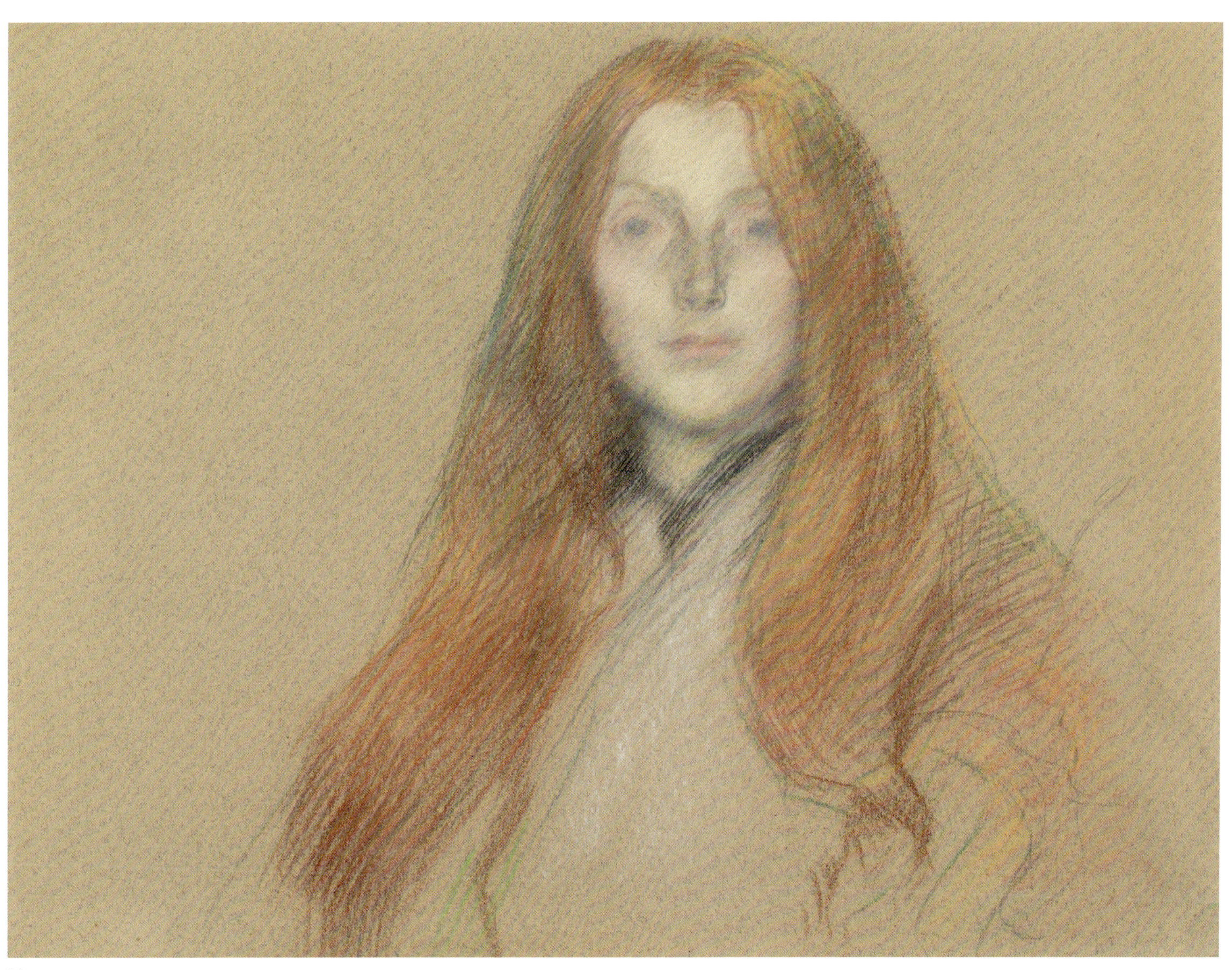

53

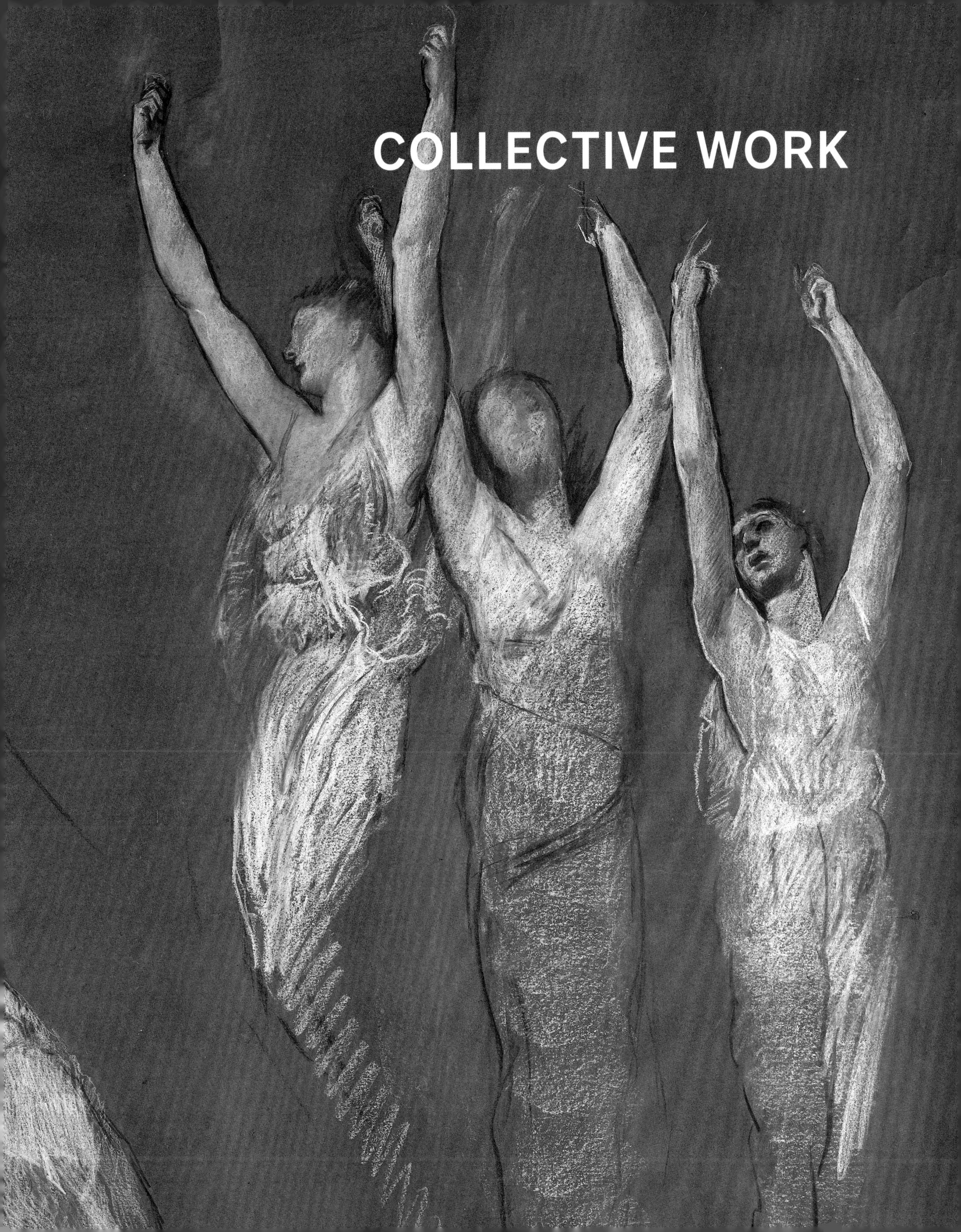

COLLECTIVE WORK

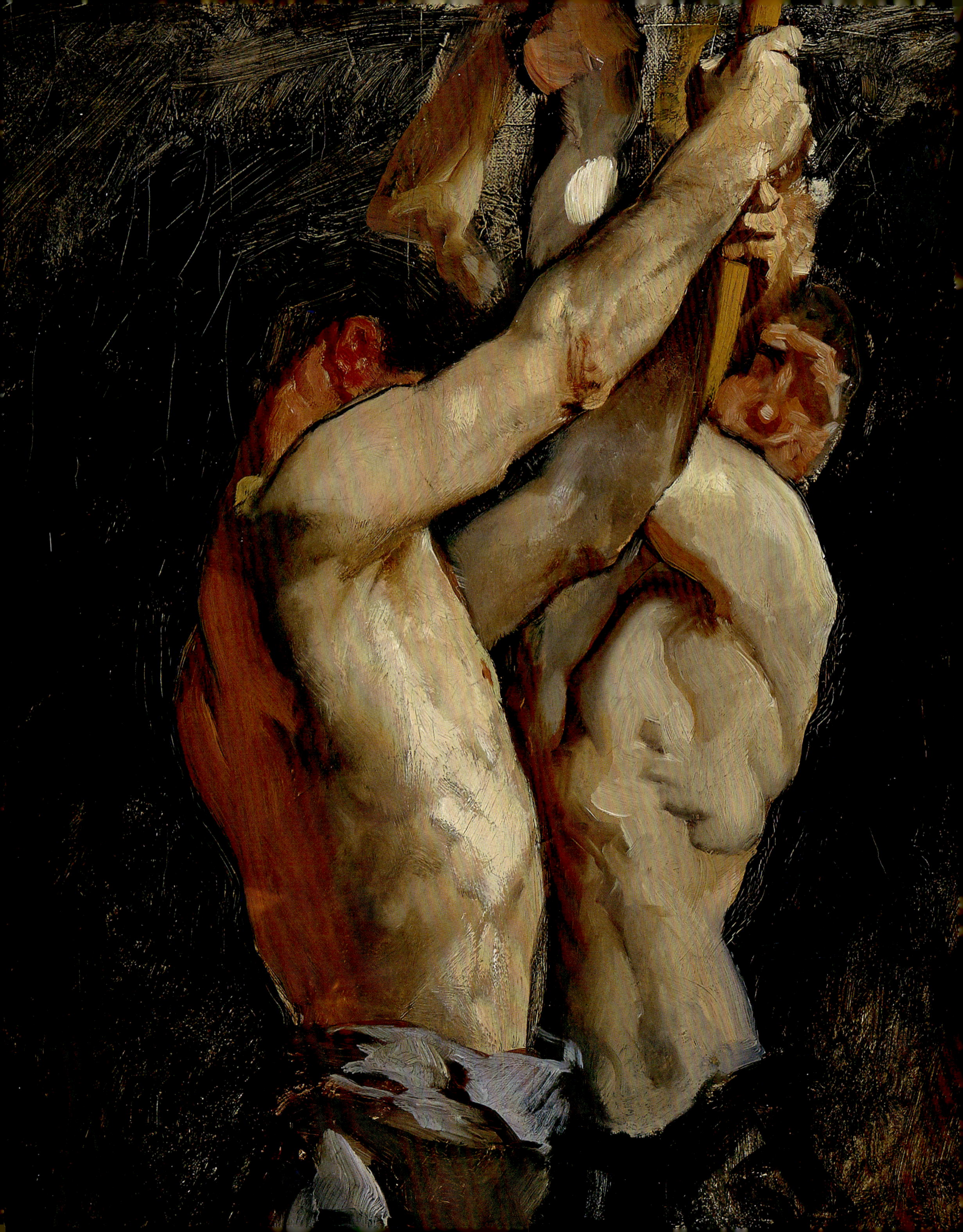

Figures in art of the American Renaissance work together. Scenes of positive morality consistently depict groups of people collaborating. In an age defined by industrial labor, that character may be unsurprising. Like assembly lines, movement and gesture are orchestrated and cadenced, with bodies aligned in harmonious arrays, untroubled by the cares of poverty, fatigue, or injury.

In his study for *The Spirit of Vulcan: Genius of the Workers in Iron and Steel* (cat. 54) in the Pennsylvania State Capitol, Edwin Austin Abbey depicts ironworkers around an anvil, their hammers raised to strike in succession to form a ship's rudder post, showing both dramatic suspension of impending action and visceral representation of straining torsos.[1] The paint in the background runs around them in rivulets, as if molten, and their leather aprons blend into their bodies. The figures are lit by the glow of the furnace at left, the paint casting itself into skin, bone, and muscle.

An industrial conceit depicting preindustrial technology, Abbey's painting ennobles cooperative effort to create a reassuring vision of labor. Despite the growth of monopolies and their abuse of workers through long hours for low pay in dangerous conditions, the composition heroizes collective toil and documents mutual responsibility and reliance. The competency of the team is what makes the work graceful and efficient. Without that community, Abbey's well-honed system would not function.

His study of miners (cat. 55), created for the adjacent lunette *Science Revealing the Treasures of the Earth*, is more sequential, showing a timelapse of a group whose movements are cautious and considered. This is not a march but a climb, characterized by uncertainty and risk. Studies such as this reveal the effort Abbey invested into group dynamics and developing the figures' psychological as well as physical energy. These are vital, strong young laborers, not industrialists, and their exertion is inspired by muses, not bosses. Notably, the figures descend below the edge of the composition, reaching into the area occupied by viewers looking up at the mural above. That space—the lower levels of the Pennsylvania capitol's rotunda—is both the mine and the resource that the workers explore.

Abbey made laborers his heroes. Similar scenes—including his mural *The Apotheosis of Pennsylvania*—equate groups of workers with regiments of soldiers. A common narrative after the Civil War was of men who had left farms for battle and then returned to work in factories. Abbey's ironworkers wear comparable aprons and move with the practiced coordination of a military drill. Such diligence celebrated ordinary citizens whose exertions powered the country's new industries.

The smooth calibration of Abbey's scene is not only moral but efficient. The coordination of labor, the figures' extended limbs and movements, reflect the increasingly streamlined activities of the factory floor. Led by figures like Frederick W. Taylor,

CAT. 54 Edwin Austin Abbey (American, 1852–1911, HON. 1897)

Figure Study for *The Spirit of Vulcan: Genius of the Workers in Iron and Steel* in the Pennsylvania State Capitol, ca. 1902–8

Oil on canvas, 30 × 40 in. (76.2 × 101.6 cm)
Yale University Art Gallery, New Haven, Conn., Edwin Austin Abbey Memorial Collection, 1937.1365

CAT. 55 Edwin Austin Abbey (American, 1852–1911, HON. 1897)

Compositional Study for *Science Revealing the Treasures of the Earth* in the Pennsylvania State Capitol, 1905

Charcoal and chalk on paper, 30¾ × 22⅜ in. (78.1 × 56.8 cm)
Yale University Art Gallery, New Haven, Conn., Edwin Austin Abbey Memorial Collection, 1937.1453

Detail of cat. 54

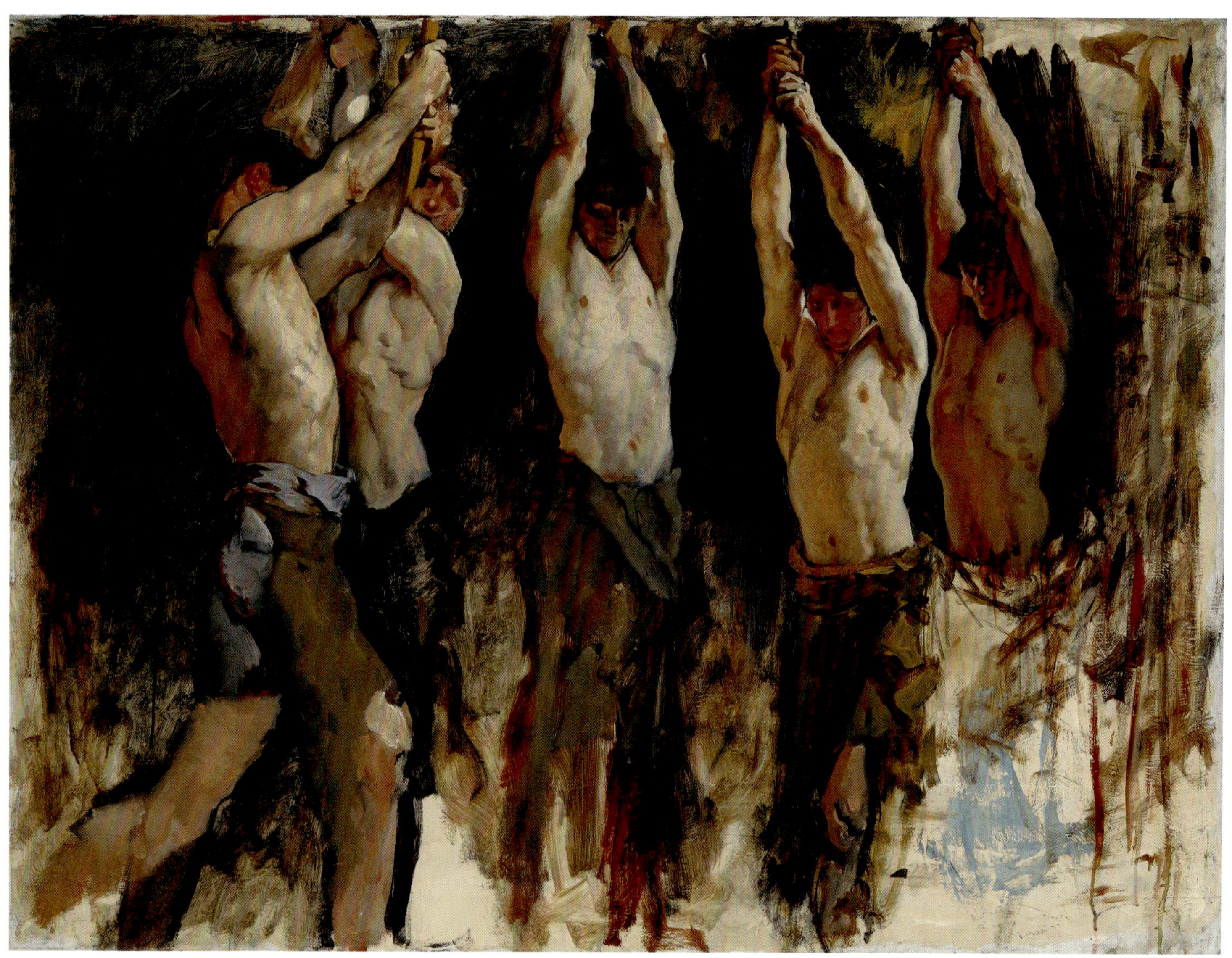

54

late nineteenth-century industrial manufacturers grew obsessed with efficiency. Abbey's painting appears to equate the smooth, natural motion of hand-crafted labor with the ergonomic controls that were increasingly enforced on workers to increase production.

NOTE

1. A 2022 article suggests that their efficiency may not spare the laborers—as Abbey depicts them—work-related ailments; Paul J. Nicholson, "Edwin Austin Abbey, *The Spirit of Vulcan, Genius of the Workers in Iron and Steel*, c. 1902–08," *Occupational Medicine* 72, no. 5 (June 2022): 286–88.

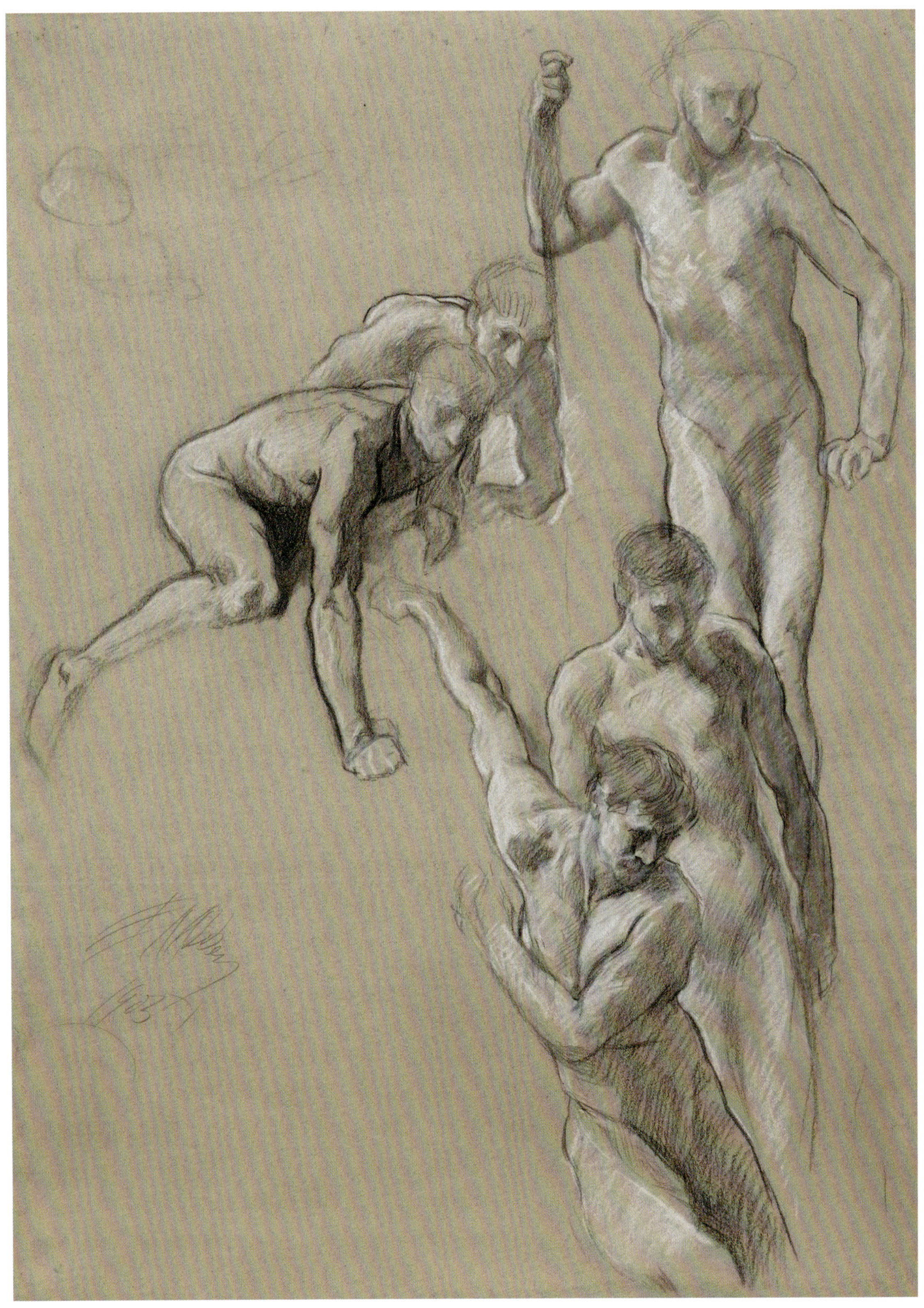

55

Heaven

Visions of heaven created during the American Renaissance were characterized by harmonious social order, but not discipline. John Singer Sargent's study for the mural *Heaven* in the Boston Public Library (cat. 56), already visited here in a study of clasping hands (see cat. 43), depicts pairs of harpists interwoven with figures that move through the procession. Although aligned, the figures are not standardized. Instead, they wend fluidly in coordinated but individual movements. For Sargent and his peers, vital, organic humanism was the ideal of society and a template for the afterlife. The dancers hold hands and support one another as they assist others, one at the center and one at lower right (and possibly a third, at far left), raising them skyward. The youthful strength and vitality of the attendants represent not winged angels but symbolic inhabitants of heaven, working in close coordination.

Edwin Austin Abbey's oil study for his lunette *The Spirit of Light* (cat. 57) in the Pennsylvania State Capitol shows a comparable group of allegorical figures aligned in controlled asymmetry. Bearing characteristics of his painted study of ironworkers at an anvil for *The Spirit of Vulcan* (see cat. 54) and Sargent's *Heaven*, Abbey's large-scale chalk and charcoal drawing focuses attention on the rhythm and spacing of the two ascending groups, each figure, in turn, reaching upward with an extension and lightness intended to echo the ephemeral characteristics of gas flame that they symbolize. Abbey's veils of white chalk unify the figures and avoid any sense of real weight or mass. Several of the lower bodies appear to dissolve into space rather than solidify into legs, suggesting uncertainty about whether Abbey considered using the figures themselves as the sources of light, rather than the flames they ultimately hold atop their fingertips in the final mural. Irrespective, the study is evidence that Abbey took every stage of creative development seriously and considered each study as an independent artwork with its own ideas and priorities.

CAT. 56 John Singer Sargent (American, born Italy, 1856–1925, LL.D. 1916)

Study for *Heaven* in *The Triumph of Religion* in the Boston Public Library, ca. 1909–14

Oil on canvas, 33¼ × 66¼ in. (84.5 × 168.3 cm)
Smith College Museum of Art, Northampton, Mass., Gift of Mrs. Dwight W. Morrow (Elizabeth Cutter, class of 1896), 1932.14.2

CAT. 57 Edwin Austin Abbey (American, 1852–1911, HON. 1897)

Study for *The Spirit of Light* in the Pennsylvania State Capitol, ca. 1902–8

Chalk and graphite on dark brown wove paper, 60 × 84 in. (152.4 × 213.4 cm)
Yale University Art Gallery, New Haven, Conn., Edwin Austin Abbey Memorial Collection, 1937.1525

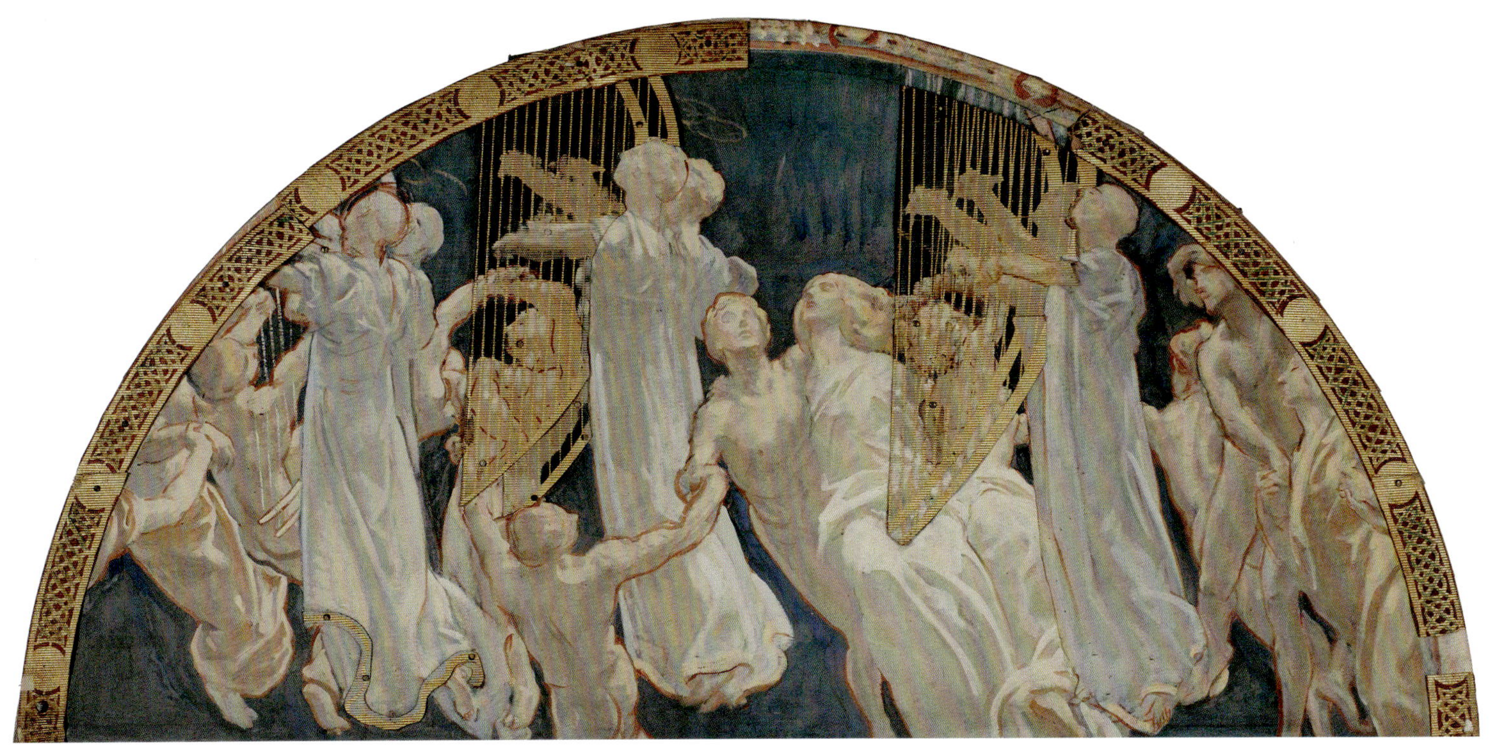

56

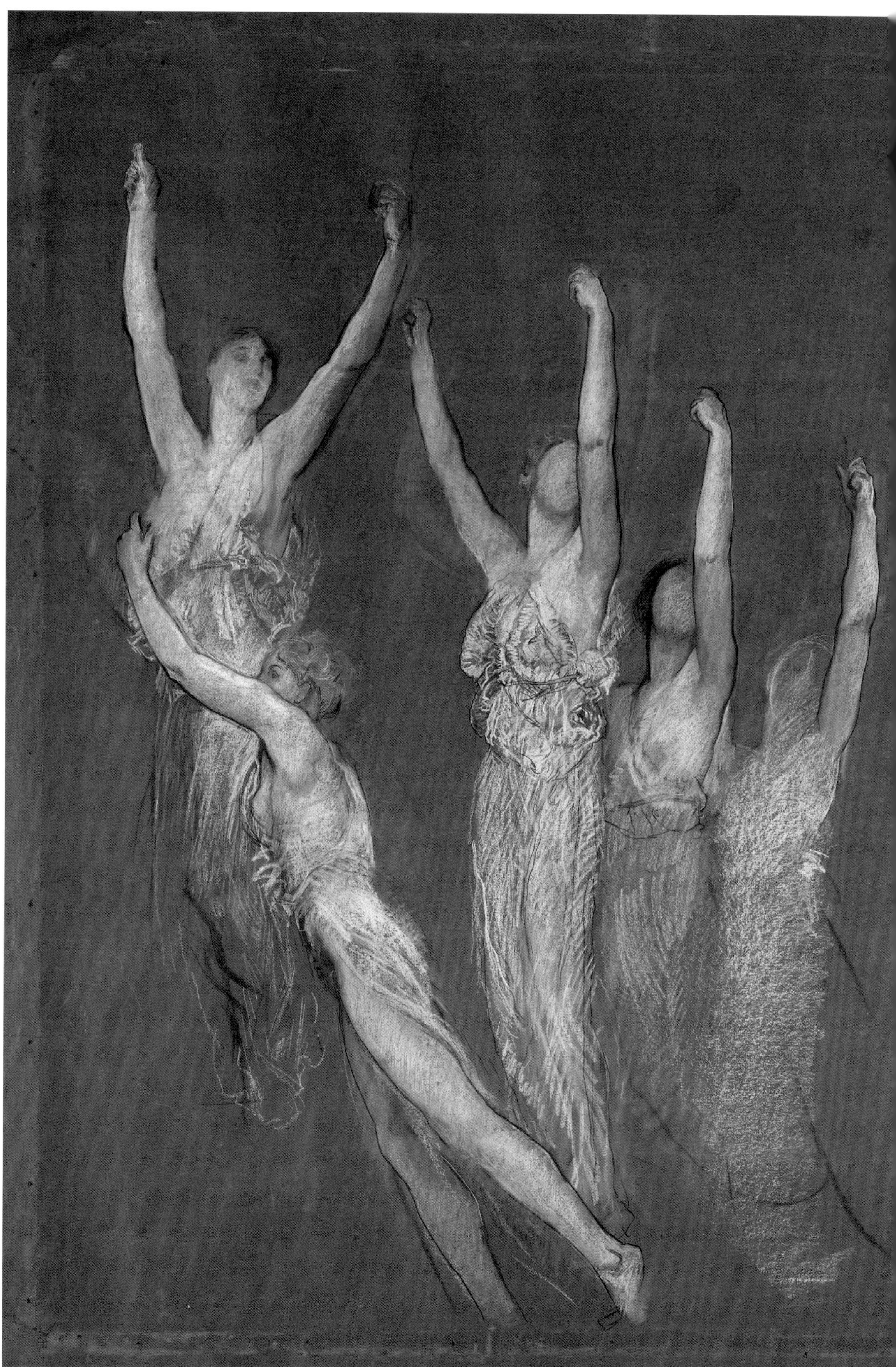

57

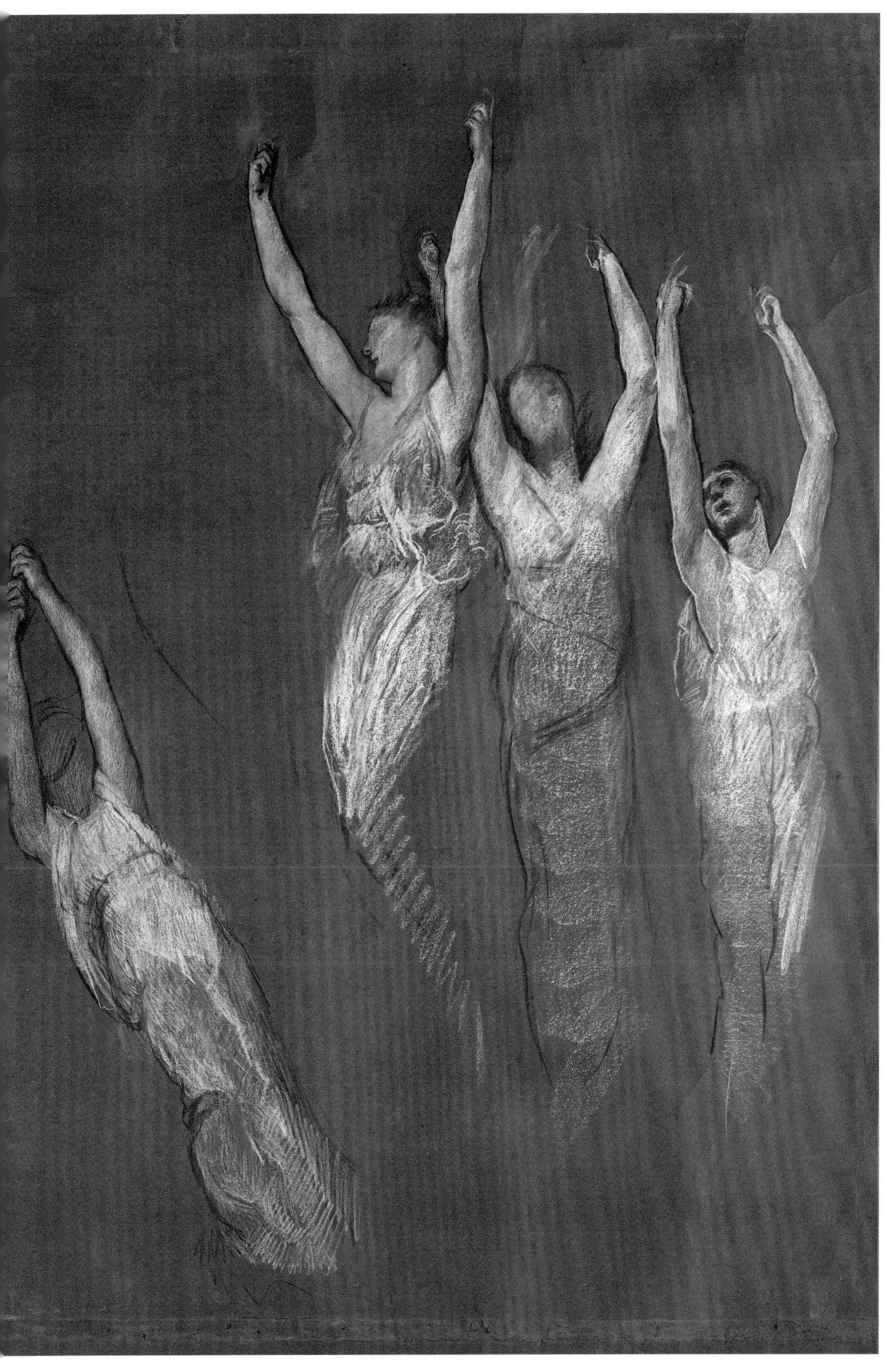

Matriarchs

Maternal allegories were abundant during the American Renaissance and held special resonance as symbols of peace, especially during the mid-1910s when the realities of world war became evident. Powerful mother and goddess figures demonstrated benevolence and firmness as well as strength in the potential for physical intervention. Grim determination characterizes their demeanor, as seen in several depictions of Alma Mater, of which Edwin Howland Blashfield's allegorical drawing is representative (cat. 58). The large throne increases her physical form, and the prominent musculature of her visible arm indicates a prowess atypical of the conventional ideals of femininity popular at the turn of the twentieth century. Instead, strength and determination are fluid attributes of the time, reassigned where needed.

Working within the context of World War I, Violet Oakley recast the central figure of her decoration for the Senate chamber in the Pennsylvania State Capitol as the final title of the mural reveals: *International Understanding and Unity*. Powerful and oversized, the woman in her pair of studies

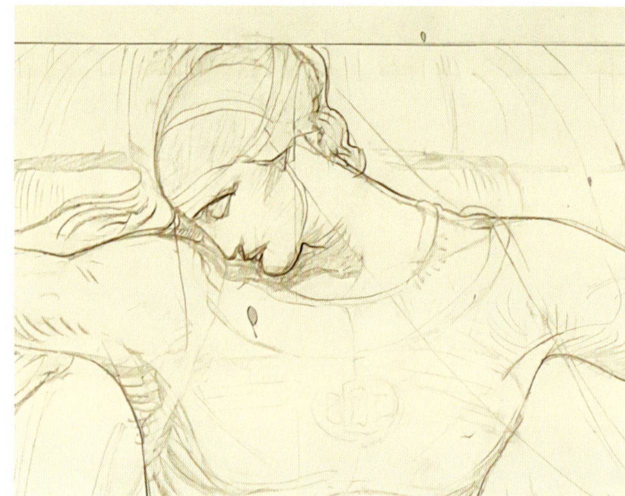

(cats. 59–60; detail of cat. 59 above) extends a protective, sheltering embrace derived from historical Christian Madonnas. She is more stylized than was typical in earlier art of the American Renaissance, looking ahead to the more archaic forms revived in the wake of the war. But Oakley's Harrisburg murals are perhaps the most directly progressive of the period. A social reformer, Oakley championed women's leadership and insisted on

CAT. 58 Edwin Howland Blashfield (American, 1848–1936)
Figure Study, ca. 1910
Charcoal and pencil on paper, 39 13/16 × 26 in. (101.1 × 66 cm)
Williams College Museum of Art, Williamstown, Mass., Gift of Grace Hall Blashfield and Mrs. William Cary Brownell, 38.7

CAT. 59 Violet Oakley (American, 1874–1961)
Figure Study of *Unity* for *International Understanding and Unity* in the Pennsylvania State Capitol, ca. 1916
Graphite on paper, 10 × 20 in. (25.4 × 50.8 cm)
Pennsylvania Capitol Preservation Committee, Pittsburgh, 82.78.319

CAT. 60 Violet Oakley (American, 1874–1961)
Study for *International Understanding and Unity* in the Pennsylvania State Capitol, ca. 1912
Tempera and gold leaf on panel, 15 5/8 × 19 5/8 in. (39.7 × 49.9 cm)
Westmoreland Museum of American Art, Greensburg, Pa., Gift of Diana and Peter Jannetta, 2005.28

CAT. 61 Gari Melchers (American, 1860–1932)
Study for *Peace* in the Library of Congress, ca. 1900
Charcoal with white and sanguine chalk on paper, 31 3/8 × 43 1/4 in. (79.7 × 109.9 cm)
Carnegie Museum of Art, Pittsburgh, Andrew Carnegie Fund, 06.17

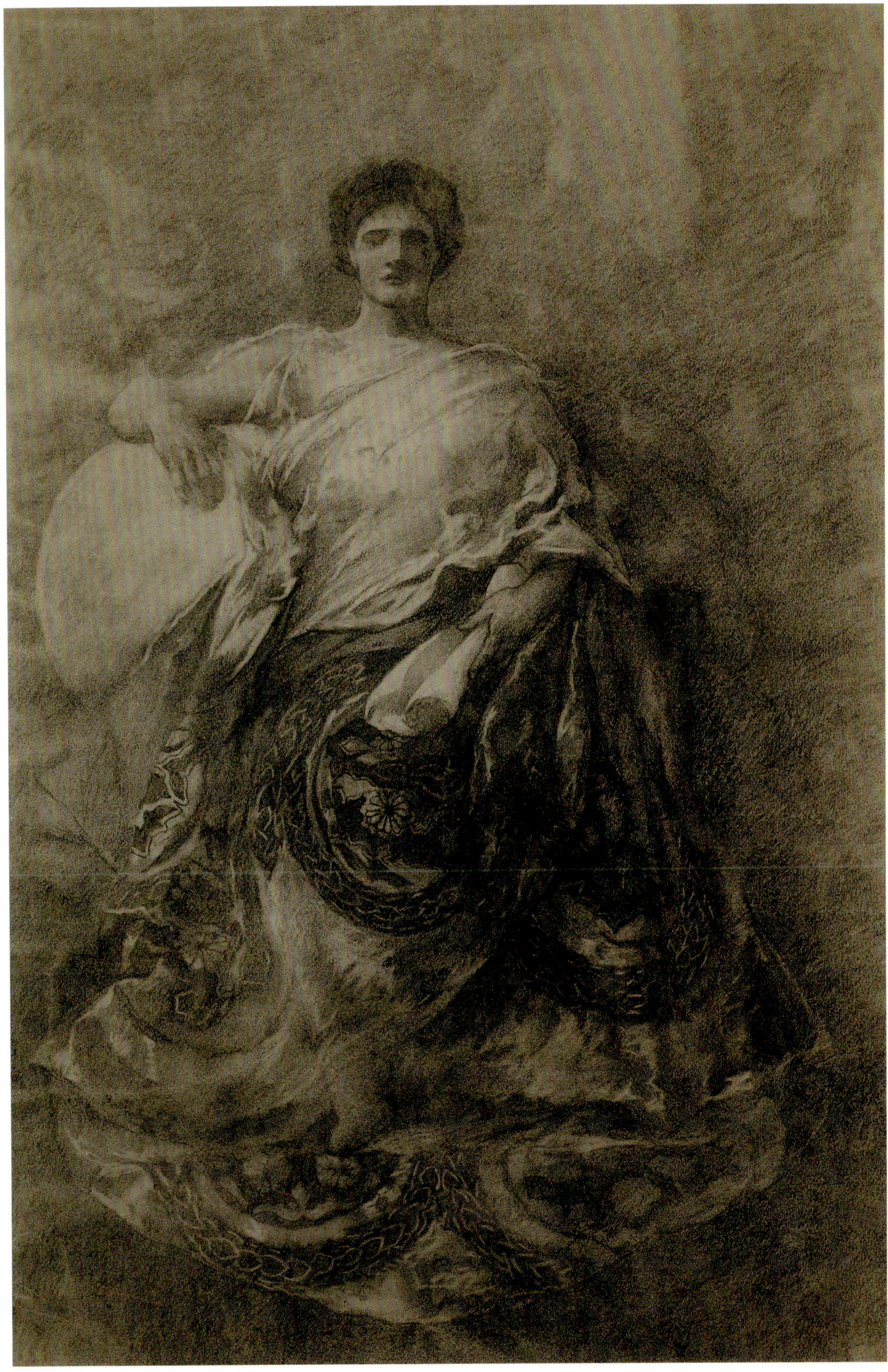

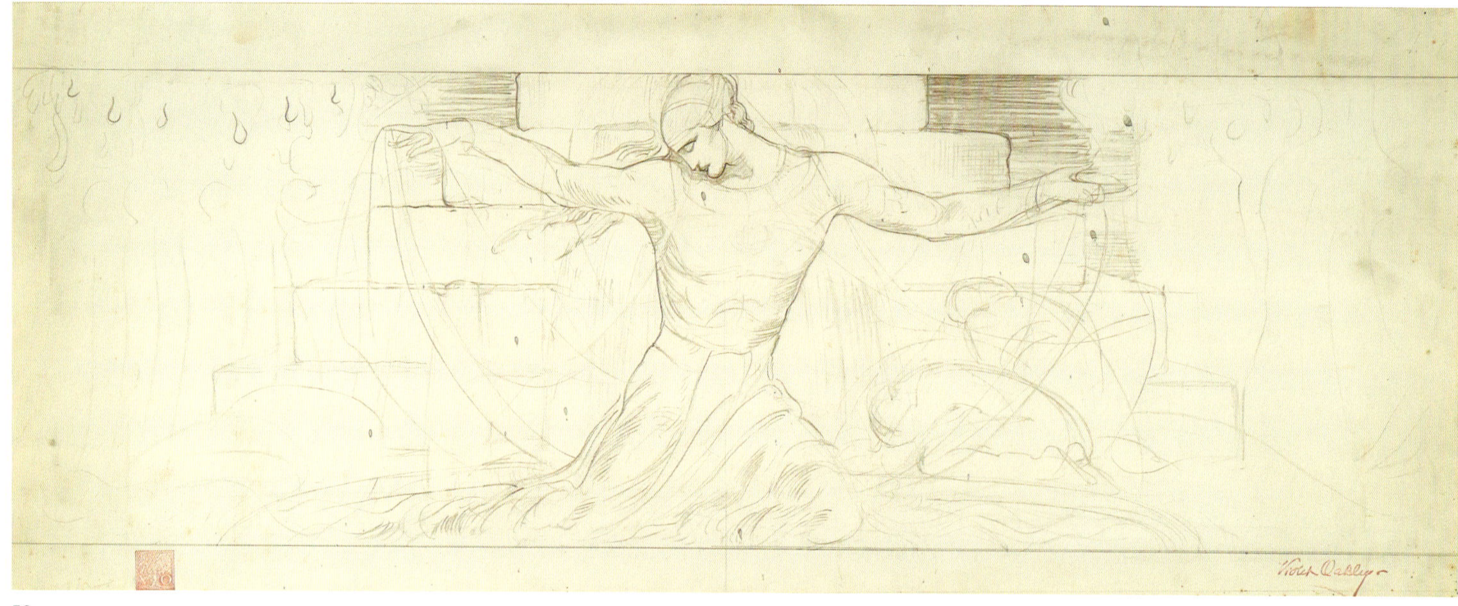

59

the same compensation as her male peers when she was offered the commission to complete the Pennsylvania statehouse's decoration after Edwin Austin Abbey's death in 1911. A commission initially devoted to the creation and preservation of the Union became, in Oakley's hands, a call for moral and global leadership in the model of maternal care.

Two decades earlier, at the Library of Congress, the spirit was less urgent. Gari Melchers's drawing (cat. 61) for his mural *Peace* portrays a group of four men carrying a litter, on which rests a female devotional sculpture in the final composition. With seriousness but not exactly reverence, the procession is depicted as a motley assortment lacking a coordinated attitude. Described with virtuosity and vigor, the figures are individual and full of eccentric character. The procession may be one of worship of a divine mother of peace, but the actors are blithe, conveying the moral drift of peacetime.

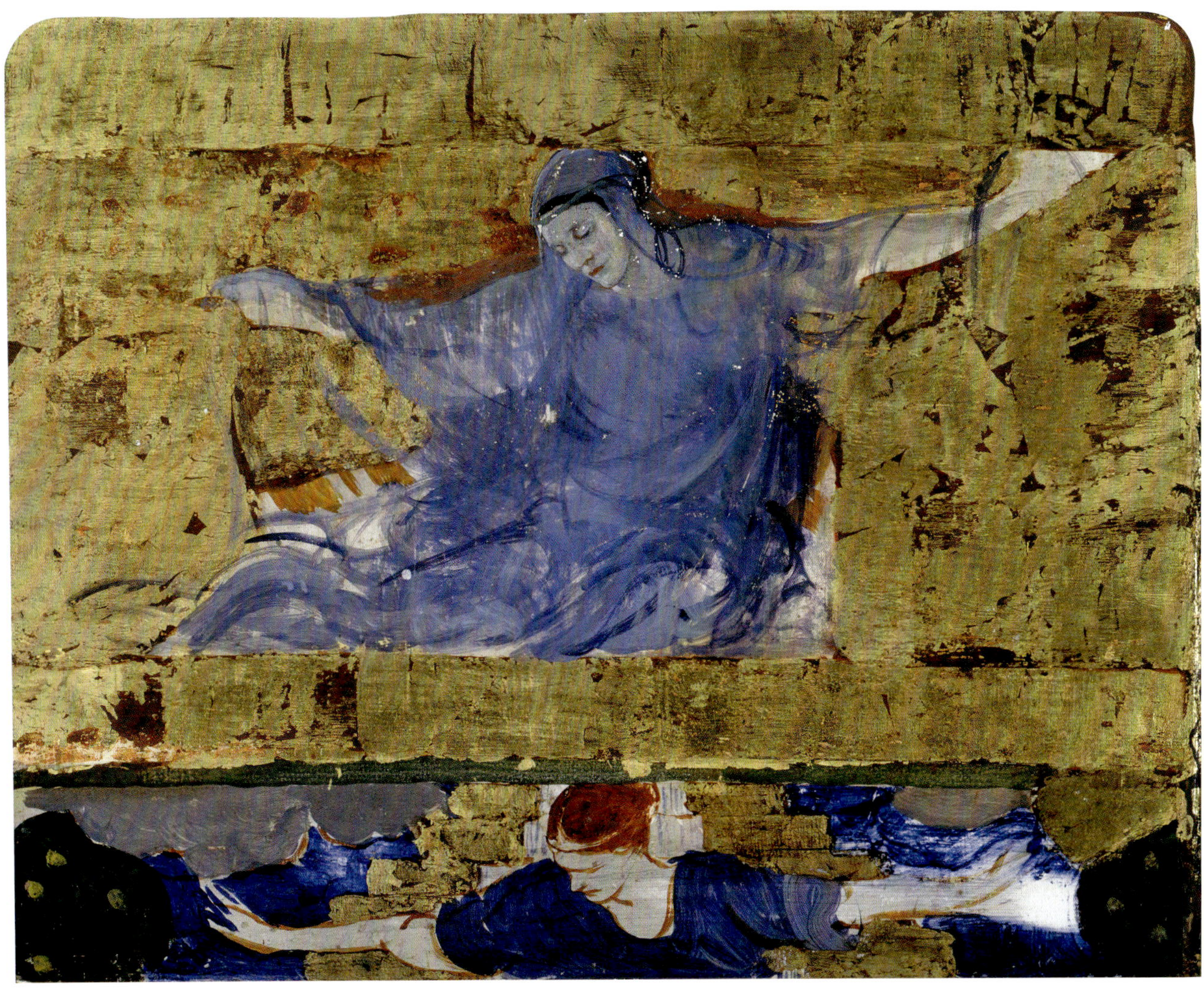

60

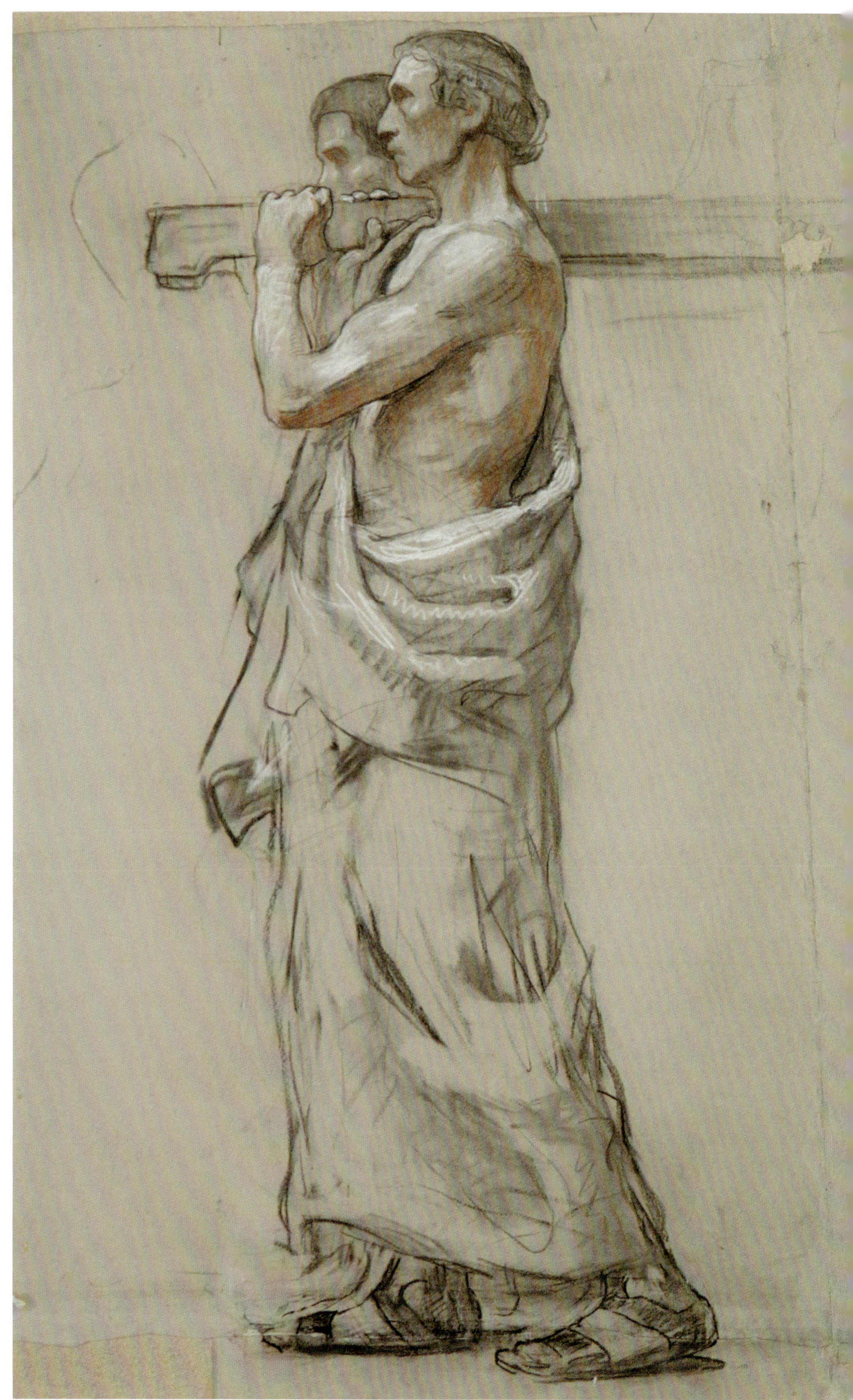

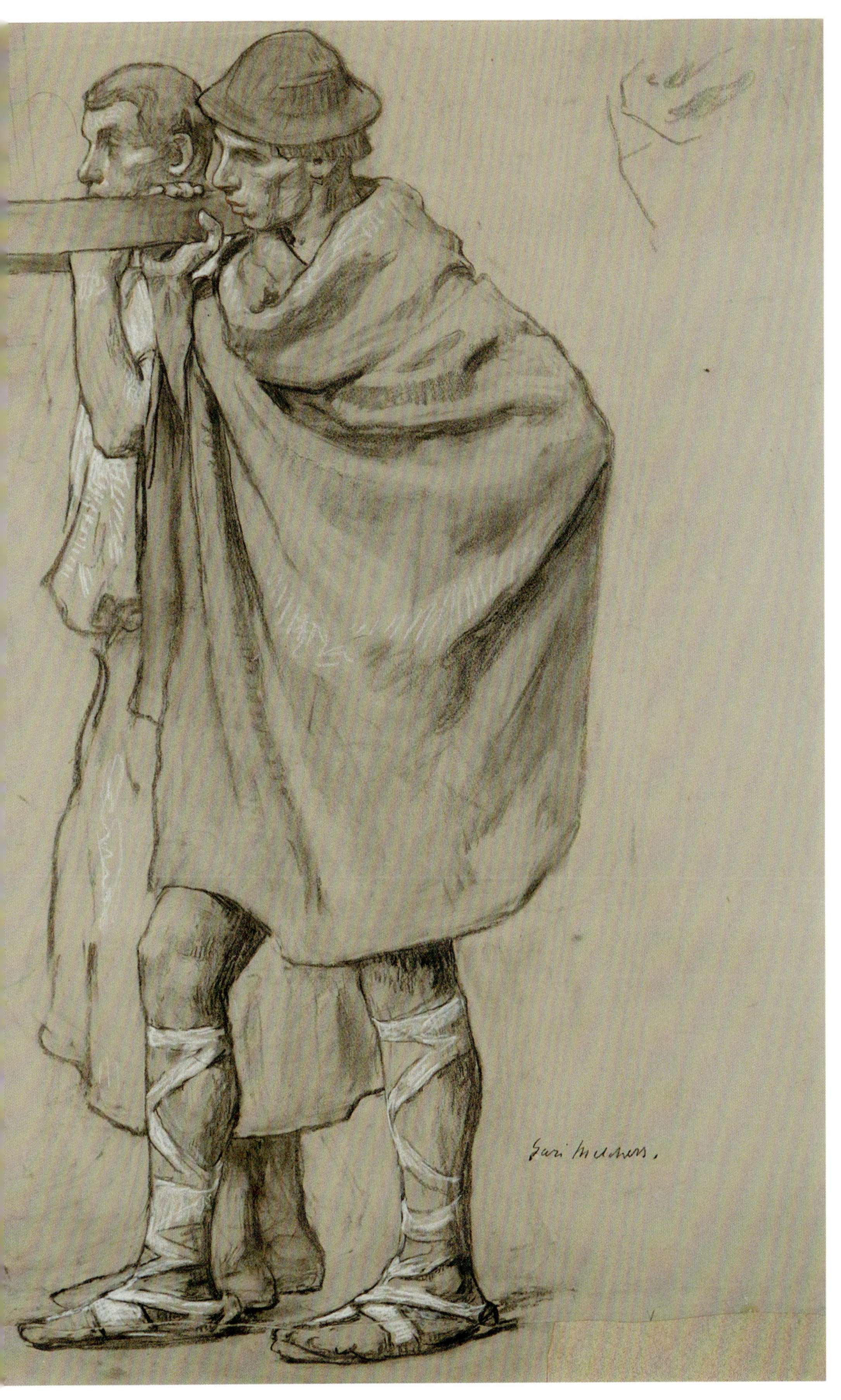
Gari Melchers.

Audience

The collective effect produced by groups of sculptures related to public art projects of the American Renaissance is documented by photographs, illustrations, and, occasionally, paintings that depict art exhibitions and fairs. The Second Annual Exhibition of the National Sculpture Society in 1895 is here represented by Charles Courtney Curran (cat. 62). The scene records an interior exhibition space at the American Fine Arts Society Building in New York, with well-heeled visitors examining the newest artworks. Artists, too, attended these exhibitions in droves and found influence and inspiration in the work of their peers. Curran is the man standing at left.

The large plaster and bronze statues displayed in such exhibitions invited a different form of engagement than that offered by the grand civic spaces inside public buildings or at the short-lived but massively popular world's fairs, which juxtaposed the wares and art of nations from around the globe. Here, sculptures are brought together for comparison and discussion. Artists were eager to show studies and reductions of their large-scale works. Even the modern French master Auguste Rodin is featured in this presentation; his bronze head of Saint John the Baptist is displayed at left, above the three seated figures. In these venues, audiences could contemplate the artists' process and ideas as expressed through the body, rather than their relationship to the architecture or function of the building for which they were created. In this space their work is art rather than decoration, and a sympathetic, informed audience could study and compare their accomplishments alongside the creations of their peers.

CAT. 62 Charles Courtney Curran (American, 1861–1942)

At the Sculpture Exhibition, 1895

Oil on canvas, 18 × 22 in. (45.7 × 55.9 cm)
Yale University Art Gallery, New Haven, Conn., Stephen Carlton Clark, B.A. 1903, Fund, 1973.103

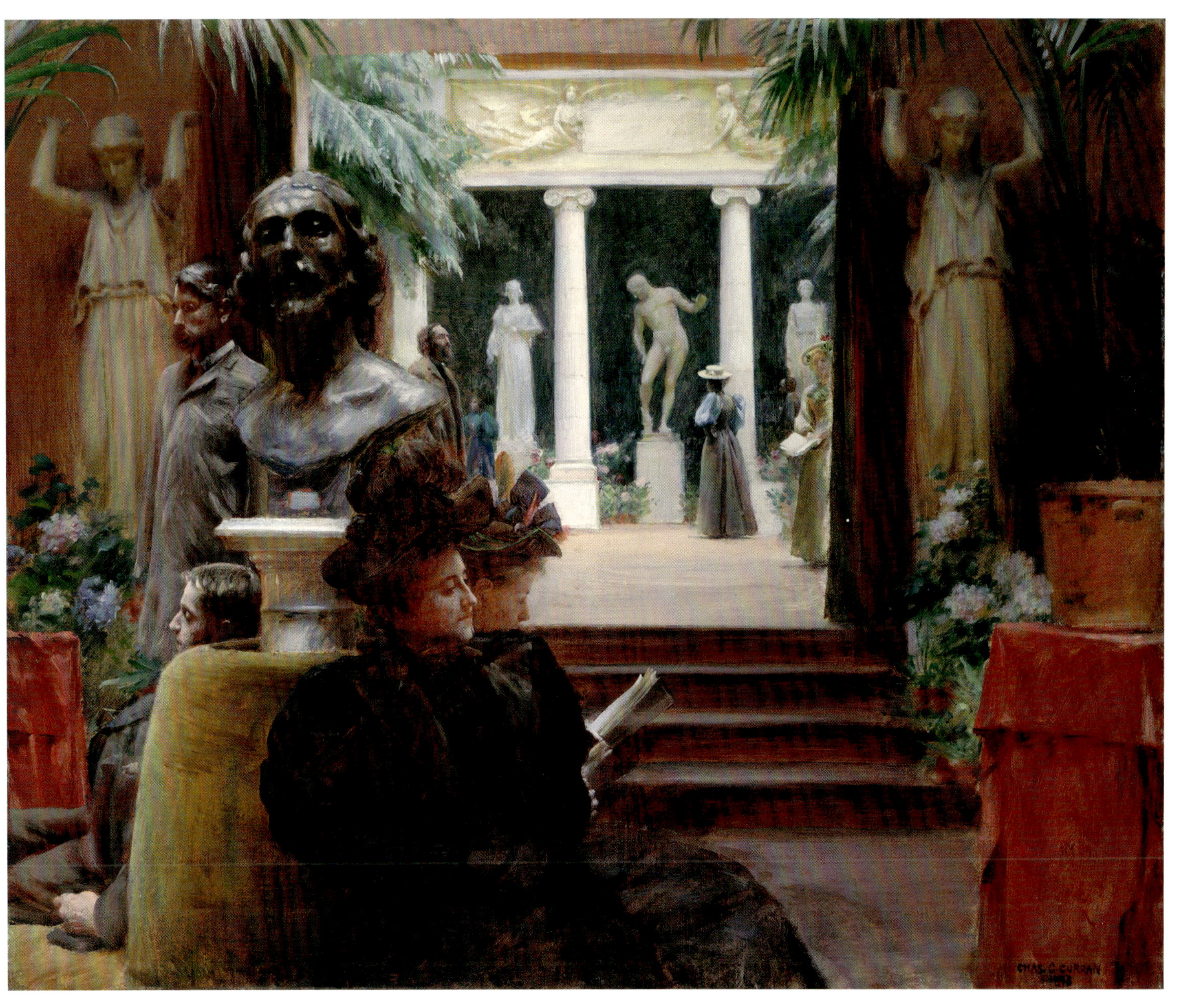
CHAS. C. CURRAN

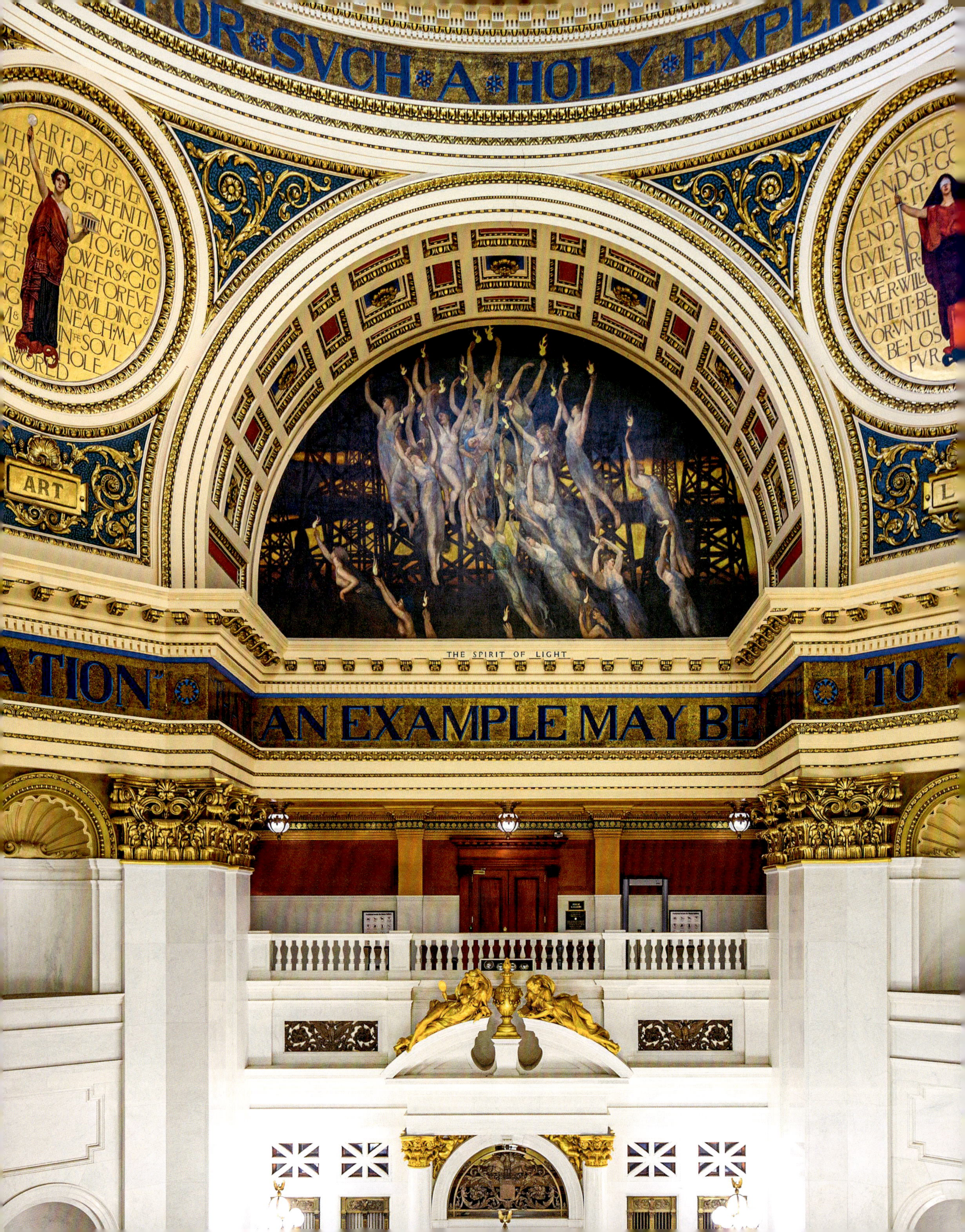

FOR SVCH A HOLY EXPER
ART
THE SPIRIT OF LIGHT
ATION"
TO
AN EXAMPLE MAY BE

Mural Painting and the Nineteenth-Century Civic Imagination:

ART, INNOVATION, AND SCIENCE

JOSEPHINE W. RODGERS

The end of the Civil War was a defining moment in U.S. history, marking a time of great change not just in society but in art as well. Following the surrender of Confederate troops on the battlefield, a long period of economic stimulus and rebirth began. In this era known as Reconstruction, which the historian Eric Foner has described as "the Second Founding," the federal government attempted to resolve key problems inherent in the Constitution, notably establishing equal economic opportunities and protection for all.[1] It was at this time that the concept of a national citizenship emerged—one independent of race and connected with the rights of individuals. To establish a sense of unity and self-definition among Americans, federal and state legislatures supported a range of nation-building initiatives, including the construction of state capitols, courthouses, libraries, and train stations. As civic buildings spread throughout the country, each project assembled a massive workforce that included the labor of previously enslaved people, war veterans, and immigrants. Artists were commissioned to decorate the interiors of these grand structures, which were imbued with physical as well as ideological functions. The republic had suffered its most divisive crisis since the Revolution, and its citizens sought reassurance that the nation's integrity remained.

A generation of painters and sculptors, among them Edwin Austin Abbey, Edwin Howland Blashfield, and Kenyon Cox, answered the call for art that could address the struggles of the day. These men and women became agents of change, responding to the tension to correlate a revised vision of America's heroic spirit with the realities of a postbellum United States. They tested their talents and reshaped narratives as they executed monumental civic-art programs. Largely through their efforts, mural panting emerged as a dominant—and distinctively American—art form, one that they and others hoped would

The grand staircase in the rotunda of the Pennsylvania State Capitol with Edwin Austin Abbey's mural *The Spirit of Light*

"educate" the public by projecting current ideals: the power of democracy and scientific innovation, combined with a desire to establish a new understanding of American citizenship and shared identity. The commissions, often encumbered by rigid time constraints, pressured artists to develop novel techniques and methods. Inspired by historic art, a range of traditions, and progressive ideals, their work served to redefine America's place in history.

The mural cycles created for the Library of Congress and the Pennsylvania State Capitol, in particular, invite us to consider not only the contradictory realities of American experience in the late nineteenth and early twentieth centuries but also how artists imagined the role of science and the individual in society. An examination of the artists' practice allows for a renewed appreciation of their ambitions and the struggles they faced when shaping a visual language that would captivate and unify a divided public. The new mural movement cultivated a shared aesthetic focused on the body to adorn public buildings across the country, essentially creating a national school of art. The narratives promoting American leadership in both the arts and sciences that were depicted in these compositions—as well as what these works omit—reveal how progress depended on the creation of a new mythology tied to the sciences. The presence, significance, and implications of scientific exploration in the murals call attention to the need to develop a new approach to the public art of this period. Such artworks provided an encompassing visual experience for viewers that engaged all of the senses in a quest to evoke specific responses and, perhaps more important, instruct the public at large.

The Library of Congress: Narratives of American Scientific Progress

The ideas of civic art, national identity, and reunification in post–Civil War America had entered public and political discourse with the 1876 Centennial Exhibition in Philadelphia celebrating the hundredth anniversary of the Declaration of Independence.[2] But it was at the 1893 World's Columbian Exposition in Chicago that "magnificent mural paintings,"[3] as they were described at the time, presenting American history and culture were introduced to a massive audience. Murals by Blashfield, Cox, and many other artists decorated the interiors of structures custom-built for the fair, which was visited by more than 27 million people during its run from May 1 to October 30.[4] By the time a new building for the Congressional library collection was being planned in Washington, D.C., the success and leadership role of Blashfield and Cox qualified them to participate in the most ambitious commission for an interior-design scheme in the nation.

Appointed Librarian of Congress by President Lincoln in 1864, Ainsworth Rand Spofford was determined to transform the library into a national institution, one that emulated the British Museum in London and the Bibliothèque

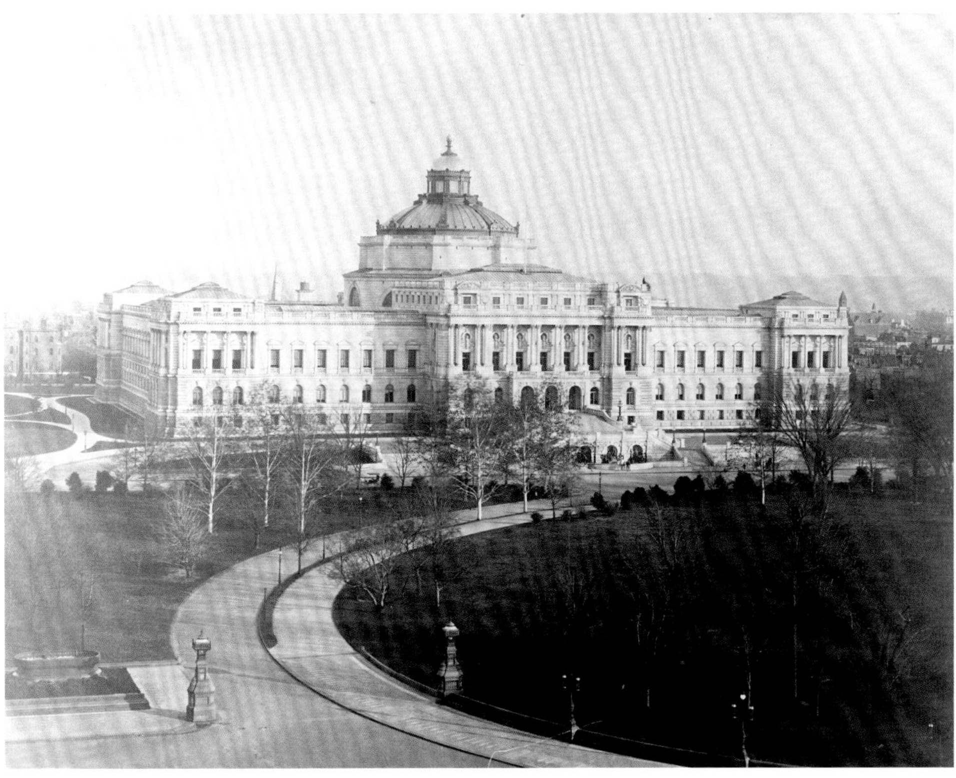

FIG. 1. Frontispiece, "The Library of Congress," *Handbook of the Library of Congress* (Boston: Curtis and Cameron, 1897)

Nationale in Paris.[5] In 1886, Congress authorized an appropriation for a new building directly across from the Capitol, and Spofford was able to gain support across the aisle with his commitment to education by providing a "book palace of the American people" (fig. 1).[6] A landmark of American architecture and innovation, the Library of Congress opened on November 1, 1897, equipped with a state-of-the-art mechanical book transportation system, telegraph and telephone lines, elevators, and electrical lighting throughout the building. Bulbs with visible filaments allowed the building to stay open after dark, a beacon drawing citizens inside at the end of their workday.

By 1893, the exterior and much of the inside construction of the library had been completed, and Edward Pearce Casey, Jr., was assigned to decorate the interiors. He approached a group of American artists to commission murals that would depict ideals associated with the country and would promote self-improvement, such as imagination, good government, justice, liberty, charity, and abundance. Casey originally selected John Singer Sargent, Edwin Austin Abbey, and James McNeill Whistler, who were already at work on their murals at the Boston Public Library. All declined because of prior commitments. After visiting the Chicago World's Fair, Casey commissioned Blashfield and Cox, among others, to execute murals throughout the building. The Library of Congress became a space of cultural agency, where library professionals,

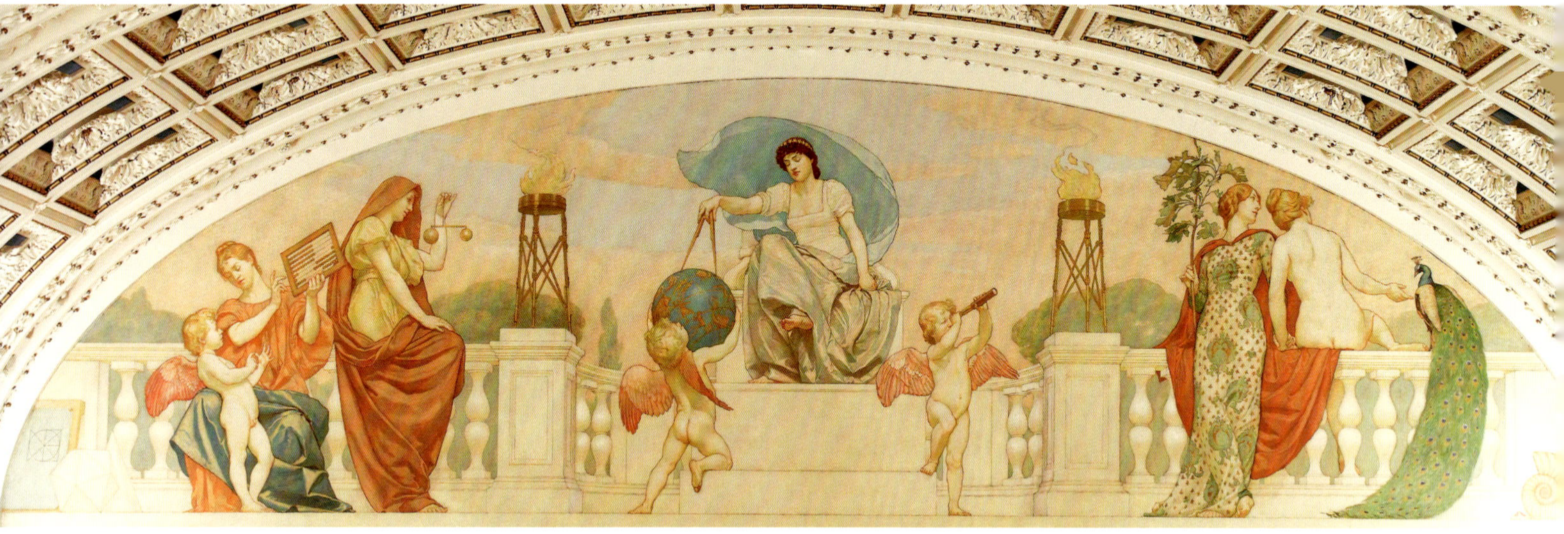

FIG. 2. View of Kenyon Cox's *Sciences* Lunette in the Library of Congress, Jefferson Building, Washington, D.C.

educational reformers, and mural painters worked together to shape citizen-building experiences. Each main room on the first and second floors was decorated with murals, totaling nineteen cycles and more than one hundred paintings. Many were painted on canvas in the artists' studios and then shipped to Washington for installation; a few were painted in situ.

Beginning in 1895, Cox worked on two lunettes titled *The Arts* and *The Sciences* (fig. 2). These were installed over the entrance to the second-floor southwest gallery, originally designed to exhibit the library's special collection of rare manuscripts. The composition of both murals follows classical principles, with attention focused on allegorical figures—each symbolizing branches of the academic fields—grouped amid attendants along a balustrade. Cox had studied in Paris with Carolus-Duran and Alexandre Cabanel, then eventually at the École des Beaux-Arts, where he was required to pass rigorous tests of technical skill in drawing. As a student, he declared to his father in a letter dated January 16, 1878, "The main reason and meaning of art is to convey to the beholder some particular impression or set of impressions . . . to choose from the scene those aspects and forms which should convey perforce to any beholder of his work the same impression which nature conveyed to him."[7] As Sally Cochrane explains, "At its core, the artistic goal [for Cox] was not to represent an objective truth of the world outside the observer, but to represent the perceptual, phenomenological truth as seen by the human observer."[8]

Cox's draftsmanship can be understood as a reflection of the history of scientific observation, and his preliminary drawings became the informing principle of his mural paintings. He believed that an artist needed an understanding of the multiple traditions, cultures, and arts across time; the only way for one to excel was to note the accomplishments of past practice. In his use of historical, anthropological, and evolutionary theories, Cox developed a highly controlled drawing technique and compositional style that engaged his audience through a mixture of classical ideals and close observation. Taking a scientific approach to art history, he strove to achieve a neoclassical universal language that would unify different people and tastes. For each project, he began with a sketch to organize the colors of the composition, followed by a sequence of drawings in a precise order; each figure was drawn to scale in the nude (as both a rough sketch and finished drawing), then outlined again. Details of the drapery were recorded in a separate finished drawing. Finally, the nude and drapery were drawn together at a scale one-quarter the size of the mural.[9]

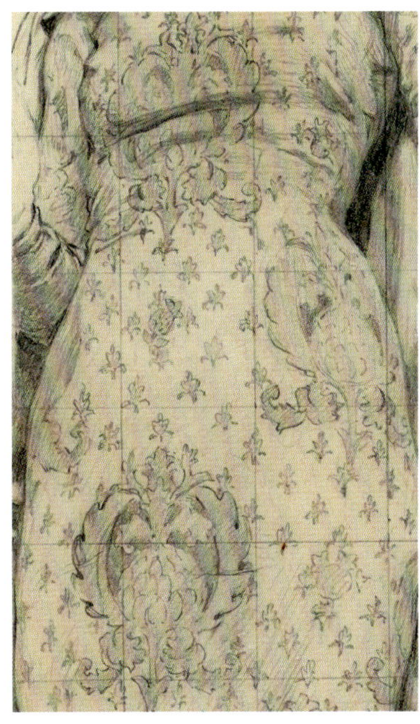

FIG. 3. Detail of cat. 78

Cox's preliminary drawings for his murals allow for a deeper understanding of his creative process and evolution of thought. He spent hours developing a suitable subject, as attested to by his many sketchbook drawings, including a drapery study for Botany created in preparation for *The Sciences* (fig. 3). In the final mural, five classical maidens personify areas of learning. Astronomy is seated in the center, her cloak swirling up behind her and forming a blue background suggestive of the firmament; with a compass, she measures distances on a celestial orb held by a winged infant while another cherub peers heavenward through a telescope. At right, Botany holds an oak branch, and Zoology gently strokes a peacock; on the left are Physics, holding a set of scales, and Mathematics, who with an abacus instructs another winged infant.

In the study, the model for Botany leans against a rail, with a slight turn in her torso that reveals the intricate patterning of the dress. Like a botanist conducting fieldwork, Cox carefully studied and recorded the geometric floral shapes. The cloak that drapes over the rail echoes the elongated branch of an oak tree in the final composition. Cox chose oak because of its role as a foundation tree species that defines ecosystems; before European settlement, it was the dominant genus in forests throughout much of the eastern United States. White oak, which is depicted in *The Sciences*, was arguably North America's most valuable hardwood species, used extensively for building construction and furniture-making throughout the nineteenth century. Old-growth oak forests that had once been prominent on the East Coast would have been decimated by the time the mural was finished in 1897. The oak species is now a symbol for the human impacts of the late 1890s, the height of the movement to relocate Indigenous peoples from their lands, of clear-cutting entire regions, and of catastrophic wildfires. The oak leaves held by Botany can thus be read as an indicator of dawning recognition of the need for land stewardship.[10]

At the turn of the twentieth century, murals created for the civic sphere played a part in forming public memory and a vocabulary for American citizens to identify with, often echoing the demands for social reform espoused by adherents of Progressive politics. The art historian Annelise K. Madsen notes

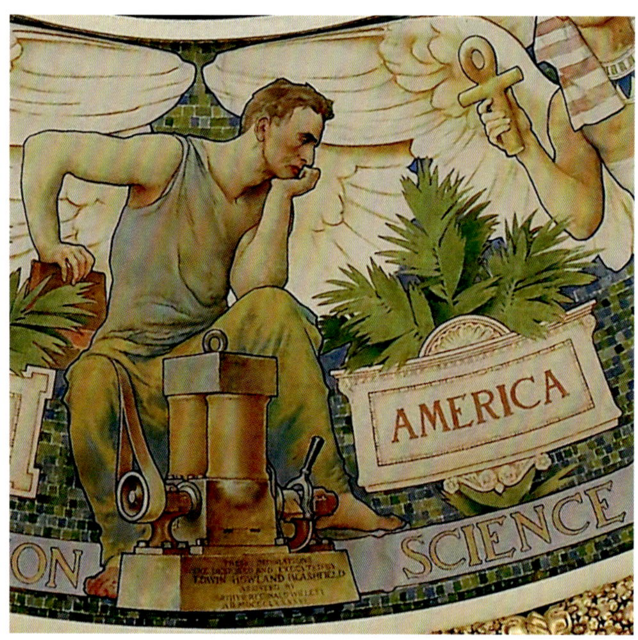

FIG. 4. Detail of Edwin Blashfield's *Evolution of Civilization* in the Library of Congress

that Blashfield's mural *The Evolution of Civilization* (see pages 170–71), which wraps around the collar of the Library of Congress's main reading room, is an important element of Progressive pedagogy, the "new education," a pathway to cultural uplift and a means to improve the welfare of the American citizen.[11] Commenting later on the project, Blashfield declared, "Municipal art is a public and municipal educator" whose "effect upon the mind—that is, of the spectator—is cumulative."[12]

Blashfield's mural program is a triumph of artistic skill, physical endurance, and creative ambition, reflecting his goal to inspire visitors in their own pursuit of knowledge. The upper reaches of the dome are adorned with a painted canvas titled *Human Understanding*, intended to capture a wide scope of learning and accomplishment. The complement mural, *The Evolution of Civilization*, depicts a ring of twelve seated male and female figures set against a mosaic pattern. Appearing in a scripted order that begins with Egypt, the allegorical grouping ends with America, represented by a male engineer wearing an apron, his chin resting in one palm and his opposite arm holding a book. Directly underneath is a band containing the word "Science" (fig. 4).

Presented as the heir to historic knowledge and the promise of progress, America is shown as both a laborer and an engineer, dressed in "the garb of the machine-shop," with an Edison electric dynamo at his feet.[13] As the art historian Sarah J. Moore explains, "This conflation of worker/engineer acts as a visual performance of the transformative power of education and knowledge—worker becomes engineer—and privileges technology as the source of and site of American progress and national identity."[14] Deprived of its mechanical function, the dynamo in Blashfield's mural acts as an emblem commemorating early electrical technologies, pioneering inventors, and American contributions to the advancement of electricity. Blashfield has constructed a linear narrative that canonizes the dynamo as the culmination of American scientific progress, whose lineage can be traced directly to the ancient Egyptians. Mimicking the patent plaque on the original machine, the artist proudly declares: "These decorations were designed and executed by EDWIN HOWLAND BLASHFIELD, assisted by ARTHUR REGINALD WILLETT, A.D. MDCCCLXXXXVI."

The Evolution of Civilization was designed to present a tangible ideal of progress amid the powerful changes to American society brought on by immigration, industrialization, corporate capitalism, and economic instability. Scholars have noted that the new library building was a triumph because it gave all Americans access to the national collection. Standing beneath the murals today, however, we must ask: Who built the Library of Congress rotunda and main reading room?

Photographs and meticulous records that survive in the Library of Congress Archives make it possible to reconstruct the networks of artists and laborers that collaborated on the project (fig. 5). Employment reference letters and interview notes offer an unparalleled glimpse into the individual stories of the men hired as well as the economic strife facing Civil War veterans, Irish and Italian immigrants, and freed Black men who applied to work on the site.[15] During the interviews, staff from the Office of Building recorded the applicant's overall appearance, including ethnicity and race. The adjectives used to describe the laborers—industrious, stout, sober, active, willing, faithful, obedient, tough, intelligent, good soldier, good citizen of the city, worthy comrade, valuable—define a moment when the fate of the country was placed in the hardworking hands of its laboring class. These characteristics are immortalized within Blashfield's mural, in which the male body is presented as strong, intelligent, able—a harbinger for America's scientific achievement.

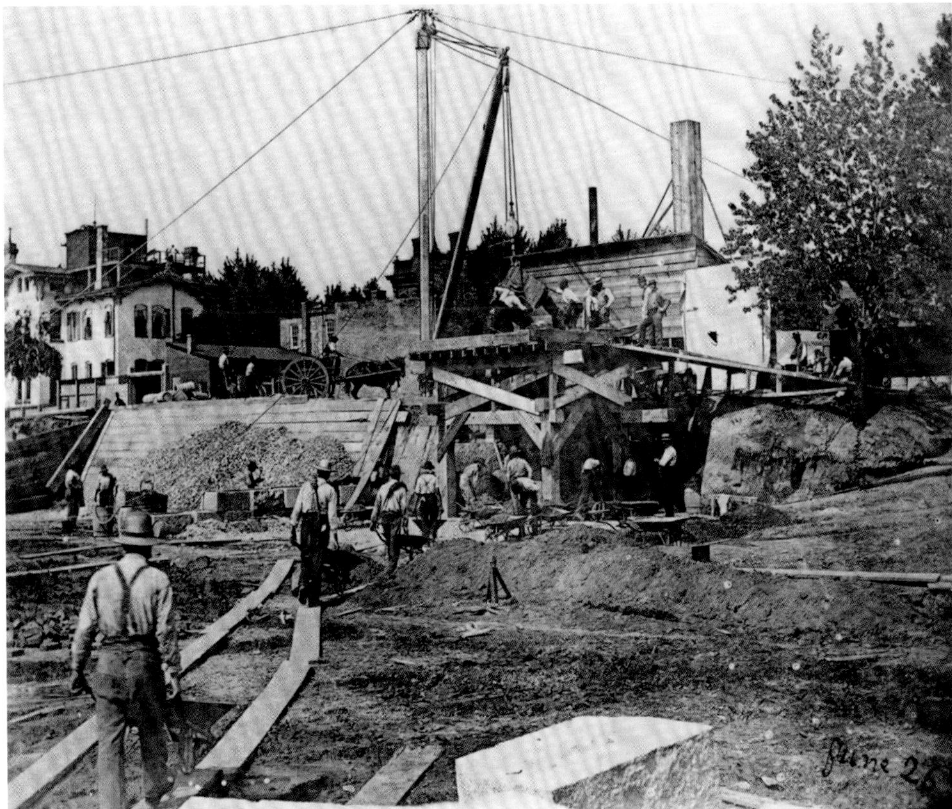

FIG. 5. Men working on the foundation of the Library of Congress, 1892. Library of Congress Prints and Photographs Division

PAGES 170–71: View of Edwin Howland Blashfield's *Evolution of Civilization*, Library of Congress, Washington, D.C.

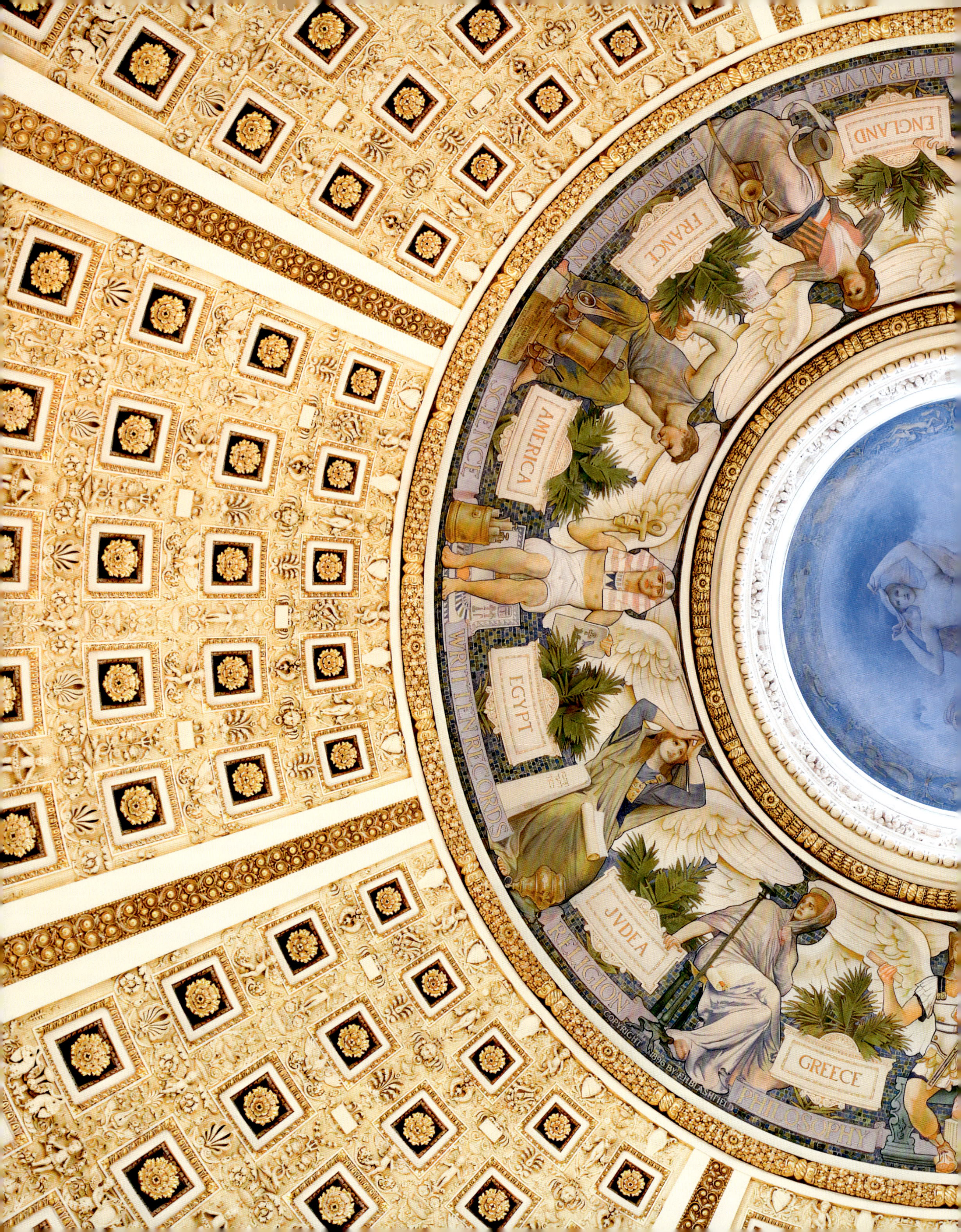
LITERATVRE
ENGLAND
EMANCIPATION
FRANCE
SCIENCE
AMERICA
WRITTEN RECORDS
EGYPT
RELIGION
JVDEA
COPYRIGHT 1896 BY E.H.BLASHFIELD
GREECE
PHILOSOPHY

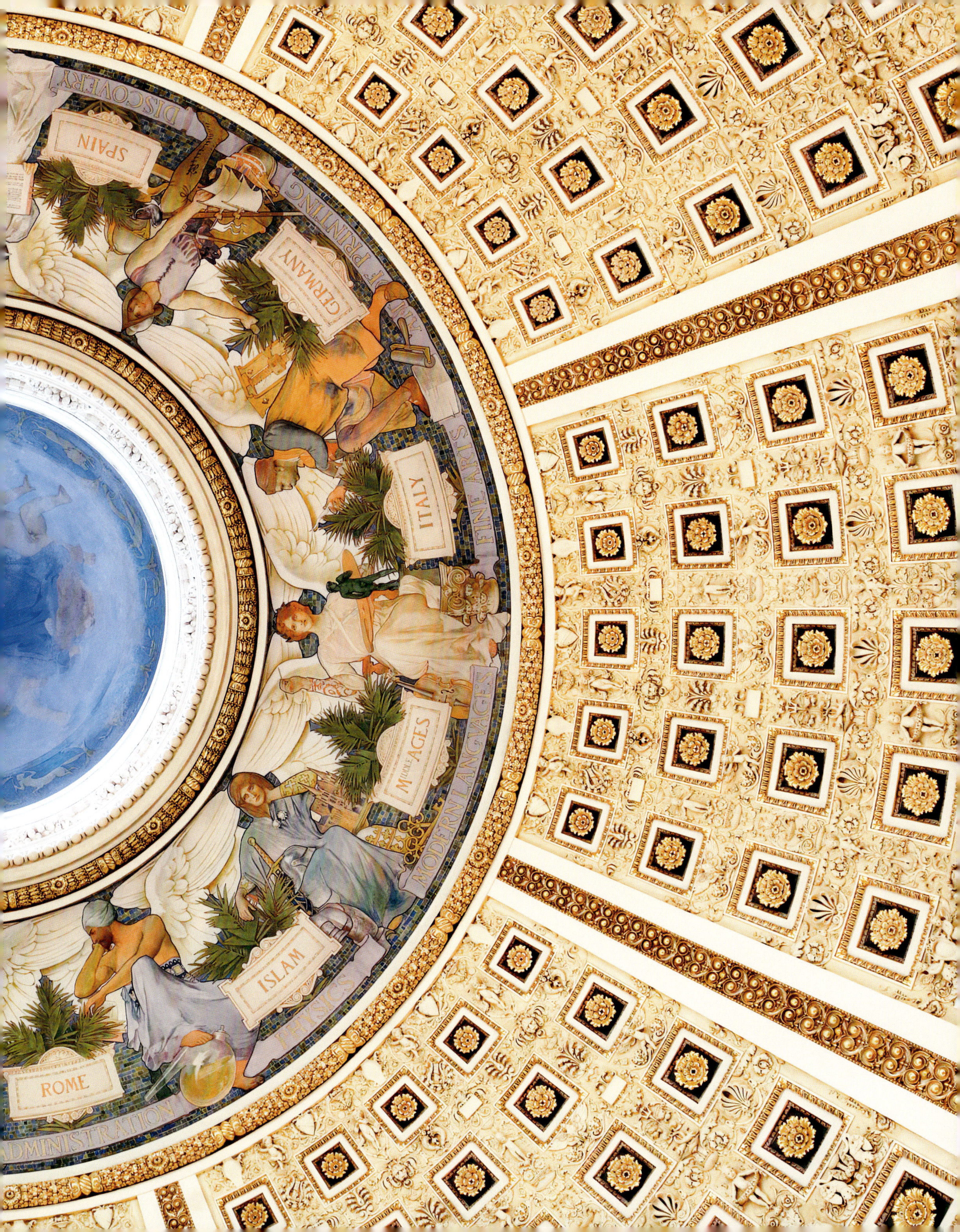
DISCOVERY
SPAIN
PRINTING
GERMANY
FINE ARTS
ITALY
MODERN LANGUAGES
AGES
ISLAM
PHYSICS
ROME
ADMINISTRATION

The Pennsylvania State Capitol: Origins of the Oil Industry in *The Spirit of Light*

The late nineteenth century was the most intense period of population growth, industrialization, and deforestation in U.S. history. The radical shift in the natural environment associated with the industrial revolution was also a crisis of culture and civic imagination. American artists such as Thomas Cole, Frederic Edwin Church, and Asher Brown Durand depicted a primordial landscape as sanctified, unspoiled, and the source of American identity. These artists attempted to show how American progress depended on a new mythology tied to the land, which differed from the classical contempt for woodland barbarism and the Puritan legacy that equated the forest with pagan beliefs. Dominance over both the American imagination and American natural resources became imperative for the success of industry and the government during Reconstruction. What had begun as an artistic response to scientific progress at the World's Columbian Exposition was continued at the Boston Public Library and carried further in the Library of Congress. By the turn of the twentieth century, decades of agriculture and industry had caused deforestation throughout the East; "electro-mania" was sweeping the nation while scientific innovations and the production of kerosene changed the daily routines of Americans countrywide.[16]

Designed at the height of the American Renaissance, the Pennsylvania State Capitol was described by President Theodore Roosevelt as "the handsomest State Capitol I have ever seen" at its dedication ceremony October 4, 1906.[17] As you enter the building and ascend the staircase to the legislative chambers, you come to a grand main rotunda, for which Edwin Austin Abbey developed a series of four murals: *The Spirit of Religious Freedom*, *The Spirit of Vulcan: Genius of the Workers in Iron and Steel*, *Science Revealing the Treasures of the Earth*, and *The Spirit of Light* (see page 162). Together, the paintings champion American engineering achievements as pillars of Pennsylvania society, but they also capture glimpses of an era grappling with climate science and industrial impacts on the environment.

Each of the murals was painted with oil on canvas in Abbey's studio and then set into the architectural lunettes, which measure approximately thirty-eight by twenty-two feet. Letters between Abbey and Blashfield discuss concerns about building scaffolding and the painting supplies needed for such large canvases, but they do not reveal exactly how Abbey chose and developed his subjects. The largest number of preparatory studies in the Yale University Art Gallery collection relate to *The Spirit of Light* (fig. 6). The final mural portrays an image of the Pennsylvania landscape covered with outdated mid-nineteenth-century oil derricks while in the foreground a group of allegorical figures emerge from the earth holding flames aloft. The invention of kerosene—a new

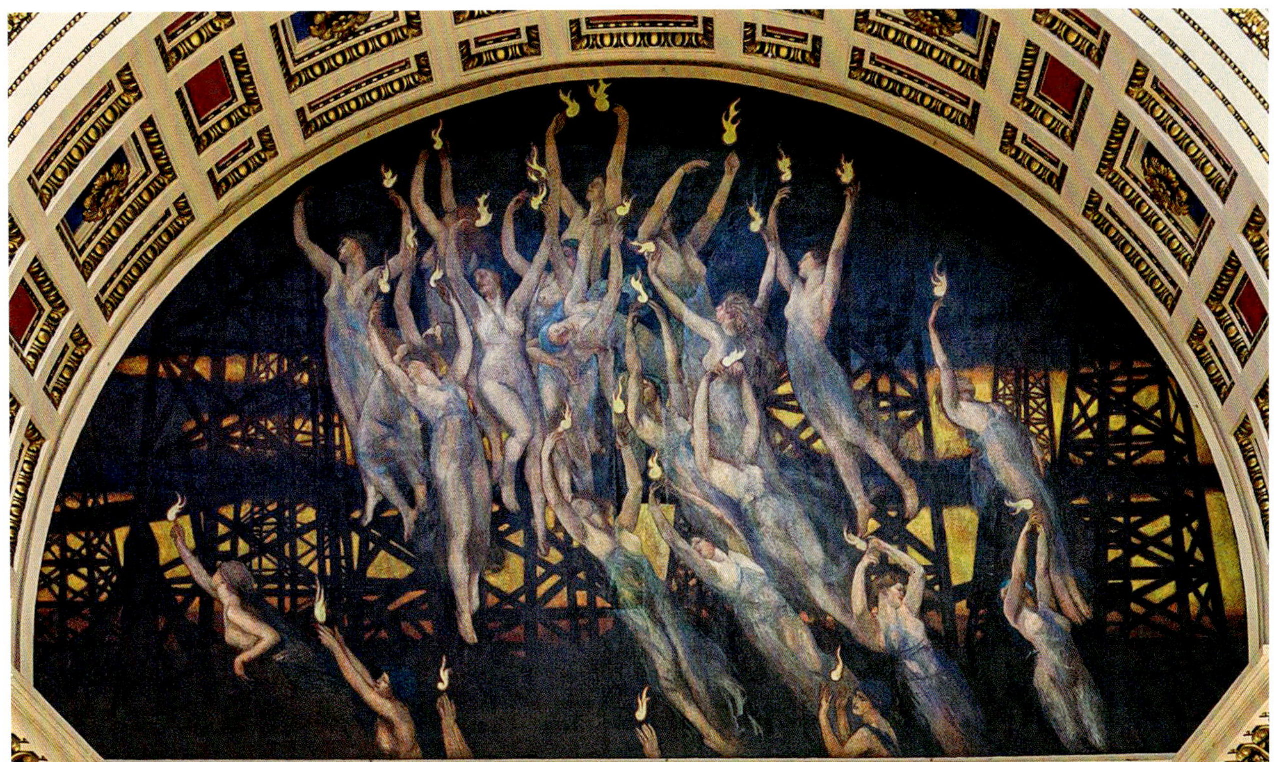

FIG. 6. View of Edwin Austin Abbey's lunette *The Spirit of Light* in the Pennsylvania State Capitol

source of light—is venerated here as a pivotal example of scientific innovation and the origin of the American oil industry.

In his choice to incorporate a history of oil extraction into the scheme for the state capitol, Abbey was surely influenced by the lasting effects of colonization and industry on the landscape. He was particularly interested in how narratives or myths had constructed a history of Pennsylvania. Throughout his murals in the rotunda, the state of Pennsylvania is described as a cosmographic territory—an amalgam of Indigenous and colonial mythology—defined by celestial, terrestrial, and aquatic elements. The tension between the visible landscape and what lies beneath is increasingly clear, manifesting in social, economic, and environmental ruptures that bring this complexity to light. In the 1800s, the expansion of railroads connected existing cities and created new towns across the region. The effects on the land were significant and often devasting. Transporting raw goods along rivers led to unprecedented pollution of major waterways. Sparks and cinders emitted by the stacks of passing locomotives burned tens of thousands of acres. The Pennsylvania timber industry left mountainsides scattered with rubble, dead stumps, dry branches, and saplings, laying waste to vast areas each year. Debris and complications from commercial exploitation commonly caused catastrophic flooding and uncontrollable wildfires, such as the one seen in Oil City on Sunday June 5, 1892.[18] In that

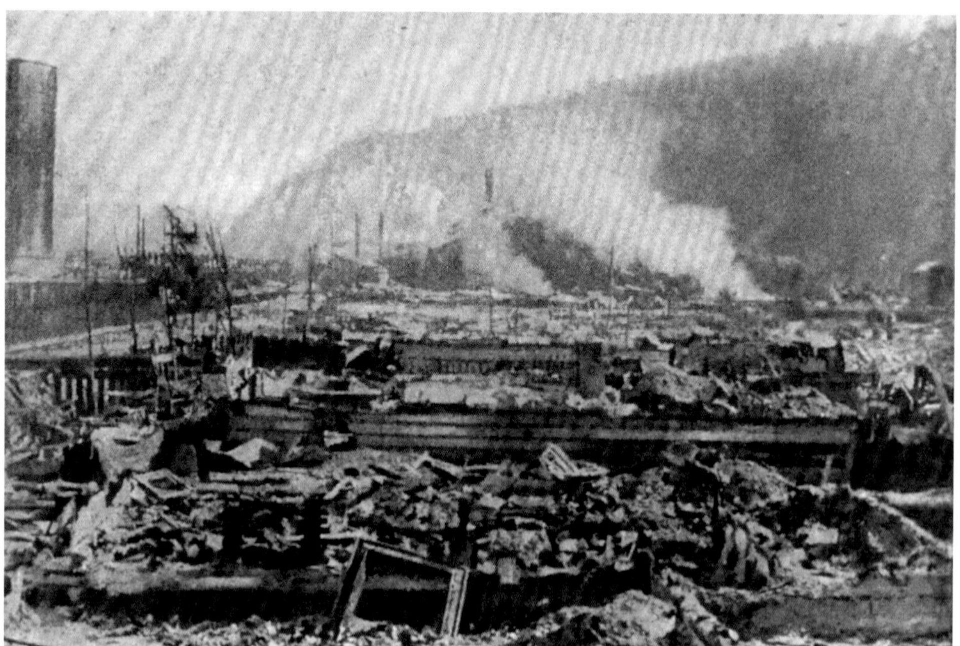

FIG. 7. "Scene at Oil City after the Disaster on June 5, 1892," from John J. McLaurin, *Sketches in Crude-Oil* (Philadelphia, 1898)

incident, high water from the Allegheny River caused a leak in a petroleum storage tank, and the oil caught fire as it floated onto the creek. The explosion sent flames seventy feet into the air, followed by a second, and then a third blast, which left sixty people dead and hundreds injured (fig. 7).

Earlier American artists such as George Inness strove to capture the complexity of this environmental change while establishing new traditions of landscape painting. The art historian Rachael DeLue has proposed that Inness's landscapes should be understood as allusions as well as a model of vision, explaining that "allusion took on a new form and purpose, becoming less about the relation of an artist to his artistic precursors and more about the interaction between a painting and its beholder." For Inness, looking at nature and at paintings was a matter of memory. In *The Lackawanna Valley*, he shows a young man reclining in the left foreground, his back to the viewer and his feet intersecting a path that originates in the viewer's space (fig. 8). The man's gaze reproduces ours as we look at the landscape of northeastern Pennsylvania. The open farmland acts as a "point of repose" on which the eye may rest—serving both as a virtual beholder and that beholder's visual experience. DeLue argues that it was the structure of perception (allusion, recollection, disorientation) evoked by Inness's landscapes, or what he seems to be proposing should happen when viewing his paintings, that laid the groundwork for the expansion of the power of vision.[19] Memory reconfigured time and space.

A nineteenth-century viewer would have also applied memories of environmental destruction or dispossession to this scene. The historian Steven Stoll

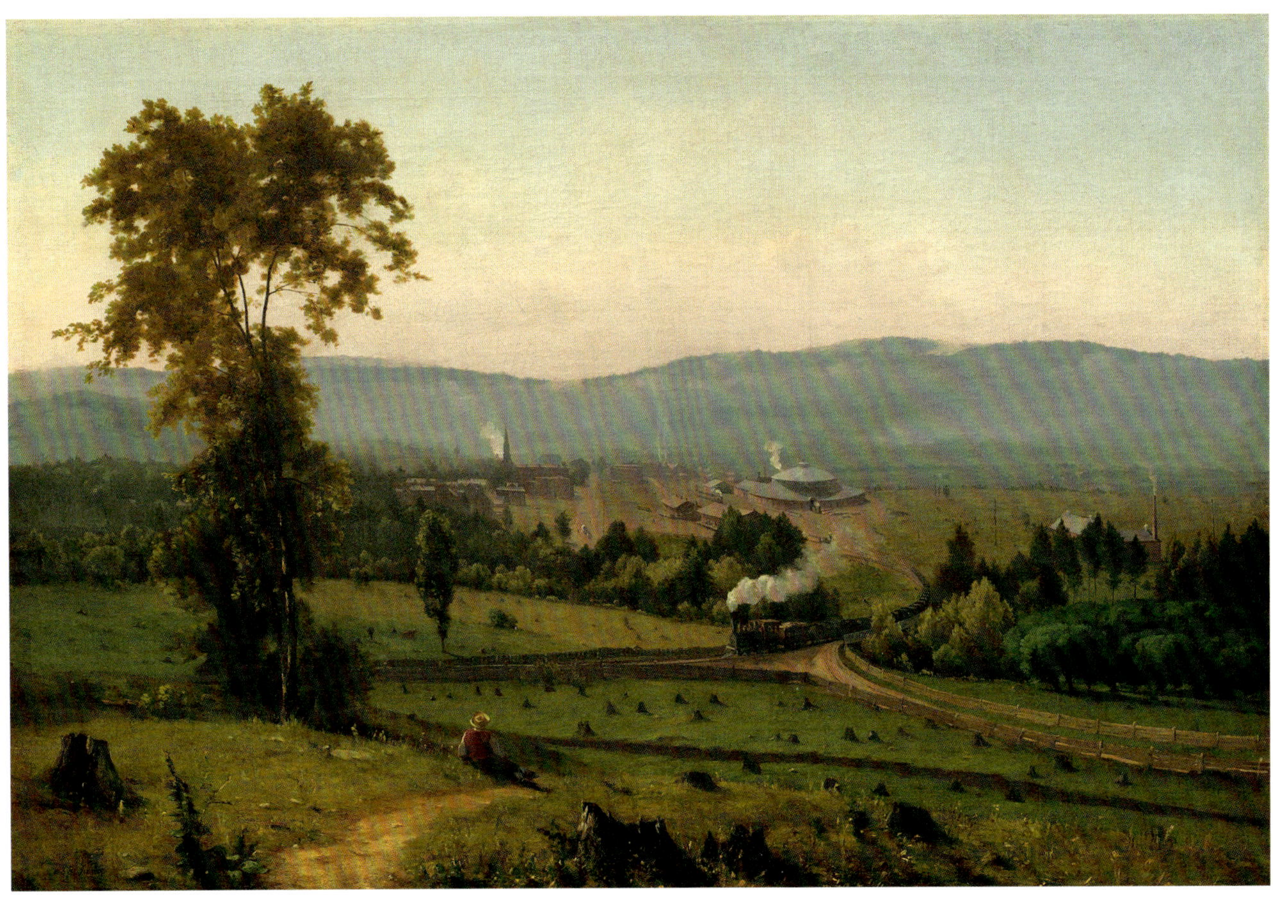

FIG. 8. George Inness, *The Lackawanna Valley*, ca. 1856. Oil on canvas, 33⅞ × 50³⁄₁₆ in. (86 × 127.5 cm). National Gallery of Art, Washington, D.C., Gift of Mrs. Huttleston Rogers, 1945.4.1

discusses the effects of agrarian dispossession in Inness's 1883 painting *Short Cut, Watchung Station, New Jersey* (fig. 9).[20] The locomotive at the center almost looks like a natural element of the landscape as it travels across the horizon. The woman seated in a field watches it go by as a man with a cane crosses a wooden bridge. Inness chose to depict the rural poor, who increasingly lost or sold their land to join the urban working classes.

Abbey responded to these same fundamental changes by embracing a new relationship between painting and beholder, establishing a provocative style of mural painting to confront the harsh realities of environmental dispossession. Upon accepting the capitol commission in 1902, he described his ambition to the architect of the building, Joseph Miller Huston:

> My belief [is] that in the decoration of wall spaces lies the great future of art in America. I would prove my faith by devoting my best energies to this branch of my profession, and not least, because of the pride I should feel in placing this most important work of my life in the Capitol of my native State.[21]

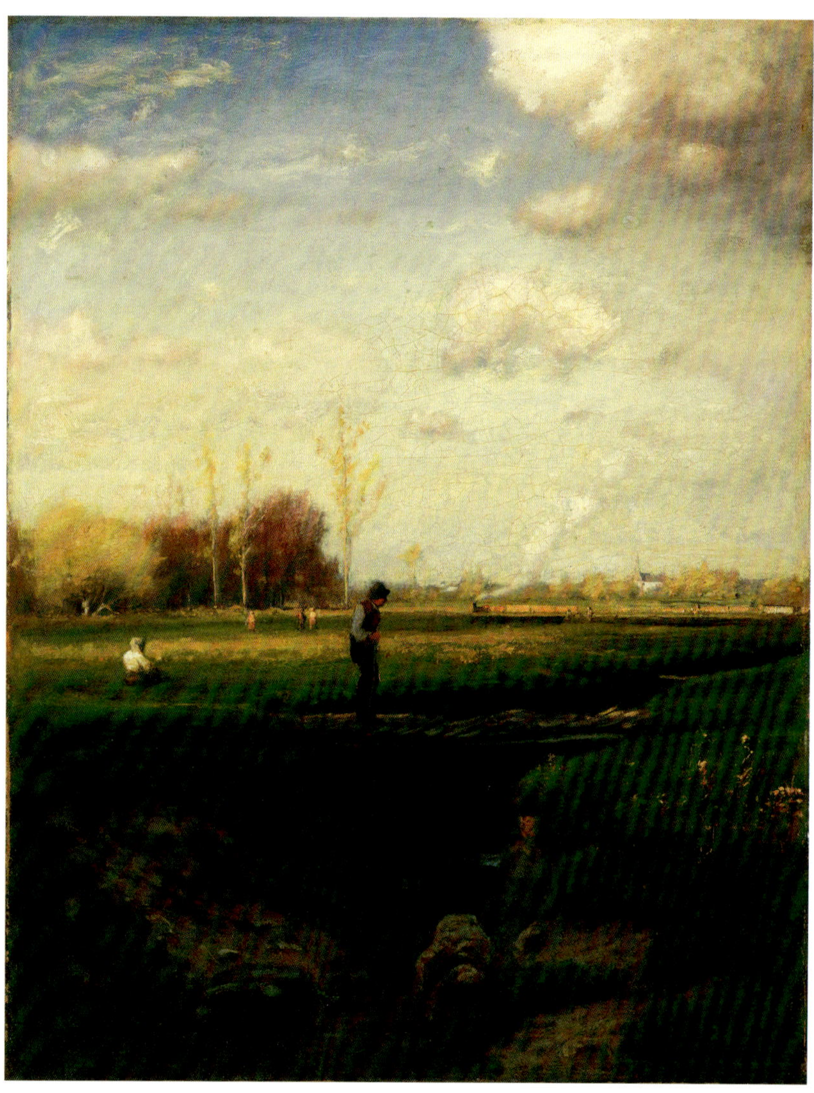

FIG. 9. George Inness, *Short Cut, Watchung Station, New Jersey*, 1883. Oil on canvas, 37⅝ × 29⅛ in. (95.6 × 74 cm). Philadelphia Museum of Art, purchased with the W. P. Wilstach Fund, 1895, W1895-1-5

Yet despite his acceptance, he objected to Huston's original mural scheme:

> I noted what you say about "allegories" but there are certain spaces where realistic subjects are as absolutely needed. It is far easier to do realistic things than abstractions of allegories—that is, for me—but I should decline to paint realistic subjects for spaces where they are inappropriate.[22]

The art historian Kathleen Foster contends that the monumentality of the commission forced Abbey to revise his artistic process and develop a contemporary symbolic narrative.[23] *The Spirit of Light* is a modern allegory that documents the development of a carbon economy, situating the oil industry at the intersection of political history, socioeconomic change, and ecological impact. Within a larger tapestry of stories, including myths of discovery, the mural draws on the viewer's own memory and interpretation of a history that prioritized economic growth and competition over environmental concerns. While developing the composition, Abbey had requested research material from Huston, including a written history of the oil industry in Pennsylvania, photographs of petroleum extraction, and a federal census report with a geological study. Surviving correspondence reveals that Huston sent Abbey issues of *Scientific American* magazine and was in contact with Orville Waring, a close colleague of John D. Rockefeller at the Standard Oil Company, to gather materials for the artist.[24] Although no records exist to reveal exactly what Abbey received, he clearly understood the cultural significance of documenting the short-lived Pennsylvania oil boom within the new state capitol.

The long and convoluted history of petroleum extraction is marked by technological milestones, both conceptual and material, from multiple contributors.[25] For millennia, petroleum appeared on the surface of springs throughout northwestern Pennsylvania, where it was used by Indigenous peoples in myriad ways—including as an adhesive for tools, to fuel torches, and for waterproofing vessels. Petroleum did not become a common illuminant in America until the mid-nineteenth century, when experiments in refining the raw material finally proved successful. Failed attempts to convert crude petroleum into a safe burning oil, or kerosene (derived from the Greek, meaning "wax" and "oil"), produced a strong odor and dark-colored smoke. In 1854, George Bissell hired Professor Benjamin Silliman, Jr., of Yale College to analyze a quantity of petroleum. The chemistry professor applied fractional distillation to the raw material (a chemical process used for the first time in America by his father, Benjamin Silliman, Sr.) and developed an economically viable method to distill kerosene from petroleum. In 1855, the younger Silliman published "Report on the Rock Oil, or Petroleum, from Venango Co., Pennsylvania" to market his odorless and clear "water white" kerosene illuminant oil. By the early 1900s, kerosene was the most common illuminant in rural America.

Soon afterward, the overwhelming demand for petroleum led to the development of an unprecedented, violent, and lawless industry in Pennsylvania; production peaked in 1891, when the state produced 31 million barrels of oil.[26] In numerous published accounts, Edwin Drake was exalted as the first American to establish a large mechanical oil well in Titusville, Pennsylvania, in 1859. Entrepreneurs strove to make a profit in the region, and farmers leased their land in the hope of earning additional income. Thousands of wooden wells covered the valleys and hills—most yielded no profit and remained abandoned for decades. On October 12, 1867, *Scientific American* published this account from a correspondent who had visited the region:

> At Petroleum Center, PA about one well in six is in operation. From the high hill west of the town you can see half a dozen villages and more than two thousand wells, some new, but many more utterly abandoned. The business has now passed entirely out of the hands of speculators, and is conducted in an orderly way, by "solid" and intelligent men, and with improved methods.[27]

A similar scene describing a small flame, or "bloomer," was documented in 1873, indicating that only a single derrick was functional in the landscape.

In March 1908, Abbey's final canvases were exhibited in the east gallery of the University of London Imperial College before being permanently installed in the dome of the Pennsylvania State Capitol. A critic who attended the exhibition commented:

> [Abbey] has converted the hardest of prose—the coal mining, metal working and oil production of Pennsylvania—into poetry. The toilsome industries and material interests of his native state have inspired him with noble conceptions and visions of beauty, and year after year he has gone on working until every canvas is spiritualized with significance and transfigured with beauty.[28]

How can a painting of female figures floating amid mid-nineteenth-century wooden oil derricks translate or inspire an experience of "spiritualized significance" or "transfigured beauty" for a viewer? An examination of studies related to *The Spirit of Light* provides some clues.

One preparatory study for the mural articulates an essential shift in the narrative of the composition (see cat. 35). We see that Abbey paused while painting, leaving the work unfinished, as two separate compositions took hold of his imagination: one depicting the oil industry (focusing on the celestial figures in flight), the second showing the coal industry (focusing on the "treasures" of the earth). Across a canvas measuring roughly forty-four by seventy-five inches, Abbey portrays a group of celestial female figures draped in classical robes moving through a storm of dark clouds or oil-infused gases. The diluted paint is "dim and sooty"—similar to those early experiments to produce a clear illuminant by burning petroleum oil. In the foreground, two figures emerge from the earth's core, bringing with them a natural element of *pure white light* (fig. 10), represented as thick, layered oil paint.[29] While in flight, the women carry fragments of the light across the canvas to illumine the dark, atmospheric sky.

On the surface of his pastel drawings, Abbey achieved an effect that shows light as ephemeral matter. In another study, offering a poetic suggestiveness of the female form, each element helps enhance the depth and clarity of the young model's body (see cat. 42). Outlined in black chalk and heightened with a range of pastel pigments, her torso emerges as if three-dimensional; the application of more than ten distinct textured pigments creates a luminous effect. Her body is transmuted into refined petroleum, appearing as if illuminated from within by a vibrant "water white" glow. Traditionally, the classical art-historical motif of the female nude was designed to invite the illusion of physical possession and touch. For Abbey, this tension exaggerates the paradoxical nature of light, oil, and the human spirit. The result is a new, balanced dimension of materiality and illusion, an effect that is retained in the final mural.

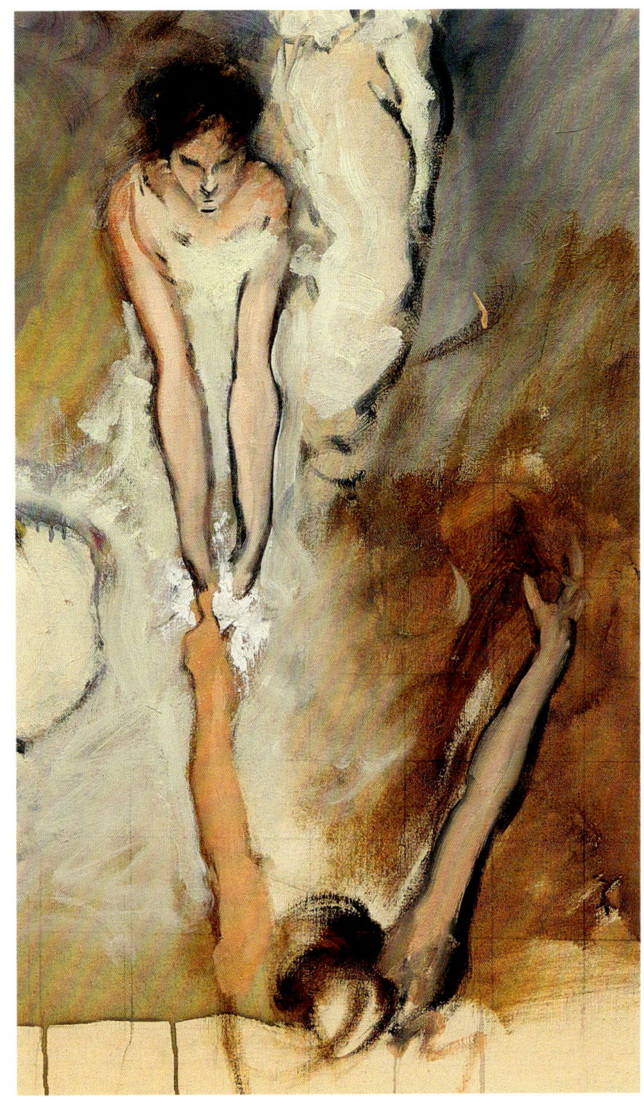

FIG. 10. Detail of cat. 35

In his choice to depict *The Spirit of Light* as a historic landscape—a hillside scattered with outdated mid-nineteenth-century machinery—Abbey engaged the transformative power of memory and strove to capture a permanent place within the minds of the American public. In the age of psychological analysis, science pushed the boundaries of pictorial representation to distinguish the physical nature of the body from the imaginative power of the mind.[30] James McNeill Whistler's innovative paintings, such as *Nocturne in Blue and Silver*, are an investigation into what it meant to physically see and intellectually interpret the world (fig. 11). Whistler was part of Abbey's artistic circle in London, and correspondence between the men exposes their mutual artistic understanding. Abbey also had strong ties to the American philosopher William James, who in 1879 wrote "The Spatial Quale," a first attempt to articulate his views on the primacy of vision as a physical, bodily experience, separate from the image that is complemented by the mind.[31]

Whistler and Abbey understood that, at its core, aesthetic appreciation was a sensate experience. In their atmospheric landscapes, both artists prioritized the prolonged study of their subject. The background of *The Spirit of Light* is full of crisscrossing wooden beams that make it impossible to distinguish which rig each belongs to. The timbers form abstracted spaces that create an immersive, compelling visual experience. Looking up at this backdrop of historic machinery, early twentieth-century audiences would have recognized, rising from the earth, the overlapping and fragmented flames of kerosene.

FIG. 11. James McNeill Whistler, *Nocturne in Blue and Silver*, 1872–78. Oil on canvas, 17½ × 24 in. (44.5 × 61 cm). Yale Center for British Art, New Haven, Conn., Paul Mellon Fund, B1994.19

The terms "positively romantic," "spiritualized significance," and "transfigured beauty" refer to an aesthetic experience that contemporaneous writers would have had in front of *The Spirit of Light*. The metaphysical bodies of kerosene and the abundant oil derricks were culturally significant to the period—symbols of ambition and power. Abbey's preparatory studies allow twenty-first-century viewers to grasp the artist's intent while imprinting our own contemporary ideals and perspectives onto his art. Abbey does not disguise the harsh reality (or environmental dispossession) that was needed to achieve a seemingly endless flow of light. This quandary remains a reality today in Pennsylvania, whose rural countryside is still covered with abandoned wells. In front of *The Spirit of Light*, recognizing the allegorical figures as kerosene or reorienting the structure of the derricks does not simply aestheticize an industrial landscape, portraying it as beautiful. Rather, it immerses the viewer within the Pennsylvania environment at the peak of the nineteenth-century oil boom. This is the origin of the American carbon economy. Abbey developed a compelling style of mural painting that fractured and foreshortened perspective to engage his audience in a personal, imaginative, and historical experience. Today the composition challenges our notion of sight and knowledge of history as we currently know it, allowing reflection about national narratives of scientific progress while addressing the continued failure to mediate an environmental crisis that has endured for more than a century.

NOTES

1. Eric Foner, *The Second Founding: How the Civil War and Reconstruction Remade the Constitution* (New York: W. W. Norton, 2019), 6.
2. See Kimberly Orcutt, *Power and Posterity: American Art at Philadelphia's 1876 Centennial Exhibition* (University Park: Penn State University Press, 2017).
3. "Story of the Fair," *Chicago Tribune*, November 1, 1893.
4. "U.S. Census Bureau History: 1893 Chicago World's Fair," United States Census Bureau, accessed January 17, 2024, https://www.census.gov/history/www/homepage_archive/2018/may_2018.html.
5. Bates Lowry, *Building a National Image: Architectural Drawings for the American Democracy, 1789–1912* (Washington, D.C.: National Building Museum, 1985), 66. See also Frances M. Brousseau, "The Library of Congress, 1873–1897: The Building, Its Architects, and the Politics of Nineteenth-Century Architectural Practice" (Ph.D. diss., University of Delaware, 1998), 428–35.
6. Ainsworth R. Spofford, "The Function of a National Library," in *Handbook of the New Library of Congress*, comp. Herbert Small (Boston: Curtis and Cameron, 1897), 123–28.
7. Kenyon Cox to his father, January 16, 1878; in Kenyon Cox, *An American Art Student in Paris: The Letters of Kenyon Cox, 1877–1882*, ed. H. Wayne Morgan (Kent, Ohio: Kent State University Press, 1986), 57–58.
8. Sally Fama Cochrane, "Science at the Nineteenth-Century École des Beaux-Arts" (Ph.D. diss., Princeton University, 2023), 8.
9. Richard Murray, "Kenyon Cox and the Art of Drawing," *Drawing* 3, no. 1 (May–June 1981): 5.
10. Sketchbook rubbings and drawings of oak leaves that are now part of the Cooper Hewitt, Smithsonian Design Museum collection offer a rare glimpse of the artist at work (acc. nos. 1984-86-3-7 and 1984-86-3-16). For more on oaks, see Edward Lee Greene, *Illustrations of West American Oaks* (San Francisco: Bosqui Engraving and Printing Co., 1889); Marc D. Abrams, "Where Has All the White Oak Gone?" *BioScience* 53, no. 10 (October 2003); and Brice B. Hanberry and Gregory J. Nowacki, "Oaks Were the Historical Foundation Genus of the East-Central United States," *Quaternary Science Reviews* 145 (2016): 94–103. See also Ned Blackhawk, *The Rediscovery of America: Native Peoples and the Unmaking of U.S. History* (New Haven, Conn.: Yale University Press, 2023).
11. Annelise K. Madsen, "Civic Primer: Mural Painting's New Education at the Library of Congress," *American Art* 26, no. 2 (Summer 2012): 73.
12. Edwin Howland Blashfield, "A Word for Municipal Art," *Municipal Affairs: A Quarterly Magazine Devoted to the Consideration of City Problems from the Standpoint of the Taxpayer and Citizen* 3 (December 1899): 582–93.
13. Spofford, "National Library," 140. Building on decades of experimentation by early international electrical engineers, Thomas Edison received a U.S. patent for his

incandescent light bulb in 1879 and a second in 1882 for the dynamo, which produced electric generation for larger distribution. Brought to New York City in the 1880s, Edison's company had spread the dynamos rapidly to cities and towns across the United States and Europe by the turn of the twentieth century. See *Scientific American* 65, no. 4 (July 25, 1891): 47. See also Henry Adams, *The Education of Henry Adams* (New York: Modern Library, 1931), 380; his chapter "The Dynamo and the Virgin" discusses the Great Exposition of 1900 in Paris and is a reflection of the sources and significance of power.

14. Sarah J. Moore, "Our National Monument of Art: Constructing and Debating the National Body at the Library of Congress," *Library Quarterly* 80, no. 4 (October 2010): 347.
15. See Bernard Green Papers, Library of Congress Archives, Washington, D.C. A hand-drawn spreadsheet titled "Table of Services" dated May 10, 1895, lists the jobs filled on that day and the pay rate for each position. The architect was paid 250 percent more than the two hundred–plus labors assigned to the site. When petitions for employment were received by the Office of Building, each was stamped with a date and assigned an application number; if the applicant was hired, the name and an address were typed under the application number and filed with additional handwritten notes from the interview. Special consideration was given to men with experience; for example, the freed Black man Fred Warren received the comments "Hod Carrier" and "looks like an A 1 workman"; Warren was recommended by the Superintendent of the Metropolitan Police, W. G. Moore, as "sober, reliable, and honest." Another application, that of the freed Black man Reisin M. Shipley, was marked with recognition because Senator W. B. Allison wrote that he was a "strong intelligent young man" who was also a student at Howard University.
16. W. M. Williams, "Electro-mania," *Scientific American Supplement* 14, no. 344 (August 1882): 5490.
17. "60,000 Visited the New Capitol," *Harrisburg (PA) Daily Independent*, October 5, 1906.
18. *New York Times*, June 6, 1892. See also Harold F. Williamson, *The American Petroleum Industry: The Age of Energy, 1899–1959* (Evanston, Ill.: Northwestern University Press, 1959).
19. Rachel DeLue, *George Inness and the Science of Landscape* (Chicago: University of Chicago Press, 2004), 75.
20. Steven Stoll, "Nowhere, Fast: George Inness's Short Cut and Agrarian Dispossession," *Environmental History* 18 (October 2013): 787.
21. Abbey to Joseph Miller Huston, July 21, 1902, Huston Personal Papers, Pennsylvania Capitol Preservation Committee, Harrisburg (hereafter "PCPC"). See also *The Pennsylvania Capitol: A Documentary History* (Princeton, N.J.: Heritage Studies, 1987), 340.
22. Abbey to Huston, July 21, 1902, PCPC.
23. Kathleen Foster and Michael Quick, *Edwin Austin Abbey (1852–1911)* (New Haven, Conn.: Yale University Art Gallery, 1973), 17.
24. Huston to Abbey, December 19, 1903, PCPC. This letter is a rare example that mentions a specific narrative for the lunette: "Enclosed I send you a description of one of the Bessemer Converter already contained in the Scientific American mailed to you this week. The Steel men say this is a magnificent scene at night, a plant of this kind is in full operation at the Penna. Steel Works and the red flame at night is perceptible even at the Capitol."
25. Ida Minerva Tarbell, *The History of the Standard Oil Company* (London: William Heineman, 1904), 4; and E. J. Babcock, *Investigations of Kerosene Oils and Gasolines* (Grand Forks: School of Mines, University of North Dakota, 1907). Myths of Edwin Drake's ingenuity persist

today and were solidified by histories of the industry written in the twentieth century; see Ernest C. Miller, *Pennsylvania's Oil Industry* (Gettysburg: Pennsylvania History Studies, 1959), 16. See also Robert Strauss, "Oil Makes a Comeback in Pennsylvania," *New York Times*, April 22, 2015. On the Silliman family's connection to slavery, including discussion of a freed Black man named Robert M. Park who contributed substantially to Silliman Jr.'s scientific work, see David W. Blight, *Yale and Slavery: A History* (New Haven, Conn.: Yale University Press, 2024), esp. 121.

26. Miller, *Pennsylvania's Oil Industry*, 4.
27. *Scientific American* 17, no. 15 (October 12, 1867): 23.
28. "I.N.F.," unidentified newspaper clipping, Fairford, Gloucestershire, March 13, 1908, PCPC; *The Pennsylvania Capitol: A Documentary History* (Princeton, N.J.: Heritage Studies, 1987), 341.
29. Babcock, *Kerosene Oils*, 4–5. This publication offers a guide to evaluating kerosene based on government standards. The term "water white" is used to distinguish the character of the oil.
30. Abbey is part of what Caroline Arscott describes as an aesthetic turn in late nineteenth-century British art; Caroline Arscott, "Subject and the Object in *Whistler: The Context of Physiological Aesthetics*," in Lee Glazer and Linda Merrill, eds., *Palaces of Art: Whistler and the Art Worlds of Aestheticism* (Washington, D.C.: Freer Gallery of Art, 2011).
31. William James, "The Spatial Quale," *Journal of Speculative Philosophy* 13, no. 1 (January 1879): 64–87. See also Martin J. Farrell, "Space Perception and William James's Metaphysical Presuppositions," *History of Psychology* 14, no. 2 (August 2011): 158–73. In the article, James defines a quale as a quality, or property, as perceived or experienced by a person and argues that there is a basic sensory understanding of space that precedes ideas of measurements and relative distance. In later writings, he expanded the idea that the subject does not impose the structure of the experience, but that the subject is found through the flux of experience.

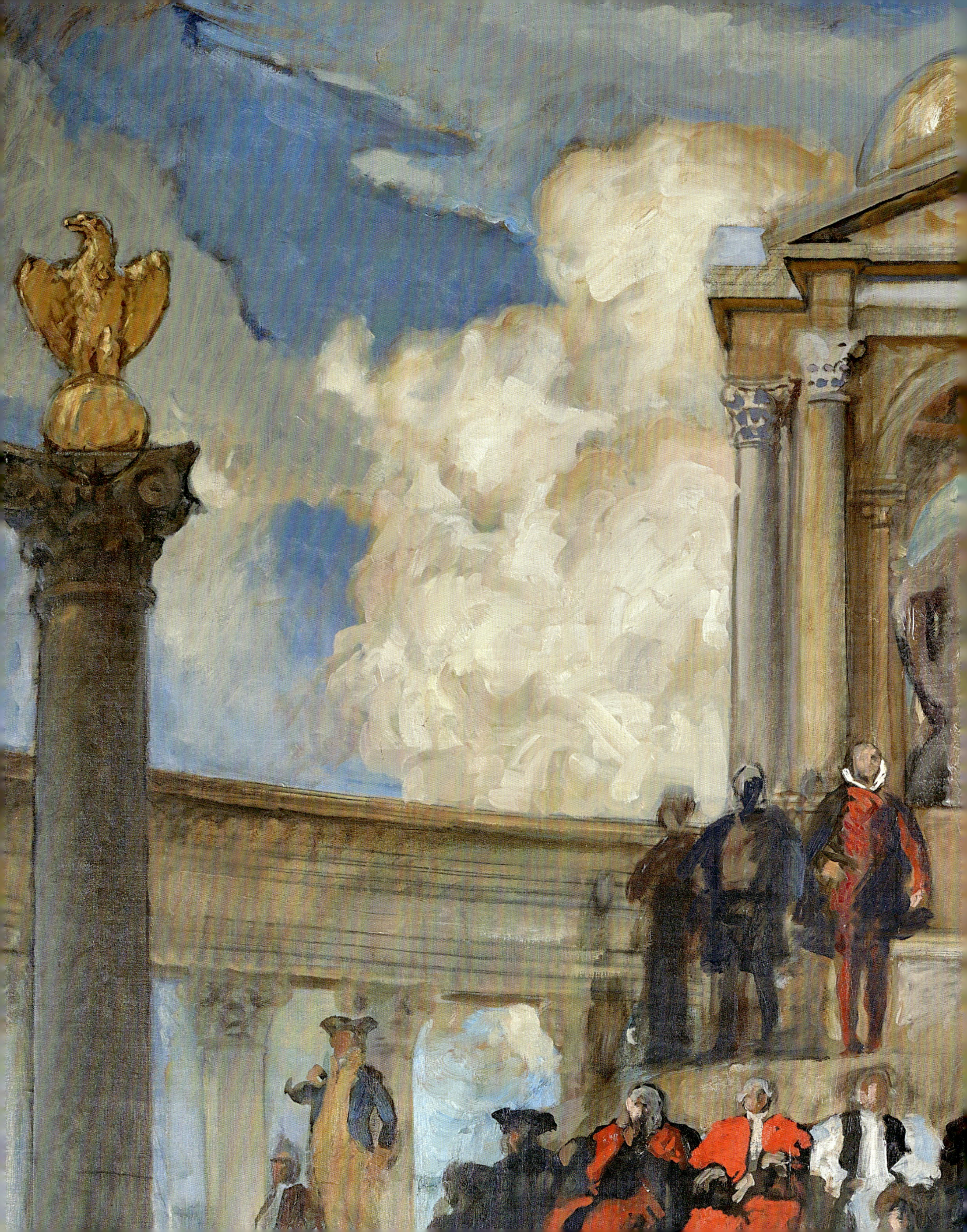

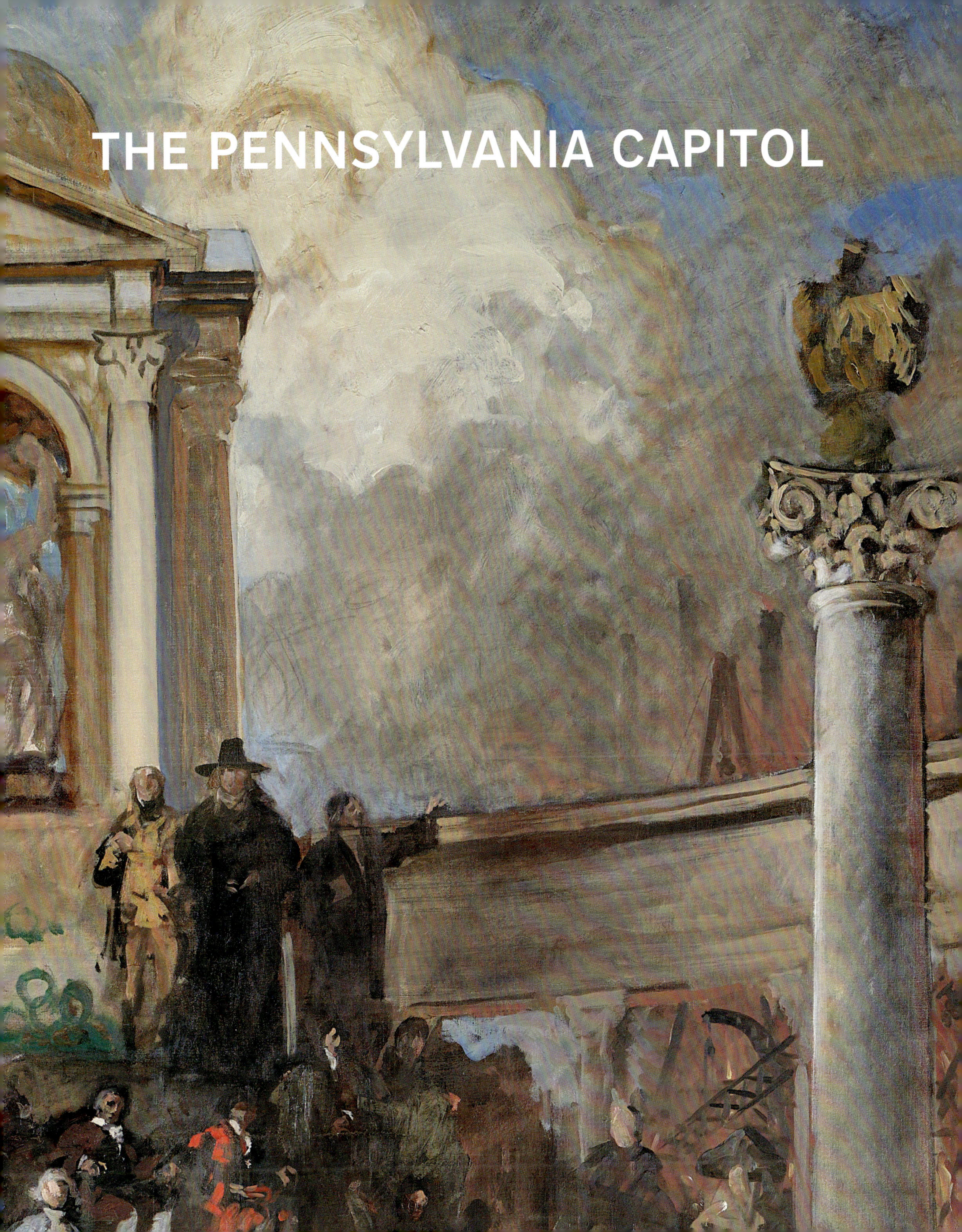

THE PENNSYLVANIA CAPITOL

The first Pennsylvania State Capitol in Harrisburg was destroyed by fire in 1897, leaving the government of the growing commonwealth in need of a home. Construction on a new site began in 1902. Designed by the Philadelphia architect Joseph Huston, the building was intended to celebrate and recognize Pennsylvania's recent emergence as an industrial power and to document its history, reaching back to its colonial charter of 1681. Among the artists involved, three are primary: the painters Edwin Austin Abbey and Violet Oakley and the sculptor George Grey Barnard. For Abbey, who had only just installed his final mural panels in the Boston Public Library, the commission to be the primary artistic interpreter of his home state's new capitol was persuasive. His efforts would be cut short by his death in 1911, leading Oakley to expand her work, which she completed in 1927.

With its dome modeled on Michelangelo's design for Saint Peter's Basilica in the Vatican, Huston's vision for the new capitol harbored an

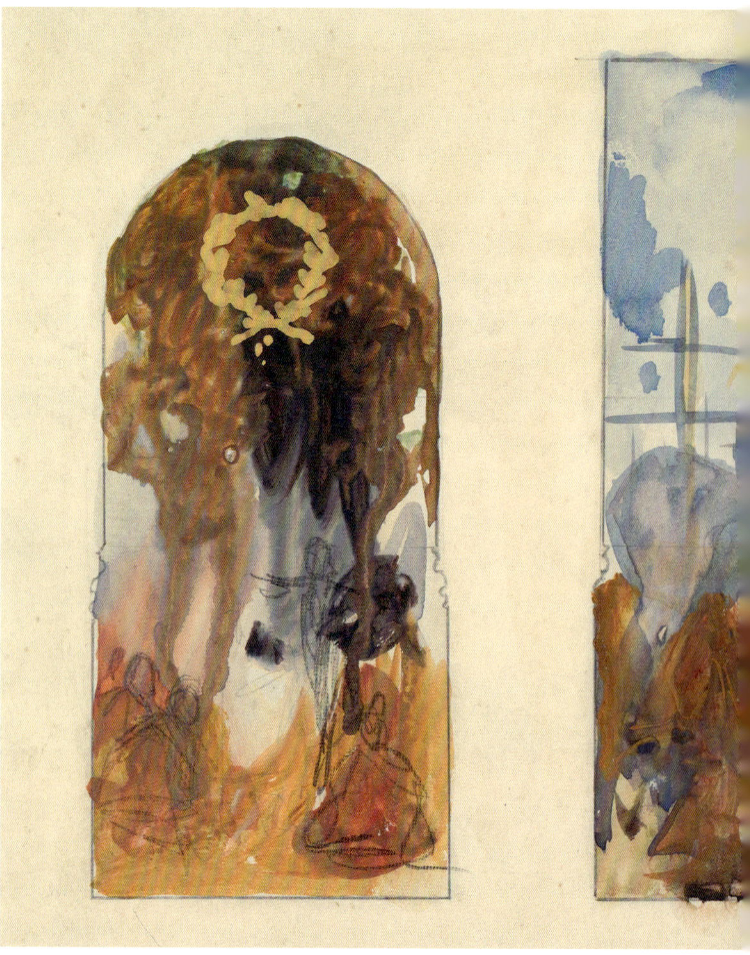

63

CAT. 63 Edwin Austin Abbey (American, 1852–1911, HON. 1897)

Compositional Studies for *Penn's Treaty with the Indians*, *The Apotheosis of Pennsylvania*, and *Reading of the Declaration of Independence* in the Pennsylvania State Capitol, ca. 1909–11

Graphite, watercolor, and gouache on paper, 7½ × 20$\frac{5}{16}$ in. (19.1 × 51.6 cm)
Yale University Art Gallery, New Haven, Conn., Edwin Austin Abbey Memorial Collection, 1937.1686

CAT. 64 Edwin Austin Abbey (American, 1852–1911, HON. 1897)

Study for *The Apotheosis of Pennsylvania* in the Pennsylvania State Capitol, ca. 1909–11

Oil on canvas, 68 × 68 in. (172.7 × 172.7 cm)
Yale University Art Gallery, New Haven, Conn., Edwin Austin Abbey Memorial Collection, 1937.1685

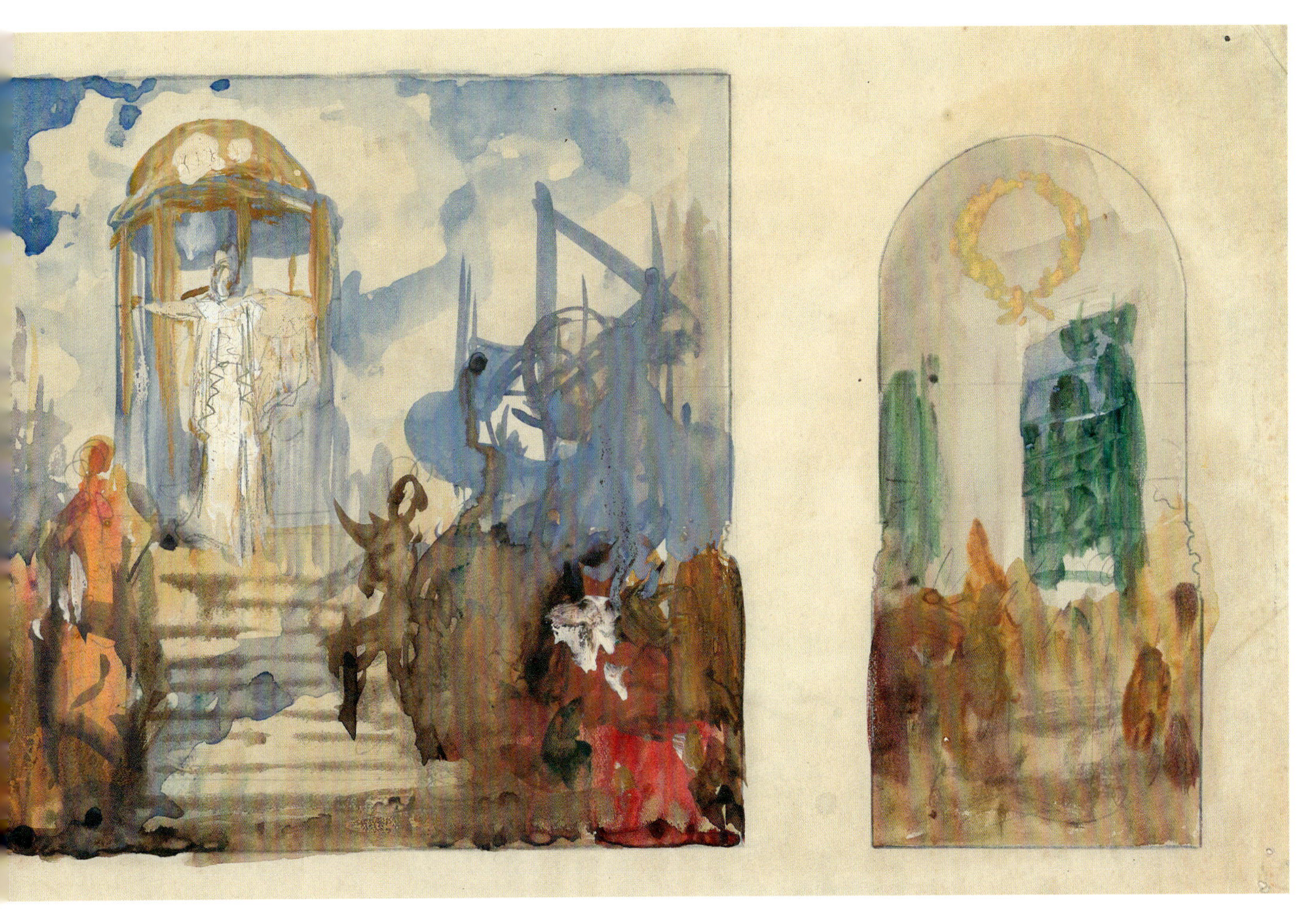

impressive ambition, seeking to rival Europe's great landmarks. Recent history was also close at hand. Situated less than forty miles from Gettysburg, where the tide of the Civil War turned against the Confederacy in the summer of 1863, Harrisburg had witnessed the conflict at close quarters. Aspiration and memory mingled in the artistic program of the building and informed the ambitious murals that Abbey formulated to decorate the seat of state government.

For Abbey, the transition to a new project called for a new method. Shifting from his background as an illustrator and theatrical storyteller, he developed a Symbolist practice based in the potential of the body to represent ideas. He continued to research his subjects intensively, but his creative focus now balanced detailed costume studies and the nude. For academically trained artists, study from the nude was the foundation of their work and the basis of their understanding of artistic practice, but Abbey had trained informally, as an illustrator. Where a library was an excellent environment in which to focus on narrative subjects, he felt that the Pennsylvania capitol called for the language of allegory.

Abbey began work on the commission with four lunettes for the capitol's central rotunda and, initially, three compositions for the House of Representatives chamber, including the forty-by-forty-foot *Apotheosis of Pennsylvania* above the Speaker's rostrum (see page 290). The three-part compositional watercolor study (cat. 63) for the primary wall of the House chamber shows how much the artist changed and elaborated the composition over time. Moving from a simpler conception of the central scene, the final mural reverses the movement of the figures; rather than showing them climbing the steps, Abbey instead faced the historical actors of Pennsylvania out toward the House, arranging the recognizable faces of the state's past leaders in a pantheon of memory. A large oil study (cat. 64) offers a sense of the complexity of the final historical portrait, surmounted by the allegorical Genius of State, that extends down to the Union soldiers at lower left and miners at lower right. Below them, elected representatives conduct the people's business, heirs of the historical genealogy overhead that puts them, literally, into perspective.

William Penn presided over the first colonial assemblies of Pennsylvania, making him not only the founder of the colony but also the forerunner of the Speaker of the House in an early trial of democratic principles. By elevating the Speaker's chair into the physical space of the painting, the architect collaborated to create a contemporary frame around the past that would unfold perpetually in its foreground, in constant dialogue. As the central figure in Abbey's composition, perched directly over the then-current Speaker's head, Penn appears to stride directly into the real space of the chamber. In contrast, the large structures of a shipyard and oil derricks in the early watercolor recede, despite interim studies in which Abbey contemplated developing structure, energy, and color from these background elements. Instead, their themes emerged more prominently in his lunettes for the rotunda.

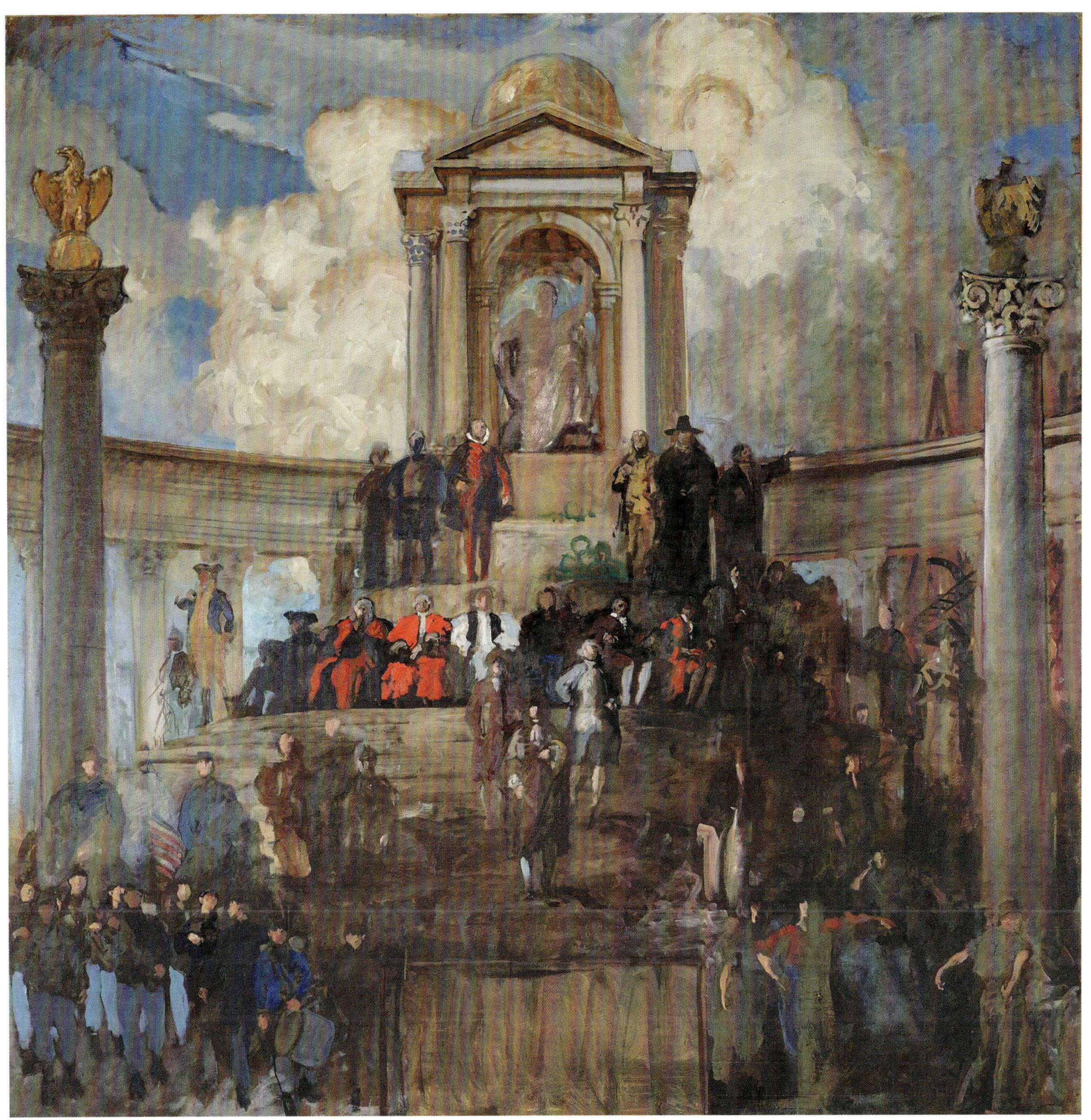

64

Key Figures

Edwin Austin Abbey's compositional drawing for *The Apotheosis of Pennsylvania* (cat. 65) offers little sense of the concentrated effort he made to create a memorable series of romanticized historical portraits, including those of the frontiersman Daniel Boone and the explorer Sir Walter Raleigh. Born in 1734 and raised a Quaker in Pennsylvania, Boone was an admired figure of self-reliance, patriotism, and ingenuity in the era of the American Revolution. Abbey's pastel portrait (cat. 66) focuses on Boone's reputation as a person at ease in nature, coexisting between settler and Indigenous communities and traditions despite the many conflicts and wars during his lifetime. Swathed in fur and hides, Boone displays a pose of casual confidence, the intermingling of browns and oranges in his garments amplifying their softness and comfort. Abbey accentuates Boone's modesty, showing him comfortable in his self-fashioned clothing even among the formal dress of the other figures beside him, including Walter Raleigh, ostentatious in his courtly finery.

Raleigh's vivid red, violet, and pink clothing is a study in sensuality as well, but of a different order than Boone's (cat. 67). Elizabethan historical dress was Abbey's specialty, and his early reputation rested on his illustrations for the works of William Shakespeare, a contemporary of Raleigh. Abbey's vast collection of historic and reproduction costumes was assembled or made to order for his illustrations and theater designs. Raleigh's ties to Pennsylvania were few, but he was intermittently credited with charting the Delaware River, which, along with his well-known charisma, may have been the basis for his inclusion in Abbey's *Apotheosis*. Abbey spared no effort in presenting Raleigh in sartorial elegance, a remarkable contrast to Boone that reflected the artist's own experience and interests more than the subject's prominence in Pennsylvania history.

CAT. 65 Edwin Austin Abbey (American, 1852–1911, HON. 1897)
Study for *The Apotheosis of Pennsylvania* in the Pennsylvania State Capitol, ca. 1909–11
Charcoal and pastel on tracing paper, 64 × 97½ in. (162.6 × 247.7 cm)
Yale University Art Gallery, New Haven, Conn., Edwin Austin Abbey Memorial Collection, 1937.1695

CAT. 66 Edwin Austin Abbey (American, 1852–1911, HON. 1897)
Study for Daniel Boone in *The Apotheosis of Pennsylvania* in the Pennsylvania State Capitol, ca. 1909–11
Pencil, black chalk, and pastel on dark gray-brown paper, 28 × 22 in. (71.1 × 55.9 cm)
Yale University Art Gallery, New Haven, Conn., Edwin Austin Abbey Memorial Collection, 1937.1610

CAT. 67 Edwin Austin Abbey (American, 1852–1911, HON. 1897)
Study for Sir Walter Raleigh in *The Apotheosis of Pennsylvania* in the Pennsylvania State Capitol, ca. 1909–11
Pencil, black chalk, and pastel on dark gray-green paper, 28½ × 22½ in. (72.4 × 57.2 cm)
Yale University Art Gallery, New Haven, Conn., Edwin Austin Abbey Memorial Collection, 1937.1626

CAT. 68 Violet Oakley (American, 1874–1961)
Studies for a Prostitute for *International Understanding and Unity* in the Pennsylvania State Capitol, ca. 1916
Graphite on paper, 15¼ × 11¼ in. (38.7 × 28.6 cm)
Pennsylvania Capitol Preservation Committee, Harrisburg, 82.78.227

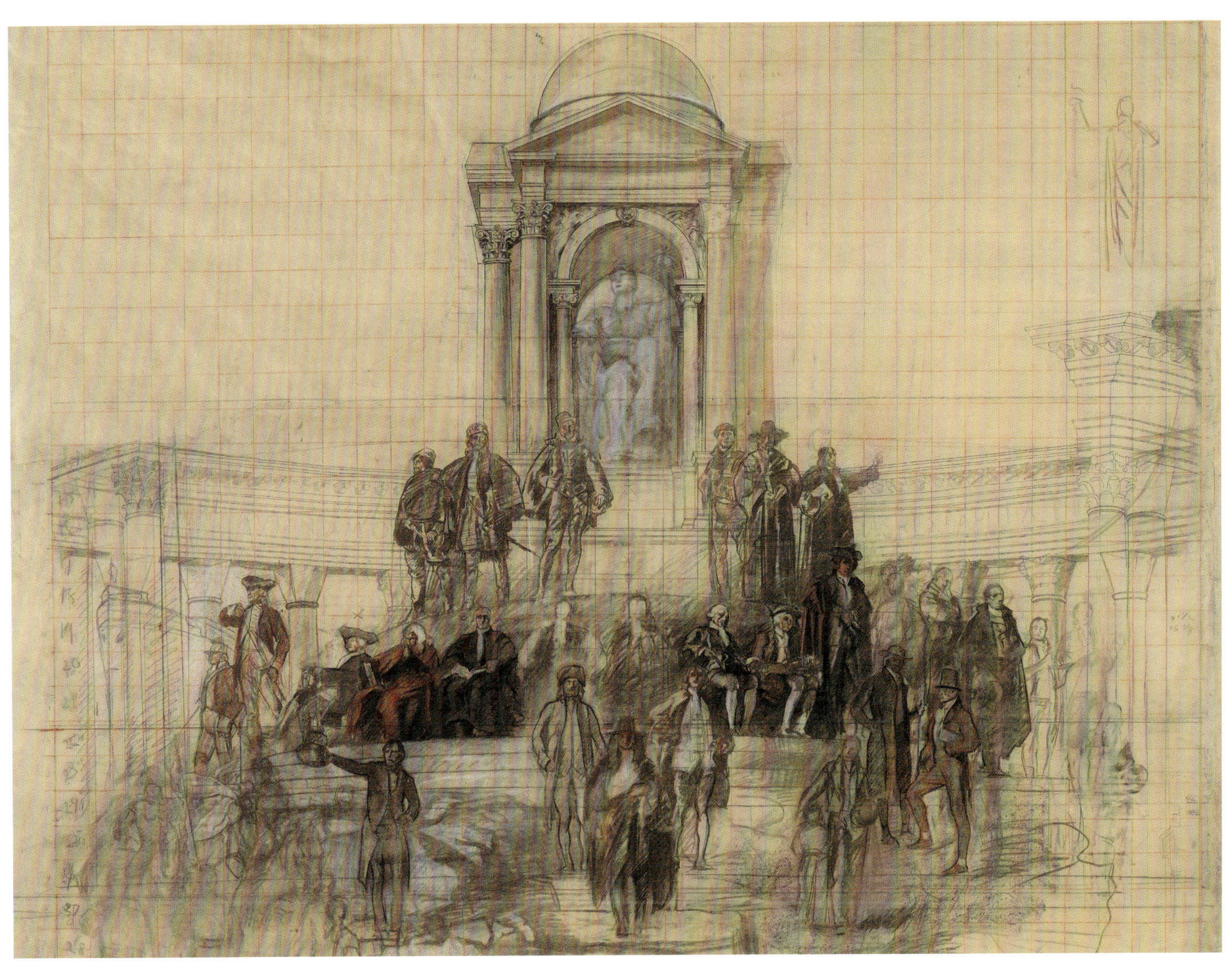

65

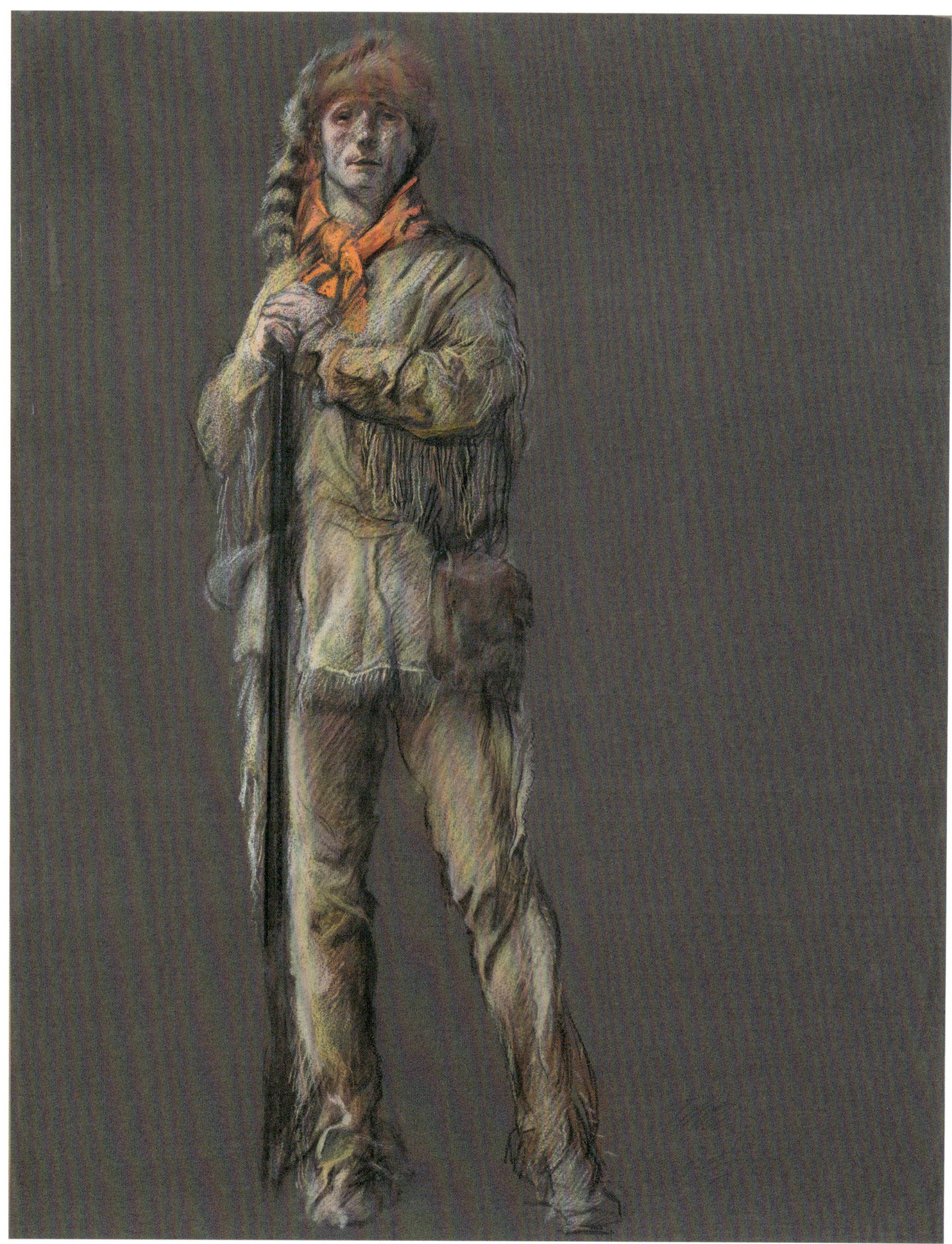

66

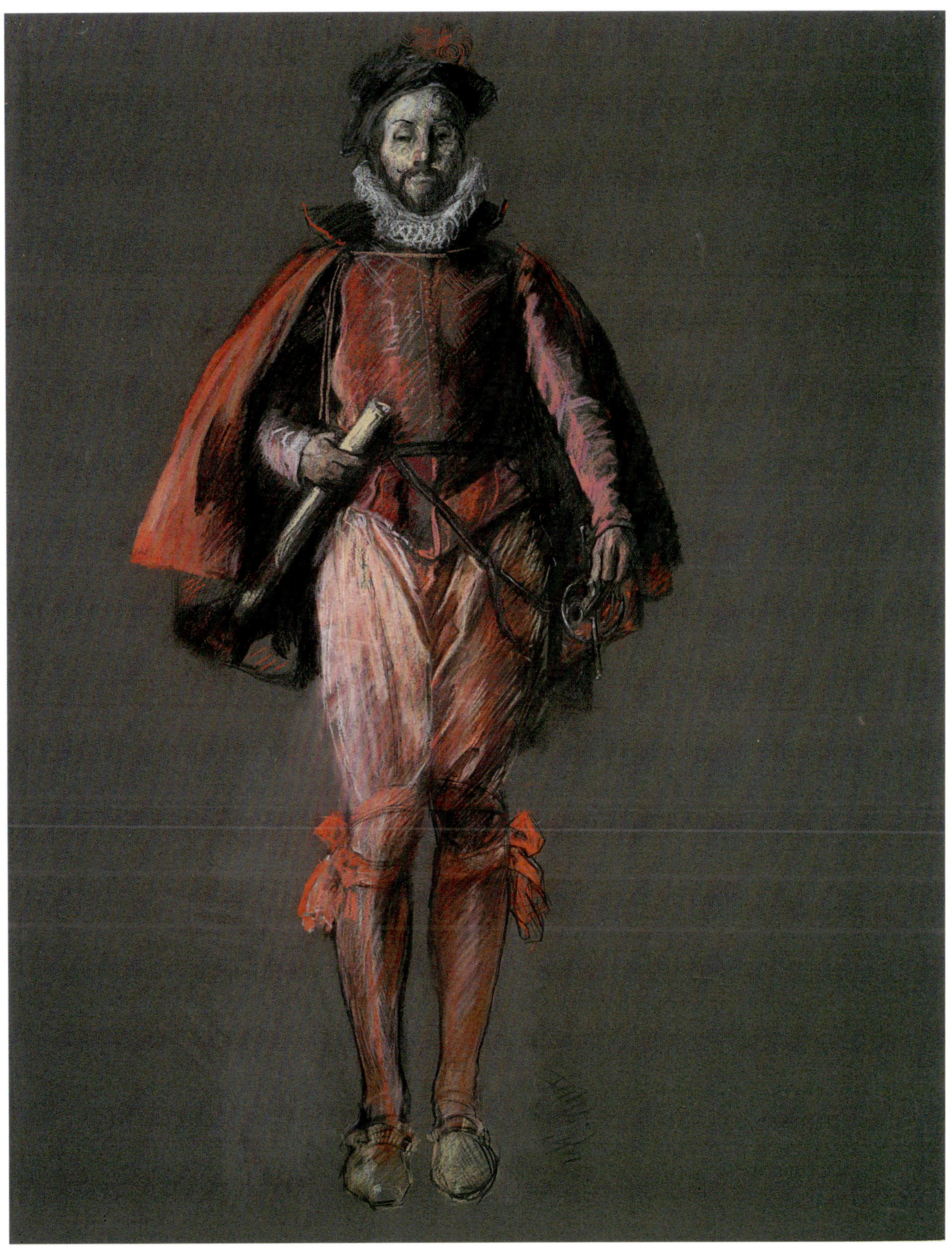

67

Violet Oakley's representations of history were of a different order—she forthrightly depicted the injustice of slavery and the efforts of Quaker and abolitionist leaders to resist it. Among the inclusions in her *International Understanding and Unity* mural for the capitol's Senate chamber is the figure of a prostitute. The pose that Oakley chose for the woman is remarkable in its grace and inward turn. Here is a figure that requires explanation to identify, but her struggle is evident in her downcast face and shrinking posture. In the preparatory drawing (cat. 68), she stands alone to suffer the isolation of social ostracism; her emotional distress extends to her physical withdrawal from the central space of the page. Both Abbey and Oakley used sensualism to create empathy and animate history for their contemporaries, asserting relevance and human understanding, but their methods and subjects are a striking contrast.

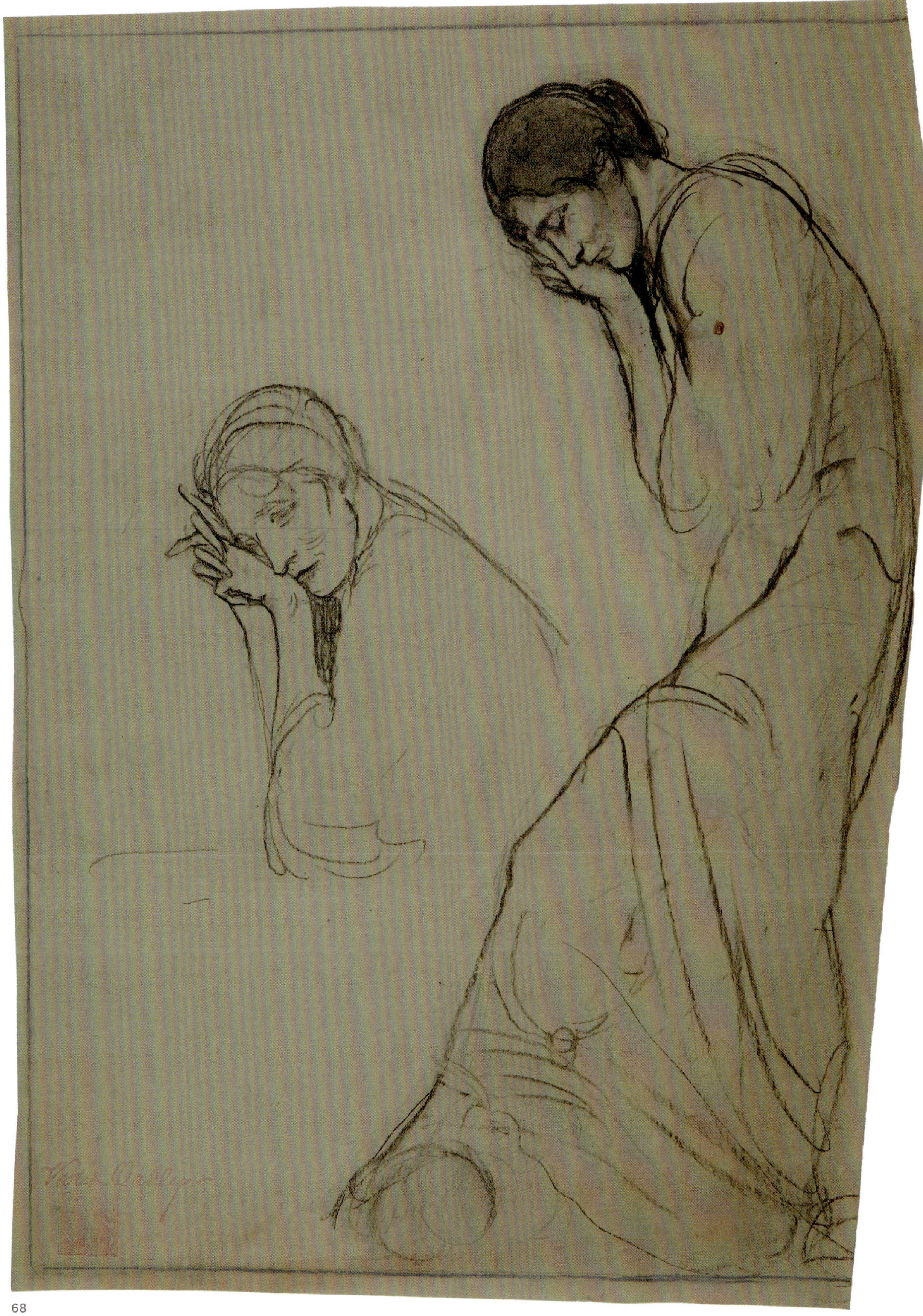

Spirits

Edwin Austin Abbey's synesthetic depictions of figures ascending, twisting, and reaching held his attention through dozens of studies for *The Spirit of Light* at different scales and in varied media. Unlike most of his peers, who concentrated on one or two types of study and medium, Abbey used nearly every available tool to develop his subjects. Even relative to his normally extensive preparatory practice, however, the figures for *The Spirit of Light* captured an extraordinary amount of his time and energy. As he strove to communicate the essential properties of a gas flame, the element that the figures represent, their movements and exchanges edged closer to dance and the balletic orchestration of bodies in motion.

CAT. 69 Edwin Austin Abbey (American, 1852–1911, HON. 1897)

Compositional Study for *The Spirit of Light* in the Pennsylvania State Capitol, ca. 1902–8

Oil on canvas, 23¾ × 35½ in. (60.3 × 90.2 cm)
Yale University Art Gallery, New Haven, Conn., Edwin Austin Abbey Memorial Collection, 1937.1501

CAT. 70 Edwin Austin Abbey (American, 1852–1911, HON. 1897)

Figure Study for *The Spirit of Light* in the Pennsylvania State Capitol, ca. 1902–8

Oil on canvas, 89¼ × 25⅜ in. (226.7 × 64.5 cm)
Yale University Art Gallery, New Haven, Conn., Edwin Austin Abbey Memorial Collection, 1937.1484

CAT. 71 Edwin Austin Abbey (American, 1852–1911, HON. 1897)

Figure Study for *The Spirit of Light* in the Pennsylvania State Capitol, ca. 1902–11

Charcoal and chalk on paper, 35¾ × 24⅛ in. (90.8 × 61.3 cm)
Yale University Art Gallery, New Haven, Conn., Edwin Austin Abbey Memorial Collection, 1937.1879

An early oil study (cat. 69) demonstrates ideas that Abbey initially developed and would gradually pull apart into two separate compositions. The figures at lower right emerging from the earth and the landscape they inhabit would eventually become the subjects of a different lunette: *Science Revealing the Treasures of the Earth*. The three female spirits reaching into, and up from, the ground would transform into a group of male miners (see cat. 54). The fluidity with which Abbey adapted his compositions suggests that his foremost artistic priority was the arrangement of bodies and their interactions, rather than the subject they depicted. Theme, gender, clothing, and other details came after the essential arrangement of figures in space and their dynamic interactions. Abbey's studies for *The Spirit of Light* exceeded the necessity of thematic development and convey his investment in the works themselves.

The oil study of two figures ascending in a narrow pillar against a golden sunset conveys a vivid sense of their interaction, coiling upward (cat. 70). It also represents Abbey's progression from nude to dressed, as if an evolution of clothing echoed the refinement or transmutation of an abstract idea into corporeal form. Insight also develops from the reiterated movements in an early charcoal drawing for this group (cat. 71). The individual figures materialize against one another, conveying their languid movements as well as their spatial interactions. This Raphael-esque drawing offers an essence of movement and fluent line that would carry through Abbey's development of the composition from sketch to mural.

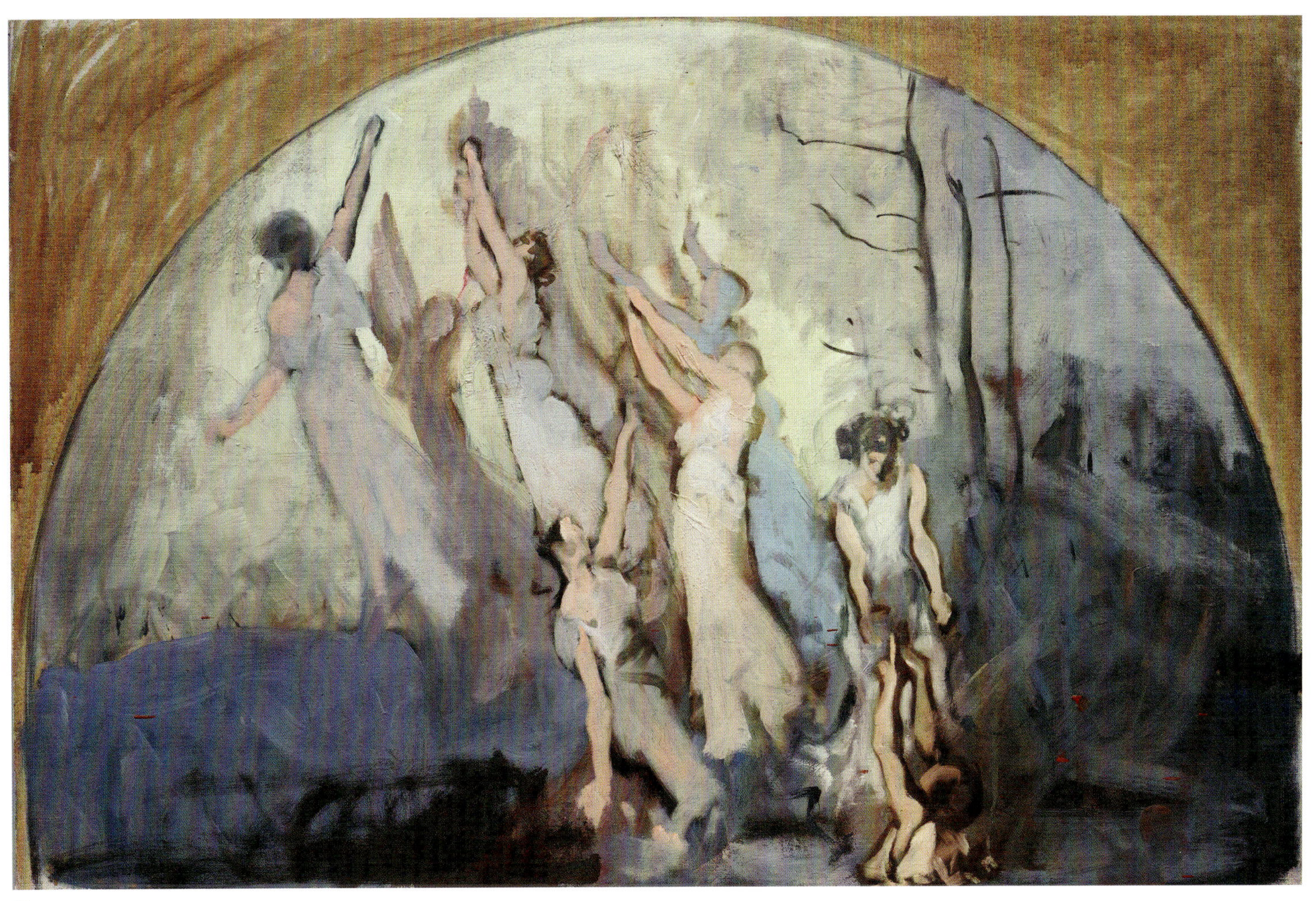

69

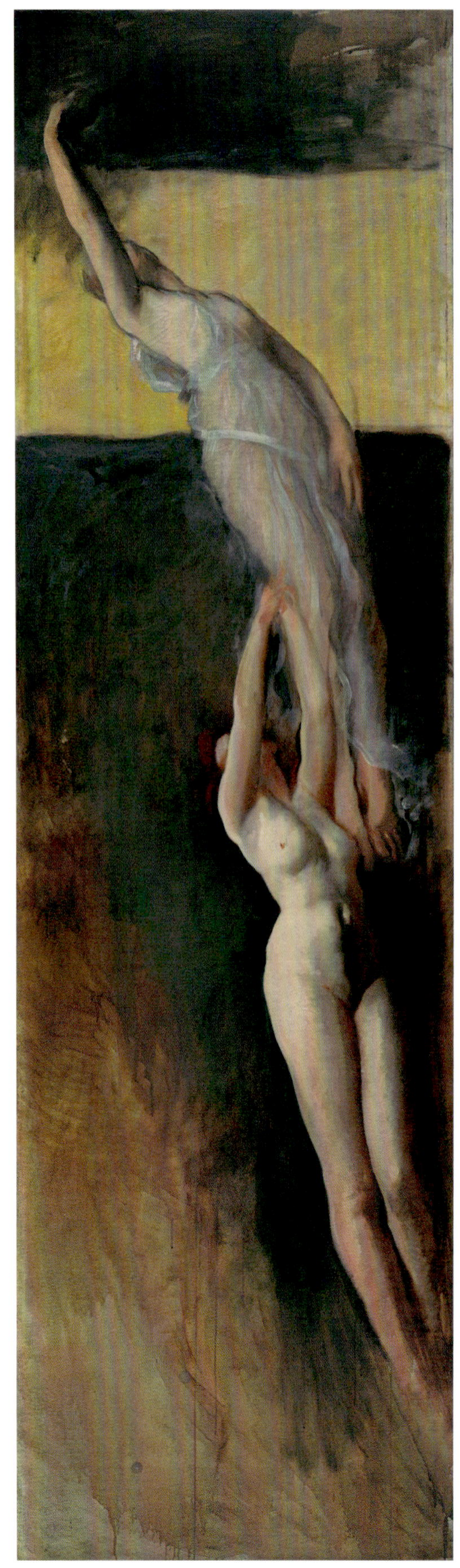

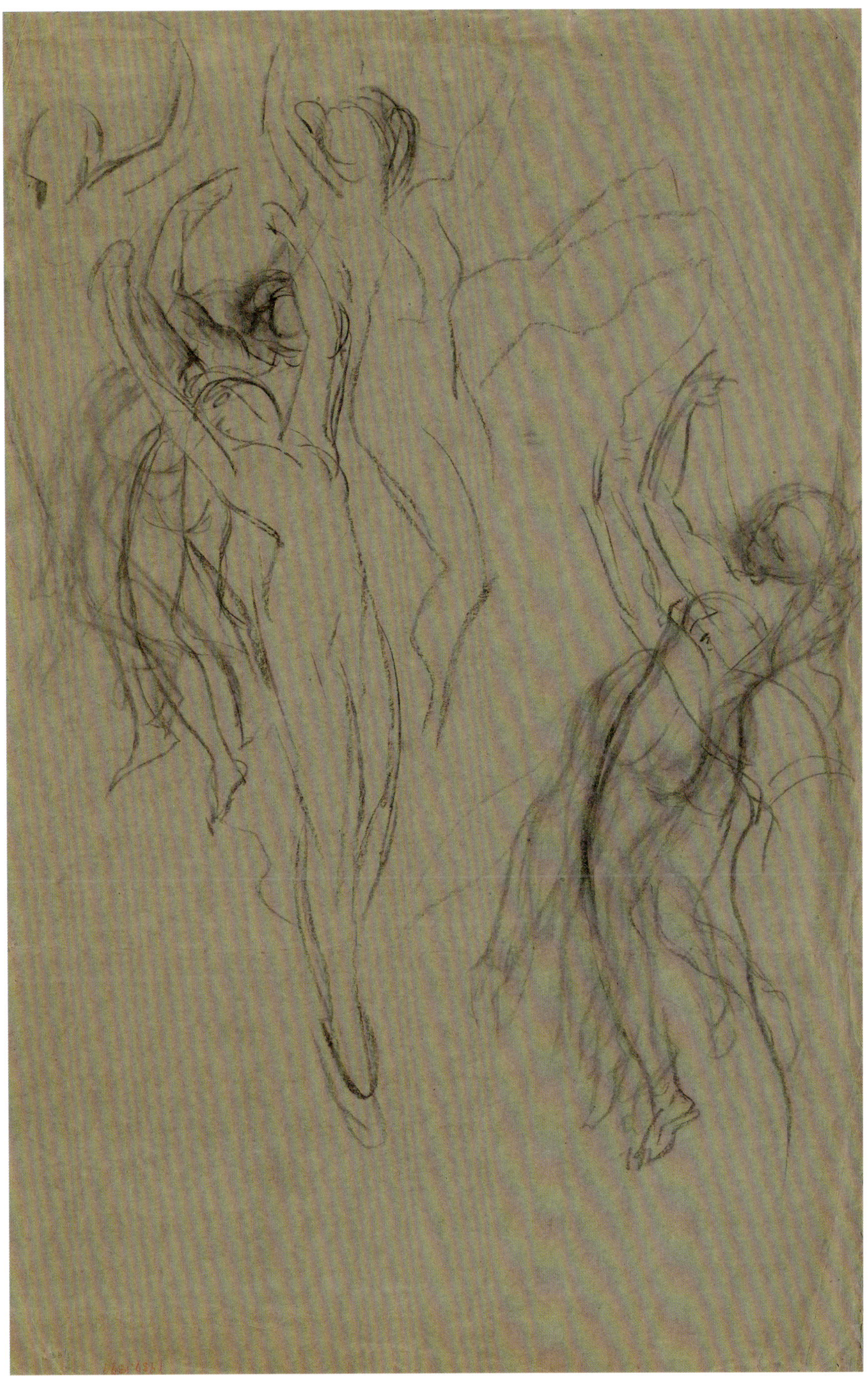

71

Descent

Inside the rotunda of the Pennsylvania State Capitol, the upward, attenuated movement of Edwin Austin Abbey's figures in *The Spirit of Light* contrasts with the descending miners exploring the earth below in the adjacent mural, *Science Revealing the Treasures of the Earth*. Artists of the American Renaissance often portrayed a Manichaean world of good and evil, and Abbey's scenes divide into essential pairs: here, up and down, spirit and earth. In the present day, the release of carbon from the earth has ominous overtones. At the dawn of the twentieth century, however, natural resources and the technology they fueled promised stability and liberation from the onerous toil and insecurity of preindustrial life.

Abbey carefully researched his subject for *Science Revealing the Treasures of the Earth*, soliciting information about the landscapes where coal formations were found in England and the United States as well as the technologies of extraction. His early sketchbook drawings for the composition show the figural group cresting a ridge before climbing down into a crevasse, while a second drawing highlights the allegorical figure of Science pointing the way (cat. 72). The graphite drawing of the miners is heavily wrought, with pressure from the pencil deeply inscribing contours and dense hatching that render the scene dark and expressive. It stands in contrast to the second, with its lighter touch and more fluid contours of the muses in the sky above.

Abbey's grouping is not as interdependent—or mutually supportive—as it would become in the final mural. Most of the figures move on their own, in succession. Over time, the downward movement of the righthand miners developed into a nearly vertical descent, increasingly exaggerating the plunge below the sight edge of the composition. Like his *Apotheosis of Pennsylvania*, in which the miners burrow directly beneath the altar of the Genius of State, here they move as if beyond the frame of the painting.

CAT. 72 Edwin Austin Abbey (American, 1852–1911, HON. 1897)

Two Studies for *Science Revealing the Treasures of the Earth*, n.d.

Graphite, pen and ink, watercolor, and colored pencils on wove paper, 7 × 10 in. (17.8 × 25.4 cm)
Yale University Art Gallery, New Haven, Conn., Edwin Austin Abbey Memorial Collection, 1937.4362

Detail of cat. 72

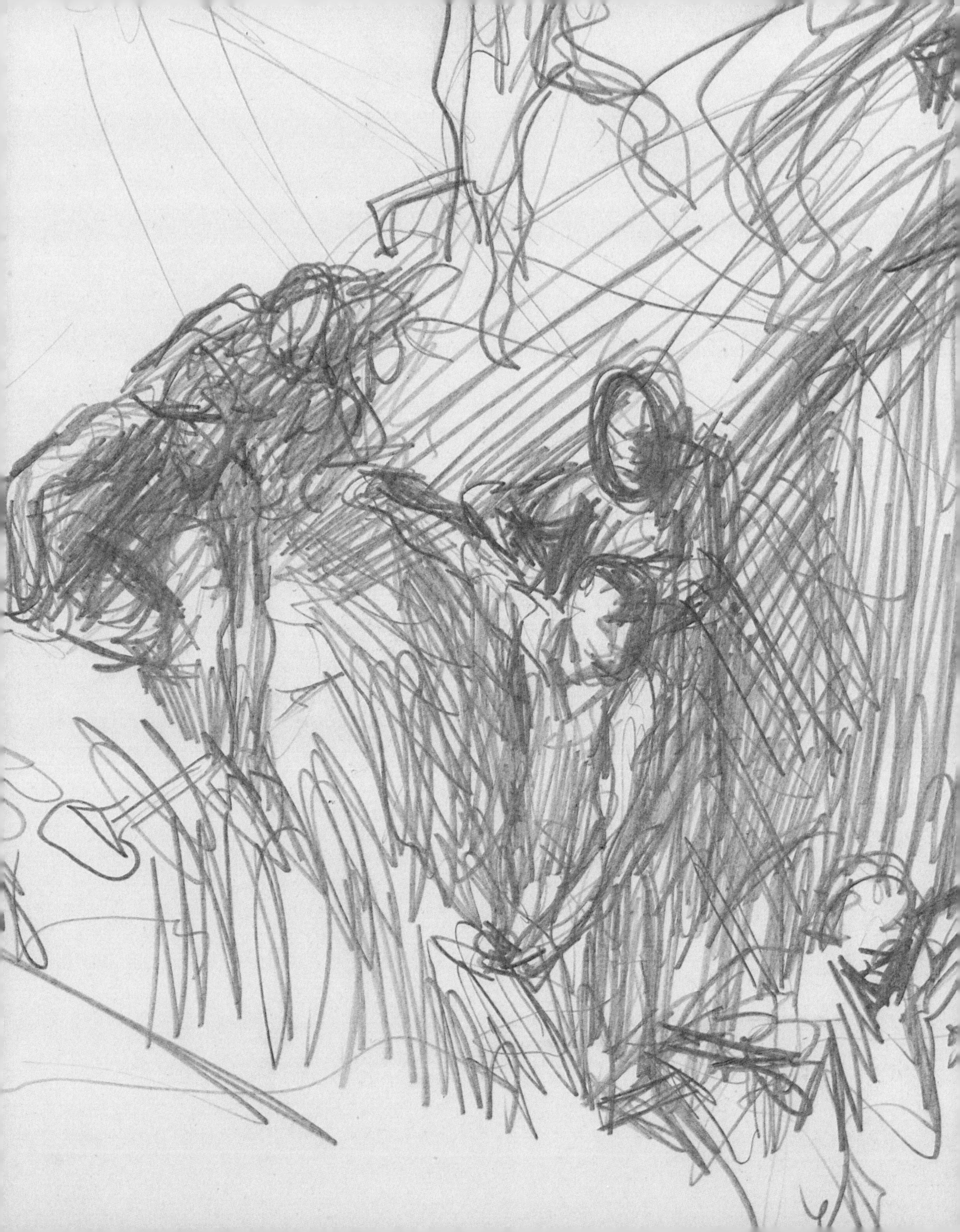

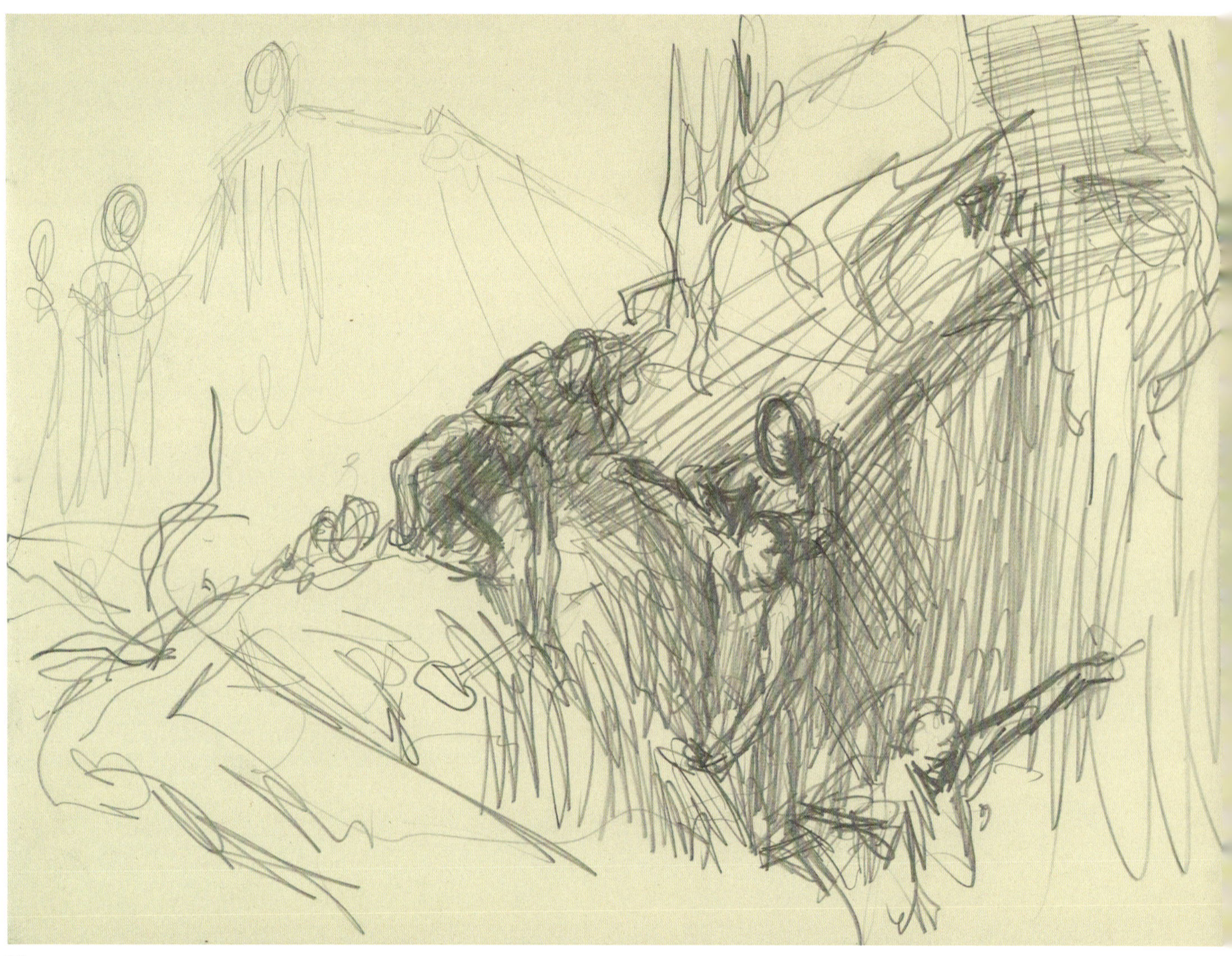

72

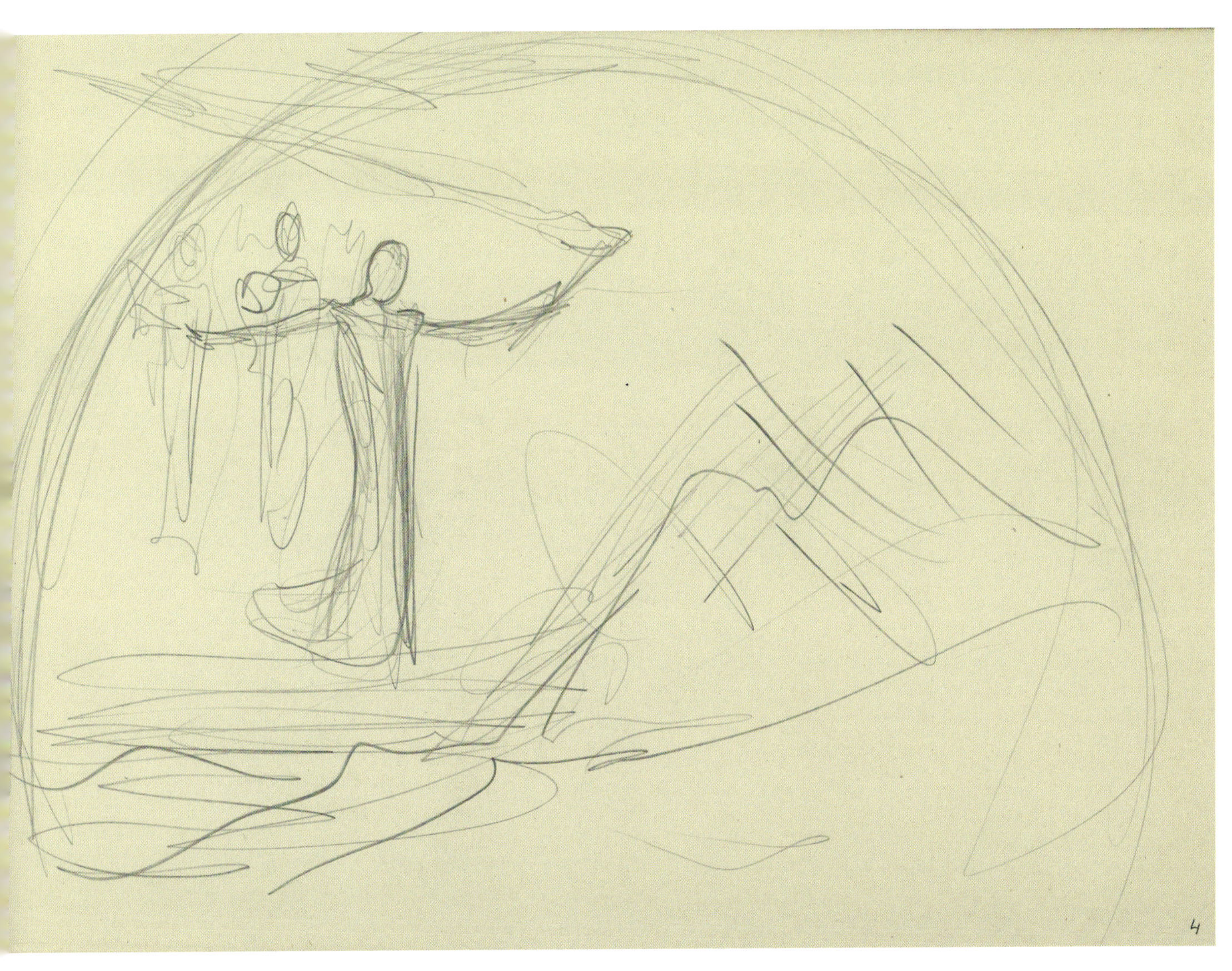
4

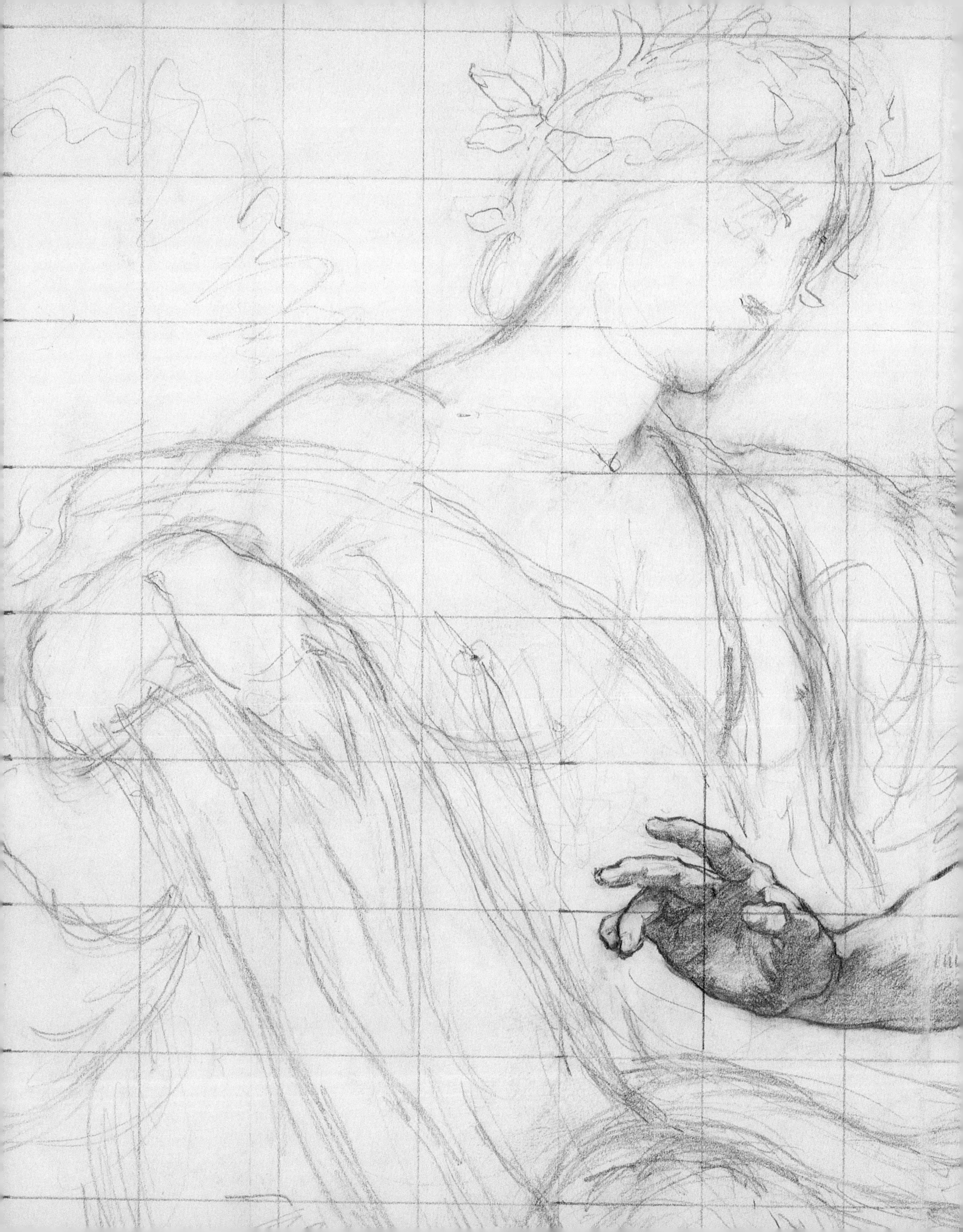

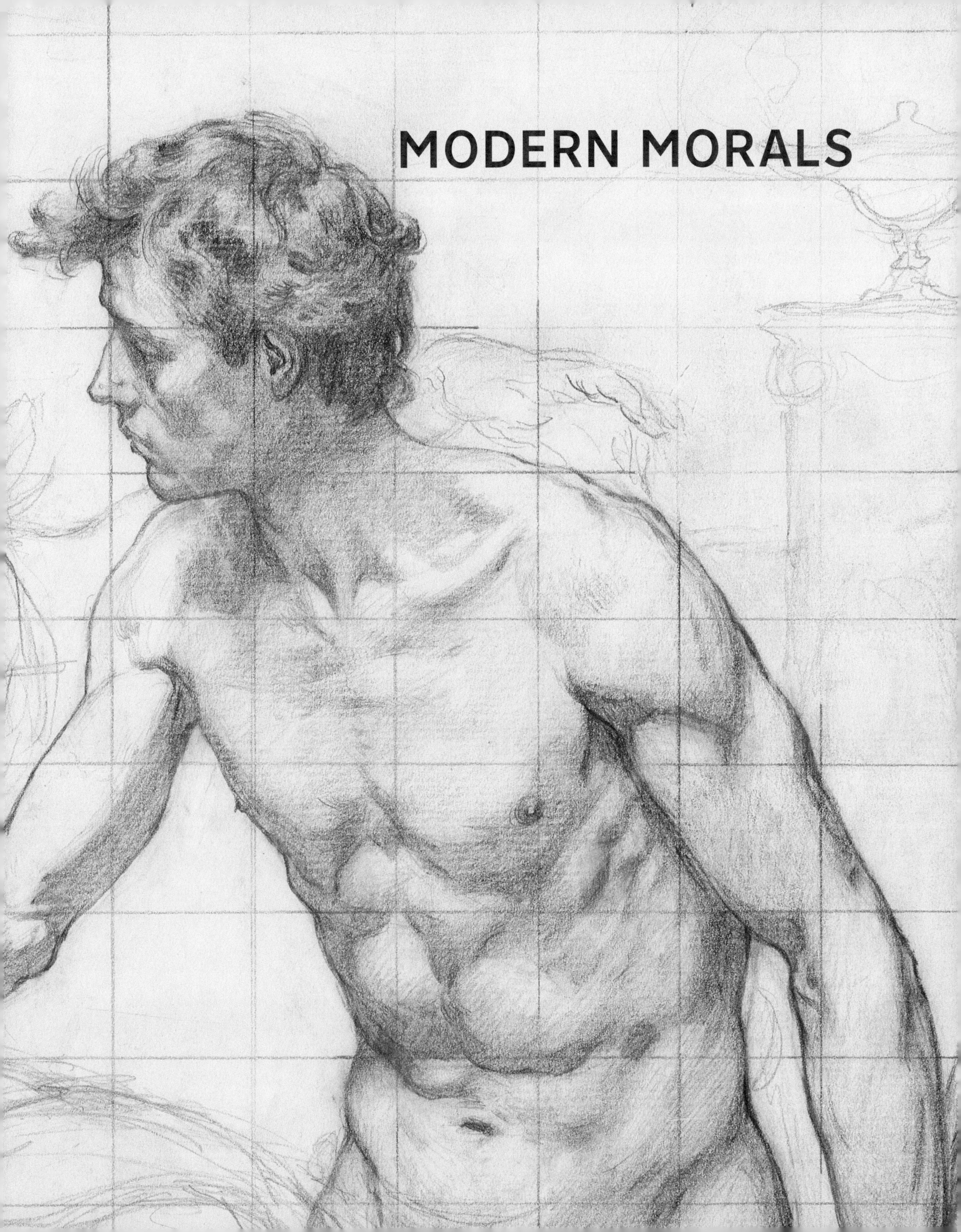

MODERN MORALS

HIGH ABOVE NEW YORK'S OLD MADISON SQUARE Garden on Madison Square Park shone one of the late nineteenth century's most scandalous and beguiling figures: Augustus Saint-Gaudens's gilded thirteen-foot-tall *Diana of the Tower*. A shining beacon overlooking the city and lit by arc lights at night, the nude goddess was a startling contrast to Frédéric Auguste Bartholdi's Statue of Liberty, a gift from the French people recently installed in 1886, standing sentinel in New York Harbor.

Which was America? The principled, moral leader or the sensual, lustrous mirage? Amid the furious growth of New York City at the end of the nineteenth century, both images, among others, held some sway and were in constant tension. Moral reformers battled for the souls of the intemperate, and capitalist showmen offered every form of temptation to urban dwellers. Bodies were the subject of a wide debate about the nature of the country that played out in public.

Ultimately, there was not one America, nor was there one civic imagination. Erecting a monumental golden nude above a bustling urban center was a bold commercial strategy in a nation that remained deeply uncomfortable with depictions of the body. The sensuality and allure of material and surface—the essence of its skin-deep Gilded Age—created by Saint-Gaudens extended to the many reductions of the sculpture (cat. 73) that a ready market demanded.

The iconic power of *Diana* made it the subject of controversy as well as popularity. If they wanted fame and fortune, artists like Saint-Gaudens had to navigate between the interests of social conservatives and capitalists without becoming an exclusive representative of either. The modernity of such works manifests in their participation in popular debate, openly—some said wantonly—highlighting the rich sensualism of the era. Although the abundance of moralizing subjects in public commissions eclipsed the number of commercial monuments, the latter represented an essential undercurrent.

CAT. 73 Augustus Saint-Gaudens (American, born Ireland, 1848–1907, HON. 1905)

Diana, 1895

Bronze, 21 × 19 × 5 in. (53.3 × 48.3 × 12.7 cm)
Yale University Art Gallery, New Haven, Conn., Purchased with the Leonard C. Hanna, Jr., Class of 1913, Katharine Ordway, and Friends of American Arts Acquisition Funds, 2008.88.1

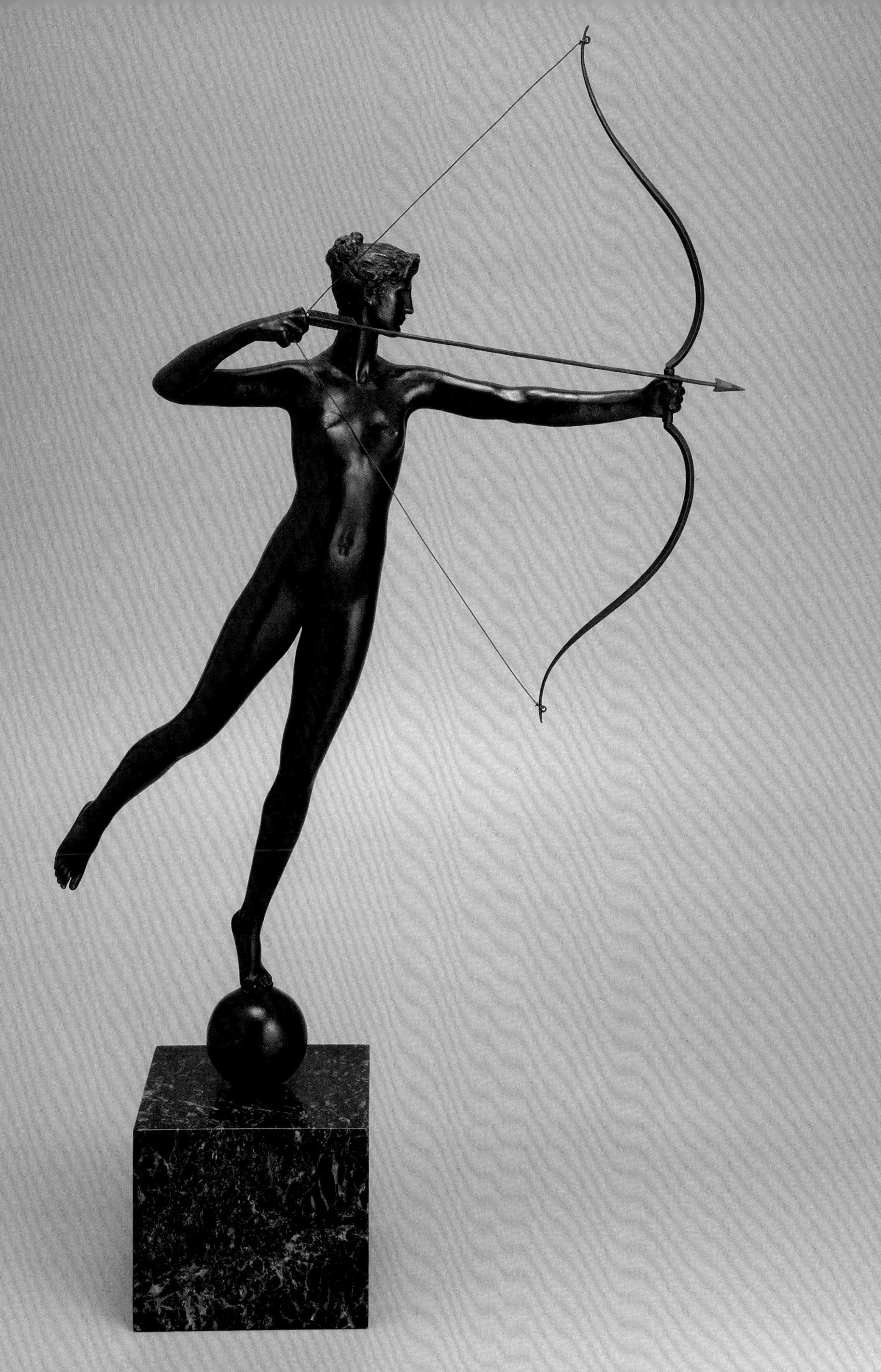

Technologies

Technology may be considered the defining allegory of the American Renaissance, a new stalwart among the muses. Often presented as muscular and female, the figure offered a rare elision of physical traits and symbolic attributes. Electricity—represented by wires, lightning, the telegraph, or other machinery—was perhaps the primary manifestation of technology. Among New York's most prolific muralists, Henry Siddons Mowbray painted *Muse of Electricity* with a note of historical nostalgia by depicting eighteenth-century Leyden jars rather than more modern devices to represent the present day (cat. 74). For his 1897 commission to decorate the main stair hall of the Boston Public Library (see pages 82–83), France's leading muralist Pierre Puvis de Chavannes presented telephone (or telegraph) wires and poles as emblems of the field of physics, across which, he said, "'Speech flashes through space, and swift as lightning bears tidings of good and evil.'"[1] Not to be misunderstood, the mural features a bolt of lightning above the horizon.

For the 1893 World's Columbian Exposition in his native Chicago, James Carroll Beckwith portrayed a combination of a telephone and stock ticker, rendered here in a graphite study (cat. 75). Surrounded by distant voices and real-time market updates, his allegory offers an early representation of the ubiquity and urgency of instantaneous communication in the modern age. Beckwith's representation is fully developed and prescient of the network of information and news that would increasingly define modernity. The floating ticker tape swirls around the sturdy woman's legs, an ephemeral layer of clothing as she confidently steps forward, a figure of action.

NOTE

1. Quoted in Cecilia Waern, "Puvis De Chavannes in Boston," *Atlantic Monthly* 79, no. 472 (February 1897): 253.

CAT. 74 Henry Siddons Mowbray (American, born Egypt, 1858–1928)
Study for *Muse of Electricity* in the Collis P. Huntington Mansion, New York, 1893
Oil on canvas, 39½ × 78¾ in. (100.3 × 200 cm)
Yale University Art Gallery, New Haven, Conn., Gift of Archer M. Huntington, HON. 1897, 1926.105

CAT. 75 James Carroll Beckwith (American, 1852–1917)
The Telephone and the Ticker, Study for *Electricity as Applied to Commerce* in the Manufactures and Liberal Arts Building, World's Columbian Exposition, Chicago, 1892
Black chalk and graphite on off-white laid paper, 24⁹⁄₁₆ × 18⁹⁄₁₆ in. (62.4 × 47.1 cm)
Cooper Hewitt, Smithsonian Design Museum, New York, Gift of J. Carroll Beckwith, 1915-2-6

Detail of cat. 74

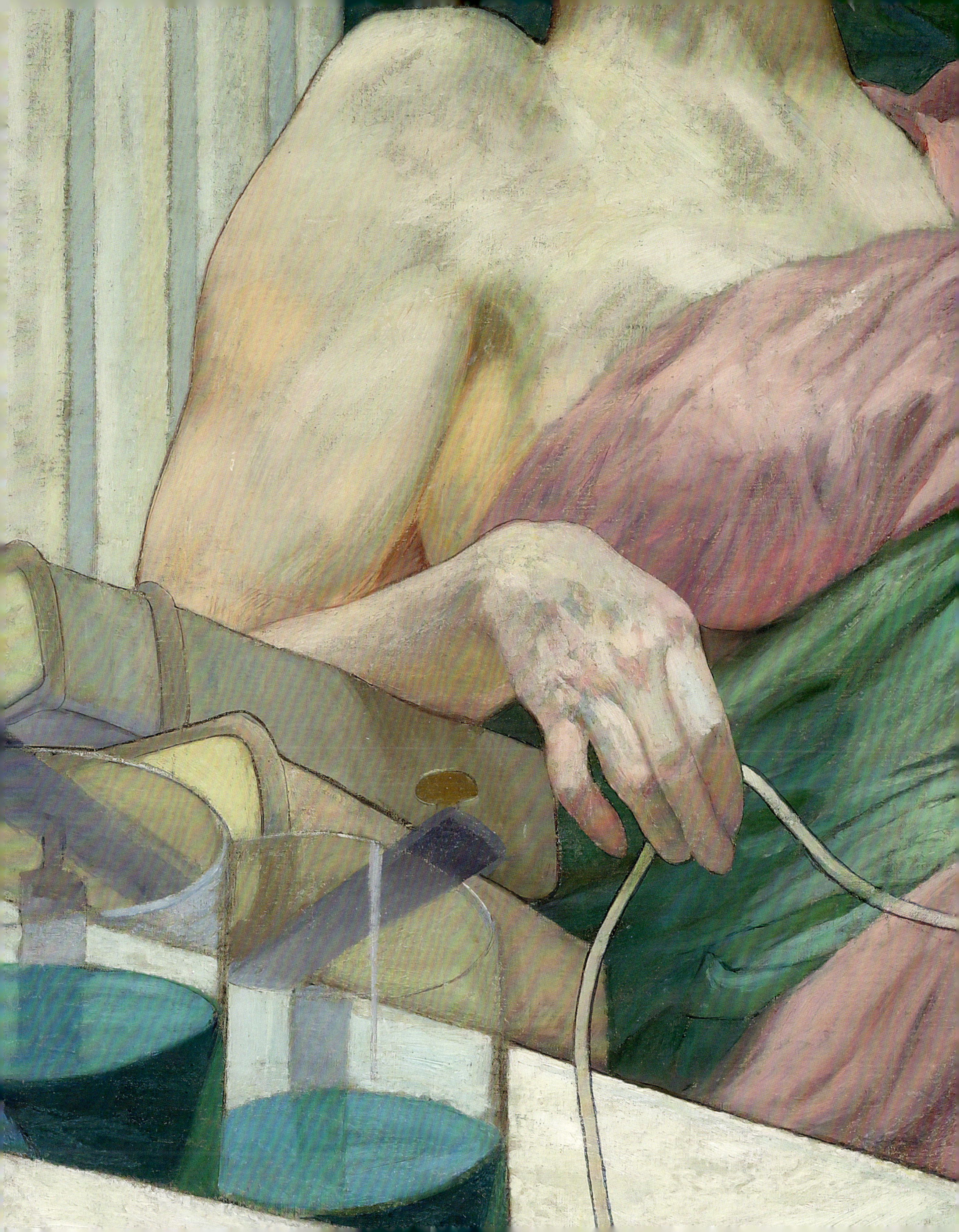

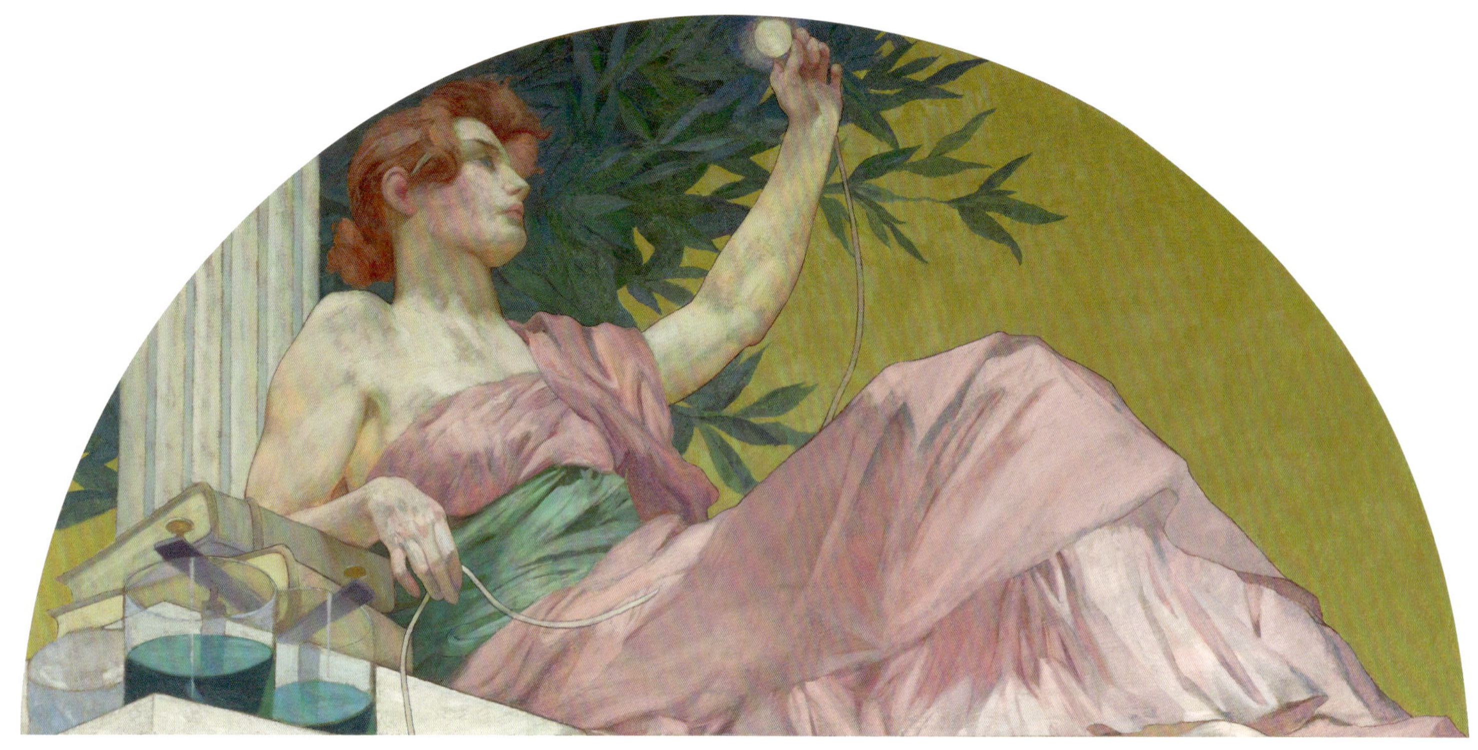

74

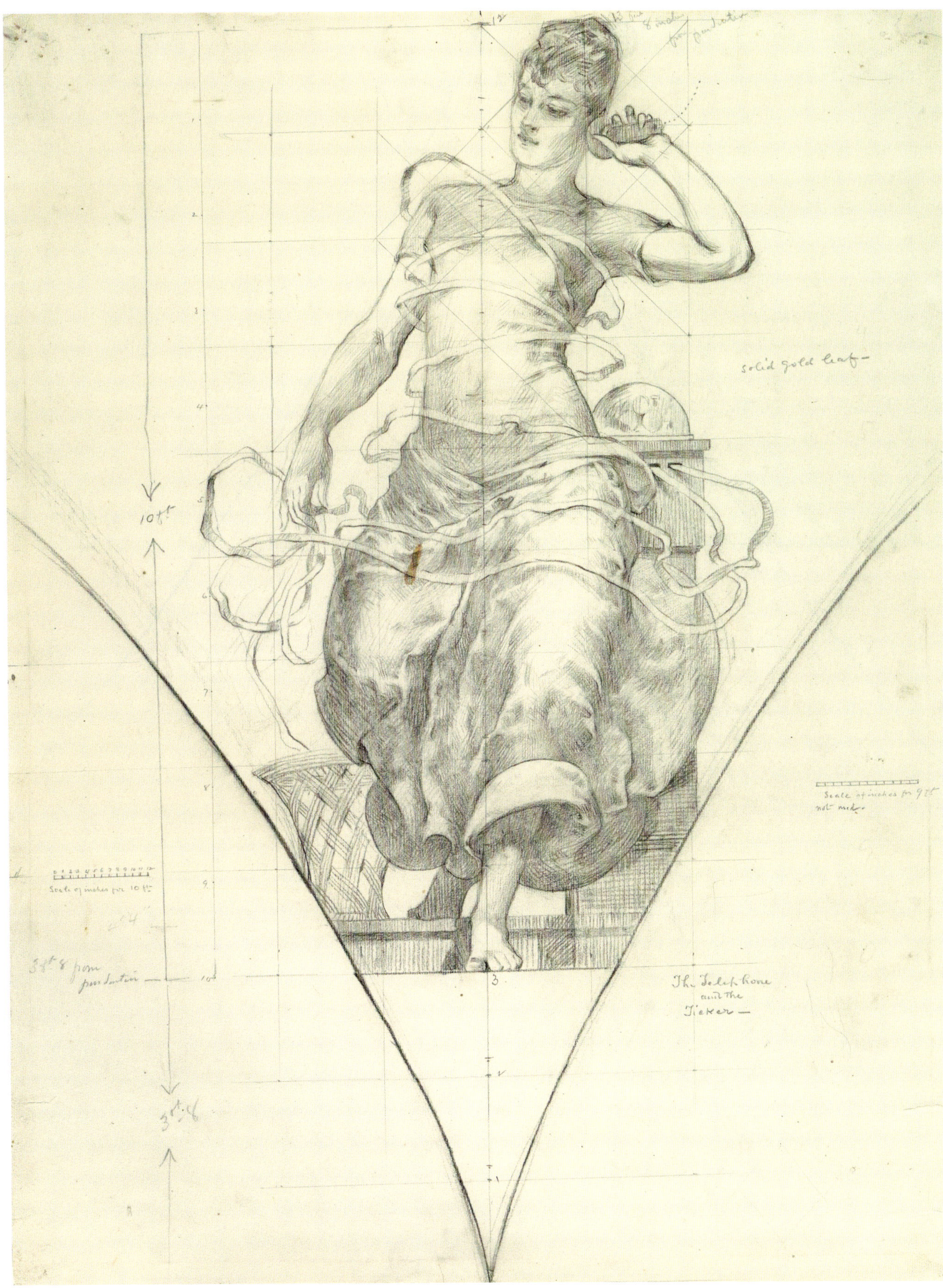

10 ft
solid gold leaf—
Scale of inches for 10 ft
The Telephone and the Ticker—

75

Science

In American civic spaces, including the Library of Congress, allegories of Science were most often aligned with the United States in emblematic surveys of Western civilization and intellectual tradition. In histories, however, the country's early nature was associated with religious liberty, either by escaping persecution in Europe or creating a new, more tolerant society, especially in Pennsylvania.

For the Pennsylvania State Capitol commission, Edwin Austin Abbey presented the origins of the nation in *The Spirit of Religious Liberty*, his central lunette for the rotunda, facing the main entrance. One of his adjacent roundels for the same space suggests a different emphasis than liberty. Science, fully veiled, presents its gifts, as seen in the oil study (cat. 76). Where the adjacent roundel for Religion is zealous and aggressive, Science is presented as mysterious and generous. This evolution placed the nation's rising power in the latter's hands.

Kenyon Cox's drawing (cat. 77) for the mural *Science Instructing Industry*, at Case Western Reserve University in Cleveland, also features the role of science in the country's identity. The clothed female allegory is lightly drawn, a prelude to her painted form in flowing white robes, which contrast with the mostly nude laborer, Industry, who is described more specifically. Science holds a book in her right hand and draws Industry to look into it. Industry reaches with his right hand, seemingly to touch the book of knowledge. The contrast in approach seems to mirror the figures' different natures—understanding and action.

In a separate costume study for the figure of Botany (cat. 78), which appears in *The Sciences* mural at the Library of Congress, Cox further demonstrates his capacity for descriptive detail, as seen in the embroidered dress. Here, too, he differentiates the elaborately patterned fabrics from the description of the body, which is almost entirely omitted.

CAT. 76 Edwin Austin Abbey (American, 1852–1911, HON. 1897)

Study for the *Science* Roundel in the Pennsylvania State Capitol, ca. 1902–8

Oil on canvas, 30 × 29¾ in. (76.2 × 75.6 cm)
Yale University Art Gallery, New Haven, Conn., Edwin Austin Abbey Memorial Collection, 1937.1817

CAT. 77 Kenyon Cox (American, 1856–1919)

Study for *Science Instructing Industry*, 1898

Graphite on off-white laid paper mounted on Egyptian linen, 14⅞ × 19 7/16 in. (37.8 × 49.4 cm)
The Metropolitan Museum of Art, New York, Francis Lathrop Fund, 1950, 50.101.2

CAT. 78 Kenyon Cox (American, 1856–1919)

Drapery Study for Botany in *The Sciences* in the Library of Congress, ca. 1896

Graphite on paper, 24 × 18 in. (61 × 45.7 cm)
Library of Congress, Washington, D.C.

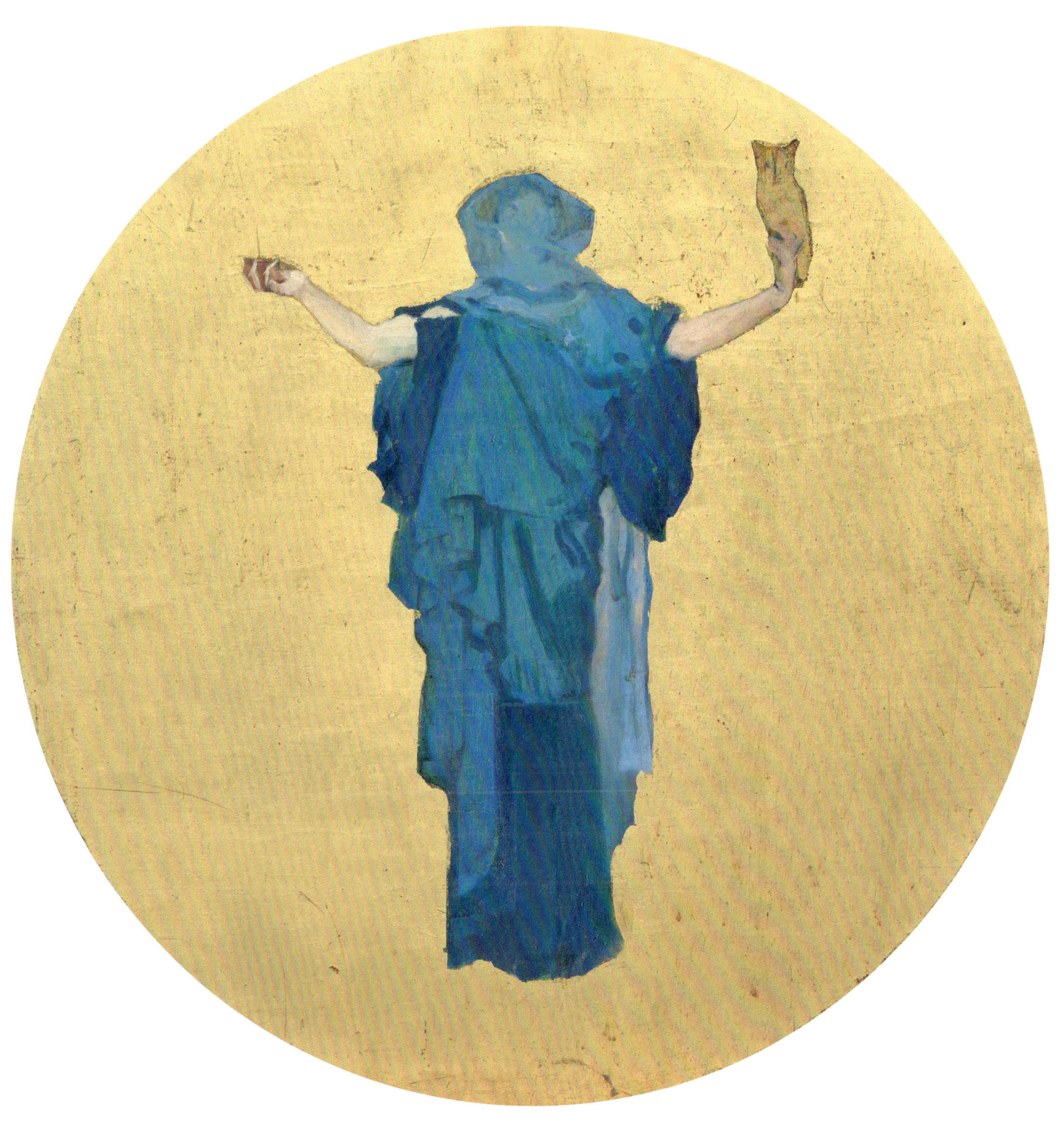

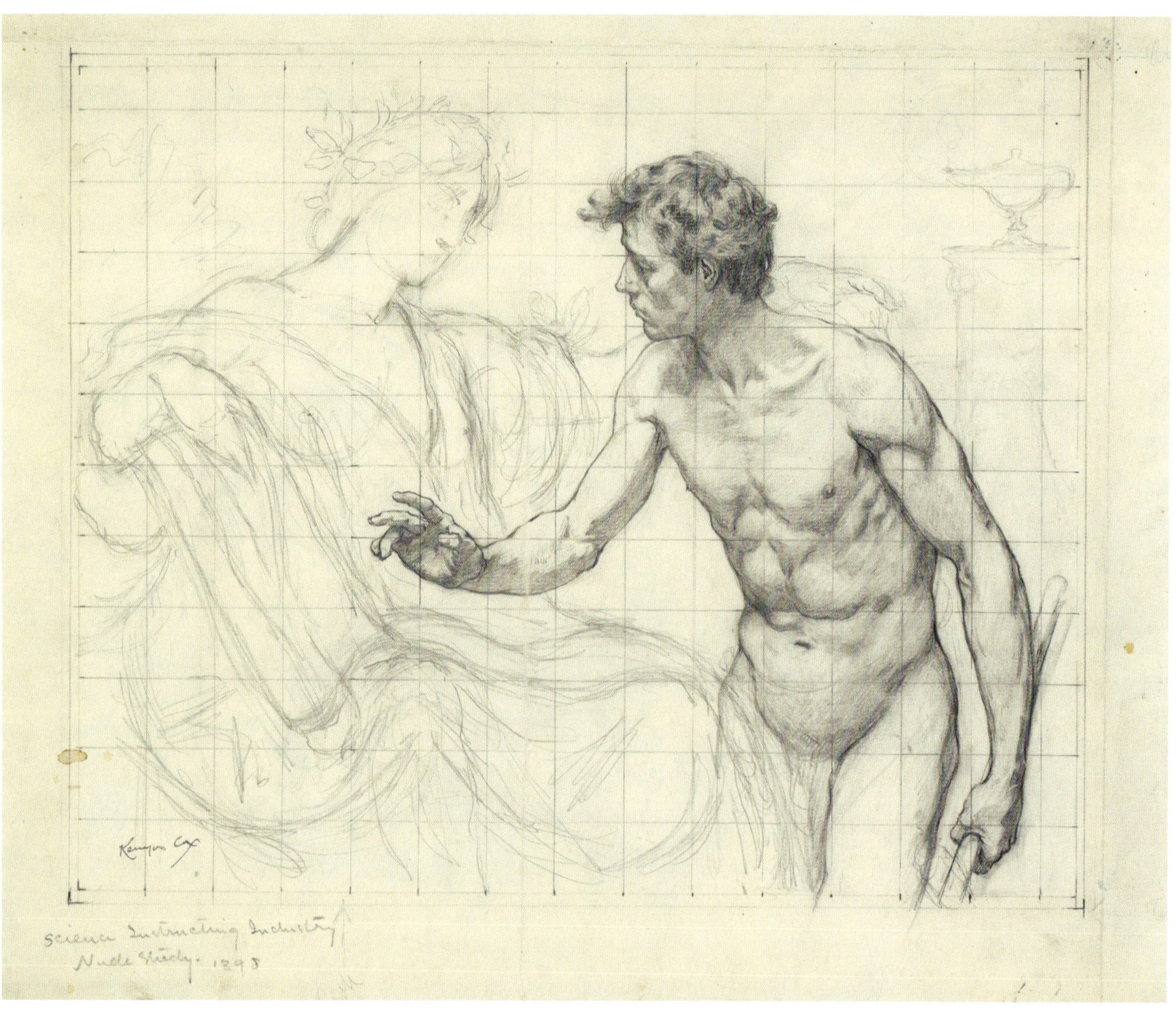

77

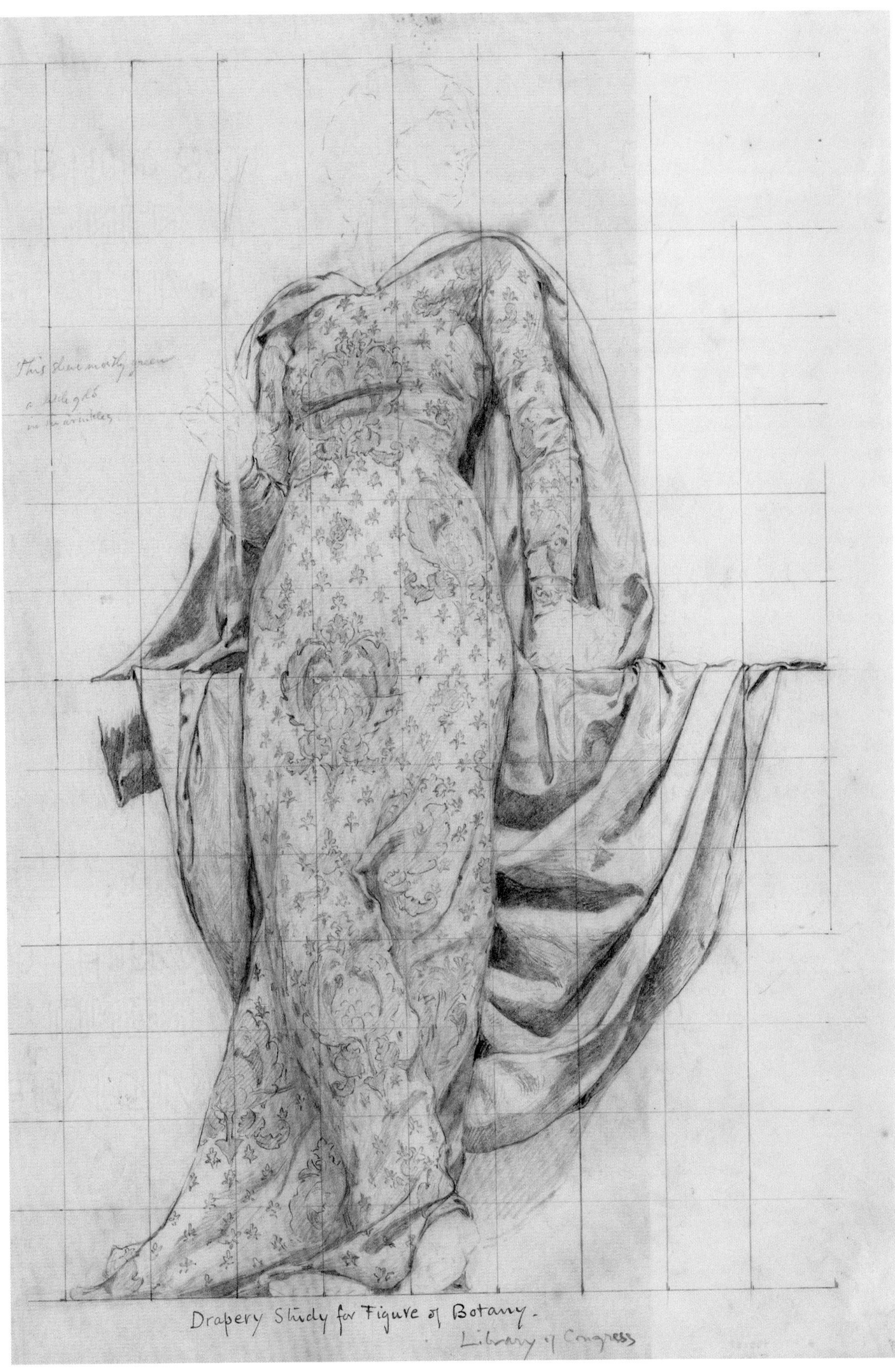
Drapery Study for Figure of Botany.
Library of Congress

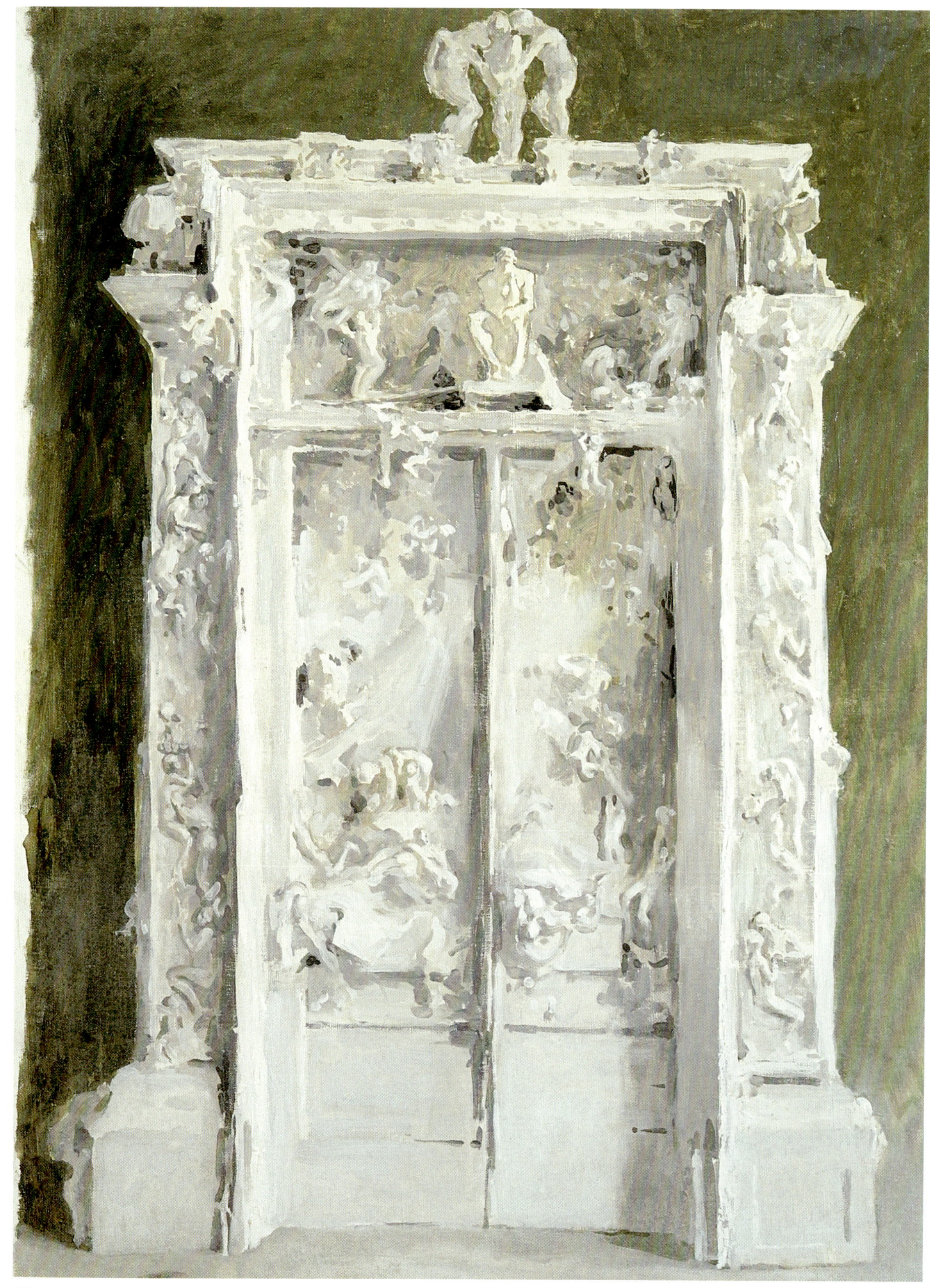

79

Style

American Renaissance painters and sculptors admired the sensualism of the French sculptor Auguste Rodin as well as the vitality of the New Sculpture movement in Britain. Rooted in the Italian Renaissance inspiration of Michelangelo, Rodin's romantic realism employed an appearance of incompletion to look both ways: to Renaissance humanism as well as modernist materialism. For American artists seeking a vibrant contemporary feeling, whether called modernist or not, Rodin and New Sculpture offered wellsprings.

Gari Melchers, when invited to illustrate an article on Rodin's career, devoted himself with astonishing concentration to painting the sculptor's celebrated *Gates of Hell*. Notoriously complicated and detailed in its many narrative anecdotes, Rodin's work is not easy to summarize visually, but Melchers attempted to record the massive plaster doors with a sense of active surface, every inch covered with figures, rather than minute detail. A study in the virtuosic play of light and shadow, Melchers's oil (cat. 79) is a remarkably concise characterization of the rich tactility of Rodin's unfinished work. Many American artists turned to Rodin for stylistic inspiration as they undertook projects that sought to feature a vital, expressive figure as the basis of their practice. Kenyon Cox's drawn figure of Science is one example (cat. 80), recasting Rodin's *Thinker* as a model for the pose of his own contemplative nude.

Rodin continued to influence American artists throughout the American Renaissance, including at its end. The Italian immigrant sculptor Onorio

CAT. 79 Gari Melchers (American, 1860–1932)
Study after Auguste Rodin's *Gates of Hell*, ca. 1895
Oil on canvas, 25¾ × 21⅜ in. (65.4 × 54.3 cm)
Gari Melchers Home and Studio at the University of Mary Washington, Va., 1942.1.1342

CAT. 80 Kenyon Cox (American, 1856–1919)
Study for Science in *The Progress of Civilization* in the Iowa State Capitol, 1905
Graphite on laid paper, 15 15/16 × 11 3/16 in. (40.5 × 28.4 cm)
National Gallery of Art, Washington, D.C., John Davis Hatch Collection, 1979.20.21

CAT. 81 Onorio Ruotolo (American, born Italy, 1888–1966)
The Doomed, 1917
Painted plaster, 28¾ × 8½ in. (73 × 21.6 cm)
Cantor Arts Center at Stanford University, Calif., Gift of Lucio and Marcia Ruotolo, 1996.67

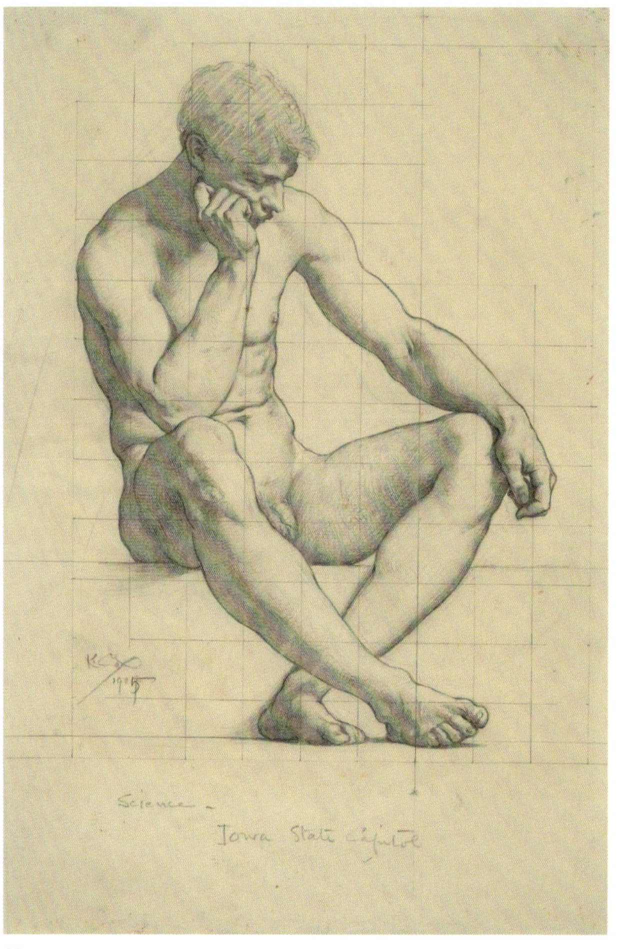

80

Ruotolo carried forward Rodin's expressive humanism to the threshold of the next phase of American modernism, when essentialization became the focus of sculptors, who distilled ideas and stripped them of unnecessary detail. Ruotolo's plaster sculpture titled *The Doomed* (cat. 81) records the artist's seriousness and intensity of engagement with the expressive body, pointing to a different path for modernist sculpture than the one that followed. The subject was capital punishment, a practice Ruotolo condemned. Convinced of the inhumanity of the death penalty, he created *The Doomed* as an act of defiance, intending it to one day stand at the site of the death chamber at Sing Sing prison in New York when the practice was finally abandoned, an outcome he viewed as an inevitability. Rodin's expressive practice provided Ruotolo with a model for portraying the ineffable: the lost hope and humanity of the condemned. His powerful distillation and moral clarity promised the beginnings of a new phase of activist civic art that did not follow, disrupted by World War I.

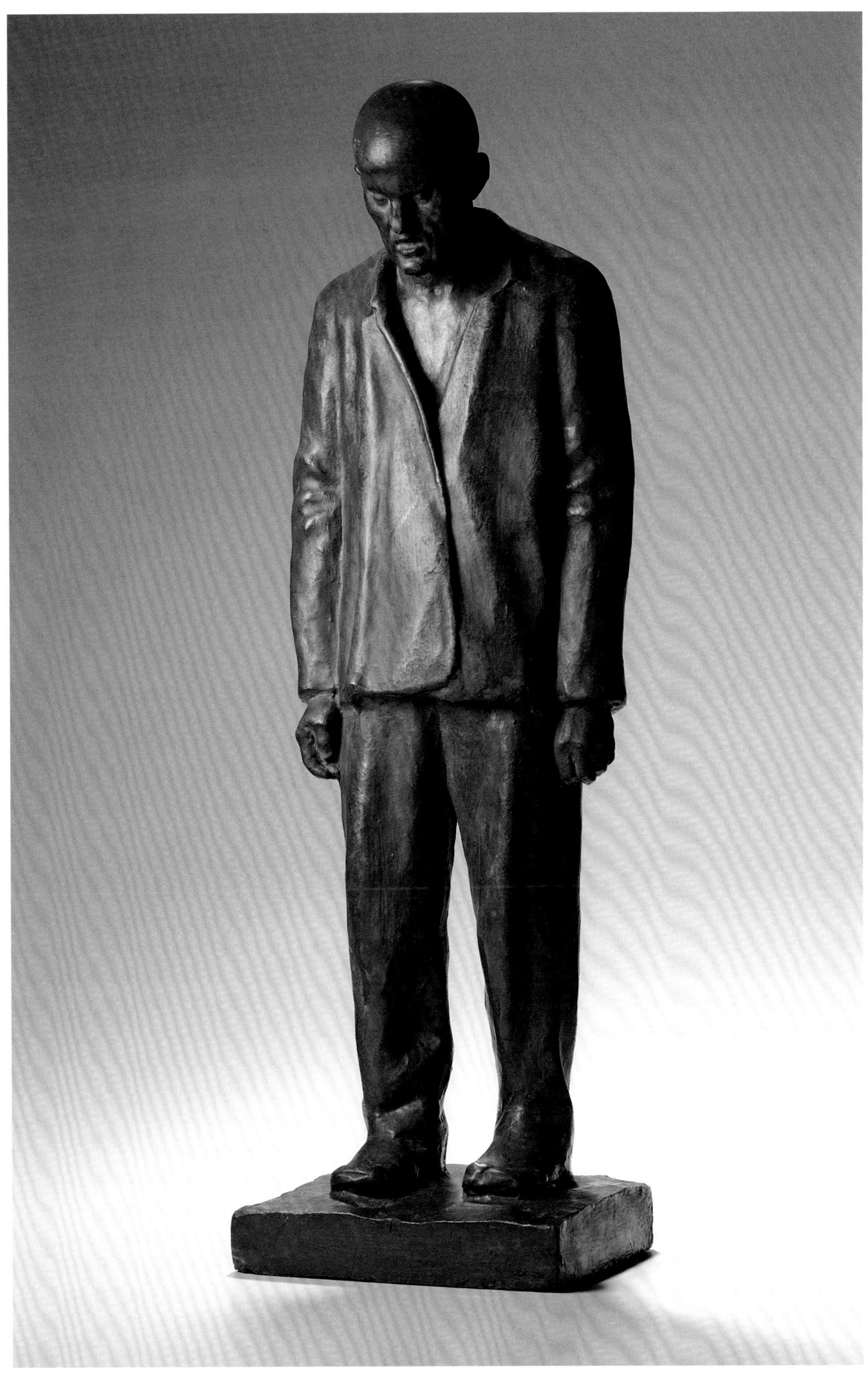

Pain

Of the array of physical and mental states explored by artists of the American Renaissance, pain is perhaps the most visually distinct. Awkward poses interrupt fluid visual movement through a composition and enforce lingering attention. Pain has a lasting effect and results in some of the most enduring visual impressions in murals of this period. Contorting the body into unnatural configurations invokes sympathetic discomfort in the viewer, creating disproportionate engagement. Such controlled disruption is a modern tool in the sense of managing the viewer's eye and attention by stimulating psychological response.

John Singer Sargent's lunette *Hell* for the Boston Public Library contains more misery than most. It draws on a long iconographic tradition of portraying hell, including works by such artists as Michelangelo and Rodin, as a writhing mass of tortured bodies. Recent attention to Sargent's charcoal drawings has concentrated on the luxuriant representations of his nudes, but his depictions of violence point to another dynamic. The screaming man at the center of an oil study for the Boston lunette (cat. 82) portrays muscular tension and discomfort through his facial expression and twisting hands. The tortured soul's expressive response to pain is a different type from Sargent's charcoal drawings, which show a broader expressive range.

CAT. 82 John Singer Sargent (American, born Italy, 1856–1925, LL.D. 1916)

Study for *Hell* in *The Triumph of Religion* in the Boston Public Library, ca. 1909–14

Oil on canvas, 33¼ × 66¼ in. (84.5 × 168.3 cm)
Smith College Museum of Art, Northampton, Mass., Gift of Mrs. Dwight W. Morrow (Elizabeth Cutter, class of 1896), 1932.14.1

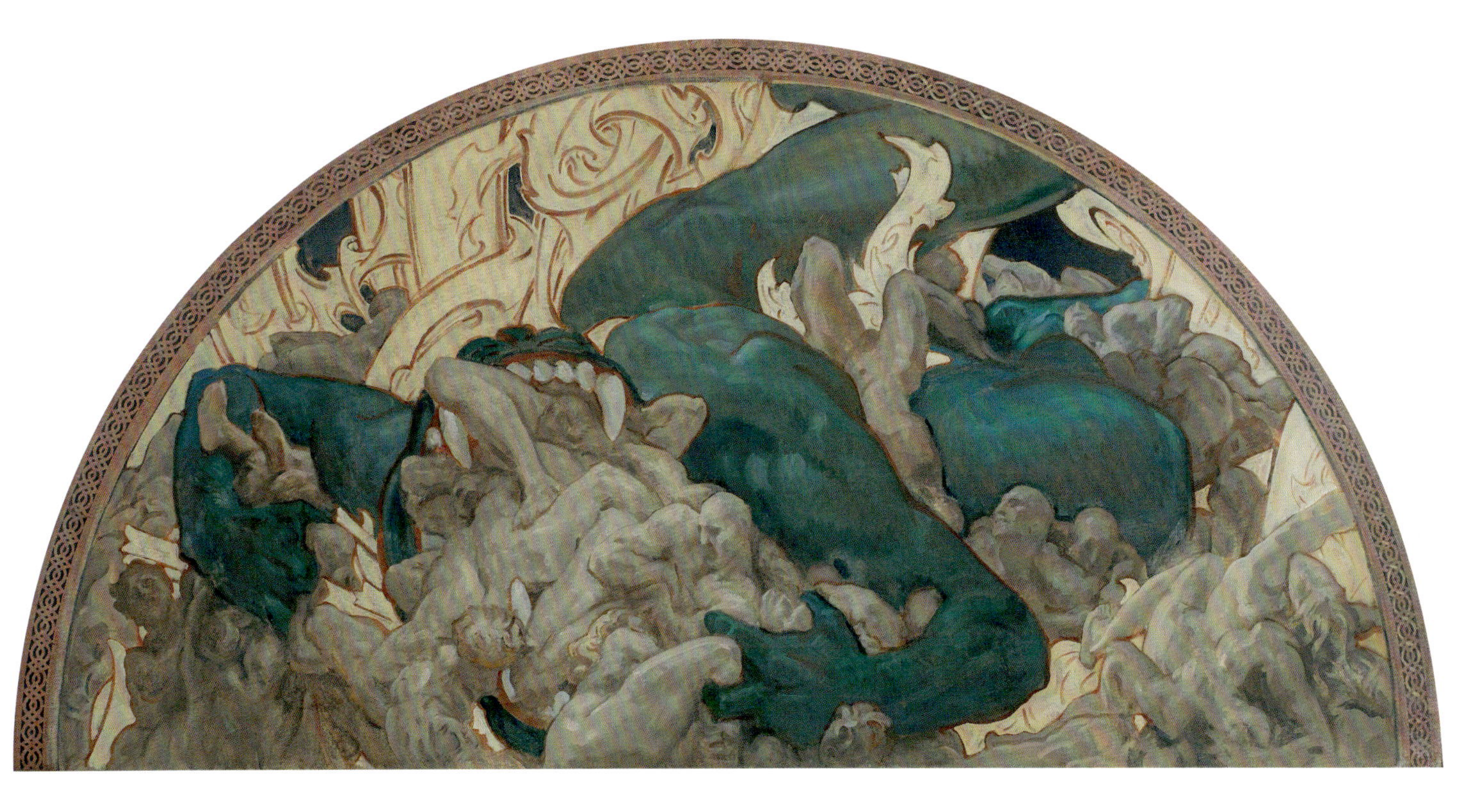

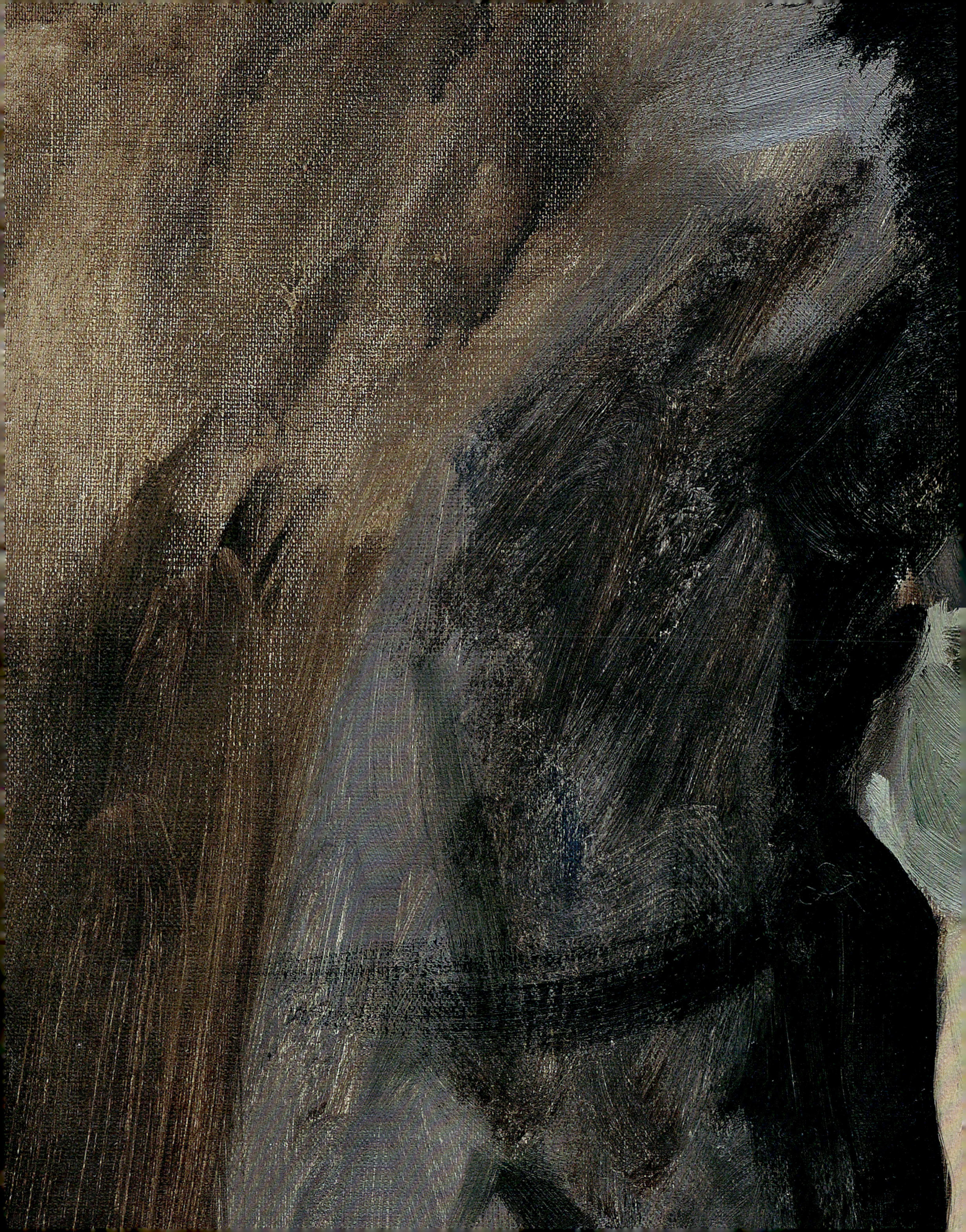

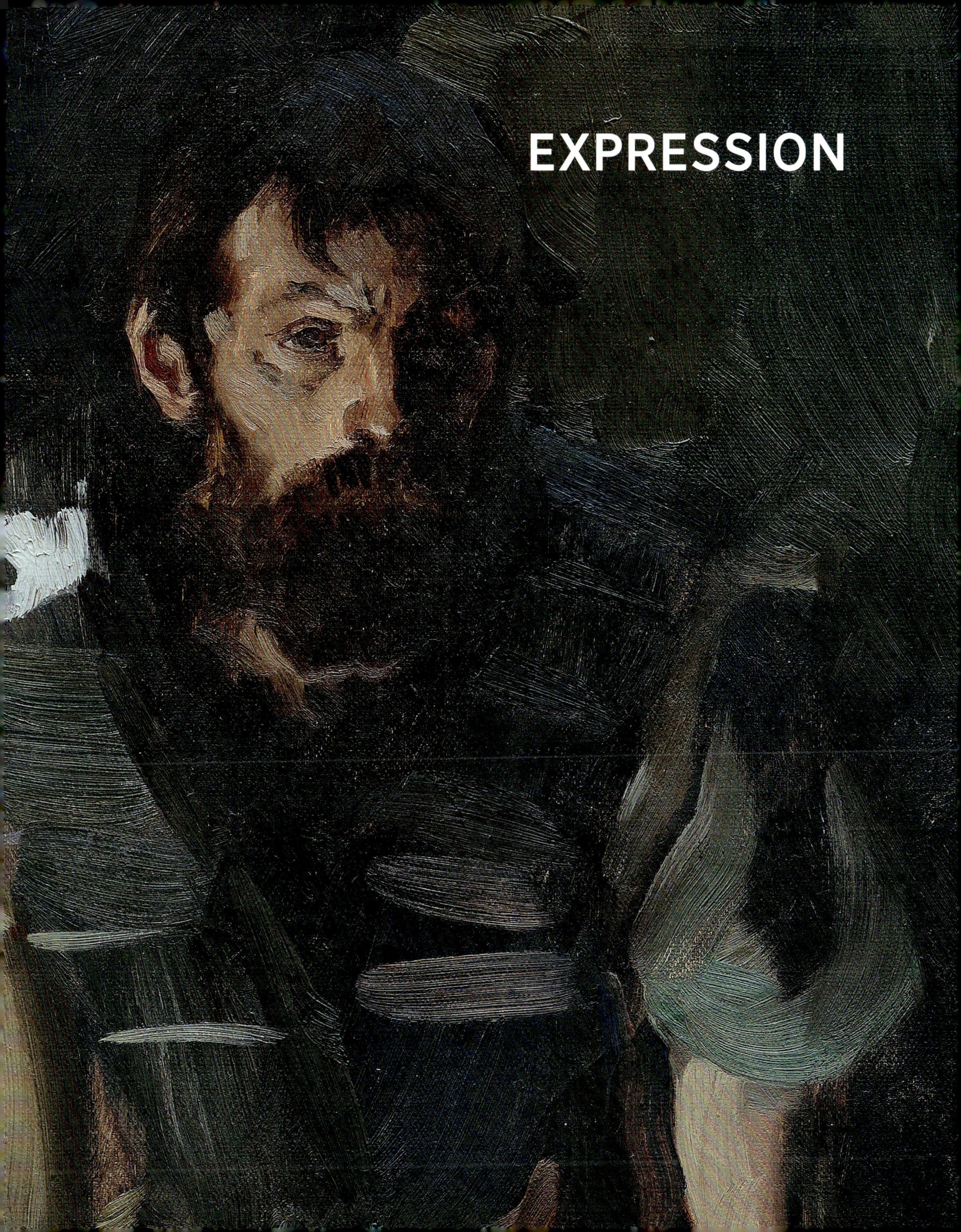

EXPRESSION

THE LIFE-SIZE FIGURE THAT AUGUSTUS SAINT-GAUDENS created in memory of Marian "Clover" Hooper Adams for Rock Creek Cemetery in Washington, D.C., is lost in contemplation. Responding to Rodin's nude *Thinker*, Saint-Gaudens's monument is at once more intimate and more evocative. The Adams Memorial translates the visceral physical engagement with media found in artists' studies to full, life size (cat. 83). Set in a cemetery, the original sculpture presides over a quiet, secluded enclosure designed by architect Stanford White, a friend of both Saint-Gaudens and the grieving widower Henry Adams. It is a space of private meditation and reflection rather than public presentation, a notable and widely admired change of register shaped by the circumstances of Clover Adams's death by suicide. The weighty robes shroud the figure's thoughts as well as its body, creating mystery—not so much an allegory as an emblem of inner life. In the presence of the quiet, unknowable figure, mourners and visitors are invited to consider their own thoughts, feelings, and existence rather than the life of a single individual. Even the sex of this silent interlocutor is opaque—or simply irrelevant, part of a universal human experience.

Saint-Gaudens's veiled form contrasts sharply with the outward representation of human emotion in Edwin Austin Abbey's study for the three Marys grieving Jesus (cat. 84). Also veiled, Abbey's figure bites her robe in anguish; her features and hand, ghostly white, are a powerful contrast. The simplicity of Abbey's composition renders the figure's expression more emphatic by concentrating focus on her face. The tactility of the media, set against a dark sheet of paper, adds a rich velvet depth to the shadows, similar to the contemporaneous work of Franz von Stuck, Arnold Böcklin, and other European Symbolists. The contrast between Abbey's intense emotion and Saint-Gaudens's withdrawal invites reflection about the meaning of the human figure in this period, when amplified feeling and its absence each contributed meaningfully to the body's range and resonance as a motif.

CAT. 83 Augustus Saint-Gaudens (American, born Ireland, 1848–1907, HON. 1905)

Adams Memorial, modeled 1886–91, cast 1969

Bronze, 69⅞ × 39⅞ × 44½ in. (177.4 × 101.4 × 112.9 cm)
Smithsonian American Art Museum, Washington, D.C., Museum purchase, 1970.11

CAT. 84 Edwin Austin Abbey (American, 1852–1911, HON. 1897)

Study for Mary, the Wife of Cleophas, for *The Three Marys*, ca. 1906–10

Charcoal heightened with white and orange chalk on dark gray-green paper, 28½ × 22 15/16 in. (72.4 × 58.3 cm)
Yale University Art Gallery, New Haven, Conn., Edwin Austin Abbey Memorial Collection, 1937.2886

Detail of cat. 84

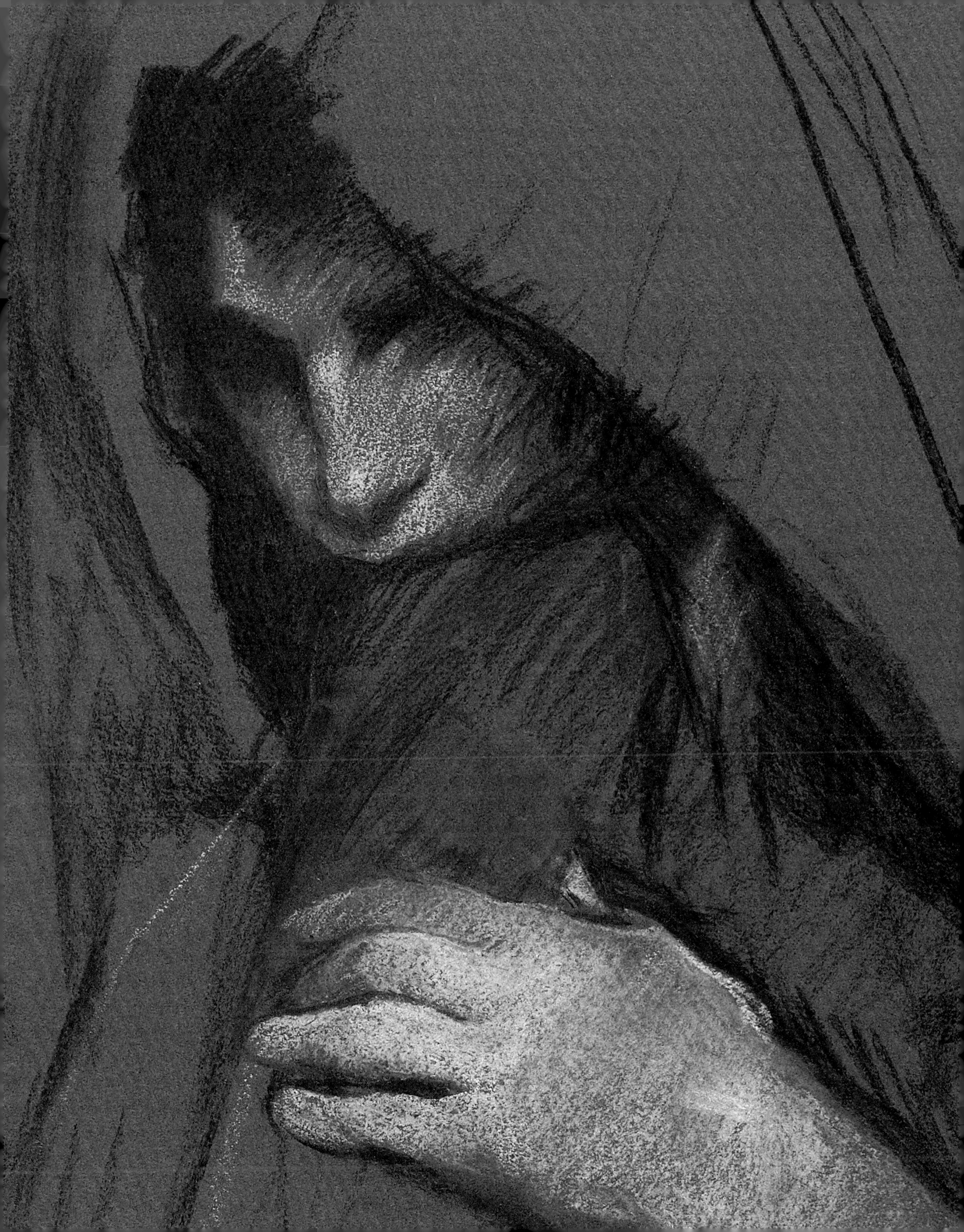

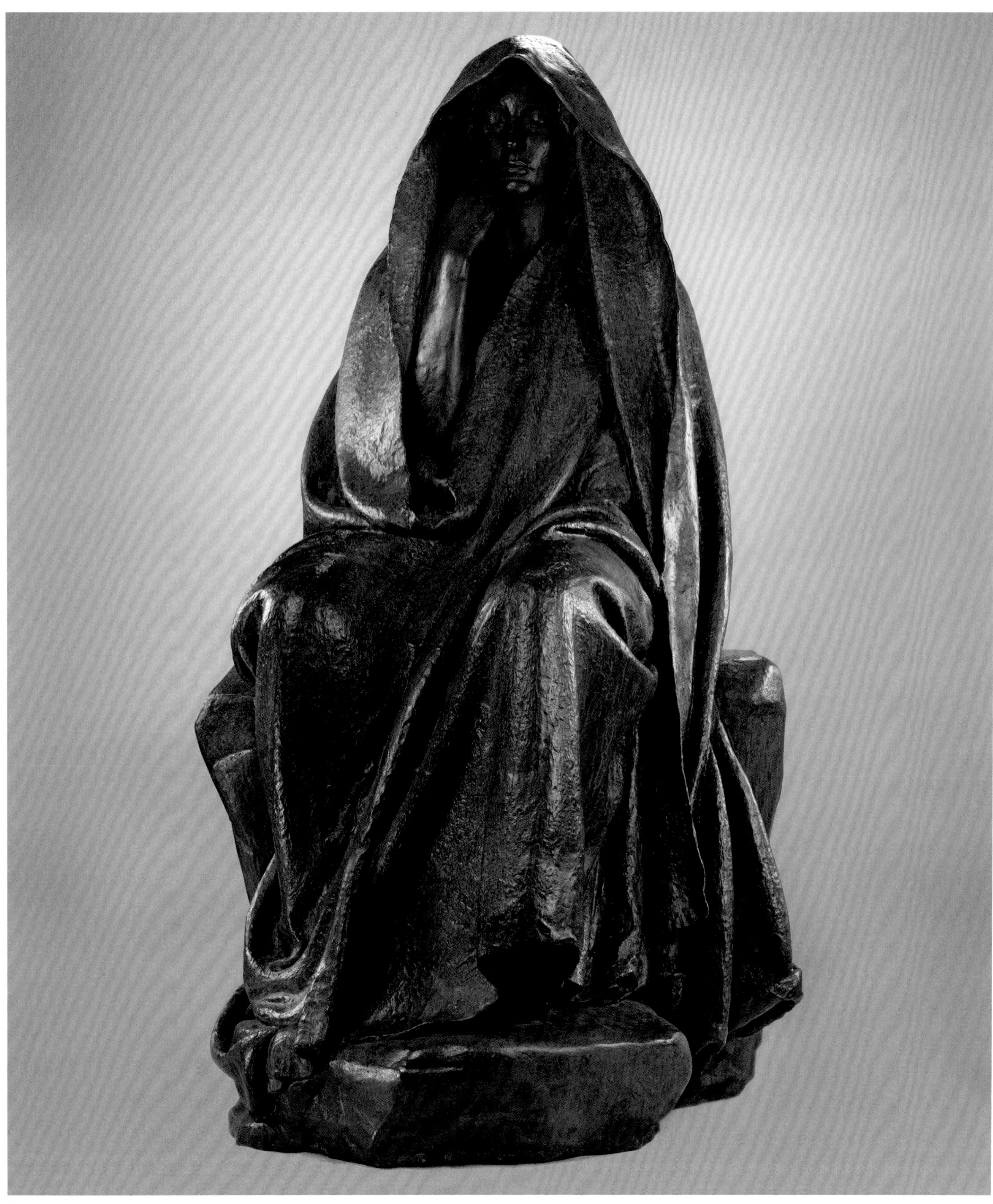

83

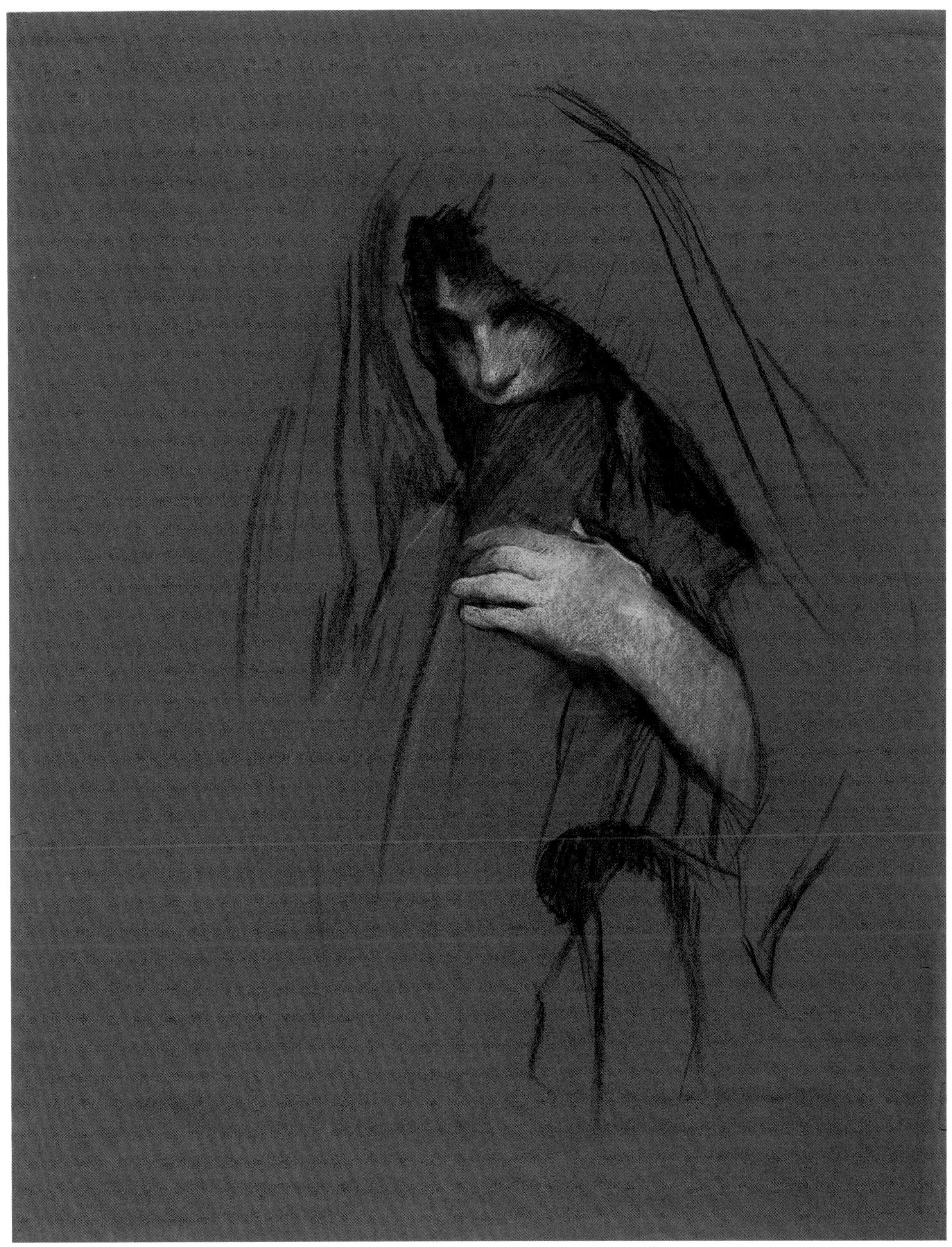

84

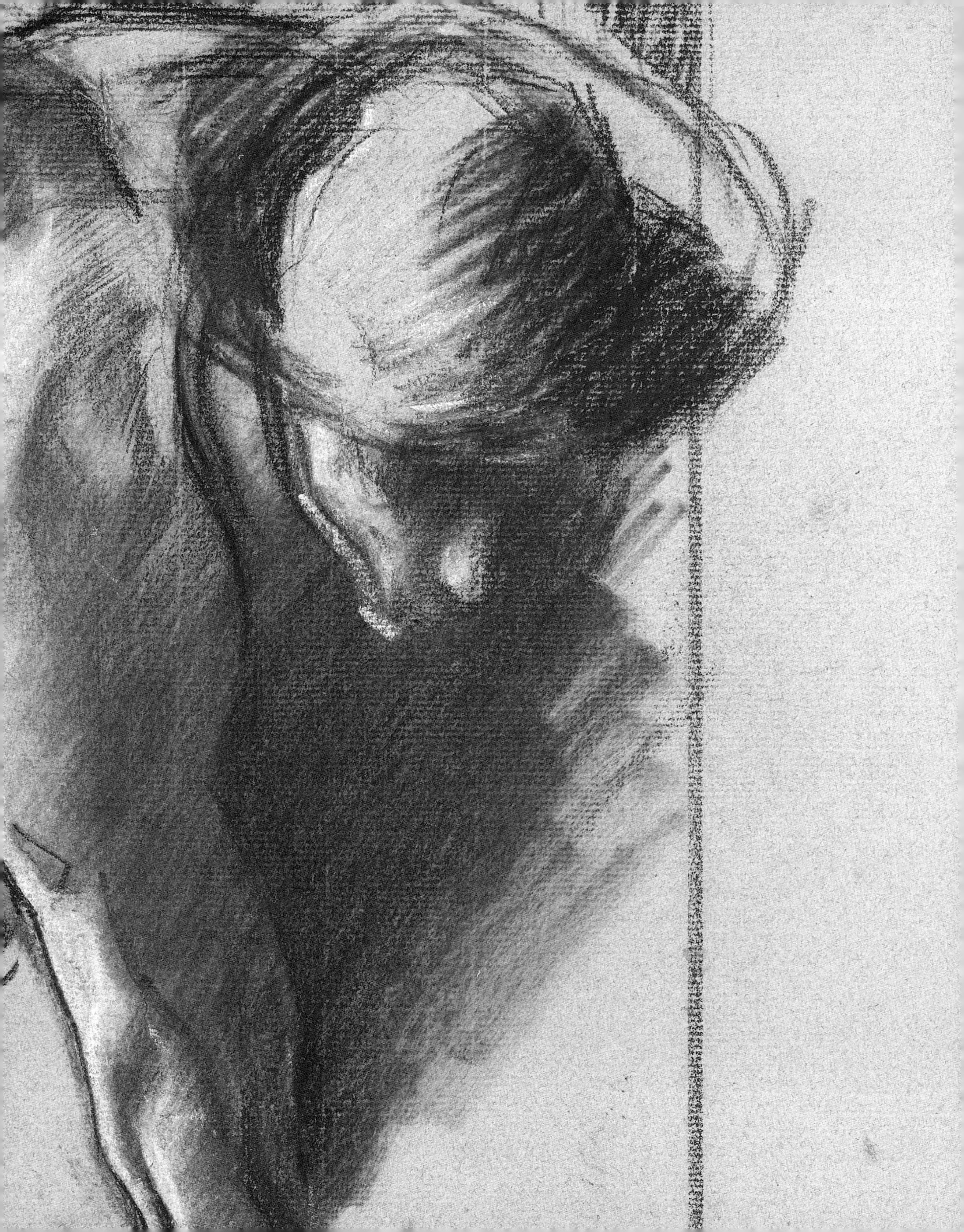

Void

Isolated from their broader company, Edwin Austin Abbey's individual figure studies at times adopt a remarkably self-absorbed emotional aspect, comparable to Saint-Gaudens's Adams Memorial (see cat. 83). Alongside Abbey's incorporation of dark spaces and voids, the studies fall into introspection, even in the midst of active movement. The remarkable power of the miner in his drawing for the mural *Science Revealing the Treasures of the Earth* in the Pennsylvania State Capitol is multidimensional (cat. 85). The abruptness of its angles and bent knee resemble Sargent's screaming man in his *Hell* lunette for the Boston Public Library, but the rich blackness beneath Abbey's figure has an exaggerated intensity. It is insistent and complete as a void, drawing the viewer's eye into its depth and space outside the body.

Similarly, the expression of disorientation and fear on the face of the kneeling knight (cat. 86), perhaps related to Abbey's *Holy Grail* murals for the Boston Public Library, creates a psychologically resonant space. The figure's extended white arms appear skeletal, contrasting starkly with the darkened interior. His pose is inscrutable, as is his expression directed outward, but their intensity engages the viewer and, absent other narrative details, invites speculation about the wider context. These figures balance narrative gesture and storytelling with expressive power and emotive resonance, as the artist elicits viewer engagement through his evocative spaces and symbolic subjects.

The American Renaissance witnessed growth in the study of human psychology, notably by William James, whose brother Henry was a close friend of Abbey's, as well as psychoanalysis in the work of Sigmund Freud. The power of Abbey's figure studies to engage feeling, using such formal devices as shadowed voids and archetypal forms that resonate with common human experience, increasingly engages viewers with symbols, rather than stories.

CAT. 85 Edwin Austin Abbey (American, 1852–1911, HON. 1897)

Study of a Miner for *Science Revealing the Treasures of the Earth* in the Pennsylvania State Capitol, 1904

Charcoal and chalk on gray paper, 19 × 24⅝ in. (48.3 × 62.5 cm)
Yale University Art Gallery, New Haven, Conn., Edwin Austin Abbey Memorial Collection, 1937.1444

CAT. 86 Edwin Austin Abbey (American, 1852–1911, HON. 1897)

Figure Study, possibly for *The Quest and Achievement of the Holy Grail* in the Boston Public Library, ca. 1895

Oil on canvas, 25¾ × 21½ in. (65.4 × 54.6 cm)
Yale University Art Gallery, New Haven, Conn., Edwin Austin Abbey Memorial Collection, 1937.2502

Detail of cat. 85

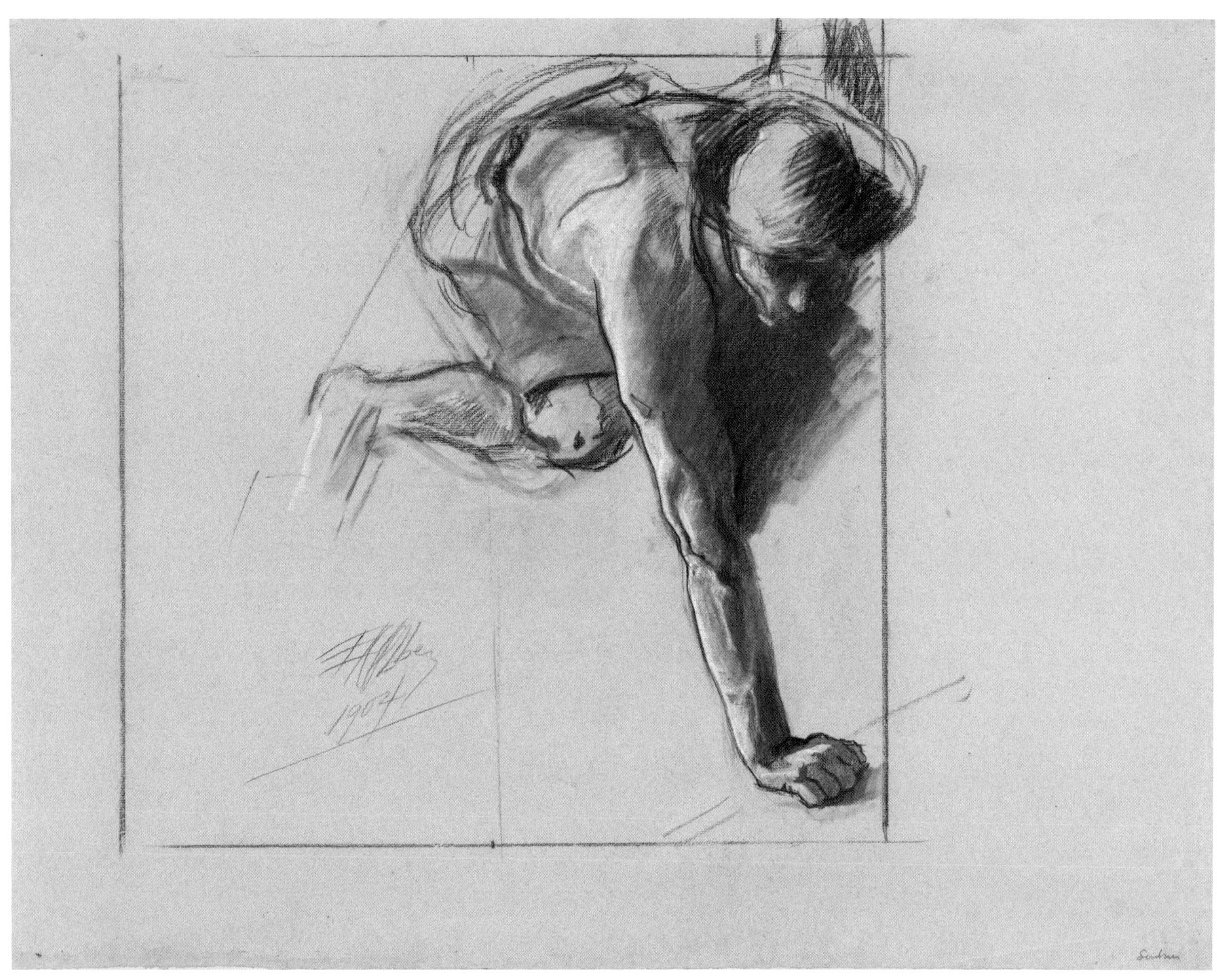

85

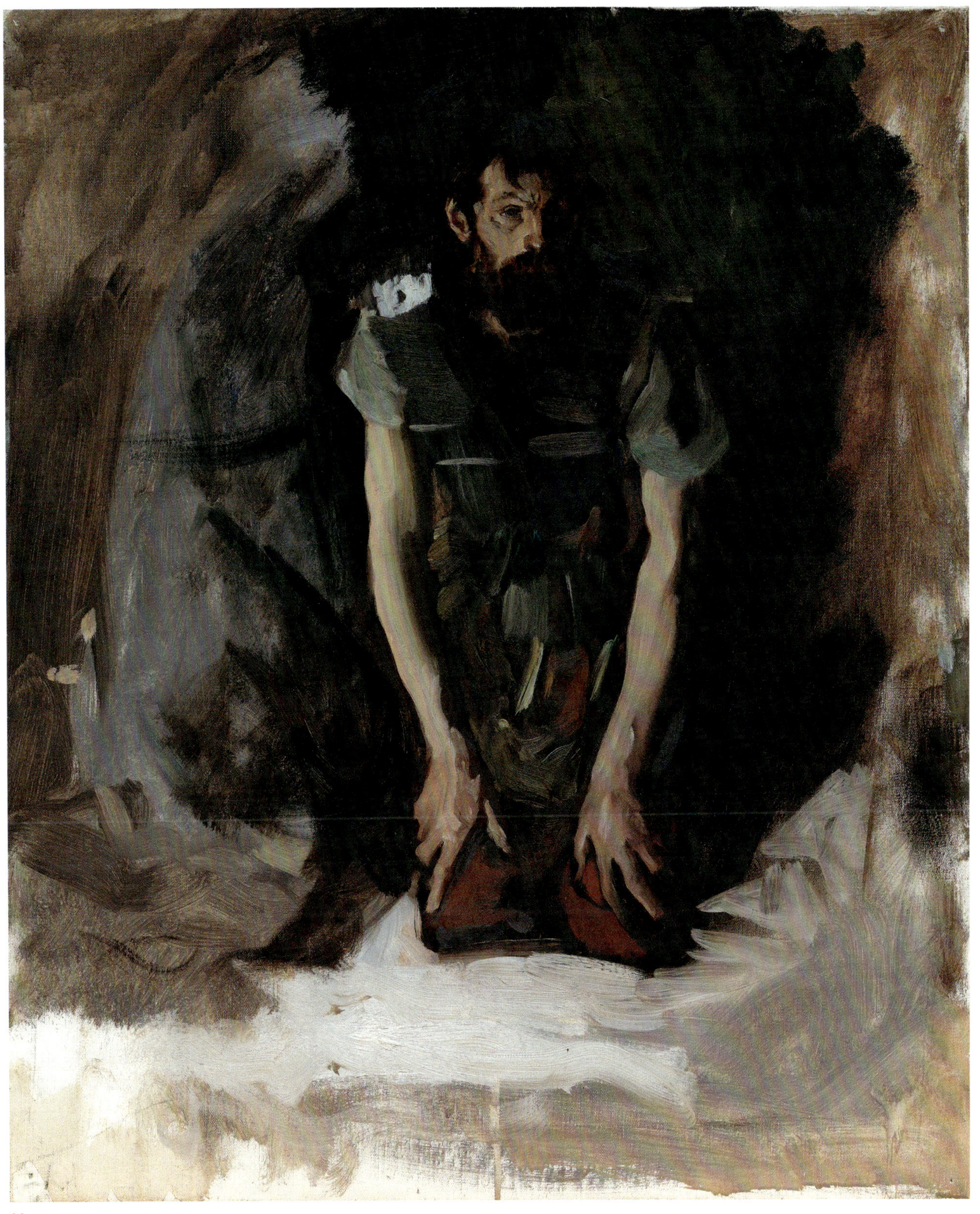

86

Intensity

In these two drawings, the artists amplify feeling to center the viewer's attention, not unlike using a subject's physical pain to disrupt visual movement. Rather than addressing viewers or confronting them, however, the figures turn away and conceal themselves within closed forms. The shame felt by Gari Melchers's nude (cat. 87) induces her to clutch her face and leg and shrink away. Her gesture, nudity, and defenselessness are compounded by the artist's contours and densely rubbed shadows. Distinct in style as well as subject from Melchers's normal practice, the drawing presents an abbreviated shorthand that is as agitated as the figure and seems to complement her mental state.

Violet Oakley's drawing (cat. 88) is more consistent with the fluidity of her wider practice. The woman's expression is less legible, but her closed eyes and gathered hands that touch her face create an impression of reassurance. The abbreviated *japoniste* character of her robe focuses attention on the more detailed, defined, and controlled area around the face, haloed by rich black hair. The blousing robe buffers the head, seeming to shelter it protectively. Both studies conform style to the sitter's psychological state, creating an expressive complement that describes a world of emotion.

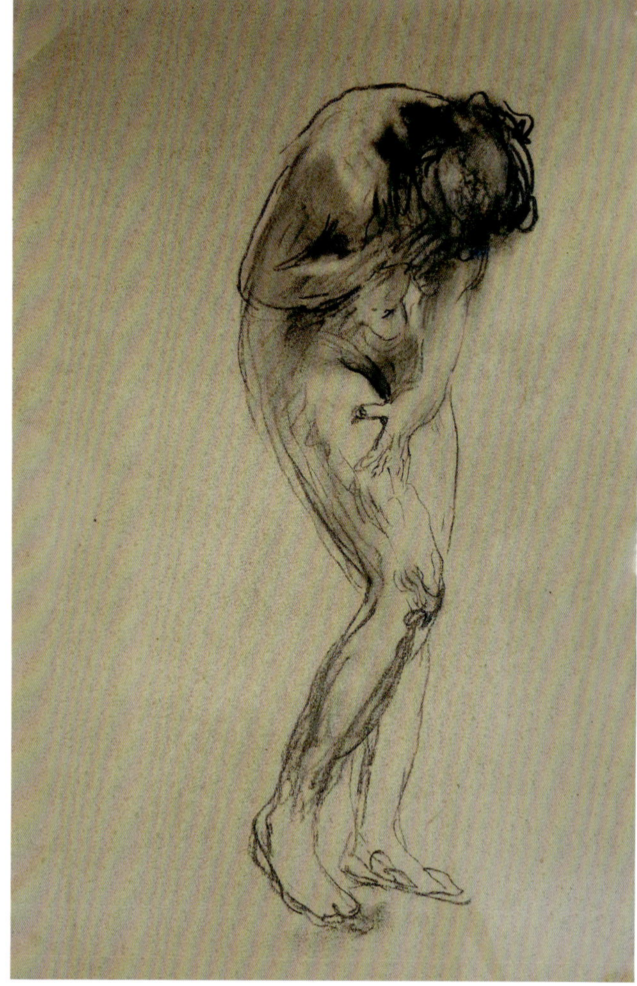

87

CAT. 87 Gari Melchers (American, 1860–1932)

Nude, n.d.

Charcoal on paper, 18 × 12 in. (45.7 × 30.5 cm)
Gari Melchers Home and Studio at the University of Mary Washington, Va., 1942.1.0002

CAT. 88 Violet Oakley (American, 1874–1961)

Figure Study of a Woman, n.d.

Graphite on paper, 16 × 10 in. (40.6 × 25.4 cm)
Pennsylvania Capitol Preservation Committee, Harrisburg, 82.78.245

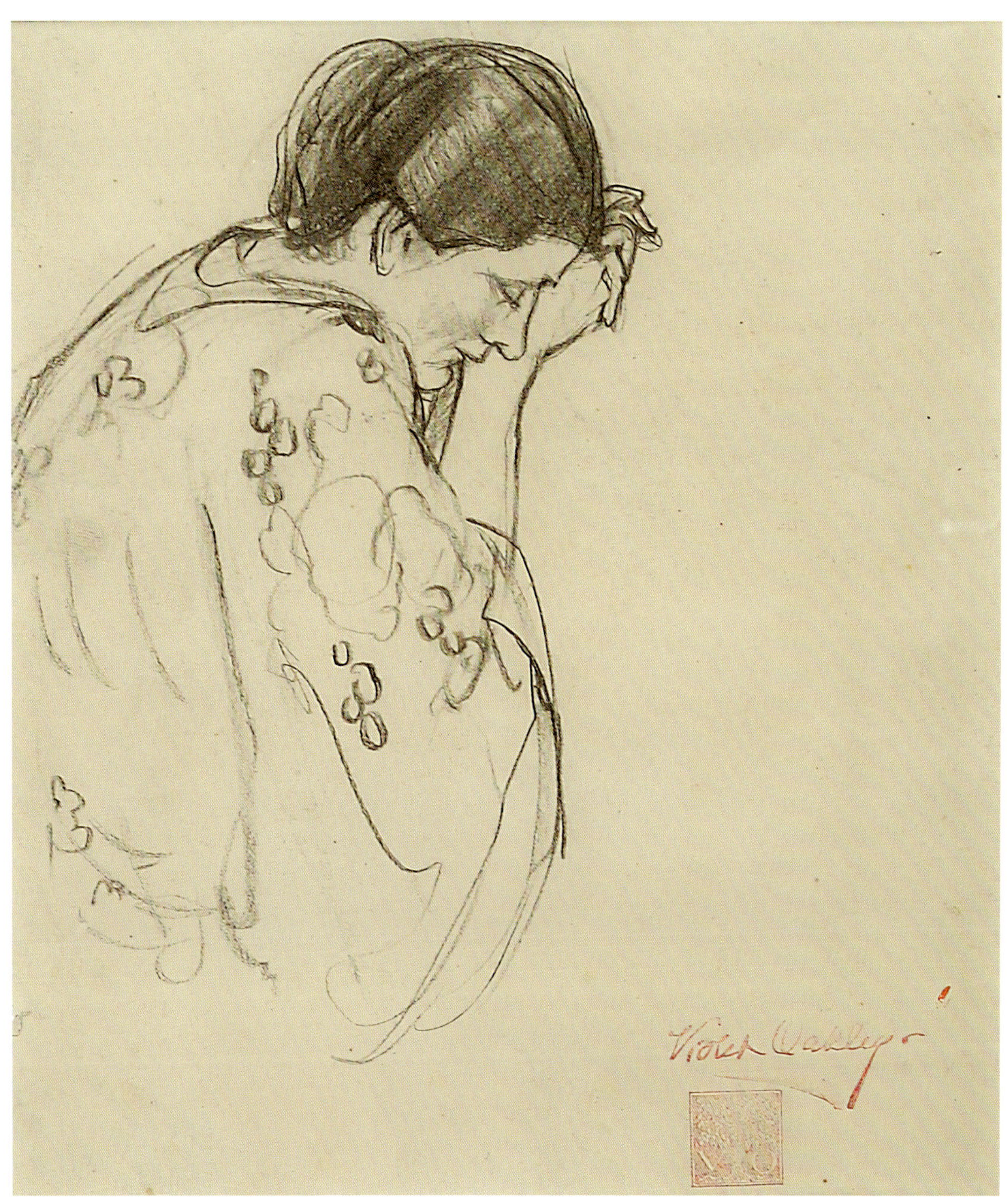

88

PAGES 234–35: The Senate chamber in the Pennsylvania State Capitol, showing Violet Oakley's murals

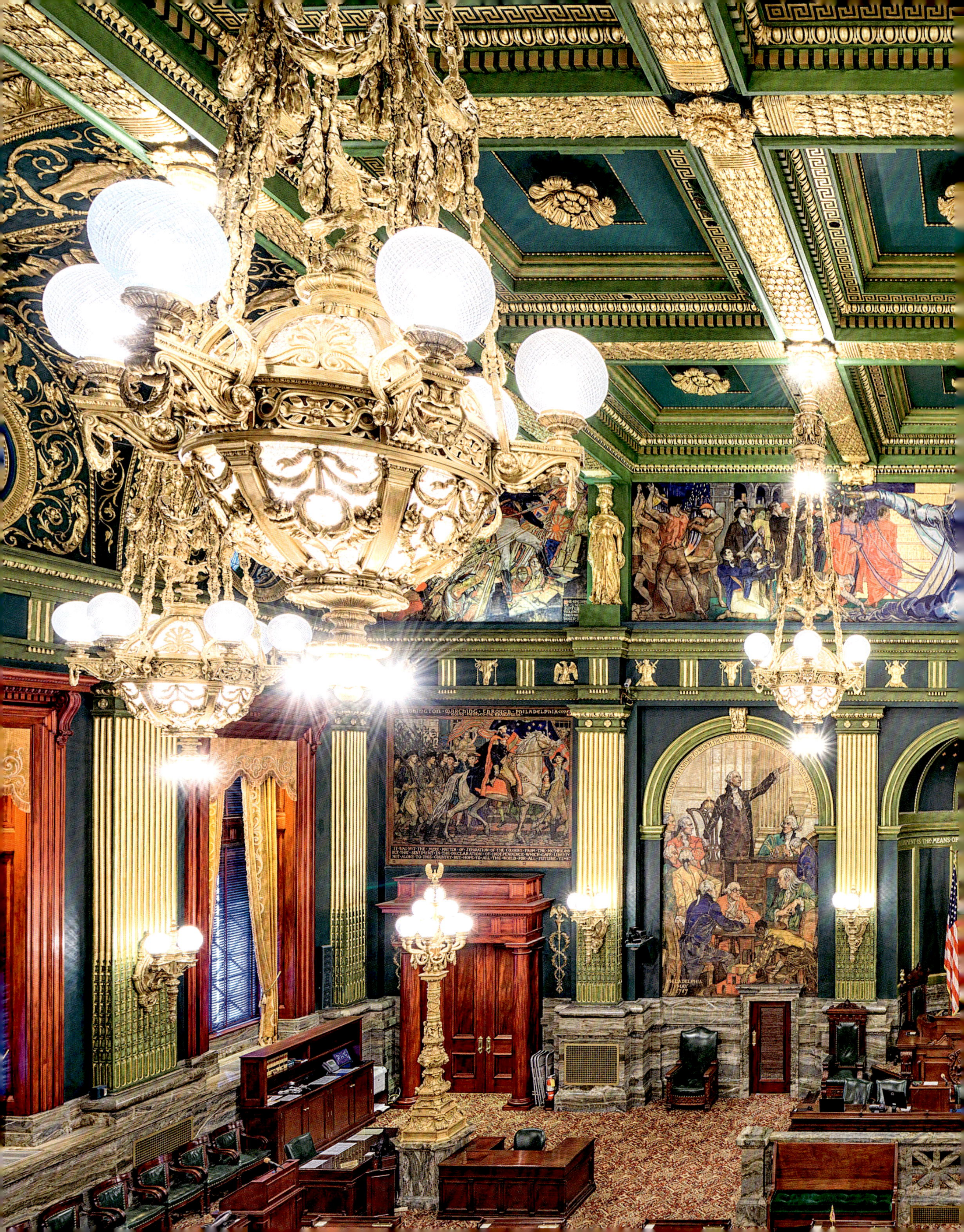
MARCHING · THROUGH · PHILADELPHIA
IT · WAS · NOT · THE · MERE · MATTER · OF · SEPARATION · OF · THE · COLONIES · FROM · THE · MOTHERLAND
BUT · THAT · SENTIMENT · IN · THE · DECLARATION · OF · INDEPENDENCE · WHICH · GAVE · LIBERTY
NOT · ALONE · TO · THIS · COUNTRY · BUT · HOPE · TO · ALL · THE · WORLD · FOR · ALL · FUTURE · TIME

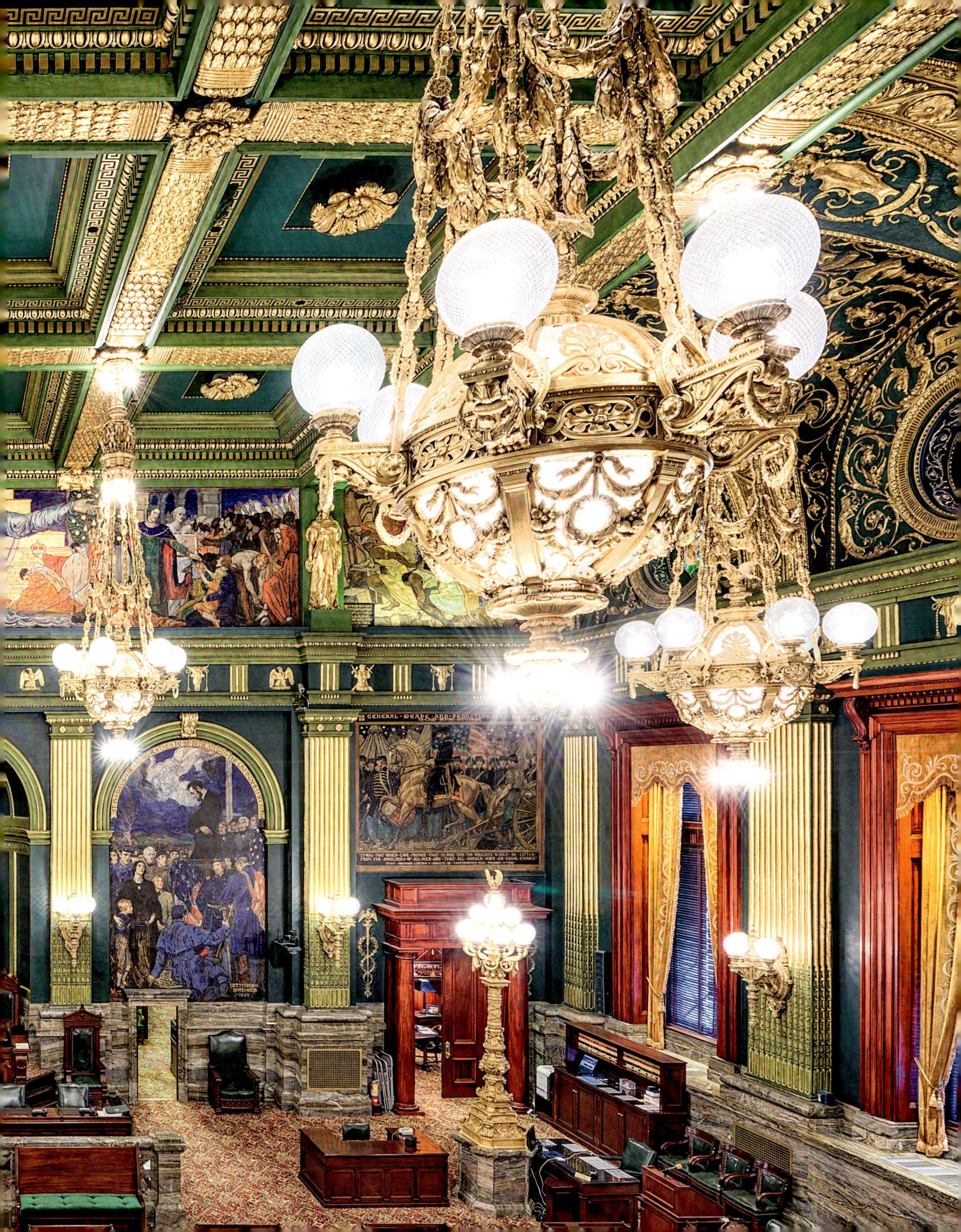
GENERAL · MEADE · AND
"IT WAS THAT WHICH GAVE PROMISE THAT IN DUE TIME THE WEIGHTS WOULD BE LIFTED FROM THE SHOULDERS OF ALL MEN AND THAT ALL SHOULD HAVE AN EQUAL CHANCE"

Broken

Charles Grafly's study for the head of War (cat. 89) is marked by its broken nose, another echo of the models of Michelangelo and Rodin (see page 220). The bald head looks down, reflecting on the violence he has visited as well as the violence he has suffered. Marked by a loss of wholeness and scarred by an unknown blow, the figure presents the irreversible, irrecoverable loss that war has written on its body. Like the violence of the Civil War and its indescribable nature, presentations of its history and impacts relied largely on indirection and allusion. Grafly's memorial to General George Gordon Meade, who led the Union army at the Battle of Gettysburg, is marked by the stylistic change that occurred at the end of the American Renaissance: a shift in focus to more stylized, archaic bodies that resist empathy, focusing instead on resolve and strength, hegemonic attributes that signal a difference of meaning and cultural value. Yet Grafly's depiction retains a lingering sense of the individual body marked by life experience, which distinguished the period and its art.

Likewise, revisiting the unwieldy body of Abraham Lincoln in Violet Oakley's study (cat. 90), made for her late commission for the Senate chamber in the Pennsylvania State Capitol, reveals how his bent silhouette had become an archetype of the nation's visual imagination. Lincoln's stooped form was emblematic both of the burdens he carried and his eventual sacrifice, standing in for the many dead at Gettysburg and through the length of the war. Like so many of the most expressive figures of the era, his energy turns inward in meditation. In Oakley's formulation, as he contemplates the Gettysburg Address that inaugurated a cemetery at the battlefield, Lincoln seems to reflect on the country's fate as much as his own.

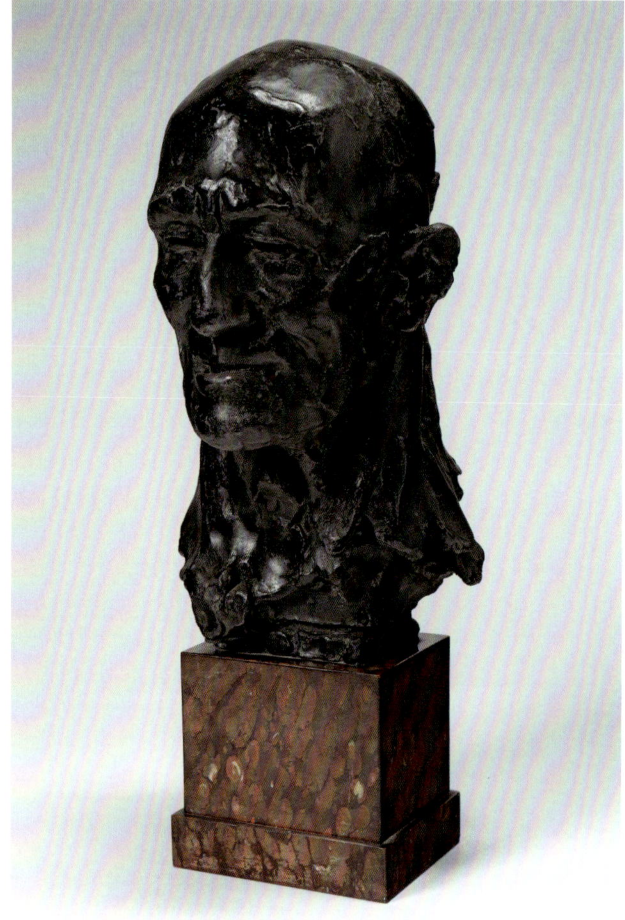

89

CAT. 89 Charles Grafly (American, 1862–1929)
Head of War, Study for the George Gordon Meade Memorial, Washington, D.C., 1921

Bronze, 22¼ × 9 × 9 in. (56.5 × 22.9 × 22.9 cm)
The Art Institute of Chicago, Mrs. Keith Spaulding Purchase Prize, 1924.957

CAT. 90 Violet Oakley (American, 1874–1961)
Study of Abraham Lincoln for *The Gettysburg Address, 1863* in the Pennsylvania State Capitol, 1916

Charcoal and chalk on paper, 22 × 11 in. (55.9 × 27.9 cm)
The State Museum of Pennsylvania, Harrisburg, 82.78.56

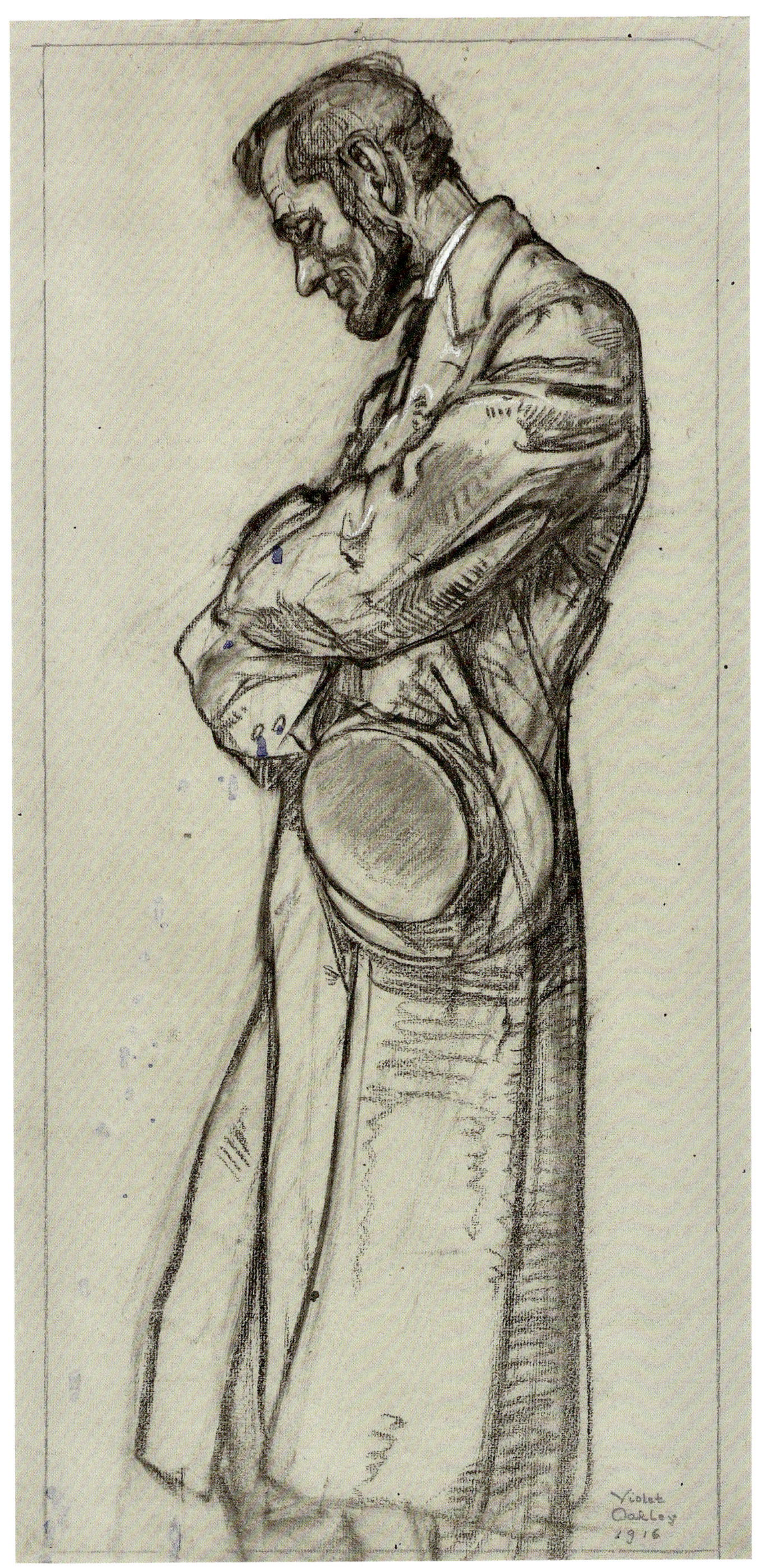
Violet
Oakley
1916

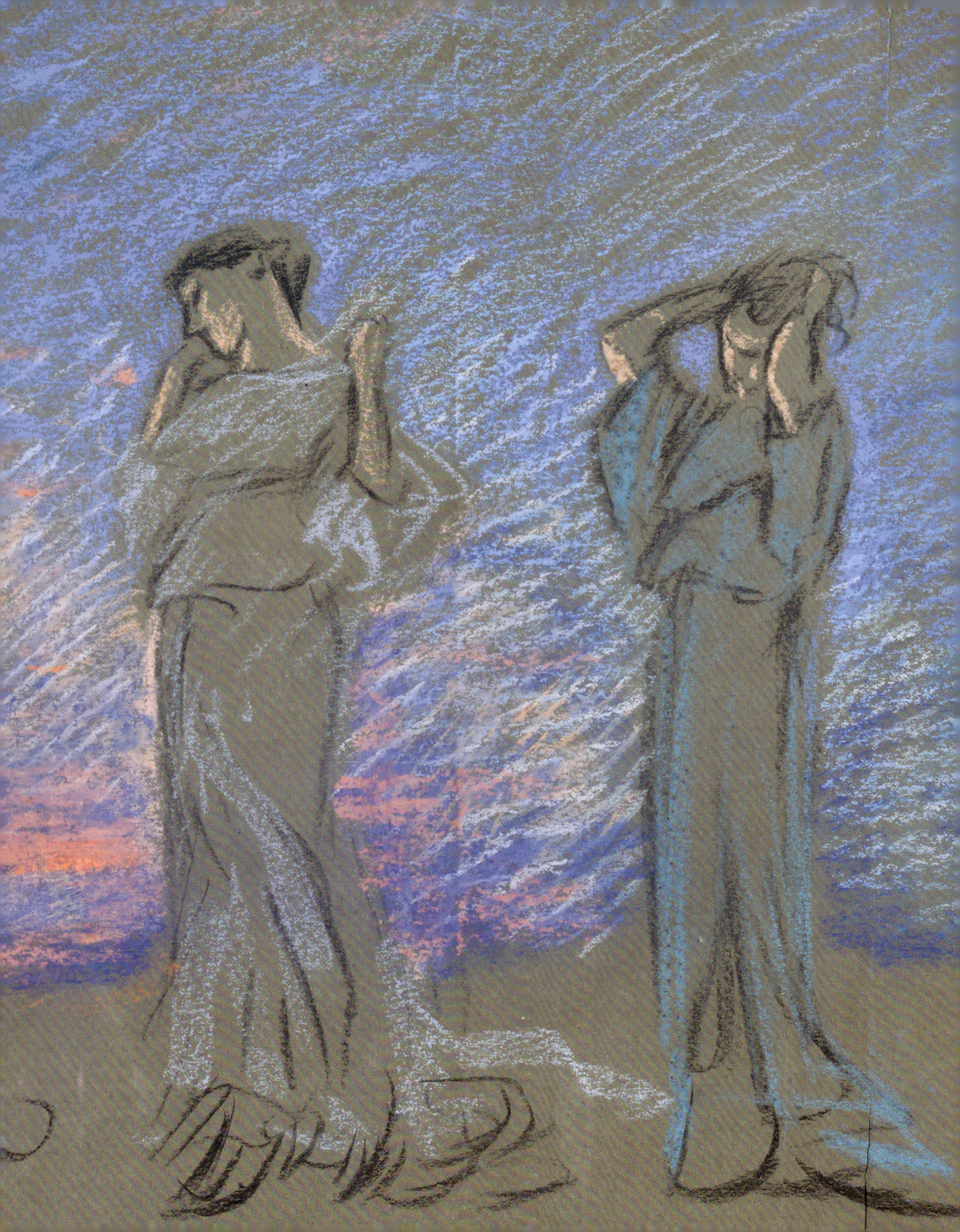

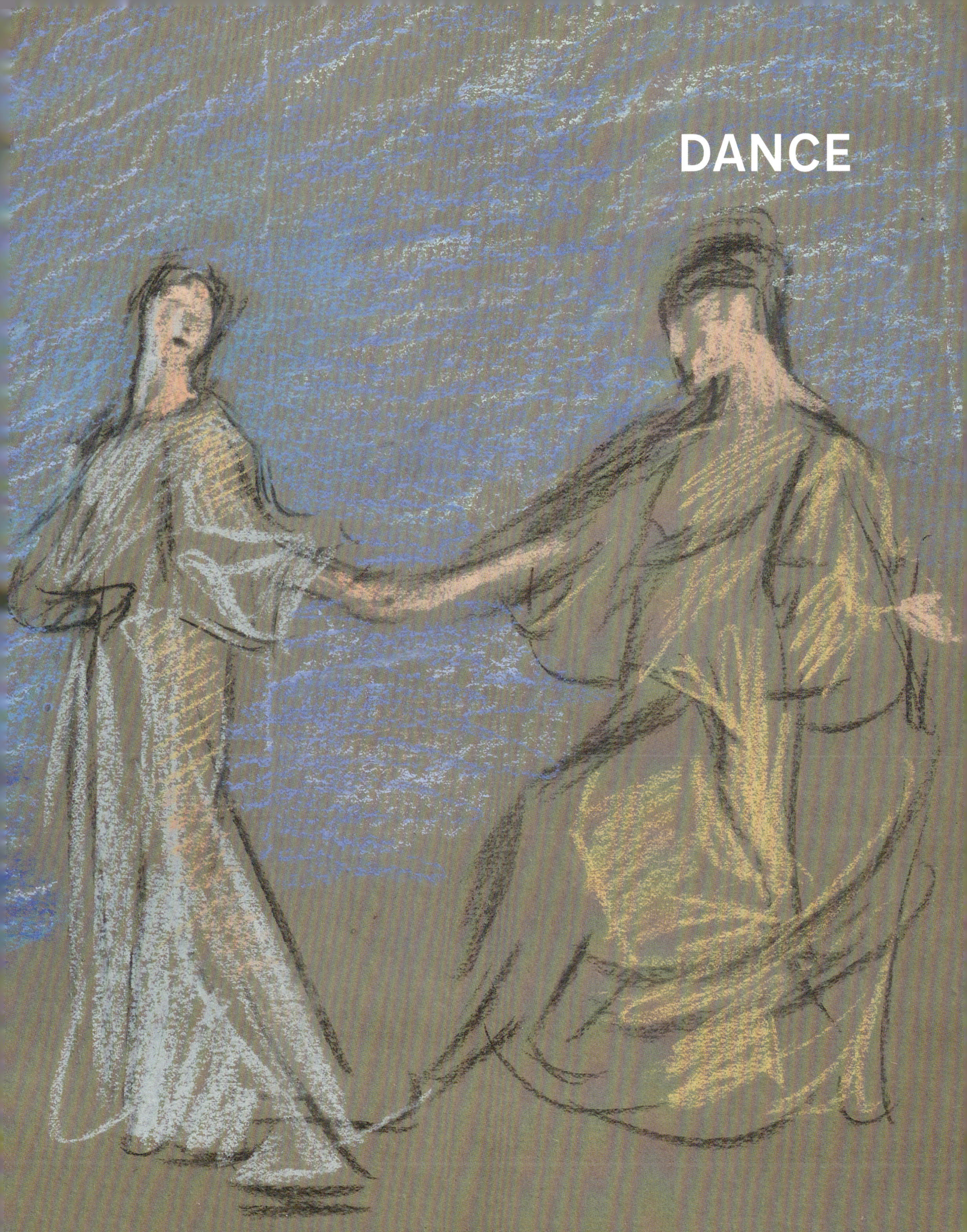

DANCE

Modern dance emerged around the turn of the twentieth century as a new and experimental medium; it often intersected with fine art and naturally centered the human body in public, if not civic, displays. Charismatic dancers and choreographers like Isadora Duncan, Loïe Fuller, Vaslav Nijinsky, Anna Pavlova, and Ruth St. Denis sought serious consideration for their art, combining diverse popular and balletic forms into new syntheses. So complete was their success that the sociologist Havelock Ellis observed in 1923 that "all human work, under natural conditions, is a kind of dance."[1]

Meta Vaux Warrick Fuller took up the vital and expressive language of dance in her *Danse Macabre* (cat. 91). The sculpture features five figures massing together in swirling robes that recall the oversized silk costumes and movements of Loïe Fuller, who had choreographed a dance to Camille Saint-Saëns's 1874 tone poem of the same title in 1911.[2] Modernizing a medieval Christian tradition and artistic subject, Fuller's figures evoke the dead, summoned from their graves on Halloween to dance through the night to the sound of Death's dissonant violin. Typically depicted as skeletons in art—both medieval and modern—here the dead are embodied spirits, closer in form and fluid movement to modern dancers. The dissonance of the subject and Saint-Saëns's modern musical recasting of the medieval tradition were the subject of extended discussion in the Boston Symphony Orchestra's program when it performed Saint-Saëns's *Danse Macabre* in 1910, by which time the artist was living in neighboring Framingham.

During the first years of the twentieth century, Fuller created a series of monuments to African American identity, history, and experience. Although she received relatively few public commissions, she entered competitions and created maquettes that directly address the subjects and recall the discrimination she faced as an African American woman in both the United States and France. Influenced by her studies with Auguste Rodin, Fuller employed the modern forms of her time—in art and dance—and created works dedicated to emancipation, victims of lynching, and African heritage that earned attention in her lifetime.[3]

Fuller's embrace of modern dance resounds with the work of her contemporaries. Edwin Austin Abbey's pastel figure study (cat. 92) for the figure of eight a.m. in his large ceiling mural *The Hours* at the Pennsylvania State Capitol describes swirling movement. The combination of stumping across the body, where the clothes are pulled taut, contrasts with the looser and separated strokes where the draperies move away from the figure more freely, echoing the liberated, natural movement embraced by Isadora Duncan. In 1899–1900, during a formative phase of her career,

CAT. 91 Meta Vaux Warrick Fuller (American, 1877–1968)

Danse Macabre, 1914

Painted plaster, 14 × 15 × 10 in. (35.6 × 38.1 × 25.4 cm)
Danforth Art Museum at Framingham State University, Mass., Gift of the Meta V. W. Fuller Trust, 2006.312

CAT. 92 Edwin Austin Abbey (American, 1852–1911, HON. 1897)

Study for Eight A.M. in *The Hours* in the Pennsylvania State Capitol, 1904

Pastel on brown paper, 17 7/16 × 11 in. (44.3 × 27.9 cm)
Yale University Art Gallery, New Haven, Conn., Edwin Austin Abbey Memorial Collection, 1937.3356

CAT. 93 Edwin Austin Abbey (American, 1852–1911, HON. 1897)

Figure Study, n.d.

Colored chalks on colored wove paper, 14 7/8 × 11 1/2 in. (37.8 × 29.2 cm)
Yale University Art Gallery, New Haven, Conn., Edwin Austin Abbey Memorial Collection, 1937.4094

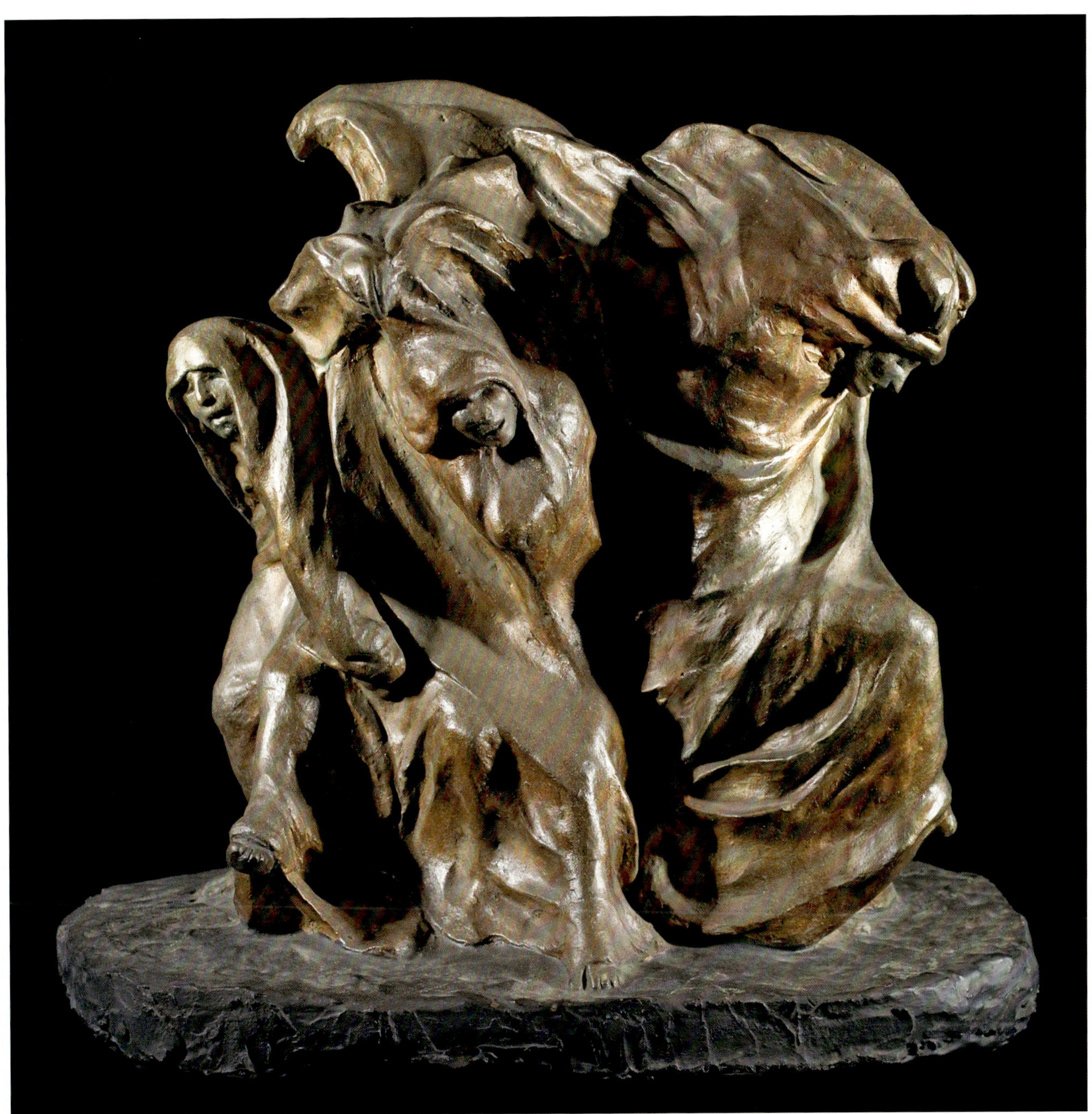

91

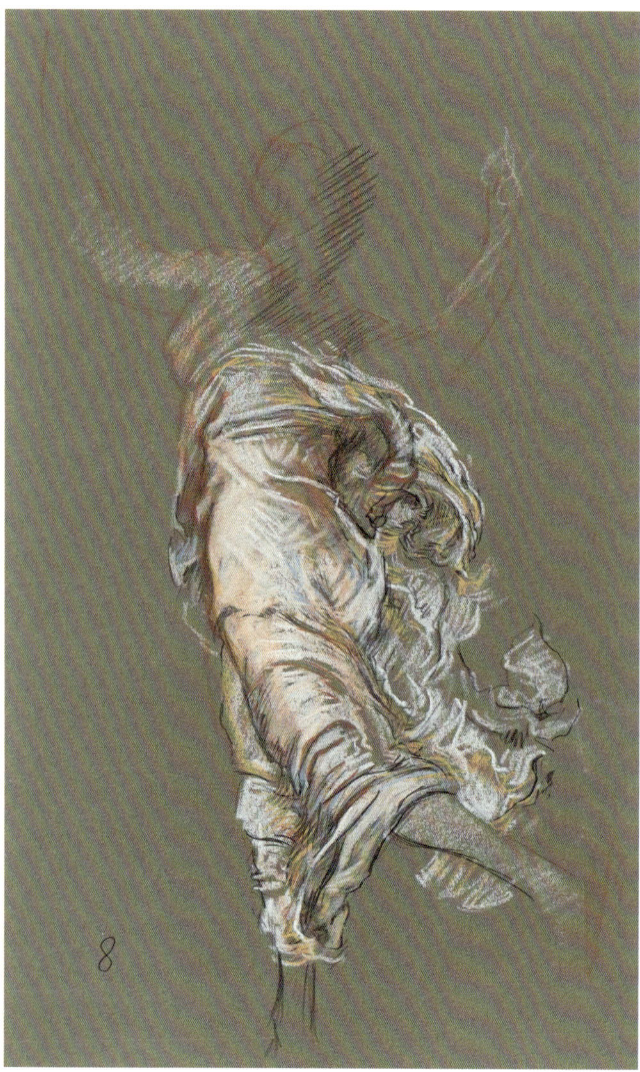

92

Duncan conducted research for her works in the British Museum, as Abbey did, and was active in London's Shakespearean community centered at the Lyceum Theater, where she and Abbey may also have crossed paths.[4] The body of Abbey's dancer is described with only a light sanguine contour and simple hatching, separating it in both color and application from the more fully rendered clothing. Equally expressive is his pastel sketch of a head and shoulders (cat. 93). The hair appears to blow upward as if flying in the wind, and the prominence of the graceful, deeply outlined neck suggests a dancer's self-aware posture, giving the impression of dramatic performance. The free, energetic movement of Fuller's and Abbey's figures is characteristic of later works of the American Renaissance, simultaneously drawing on the dynamic language of dance and the expressive power of contemporary Symbolist art in Europe and America.

NOTES

1. Havelock Ellis, *The Dance of Life* (1923; rev. ed., New York: The Modern Library, 1929), 58.
2. Margaret H. Harris and Sally R. Sommer, comps., "Choreochronicle of Loie Fuller," in Don McDonagh, *The Complete Guide to Modern Dance* (New York: Doubleday, 1976), 24. No family relationship between artist and dancer has been documented.
3. Among her projects, see the discussion of her *Emancipation* (1913) in Renée Ater, *Remaking Race and History: The Sculpture of Meta Warrick Fuller* (Berkeley: University of California Press, 2011), 73–100; and her monument to Mary Turner (1919) in Caitlin Beach, "Meta Warrick Fuller's Mary Turner and the Memory of Mob Violence," *Nka: Journal of Contemporary African Art*, no. 36 (May 2015): 16–27.
4. Dorée Duncan, Carol Pratl, and Cynthia Splatt, eds., *Life into Art: Isadora Duncan and Her World* (New York: W. W. Norton, 1993), 36–38.

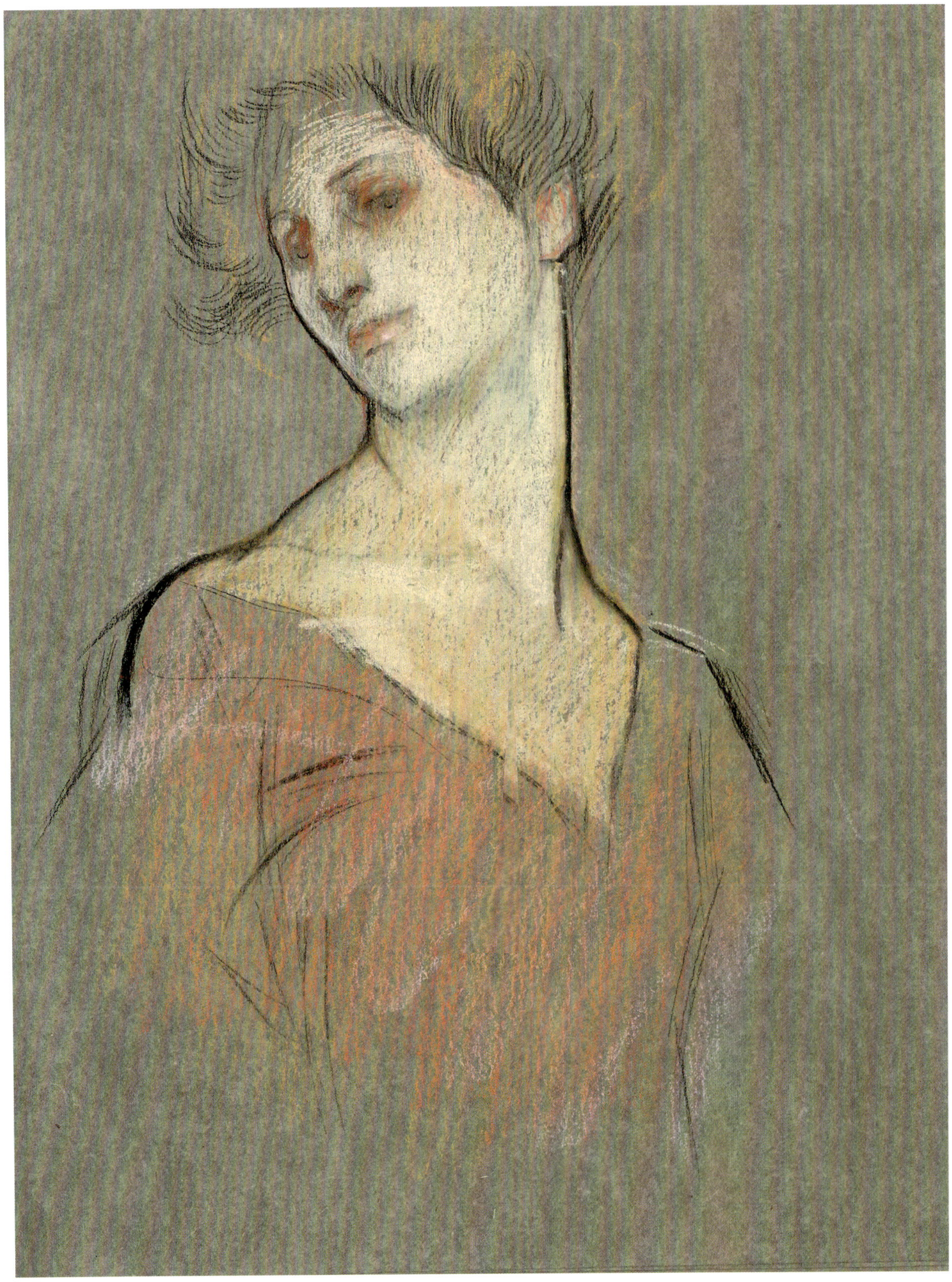

93

Vitality

Evelyn Beatrice Longman's victorious young athlete broke from traditional representations of Victory as a female figure and so impressed organizers of the Louisiana Purchase Exposition of 1904 that it was moved from an ancillary building to the top of the main Festival Hall. It became the icon of the fair, simultaneously launching the artist's career and professional reputation as a public sculptor.[1] The image remained a touchstone of Longman's oeuvre and was popular in later reductions. She made this version (cat. 94), one of the first and largest of the casts, as a gift to the Art Institute of Chicago, where she had studied.

The vitality of the sculpture was what drew critics' attention. Raised high on his toes, Victory seems to overbalance in his celebration. His cuirass is modeled to his lanky form, and his cloak wraps around him in the wind. The liveliness of the surface and the sculpture's gravity-defying extension use bronze to its full potential, beyond what carved stone or clay would permit. For American audiences, the athlete represents a new generation: too young to have served in the Civil War, his athletic accomplishments unimpeded by the call to fight. His cuirass, greaves, and cape, along with laurel and oak leaves—symbols of victory—lightly dress the modern, awkwardly juvenile figure in classical style, like Augustus Saint-Gaudens's *Diana of the Tower*, but acceptably clothed.

NOTE

1. Margaret Samu, "Evelyn Beatrice Longman: Establishing a Career in Public Sculpture," *Woman's Art Journal* 25, no. 2 (Autumn 2004/Winter 2005): 9.

CAT. 94 Evelyn Beatrice Longman (American, 1874–1954)

Study for *Victory*, modeled 1903, cast 1905

Bronze, 49½ × 19 × 16 in. (125.7 × 48.3 × 40.6 cm)
The Art Institute of Chicago, Gift of the artist, 1906.128

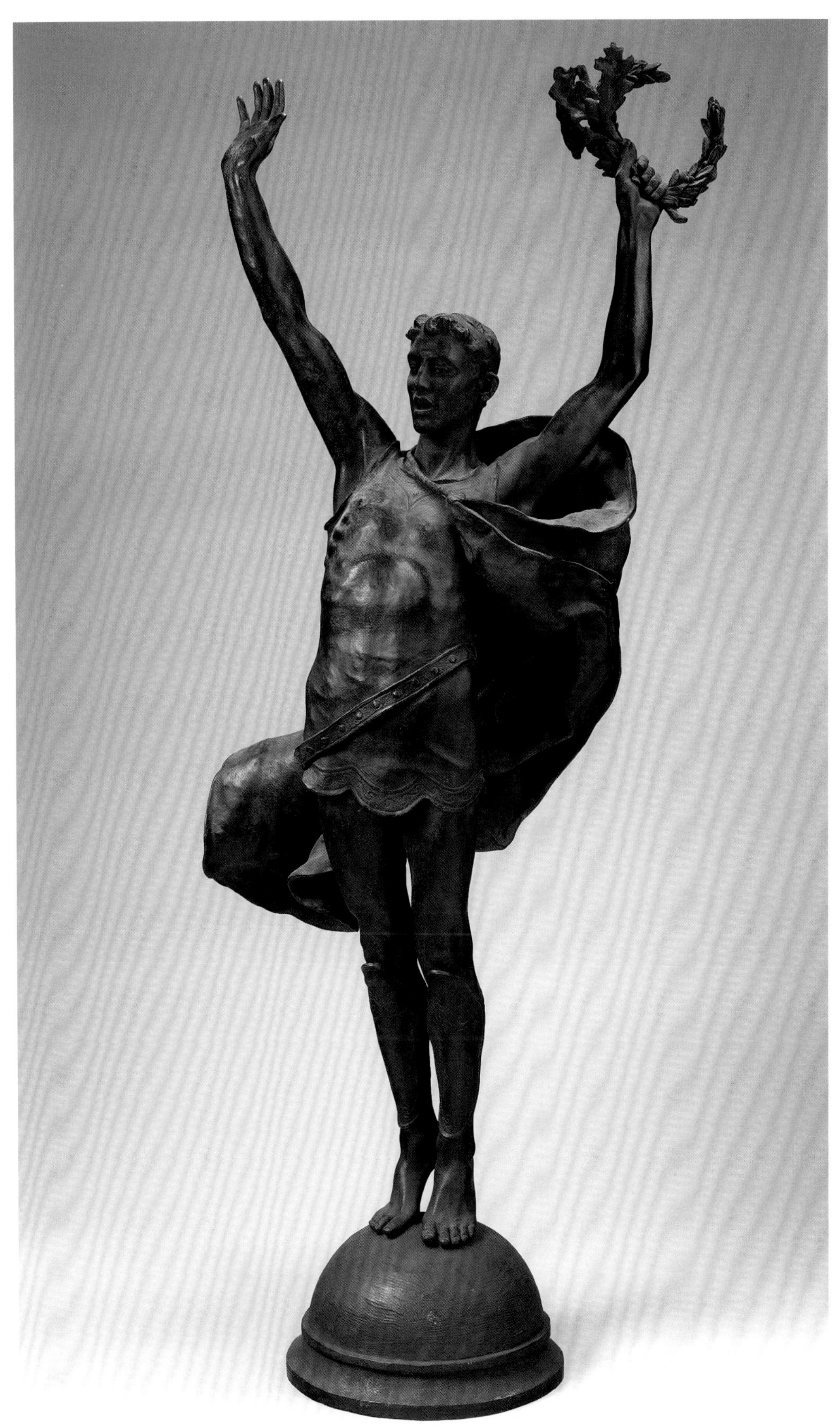

Control

Conceived as one of a pair of monumental sculptures for the south entrance to Prospect Park in Brooklyn, this cast of Frederick William MacMonnies's *Horse Tamer* (cat. 95) captures the astonishing power and strength of the huge Andalusian (possibly Normandy) stallions that the artist purchased as models and photographed extensively as the basis for their poses. The small rider seems hardly capable of controlling the pair of animals, which are allegories, according to the work's early title, *The Triumph of Mind over Brute Force*.[1] The sculpture exemplifies the vertiginous change that was happening in America throughout the period, ever on the cusp of chaos. "I do not see how they could be improved upon," the sculptor Lorado Taft observed of the horses in 1900, when the full-scale pair was first exhibited at the Paris Exposition flanking Augustus Saint-Gaudens's Sherman Monument.[2]

John Singer Sargent's charcoal study (cat. 96) of a torso for one of the figures in his mural *Apollo and His Chariot with the Hours* in the Museum of Fine Arts, Boston is a remarkably concise expression of an idea similar to that of MacMonnies's. In Sargent's scene, the hours (male here, unlike those in Edwin Austin Abbey's composition for the Pennsylvania State Capitol) dance around and among the horses and chariot that Apollo pilots, all seemingly on the edge of falling away. In his drawing, Sargent focuses our attention on the relationship between the parts of the body, including how the arms align with the turning torso and how light and shadow move across the surface of the body—a dancer's pose, certainly. Despite careful preparations, little of the sense of definition and control that he developed in the studies carried over into the final oil painting. Sargent and MacMonnies sought to define the figure reaching its limits and capture the essence of the body in action. Both artists present an engaging expression of barely exercised control, distilling the anxieties of their time.

CAT. 95 Frederick William MacMonnies (American, 1863–1937)

The Horse Tamer, ca. 1894–99

Bronze, H. 38½ in. (97.8 cm)
Private collection

CAT. 96 John Singer Sargent (American, born Italy, 1856–1925, LL.D. 1916)

Study for *Apollo and His Chariot with the Hours* in the Museum of Fine Arts, Boston, ca. 1921–25

Black chalk and charcoal on paper, 16 9/16 × 20 7/8 in. (42.1 × 53 cm)
Yale University Art Gallery, New Haven, Conn., Gift of Miss Emily Sargent and Mrs. Francis Ormond, through Thomas A. Fox, 1929.264

NOTES

1. Mary Smart, *A Flight with Fame: The Life and Art of Frederick MacMonnies (1863–1937)* (Madison, Conn.: Sound View, 1996), 177–78. See also Ethelyn Adina Gordon, "The Sculpture of Frederick William MacMonnies: A Critical Catalogue" (Ph.D. diss., Institute of Fine Arts, New York University, 1998), 357–61.
2. Lorado Taft, "American Sculpture at the [Paris] Exposition, II," *Brush and Pencil* 6, no. 5 (August 1900): 211.

Detail of cat. 95

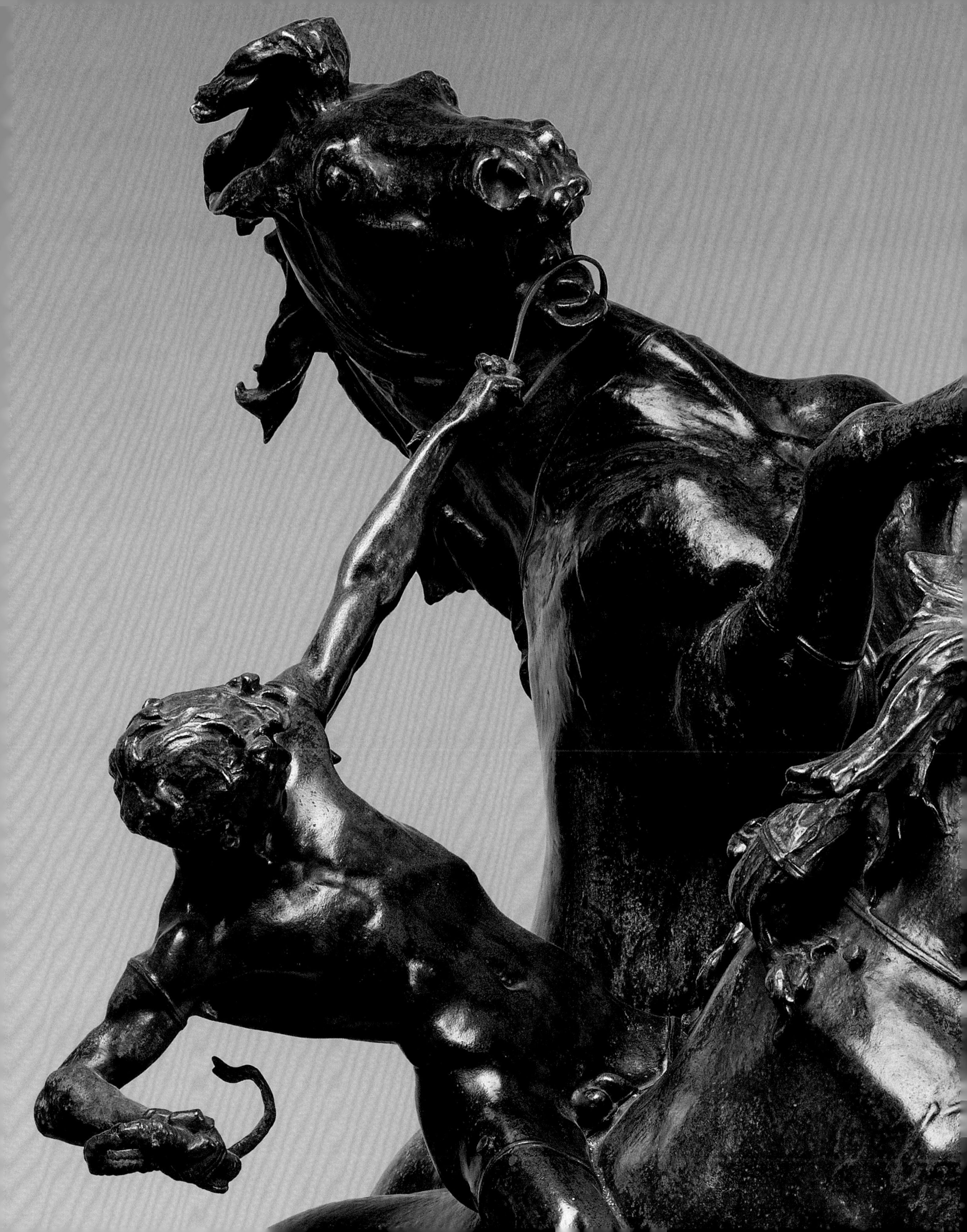

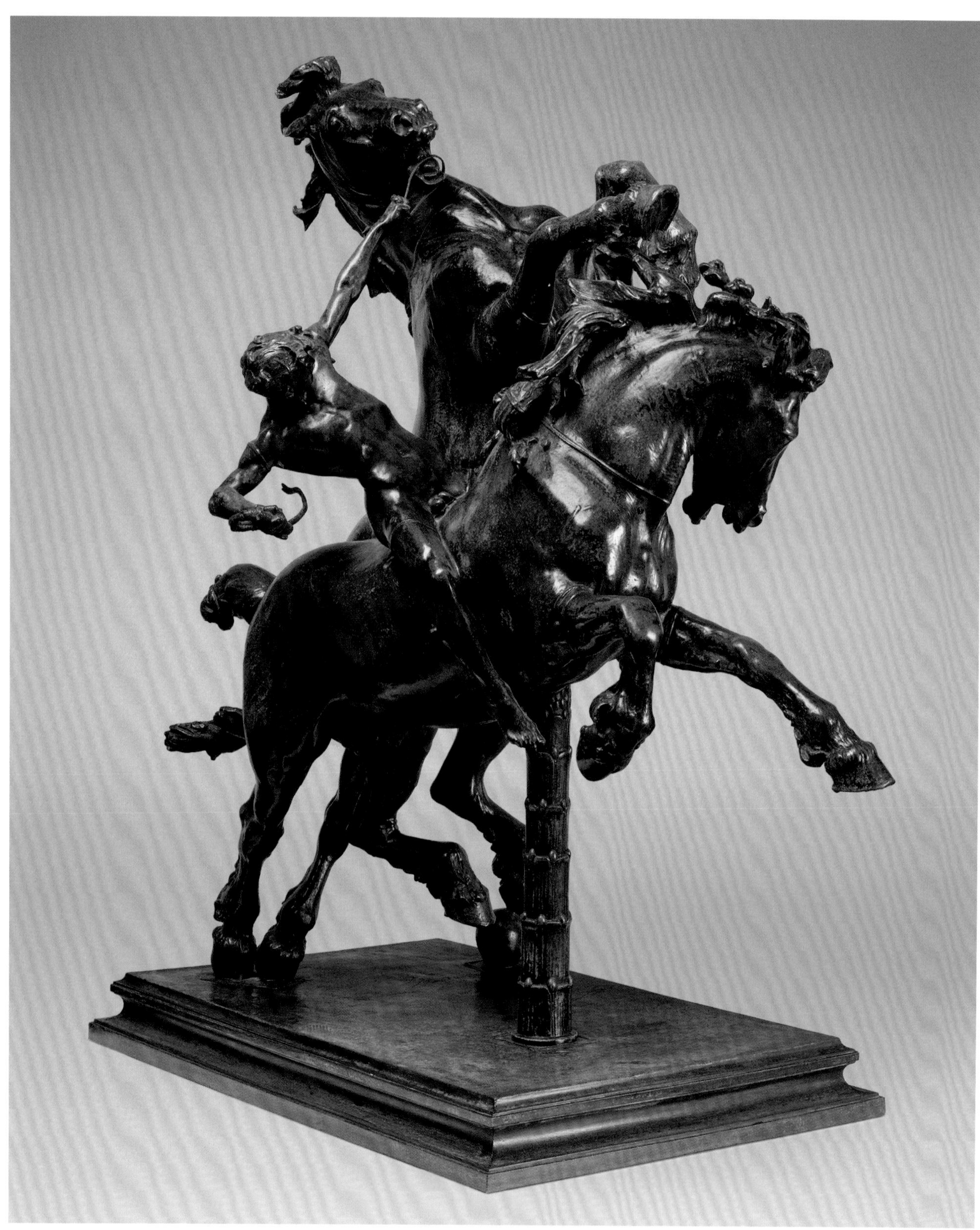

95

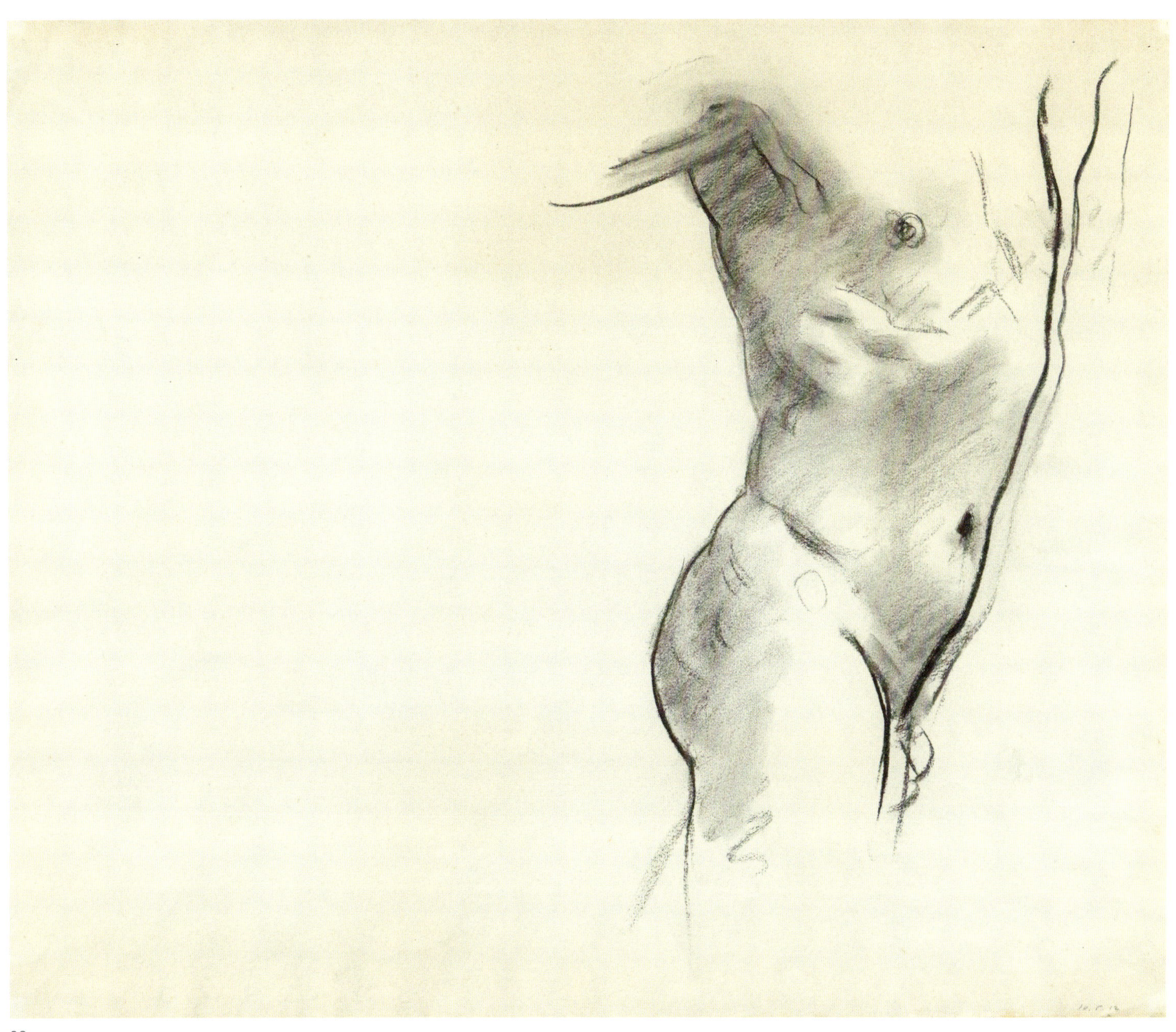

96

Grace

The opposite of nearly losing control is the discipline of poise. In these two studies, Edwin Austin Abbey and John Singer Sargent record figures arrayed in gracious stances of stability. The sensibility of both drawings approximates sculpture, studying the volumes of the body in space. Absent movement, however, static forms such as these appear to have had relatively few applications in the American Renaissance, which valued action and energy over composure. Because of its often dynamic volumes and mannered contortions, the era may be better characterized as the American Baroque. More emphatic than naturalistic, both Abbey and Sargent rarely focused on static, stable figures. Abbey's worker stands at the far side of the composition for *The Spirit of Vulcan*, isolated from the primary action and subject of the group hammering at an anvil (cat. 97). This figure waits to feed sheets of raw metal into the furnace.[1]

The figure in Sargent's study (cat. 98) diverges from the final arrangement, assuming it has been accurately identified, portraying stability that would not characterize the finished pose. In the mural in the Museum of Fine Arts, Boston, Perseus rides a rearing Pegasus; he holds the severed head of Medusa and twists around fully while looking in the opposite direction. Not at all cast in a pose of composure, Perseus is the image of dynamic torsion, combining aversion and extension. Sargent apparently settled on a more energetic configuration than this one, moving away from its static discipline toward vigorous animation. Grace had an important role to play in the American Renaissance, but it manifested in the context of dynamic movement not equipoise.

NOTE

1. A nearly identical drawing of one of the figures by Sargent, titled *At the Forge*, reproduced in Evan Charteris's biography, suggests that the artists' close creative relationship continued long after their time as studio-mates in the early 1890s; Charteris, *John Sargent* (New York: Charles Scribner's Sons, 1927), 116.

CAT. 97 Edwin Austin Abbey (American, 1852–1911, HON. 1897)

Figure Study for *The Spirit of Vulcan: Genius of the Workers in Iron and Steel* in the Pennsylvania State Capitol, 1902–8

Black and white chalk on dark green wove paper, 28 7/16 × 22 7/16 in. (72.2 × 57 cm)
Yale University Art Gallery, New Haven, Conn., Edwin Austin Abbey Memorial Collection, 1937.1385

CAT. 98 John Singer Sargent (American, born Italy, 1856–1925, LL.D. 1916)

Study for *Perseus on Pegasus Slaying Medusa* in the Museum of Fine Arts, Boston, ca. 1921–25

Black chalk and charcoal on paper, 24 13/16 × 18 11/16 in. (63 × 47.5 cm)
Yale University Art Gallery, New Haven, Conn., Gift of Miss Emily Sargent and Mrs. Francis Ormond, 1929.286

Detail of cat. 97

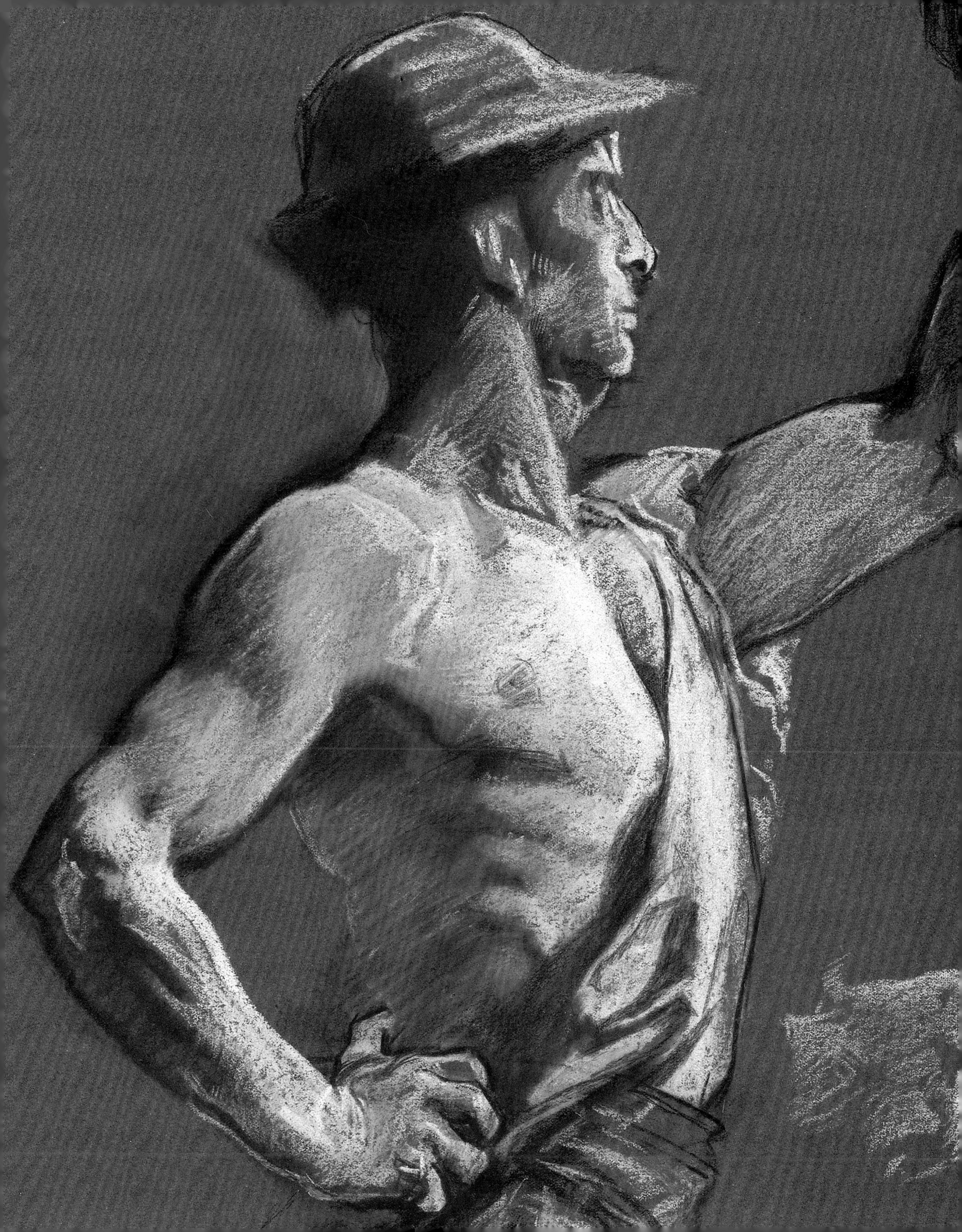

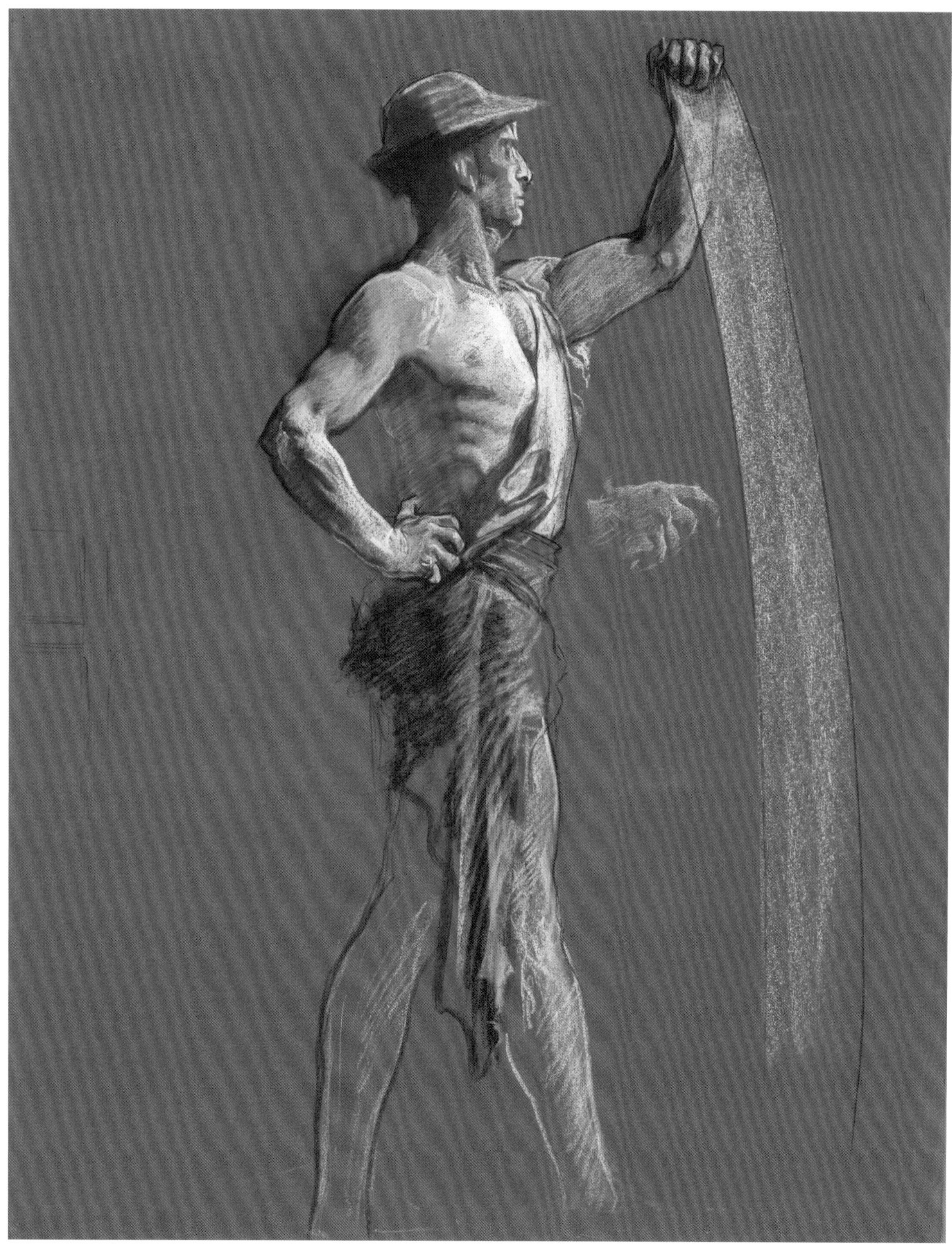

97

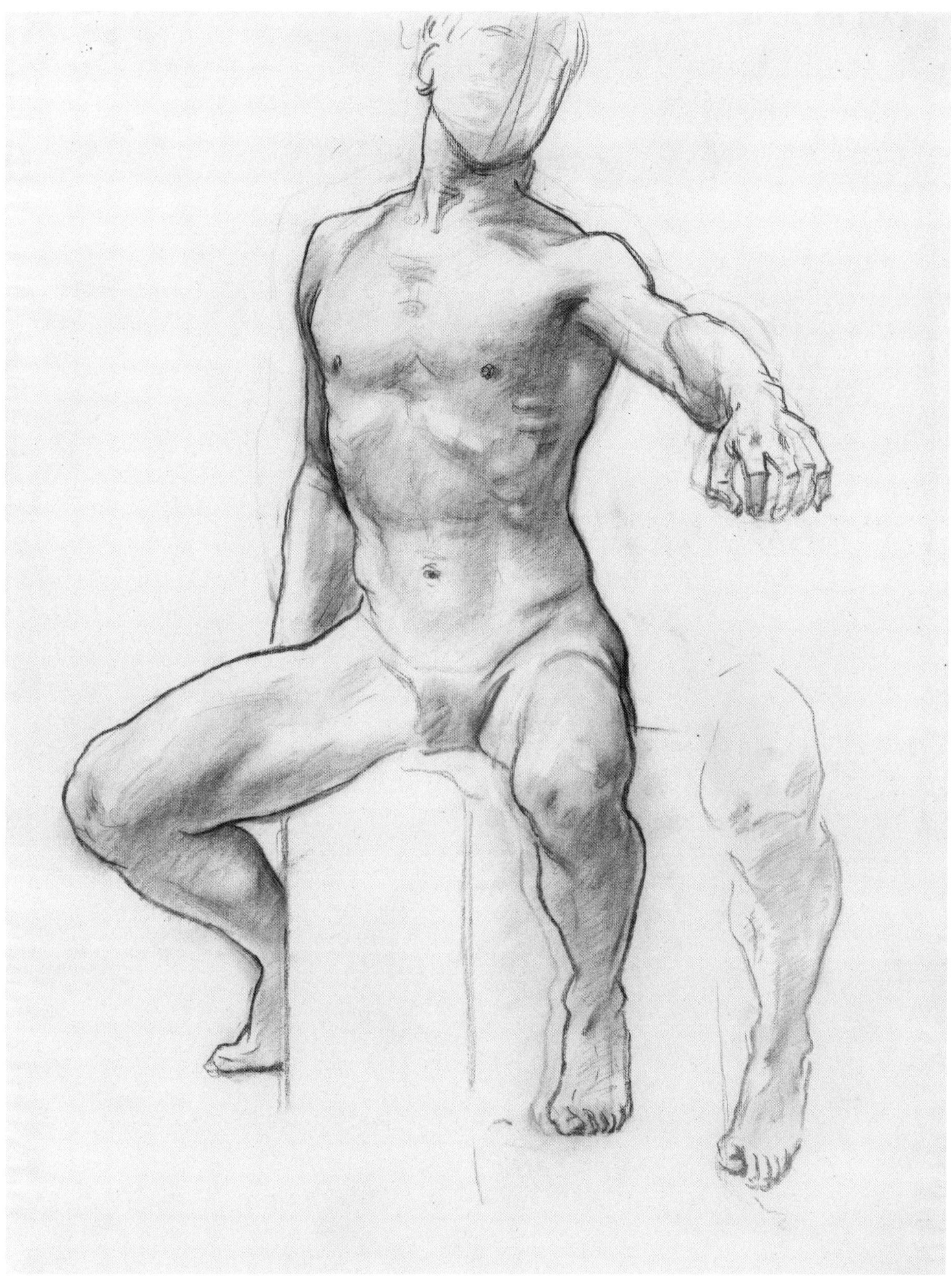

98

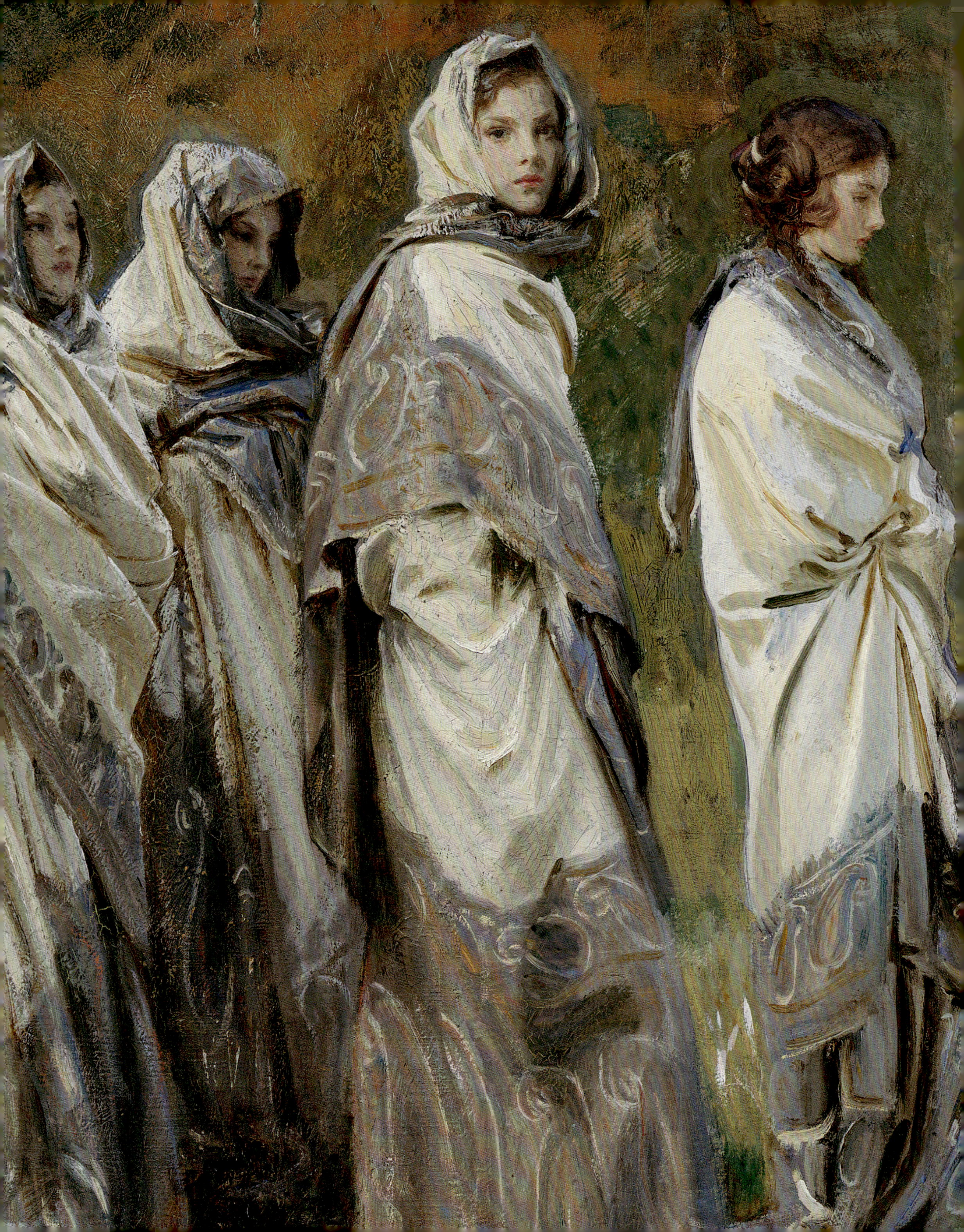

Procession

Edwin Austin Abbey's conception for his last mural, *The Hours*, developed fitfully and was apparently adapted from a different format: a lateral frieze. In a pen-and-ink study from his sketchbook (cat. 99), Abbey presented the transition from night, portrayed as heavily cloaked figures under the moon and stars, to daytime, represented by figures dancing in a light dress. Similarly, a pastel (cat. 100) presents an advanced iteration of the palette and clothing featured in the final work, with the same succession of figures (starting from midnight beneath the moon) as in the sketchbook. Abbey was evidently engaged by the initial formulation, though the venue for which it was intended remains unidentified. The early idea lent itself to adaption for the ceiling in the House of Representatives chamber of the Pennsylvania State Capitol, likely because it was partially developed when the additional commission arose to fill a space originally designed as a skylight. Despite Abbey's many existing commitments, *The Hours* would become a primary focus of his last years.

Abbey's interest in friezes was shared by his friend John Singer Sargent, whose *Cashmere* (cat. 101) depicts a comparable procession; his earlier *Frieze of the Prophets* for the Boston Public Library was considered a highlight of the commission. *Cashmere* was painted around 1908, the same year that Abbey received *The Hours* commission for Harrisburg, and both works share a succession of poses that can be interpreted as a time-lapse. The two artists, who were neighbors and regular dinner companions on Tite Street in London, would have known about their respective works and progress. They had shared inspiration, props, and models since the early 1890s, when both artists began their commissions for the Boston Public Library.

CAT. 99 Edwin Austin Abbey (American, 1852–1911, HON. 1897)
Sketchbook Study for *The Hours*, ca. 1908
Graphite, pen and ink, watercolor, and black chalk on laid paper, 13⅜ × 20⅝ in. (34 × 52.4 cm)
Yale University Art Gallery, New Haven, Conn., Edwin Austin Abbey Memorial Collection, 1937.4091

CAT. 100 Edwin Austin Abbey (American, 1852–1911, HON. 1897)
Study for *The Hours* in the Pennsylvania State Capitol, ca. 1904–11
Pastel on gray paper on cardboard, 19½ × 55½ in. (49.5 × 141 cm)
Yale University Art Gallery, New Haven, Conn., Edwin Austin Abbey Memorial Collection, 1937.1712

CAT. 101 John Singer Sargent (American, born Italy, 1856–1925, LL.D. 1916)
Cashmere, ca. 1908
Oil on canvas, 28 × 43 in. (71.1 × 109.2 cm)
Private collection

Detail of cat. 101

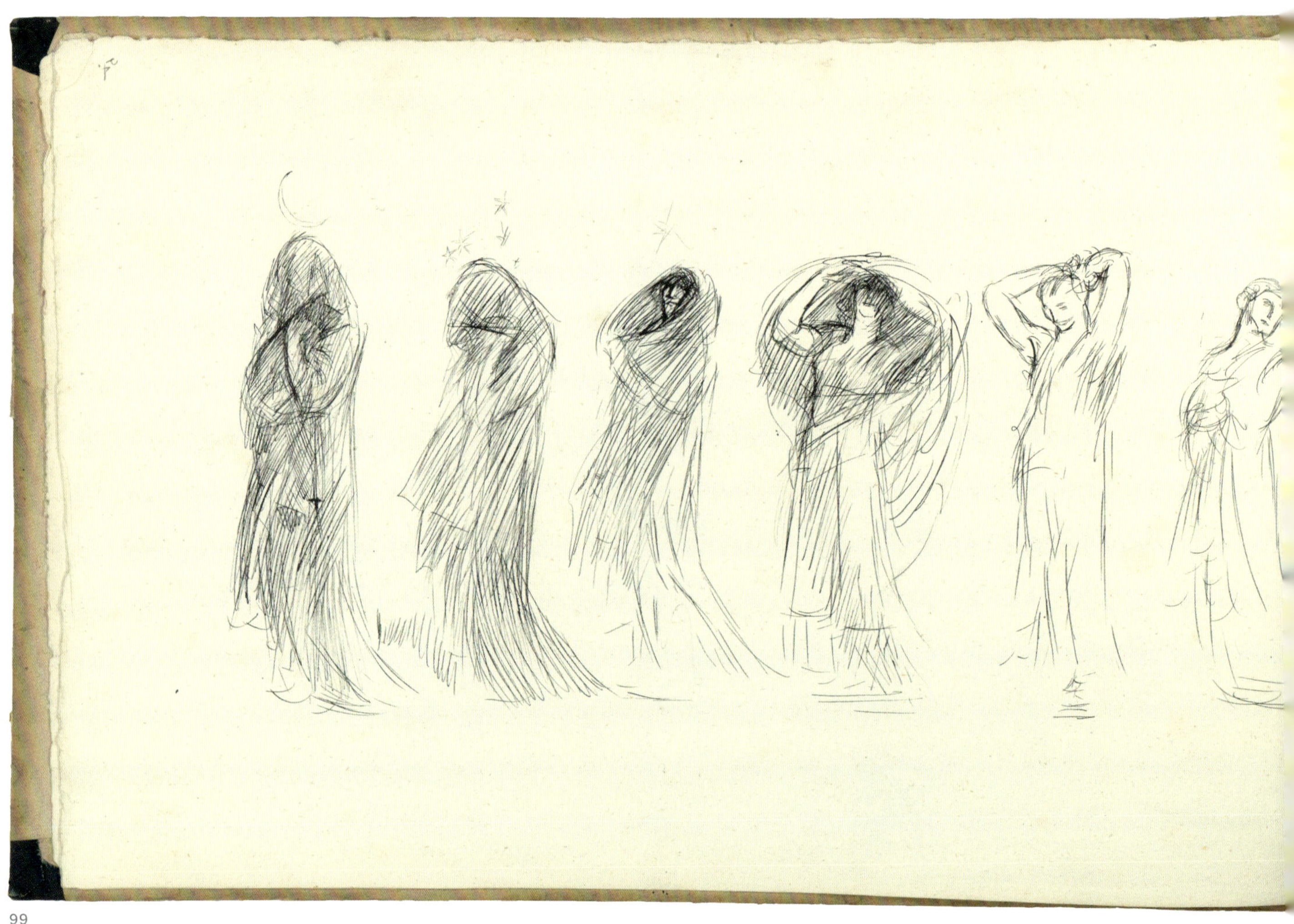

99

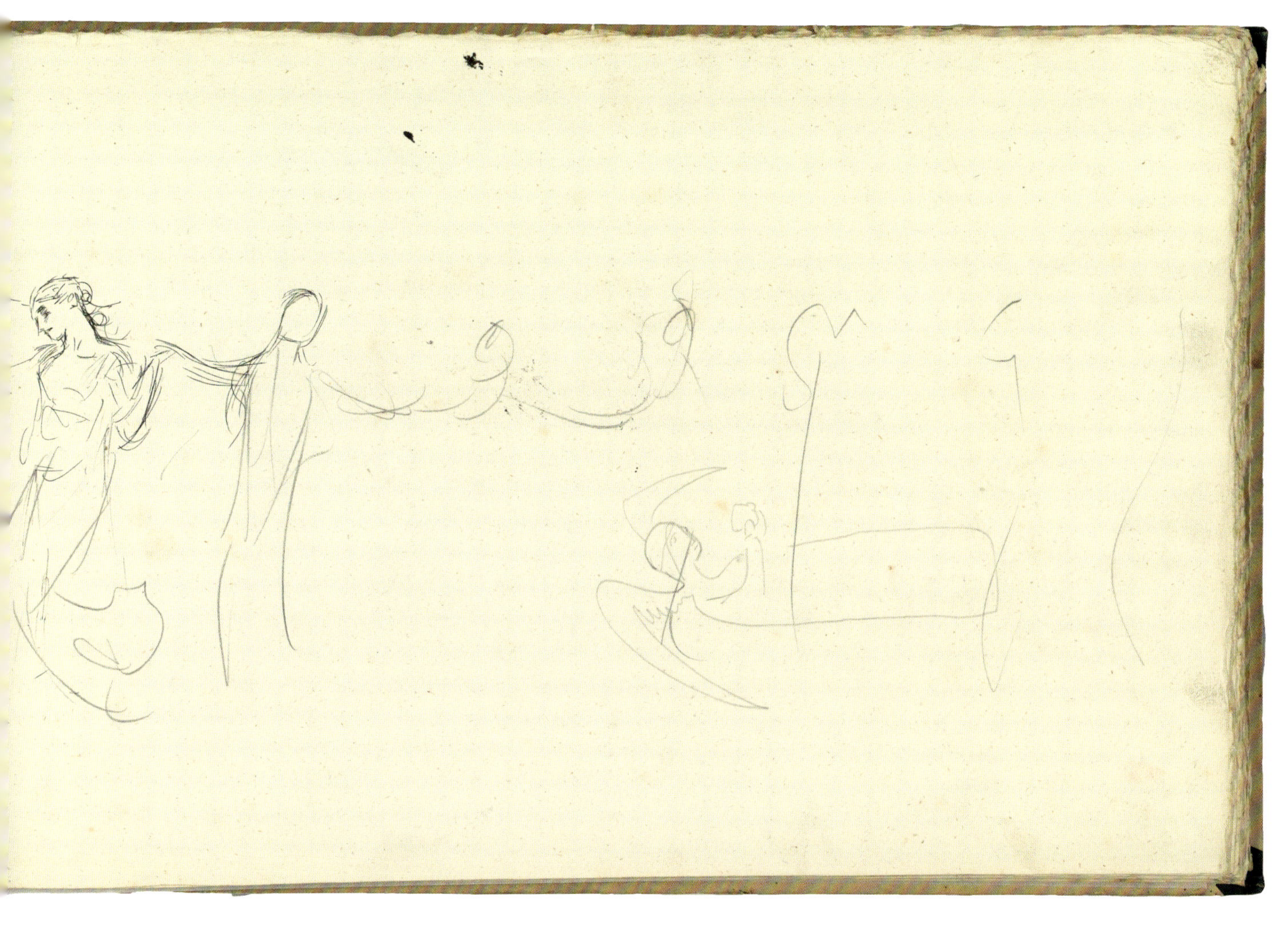

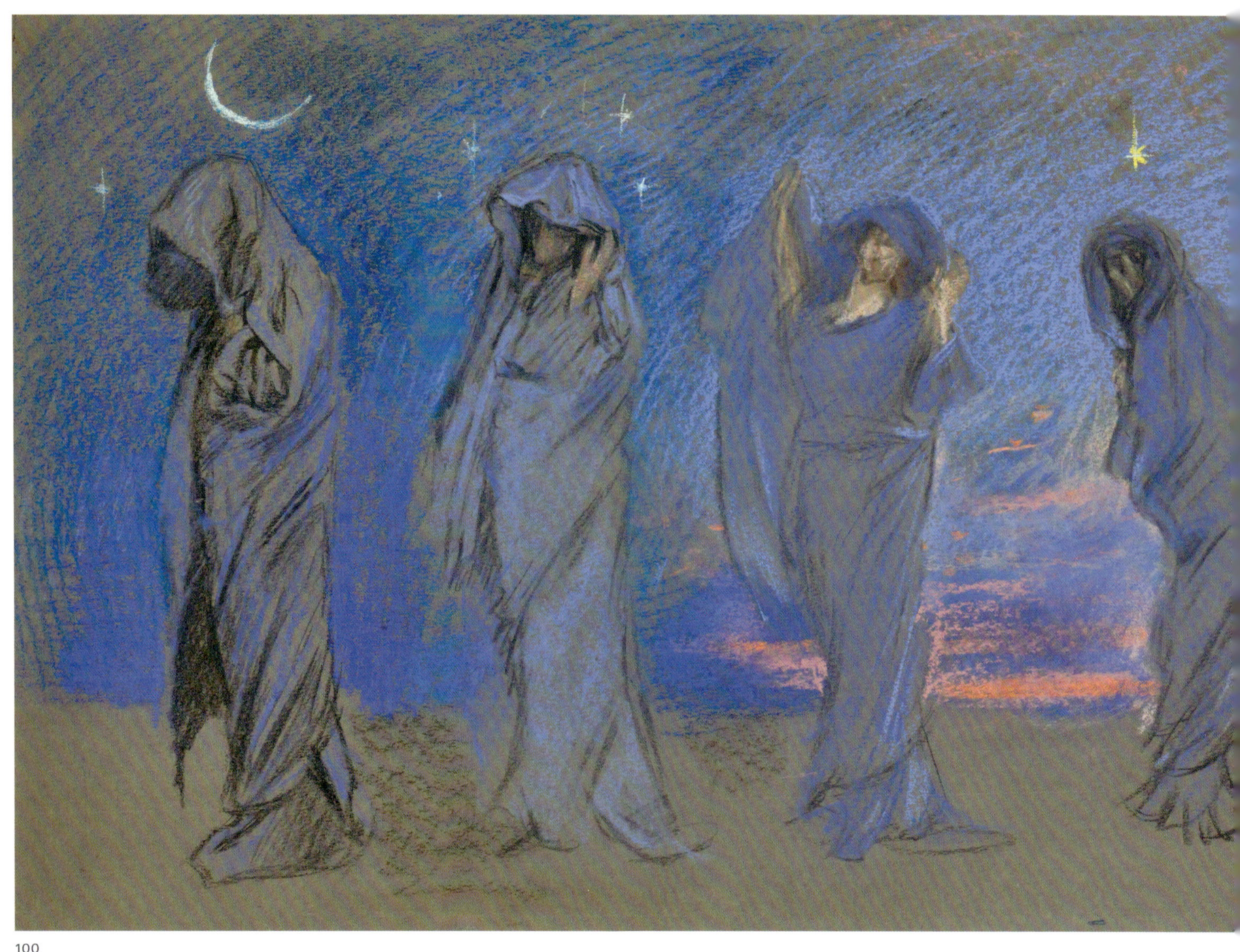

100

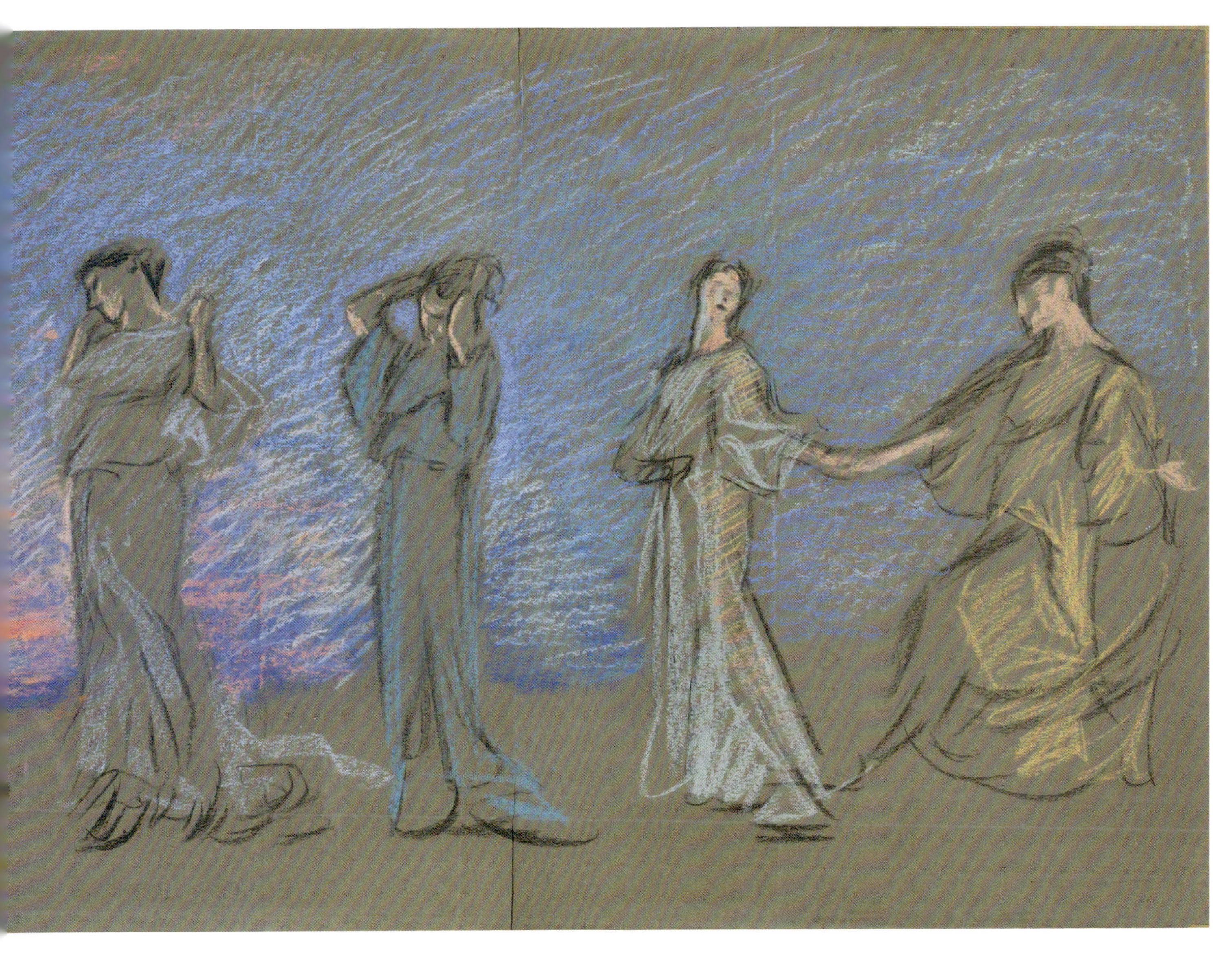

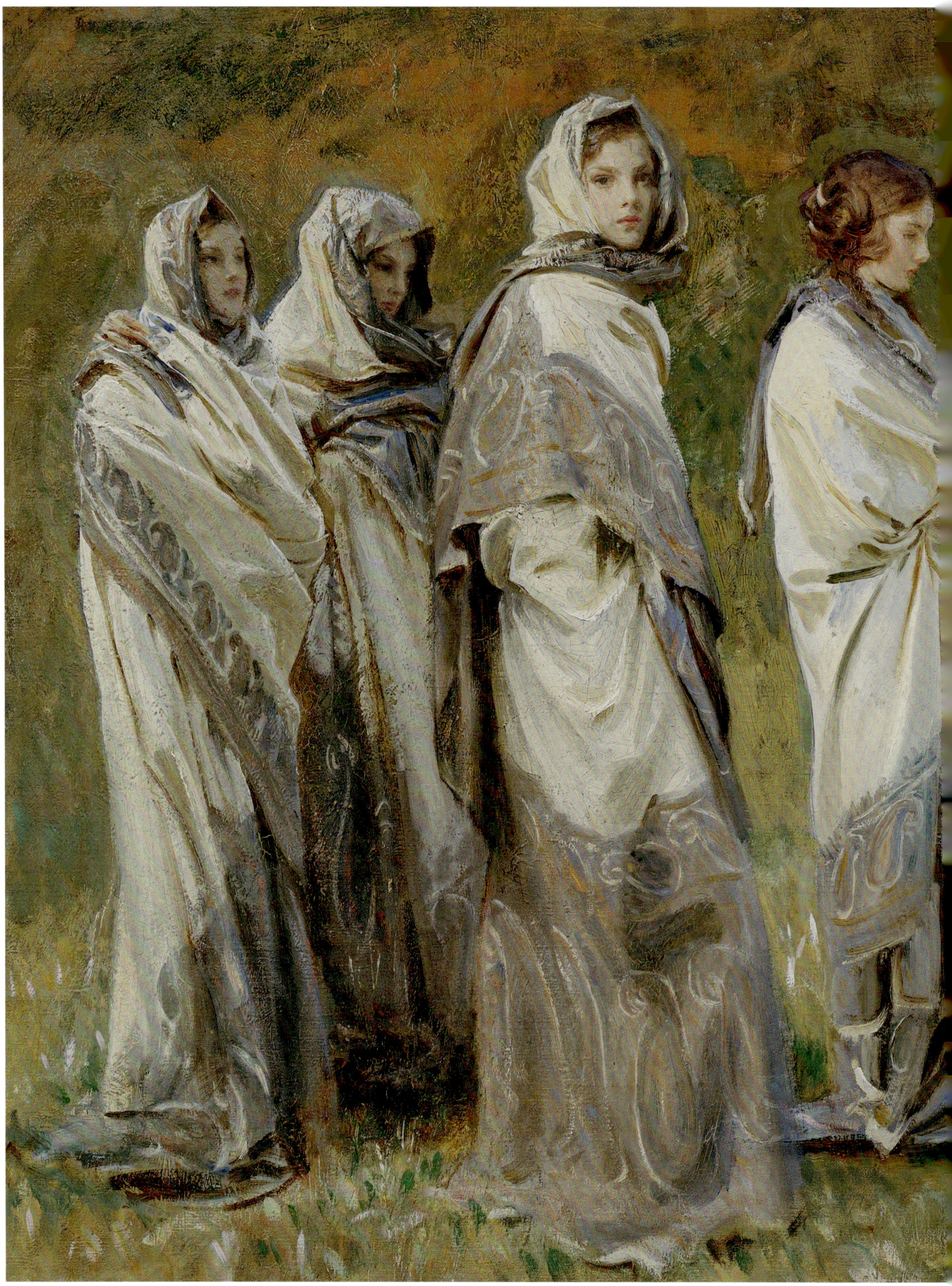

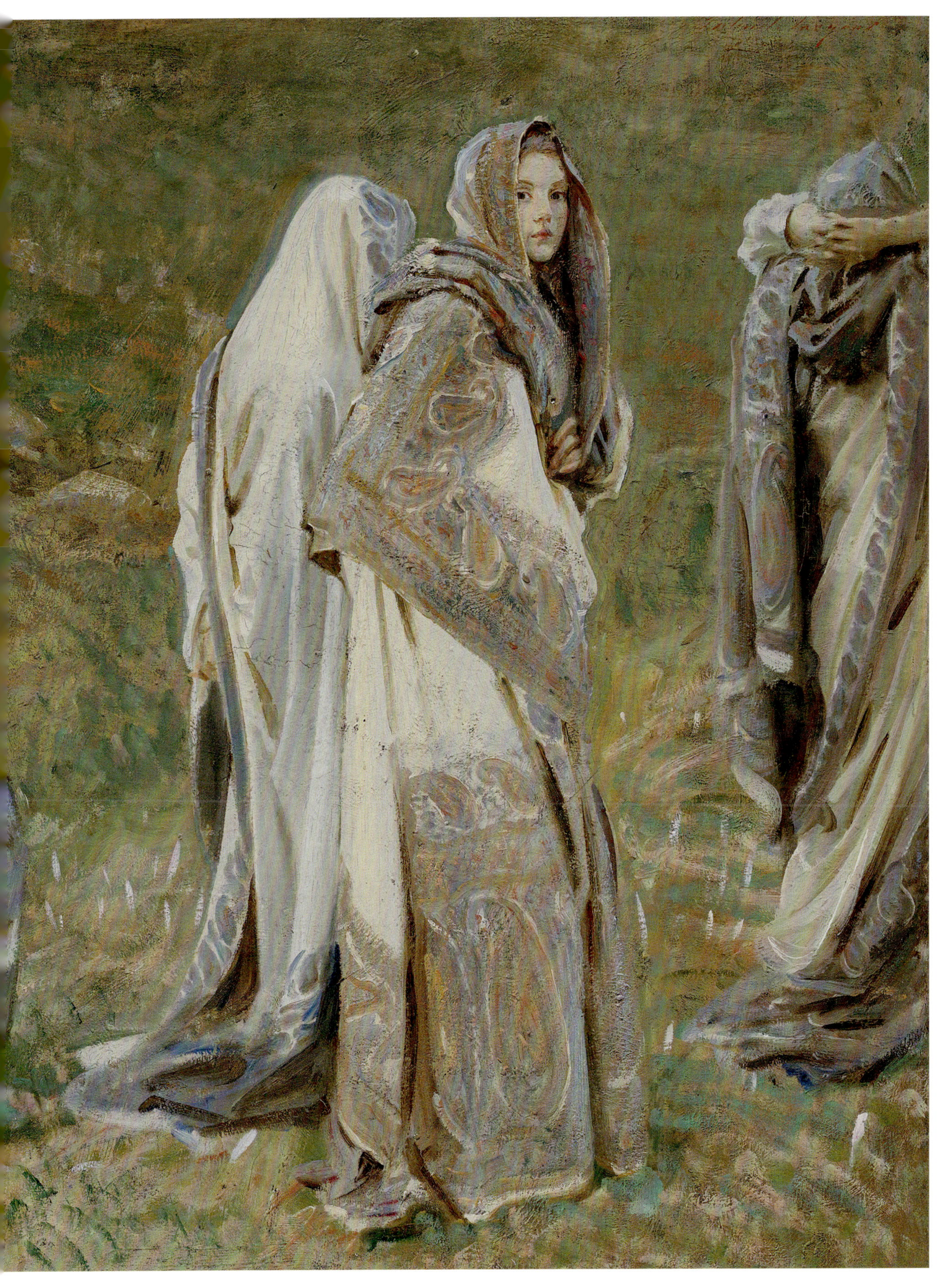

Experiments

Edwin Austin Abbey's compositional studies for *The Hours* record his interest in rhythm, color transitions, interactions among figures, and their orientation. Feet in or feet out? The broadest, and perhaps earlier, of these two studies (cat. 102), which lacks stars, celestial bodies, or constellations, shows that he explored having the figures facing out rather than in—a dramatic difference in effect. The daylight hours are all nude, focusing attention on their movements instead of their clothing. The lightly rendered and dark-contoured figures call to mind the joyful dancers of Henri Matisse from the same era, echoing Abbey's artistic priorities of decorative conception and expressive character.[1] Abbey traveled to Paris each year to see the latest exhibitions and certainly admired recent art, though Matisse is not mentioned in his personal papers or early biographies.

The later study (cat. 103) explores different aspects of the composition, especially color and interaction among the figures. Abbey needed to determine proportions and movements to fit all the hours into the space. Both iterations offer details of his process, as he thought about and explored ideas heuristically, trying them out in study after study. As these works document, he made messes and mistakes, revised in progress, and then continued or abandoned each version in turn, likely revisiting some from time to time. A remarkable quality of *The Hours* is the sheer number of surviving oil studies related to the composition and each figure in it. Pastels were a close second, also allowing vivid color development. Each trial brought Abbey closer to the final composition.

NOTE

1. The large 1909 version of Matisse's *Dance (I)* (Museum of Modern Art, 201.1963) is itself a study. The composition derived from Matisse's earlier *Joy of Life* (1905–6; Barnes Foundation, BF719), which he developed with inspiration from Pierre Puvis de Chavannes, describing the coloring of *Dance (I)* as "à la Puvis"; Stephanie D'Alessandro and John Elderfield, *Matisse: Radical Invention, 1913–1917*, exh. cat. (Chicago: The Art Institute of Chicago, 2010), 48.

CAT. 102 Edwin Austin Abbey (American, 1852–1911, HON. 1897)

Study for *The Hours* in the Pennsylvania State Capitol, ca. 1904–11

Oil on canvas, 36 × 36 in. (91.4 × 91.4 cm)
Yale University Art Gallery, New Haven, Conn., Edwin Austin Abbey Memorial Collection, 1937.1717

CAT. 103 Edwin Austin Abbey (American, 1852–1911, HON. 1897)

Study for *The Hours* in the Pennsylvania State Capitol, ca. 1904–11

Oil on canvas, 36 × 36 in. (91.4 × 91.4 cm)
Yale University Art Gallery, New Haven, Conn., Edwin Austin Abbey Memorial Collection, 1937.1715

Detail of cat. 102

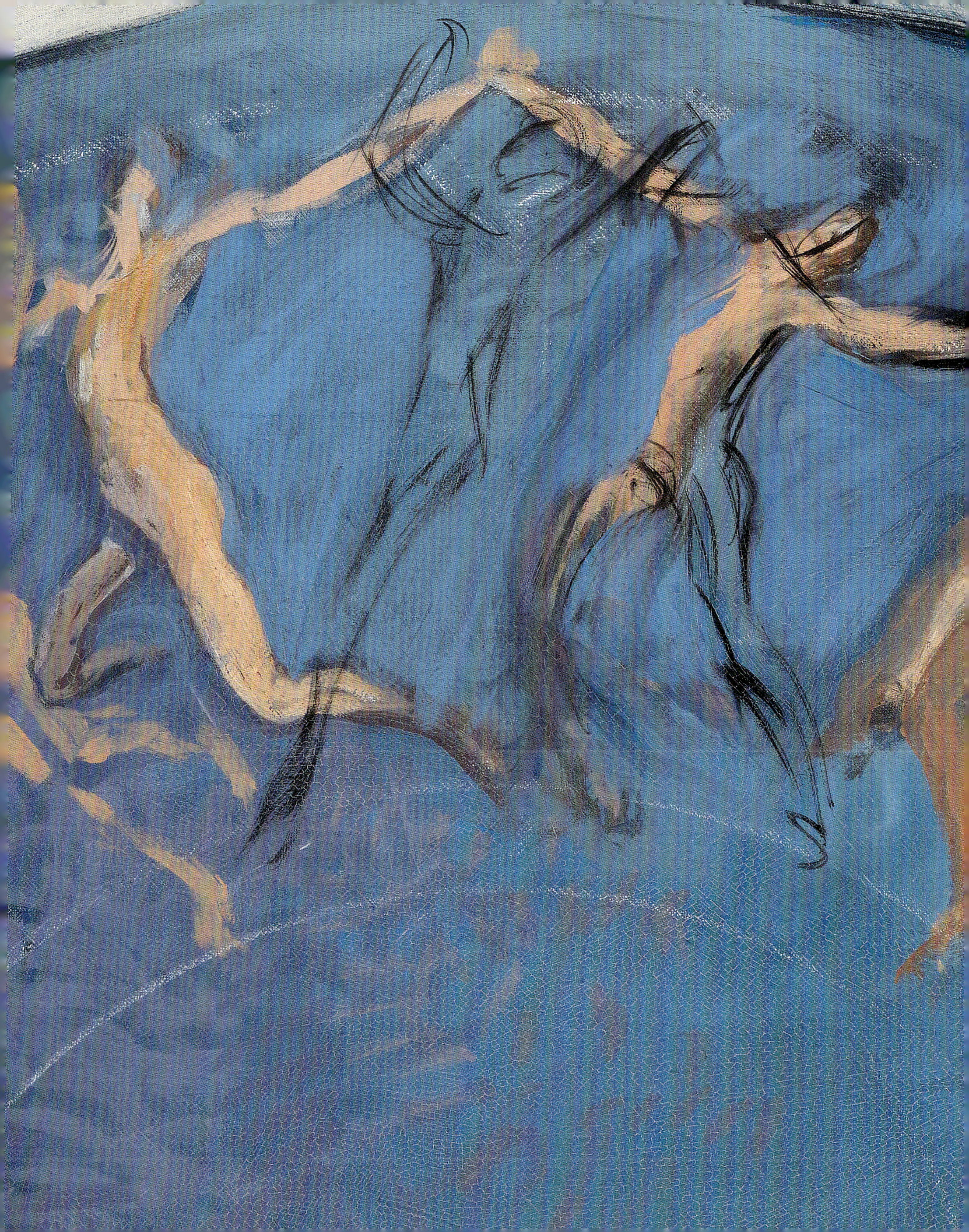

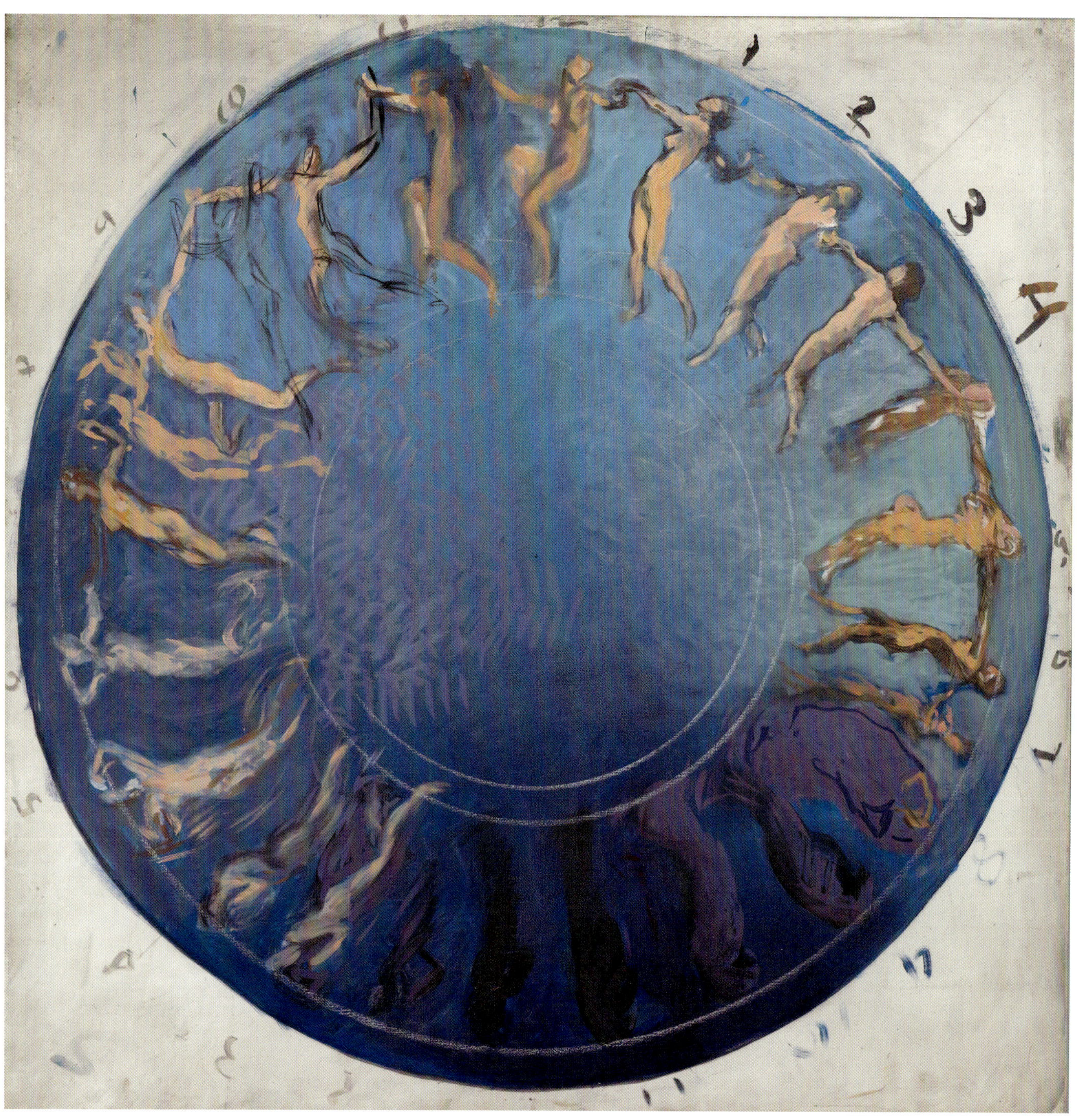

102

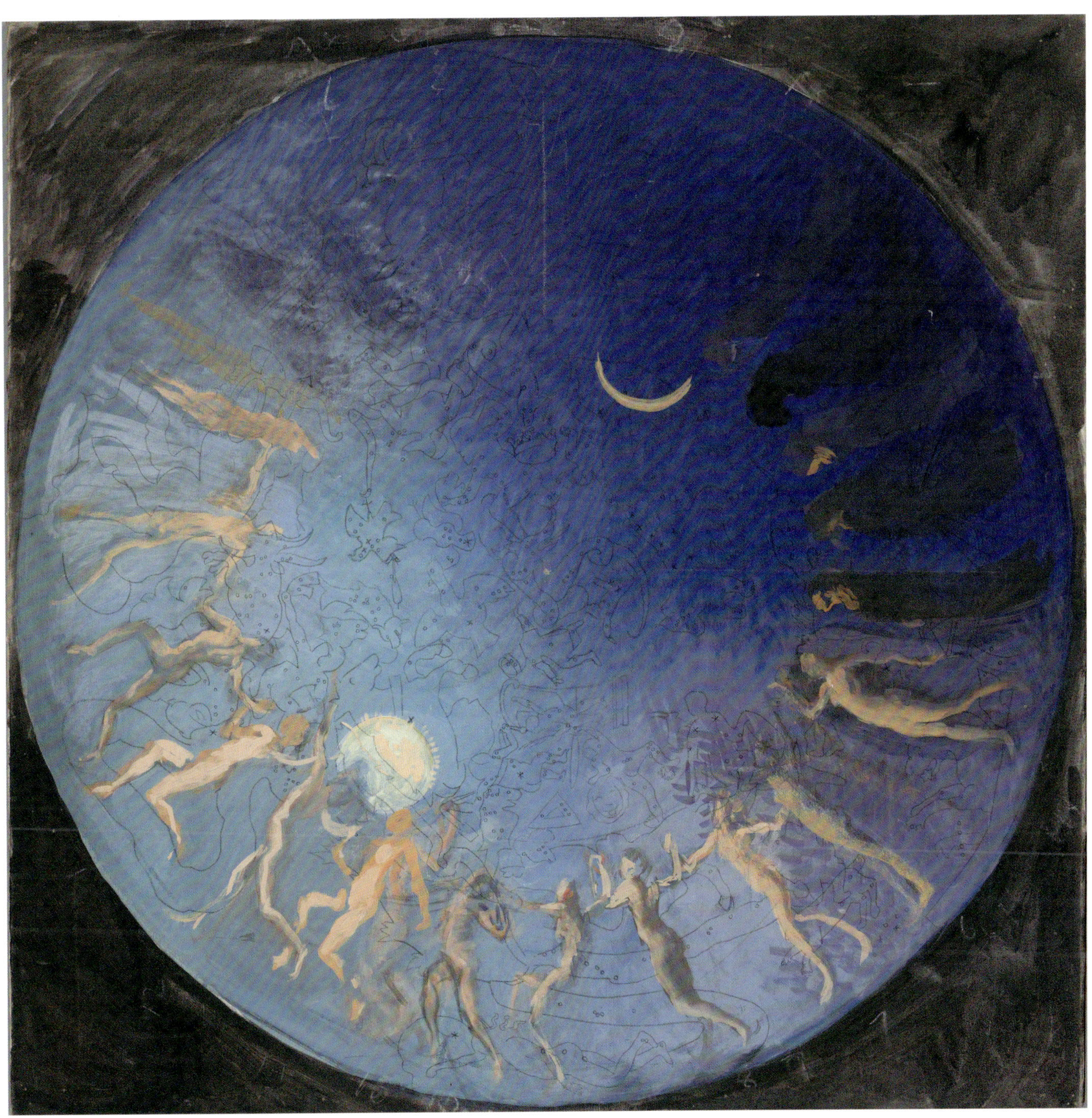

103

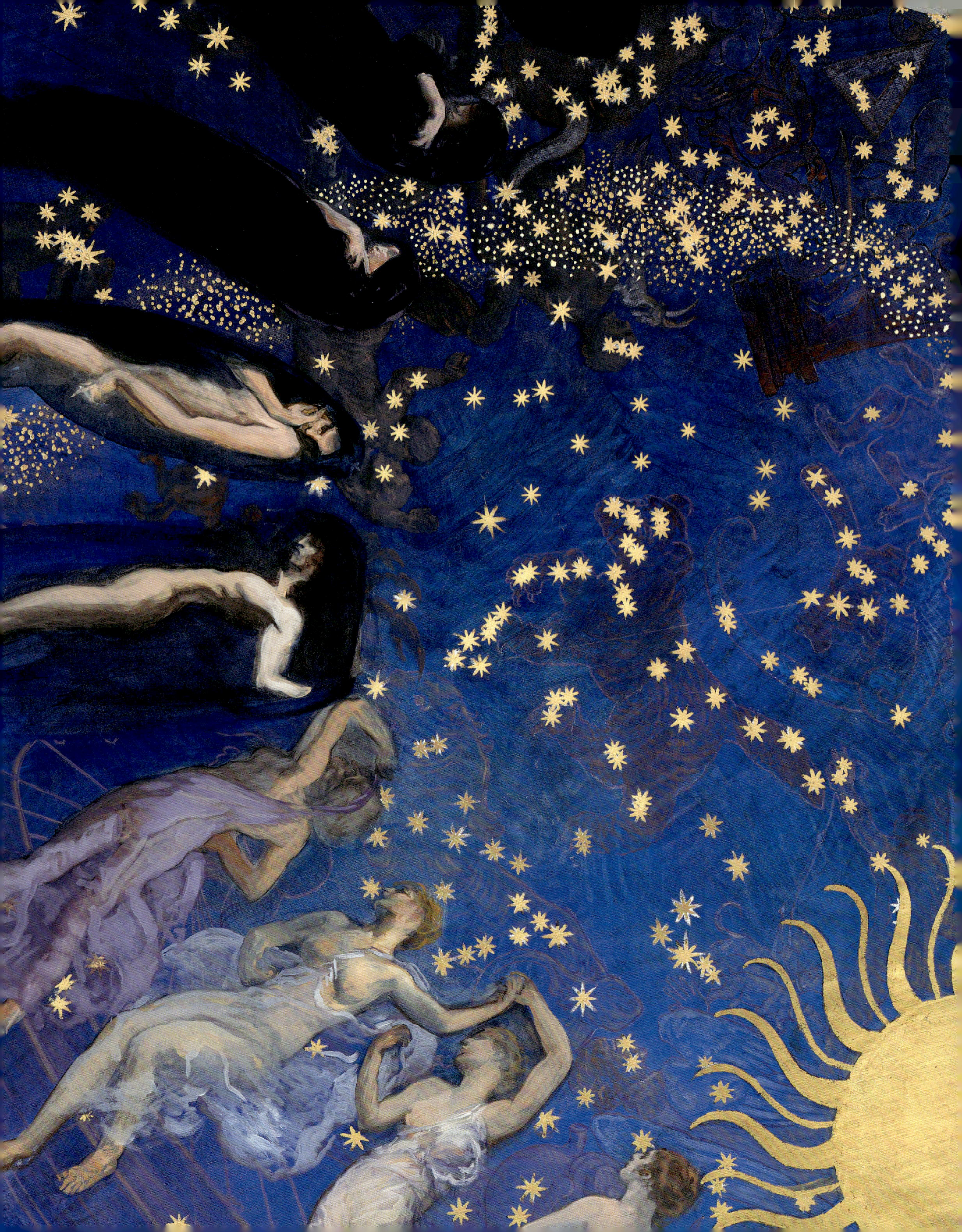

THE HOURS

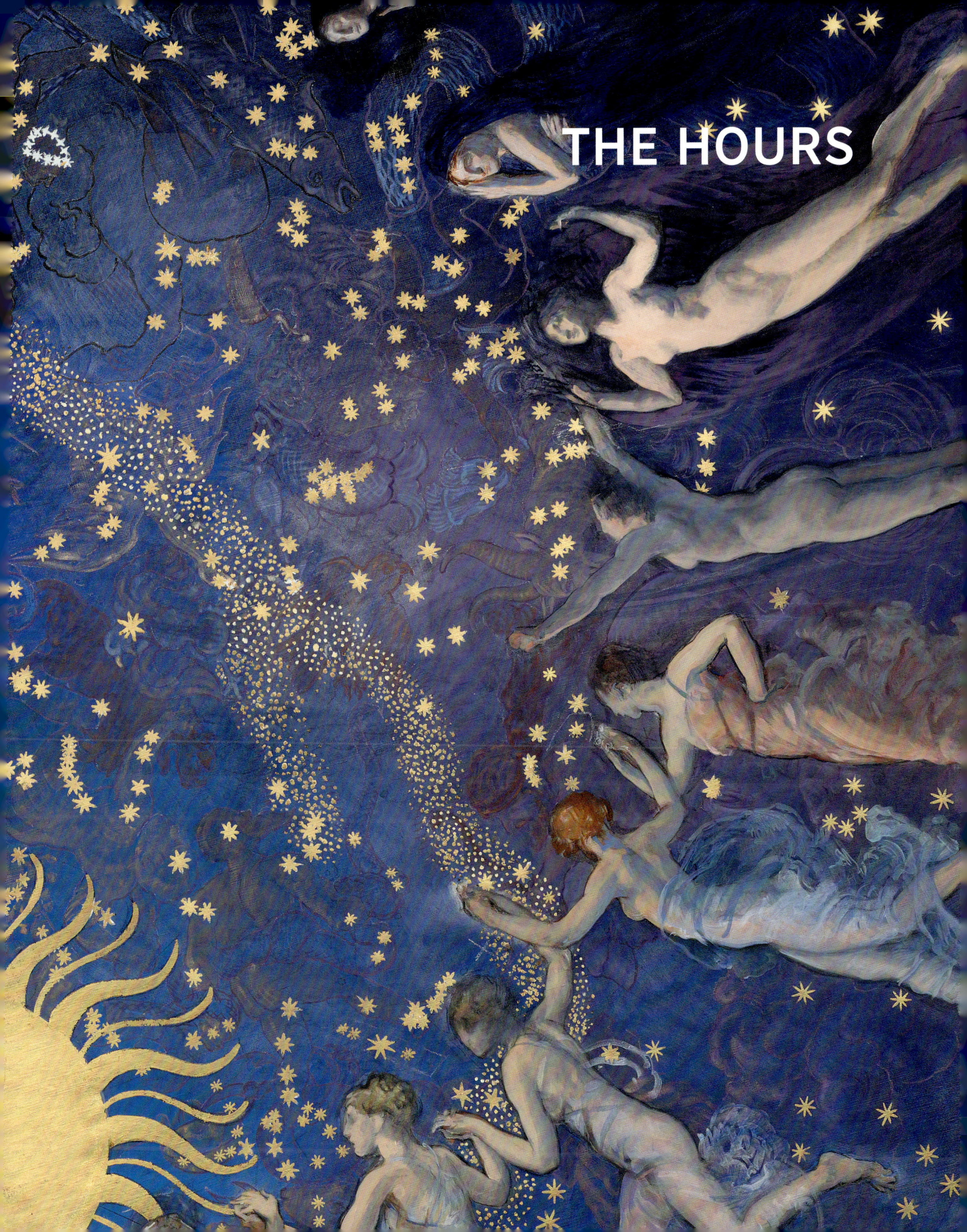

THIS LAST, HALF-SCALE STUDY—DESCRIBED AS A "finished study" by Edwin Austin Abbey's biographer E. V. Lucas—records the artist's last thoughts before progressing to the twenty-four-foot-diameter canvas for *The Hours*.[1] Revisions are everywhere, and yet still he would significantly change the presentations of the sun and moon in the final version. As they were from the outset, Abbey's nocturnal figures are shrouded, and the daylight figures move freely in their light, diaphanous robes that reveal their dancing bodies. Abbey dedicated himself to thoroughly understanding his figures and their interactions, and he developed new methods of working that would enable him to shift readily between orders of magnitude.[2]

The Hours was Abbey's most Symbolist work, a change in emphasis, subject, and style from the visual storytelling of his early career as a magazine illustrator. The dramatic forms of the hours of night are especially redolent of Symbolist foreboding and psychological intensity, with their bodies concealed and their gender opaque. Seeking to distance himself from his professional beginnings—though his sketchbooks show that he still relied on the pen-and-ink drawings that gave him his start—Abbey moved further and further into other media and the defining subject of fine art: the figure.

During the American Renaissance, mural painting was extolled as the highest art form, and Abbey sought to reach its greatest accomplishment. The recognition that he received in both America and England, where he was credited with revitalizing the practice of mural painting after its decades-long hiatus, demonstrates his success and remarkable achievement.[3] With *The Hours*, Abbey embraced Henry James's early perception that "life itself is his subject."[4]

NOTES

1. Edward Verrall Lucas, *Edwin Austin Abbey, Royal Academician: The Record of His Life and Work* (London: Methuen, 1921), 2:471.
2. Ernest Board, who apprenticed with Abbey, described his "Harrisburg methods," including making lantern slides of individual figure studies and then projecting them onto the canvas at night in order to trace their contours with charcoal; Lucas, *Abbey*, 2:441.
3. In 1902, the critic Hermann Muthesius put Abbey at the head of a new "Neo-Pre-Raphaelite" school of British mural painting; cited in Clare A. P. Willsdon, *Mural Painting in Britain, 1840–1940: Image and Meaning* (Oxford: Oxford University Press, 2000), 96–97.
4. James's 1886 review of Abbey's work in *Harper's Weekly* is cited in Lucas, *Abbey*, 1:161.

CAT. 104 Edwin Austin Abbey (American, 1852–1911, HON. 1897)

Study for *The Hours* in the Pennsylvania State Capitol, ca. 1909–11

Oil on canvas, DIAM. 150 in. (381 cm)
Yale University Art Gallery, New Haven, Conn., Edwin Austin Abbey Memorial Collection, 1937.1716

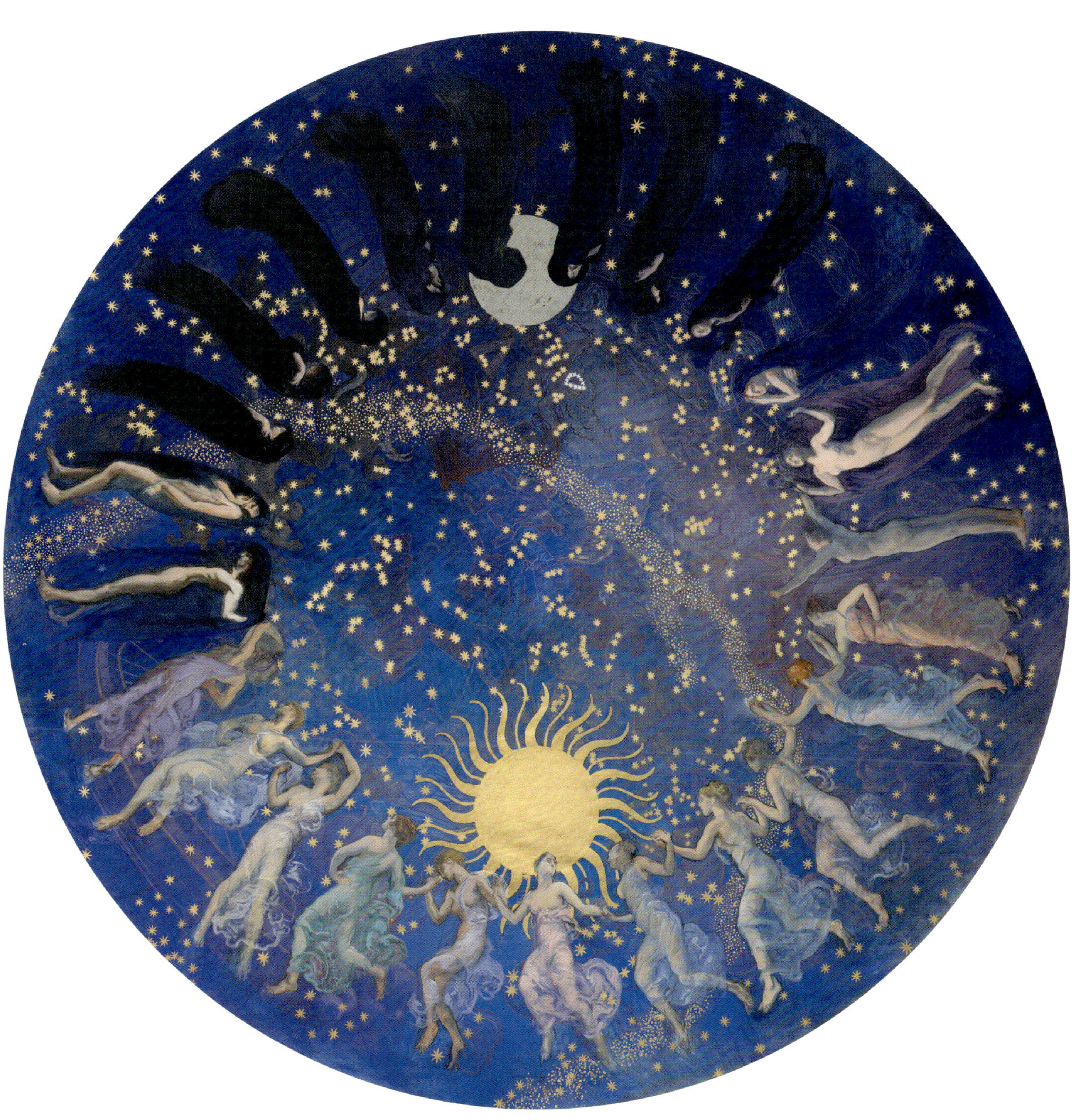

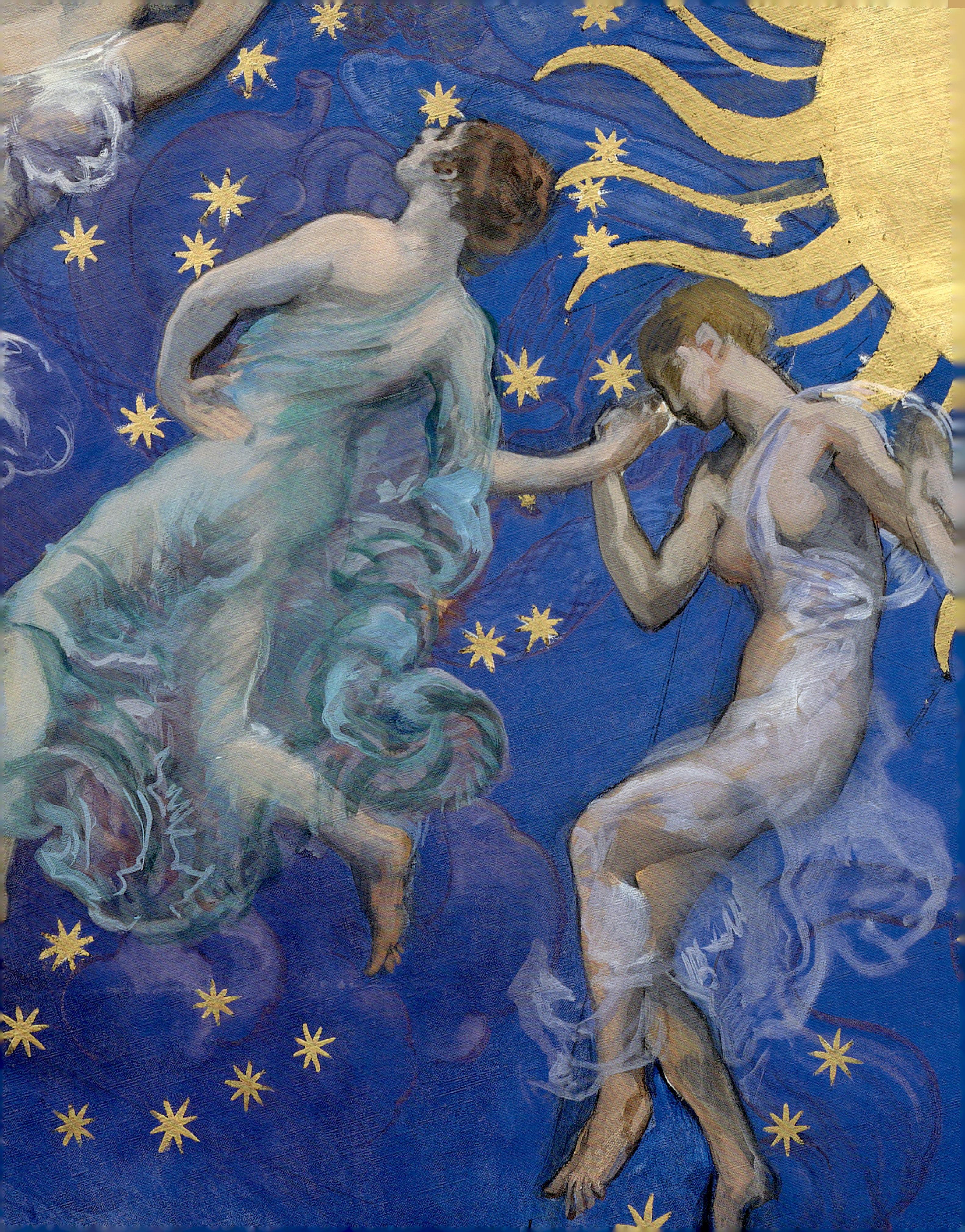

Creating "The Hours":

EDWIN AUSTIN ABBEY'S PROCESS AND MATERIALS

KELSEY WINGEL

Beginning in 1907, Edwin Austin Abbey wrote repeatedly to Joseph Huston, architect of the Pennsylvania State Capitol in Harrisburg, imploring him to return the artist's preparatory studies. Upon Huston's request, earlier that year Abbey had sent several compositional studies and color schemes for the interior spaces he had been commissioned to decorate, including the House, Senate, and Supreme Court chambers. Abbey explained that his sketches contained "notes of ideas which I wish to use in my work for the Capitol, and without them I am much embarrassed."[1] Still without them in 1911, an increasingly frustrated Abbey enlisted the help of Dr. James William White, his representative for the Harrisburg commission, writing, "I am greatly hoping that you may be able to get for me those sketches from Huston—I can't imagine what he wants with them, and they are, although slight, invaluable to me, as the first notes one makes always are."[2]

What, one might ask, was so invaluable about these early studies, and what did Abbey hope to gain by retrieving them years later? Considering Abbey's singular creative process, the answer comes easily: that fleeting original idea for a composition, miraculously captured on paper or canvas. Abbey's process was remarkably nonlinear, and in its early stages it was guided almost exclusively by the vagaries of his imagination. He once reflected, "While I am waiting to discover the details of one design numerous other designs will have suggested themselves, or some details or movement I may have been groping for, for a year, may appear out of the mist." What followed the (often unexpected) arrival of this artistic vision were years of historical research and the creation of dozens of preparatory works in watercolor, charcoal, oil, and pastel to develop and refine each composition. And although that composition may be drastically transformed over the course of months and years, the studies that captured the "floating idea"[3]—that key representation of the artist's ultimate intent—were essential inspirational fuel throughout Abbey's creative process.

The vital role of Abbey's imagination in the conception and development of his mural paintings aligns his artistic practice with that of artists of the American Renaissance, who sought to revive the inventive genius of the Italian Renaissance through the creation of magnificent civic spaces for the country's growing cities.[4] New and purposeful collaborations between painters, sculptors, and architects sought to infuse these harmoniously aligned arts into the libraries, train stations, and capitols daily encountered by the public. Befitting the longevity of the buildings they adorned, mural paintings aimed to celebrate enduring American values and history in a visual language both readily understandable to their audience and appropriate to the architectural style and function of the spaces they completed. As the painter Charles M. Shean noted, if mural painting in the United States "is ever to become vital and living, . . . it must cease to bedizen and bedeck. It must become more than an academic echo, a Renaissance reminiscence. The artist must learn to make the walls of our public buildings splendid with pictured records of American exploit and achievement, of American industry and commerce, of American life and culture."[5]

Abbey heeded this rousing appeal as he began preparing studies for his last mural commission for the Pennsylvania State Capitol in 1902. The rotunda, the first space he completed, features four allegorical lunettes celebrating Pennsylvania's oil, steel, and coal industries, as well as the state's history of religious freedom. In his subsequent murals for the House of Representatives chamber, he masterfully integrated allegory with historical figures and events of local significance to convey what Pennsylvania contributed to the birth and prosperity of a nation. On the south wall (see page 290), behind the Speaker's rostrum and facing the representatives, Abbey painted three large murals. At the center is the thirty-five-foot-square *Apotheosis of Pennsylvania*, featuring notable men in state history positioned on the steps of a temple to the enthroned Genius of State. On either side, two murals, each measuring twenty-four by twelve feet, commemorate events of local and national importance: *Penn's Treaty with the Indians* and *The Reading of the Declaration of Independence*. As the definitive voice in the scale and placement of these murals, as well as the designer of the blue-and-gold color scheme and architectural ornament, Abbey possessed unparalleled control over the decorative and symbolic unity of this ultimately magnificent chamber. What he may not have anticipated during the invention of his elaborate mural scheme was the elimination of a leaded-glass dome skylight and the additional commission of a twenty-four-foot circular ceiling painting in its place.[6] Completed during the last years of his life, the resulting mural, *The Hours* (see pages 276–77), is Abbey's only ceiling painting and, perhaps, his most symbolically complex and imaginative composition.

The Hours depicts twenty-four women, personifications of the hours in a day, traveling around the perimeter of a sky filled with the constellations of the

Northern Hemisphere. The daytime hours wear billowing, cloudlike drapery and gracefully dance with one another from dawn into evening. At six p.m., they cover themselves with black cloaks and proceed solemnly and solitarily into the night. The gilded sun and moon, positioned behind the hours of noon and midnight, respectively, face each other across the canvas as they progress through the zodiac belt, which is painted above the heads of the figures. The Milky Way sweeps across the composition, and a comet punctures the deep-purple sky.

Painted between 1909 and 1911, *The Hours* is the product of the knowledge, discernment, and technical skill Abbey acquired while creating more than one hundred preparatory studies for this composition. At its most foundational, the act of making a study was a vehicle for Abbey to transmit his ideas from mental visualization to physical form. The process was often psychologically taxing and physically arduous, as the artist once expressed: "I do work pretty hard, I think, but I only feel it when I scrub and paint and scrape and cannot get what I see in my mind."[7] Abbey's studies are captivating representations of both his intentions and his state of mind: moments of thought communicated and preserved through his materials. The process of creating a study was also an opportunity for Abbey to gain facility with his artistic materials and explore the expressive power of color, fluidity, texture, and gloss. After its creation, the study served an equally vital role in propelling his creative process forward. Studies served as references for the design, palette, and scale of the final mural painting, as well as inspiration for the making of other preparatory works. What each study contributed to the development of an idea can be singularly unlocked through close examination of its materials, in terms of both its creation and its later use in Abbey's studio. When considered together, Abbey's preparatory studies for *The Hours* provide invaluable insight into his artistic motivations and the progression of his thoughts, illuminating how he came to realize, in his words, "one of the most successful designs I've ever made."[8]

A testament to how dramatically Abbey's compositions could evolve, the dynamic circular format of *The Hours* may have first been conceptualized as a frieze, perhaps years before he received the Harrisburg commission. In a pen-and-ink drawing in his sketchbook, Abbey depicts a procession of figures moving from right to left across a spread of two pages (fig. 1). On the right, the daytime hours are sparsely sketched, their presence only suggested by swift circles for the heads and sweeping lines to indicate joined hands.

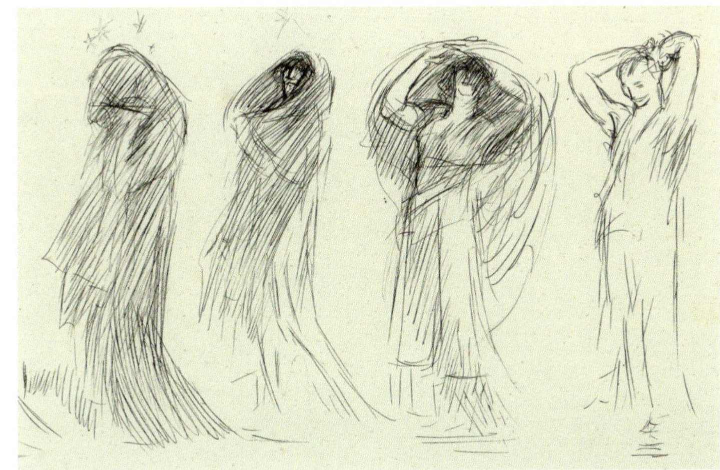

FIG. 1. Detail of cat. 99

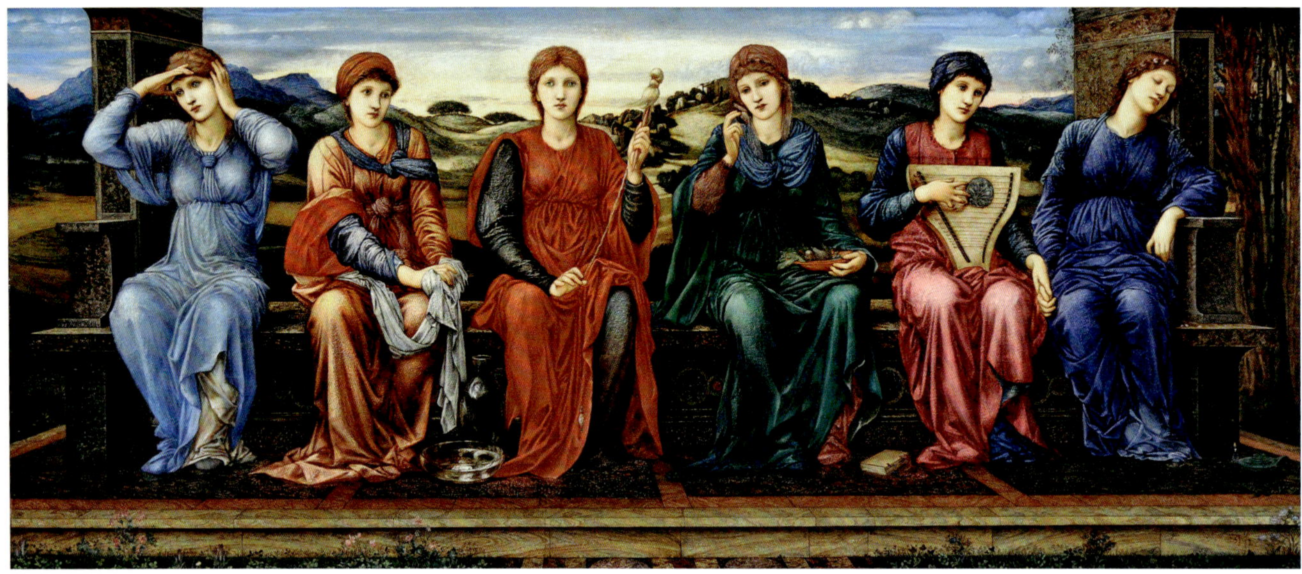

FIG. 2. Edward Burne-Jones, *The Hours*, 1870–82. Oil on canvas, 34 × 72¼ in. (86.5 × 183.5 cm). Graves Gallery, Sheffield Museum Trust

The nighttime hours are more fully realized, revealing Abbey's initial interest in the formal beauty and mystery of the shrouded figure. As they are progressively enveloped, the bodies recall a funeral procession. Created through the diagonal strokes for the drapery, a fluid leftward movement carries the figures across the page, even as each appears frozen in midaction. While Abbey references well-established depictions of night and death, his rendering of movement is strikingly photographic.

The rhythmic, decorative effect of the body in a progression of arrested motions is even more fully realized in a pastel study of primarily the nighttime hours, also arranged in a frieze (see cat. 100). Here, Abbey has further developed the symbolism, depicting the changing sky and swathing each figure in a different color representative of the time of day, the last hour enshrouded in the most somber of hues. A crescent moon and clusters of stars hover poetically above. In the poignant contrast between the joined hands of the daytime hours and the solitary state of those of the night, Abbey conveys that wherever these bodies are going, whether to sleep or to death, they go alone.

For painters of the Gilded Age, especially those of the Decorative, Symbolist, and Aesthetic schools, abstract themes such as death, hope, and love as embodied by the human figure were explored with renewed interest. Measured reflections on the passage of time were often represented in classically inspired, friezelike compositions, as in Edward Burne-Jones's painted version, exhibited at the Grosvenor Gallery in 1883 (fig. 2). Here, time is depicted as six seated women, arranged horizontally and each engaged in an activity or holding an emblem representative of a particular time of day. Burne-Jones developed the symbolism through not merely iconography but also the formal qualities of color. As he explained in a letter to Eleanor Warren, Lady Leighton, "Every little lady besides the proper colour of her own frock wears a lining of the color of the hour before her and a sleeve of the hour coming after—so that Mr. Whistler could, if he liked, call it a fugue."[9]

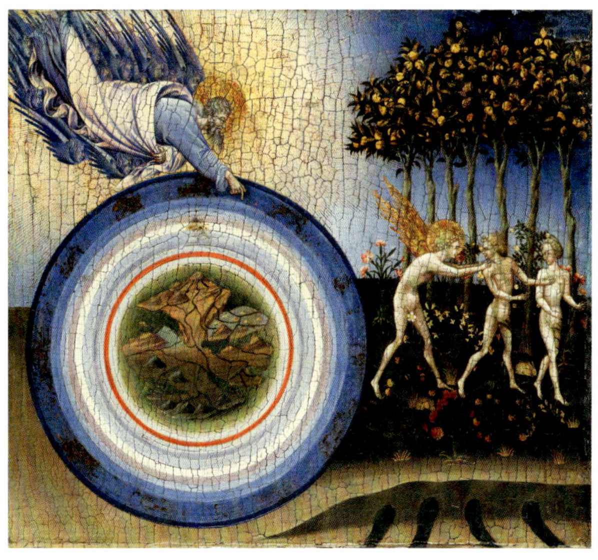

FIG. 3. Giovanni di Paolo, *The Creation of the World and the Expulsion from Paradise*, 1445. Tempera and gold on wood, 18¼ × 20½ in. (46.4 × 52.1 cm). The Metropolitan Museum of Art, New York, 1975.1.31

Abbey's similar interest in the symbolic, metrical power of color is apparent throughout his preparatory studies. In perhaps his earliest painted study to depict a circular composition, he embraced a palette resembling that of Burne-Jones, using hues reminiscent of medieval paintings and stained glass to suggest a mystical space (see cat. 30). All twenty-four hours have been painted in prismatic draperies, warm hues for the day and cool for the night; they are organized not in a frieze but around the perimeter of a deep blue sky that incorporates six zodiac constellations, the sun, the moon, and stars. His hours are spritely, closer to the visual tradition of the Horae in ancient and Renaissance depictions of the hours. For Abbey and his contemporaries, the most recognized example was likely the Hours of Raphael, rediscovered in the nineteenth century from an engraving of the ceiling of the Sala del Camino in the Borgia Apartments at the Vatican.[10]

This highly ordered, spherical composition recalls structured depictions of the cosmos in medieval paintings and illuminations, such as Giovanni di Paolo's fifteenth-century predella *The Creation of the World and the Expulsion from Paradise* (fig. 3). Abbey's even spacing of the hours and the addition of an interior circle of zodiac figures, painted in gold against a background of deep blue, reference the rings of a divinely organized understanding of the universe. In placing his figural depiction of a day against a sky, Abbey's study advances far beyond a portrayal of time. Drawing on established traditions of using blue and gold to depict sacred spaces, his composition asks the viewer to consider the role of divine influence over not just the course of a day but also a seemingly predetermined and unending cycle of human existence, represented by the cosmos beyond.

Abbey's inward-facing figures complement the circular form of his painting, now clearly intended for a ceiling mural. Consideration of the unique architectural volume of the House chamber likely influenced Abbey's developing conception of *The Hours* as a celestial space, for the depiction of heavenly realms on domes and ceilings is well established in the history of art. Even in the early stages of design, Abbey carefully considered the architecture of the chamber; the graphite circle around the painting references the elaborate ornamentation of the ceiling. Sketched in pencil in the lower-right corner, Abbey has planned the scale of his successive studies.

PAGES 276–77: The rotunda of the Pennsylvania State Capitol, showing Abbey's *Hours*

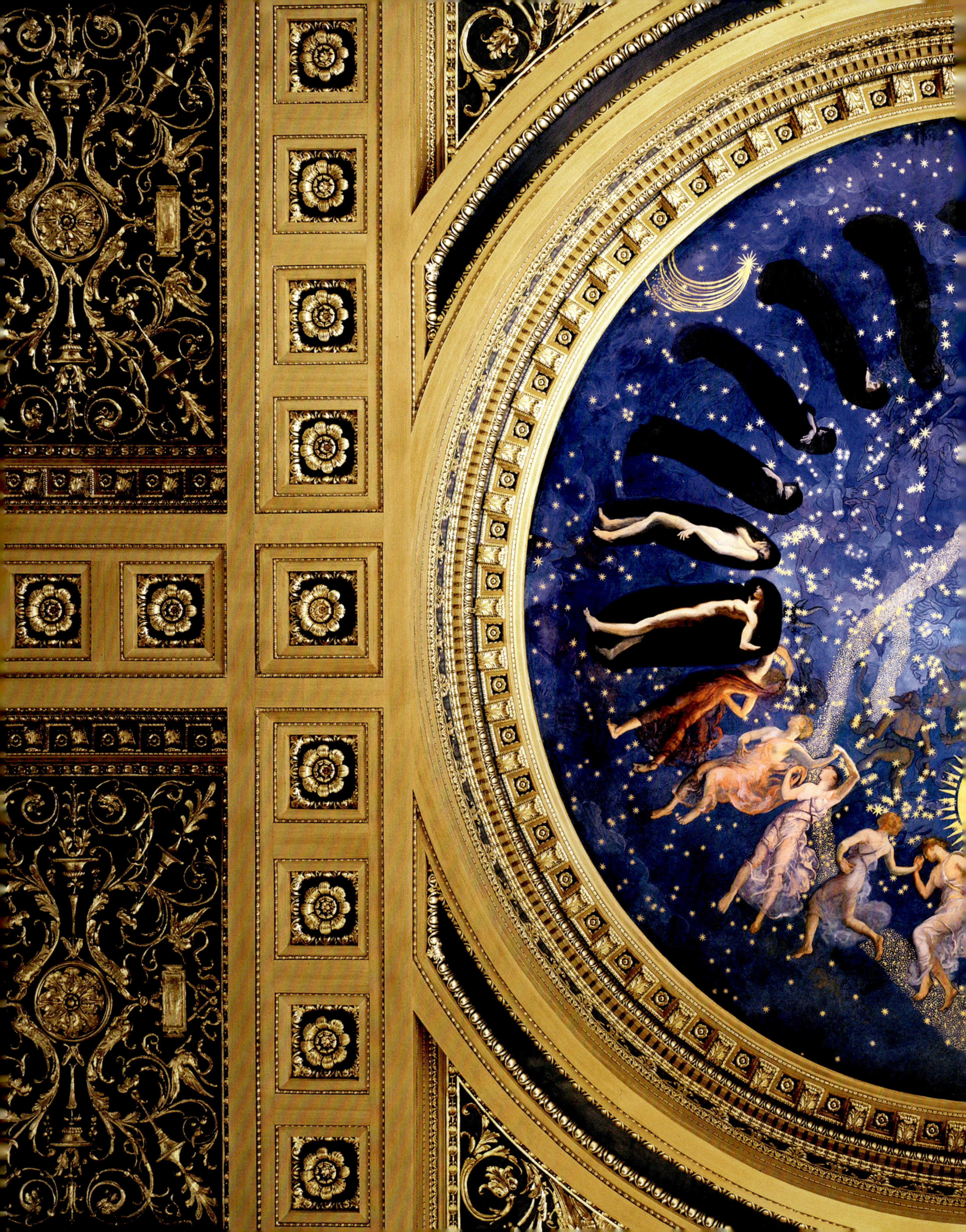

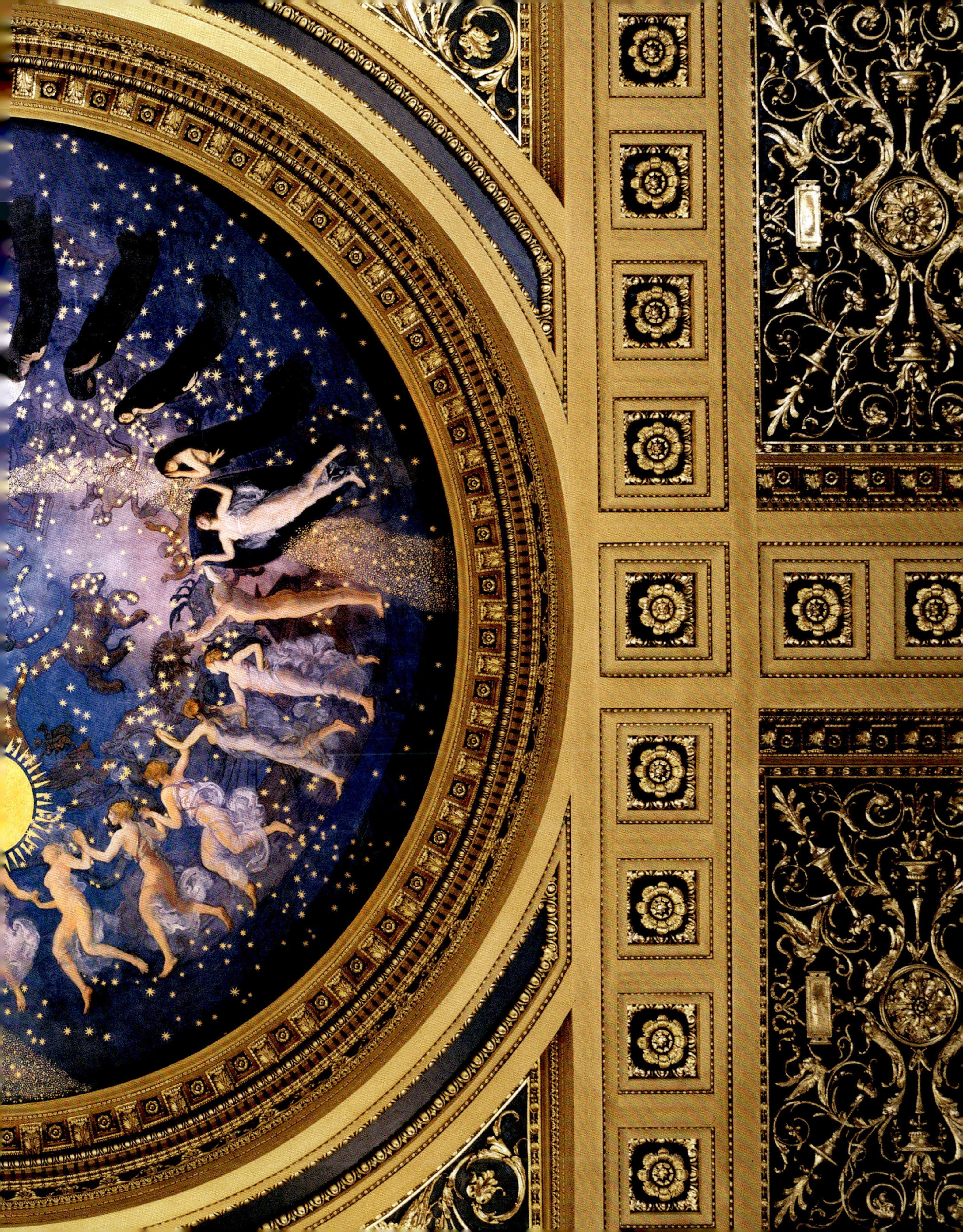

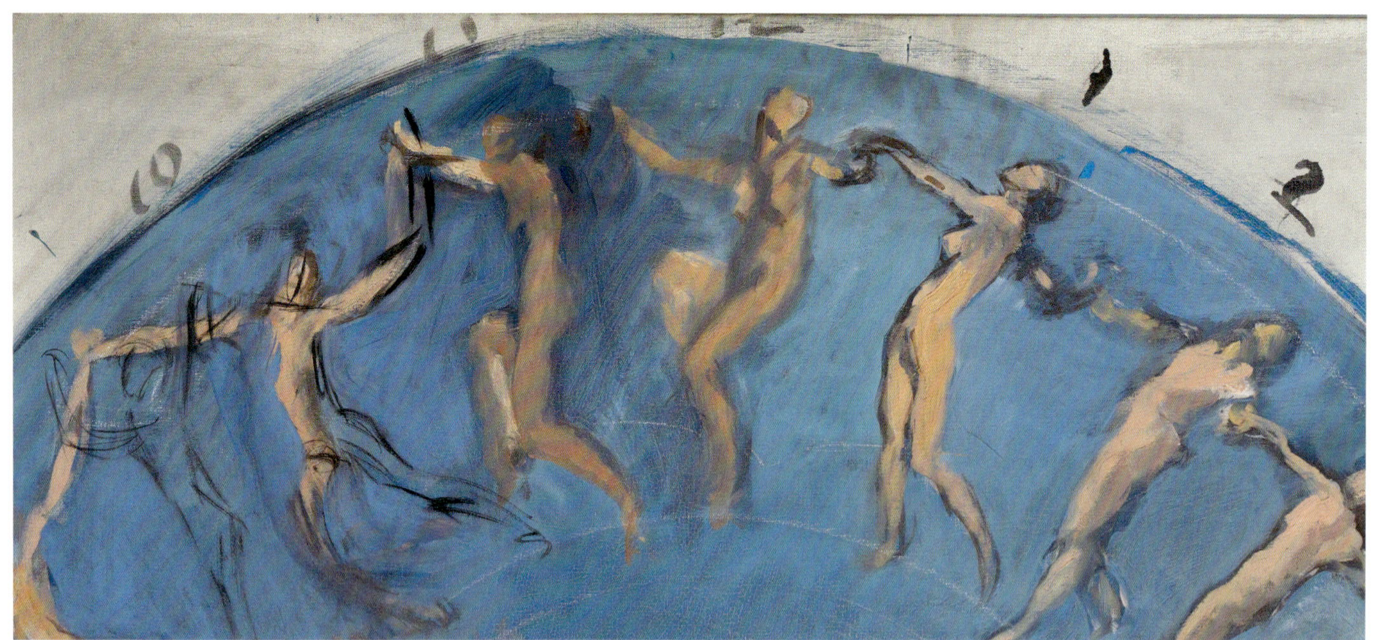

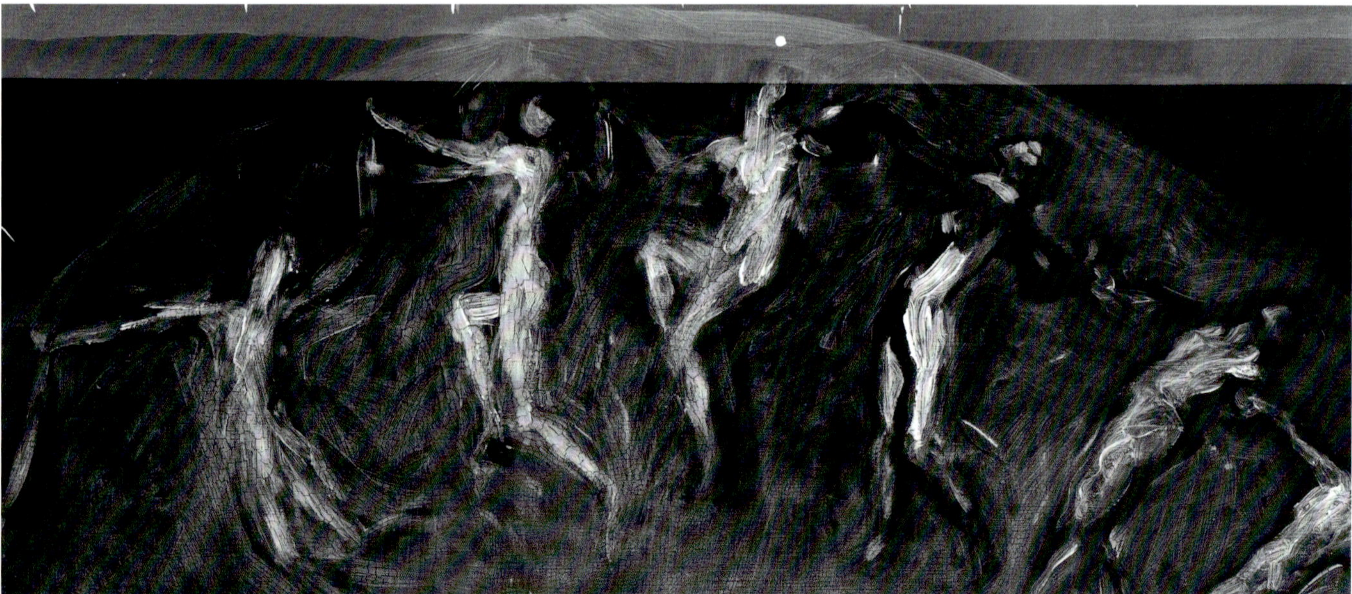

FIG. 4 (TOP). Detail of cat. 102

FIG. 5 (BOTTOM). X-radiograph of fig. 4 captured at 25 kV, 4.5 mA, 20 sec

In tension with the palpable mysticism of this study is another early preparatory painting, perhaps developed concurrently, that celebrates the beauty and expressiveness of the human body (see cat. 102). Nothing could stand in greater contrast to the clothed goddesses than the strikingly modern nude figures Abbey painted in a study carefully scaled to one-eighth the size of the final mural. Now positioned outward and periodically illuminated by a golden light, Abbey's day hours radiate lighthearted joy as they playfully pull one another forward, eventually beginning to leap and dance. Abbey returns to the theme of the night hours, bathed in the cool light of evening, actively wrapping themselves in black and purple drapery. The emotions conveyed through their bodies are ones that we recognize, and more than Abbey's previous studies, they invoke a strong sympathetic response within the viewer. We can relate (or aspire to relate) to the feeling of cheerfully awakening to the warmth of the sun on our faces, to living a productive and active day; to the satisfaction of being tired and enjoying peaceful repose, and to the expectation of awakening to yet another day.

The almost exuberant mood of this painting is partially created though Abbey's lively brushwork and lighter palette (fig. 4). The rapid and easy elegance of the bold application of paint, brushed wet into wet with impasto, suggests that Abbey worked quickly, perhaps largely from his imagination during one of his "fillips or bursts of intelligence," as he described them.[11] Indeed, there is little evidence of underdrawing, and the X-radiograph highlights the extent to which Abbey confidently rendered the highlights on the figures and laid in the background around them (fig. 5). The X-radiograph reveals alterations to the arms and heads of the figures of ten a.m. and eleven a.m. but little other evidence of compositional change. The seemingly spontaneous and easy execution of this study clearly presents Abbey's developing ideas about the figures' potential to represent fundamental and unchanging human emotions and experience.

The new and compelling vitality evident in this study appears to have catalyzed the making of many drawings of individual figures as Abbey sought to explore the emotional impact of the body's movement and to define the characteristic pose for each hour. These drawings—in graphite, charcoal, and chalk on paper ranging from red to blue—were likely done directly from a model. They fill the page with a similarly unbridled energy channeled in his painted study, revealing Abbey's intent to represent spirit through movement. The facial features in many of his drawings are poorly defined, with the action of the body instead bearing the expressive weight. Abbey likely began to resolve the position of each hour through graphite sketches (fig. 6), later exploring the fall of light and shadow across musculature through chalk and charcoal studies (fig. 7). This process aligns with what Ernest Board, one of

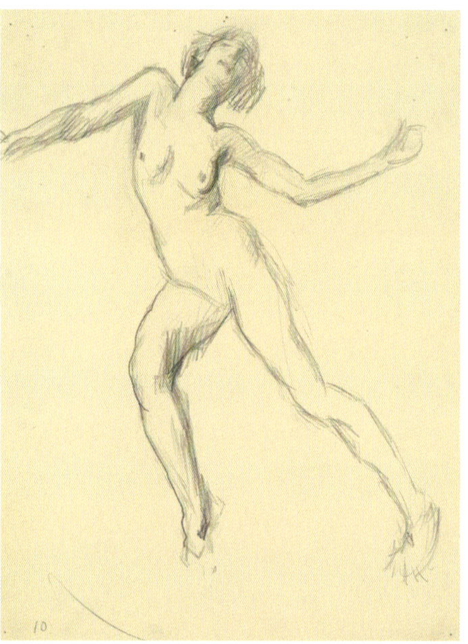

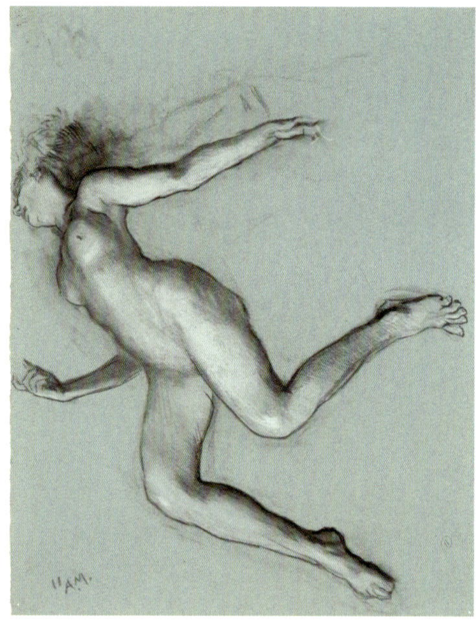

FIG. 6. Edwin Austin Abbey, Study for Ten A.M. for *The Hours*, 1904–11. Graphite on cream wove paper, $13\frac{7}{16} \times 10\frac{1}{16}$ in. (34.1 × 25.6 cm). Yale University Art Gallery, New Haven, Conn., Edwin Austin Abbey Memorial Collection, 1937.1739

FIG. 7. Edwin Austin Abbey, Study for Eleven A.M. for *The Hours*, 1904–11. Black and white chalk on green laid paper, $24\frac{7}{16} \times 18\frac{7}{8}$ in. (62 × 48 cm). Yale University Art Gallery, New Haven, Conn., Edwin Austin Abbey Memorial Collection, 1937.1741

Abbey's studio assistants, recalled of his mural painting practice: "His process of evolving each subject, started perhaps with the merest pencil sketch in a sketch book or a small oil study; this would pass through various phases of elimination or refining, often with the help of little groups of mannikins set up, arranged and rearranged until the required composition was obtained. Then careful studies of each figure were done in charcoal, pastel, or paint from the living model."[12]

In a very different manner from the rapid paint application seen in figure 4, Abbey's premeditated approach to the creation of another painted study of identical size reveals his intent to synthesize an extraordinary amount of thought, research, and preparation into a design growing in symbolic complexity (fig. 8). Different passages of this unfinished study demonstrate distinct stages in Abbey's painting process. He first applied the paint of the sky with feathered transitions between the deep purple night and the bright blue of day. He let these layers dry and then, using black dry media, carefully traced a map of the constellations of the Northern Hemisphere, greatly expanding the iconography beyond the zodiac. Abbey next drew the figures in white chalk before painting them, demonstrated by the unfinished passage at the top of the painting. The hours appear to have been painted concurrently with, or with the direct aid of, his figure drawings, an observation supported not only by similarities in the bodily positions in this painting and several graphite drawings but also through physical evidence on the studies themselves. The study detailed in figure 8 has more than fifty pinholes, suggesting that Abbey attached drawings directly to his canvas while painting (fig. 9).[13] Many of

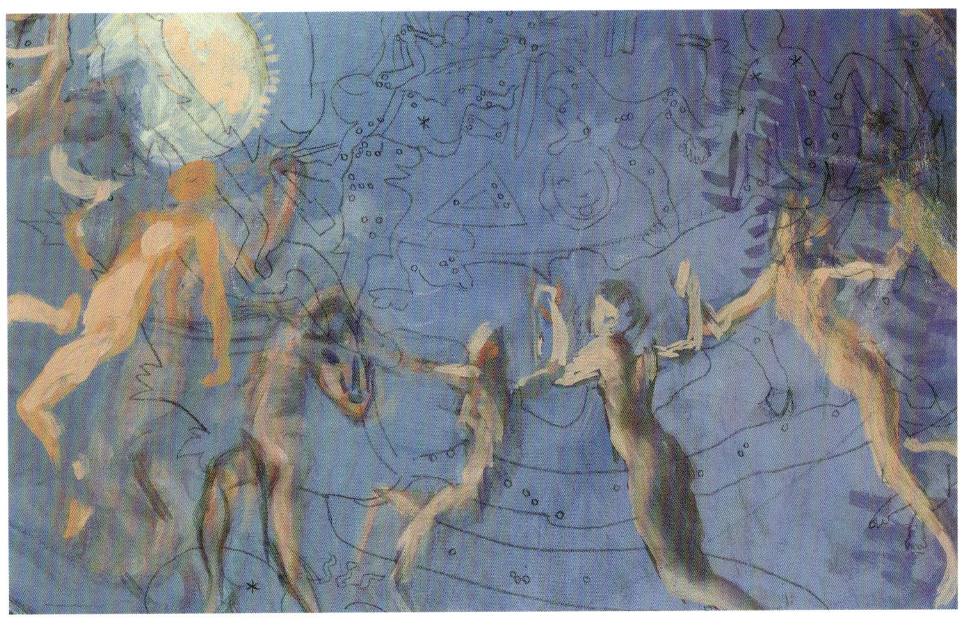

FIG. 8. Detail of cat. 103

his figural drawings also display pinholes in their upper corners and edges, evidence that they were actively used in the creation of other preparatory works (fig. 10).

Yet despite the guidance and inspiration that Abbey likely gained from his preparatory drawings, this study (see cat. 103) suggests that painting the figures remained a challenging process. Passages of scratching, gouging, and abrasion in the paint layers reveal the extent to which he scraped away and repainted his figures, occasionally also amending their positions with black lines. Abbey struggled to define their movements, especially the graceful rhythm of the linking limbs of the daytime hours. The edges of the painting are a jumble of chalk numbers, partially rubbed away and added while the painting was oriented in different positions. The night hours are only partially painted, indicating that Abbey may not have fully conceived of this portion of the painting. One also wonders if, as he worked to build symbolism and refine the formal qualities of his mural, he was dissatisfied with the crowded, hectic energy the composition was acquiring, causing him to leave the work incomplete and returning his attention to the individual figure to establish greater visual clarity.

This same study also combines the mysticism of his earliest painted study (see cat. 30) with the modern dancelike movement of the figures in his later study (see cat. 102). But here the lighthearted mood has been replaced by a more subdued feeling, and the palette has once again acquired a tonal richness. Although the figures appear against a sky that still represents day and night, the physical qualities of the paint have changed drastically. In sharp contrast to

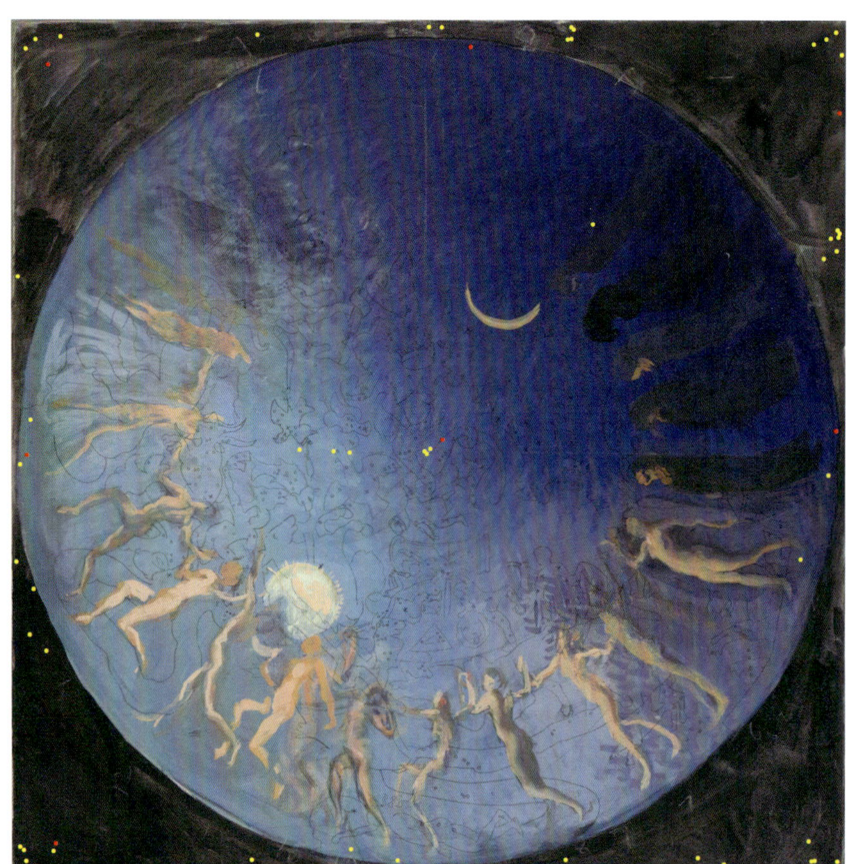

FIG. 9. Cat. 103, showing location of pinholes made before paint was applied (red) and after paint was dry (yellow)

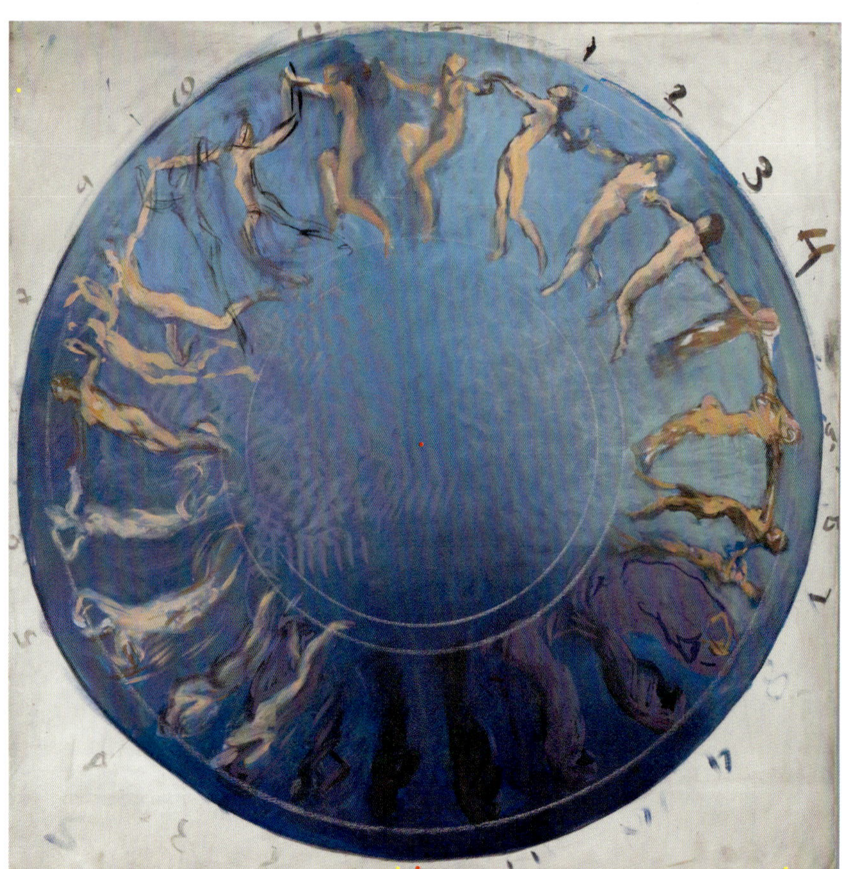

FIG. 10. Cat. 102, showing location of pinholes made before paint was applied (red) and after paint was dry (yellow)

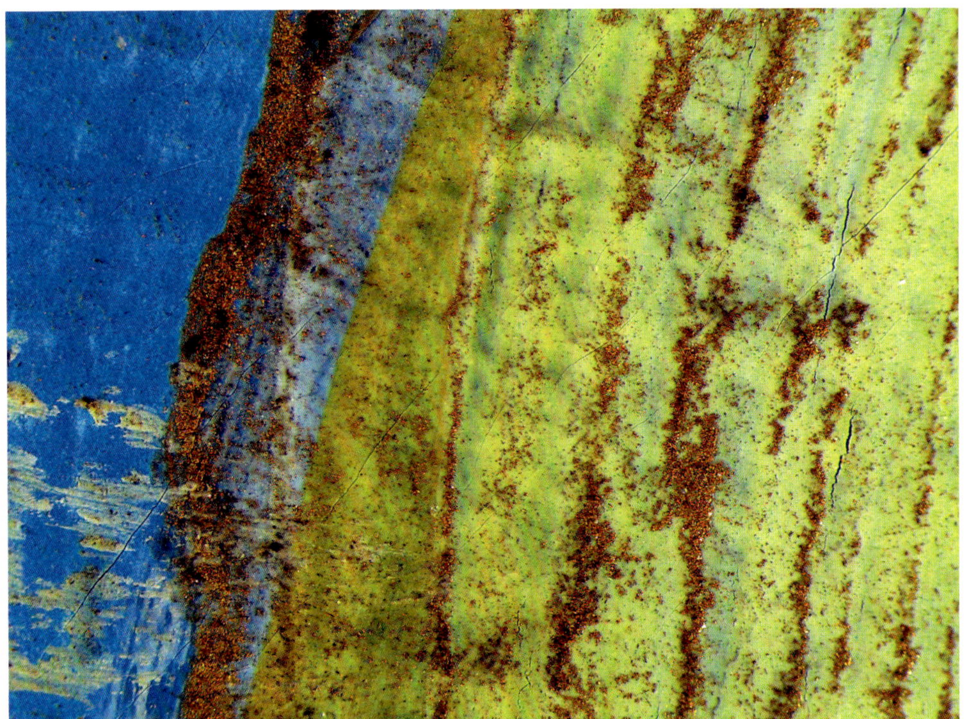

FIG. 11. Photomicrograph of metallic particles applied over sun in cat. 103, photographed at 160x magnification

the vigorous, impastoed brushwork seen in figure 4, this night sky is painted with a smoother, deeper, and more transparent purple paint, adding solemnity, gravity, and mystery to the composition. The night hours are rendered in thin whispers of black paint that almost dissolve into the sky, with no discernible detail or movement in their draperies. The day hours are painted in a flatter, nearly matte medium that resembles gouache or tempera more than oil. As Abbey began to experiment with the physical qualities of his paint and more thoroughly explore its symbolic impact, he also considered other surface effects. The subtle presence of metallic particles applied over the sun suggests that he was pondering the visual impression of gilded celestial bodies (fig. 11).

This study further reveals Abbey's conception of his ceiling painting, in that moment, as a recessive and immersive space. He painted the corners black, eliminating the white ground that keeps the viewer's gaze close to the surface. The impact is dramatic: like looking through a telescope, the viewer is absorbed into a vast celestial space. He also advanced the iconography of the sky, including not just the zodiacs, sun, and moon but also drawing many more constellations. The detailed yet slightly stiff rendering of these suggests that they were traced from another source. A preparatory drawing on a transparent woven support (fig. 12) reveals that the constellations in this study and the final mural were traced from a planisphere of the northern celestial hemisphere by the German mathematician Peter Apian (fig. 13).[14] First published as an

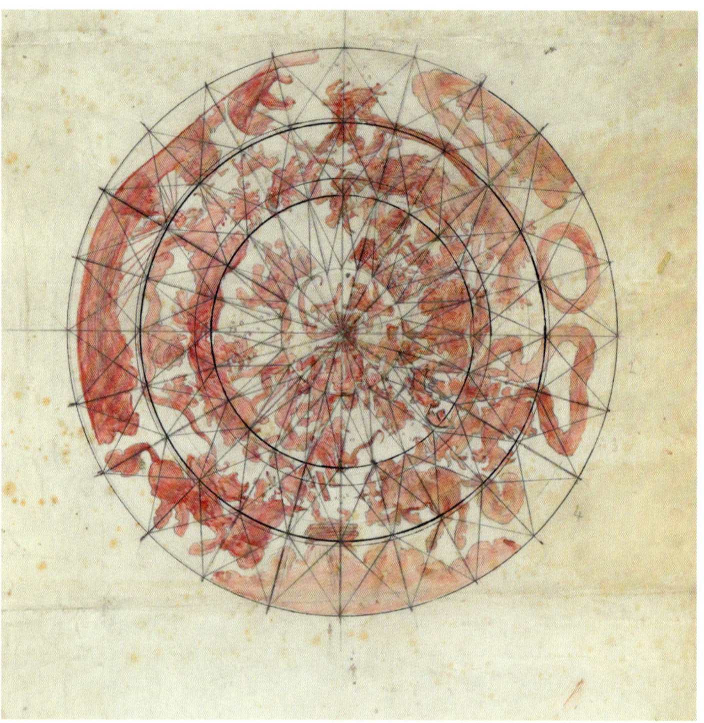

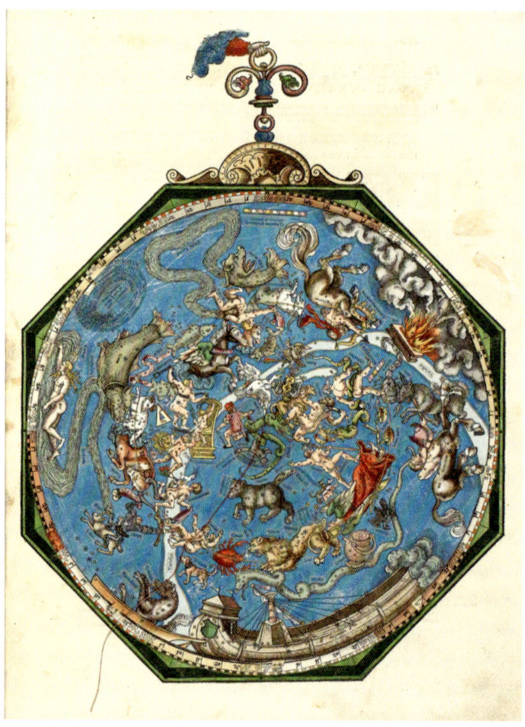

FIG. 12. Edwin Austin Abbey, Compositional Study with Zodiac Figures for *The Hours*, 1904–11. Graphite, ink, and watercolor on transparent fabric, 14 × 13⅛ in. (35.6 × 33.4 cm). Yale University Art Gallery, New Haven, Conn., Edwin Austin Abbey Memorial Collection, 1937.4329

FIG. 13. Peter Apian, *Planisphere of Northern Celestial Hemisphere*, in *Astronomicum Caesareum*, 1540. Fitzwilliam Museum University of Cambridge, Bequeathed by Frank McClean, PB 18-202

independent map in 1536 and later included in his book *Astronomicum Caesareum* (1540), Apian's celestial map features the forty-eight Ptolemaic constellations of the classical world and the Milky Way.[15]

Abbey was surely drawn to the stylized beauty and Renaissance aesthetics of Apian's planisphere, some copies of which feature a hand-colored blue sky and gilded stars, but he must also have been aware of the symbolic significance of the perspective it represented.[16] Abbey had selected a geocentric, or earth-centered, view of the universe. Only three years after the publication of Apian's planisphere, Nicolaus Copernicus proposed that the sun, not the earth, was at the center of the solar system, initiating a fundamental shift in the understanding of the universe and humankind's place within it. Humanity was no longer the center of the known cosmos, but in Abbey's vision for *The Hours*, as in Giovanni di Paolo's *Creation of the World*, the human experience remains at its center.

Apian's map proved vitally important to the compositional development of *The Hours*, serving as the foundation for the constellations, whose placement aligns nearly perfectly across Abbey's subsequent painted studies. Abbey revisited his tracing of the map to add black radiating lines, rings of various sizes, numbers, and crosses, effectively using it as a framework to organize *The Hours* and build symbolism. The impact of the map is perhaps most appreciable in Abbey's twelve-foot-six-inch-diameter half-scale study for the final mural (see cat. 104), which still bears traces of radiating charcoal lines, rings, and crosses. In connecting the surviving concentric traces, we can observe how he used the map to plan the figures' ultimate location and scale.

Both the materials and the painting technique Abbey used to create the half-scale study suggest that he had nearly finalized his composition. Because of its large size, Abbey painted on a heavyweight canvas, likely made for mural painting, that was prepared with a lead-white ground and then stretched on a circular strainer, likely in his studio.[17] By this later stage in his career, Abbey had abandoned the use of a grid to transfer his designs to the immense canvases. He instead photographed his studies and projected them with a magic lantern onto the canvas, tracing the outlines of the figures in charcoal.[18] He seems to have used this method in the half-scale study, evidenced by the lack of grid lines and the manner in which the blue background paint was applied around precise reserves intended for the figures, seen near the clasping hands of the figures for one and two p.m. (see page 270). Abbey initially painted the day hours without drapery, fully realizing each body on its own and using the brightness of the white ground to maximum effect in rendering the skin tones, especially the passages of the body warmed by sunlight. Similar to his use of the tonality of the paper as a midtone to build his figural drawings, Abbey underpainted the figures in a transparent brown midtone. He then applied the warmest passages of pink and orange paint. Next, the outline of the figure was reinforced with heavy charcoal lines, and the darkest shadows were established. Last came a succession of cool, bright scumbles of opaque paint to finish the figure. In his final layers of paint, Abbey's brushwork is uncharacteristically linear, often applied in a series of visible lines and cross-hatchings almost reminiscent of egg tempera paint application. After completing each body, Abbey clothed the day hours in diaphanous drapery, sometimes adding more flesh tones on top to preserve the appearance of sheer fabric. Separately from his nude figure drawing, he also completed pastel studies for the day hours that concentrated on rendering the windswept movement of the drapery around the body (fig. 14). These pastels, completed in 1909, likely served as critical references while painting the half-scale study and final mural.

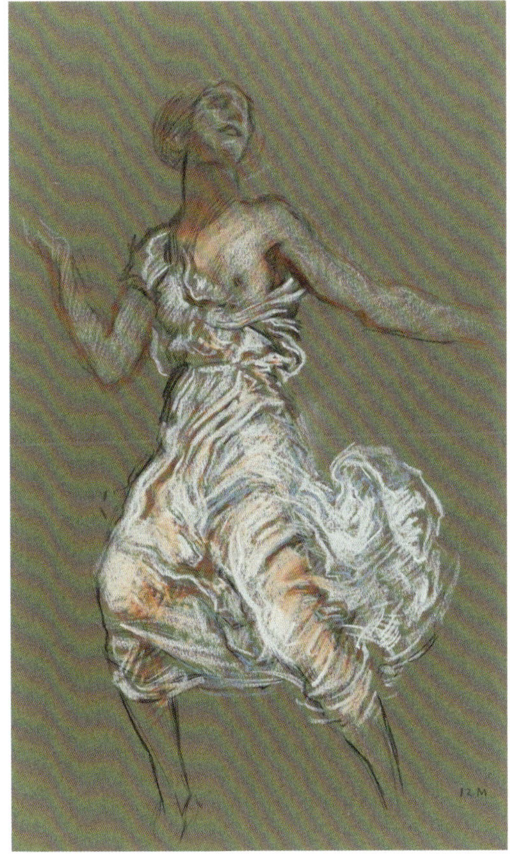

FIG. 14. Edwin Austin Abbey, Study for Noon in *The Hours*, 1909. Pastel on paper, 17 7/16 × 10 15/16 in. (44.3 × 27.8 cm). Yale University Art Gallery, New Haven, Conn., Edwin Austin Abbey Memorial Collection, 1937.3359

Despite the apparent influence of High Renaissance and classical bodies—the figure of noon, for example, appears directly inspired by the pediment sculpture of Iris from the Parthenon (now in the collection of the

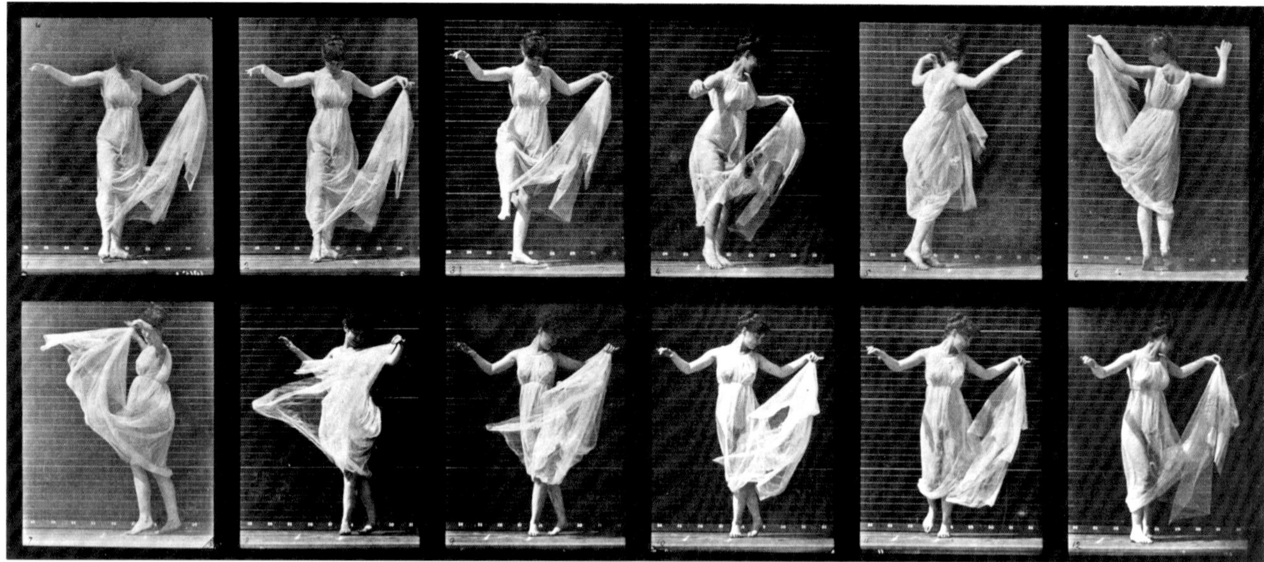

FIG. 15. Eadweard Muybridge, *Dancing (Fancy)*, 1872–85. Collotype on white wove paper, 7¼ × 16½ in. (18.4 × 41.7 cm). The Royal Academy of Arts, London, 04/2693

British Museum)—Abbey's hours are distinctly modern. Their classical drapery denotes them as goddesses, but they do not possess the stately poise of Raphael's nor the serene remoteness of those of Burne-Jones. Rather, they are individuals carefully conceived to appear caught in graceful midaction, more reminiscent of the dancing motion studies of Eadweard Muybridge (fig. 15). Abbey's reference to this evocatively modern mode of figural representation establishes his hours as maidens of the modern age, rendered with ideal beauty but also a scientific specificity unique to photography.

Unlike the day hours, whose movements appear independent and nonsequential, the subtle movements of the night hours are a measured progression into slumber, their increasing stillness balancing the dancing movements of the day hours. As the evening hours advance, their steadily emaciated and masculine bodies become hidden by black drapery (fig. 16). Abbey paints the drapery in bold, broad strokes that seem drawn from the night sky, as if they were clothing themselves in the dark cosmos. Increasingly consumed by their mantles, their faces drift into a semiconscious and, finally, unconscious state. The heads bend deeper into slumber, the body loses its presence, and the mysterious world of the mind dominates. In the gradual retreat of the body and suppression of all movement, Abbey evokes the activity of the interior world of dreams and the unconscious.

Yet even more than a dreamworld, the shrouded hours, especially the figure of midnight poignantly silhouetted against the moon (fig. 17), recall personifications of Death. This association prompts us to contemplate not just the cycle of the hours, days, and months—all depicted in the composition—but also the cycle of human life. The early-morning hours, corpselike in their pallor,

FIG. 16. Detail of cat. 104

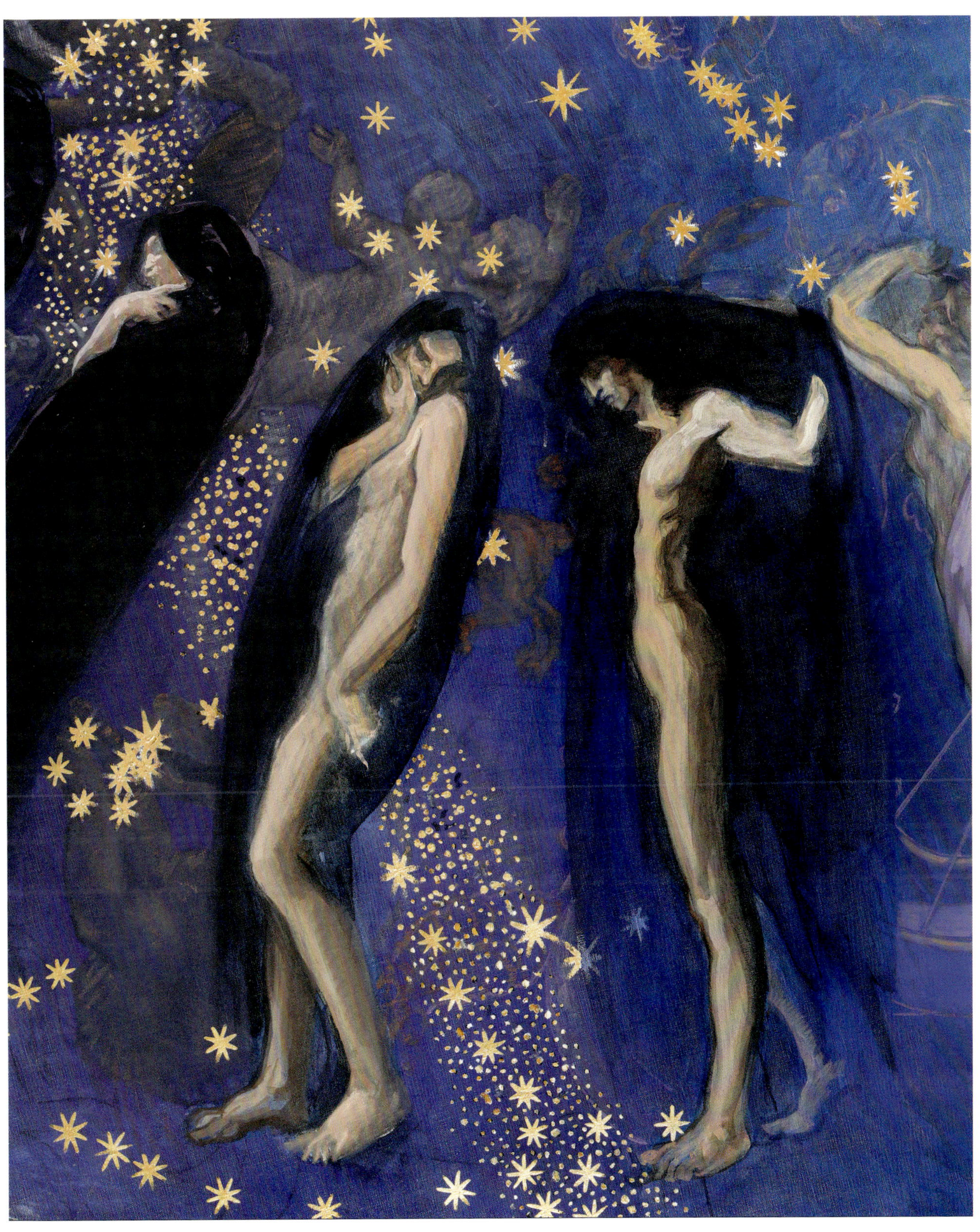

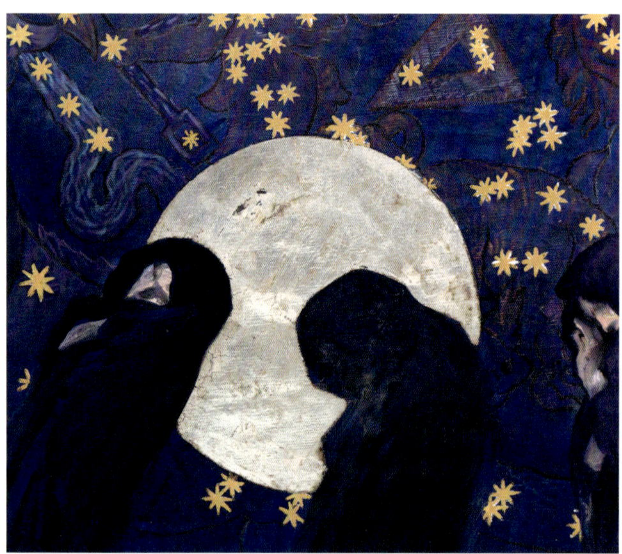

FIG. 17. Detail of cat. 104

lift their heads toward the sun, reawakening and receiving new life. Perhaps tellingly, these hours' faces are the most detailed of all of Abbey's figures. Unlike the day hours, he explored the psychology of his night figures through increased attention to their facial features and the subtle movements of their heads, conveying the waning importance of the body and the ascendancy of the mind and spirit.

As Abbey refined the iconography in the half-scale study, the evolution of the physical qualities of his materials contribute ever more to the symbolic power of the painting and enhance our emotional response. The background has transformed drastically again: it retains the constellation figures but is much less a depiction of day and night and more a representation of a celestial realm. Painted with subtler gradations between deep cobalt and ultramarine, the expanses of velvety blue paint envelop the viewer and saturate our visual field. When united with the reflective golden stars, it begs comparison to sacred, heavenly spaces, such as the early fourteenth-century frescoed ceiling of Giotto di Bondone for the Scrovegni Chapel in Padua.

The creation of this matte, warm surface was of paramount importance to Abbey. When painting the final mural, he related to a friend, "I've used several tons of costly blue paint on it—painted it all in the mat colours. . . . Their great pull is their luminosity, and as there is no oil in them to get yellow—only wax—I don't see why they should not stay luminous."[19] Achieving a surface that appeared to glow from within was likely the artist's primary motivation in choosing a wax-based medium. Particularly for a ceiling painting, Abbey also would have wished to avoid the surface reflections that a glossier medium might impart, potentially obscuring the legibility of the composition and inhibiting the viewer's unmediated response to the beauty of brilliant pigment on canvas. Scientific analysis of the half-scale study has revealed that the medium of the blue background contains a mixture of wax, resin, and oil, suggesting that Abbey began to experiment with adding wax to the paint layers at this point in his artistic process.[20]

The stirring complements to the rich and softly matte background of *The Hours* half-scale study are the shimmering celestial bodies, gilded with gold and silver leaf.[21] The use of such materials on a preparatory study must have been a significant expense, but one that Abbey believed necessary to evaluate their visual impact before embarking on creating the final mural. Abbey dedicated equal attention to the surface qualities of the metal leaf as to his paint

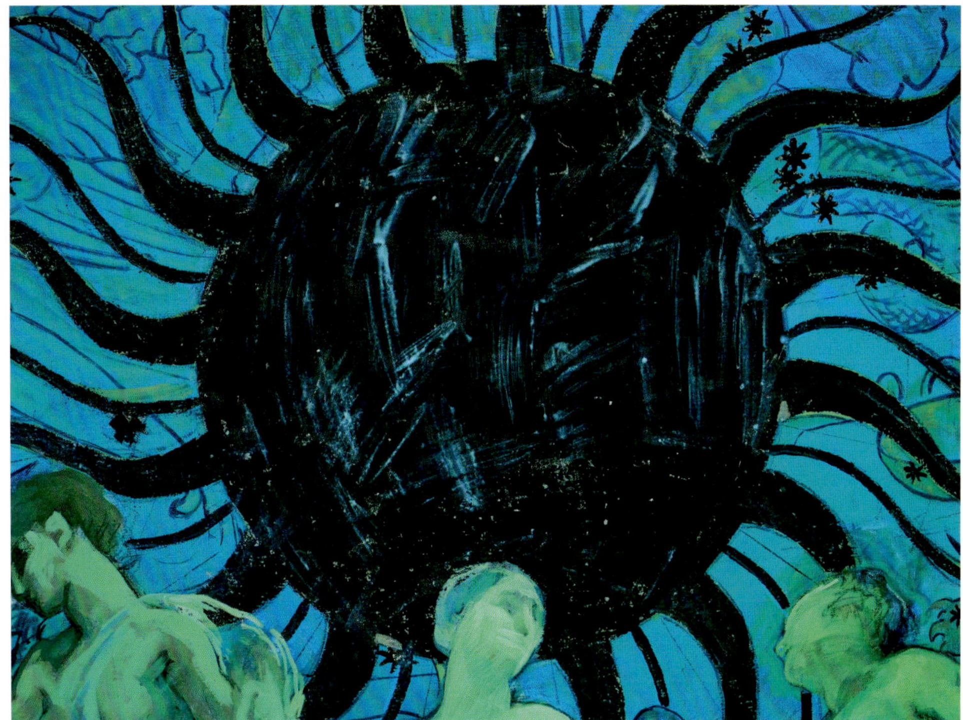

FIG. 18. Detail of cat. 104 under ultraviolet light, showing the matte coating applied to the sun

layers, applying a matte coating on both the sun and the moon to reduce their reflectivity and to achieve balance with the velvety background. This coating is visible under ultraviolet light as a highly fluorescent layer, applied in loose but purposeful strokes (fig. 18).

Abbey's careful attention to the physical qualities and composition of his materials, especially their texture, color, and surface, demonstrates his engagement with Aestheticism and the wider decorative painting movement in Britain and America. Muralists such as Pierre Puvis de Chavannes and John La Farge were reported to have used wax as either an additive or a primary medium in their murals, both to achieve a matte appearance similar to fresco paintings and to ensure durability. Frederic Lord Leighton, a close friend of Abbey's, recommended the wax-based spirit fresco technique to artists involved in the Royal Exchange Commission, for which Abbey painted a mural between 1896 and 1904. Although the primary impetus for its invention was to devise a more stable, moisture-resistant medium for wall painting, the spirit fresco technique also helped muralists achieve a "luminous effect" and "dead surface" in sympathy with the aesthetic aims of the contemporary mural movement in Britain.[22] Abbey was reported to have incorporated wax into his paint for the *Quest and Achievement of the Holy Grail* murals at the Boston Public Library, and ceresine wax was identified in the lunettes he painted for the rotunda of the Pennsylvania State Capitol.[23]

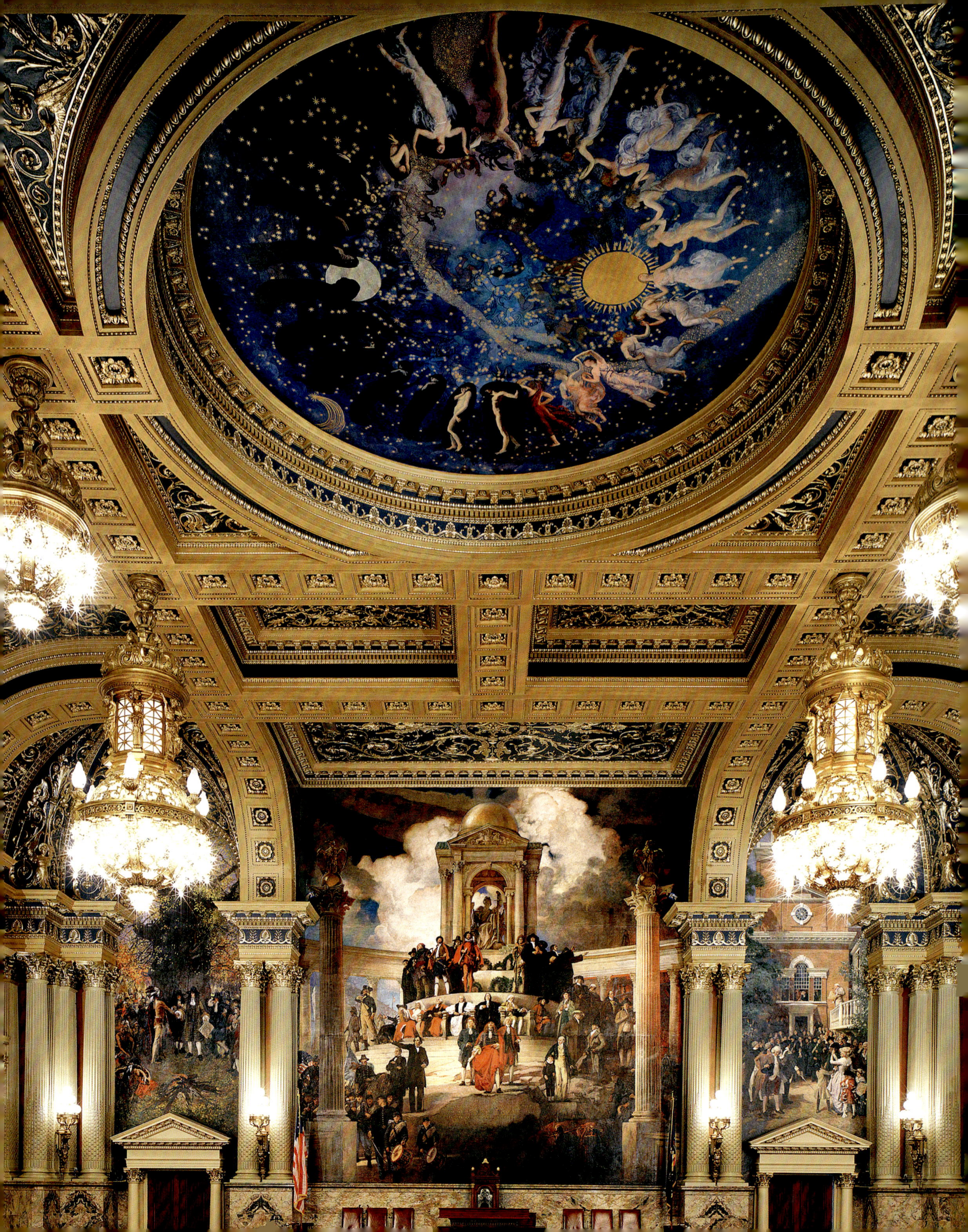

For the final full-scale mural, Abbey made two compositional alterations: he painted a mirror image of Apian's star map, flipping it on the vertical axis, and he added a comet. Easily overlooked, the change to the planisphere served at least two significant symbolic purposes. First, it harmonized the movement of the sun and moon through the zodiac over the course of a year with the clockwise movement of the figures. Second, it changed the perspective from Apian's external view, looking onto the celestial sphere from the outside, to an internal view that contemplates the sky from earth. The viewer's experience is thus transformed—now looking up at the sky from an earthly perspective, we become a participant in the act of gazing into the heavens.

The inclusion of a comet between the nighttime hours of nine and ten is a more puzzling addition. The scholar Patricia Likos Ricci has postulated that it is a representation of Halley's Comet, which arrives in our solar system roughly every seventy-six years and returned in 1910, just as Abbey was finalizing his ceiling mural.[24] This theory is compelling. Just as Giotto's depiction of Halley's Comet in his Scrovegni Chapel frescos references their creation in the early fourteenth century, its inclusion in *The Hours* signifies the historic creation of a capitol for Pennsylvania in the early twentieth century.[25] The cyclical poetry of this contemporary event was likely not lost on Abbey.

If *The Hours* functions as a heavenly dome for the House chamber, we must ask what Abbey considered sacred about this space and what he hoped to convey to the legislators on the floor below. When considered alongside the south wall murals and within the architectural splendor of the chamber, Abbey's ceiling alludes to the fated birth of a great nation. The sun, oriented on the right side of the chamber, casts its light diagonally across *The Apotheosis*, in which the Genius of State, enthroned within her own domed temple, gazes upward, perhaps seeking guidance or inspiration from above. Noting the achievements of the men gathered on the steps, laboring in the mines, and marching to the aid of the Union, we are reminded of our ability to carve a place in American legend. Faced with slabs of unfinished stone, viewers are invited to make their mark in a quintessentially American call to individual action. On either side, *Penn's Treaty with the Indians* and *The Reading of the Declaration of Independence* commemorate two vital documents in U.S. history, the first of which was greatly supported by the Pennsylvania House of Representatives (then known as the Provincial Assembly). Acting as legislative pillars for the chamber, these murals remind the representatives of their distinguished history and their current responsibility as participants in the democratic system.

Through the beauty of its materials and carefully developed iconography, *The Hours* urges both reflection and action. Considered within the symbolic scheme of the chamber, Abbey's ceiling painting declares that the stars have aligned over Pennsylvania, gathering extraordinary minds, military strength,

The House of Representatives chamber of the Pennsylvania State Capitol, showing Abbey's south wall murals, including *The Apotheosis of Pennsylvania* and *The Hours*

and natural resources. But in his poetic vision of the course of life, Abbey also declares that our ability to complete the steps leading to the Genius of State depends on the actions of our hours.

NOTES

1. Edward Verrall Lucas, *Edwin Austin Abbey, Royal Academician: The Record of His Life and Work* (London: Methuen, 1921), 2:475. Edwin Austin Abbey to Joseph Huston via unknown proxy, January 29, 1908, Joseph Huston Personal Papers, Pennsylvania Capitol Preservation Committee, Harrisburg (hereafter "Huston Papers, PCPC").
2. Lucas, *Abbey*, 2:475. It is unknown whether Abbey ever received the sketches back from Huston.
3. Lucas, *Abbey*, 2:381–82.
4. See *The American Renaissance: 1876–1917*, exh. cat. (Brooklyn, N.Y.: Brooklyn Museum, 1979); and Bailey Van Hook, *The Virgin and the Dynamo: Public Murals in American Architecture, 1893–1917* (Athens: Ohio University Press, 2003).
5. Charles M. Shean, "The Decoration of Public Buildings: A Plea for Americanism in Subject and Ornamental Detail," *Municipal Affairs* 5, no. 3 (September 1901): 712.
6. Architectural changes to the House of Representatives Chamber are described in chapter 3 of *The Pennsylvania Capitol: A Documentary History* (Princeton, N.J.: Heritage Studies, 1987), 1:99–234. A letter between Abbey and Huston reveals that Abbey expanded the diameter of the painting from eighteen to twenty-four feet, agreeing to do so at his own expense; Huston to Abbey, January 16, 1906, Huston Papers, PCPC.
7. Lucas, *Abbey*, 2:313.
8. Ibid., 1:436. Abbey's practice of pinning his studies to his canvases is described in ibid., 2:283–84.
9. Georgiana Burne-Jones, *Memorials of Edward Burne-Jones* (London: Macmillan, 1906), 127–28.
10. Mary E. Williams, *The Hours of Raphael in Outline Together with the Ceiling of the Hall Where They Were Originally Painted* (Boston: Little, Brown, 1891), 9–19 and accompanying plates.
11. Lucas, *Abbey*, 1:187.
12. Ibid., 2:441.
13. Ibid., 2:283–84.
14. The planisphere that Abbey painted in *The Hours* was first identified and published in Patricia Likos Ricci, "Edwin Austin Abbey's *The Passage of the Hours*: Astronomy as History," *Astronomical Society of the Pacific Conference Series* 501 (2015): 51–52. It is unknown which manuscript Abbey copied, but several copies of the *Astronomicum Caesareum* were likely in public and private collections in or near London at the beginning of the twentieth century. For a list of all known copies of this manuscript, see Owen Gingerich, "A Survey of Apian's *Astronomicum Caesareum*," in *Peter Apian: Astronomie, Kosmographie und Mathematik am Beginn der Neuzit: mit Ausstellungskatalog*, ed. Karl Röttel (Eichstätt, Germany: Polygon, 1995), 113–22.
15. Deborah J. Warner, *The Sky Explored: Celestial Cartography, 1500–1800* (New York: Alan R. Liss, 1979), 10.
16. Gingerich, "Survey of *Astronomicum Caesareum*," 114. Copies of these hand-colored versions are in the collections of the Fitzwilliam Museum at the University of Cambridge (accessioned 1904) and St. Johns Library at Oxford University (accessioned 1635).
17. The half-scale study for *The Hours* is painted on a single plain-weave canvas with an open weave. The canvas has a thread count of 26 by 22 threads per inch. The ground

layer was analyzed with portable X-ray fluorescence spectroscopy (p-XRF) and was found to contain lead, indicating the use of lead white in the ground layer. Analysis was performed by Dr. Marcie Wiggins and Dr. Pablo Londero at Yale University's Institute for the Preservation of Cultural Heritage (IPCH).

18. Lucas, *Abbey*, 2:441.
19. Ibid., 2:466.
20. A sample of the blue background paint from the study was analyzed with Pyrolysis-gas chromatography-mass spectrometry (Py-GC/MS) and was found to contain drying oil, beeswax, and pine resin. Analysis performed by Dr. Anikó Bezur at Yale University's IPCH.
21. The gold leaf and silver leaf were applied with a mordant gilding technique. The metal leaf was characterized with XRF by Dr. Pablo Londero and Dr. Marcie Wiggins at Yale University's IPCH.
22. Van Hook, *The Virgin and the Dynamo*, 6, 77; Lance Mayer and Gay Myers, *American Painters on Technique: 1860–1945* (Los Angeles: J. Paul Getty Museum, 2013), 63–67; and Clare A. P. Willsdon, *Mural Painting in Britain, 1840–1940: Image and Meaning* (Oxford: Oxford University Press, 2000), 64–65. The spirit fresco medium, developed by Thomas Gambier Parry in 1859, consisted of copal, white wax, gum elemi resin, turpentine, and oil of spike lavender applied to a dry plaster wall (394); see Thomas Gambier Parry, *Spirit Fresco Painting: An Account of the Process* (London, 1883), 1.
23. See Lucas, *Abbey*, 1:247; and Susanne Brendel Pandich, "Restoration of the Abbey Murals at the Pennsylvania State Capitol," *APT Bulletin: The Journal of Preservation Technology* 24, no. 1 (1992): 15.
24. Patricia Likos Ricci, "Edwin Austin Abbey's *The Passage of the Hours*: Astronomy as History," in *Inspiration of Astronomical Phenomena VIII: City of Stars*, ed. Brian P. Abbott (New York: American Museum of Natural History, 2013), 54.
25. For an examination of the depiction of Halley's Comet in Giotto's Scrovegni Chapel frescoes, see Roberta J. M. Olson, "Giotto's Portrait of Halley's Comet," *Scientific American* 240, no. 5 (May 1979): 160–71.

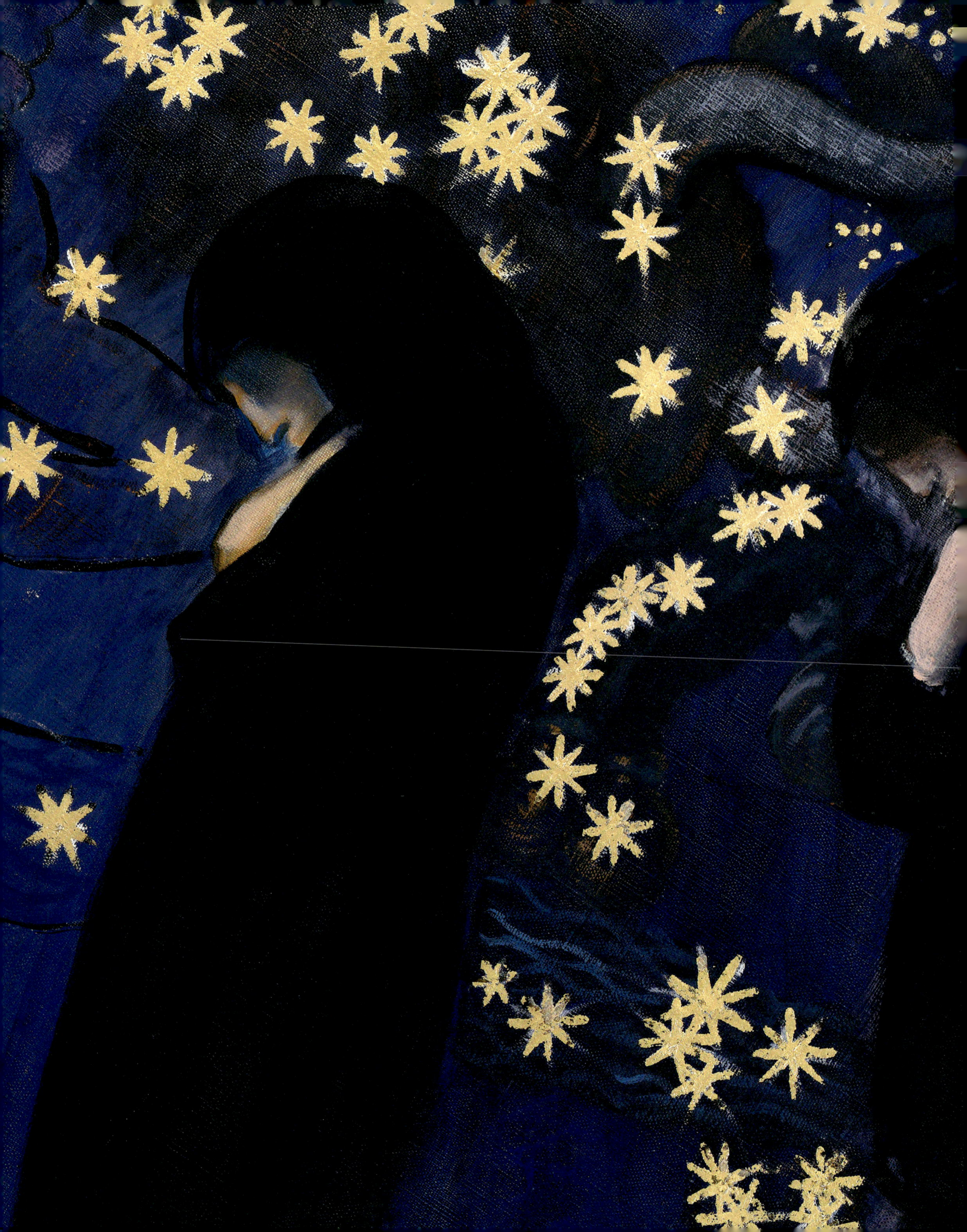

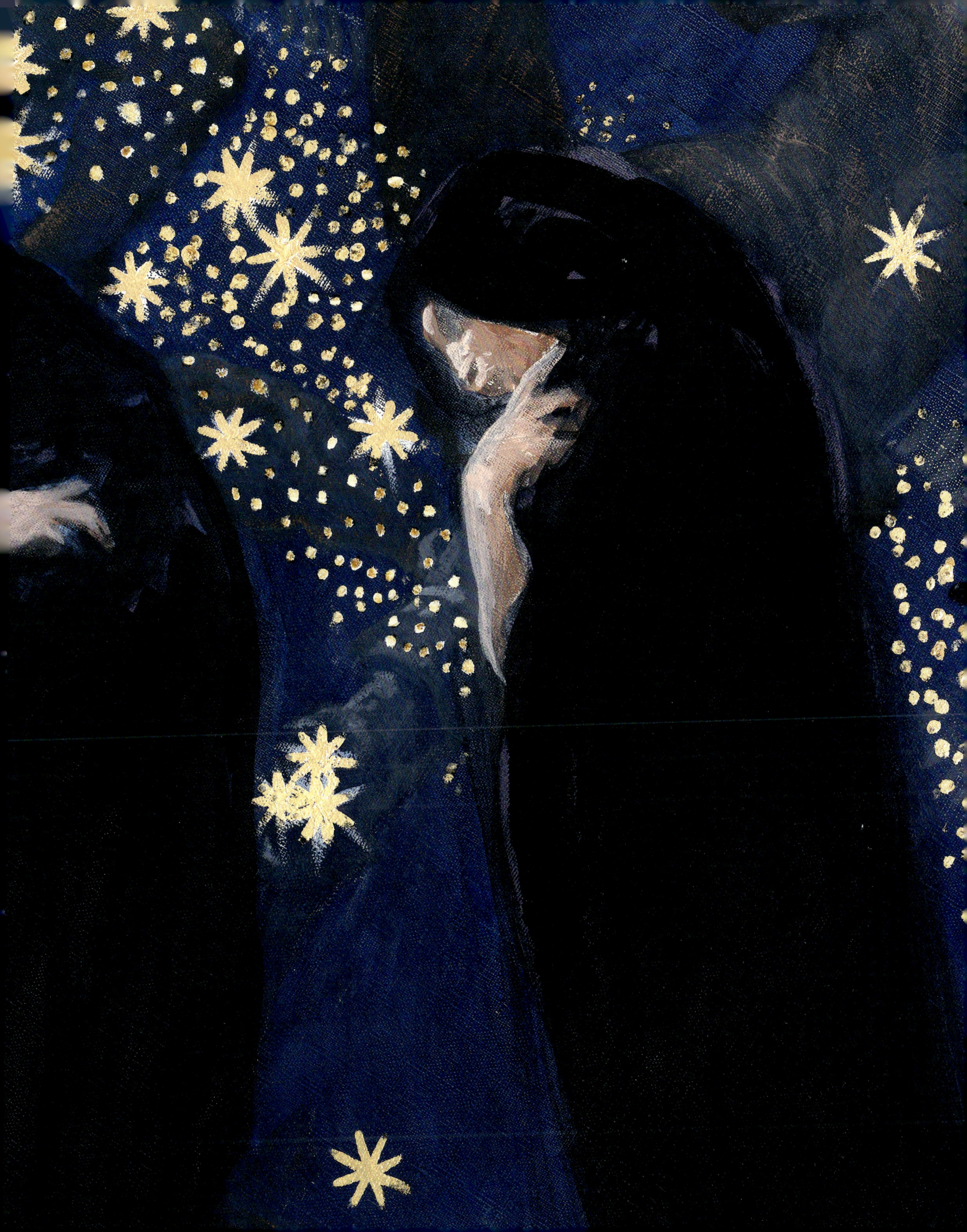

Index

Page numbers in *italics* refer to illustrations.

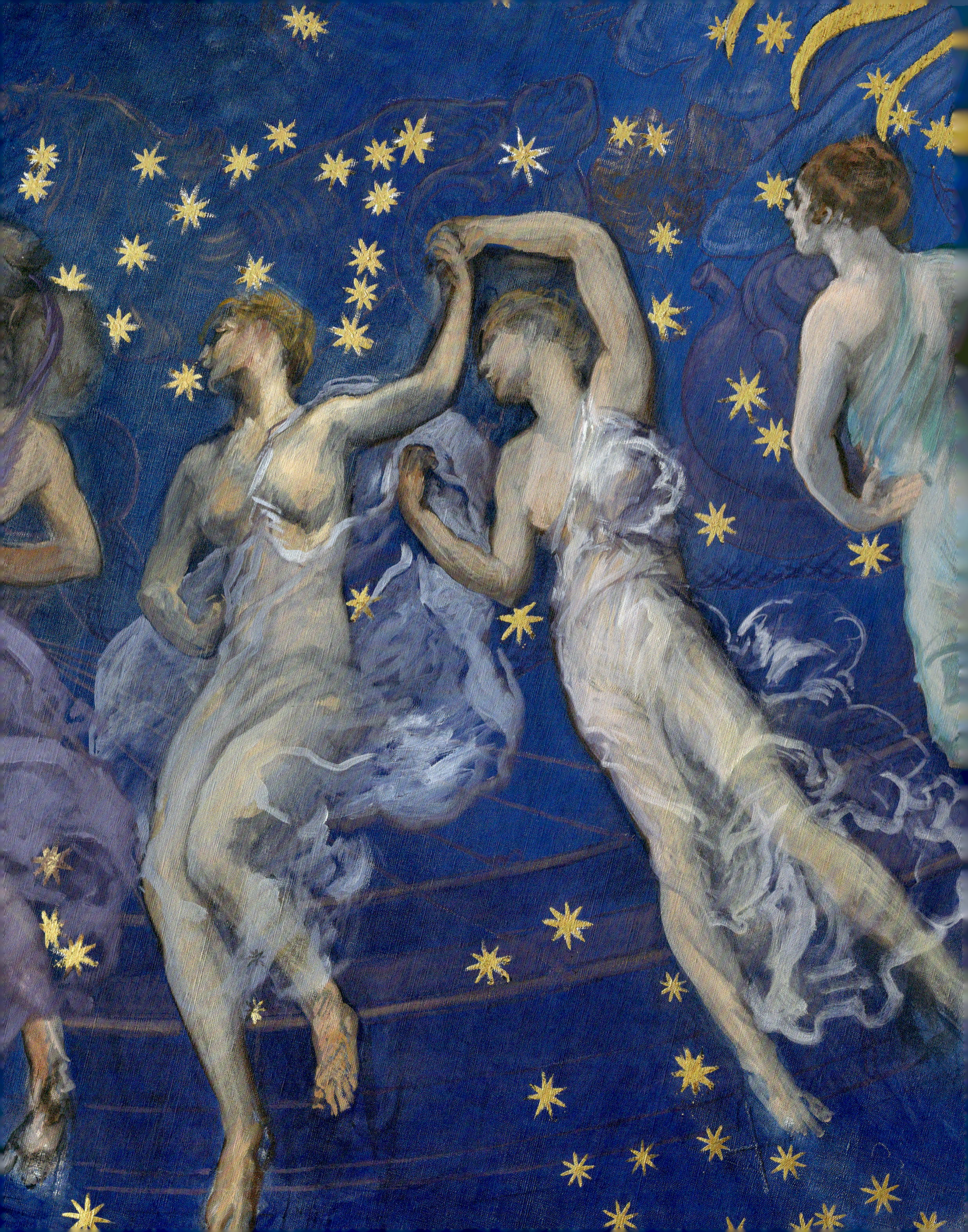

Photography Credits

Every effort has been made to credit the artists and the sources; if there are errors or omissions, please contact the Yale University Art Gallery so that corrections can be made in subsequent editions. All images courtesy Visual Resources Department, Yale University Art Gallery, unless otherwise noted.

Endpapers (detail of cat. 43): President and Fellows of Harvard College

Frontmatter: pp. 4–5 (details of cats. 18–19): Jim Gipe/Pivot Media and Stephen Petegorsky; p. 21, fig. 2: Photo © 2024 Museum of Fine Arts, Boston

AFTER LIFE: cat. 1 (p. 27): Courtesy Toledo Museum of Art; cat. 3 (p. 32): Photograph © 2024 Museum of Fine Arts, Boston; cat. 5 (pp. 36–37): Bowdoin College Museum of Art, Brunswick, Maine; cat. 6 (p. 38): Courtesy Library of Congress Prints and Photographs Division, Washington, D.C.; cat. 7 (p. 39): Photo © Smithsonian Institution; cat. 9 (p. 43; detail p. 41): Courtesy the State Museum of Pennsylvania, Pennsylvania Historical and Museum Commission

MODELS: cat. 12 (p. 51): © The Metropolitan Museum of Art. Art Resource, N.Y.; cat. 14 (p. 55): © The Metropolitan Museum of Art. Art Resource, N.Y.; cat. 15 (p. 56): Photo © 2024 Museum of Fine Arts, Boston; cats. 18–19 (p. 61): Jim Gipe/Pivot Media and Stephen Petegorsky

Live One's Life as a Work of Art: p. 68, fig. 4: Courtesy the Pennsylvania Academy of the Fine Arts, Philadelphia; p. 69, fig 5: © Center for Creative Photography, The University of Arizona Foundation; p. 71, fig. 7: Courtesy Boston Public Library. Photo © Sheryl Lanzel; p. 71, fig. 8: The Art Institute of Chicago/Art Resource, NY; p. 72, fig. 9: Courtesy Boston Public Library. Photo © Sheryl Lanzel

THE BOSTON PUBLIC LIBRARY: pp. 82–83: Courtesy Boston Public Library. Photo © Sheryl Lanzel; cat. 27 (p. 96): Photo © 2024 Museum of Fine Arts, Boston; pp. 100–101: Photo: Aram Boghosian for the Boston Public Library

VITAL ENERGY: cat. 36 (p. 116): Courtesy National Gallery of Art, Washington, D.C.; cat. 37 (p. 117): © The Metropolitan Museum of Art. Art Resource, N.Y.: cats. 38–39 (pp. 118–19; detail p. 115): President and Fellows of Harvard College; cat. 40 (p. 121): © The Metropolitan Museum of Art/Art Resource, N.Y.

TOUCH: cat. 43 (p. 127): President and Fellows of Harvard College; cat. 44 (p. 130, detail p. 128): The Art Institute of Chicago/Art Resource, N.Y.; cat. 45 (p. 131; detail pp. 124–25); cats. 46–47 (pp. 133, 135): Courtesy National Gallery of Art, Washington; cat. 48 (p. 136): Courtesy the State Museum of Pennsylvania, Pennsylvania Historical and Museum Commission; cat. 49 (p. 137): Carnegie Museum of Art, Pittsburgh, Pa./Art Resource, N.Y.; cat. 50 (p. 139): Courtesy of Gari Melchers Home and Studio at the University of Mary Washington; cat. 51 (p. 141): Photo © Smithsonian Institution

COLLECTIVE WORK: cat. 56 (p. 151): Courtesy Smith College Museum of Art; cat. 58 (p. 155): Jim Gipe/Pivot Media; cat. 59 (p. 156): Courtesy the State Museum of Pennsylvania, Pennsylvania Historical and Museum Commission; cat. 60 (p. 157): Courtesy Westmoreland Museum of American Art; cat. 61 (pp. 158–59): Carnegie Museum of Art, Pittsburgh, Pa./Art Resource, N.Y.

Mural Painting and the Nineteenth-Century Civic Imagination: p. 162: Sean Pavone/Alamy Stock Photo; pp. 168, 170–71: Alpha Stock/Alamy Stock Photo; p. 173, fig. 6: Brian Hunt & Pennsylvania Capitol Preservation Committee; p. 175, fig. 8: Courtesy National Gallery of Art, Washington, D.C.; p. 176, fig. 9: Courtesy Philadelphia Museum of Art; p. 180, fig. 11: Yale Center for British Art

THE PENNSYLVANIA CAPITOL: cat. 68 (p. 195): Courtesy the State Museum of Pennsylvania, Pennsylvania Historical and Museum Commission

MODERN MORALS: cat. 75 (p. 211): Photo © Smithsonian Institution; cat. 77 (p. 214; detail pp. 204–5): © The Metropolitan Museum of Art/Art Resource, N.Y.; cat. 78 (p. 215): Courtesy Library of Congress Prints and Photographs Division, Washington, D.C.; cat. 79 (p. 216): Courtesy of Gari Melchers Home & Studio at the University of Mary Washington; cat. 80 (p. 217): Courtesy National Gallery of Art, Washington, D.C.; cat. 82 (p. 221): Courtesy Smith College Museum of Art

EXPRESSION: cat. 87 (p. 232): Courtesy of Gari Melchers Home & Studio at the University of Mary Washington; cat. 88 (p. 233): Courtesy the State Museum of Pennsylvania, Pennsylvania Historical and Museum Commission; pp. 234–35: Sean Pavone/Alamy Stock Photo; cat. 89 (p. 236): The Art Institute of Chicago/Art Resource, N.Y.; cat. 90 (p. 237): Courtesy the State Museum of Pennsylvania, Pennsylvania Historical and Museum Commission

DANCE: cat. 91 (p. 241): Courtesy of the Danforth Art Museum at Framingham State University; cat. 94 (p. 245): The Art Institute of Chicago/Art Resource, N.Y.; cat. 95 (p. 248; detail p. 247): Photo: Christopher Gardner; cat. 101 (pp. 260–61; detail p. 254): Photo © 2024 Museum of Fine Arts, Boston

Creating "The Hours": p. 274, fig. 2: © Sheffield Museum Trust; p. 275, fig. 3: © The Metropolitan Museum of Art. Art Resource, N.Y. Photo: Malcolm Varon; pp. 276–77: © Robert Benson Photography; p. 284, fig. 13: © The Fitzwilliam Museum, University of Cambridge; p. 286, fig. 15: Royal Academy of Arts, London; Photo: John Hammond; p. 290: © Robert Benson Photography

Published in conjunction with the exhibition
The Dance of Life: Figure and Imagination in American Art, 1876–1917
Yale University Art Gallery
September 6, 2024–January 5, 2025

Exhibition and publication made possible by Jerald Dillon Fessenden, B.A. 1960; Clifford Ross, B.A. 1974; the Henry Luce Foundation; the Mr. and Mrs. Raymond J. Horowitz Foundation for the Arts, Inc.; the Wyeth Foundation for American Art; the Rosalee and David McCullough Fund; the Eugénie Prendergast Fund for American Art, given by Jan and Warren Adelson; the Mr. and Mrs. Raymond J. Horowitz Foundation for the Arts Fund; and the Friends of American Arts at Yale Exhibition and Publication Endowment Funds.

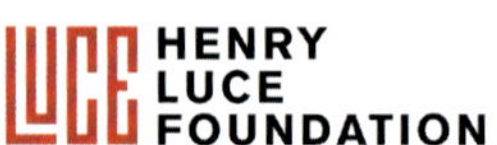

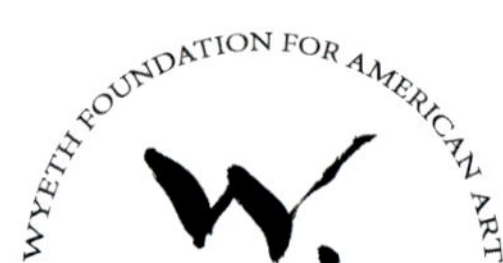

Produced by the Yale University Art Gallery
Tiffany Sprague, Director of Publications and Editorial Services
Annika Fisher, Assistant Editor
Mary Ellen Wilson, Assistant Editor
Grace Zhou, Editorial and Production Assistant
Kathleen Mylen-Coulombe, Rights and Reproductions Coordinator

Project Manager: Mary Ellen Wilson
Designer: Laura Lindgren
Proofreader: Annika Fisher
Indexer: Theresa Duran

Typeset in Sedan and Nort
Printed by Meridian Printing, East Greenwich, R.I.

First printing

Yale University Art Gallery
1111 Chapel Street
P.O. Box 208271
New Haven, CT 06520-8271
artgallery.yale.edu/publications

Distributed by Yale University Press
302 Temple Street
P.O. Box 209040
New Haven, CT 06520-9040
yalebooks.com/art

Library of Congress Control Number: 2024934537

ISBN: 978-0-300-25645-1

Cover (front and back): Details of cat. 104
Details: endpapers: cat. 43; pp. 2–3: cat. 100; pp. 4–5: cats. 18–19; p. 6: cat. 69; p. 14: cat. 28; p. 16: cat. 103; pp. 24–25, 42: cat. 9; p. 40: cat. 13; pp. 44–45: cat. 17; p. 46: cat. 11; p. 50: cat. 13; p. 54: cat. 16; p. 62: cat. 62; pp. 76–77: cat. 26; p. 80: cat. 20; p. 84: cat. 21; p. 88: cat. 24; p. 92: cat. 25; pp. 102–3: cat. 29; p. 108: cat. 34; p. 115: cat. 119; pp. 124–25: cat. 45; p. 128: cat. 44; p. 132: cat. 47; pp. 144–45: cat. 57; p. 146: cat. 54; p. 154: cat. 59; pp. 184–85: cat. 64; p. 201: cat. 72; pp. 204–5: cat. 77; p. 209: cat. 74; pp. 222–23: cat. 86; p. 225: cat. 84; p. 228: cat. 85; pp. 238–39: cat. 100; p. 247: cat. 95; p. 251: cat. 97; p. 254: cat. 101; p. 263: cat. 102; pp. 266–67, 270, 294–95, 302: cat. 104

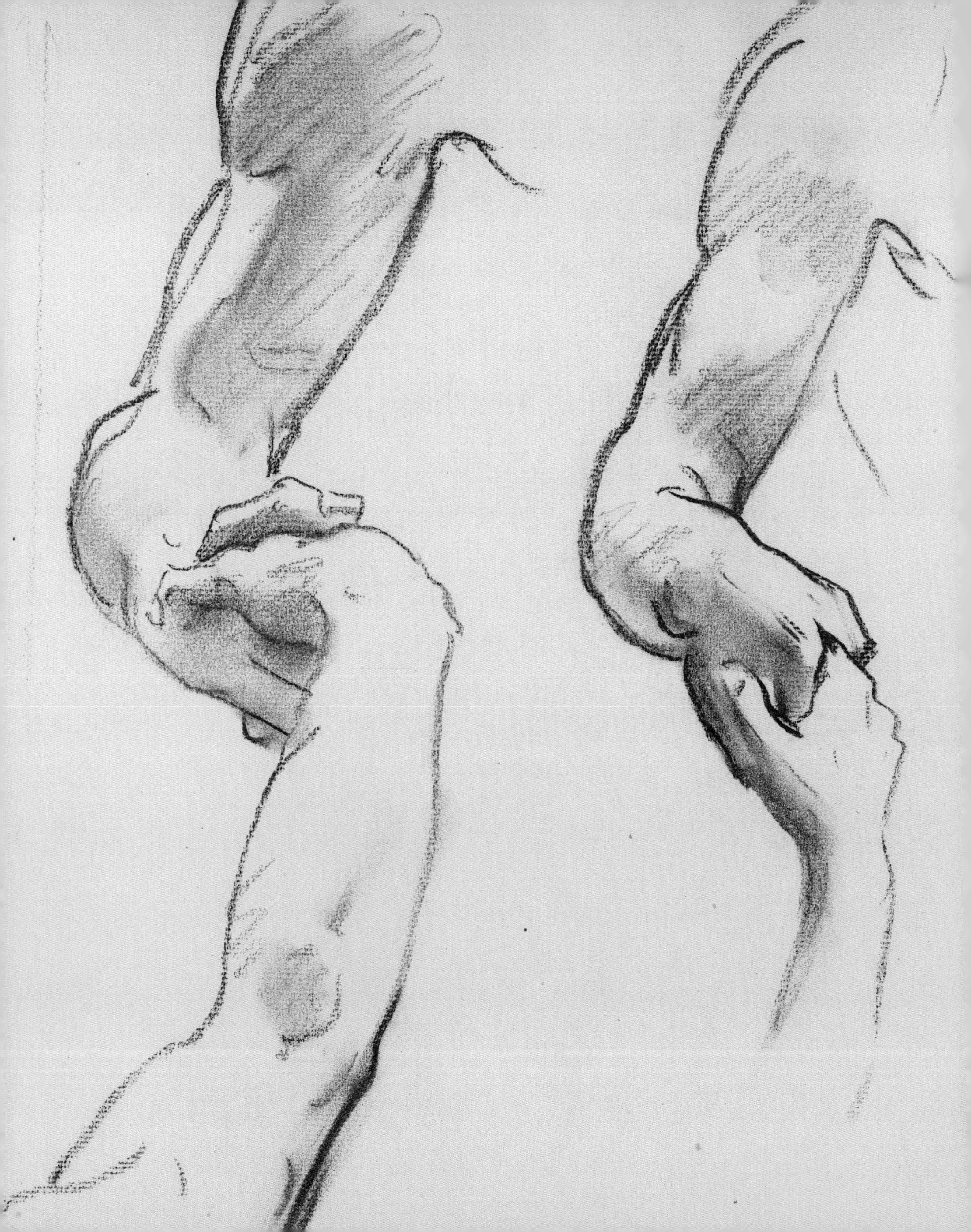